THE NEW TESTAMENT
IN MODERN ENGLISH
FOR SCHOOLS

J. B. PHILLIPS

The New Testament in Modern English

FOR SCHOOLS

BLES · COLLINS

Printed in Great Britain by
Cox & Wyman Ltd, Reading
for the publishers
Geoffrey Bles Ltd
52 Doughty Street, London, WC1
and distributed by
William Collins Sons & Co. Ltd
144 Cathedral Street, Glasgow, C4

This edition for schools
first published October 1959
Reprinted February and May 1960
Revised edition October 1960
Reprinted May and October 1962
June and September 1963
March and July 1964
October 1965

I DEDICATE
THIS TRANSLATION TO
VERA
MY WIFE AND
FINEST CRITIC

TRANSLATOR'S FOREWORD

The essential principles of translation

THERE seem to be three necessary tests which any work of transference from one language to another must pass before it can be
classed as good translation. The first is simply that it must not
sound like a translation at all. If it is skilfully done, and we are
not previously informed, we should be quite unaware that it *is*
a translation, even though the work we are reading is far distant
from us in both time and place. That is a first, and indeed fundamental test, but it is not by itself sufficient. For the translator himself may be a skilful writer, and although he may have conveyed
the essential meaning, characterisation and plot of the original
author, he may have so strong a style of his own that he completely changes that of the original author. The example of this
kind of translation which springs most readily to my mind is
Fitzgerald's *Rubáiyát of Omar Khayyám*. I would therefore make
this the second test: that a translator does his work with the least
possible obtrusion of his own personality. The third and final test
which a good translator should be able to pass is that of being able
to produce in the hearts and minds of his readers an effect equivalent to that produced by the author upon his original readers.
Of course no translator living would claim that his work successfully achieved these three ideals. But he must bear them in mind
constantly as principles for his guidance.

Translation as interpretation

This seems to me to be the right place to set down a justification
for my own methods. As I have frequently said, a translator is not
a commentator. He is usually well aware of the different con-
notations which a certain passage may bear, but unless his work
is to be cluttered with footnotes he is bound, after careful consideration, to set down what is the most likely meaning. Occasion-
ally one is driven into what appears to be a paraphrase, simply
because a literal translation of the original Greek would prove
unintelligible. But where this has proved necessary I have always

been careful to avoid giving any slant or flavour which is purely of my own making. That is why I have been rather reluctant to accept the suggestion that my translation is "interpretation"! If the word interpretation is used in a bad sense, that is, if it is meant that a work is tendentious, or that there has been a manipulation of the words of New Testament Scripture to fit some private point of view, then I would still strongly repudiate the charge! But "interpretation" can also mean transmitting meaning from one language to another, and skilled interpreters in world affairs do not intentionally inject any meaning of their own. In this sense I gladly accept the word interpretation to describe my work. For, as I see it, the translator's function is to understand as fully and deeply as possible what the New Testament writers had to say and then, after a process of what might be called reflective digestion, to write it down in the language of the people today. And here I must say that it is essential for the interpreter to know the language of both parties. He may be a first-class scholar in New Testament Greek and know the significance of every traditional crux, and yet be abysmally ignorant of how his contemporaries outside his scholastic world are thinking and feeling.

Words and their context

After reading a large number of commentaries I have a feeling that some scholars, at least, have lived so close to the Greek Text that they have forgotten their sense of proportion. I doubt very much whether the New Testament writers were as subtle or as self-conscious as some commentators would make them appear. For the most part I am convinced that they had no idea that they were writing Holy Scripture. They would be, or indeed perhaps are, amazed to learn what meanings are sometimes read back into their simple utterances! Paul, for instance, writing in haste and urgency to some of his wayward and difficult Christians, was not tremendously concerned about dotting the "i's" and crossing the "t's" of his message. I doubt very much whether he was even concerned about being completely consistent with what he had already written. Consequently, it seems to me quite beside the point to study his writings microscopically, as it were, and deduce hidden meanings of which almost certainly he was unaware. His letters are alive, and they are moving—in both senses of that word —and their meaning can no more be appreciated by cold minute examination than can the beauty of a bird's flight be appreciated by dissection after its death. We have to take these living New Testament documents in their context, a context of supreme urgency and often of acute danger. But a word is modified very considerably by the context in which it appears, and where a translator fails to realise this, we are not far away from the result of an electronic word transmuter! The translators of the Authorised Version were certainly not unaware of this modification, even though they had an extreme reverence for the actual words of Holy Writ. Three hundred years ago they did not hesitate to translate the Greek word EKBALLO by such varying expressions as *put out, drive out, bring forth, send out, tear out, take out, leave out, cast out*, etc., basing their decision on the context. And as a striking example of their translational freedom, in Matthew 27: 44 we read that the thieves who were crucified with Jesus "cast the same in his teeth", where the Greek words mean simply, "abused him".

The translator must be flexible

I feel strongly that a translator, although he must make himself as familiar as possible with New Testament Greek usage, must steadfastly refuse to be driven by the bogey of consistency. He must be guided both by the context in which a word appears, and by the sensibilities of modern English readers. In the story of the raising of Lazarus, for example, Martha's objection to opening the grave would be natural enough to an Eastern mind. But to put into her lips the words, "by this time he's stinking", would sound to Western ears unpleasantly out of key with the rest of that moving story. Similarly, we know that the early Christians greeted one another with "an holy kiss". Yet to introduce such an expression into a modern English translation immediately reveals the gulf between the early Christians and ourselves, the very thing which I as a translator am trying to bridge. Again, it is perfectly true, if we are to translate literally, that Jesus said, "Blessed are the beggars in spirit". In an Eastern land, where the disparity between rich and poor was very great, beggars were common. But it is to my mind extremely doubtful whether the word "beggar" in our Welfare State, or indeed in most English-speaking countries, conjures up the mental image which Jesus intended to convey to his hearers. It was not the social misfit or the work-shy, spiritually speaking, but the one who was obviously and consciously in need whom Jesus describes as "blessed" or "happy".

The use of insight and sympathy

Perhaps a few words about the kind of technique which I have adopted may be introduced here. I have found imaginative sympathy, not so much with words as with people, to be essential. If it is not presumptuous to say so, I attempted, as far as I could, to think myself into the heart and mind of Paul, for example, or of Mark or of John the Divine. Then I tried further to imagine myself as each of the New Testament authors writing his particular message for the people of today. No one could succeed in doing this superlatively well, if only because of the scantiness of our knowledge of the first century A.D. But this has been my ideal, and that is why consistency and meticulous accuracy have sometimes both been sacrificed in the attempt to transmit freshness and life across the centuries. The cross-headings which appear throughout the book are meant to make it both more readable and more intelligible; at the same time they are intended to be quite unobtrusive and can easily be ignored. But, by the use of these headings, solid and rather forbidding slabs of continuous writing (such as appear in the Greek Text) are made more assimilable to the modern reader, whose reading habits have already been "conditioned" by the comparatively recent usage of clear punctuation, intelligent paragraphing and good printer's type.

Acknowledgments

Although I have worked directly in this translation from the best available Greek Text, it would be ungracious to forget the very many people who have made the work possible. I think first of the textual critics, whose patient work gives us a text to work from which is as near as possible to that of the original writers. I am most grateful to them, as all translators must be, and I should also like to express my thanks to the numerous commentators whose works I have consulted again and again. As will be gathered from what I have said above, I have not always agreed with them, but they have informed my mind and stimulated my thoughts many times. The painstaking work of commentators, to put it at its lowest, saves the translator from being over-facile or slipshod! Again, although it would be impossible to supply a full list, I am extremely grateful to the many people—including first-rate scholars, hard-working parish priests, busy ministers, doctors, scientists, missionaries, educationists, elderly saints and lively young people—who have, over the years, written me hundreds of letters, the great majority of which were constructive and useful. Their help has been invaluable.

It has been my practice not to consult other modern translations until my own version has been finished. I do not therefore owe anything directly to any contemporary translator, much as I admire the work of Dr. J. W. C. Wand and Dr. E. V. Rieu of this country, and Dr. Edgar J. Goodspeed of the United States of America. But none of us who translates today can be unaware of the trail that was blazed for us near the beginning of this century by such pioneers as Dr. R. F. Weymouth and Dr. James Moffatt. We cannot but admit that we are in a much more favourable position because such men had the courage to break a centuries-old tradition, and translate into contemporary English.

I am particularly grateful to Dr. C. S. Lewis, to whom I sent a copy of my version of Paul's letter to Colossae when I first began the work of translating. He wrote back giving me great encouragement. And later, after many disappointments, when I eventually found a publisher in Mr. Geoffrey Bles, Dr. Lewis not only supplied the admirable title *Letters to Young Churches* but wrote an Introduction which played no small part in launching that book.

I find myself therefore indebted to all kinds of people of different nationalities and different denominations. Not the least of my gratitude is evoked by the assurance that has grown within me that here in the New Testament, at the very heart and core of our Faith, Christians are far more at one than their outward divisions would imply. From this unquestionable evidence of fundamental unity I derive not only great comfort but a great hope for the future.

J. B. PHILLIPS

SWANAGE, DORSET,
1958

PREFACE TO THE SCHOOLS' EDITION

WHEN I began the work of translating Paul's epistles in 1941 I certainly had no idea either that my efforts would be published or that I should eventually translate the whole New Testament. I wrote for the young people who belonged to my youth club, most of them not much above school-leaving age, and I undertook the work simply because I found that the Authorised Version was not intelligible to them. My primary aim was not in any sense to compete with the version of 1611, but to communicate to young people inspired truths of which they were almost entirely ignorant.

It is, then, with the greatest possible pleasure that I welcome this schools edition of my whole translational work. It is as though the wheel had come full circle after eighteen years and once more I find myself using modern language to communicate ancient truths to young people.

Before ordination I had myself a short experience as a schoolmaster, and in each of the four parishes in which I have served there have been Church schools and sometimes State schools as well. My contact with these schools has greatly increased my respect for the teaching profession, not least for those who undertake the extremely difficult task of conveying the meaning of essential Christianity to the young mind. In my view we are starting off on the wrong foot if, in teaching Scripture, we insist on using language which is nearly three hundred and fifty years old. I would myself be among the first to admire and marvel at the beauty, the majesty and the moving rhythms of that version to which we of older generations are accustomed. But if the true meaning and relevance of the New Testament message is blunted and masked by archaic language, then I think we must, at least in our first approach, use language which is intelligible to modern children. There is a peculiar danger here: if school prayers and scripture readings are invariably couched in outdated language, then it is very unlikely that the children will think of God as in any sense contemporary, and it is probable that they will tend to regard the New Testament story as a holy legend far away and long ago. If we are to help in the development of Christian citizens for the future it is imperative that we teach the New Testament as containing spiritual essentials for modern living. If this book helps that admirable army of teachers in the vital art of communicating what I believe to be most urgent to communicate, then one of my greatest hopes will be realised.

May I add a short practical note? In order to make this translation more useful for schools the verse numbers of the Authorised Version have been printed in the margin. There are some cases where the sense of two or three verses has been combined, and a few where, for the sake of clarity, a phrase from one verse has been transferred to another. Here the Authorised Version verse numbers have been retained, but it will be quite obvious what has happened. In some instances, particularly in *The Gospels*, a verse will be found to be omitted altogether in my version. The reason for this is simply that I have worked from later and more reliable Texts than those available to the translators of 1611. One verse has been transferred, that is, Revelation 18, *14*, and here there is an explanatory footnote.

J. B. PHILLIPS

1959

CONTENTS

CONTENTS

MAPS

THE GOSPELS

The Gospel of Matthew

Early tradition ascribed this Gospel to the apostle Matthew, but scholars nowadays almost all reject this view.

The author, whom we still can conveniently call Matthew, has plainly drawn on the mysterious "Q", which may have been a collection of oral traditions. He has used Mark's Gospel freely, though he has rearranged the order of events and has in several instances used different words for what is plainly the same story. The style is lucid, calm and "tidy". Matthew writes with a certain judiciousness as though he himself had carefully digested his material and is convinced not only of its truth but of the divine pattern that lies behind the historic facts.

Matthew is quite plainly a Jew who has been convinced of Jesus' messianic claim. It is probable that he is writing primarily for fellow Jews. The frequent references to the Old Testament, the sense that Jesus' primary mission is to the "lost sheep" of the house of Israel and the implication that the Church, founded on the rock of Peter's faith, is the new Israel, all bear the marks of a converted Jew writing for fellow Jews. He attempts to convey a logical conviction that the new teaching was not only prophesied in the old but does in fact supersede it in the divine plan.

If Matthew wrote, as is now generally supposed, somewhere between the years 85 and 90, this Gospel's value as a Christian document is enormous. It is, so to speak, a second generation view of Jesus Christ the Son of God and the Son of Man. It is being written at that distance in time from the great event where sober reflection and sturdy conviction can perhaps give a better balanced portrait of God's unique revelation of himself than could be given by those who were so close to the light that they were partly dazzled by it.

1

CHAPTER 1

The ancestry of Jesus Christ

1 THIS is the record of the ancestry of Jesus Christ who was the
2 descendant of both David and Abraham:

   Abraham was the father of Isaac, who was the father of Jacob,
3 who was the father of Judah and his brothers, who was the father
   of Perez and Zerah (whose mother was Tamar). Perez was the
4 father of Hezron, who was the father of Ram, who was the father
   of Amminadab, who was the father of Nahshon, who was the
5 father of Salmon, who was the father of Boaz (whose mother was
   Rahab). Boaz was the father of Obed (whose mother was Ruth),
6 and Obed was the Father of Jesse, who was the father of King
   David, who was the father of Solomon (whose mother was Uriah's
7 wife). Solomon was the father of Rehoboam, who was the father
8 of Abijah, who was the father of Asa, who was the father of
   Jehoshaphat, who was the father of Joram, who was the father
9 of Uzziah, who was the father of Jotham, who was the father of
10 Ahaz, who was the father of Hezekiah, who was the father of
   Manasseh, who was the father of Amon, who was the father of
11 Josiah, who was the father of Jechoniah and his brothers, at the
   time of the deportation to Babylon.
12   After the Babylonian exile Jechoniah was the father of Shealtiel,
13 who was the father of Zerubbabel, who was the father of Abiud,
14 who was the father of Eliakim, who was the father of Azor, who
   was the father of Sadoc, who was the father of Achim, who was
15 the father of Eliud, who was the father of Eleazar, who was the
16 father of Matthan, who was the father of Jacob, who was the father
   of Joseph, who was the husband of Mary, the mother of Jesus
   Christ.
17   The genealogy of Jesus Christ may thus be traced for fourteen
   generations from Abraham to David, fourteen from David to the
   deportation to Babylon, and fourteen more from the deportation
   to Christ himself.

His birth in human history

18   The birth of Jesus Christ happened like this. When Mary was
   engaged to Joseph, just before their marriage, she was discovered
19 to be pregnant—by the Holy Spirit. Whereupon Joseph, her
   future husband, who was a good man and did not want to see her

2

disgraced, planned to break off the engagement quietly. But while 20
he was turning the matter over in his mind an angel of the Lord
appeared to him in a dream and said, "Joseph, son of David, do
not be afraid to take Mary as your wife! What she has conceived
is conceived through the Holy Spirit, and she will give birth to a 21
son, whom you will call Jesus ('the Saviour') for it is he who will
save his people from their sins."

All this happened to fulfil what the Lord has said through the 22
prophet—

> Behold, the virgin shall be with child, and shall bring forth 23
> a son, and they shall call his name Immanuel. ("Immanuel"
> means "God with us.")

When Joseph woke up he did what the angel had told him. He 24
married Mary, but had no intercourse with her until she had given 25
birth to a son. Then he gave him the name Jesus.

CHAPTER 2

Herod, suspicious of the new-born king, takes vindictive precautions

JESUS was born in Bethlehem, in Judaea, in the days when Herod 1
was king of the province. Not long after his birth there arrived
from the east a party of astrologers making for Jerusalem and
enquiring as they went, "Where is the child born to be king of the 2
Jews ? For we saw his star in the east and we have come here to pay
homage to him."

When King Herod heard about this he was deeply perturbed, 3
as indeed were all the other people living in Jerusalem. So he 4
summoned all the Jewish scribes* and chief priests together and
asked them where "Christ" should be born. Their reply was: "In 5
Bethlehem, in Judea, for this is what the prophet wrote about the
matter—

> And thou Bethlehem, land of Judah, 6
> Art in no wise least among the princes of Judah:
> For out of thee shall come forth a governor,
> Which shall be shepherd of my people Israel."

Then Herod invited the wise men to meet him privately and 7
found out from them the exact time when the star appeared. Then 8
he sent them off to Bethlehem saying, "When you get there, search
for this little child with the utmost care. And when you have found
him come back and tell me—so that I may go and worship him too."

* See note 1, page 551.

9 The wise men listened to the king and then went on their way to Bethlehem. And now the star, which they had seen in the east, went in front of them as they travelled until at last it shone
10 immediately above the place where the little child lay. The sight of the star filled them with indescribable joy.
11 So they went into the house and saw the little child with his mother Mary. And they fell on their knees and worshipped him. Then they opened their treasures and presented him with gifts— gold, incense and myrrh.
12 Then, since they were warned in a dream not to return to Herod, they went back to their own country by a different route.
13 But after they had gone the angel of the Lord appeared to Joseph in a dream and said, "Get up now, take the little child and his mother and escape to Egypt. Stay there until I tell you. For Herod means to seek out the child and kill him."
14 So Joseph got up, and taking the child and his mother with him
15 in the middle of the night, set off for Egypt, where he remained until Herod's death.

This again is a fulfilment of the Lord's word spoken through the prophet—

Out of Egypt did I call my son

16 When Herod saw that he had been fooled by the wise men he was furiously angry. He issued orders, and killed all the male children of two years and under in Bethlehem and the surrounding district—basing his calculation on his careful questioning of the wise men.
17 Then Jeremiah's prophecy was fulfilled:
18 A voice was heard in Ramah,
Weeping and great mourning,
Rachel weeping for her children;
And she would not be comforted, because they are not.

Jesus is brought to Nazareth

19 But after Herod's death an angel of the Lord again appeared to
20 Joseph in a dream and said, "Now get up and take the infant and his mother with you and go into the land of Israel. For those who sought the child's life are dead."
21 So Joseph got up and took the little child and his mother with
22 him and journeyed towards the land of Israel. But when he heard that Archelaus was now reigning as king of Judaea in the place of

his father Herod, he was afraid to enter the country. Then he received warning in a dream to turn aside into the district of Galilee and came to live in a small town called Nazareth— *23* thus fulfilling the old prophecy, that he should be called a Nazarene.

CHAPTER 3

The prophesied "Elijah": John the Baptist

In due course John the Baptist arrived, preaching in the *1* Judaean desert: "You must change your hearts—for the kingdom *2* of Heaven has arrived!"

This was the man whom the prophet Isaiah spoke about in the *3* words:

> The voice of one crying in the wilderness,
> Make ye ready the way of the Lord,
> Make his paths straight.

John wore clothes of camel-hair with a leather belt round his *4* waist, and lived on locusts and wild honey. The people of Jerusalem and of all Judaea and the Jordan district flocked to him, and *5* were baptised by him in the river Jordan, publicly confessing their *6* sins.

But when he saw many Pharisees and Sadducees* coming for *7* baptism he said: "Who warned you, you serpent's brood, to escape from the wrath to come? Go and do something to show *8* that your hearts are really changed. Don't suppose that you can *9* say to yourselves, 'We are Abraham's children', for I tell you that God could produce children of Abraham out of these stones!

"The axe already lies at the root of the tree, and the tree that *10* fails to produce good fruit will be cut down and thrown into the fire. It is true that I baptise you with water as a sign of your *11* repentance, but the one who follows me is far stronger than I am —indeed, I am not fit to carry his shoes. He will baptise you with the fire of the Holy Spirit. He comes all ready to separate the *12* wheat from the chaff and very thoroughly will he clear his threshing-floor—the wheat he will collect into the granary and the chaff he will burn with a fire that can never be put out."

* See note 1, page 551.

5

John baptises Jesus

13 Then Jesus came from Galilee to the Jordan to be baptised by
14 John. But John tried to prevent him. "I need you to baptise *me*",
15 he said. "Surely *you* do not come to me?" But Jesus replied, "It
is right for us to meet all the Law's demands—let it be so
now."

16 Then John agreed to his baptism. Jesus came straight out of the
water afterwards, and suddenly the heavens opened and he saw
the Spirit of God coming down like a dove and resting upon him.

17 And a voice came out of Heaven saying, "This is my dearly-loved
Son, in whom I am well pleased."

CHAPTER 4

Jesus faces temptation alone in the desert

1 THEN Jesus was led by the Spirit up into the desert, to be
2 tempted by the devil. After a fast of forty days and nights he was
very hungry.

3 "If you really are the Son of God," said the tempter, coming to
him, "tell these stones to turn into loaves."

4 Jesus answered, "The scripture says 'Man shall not live by
bread alone, but by every word that proceedeth out of the mouth
of God'."

5 Then the devil took him to the holy city, and set him on the
6 highest ledge of the Temple. "If you really are the Son of God,"
he said, "throw yourself down. For the scripture says—

He shall give his angels charge concerning thee:
And on their hands they shall bear thee up,
Lest haply thou dash thy foot against a stone."

7 "Yes," retorted Jesus, "and the scripture also says 'Thou shalt
not tempt the Lord thy God'."

8 Once again the devil took him to a very high mountain, and
from there showed him all the kingdoms of the world and their
9 magnificence. "Everything there I will give you," he said to him,
"if you will fall down and worship me."

10 "Away with you, Satan!" replied Jesus, "the scripture says,
Thou shalt worship the Lord thy God, and him only shalt
thou serve."

11 Then the devil let him alone, and angels came to him and took
care of him.

6

Jesus begins his ministry, in Galilee, and calls his first disciples

Now when Jesus heard that John had been arrested he went 12
back to Galilee. He left Nazareth and came to live in Capernaum, 13
a lake-side town in the Zebulun-Naphtali territory. In this way 14
Isaiah's prophecy came true:

> The land of Zebulun and the land of Naphtali, 15
> Toward the sea, beyond Jordan,
> Galilee of the Gentiles,
> The people which sat in darkness 16
> Saw a great light,
> And to them which sat in the region and shadow of death,
> To them did light spring up.

From that time Jesus began to preach and to say, "You must 17
change your hearts—for the kingdom of Heaven has arrived."

While he was walking by the lake of Galilee he saw two 18
brothers, Simon (Peter) and Andrew, casting their large net into
the water. They were fishermen, so Jesus said to them, 19
"Follow me and I will teach you to catch men!"

At once they left their nets and followed him. 20

Then he went further on and saw two more men, also brothers, 21
James and John. They were aboard the boat with their father
Zebedee repairing their nets, and he called them. At once they 22
left the boat, and their father, and followed him.

Jesus teaches, preaches and heals

Jesus now moved about through the whole of Galilee, teaching 23
in their synagogues and preaching the good news about the
kingdom, and healing every disease and disability among the
people. His reputation spread throughout Syria, and people 24
brought to him all those who were ill, suffering from all kinds of
diseases and pains—including the devil-possessed, the insane and
the paralysed. He healed them, and was followed by enormous 25
crowds from Galilee, the Ten Towns, Jerusalem, Judaea, and
from beyond the river Jordan.

CHAPTER 5

Jesus proclaims the new values of the kingdom

WHEN Jesus saw the vast crowds he went up the hill-side and 1
after he had sat down his disciples came to him.

7

2 Then he began his teaching by saying to them,

3 "How happy are the humble-minded, for the kingdom of Heaven is theirs!

4 "How happy are those who know what sorrow means, for they will be given courage and comfort!

5 "Happy are those who claim nothing, for the whole earth will belong to them!

6 "Happy are those who are hungry and thirsty for goodness, for they will be fully satisfied!

7 "Happy are the merciful, for they will have mercy shown to them!

8 "Happy are the utterly sincere, for they will see God!

9 "Happy are those who make peace, for they will be known as sons of God!

10 "Happy are those who have suffered persecution for the cause of goodness, for the kingdom of Heaven is theirs!

11 "And what happiness will be yours when people blame you and ill-treat you and say all kinds of slanderous things against you

12 for my sake! Be glad then, yes, be tremendously glad—for your reward in Heaven is magnificent. They persecuted the prophets before your time in exactly the same way.

13 "You are the earth's salt. But if the salt should become tasteless, what can make it salt again? It is completely useless and can only be thrown out of doors and stamped under foot.

14 "You are the world's light—it is impossible to hide a town built
15 on the top of a hill. Men do not light a lamp and put it under a bucket. They put it on a lamp-stand and it gives light for everybody in the house.

16 "Let your light shine like that in the sight of men. Let them see the good things you do and praise your Father in Heaven.

Christ's authority surpasses that of the Law

17 "You must not think that I have come to abolish the Law or the Prophets; I have not come to abolish them but to complete
18 them. Indeed, I assure you that, while Heaven and earth last, the Law will not lose a single dot or comma until its purpose is
19 complete. This means that whoever now relaxes one of the least of these commandments and teaches men to do the same will himself be called least in the kingdom of Heaven. But whoever teaches and practises them will be called great in the kingdom of
20 Heaven. For I tell you that your goodness must be a far better

thing than the goodness of the scribes and Pharisees before you can set foot in the kingdom of Heaven at all!

"You have heard that it was said to the people in the old days, 21 'Thou shalt not murder', and anyone who does so must stand his trial. But I say to you that anyone who is angry with his brother 22 must stand his trial; anyone who contemptuously calls his brother a fool* must face the supreme court; and anyone who looks down on his brother as a lost soul is himself heading straight for the fire of destruction.

"So that if, while you are offering your gift at the altar, you 23 should remember that your brother has something against you, you must leave your gift there before the altar and go away. Make 24 your peace with your brother first, then come and offer your gift. Come to terms quickly with your opponent while you have the 25 chance, or else he may hand you over to the judge and the judge in turn hand you over to the officer of the court and you will be thrown into prison. Believe me, you will never get out again till 26 you have paid your last farthing!

"You have heard that it was said to the people in the old days, 27 'Thou shalt not commit adultery.' But I say to you that every man 28 who looks at a woman lustfully has already committed adultery with her—in his heart.

"Yes, if your right eye leads you astray pluck it out and throw 29 it away; it is better for you to lose one of your members than that your whole body should be thrown on to the rubbish-heap.

"Yes, if your right hand leads you astray cut it off and throw it 30 away; it is better for you to lose one of your members than that your whole body should go to the rubbish-heap.

"It also used to be said that whoever divorces his wife must 31 give her a proper certificate of divorce. But I say to you that 32 whoever divorces his wife except on the ground of unfaithfulness is making her an adulteress. And whoever marries the woman who has been divorced also commits adultery.

"Again, you have heard that the people in the old days were 33 told—'Thou shalt not forswear thyself, but shalt perform unto the Lord thine oaths', but I say to you, don't use an oath at all. Don't 34 swear by Heaven for it is God's throne, nor by the earth for it is 35 his footstool, nor by Jerusalem for it is the city of the great king. No, and don't swear by your own head, for you cannot make a 36 single hair—white or black! Whatever you have to say let your 37

* See note 2, page 551.

'yes' be a plain 'yes' and your 'no' be a plain 'no'—anything more than this has a taint of evil.

38 "You have heard that it used to be said 'An eye for an eye and a
39 tooth for a tooth', but I tell you, don't resist the man who wants to harm you. If a man hits your right cheek, turn the other one to
40 him as well. If a man wants to sue you for your coat, let him have
41 it and your overcoat as well. If anybody forces you to go a mile
42 with him, do more—go two miles with him. Give to the man who asks anything from you, and don't turn away from the man who wants to borrow.

43 "You have heard that it used to be said 'Thou shalt love thy
44 neighbour and hate thine enemy', but I tell you, Love your
45 enemies, and pray for those who persecute you, so that you may be sons of your Heavenly Father. For he makes his sun rise upon evil men as well as good, and he sends his rain upon honest and dishonest men alike.

46 "For if you love only those who love you, what credit is that
47 to you? Even tax-collectors do that! And if you exchange greetings only with your own circle, are you doing anything excep-
48 tional? Even the pagans do that much. No, you are to be perfect, like your Heavenly Father.

CHAPTER 6

The new life is not a matter of outward show

1 "BEWARE of doing your good deeds conspicuously to catch men's eyes or you will miss the reward of your Heavenly Father.

2 "So, when you do good to other people, don't hire a trumpeter to go in front of you—like those play-actors in the synagogues and streets who make sure that men admire them. Believe me, they
3 have had all the reward they are going to get! No, when you give to charity, don't even let your left hand know what your right
4 hand is doing, so that your giving may be secret. Your Father who knows all secrets will reward you.

5 "And then, when you pray, don't be like the play-actors. They love to stand and pray in the synagogues and at street-corners so that people may see them at it. Believe me, they have had all
6 the reward they are going to get. But when you pray, go into your own room, shut your door and pray to your Father privately.
7 Your Father who sees all private things will reward you. And when you pray don't rattle off long prayers like the pagans who

think they will be heard because they use so many words. Don't 8
be like them. After all, God, who is your Father, knows your
needs before you ask him. Pray then like this— 9

Our Heavenly Father, may your name be honoured;
May your kingdom come, and your will be done on earth as it 10
is in Heaven.
Give us this day the bread we need, 11
Forgive us what we owe to you, as we have also forgiven those 12
who owe anything to us.
Keep us clear of temptation, and save us from evil. 13

Forgiveness of fellow-man is essential

"For if you forgive other people their failures, your Heavenly 14
Father will also forgive you. But if you will not forgive other 15
people, neither will your Heavenly Father forgive you your
failures.

"Then, when you fast, don't look like those miserable play- 16
actors! For they deliberately disfigure their faces so that people
may see that they are fasting. Believe me, they have had all their
reward. No, when you fast, brush your hair and wash your face 17
so that nobody knows that you are fasting—let it be a secret 18
between you and your Father. And your Father who knows all
secrets will reward you.

Put your trust in God alone

"Don't pile up treasures on earth, where moth and rust can spoil 19
them and thieves can break in and steal. But keep your treasure 20
in Heaven where there is neither moth nor rust to spoil it and
nobody can break in and steal. For wherever your treasure is, you 21
may be certain that your heart will be there too!

"The lamp of the body is the eye. If your eye is sound, your 22
whole body will be full of light. But if your eye is evil, your 23
whole body will be full of darkness. If all the light you have is
darkness, it is dark indeed!

"No one can be loyal to two masters. He is bound to hate one 24
and love the other, or support one and despise the other. You
cannot serve God and the power of money at the same time.
That is why I say to you, don't worry about living—wondering 25
what you are going to eat or drink, or what you are going to wear.
Surely life is more important than food, and the body more important than the clothes you wear. Look at the birds in the sky. 26

They never sow nor reap nor store away in barns, and yet your Heavenly Father feeds them. Aren't you much more valuable to
27 him than they are? Can any of you, however much he worries,
28 make himself an inch taller? And why do you worry about clothes? Consider how the wild flowers grow. They neither work
29 nor weave, but I tell you that even Solomon in all his glory was
30 never arrayed like one of these! Now if God so clothes the flowers of the field, which are alive today and burnt in the stove tomorrow, is he not much more likely to clothe you, you 'little-faiths'?
31 "So don't worry and don't keep saying, 'What shall we eat,
32 what shall we drink or what shall we wear?'! That is what pagans are always looking for; your Heavenly Father knows that you
33 need them all. Set your heart on his kingdom and his goodness, and all these things will come to you as a matter of course.
34 "Don't worry at all then about tomorrow. Tomorrow can take care of itself! One day's trouble is enough for one day.

CHAPTER 7

The common sense behind right behaviour

1, 2 "DON'T criticise people, and you will not be criticised. For you will be judged by the way you criticise others, and the measure you give will be the measure you receive.
3 "Why do you look at the speck of sawdust in your brother's
4 eye and fail to notice the plank in your own? How can you say to your brother, 'Let me get the speck out of your eye', when
5 there is a plank in your own? You fraud! Take the plank out of your own eye first, and then you can see clearly enough to remove your brother's speck of dust.
6 "You must not give holy things to dogs, nor must you throw your pearls before pigs—or they may trample them underfoot and turn and attack you.
7 "Ask and it will be given to you. Search and you will find.
8 Knock and the door will be opened for you. The one who asks will always receive; the one who is searching will always find, and the door is opened to the man who knocks.
9 "If any of you were asked by his son for bread would you be
10 likely to give him a stone, or if he asks for a fish would you give
11 him a snake? If you then, for all your evil, quite naturally give good things to your children, how much more likely is it that your Heavenly Father will give good things to those who ask him?

12

"Treat other people exactly as you would like to be treated by *12*
them—this is the essence of all true religion.

"Go in by the narrow gate. For the wide gate has a broad road *13*
which leads to disaster and there are many people going that way.
The narrow gate and the hard road lead out into life and only a *14*
few are finding it.

Living, not professing, is what matters

"Be on your guard against false religious teachers, who come *15*
to you dressed up as sheep but are really greedy wolves. You can *16*
tell them by their fruit. Do you pick a bunch of grapes from a
thorn-bush or figs from a clump of thistles? Every good tree *17*
produces good fruit, but a bad tree produces bad fruit. A good *18*
tree is incapable of producing bad fruit, and a bad tree cannot produce good fruit. The tree that fails to produce good *19*
fruit is cut down and burnt. So you may know men by their *20*
fruit.

"It is not everyone who keeps saying to me 'Lord, Lord' who *21*
will enter the kingdom of Heaven, but the man who actually does
my Heavenly Father's will.

"In 'that day' many will say to me, 'Lord, Lord, didn't we *22*
preach in your name, didn't we cast out devils in your name, and
do many great things in your name?' Then I shall tell them *23*
plainly, 'I have never known you. Go away from me, you have
worked on the side of evil!'

To follow Christ's teaching means the only real security

"Everyone then who hears these words of mine and puts them *24*
into practice is like a sensible man who builds his house on the
rock. Down came the rain and up came the floods, while the *25*
winds blew and roared upon that house—and it did not fall
because its foundations were on the rock.

"And everyone who hears these words of mine and does not *26*
follow them can be compared with a foolish man who built his
house on the sand. Down came the rain and up came the floods, *27*
while the winds blew and battered that house till it collapsed, and
fell with a great crash."

When Jesus had finished these words the crowd were astonished *28*
at the power behind his teaching. For his words had the ring of *29*
authority, quite unlike those of their scribes.

CHAPTER 8

Jesus cures leprosy, and heals many other people

1 LARGE crowds followed him when he came down from the hill-
2 side. There was a leper who came and knelt in front of him. "Sir,"
3 he said, "if you want to, you can make me clean." Jesus stretched
out his hand and placed it on the leper saying, "Of course I want
to. Be clean!" And at once he was clear of the leprosy.

4 "Mind you say nothing to anybody," Jesus told him. "Go
straight off and show yourself to the priest and make the offering
for your recovery that Moses prescribed, as evidence to the
authorities."

5 Then as he was coming into Capernaum a centurion approached.
6 "Sir," he implored him, "my servant is in bed at home paralysed
and in dreadful pain."

7 "I will come and heal him," said Jesus to him.

8 "Sir," replied the centurion, "I'm not important enough for
you to come under my roof. Just give the order, please, and my
9 servant will recover. I'm a man under authority myself, and I
have soldiers under me. I can say to one man 'Go' and I know
he'll go, or I can say 'Come here' to another and I know he'll
come—or I can say to my slave 'Do this' and he'll always do it."

10 When Jesus heard this, he was astonished. "Believe me," he
said to those who were following him, "I have never found faith
11 like this, even in Israel! I tell you that many people will come from
east and west and sit at my table with Abraham, Isaac and Jacob
12 in the kingdom of Heaven. But those who should have belonged
to the kingdom will be banished to the darkness outside, where
there will be tears and bitter regret."

13 Then he said to the centurion, "Go home now, and everything
will happen as you have believed it will."

And his servant was healed at that actual moment.

14 Then, on coming into Peter's house Jesus saw that Peter's
15 mother-in-law had been put to bed with a high fever. He touched
her hand and the fever left her. And then she got up and began
to see to their needs.

16 When evening came they brought to him many who were
possessed by evil spirits, which he expelled with a word. Indeed,
17 he healed all who were ill. Thus was fulfilled Isaiah's prophecy—
Himself took our infirmities and bare our diseases.

When Jesus had seen the great crowds around him he gave 18
orders for departure to the other side of the lake. But before they 19
started, one of the scribes came up to Jesus and said to him,
"Master, I will follow you wherever you go."

"Foxes have earths, birds in the sky have nests, but the Son 20
of Man has nowhere that he can call his own," replied Jesus.

Another of his disciples said, "Lord, let me first go and bury 21
my father."

But Jesus said to him, "Follow me, and leave the dead to bury 22
their own dead."

Jesus shows his mastery over the forces of nature

Then he went aboard the boat, and his disciples followed him. 23
Before long a terrific storm sprang up and the boat was awash 24
with the waves. Jesus was sleeping soundly and the disciples went 25
forward and woke him up.

"Lord, save us!" they cried. "We are drowning!"

"What are you so frightened about, you little-faiths?" he replied. 26

Then he got to his feet and rebuked the wind and the waters
and there was a great calm. The men were filled with astonish- 27
ment and kept saying, "Whatever sort of man is this—why, even
the wind and the waves do what he tells them!"

When he arrived on the other side (which is the Gadarenes' 28
country) he was met by two devil-possessed men who came out
from among the tombs. They were so violent that nobody dared
to use that road.

"What have you got to do with us, Jesus, you Son of God?" 29
they screamed at him. "Have you come to torture us before the
proper time?"

It happened that in the distance there was a large herd of pigs 30
feeding. So the devils implored him, "If you throw us out, send 31
us into the herd of pigs!"

"Then go!" said Jesus to them. 32

And the devils came out of the two men and went into the pigs.
Then quite suddenly the whole herd rushed madly down a steep
cliff into the lake and were drowned.

The swineherds took to their heels, and ran to the town. There 33
they poured out the whole story, not forgetting what had
happened to the two men who had been devil-possessed. Where- 34
upon the whole town came out to meet Jesus, and as soon as they
saw him implored him to leave their territory.

R—N.T.—B 15

CHAPTER 9

Jesus heals in his own town

1 So Jesus re-embarked on the boat, crossed the lake, and came
2 to his own town. Immediately some people arrived bringing him
a paralytic lying flat on his bed. When Jesus saw the faith of those
who brought him he said to the paralytic, "Cheer up, my son!
Your sins are forgiven."

3 At once some of the scribes thought to themselves, "This man
4 is blaspheming". But Jesus realised what they were thinking, and
said to them, "Why must you have such evil thoughts in your
5 minds ? Do you think it is easier to say to this man, 'Your sins are
6 forgiven' or 'Get up and walk' ? But to make it quite plain that
the Son of Man has full authority on earth to forgive sins"—and
here he spoke to the paralytic—"Get up, pick up your bed and go
7, 8 home." And the man sprang to his feet and went home. When
the crowds saw what had happened they were filled with awe
and praised God for giving such power to men.

Jesus calls a "sinner" to be his disciple

9 Jesus left there and as he passed on he saw a man called Matthew
sitting at his desk in the tax-collector's office.
"Follow me!" he said to him—and the man got to his feet and
followed him.
10 Later, as Jesus was in the house sitting at the dinner-table, a
good many tax-collectors and other disreputable people came on the
11 scene and joined him and his disciples. The Pharisees noticed this
and said to the disciples, "Why does your master have his meals
12 with tax-collectors and sinners ?" But Jesus heard this and replied,
"It is not the fit and flourishing who need the doctor, but those
13 who are ill! Suppose you go away and learn what this means:
'I desire mercy and not sacrifice.' In any case I did not come to
invite the 'righteous' but the 'sinners'."

He explains the joy and strength of the new order

14 Then John's disciples approached him with the question, "Why
is it that we and the Pharisees observe the fasts, but your disciples
do nothing of the kind ?"

"Can you expect wedding-guests to mourn while they have *15* the bridegroom with them?" replied Jesus. "The day will come when the bridegroom will be taken away from them—they will certainly fast then!

"Nobody sews a patch of unshrunken cloth on to an old coat, *16* for the patch will pull away from the coat and the hole will be worse than ever. Nor do people put new wine into old wineskins *17* —otherwise the skins burst, the wine is spilt and the skins are ruined. But they put new wine into new skins and both are preserved."

Jesus heals a young girl, and several others in need

While he was saying these things to them an official came up *18* to him and, bowing low before him, said,

"My daughter has just this moment died. Please come and lay your hand on her and she will come back to life!"

At this Jesus got to his feet and followed him, accompanied by *19* his disciples. And on the way a woman who had had a haemor- *20* rhage for twelve years approached him from behind and touched the edge of his cloak.

"If I can only touch his cloak," she kept saying to herself, "I *21* shall be all right."

But Jesus turned right round and saw her. *22*

"Cheer up, my daughter," he said, "your faith has made you well!" And the woman was completely cured from that moment.

Then when Jesus came into the official's house and noticed the *23* flute-players and the noisy crowd he said, "You must all go *24* outside; the little girl is not dead, she is fast asleep."

This was met with scornful laughter. But when Jesus had *25* forced the crowd to leave, he came right into the room, took hold of her hand, and the girl got up. And this became the talk of the *26* whole district.

As Jesus passed on his way two blind men followed him with *27* the cry, "Have pity on us, Son of David!" And when he had gone *28* inside the house these two came up to him.

"Do you believe I can do it?" he said to them.

"Yes, Lord," they replied.

Then he touched their eyes, saying, "You have believed and *29* you will not be disappointed."

Then their sight returned, but Jesus sternly warned them, *30*

31 "Don't let anyone know about this." Yet they went outside and spread the story throughout the whole district.

32 Later, when Jesus and his party were coming out, they brought
33 to him a dumb man who was possessed by a devil. As soon as the devil had been ejected the dumb man began to talk. The crowds were simply amazed and said, "Nothing like this has ever been
34 seen in Israel." But the Pharisees' comment was, "He throws out these devils because he is in league with the devil himself."

Jesus is touched by the people's need

35 Jesus now travelled through all the towns and villages, teaching in their synagogues, proclaiming the gospel of the kingdom, and
36 healing all kinds of illness and disability. As he looked at the vast crowds he was deeply moved with pity for them, for they were as bewildered and miserable as a flock of sheep with no shepherd.

37 "The harvest is great enough," he remarked to his disciples,
38 "but the reapers are few. So you must pray to the Lord of the harvest to send men out to reap it."

CHAPTER 10

Jesus sends out the twelve with divine power

1 JESUS called his twelve disciples to him and gave them authority to expel evil spirits and heal all kinds of disease and infirmity.
2 The names of the twelve apostles were:

First, Simon, called Peter, with his brother Andrew;
James and his brother John, sons of Zebedee;
3 Philip and Bartholomew,
Thomas, and Matthew the tax-collector,
James, the son of Alphaeus, and Thaddaeus,
4 Simon the Patriot, and Judas Iscariot, who later turned traitor.

5 These were the twelve whom Jesus sent out, with the instructions: "Don't turn off into any of the heathen roads, and don't go
6 into any Samaritan town. Concentrate on the lost sheep of the
7 house of Israel. As you go proclaim that the kingdom of Heaven
8 has arrived. Heal the sick, raise the dead, cure the lepers, drive out devils—give, as you have received, without any charge whatever.
9 "Don't take any gold or silver or even coppers to put in your

purse; nor a knapsack for the journey, nor even a change of *10*
clothes, or sandals or a staff—the workman is worth his keep!

"Wherever you go, whether it is into a town or a village, find *11*
out someone who is respected, and stay with him until you leave.
As you enter his house give it your blessing. If the house *12,13*
deserves it, the peace of your blessing will come to it. But if it
doesn't, your peace will return to you.

"And if no one will welcome you or even listen to what you *14*
have to say, leave that house or town, and once outside it shake
off the dust of that place from your feet. Believe me, Sodom and *15*
Gomorrah will fare better in the day of judgment than that town.

He warns them of troubles that lie ahead

"Here am I sending you out like sheep with wolves all round *16*
you; so be as wise as serpents and yet as harmless as doves. But be *17*
on your guard against men. For they will take you to the courts
and flog you in their synagogues. You will be brought into the *18*
presence of governors and kings because of me—to give your
witness to them and to the heathen.

"But when they do arrest you, never worry about how you are *19*
to speak or what you are to say. You will be told at the time what
you are to say. For it will not be really you who are speaking but *20*
the Spirit of your Father speaking through you.

"Brothers are going to betray their brothers to death, and *21*
fathers their children. Children are going to betray their parents
and have them executed. You yourselves will be universally *22*
hated because of my name. But the man who endures to the
very end will be safe and sound.

"But when they persecute you in one town make your escape *23*
to the next. Believe me, you will not have covered the towns of
Israel before the Son of Man arrives. The disciple is not superior *24*
to his teacher any more than the servant is superior to his master,
for what is good enough for the teacher is good enough for the *25*
disciple as well, and the servant will not fare better than his
master. If men call the master of the household the 'Prince of
Evil', what sort of names will they give to his servants? But never *26*
let them frighten you, for there is nothing covered up which is
not going to be exposed nor anything private which will not be
made public. The things I tell you in the dark you must say in the *27*
daylight, and the things you hear in your private ear you must
proclaim from the house-tops.

They should reverence God but have no fear of man

28 "Never be afraid of those who can kill the body but are powerless to kill the soul! Far better to stand in awe of the one who has the power to destroy body and soul in the fires of destruction!

29 "Two sparrows sell for a farthing, don't they? Yet not a single sparrow falls to the ground without your Father's knowledge.

30, 31 The very hairs of your head are all numbered. Never be afraid, then—you are far more valuable than sparrows.

32 "Every man who publicly acknowledges me I shall acknow-
33 ledge in the presence of my Father in Heaven, but the man who disowns me before men I shall disown before my Father in Heaven.

The Prince of Peace comes to bring division

34 "Never think I have come to bring peace upon the earth. No,
35 I have not come to bring peace but a sword! For I have come to set a man against his own father, a daughter against her own
36 mother, and a daughter-in-law against her mother-in-law. A man's enemies will be those who live in his own house.

37 "Anyone who puts his love for father or mother above his love for me does not deserve to be mine, and he who loves son or
38 daughter more than me is not worthy of me, and neither is the
39 man who refuses to take up his cross and follow my way. The man who has found his own life will lose it, but the man who has lost it for my sake will find it.

40 "Whoever welcomes you, welcomes me; and whoever welcomes me is welcoming the one who sent me.

41 "Whoever welcomes a prophet just because he is a prophet will get a prophet's reward. And whoever welcomes a good man just
42 because he is a good man will get a good man's reward. Believe me, anyone who gives even a drink of water to one of these little ones, just because he is my disciple, will by no means lose his reward."

CHAPTER 11

WHEN Jesus had finished giving his twelve disciples these in-   *1*
structions he went on from there to teach and preach in the towns
in which they lived.

John enquires about Christ: Christ speaks about John

John the Baptist was in prison when he heard what Christ was   *2*
doing, and he sent a message through his own disciples asking the   *3*
question, "Are you the one who was to come or are we to look for
somebody else?"
Jesus gave them this reply, "Go and tell John what you see and   *4*
hear—that blind men are recovering their sight, cripples are   *5*
walking, lepers being healed, the deaf hearing, the dead being
brought to life and the good news is being given to those in need.
And happy is the man who never loses his faith in me."   *6*
As John's disciples were going away Jesus began talking to the   *7*
crowd about John:
"What did you go out into the desert to look at? A reed waving
in the breeze? No? Then *what* was it you went out to see?—a man   *8*
dressed in fine clothes? But the men who wear fine clothes live in
the courts of kings! But what did you really go to see—a prophet?   *9*
Yes, I tell you, a prophet and far more than a prophet! This is the   *10*
man of whom the scripture says—
Behold, I send my messenger before thy face,
Who shall prepare thy way before thee.
"Believe me, no one greater than John the Baptist has ever been   *11*
born of all mankind, and yet a humble member of the kingdom of
Heaven is greater than he.
"From the days of John the Baptist until now the kingdom of   *12*
Heaven has been taken by storm and eager men are forcing their
way into it. For the Law and all the Prophets foretold it till the   *13*
time of John and—if you can believe it—John himself is the   *14*
'Elijah' who must come before the kingdom. The man who has   *15*
ears to hear must use them!
"But how can I show what the people of this generation are   *16*
like? They are like children sitting in the market-place calling out
to their friends, 'We played at weddings for you but you wouldn't   *17*
dance, and we played at funerals and you wouldn't cry!' For   *18*

John came in the strictest austerity and people say, 'He's crazy!'
19 Then the Son of Man came, enjoying life, and people say, 'Look, a drunkard and a glutton—the bosom-friend of the tax-collector and the sinner.' Ah, well, wisdom stands or falls by her own actions."

Jesus denounces apathy—and thanks God that simple men understand his message

20 Then Jesus began reproaching the towns where most of his miracles had taken place because their hearts were unchanged.

21 "Alas for you, Chorazin! Alas for you, Bethsaida! For if Tyre and Sidon had seen the demonstrations of God's power which you have seen they would have repented long ago in sackcloth and
22 ashes. Yet I tell you this, that it will be more bearable for Tyre and Sidon in the day of judgment than for you.

23 "And as for you, Capernaum, are you on your way up to Heaven? I tell you you will go hurtling down among the dead! If Sodom had seen the miracles that you have seen, Sodom would
24 be standing today. Yet I tell you now that it will be more bearable for the land of Sodom in the day of judgment than for you."

25 At this same time Jesus said, "O Father, Lord of Heaven and earth, I thank you for hiding these things from the clever and
26 intelligent and for showing them to mere children. Yes, I thank you, Father, that this was your will."

27 Then he said: "Everything has been put in my hands by my Father, and nobody knows the Son except the Father. Nor does anyone know the Father except the Son—and the man to whom the Son chooses to reveal him.

28 "Come to me, all of you who are weary and over-burdened,
29 and I will give you rest! Put on my yoke and learn from me. For I am gentle and humble in heart and you will find rest for your
30 souls. For my yoke is easy and my burden is light."

CHAPTER 12

Jesus rebukes the sabbatarians

1 IT happened then that Jesus passed through the cornfields on the Sabbath day. His disciples were hungry and began picking the
2 ears of wheat and eating them. But the Pharisees saw them do it.
"There, you see," they remarked to Jesus, "your disciples are doing what the Law forbids them to do on the Sabbath."

"Haven't any of you read what David did when he and his *3*
companions were hungry?" replied Jesus, "—how he went into *4*
the house of God and ate the presentation loaves, which he and
his followers were not allowed to eat since only priests can do so?

"Haven't any of you read in the Law that every Sabbath day *5*
priests in the Temple can break the Sabbath and yet remain
blameless? I tell you that there is something more important than *6*
the Temple here. If you had grasped the meaning of the scripture *7*
'I desire mercy and not sacrifice', you would not have been so
quick to condemn the innocent! For the Son of Man is master *8*
even of the Sabbath."

Leaving there he went into their synagogue, where there *9, 10*
happened to be a man with a shrivelled hand.

"Is it right to heal anyone on the Sabbath day?" they asked
him—hoping to bring a charge against him.

"If any of you had a sheep which fell into a ditch on the *11*
Sabbath day, would he not take hold of it and pull it out?" replied
Jesus. "How much more valuable is a man than a sheep? You see, *12*
it is right to do good on the Sabbath day."

Then Jesus said to the man, "Stretch out your hand!" He did *13*
stretch it out, and it was restored as sound as the other.

But the Pharisees went out and held a meeting against Jesus *14*
and discussed how they could get rid of him altogether.

Jesus retires to continue his work

But Jesus knew of this and he left the place. *15*
Large crowds followed him and he healed them all, with the *16*
strict injunction that they should not make him conspicuous by
their talk, thus fulfilling Isaiah's prophecy: *17*

Behold, my servant whom I have chosen; *18*
My beloved in whom my soul is well pleased:
I will put my Spirit upon him,
And he shall declare judgment to the gentiles.
He shall not strive, nor cry aloud; *19*
Neither shall anyone hear his voice in the streets.
A bruised reed shall he not break, *20*
And smoking flax shall he not quench,
Till he send forth judgment unto victory.
And in his name shall the gentiles hope. *21*

Then a devil-possessed man who could neither see nor speak *22*
was brought to Jesus. He healed him, so that the dumb man could

23 both speak and see. At this the whole crowd went wild with excitement, and people kept saying, "Can this be the Son of David?"

The Pharisees draw an evil conclusion, and Jesus rebukes them

24 But the Pharisees on hearing this remark said to each other, "This man is only expelling devils because he is in league with Beelzebub, the prince of devils."

25 Jesus knew what they were thinking and said to them, "Any kingdom divided against itself is bound to collapse, and no town
26 or household divided against itself can last for long. If it is Satan who is expelling Satan, then he is divided against himself—so how
27 do you suppose that his kingdom can continue? And if I expel devils because I am an ally of Beelzebub, what alliance do your sons make when they do the same thing? They can settle that
28 question for you! But if I am expelling devils by the Spirit of God,
29 then the kingdom of God has swept over you unawares! How do you suppose anyone could get into a strong man's house and steal his property unless he first tied up the strong man? But if he did that, he could ransack his whole house.

30 "The man who is not on my side is against me, and the man
31 who does not gather with me is really scattering. That is why I tell you that men may be forgiven for every sin and blasphemy,
32 but blasphemy against the Spirit cannot be forgiven. A man may say a word against the Son of Man and be forgiven, but whoever speaks against the Holy Spirit cannot be forgiven either in this world or in the world to come!

33 "You must choose between having a good tree with good fruit and a rotten tree with rotten fruit. For you can tell a tree at once by its fruit.

34 "You serpent's brood, how can you say anything good out of your evil hearts? For a man's words depend on what fills his heart.
35 A good man gives out good—from the goodness stored in his
36 heart; a bad man gives out evil—from his store of evil. I tell you that men will have to answer at the day of judgment for every
37 careless word they utter—for it is your words that will acquit you, and your words that will condemn you!"

Jesus refuses to give a sign

38 Then some of the scribes and Pharisees said, "Master, we want
39 to see a sign from you." But Jesus told them,

"It is an evil and unfaithful generation that craves for a sign, and no sign will be given to it—except the sign of the prophet Jonah. For just as Jonah was in the belly of that great sea-monster *40* for three days and nights, so will the Son of Man be in the heart of the earth for three days and nights. The men of Nineveh will *41* stand up with this generation in the judgment and will condemn it. For they did repent when Jonah preached to them, and you have more than Jonah's preaching with you now! The Queen of *42* the South will stand up in the judgment with this generation and will condemn it. For she came from the ends of the earth to listen to the wisdom of Solomon, and you have more than the wisdom of Solomon with you now!

The danger of spiritual emptiness

"When the evil spirit goes out of a man it wanders through *43* waterless places looking for rest and never finding it. Then it says, *44* 'I will go back to my house from which I came.' When it arrives it finds it unoccupied, but cleaned and all in order. Then it goes *45* and collects seven other spirits more evil than itself to keep it company, and they all go in and make themselves at home. The last state of that man is worse than the first—and that is just what will happen to this evil generation."

Jesus and his relations

While he was still talking to the crowds, his mother and *46* his brothers happened to be standing outside wanting to speak to him. Somebody said to him, "Look, your mother and your *47* brothers are outside wanting to speak to you." But Jesus replied *48* to the one who told him, "Who is my mother, and who are my brothers?"; then with a gesture of his hand towards his disciples *49* he went on, "There are my mother and brothers! For whoever *50* does the will of my Heavenly Father is brother and sister and mother to me."

CHAPTER 13

Jesus tells the parable of the seed

IT was on the same day that Jesus went out of the house and *1* sat down by the lake-side. Such great crowds collected round him *2*

that he went aboard a small boat and sat down while all the
3 people stood on the beach. He told them a great deal in parables,
and began:

4   "There was once a man who went out to sow. In his sowing
some of the seeds fell by the road-side and the birds swooped
5 down and gobbled them up. Some fell on stony patches where
they had very little soil. They sprang up quickly in the shallow
6 soil, but when the sun came up they were scorched by the heat
7 and withered away because they had no roots. Some seeds fell
among thorn-bushes and the thorns grew up and choked the life
8 out of them. But some fell on good soil and produced a crop—
some a hundred times what had been sown, some sixty and some
9 thirty times. The man who has ears to hear should use them!"

10   At this the disciples approached him and asked, "Why do you
talk to them in parables?"

11   "Because you have been given the chance to understand the
secrets of the kingdom of Heaven," replied Jesus, "but they have
12 not. For when a man has something, more is given to him till he
has plenty. But if he has nothing even his nothing will be taken
13 away from him. This is why I speak to them in these parables;
because they go through life with their eyes open, but see
nothing, and with their ears open, but understand nothing of what
14 they hear. They are the living fulfilment of Isaiah's prophecy
which says:

> By hearing ye shall hear, and shall in no wise understand;
> And seeing ye shall see, and shall in no wise perceive:
15 > For this people's heart is waxed gross,
> And their ears are dull of hearing,
> And their eyes they have closed;
> Lest haply they should perceive with their eyes,
> And hear with their ears,
> And understand with their heart,
> And should turn again,
> And I should heal them.

16   "But how fortunate you are to have eyes that see and ears that
17 hear! Believe me, a great many prophets and good men have
longed to see what you are seeing and they never saw it. Yes, and
they longed to hear what you are hearing and they never heard it.

18, 19   "Now listen to the parable of the sower. When a man hears the
message of the kingdom and does not grasp it, the evil one comes
and snatches away what was sown in his heart. This is like the
20 seed sown by the road-side. The seed sown on the stony patches

represents the man who hears the message and eagerly accepts it. But it has not taken root in him and does not last long—the 21 moment trouble or persecution arises through the message he gives up his faith at once. The seed sown among the thorns 22 represents the man who hears the message, and then the worries of this life and the illusions of wealth choke it to death and so it produces no 'crop' in his life. But the seed sown on good soil is the 23 man who both hears and understands the message. His life shows a good crop, a hundred, sixty or thirty times what was sown."

Good and evil grow side by side in this present world

Then he put another parable before them. "The kingdom of 24 Heaven," he said, "is like a man who sowed good seed in his field. But while his men were asleep his enemy came and sowed weeds 25 among the wheat, and went away. When the crop came up and 26 ripened, the weeds appeared as well. Then the owner's servants 27 came up to him and said, 'Sir, didn't you sow good seed in your field? Where did all these weeds come from?' 'Some blackguard 28 has done this to spite me,' he replied. 'Do you want us then to go out and pull them all up?' said the servants. 'No,' he returned, 29 'if you pull up the weeds now, you would pull up the wheat with them. Let them both grow together till the harvest. And 30 at harvest-time I shall tell the reapers, 'Collect all the weeds first and tie them up in bundles ready to burn, but collect the wheat and store it in my barn.' "

The kingdom's power of growth, and widespread influence

Then he put another parable before them: "the kingdom of 31 Heaven is like a tiny grain of mustard-seed which a man took and sowed in his field. As a seed it is the smallest of them all, but 32 it grows to be the biggest of all plants. It becomes a tree, big enough for birds to come and nest in its branches."

This is another of the parables he told them: "The kingdom of 33 Heaven is like yeast, taken by a woman and put into three measures of flour until the whole lot had risen."

All these things Jesus spoke to the crowd in parables, and he 34 did not speak to them at all without using parables—to fulfil the 35 prophecy:

I will open my mouth in parables;
I will utter things hidden from the foundation of the world.

Jesus again explains a parable to his disciples

36   Later, he left the crowds and went indoors, where his disciples came and said, "Please explain to us the parable of the weeds in the field."

37   "The one who sows the good seed is the Son of Man," replied
38   Jesus. "The field is the whole world. The good seed? That is the sons of the kingdom, while the weeds are the sons of the evil one.
39   The blackguard who sowed them is the devil. The harvest is the end of this world. The reapers are angels.

40   "Just as weeds are gathered up and burned in the fire so will it
41   happen at the end of this world. The Son of Man will send out his angels and they will uproot from the kingdom everything that is
42   spoiling it, and all those who live in defiance of its laws, and will throw them into the blazing furnace, where there will be tears
43   and bitter regret. Then the good will shine out like the sun in their Father's kingdom. The man who has ears should use them!

More pictures of the kingdom of Heaven

44   "Again, the kingdom of Heaven is like some treasure which has been buried in a field. A man finds it and buries it again, and goes off overjoyed to sell all his possessions to buy himself that field.

45   "Or again, the kingdom of Heaven is like a merchant searching
46   for fine pearls. When he has found a single pearl of great value, he goes and sells all his possessions and buys it.

47   "Or the kingdom of Heaven is like a big net thrown into the
48   sea collecting all kinds of fish. When it is full, the fishermen haul it ashore and sit down and pick out the good ones for the barrels,
49   but they throw away the bad. That is how it will be at the end of this world. The angels will go out and pick out the wicked from
50   among the good and throw them into the blazing furnace, where there will be tears and bitter regret.

51   "Have you grasped all this?"
      "Yes," they replied.

52   "You can see, then," returned Jesus, "how every one who knows the Law and becomes a disciple of the kingdom of Heaven is like a householder who can produce from his store both the new and the old."

Jesus is not appreciated in his native town

53,54   When Jesus had finished these parables he left the place, and came into his own country. Here he taught the people in their own synagogue, till in their amazement they said, "Where does this man get this wisdom and these powers? He's only the carpenter's 55 son. Isn't Mary his mother, and aren't James, Joseph, Simon and Judas his brothers? And aren't all his sisters living here with us? 56 Where did he get all this?" And they were deeply offended with 57 him.

But Jesus said to them, "No prophet goes unhonoured except in his own country and in his own home!"

And he performed very few miracles there because of their lack 58 of faith.

CHAPTER 14

Herod's guilty conscience

ABOUT this time Herod, governor of the province, heard the 1 reports about Jesus and said to his men, "This must be John the 2 Baptist: he has risen from the dead. That is why miraculous powers are at work in him."

For previously Herod had arrested John and had him bound 3 and put in prison, all on account of Herodias, the wife of his brother Philip. For John had said to him, "It is not right for you 4 to have this woman." Herod wanted to kill him for this, but he 5 was afraid of the people, since they all thought John was a prophet. But during Herod's birthday celebrations Herodias' daughter 6 delighted him by dancing before his guests, so much so that he 7 swore to give her anything she liked to ask. And she, prompted 8 by her mother, said, "I want you to give me, here and now, on a dish, the head of John the Baptist!" Herod was aghast at this, but 9 because he had sworn in front of his guests, he gave orders that she should be given what she had asked. So he sent men and had 10 John beheaded in the prison. Then his head was carried in on a 11 dish and presented to the young girl who handed it to her mother. Later, John's disciples came, took his body and buried it. Then they 12 went and told the news to Jesus. When he heard it he went away 13 by boat to a deserted place, quite alone.

Jesus feeds a tired and hungry crowd

Then the crowds heard of his departure and followed him out of the towns on foot. When Jesus emerged from his retreat he 14

15 saw a vast crowd and was very deeply moved and cured the sick among them. As evening fell his disciples came to him and said, "We are right in the wilds here and it is very late. Send away these crowds now, so that they can go into the villages and buy themselves food."

16 "There's no need for them to go away," returned Jesus. "You give them something to eat!"

17 "But we haven't anything here," they told him, "except five
18 loaves and two fish." To which Jesus replied, "Bring them here to me."

19 He told the crowd to sit down on the grass. Then he took the five loaves and the two fish in his hands, and, looking up to Heaven, he thanked God, broke the loaves and passed them to his
20 disciples who handed them to the crowd. Everybody ate and was satisfied. Afterwards they collected twelve baskets full of the
21 pieces which were left over. Those who ate numbered about five thousand men, apart from the women and children.

Jesus again shows his power over the forces of nature

22 Directly after this Jesus insisted on his disciples' getting aboard their boat and going on ahead to the other side, while he himself
23 sent the crowds home. And when he had sent them away he went up the hill-side quite alone, to pray. When it grew late he was
24 there by himself while the boat was by now a long way from the shore at the mercy of the waves, for the wind was dead against
25 them. In the small hours Jesus went out to them, walking on the
26 water of the lake. When the disciples caught sight of him walking on the water they were terrified. "It's a ghost!" they said, and
27 screamed with fear. But at once Jesus spoke to them. "It's all right! It's I myself, don't be afraid!"

28 "Lord, if it's really you," said Peter, "tell me to come to you on the water."

29 "Come on, then," replied Jesus.

Peter stepped down from the boat and did walk on the water,
30 making for Jesus. But when he saw the fury of the wind he
31 panicked and began to sink, calling out, "Lord save me!" At once Jesus reached out his hand and caught him, saying, "You little-
32 faith! What made you lose your nerve like that?" Then, when
33 they were both aboard the boat, the wind dropped. The whole crew came and knelt down before Jesus, crying, "You are indeed the Son of God!"

30

When they had crossed over to the other side of the lake, they 34
landed at Gennesaret, and when the men of that place had 35
recognised him, they sent word to the whole surrounding country
and brought all the diseased to him. They implored him to let 36
them "touch just the edge of his cloak", and all those who did so
were cured.

CHAPTER 15

The dangers of tradition

THEN some of the scribes and Pharisees from Jerusalem came 1
and asked Jesus, "Why do your disciples break our ancient 2
tradition and eat their food without washing their hands properly
first?"

"Tell me," replied Jesus, "why do you break God's command- 3
ment through your tradition? For God said, 'Honour thy father 4
and thy mother', and 'He that speaketh evil of father or mother,
let him die the death.' But you say that if a man tells his parents, 5
'Whatever use I might have been to you is now given to God', then 6
he owes no further duty to his parents. And so your tradition
empties the commandment of God of all its meaning. You 7
hypocrites! Isaiah described you beautifully when he said:

This people honoureth me with their lips; 8
But their heart is far from me.
But in vain do they worship me, 9
Teaching as their doctrines the precepts of men."

Superficial and true cleanliness

Then he called the crowd to him and said, "Listen, and under- 10
stand this thoroughly! It is not what goes *into* a man's mouth that 11
makes him common or unclean. It is what comes *out* of a man's
mouth that makes him unclean."

Later his disciples came to him and said, "Do you know that 12
the Pharisees are deeply offended by what you said?"

"Every plant which my Heavenly Father did not plant will be 13
pulled up by the roots," returned Jesus. "Let them alone. They 14
are blind guides, and when one blind man leads another blind man
they will both end up in the ditch!"

"Explain this parable to us," broke in Peter. 15

"Are you still unable to grasp things like this?" replied Jesus. 16

17 "Don't you see that whatever goes *into* the mouth passes into the
18 stomach and then out of the body altogether? But the things that
come *out* of a man's mouth come from his heart and mind, and it
19 is they that really make a man unclean. For it is from a man's
mind that evil thoughts arise—murder, adultery, lust, theft,
20 perjury and blasphemy. These are the things which make a man
unclean, not eating without washing his hands properly!"

A gentile's faith in Jesus

21 Jesus then left that place and retired into the Tyre and Sidon
22 district. There a Canaanite woman from those parts came to him
crying at the top of her voice,

"Lord, have pity on me! My daughter is in a terrible state—a
devil has got into her!"

23 Jesus made no answer, and the disciples came up to him and
said, "Do send her away—she's still following us and calling
out."

24 "I was only sent," replied Jesus, "to the lost sheep of the house
of Israel."

25 Then the woman came and knelt at his feet. "Lord, help me,"
she said.

26 "It is not right, you know," Jesus replied, "to take the children's
food and throw it to the dogs."

27 "Yes, Lord, I know, but even the dogs live on the scraps that
fall from their master's table!"

28 "You certainly don't lack faith," returned Jesus, "it shall be as
you wish."

And at that moment her daughter was cured.

Jesus heals and feeds vast crowds of people

29 Jesus left there, walked along the shore of the lake of Galilee,
30 then climbed the hill and sat down. And great crowds came to
him, bringing with them people who were lame, crippled, blind,
dumb and many others. They simply put them down at his feet
31 and he healed them. The result was that the people were astonished at seeing dumb men speak, crippled men healed, lame men
walking about and blind men having recovered their sight. And
they praised the God of Israel.

32 But Jesus quietly called his disciples to him. "My heart goes out
to this crowd," he said. "They've stayed with me three days now

and have no more food. I don't want to send them home without
anything or they will collapse on the way."

"Where could we find enough food to feed such a crowd in *33*
this deserted spot?" said the disciples.

"How many loaves have you?" asked Jesus. *34*

"Seven, and a few small fish," they replied.

Then Jesus told the crowd to sit down comfortably on the *35*
ground. And when he had taken the seven loaves and the fish *36*
into his hands, he broke them with a prayer of thanksgiving and
gave them to the disciples to pass on to the people. Everybody *37*
ate and was satisfied, and they picked up seven baskets full of the
pieces left over. Those who ate numbered four thousand men *38*
apart from women and children. Then Jesus sent the crowds *39*
home, boarded the boat and arrived at the district of Magadan.

CHAPTER 16

Jesus again refuses to give a sign

ONCE the Pharisees and the Sadducees arrived together to test *1*
him, and asked him to give them a sign from Heaven. But he *2*
replied, "When the evening comes you say, 'Ah, fine weather—
the sky is red.' In the morning you say, 'There will be a storm *3*
today, the sky is red and threatening.' Yes, you know how to
interpret the look of the sky but you have no idea how to interpret
the signs of the times! A wicked and unfaithful age insists on a *4*
sign; and it will not be given any sign at all but that of the prophet
Jonah." And he turned on his heel and left them.

He is misunderstood by the disciples

Then his disciples came to him on the other side of the lake, *5*
forgetting to bring any bread with them. "Keep your eyes open," *6*
said Jesus to them, "and be on your guard against the 'yeast' of
the Pharisees and Sadducees!" But they were arguing with each *7*
other, and saying. "We forgot to bring the bread." When Jesus *8*
saw this he said to them, "Why all this argument among yourselves about not bringing any bread, you little-faiths? Don't you *9*
understand yet, or have you forgotten the five loaves and the five
thousand, and how many baskets you took up afterwards; or the *10*
seven loaves and the four thousand and how many baskets you
took up then? I wonder why you don't yet understand that I *11*

12 wasn't talking about bread at all—I told you to beware of the yeast of the Pharisees and Sadducees." Then they grasped the fact that he had not told them to beware of yeast in the ordinary sense but of the teaching of the Pharisees and Sadducees.

Peter's bold affirmation

13 When Jesus reached the Caesarea-Philippi district he asked his disciples a question. "Who do people say the Son of Man is?"

14 "Well, some say John the Baptist," they told him. "Some say Elijah, others Jeremiah or one of the prophets."

15 "But what about you?" he said to them. "Who do you say that I am?"

16 Simon Peter answered, "You? You are Christ, the Son of the living God!"

17 "Simon, son of Jonah, you are a fortunate man indeed!" said Jesus, "for it was not your own nature but my Heavenly Father

18 who has revealed this truth to you! Now I tell you that you are Peter the rock, and it is on this rock that I am going to found my

19 Church, and the powers of death will never prevail against it. I will give you the keys of the kingdom of Heaven; whatever you forbid on earth will be what is forbidden in Heaven and whatever you permit on earth will be what is permitted in Heaven!"*

20 Then he impressed on his disciples that they should not tell anyone that he was Christ.

Jesus speaks about his passion, and the cost of following him

21 From that time onwards Jesus began to explain to his disciples that he would have to go to Jerusalem, and endure much suffering from the elders, chief priests and scribes, and finally be killed; and be raised to life again on the third day.

22 Then Peter took him on one side and started to remonstrate with him over this. "God bless you, Master! Nothing like this

23 must happen to you!" Then Jesus turned round and said to Peter, "Out of my way, Satan! . . . you stand right in my path, Peter, when you look at things from man's point of view and not from God's."

24 Then Jesus said to his disciples, "If anyone wants to follow in my footsteps he must give up all right to himself, take up his cross

* See note 3, page 552.

and follow me. For the man who wants to save his life will lose it; 25
but the man who loses his life for my sake will find it. For what 26
good is it for a man to gain the whole world at the price of his
own soul? What could a man offer to buy back his soul once he
had lost it?

"For the Son of Man will come in the glory of his Father and 27
in the company of his angels and then he will repay every man for
what he has done. Believe me, there are some standing here today 28
who will know nothing of death till they have seen the Son of
Man coming as king."

CHAPTER 17

Three disciples glimpse the glory of Christ

Six days later Jesus chose Peter, James and his brother John, to 1
accompany him high up on the hill-side where they were quite
alone. There his whole appearance changed before their eyes, his 2
face shining like the sun and his clothes as white as light. Then 3
Moses and Elijah were seen talking to Jesus.

"Lord," exclaimed Peter, "it is wonderful for us to be here! If 4
you like I could put up three shelters, one each for you and Moses
and Elijah——"

But while he was still talking a bright cloud overshadowed them 5
and a voice came out of the cloud:

"This is my dearly loved Son in whom I am well pleased.
Listen to him!"

When they heard this voice the disciples fell on their faces, 6
overcome with fear. Then Jesus came up to them and touched 7
them.

"Get up and don't be frightened," he said. And as they raised 8
their eyes there was no one to be seen but Jesus himself.

On their way down the hill-side Jesus warned them not to tell 9
anyone about what they had seen until after the Son of Man had
risen from the dead. Then the disciples demanded, "Why is it, 10
then, that the scribes always say Elijah must come first?"

"Yes, Elijah does come first," replied Jesus, "and begins the 11
world's reformation. But I tell you that Elijah has come already 12
and men did not recognise him. They did what they liked with
him, and they will do the same to the Son of Man."

Then they realised that he had been referring to John the 13
Baptist.

Jesus heals an epileptic boy

14
15 When they returned to the crowds again a man came and knelt in front of Jesus. "Lord, do have pity on my son," he said, "for he is a lunatic and is in a terrible state. He is always falling into the
16 fire or into the water. I did bring him to your disciples but they couldn't cure him."
17 "You really are an unbelieving and difficult people," Jesus returned. "How long must I be with you, and how long must I put up with you? Bring him here to me!"
18 Then Jesus reprimanded the evil spirit and it went out of the boy, who was cured from that moment.
19 Afterwards the disciples approached Jesus privately and asked, "Why weren't we able to get rid of it?"
20 "Because you have so little faith," replied Jesus. "I assure you that if you have as much faith as a grain of mustard-seed you can say to this hill, 'Up you get and move over there!' and it will move—you will find nothing is impossible."
22
23 As they went about together in Galilee, Jesus told them, "The Son of Man is going to be handed over to the power of men, and they will kill him. And on the third day he will be raised to life again." This greatly distressed the disciples.

Jesus pays the Temple-tax—in an unusual way

24 Then when they arrived at Capernaum the Temple tax-collectors came up and said to Peter, "Your master doesn't pay Temple-tax, we presume?"
25 "Oh, yes, he does!" replied Peter. Later when he went into the house Jesus anticipated what he was going to say. "What do *you* think, Simon?" he said. "Whom do the kings of this world get their rates and taxes from—their own people or from others?"
26 "From others," replied Peter.
27 "Then the family is exempt," Jesus told him. "Yet we don't want to give offence to these people, so go down to the lake and throw in your hook. Take the first fish that bites, open his mouth and you'll find a coin. Take that and give it to them, for both of us."

CHAPTER 18

Jesus commends the simplicity of children

It was at this time that the disciples came to Jesus with the 1
question, "Who is really greatest in the kingdom of Heaven?"
Jesus called a little child to his side and set him on his feet in the 2
middle of them all. "Believe me," he said, "unless you change 3
your whole outlook and become like little children you will never
enter the kingdom of Heaven. It is the man who can be as humble 4
as this little child who is greatest in the kingdom of Heaven.

"Anyone who welcomes one child like this for my sake is 5
welcoming me. But if anyone leads astray one of these little chil- 6
dren who believe in me he would be better off thrown into the
depths of the sea with a mill-stone hung round his neck! Alas for 7
the world with its pitfalls! In the nature of things there must be
pitfalls, yet alas for the man who is responsible for them!

The right way may mean costly sacrifice

"If your hand or your foot is a hindrance to your faith, cut it 8
off and throw it away. It is a good thing to go into life maimed
or crippled—rather than to have both hands and feet and be
thrown on to the everlasting fire. Yes, and if your eye leads you 9
astray, tear it out and throw it away. It is a good thing to go one-
eyed into life—rather than to have both your eyes and be thrown
on the fire of the rubbish-heap.

"Be careful that you never despise a single one of these little 10
ones—for I tell you that they have angels who see my Father's
face continually in Heaven.

"What do you think? If a man has a hundred sheep and one 12
wanders away from the rest, won't he leave the ninety-nine on the
hill-side and set out to look for the one who has wandered away?
Yes, and if he should chance to find it I assure you he is more 13
delighted over that one than he is over the ninety-nine who never
wandered away. You can understand then that it is never the will 14
of your Father in Heaven that a single one of these little ones
should be lost.

Reconciliation must always be attempted

"But if your brother wrongs you, go and have it out with him 15

37

at once—just between the two of you. If he will listen to you,
16 you have won him back as your brother. But if he will not listen
to you, take one or two others with you so that everything that
17 is said may have the support of two or three witnesses. And if he
still won't pay any attention, tell the matter to the church. And
if he won't even listen to the church then he must be to you just
like a pagan—or a tax-collector!

The connection between earthly conduct and spiritual reality

18 "Believe me, whatever you forbid upon earth will be what is
forbidden in Heaven, and whatever you permit on earth will be
what is permitted in Heaven.*
19 "And I tell you once more that if two of you on earth agree in
asking for anything it will be granted to you by my Heavenly
20 Father. For wherever two or three people come together in my
name, I am there, right among them!"

The necessity for forgiveness

21 Then Peter approached him with the question, "Master, how
many times can my brother wrong me and I must forgive him?
Would seven times be enough?"
22 "No," replied Jesus, "not seven times, but seventy times seven!
23 For the kingdom of Heaven is like a king who decided to settle his
24 accounts with his servants. When he had started calling in his
accounts, a man was brought to him who owed him millions of
25 pounds. And when it was plain that he had no means of repaying
the debt, his master gave orders for him to be sold as a slave, and
his wife and children and all his possessions as well, and the money
26 to be paid over. At this the servant fell on his knees before his
master, 'Oh, be patient with me!' he cried, 'and I will pay you
27 back every penny!' Then his master was moved with pity for
him, set him free and cancelled his debt.
28 "But when this same servant had left his master's presence, he
found one of his fellow-servants who owed him a few shillings.
He grabbed him and seized him by the throat, crying, 'Pay up
29 what you owe me!' At this his fellow-servant fell down at his
feet, and implored him, 'Oh, be patient with me, and I will pay
30 you back!' But he refused and went out and had him put in prison
until he should repay the debt.

* See note 3, page 552.

58

"When the other fellow-servants saw what had happened, they 31
were horrified and went and told their master the whole incident.
Then his master called him in. 32

"'You wicked servant!' he said. 'Didn't I cancel all that debt
when you begged me to do so? Oughtn't you to have taken pity 33
on your fellow-servant as I, your master, took pity on you?' And 34
his master in anger handed him over to the gaolers till he should
repay the whole debt. This is how my Heavenly Father will 35
treat you unless you each forgive your brother from your heart."

CHAPTER 19

The divine principle of marriage

WHEN Jesus had finished talking on these matters, he left 1
Galilee and went on to the district of Judaea on the far side
of the Jordan. Vast crowds followed him, and he cured them 2
there.

Then the Pharisees arrived with a test-question. 3

"Is it right," they asked, "for a man to divorce his wife on any
grounds whatever?"

"Haven't you read," he answered, "that the one who created 4
them from the beginning made them male and female and said: 5
'For this cause shall a man leave his father and mother, and shall
cleave to his wife; and the twain shall become one flesh'? So they 6
are no longer two separate people but one. No man therefore
must separate what God has joined together."

"Then why," they retorted, "did Moses command us to give 7
a written divorce-notice and dismiss the woman?"

"It was because you knew so little of the meaning of love that 8
Moses allowed you to divorce your wives! But that was not the
original principle. I tell you that anyone who divorces his wife on 9
any grounds except her unfaithfulness and marries some other
woman commits adultery."

His disciples said to him, "If that is a man's position with his 10
wife, it is not worth getting married!"

"It is not everybody who can live up to this," replied Jesus, 11
"—only those who have a special gift. For some are incapable of 12
marriage from birth, some are made incapable by the action of
men, and some have made themselves so for the sake of the
kingdom of Heaven. Let the man who can accept what I have
said accept it."

Jesus welcomes children

13 Then some little children were brought to him, so that he could put his hands on them and pray for them. The disciples frowned
14 on the parents' action but Jesus said,

"You must let little children come to me, and you must never stop them. The kingdom of Heaven belongs to little children like
15 these!" Then he laid his hands on them and went on his way.

Jesus shows that keeping the commandments is not enough

16 Then it happened that a man came up to him and said, "Master what good thing must I do to secure eternal life?"

17 "I wonder why you ask me about what is good?" Jesus answered him. "Only one is good. But if you want to enter that life you must keep the commandments."

18 "Which ones?" he asked.

"Thou shalt do no murder, Thou shalt not commit adultery,
19 Thou shalt not steal, Thou shalt not bear false witness, Honour thy father and thy mother: and Thou shalt love thy neighbour as thyself," replied Jesus.

20 "I have carefully kept all these," returned the young man. "What is still missing in my life?"

21 Then Jesus told him, "If you want to be perfect, go now and sell your property and give the money away to the poor—you will have riches in Heaven. Then come and follow me!"

22 When the young man heard that he turned away crestfallen, for he was very wealthy.

23 Then Jesus remarked to his disciples, "Believe me, a rich man
24 will find it very difficult to enter the kingdom of Heaven. Yes, I repeat, a camel could more easily squeeze through the eye of a needle than a rich man get into the kingdom of God!"

25 The disciples were simply amazed to hear this, and said, "Then who can possibly be saved?"

26 Jesus looked steadily at them and replied, "Humanly speaking it is impossible; but with God anything is possible!"

Jesus declares that sacrifice for the kingdom will be repaid

27 At this Peter exclaimed, "Look, we have left everything and followed you. What is that going to be worth to us?"

28 "Believe me," said Jesus, "when I tell you that in the next

world, when the Son of Man shall sit down on his glorious throne, you who have followed me will also sit on twelve thrones and become judges of the twelve tribes of Israel. Every man who has *29* left houses or brothers or sisters or fathers or mother or children or land for my sake will receive it all back many times over, and will inherit eternal life. But many who are first now will be last *30* then—and the last first!

CHAPTER 20

But God's generosity may appear unfair

"For the kingdom of Heaven is like a farmer going out early *1* in the morning to hire labourers for his vineyard. He agreed with *2* them on a wage of a silver coin a day and sent them to work. About nine o'clock he went and saw some others standing *3* about in the market-place with nothing to do. 'You go to the *4* vineyard too,' he said to them, 'and I will pay you a fair wage.' And off they went. At about mid-day and again at about three *5* o'clock in the afternoon he went out and did the same thing. Then about five o'clock he went out and found some others *6* standing about. 'Why are you standing about here all day doing nothing?' he asked them. 'Because no one has employed us,' *7* they replied. 'You go off into the vineyard as well, then,' he said.

"When evening came the owner of the vineyard said to his *8* foreman, 'Call the labourers and pay them their wages, beginning with the last and ending with the first.' So those who were en- *9* gaged at five o'clock came up and each man received a silver coin. But when the first to be employed came they reckoned they *10* would get more, but they also received a silver coin a man. As *11* they took their money they grumbled at the farmer and said, *12* 'These last fellows have only put in one hour's work and you've treated them exactly the same as us who have gone through all the hard work and heat of the day!'

"But he replied to one of them, 'My friend, I'm not being *13* unjust to you. Wasn't our agreement for a silver coin a day? Take *14* your money and go home. It is my wish to give the late-comers as much as I give you. May I not do what I like with what belongs *15* to me? Must you be jealous because I am generous?'

"So, many who are the last now will be first then and the first *16* last."

Jesus' final journey to Jerusalem

17 Then, as he was about to go up to Jerusalem, Jesus took the twelve disciples aside and spoke to them as they walked along.

18 "Listen, we are now going up to Jerusalem and the Son of Man will be handed over to the chief priests and the scribes—and they

19 will condemn him to death. They will hand him over to the heathen to ridicule and flog and crucify. And on the third day he will rise again!"

20 At this point the mother of the sons of Zebedee arrived with her sons and knelt in front of Jesus to ask him a favour.

21 "What is it you want?" he asked her.

"Please say that these two sons of mine may sit one on each side of you when you are king!" she said.

22 "You don't know what it is you are asking," replied Jesus. "Can you two drink what I have to drink?"

"Yes, we can," they answered.

23 "Ah, you will indeed 'drink my drink'," Jesus told them, "but as for sitting on either side of me, that is not for me to grant—that belongs to those for whom my Father has planned it."

24 When the other ten heard of this incident they were highly indignant with the two brothers.

25 But Jesus called them to him and said,

"You know that the rulers of the heathen lord it over them and

26 that their great ones have absolute power? But it must not be so among you. No, whoever among you wants to be great must

27 become the servant of you all, and if he wants to be first among

28 you he must be your slave—just as the Son of Man has not come to be served but to serve, and to give his life to set many others free."

He restores sight to two blind men

29,30 A great crowd followed them as they were leaving Jericho, and two blind men who were sitting by the roadside, hearing that it was Jesus who was passing by, cried out, "Have pity on us, Lord,

31 you Son of David!" The crowd tried to hush them up, but this only made them cry out more loudly still, "Have pity on us, Lord, you Son of David!"

32 Jesus stood quite still and called out to them, "What do you want me to do for you?"

33 "Lord, let us see again!"

34 And Jesus, deeply moved with pity, touched their eyes. At once their sight was restored, and they followed him.

CHAPTER 21

Jesus' final entry into Jerusalem

As they approached Jerusalem and came to Bethphage and the **1**
Mount of Olives, Jesus sent two disciples ahead telling them, "Go **2**
into the village in front of you and you will at once find there an
ass tethered, and a colt with her. Untie them and bring them to
me. Should anyone say anything to you, you are to say, 'The **3**
Lord needs them', and he will send them immediately."

All this happened to fulfil the prophet's saying— **4**
    Tell ye the daughter of Zion, **5**
    Behold, thy King cometh unto thee,
    Meek, and riding upon an ass,
    And upon a colt the foal of an ass.

So the disciples went off and followed Jesus' instructions. They **6, 7**
brought the ass and the colt, and put their cloaks on them, and
Jesus took his seat. Then most of the crowd spread their own **8**
cloaks on the road, while others cut down branches from the trees
and spread them in his path. The crowds who went in front of **9**
him and the crowds who followed behind him all shouted, "God
save the Son of David! Blessed is the man who comes in the name
of the Lord! God save him from on high!"

And as he entered Jerusalem a shock ran through the whole **10**
city. "Who *is* this?" men cried. "This is Jesus the prophet," **11**
replied the crowd, "the man from Nazareth in Galilee!"

Then Jesus went into the Temple and drove out all the buyers **12**
and sellers there. He overturned the tables of the money-changers
and the benches of those who sold doves, crying— **13**

"It is written, 'My house shall be called a house of prayer.' But
you have turned it into a thieves' kitchen!"

And there in the Temple the blind and the lame came to him, **14**
and he healed them. But when the chief priests and the scribes **15**
saw the wonderful things he had done, and that children were
shouting in the Temple the words, "God save the Son of David",
they were highly indignant. "Can't you hear what these children **16**
are saying?" they asked Jesus.

"Yes," he replied, "and haven't you ever read the words, 'Out
of the mouth of babes and sucklings thou hast perfected praise'?"
And he turned on his heel and went out of the city to Bethany, **17**
where he spent the night.

His strange words to the fig-tree

18 In the morning he came back early to the city and felt hungry.
19 He saw a fig-tree growing by the side of the road, but when he got to it he discovered there was nothing on it but leaves.

"No more fruit shall ever grow on you!" he said to it, and all
20 at once the fig-tree withered away. When the disciples saw this happen they were simply amazed. "How on earth did the fig-tree wither away quite suddenly like that?" they asked.

21 "Believe me," replied Jesus, "if you have faith and have no doubts in your heart, you will not only do this to a fig-tree but even if you should say to this hill, 'Get up and throw yourself into
22 the sea', it will happen! Everything you ask for in prayer, if you have faith, you will receive."

Jesus meets a question with a counter-question

23 Then when he had entered the Temple and was in the act of teaching, the chief priests and Jewish elders came up to him and said, "What authority have you for what you're doing, and who gave you that authority?"

24 "I am also going to ask you one question," Jesus replied to them, "and if you answer it I will tell you what authority I have
25 for what I do. John's baptism, now, did it come from Heaven or was it purely human?"

At this they began arguing among themselves, "If we say, 'It came from Heaven', he will say to us, 'Then why didn't you
26 believe in him?' If on the other hand we should say, 'It was purely human'—well, frankly, we are afraid of the people—for all of them consider John was a prophet."

27 So they answered Jesus, "We do not know."

"Then I will not tell you by what authority I do these things!"
28 returned Jesus. "But what is your opinion about this? There was a man with two sons. He went to the first and said, 'Go and
29 work in my vineyard today, my son.' He said, 'All right, sir'—
30 but he never went near it. Then the father approached the second son with the same request. He said, 'I won't.' But afterwards he
31 changed his mind and went. Which of these two did what their father wanted?"

"The second one," they replied.

"Yes, and I tell you that tax-collectors and prostitutes are going into the kingdom of God in front of you!" retorted Jesus.

44

"For John came to you as a saint, and you did not believe him—— *32*
—yet the tax-collectors and the prostitutes did! And, even after
seeing that, you would not change your minds and believe him."

Jesus tells a pointed story

"Now listen to another story. There was once a man, a land- *33*
owner, who planted a vineyard, fenced it round, dug out a hole
for the wine-press and built a watch-tower. Then he let it out
to farm-workers and went abroad. When the vintage-time *34*
approached he sent his servants to the farm-workers to receive
his share of the proceeds. But they took the servants, beat up one, *35*
killed another, and drove off a third with stones. Then he sent *36*
some more servants, a larger party than the first, but they treated
them in just the same way. Finally he sent his own son, thinking, *37*
'They will respect my son.' Yet when the farm-workers saw the *38*
son they said to each other, 'This fellow is the future owner.
Come on, let's kill him and we shall get everything that he would
have had!' So they took him, threw him out of the vineyard and *39*
killed him. Now when the owner of the vineyard returns, what *40*
will he do to those farm-workers?"

"He will kill those scoundrels without mercy," they replied, *41*
"and will let the vineyard out to other tenants, who will give him
the produce at the right season."

"And have you never read these words of scripture," said Jesus *42*
to them:

The stone which the builders rejected,
The same was made the head of the corner:
This was from the Lord,
And it is marvellous in our eyes?

"Here, I tell you, lies the reason why the kingdom of God is *43*
going to be taken away from you and given to a people who will
produce its proper fruit."

When the chief priests and the Pharisees heard his parables they *45*
realised that he was speaking about them. They longed to get *46*
their hands on him, but they were afraid of the crowds, who
regarded him as a prophet.

CHAPTER 22

The kingdom is not to be lightly disregarded

1 THEN Jesus began to talk to them again in parables.
2 "The kingdom of Heaven," he said, "is like a king who
3 arranged a wedding for his son. He sent his servants to summon those who had been invited to the festivities, but they refused to
4 come. Then he tried again; he sent some more servants, saying to them, 'Tell those who have been invited, "Here is my wedding-breakfast all ready, my bullocks and fat cattle have been slaughtered and everything is prepared. Come along to the festivities."'
5 But they took no notice of this and went off, one to his farm, and
6 another to his business. As for the rest, they got hold of the
7 servants, treated them disgracefully, and finally killed them. At this the king was very angry and sent his troops and killed those
8 murderers and burned down their city. Then he said to his
9 servants, 'The wedding feast is quite ready, but those who were invited were not good enough for it. So go off now to all the
10 street corners and invite everyone you find there to the feast.' So the servants went out on to the streets and collected together all those whom they found, bad and good alike. And the hall became
11 filled with guests. But when the king came in to inspect the guests, he noticed among them a man not dressed for a wed-
12 ding. 'How did you come in here, my friend,' he said to him, 'without being properly dressed for the wedding?' And the
13 man had nothing to say. Then the king said to the ushers, 'Tie him up and throw him into the darkness outside. There he
14 can weep and regret his folly!' For many are invited but few are chosen."

A clever trap—and a penetrating answer

15 Then the Pharisees went off and discussed how they could trap
16 him in argument. Eventually they sent their disciples with some of the Herod-party to say this, "Master, we know that you are an honest man who teaches the way of God faithfully and that you are not swayed by men's opinion of you. Obviously you don't
17 care for human approval. Now tell us—'Is it right to pay taxes to Caesar or not'?"
18 But Jesus knowing their evil intention said, "Why try this trick

on me, you frauds? Show me the money you pay the tax with." 19
They handed him a coin, and he said to them, "Whose face is this 20
and whose name is in the inscription?"

"Caesar's," they said. 21

"Then give to Caesar," he replied, "what belongs to Caesar
and to God what belongs to God!"

This reply staggered them and they went away and let him 22
alone.

Jesus exposes the ignorance of the Sadducees

On the same day some Sadducees (who deny that there is any 23
resurrection) approached Jesus with this question: "Master, 24
Moses said if a man should die without any children, his brother
should marry his widow and raise up a family for him. Now, we 25
have a case of seven brothers. The first one married and died, and
since he had no family he left his wife to his brother. The same 26
thing happened with the second and the third, right up to the
seventh. Last of all the woman herself died. Now in this 'resur- 27, 28
rection', whose wife will she be of these seven men—for she
belonged to all of them?"

"You are very wide of the mark," replied Jesus to them, "for 29
you are ignorant of both the scriptures and the power of God.
For in the resurrection there is no such thing as marrying or being 30
given in marriage—men live like the angels in Heaven. And as for 31
the matter of the resurrection of the dead, haven't you ever read
what was once said to you by God himself, 'I am the God of 32
Abraham, the God of Isaac and the God of Jacob'? God is not
God of the dead but of living men!" When the crowds heard this 33
they were astounded at his teaching.

The greatest commandments in the Law

When the Pharisees heard that he had silenced the Sadducees 34
they came up to him in a body, and one of them, an expert in the 35
Law, put this test-question: "Master, what are we to consider the 36
Law's greatest commandment?"

Jesus answered him, " 'Thou shalt love the Lord thy God with 37
all thy heart, and with all thy soul and with all thy mind.' This is 38
the first and great commandment. And there is a second like it: 39
'Thou shalt love thy neighbour as thyself.' The whole of the Law 40
and the Prophets depends on these two commandments."

R—N.T.—C   47

Jesus puts an unanswerable question

41, 42   Then Jesus asked the assembled Pharisees this question: "What is your opinion about Christ? Whose son is he?"

"The Son of David," they answered.

43   "How then," returned Jesus, "does David when inspired by the Spirit call him Lord? He says—

44   The Lord said unto my *Lord*,

      Sit thou on my right hand,

      Till I put thine enemies underneath thy feet?

45   If David then calls him Lord, how can he be his son?"

46   Nobody was able to answer this and from that day on no one dared to ask him any further questions.

CHAPTER 23

He publicly warns the people against their religious leaders

1, 2   THEN Jesus addressed the crowds and his disciples. "The scribes and the Pharisees speak with the authority of Moses," he told

3   them, "so you must do what they tell you and follow their instructions. But you must not imitate their lives! For they preach

4   but do not practise. They pile up back-breaking burdens and lay them on other men's shoulders—yet they themselves will not raise

5   a finger to move them. Their whole lives are planned with an eye to effect. They increase the size of their phylacteries* and

6   lengthen the tassels of their robes; they love seats of honour at

7   dinner parties and front places in the synagogues. They love to be greeted with respect in public places and to have men call them

8   'rabbi!' Don't you ever be called 'rabbi'—you have only one

9   teacher, and all of you are brothers. And don't call any human

10   being 'father'—for you have one Father and he is in Heaven. And you must not let people call you 'leaders'—you have only one

11   leader, Christ! The only 'superior' among you is the one who

12   serves the others. For every man who promotes himself will be humbled, and every man who learns to be humble will find promotion.

13   "But alas for you, you scribes and Pharisees, play-actors that you are! You lock the doors of the kingdom of Heaven in men's faces; you will not go in yourselves neither will you allow those at the door to go inside.

---

* Phylacteries: Strips of parchment inscribed with texts from the Law, worn on the arm and forehead.

"Alas for you, you scribes and Pharisees, play-actors! You 15
scour sea and land to make a single convert, and then you make
him twice as ripe for destruction as you are yourselves.

"Alas for you, you blind leaders! You say, 'If anyone swears 16
by the Temple it amounts to nothing, but if he swears by the
gold of the Temple he is bound by his oath.' You blind fools, 17
which is the more important, the gold or the Temple which
sanctifies the gold? And you say, 'If anyone swears by the altar 18
it doesn't matter, but if he swears by the gift placed on the altar
he is bound by his oath.' Have you no eyes—which is more im- 19
portant, the gift, or the altar which sanctifies the gift? Any man 20
who swears by the altar is swearing by the altar and whatever is
offered upon it; and anyone who swears by the Temple is swearing 21
by the Temple and by him who dwells in it; and anyone who 22
swears by Heaven is swearing by the throne of God and by the
one who sits upon that throne.

"Alas for you, scribes and Pharisees, you utter frauds! For you 23
pay your tithe on mint and aniseed and cummin, and neglect the
things which carry far more weight in the Law—justice, mercy
and good faith. These are the things you should have observed—
without neglecting the others. You call yourselves leaders, and 24
yet you can't see an inch before your noses, for you filter out the
mosquito and swallow the camel.

"What miserable frauds you are, you scribes and Pharisees! 25
You clean the outside of the cup and the dish, while the inside is
full of greed and self-indulgence. Can't you see, Pharisee? First 26
wash the inside of a cup, and then you can clean the outside.

"Alas for you, you hypocritical scribes and Pharisees! You are 27
like white-washed tombs, which look fine on the outside but
inside are full of dead men's bones and all kinds of rottenness.
For you appear like good men on the outside—but inside you are 28
a mass of pretence and wickedness.

"What miserable frauds you are, you scribes and Pharisees! 29
You build tombs for the prophets, and decorate monuments for
good men of the past, and then say, 'If we had lived in the times 30
of our ancestors we should never have joined in the killing of the
prophets.' Yes, 'your ancestors'—*that* shows you to be sons indeed 31
of those who murdered the prophets. Go ahead then, and finish 32
off what your ancestors tried to do! You serpents, you viper's 33
brood, how do you think you are going to avoid being condemned to the rubbish-heap? Listen to this: I am sending you 34
prophets and wise and learned men; and some of these you will

kill and crucify, others you will flog in your synagogues and hunt
35 from town to town. So that on your hands is all the innocent
blood spilt on this earth, from the blood of Abel the good to the
blood of Zachariah, Barachiah's son, whom you murdered
36 between the sanctuary and the altar. Yes, I tell you that all this
will be laid at the doors of this generation.

Jesus mourns over Jerusalem, and foretells its destruction

37 "Oh, Jerusalem, Jerusalem! You murder the prophets and stone
the messengers that are sent to you. How often have I longed to
gather your children round me like a bird gathering her brood
38 together under her wings—and you would never have it. Now all
39 you have left is your house. I tell you that you will never see me
again till the day when you cry, 'Blessed is he who comes in the
name of the Lord!' "

CHAPTER 24

1 THEN Jesus went out of the Temple and was walking away
when his disciples came up and drew his attention to its buildings.
2 "You see all these?" replied Jesus. "I tell you every stone will be
thrown down till there is not a single one left standing upon
another."

3 And as he was sitting on the slope of the Mount of Olives his
disciples came to him privately and said, "Tell us, when will this
happen? What will be the signal for your coming and the end of
this world?"

4, 5 "Be careful that no one misleads you," returned Jesus, "for
many men will come in my name saying 'I am Christ', and they
6 will mislead many. You will hear of wars and rumours of wars—
but don't be alarmed. Such things must indeed happen, but that
7 is not the end. For one nation will rise in arms against another, and
one kingdom against another, and there will be famines and earth-
8 quakes in different parts of the world. But all that is only the
9 beginning of the birth-pangs. For then comes the time when men
will hand you over to persecution, and kill you. And all nations
10 will hate you because you bear my name. Then comes the time
when many will lose their faith and will betray and hate each
11 other. Yes, and many false prophets will arise, and will mislead

many people. Because of the spread of wickedness the love of 12
most men will grow cold, though the man who holds out to the 13
end will be saved. This good news of the kingdom will be pro- 14
claimed to men all over the world as a witness to all the nations,
and then the end will come.

Jesus prophesies a future of suffering

"When the time comes, then, that you see the 'abomination of 15
desolation' prophesied by Daniel 'standing in the sacred place'—
the reader should note this—then is the time for those in Judaea 16
to escape to the hills. A man on his house-top must not waste time 17
going into his house to collect anything; a man at work in the 18
fields must not go back home to fetch his clothes. Alas for the 19
pregnant, alas for those with tiny babies at that time! Pray God 20
that you may not have to make your escape in the winter or on
the Sabbath day, for then there will be great misery, such as has 21
never happened from the beginning of the world until now, and
will never happen again! Yes, if those days had not been cut short 22
no human being would survive. But for the sake of God's people
those days are to be shortened.

"If anyone says to you then, 'Look, here is Christ!' or 'There 23
he is!' don't believe it. False christs and false prophets are going 24
to appear and will produce great signs and wonders to mislead, if
it were possible, even God's own people. Listen, I am warning 25
you. So that if people say to you, 'There he is, in the desert!' you 26
are not to go out there. If they say, 'Here he is, in this inner room!'
don't believe it. For as lightning flashes across from east to west 27
so will the Son of Man's coming be. 'Wherever there is a dead 28
body, there the vultures will flock.'

At the end of time the Son of Man will return

"Immediately after the misery of those days the sun will be 29
darkened, the moon will fail to give her light, the stars will fall
from the sky, and the powers of heaven will be shaken. Then the 30
sign of the Son of Man will appear in the sky, and all the nations
of the earth will wring their hands as they see the Son of Man
coming on the clouds of the sky in power and great splendour.
And he will send out his angels with a loud trumpet-call and they 31
will gather together his chosen from the four winds—from one
end of the heavens to the other.

32 "Learn what the fig-tree can teach you. As soon as its branches grow full of sap and produce leaves you know that summer is
33 near. So when you see all these things happening you may know
34 that he is near, at your very door! Believe me, this generation
35 will not disappear till all this has taken place. Earth and sky will
36 pass away, but my words will never pass away! But about that actual day and time no one knows—not even the angels of
37 Heaven, nor the Son, only the Father. For just as life went on in the days of Noah so will it be at the coming of the Son of Man.
38 In those days before the flood people were eating, drinking, marrying and being given in marriage until the very day that
39 Noah went into the ark, and knew nothing about the flood until it came and destroyed them all. So will it be at the coming
40 of the Son of Man. Two men will be in the field; one is taken
41 and one is left behind. Two women will be grinding at the hand-
42 mill; one is taken and one is left behind. You must be on the alert
43 then, for you do not know when your master is coming. You can be sure of this, however, that if the householder had known what time of night the burglar would arrive, he would have been ready for him and would not have allowed his house to be broken into.
44 That is why you must always be ready, for you do not know what time the Son of Man will arrive.

Vigilance is essential

45 "Who then is the faithful and sensible servant, whom his master put in charge of his household to give the others their food at the
46 proper time? Well, he is fortunate if his master finds him doing
47 that duty on his return! Believe me, he will promote him to look
48 after all his property. But if he should be a bad servant who says
49 to himself, 'My master takes his time about returning', and should begin to beat his fellow-servants and eat and drink with drunkards,
50 that servant's master will return suddenly and unexpectedly, and
51 will punish him severely and send him off to share the penalty of the unfaithful—to his bitter sorrow and regret!

CHAPTER 25

1 "IN those days the kingdom of Heaven will be like ten brides-maids who took their lamps and went out to meet the bride-

groom. Five of them were sensible and five were foolish. The 2, 3
foolish ones took their lamps but did not take any oil with them.
But the sensible ones brought their lamps and oil in their flasks 4
as well. Then, as the bridegroom was a very long time, they all 5
grew drowsy and fell asleep. But in the middle of the night there 6
came a shout, 'Wake up, here comes the bridegroom! Out you
go to meet him!" Then up got all the bridesmaids and attended 7
to their lamps. The foolish ones said to the sensible ones, 'Please 8
give us some of your oil—our lamps are going out!' 'Oh, no,' 9
returned the sensible ones, 'there might not be enough for all of
us. Better go to the oil-shop and buy some for yourselves.' But 10
while they had gone off to buy the oil the bridegroom arrived,
and those bridesmaids who were ready went in with him for the
festivities and the door was shut behind them. Later on the rest 11
of the bridesmaids came and said, 'Oh, please, sir, open the door
for us!' But he replied, 'I tell you I don't know you!' So be on 12, 13
the alert—for you do not know the day or the time.

Life is hard for the faint-hearted

"It is just like a man going abroad who called his household 14
servants together before he went and handed his property over
to them to manage. He gave one five thousand pounds, another 15
two thousand and another one thousand—according to their
respective abilities. Then he went away.

"The man who had received five thousand pounds went out 16
at once and by doing business with this sum he made another
five thousand. Similarly the man with two thousand pounds made 17
another two thousand. But the man who had received one 18
thousand pounds went off and dug a hole in the ground and hid his
master's money.

"Some years later the master of these servants arrived and went 19
into the accounts with them. The one who had the five thousand 20
pounds came in and brought him an additional five thousand
with the words, 'You gave me five thousand pounds, sir; look,
I've increased it by another five thousand.' 'Well done!' said his 21
master, 'you're a sound, reliable servant. You've been trustworthy
over a few things, now I'm going to put you in charge of much
more. Come in and share your master's rejoicing.' Then the 22
servant who had received two thousand pounds came in and said,
'You gave me two thousand pounds, sir; look, here's two thousand more that I've managed to make by it.' 'Well done!' said 23

his master, 'you're a sound, reliable servant. You've been trust-worthy over a few things, now I'm going to put you in charge of many. Come in and share your master's pleasure.'

24 "Then the man who had received the one thousand pounds came in and said, 'Sir, I always knew you were a hard man, reap-ing where you never sowed and collecting where you never laid

25 out—so I was scared and I went off and hid your thousand pounds in the ground. Here is your money, intact.'

26 "'You're a wicked, lazy servant!' his master told him. 'You say you knew that I reap where I never sowed and collect where

27 I never laid out? Then you ought to have put my money in the bank, and when I came I should at any rate have received what

28 belongs to me with interest. Take his thousand pounds away from

29 him and give it to the man who now has the ten thousand!' (For the man who has something will have more given to him and will have plenty. But as for the man who has nothing, even his

30 'nothing' will be taken away.) 'And throw this useless servant into the darkness outside, where he can weep and wail over his stupidity.'

The final judgment

31 "But when the Son of Man comes in his splendour with all his angels with him, then he will take his seat on his glorious throne.

32 All the nations will be assembled before him and he will separate men from each other like a shepherd separating sheep from goats.

33 He will place the sheep on his right hand and the goats on his left.

34 "Then the king will say to those on his right: 'Come, you who have won my Father's blessing! Take your inheritance—the king-

35 dom reserved for you since the foundation of the world! For I was hungry and you gave me food. I was thirsty and you gave

36 me a drink. I was lonely and you made me welcome. I was naked and you clothed me. I was ill and you came and looked after me. I was in prison and you came to see me there."

37 "Then the true men will answer him, 'Lord, when did we see you hungry and give you food? When did we see you thirsty and

38 give you something to drink? When did we see you lonely and

39 make you welcome, or see you naked and clothe you, or see you ill or in prison and go to see you?'

40 "And the king will reply, 'I assure you that whatever you did for the humblest of my brothers you did for me.'

41 "Then he will say to those on his left, 'Out of my presence,

cursed as you are, into the eternal fire prepared for the devil and
his angels! For I was hungry and you gave me nothing to eat. I *42*
was thirsty and you gave me nothing to drink. I was lonely and *43*
you never made me welcome. When I was naked you did nothing
to clothe me; when I was sick and in prison you never cared about
me.'

"Then they too will answer him, 'Lord, when did we ever see *44*
you hungry, or thirsty, or lonely, or naked, or sick, or in prison,
and fail to look after you?'

"Then the king will answer them with these words, 'I assure *45*
you that whatever you failed to do to the humblest of my brothers
you failed to do to me.'

"And these will go off to eternal punishment, but the true men *46*
to eternal life."

CHAPTER 26

Jesus announces his coming death

WHEN Jesus had finished all this teaching he spoke to his *1*
disciples, "Do you realise that the Passover will begin in two days' *2*
time; and the Son of Man is going to be betrayed and crucified?"

An evil plot—and an act of love

At that very time the chief priests and elders of the people had *3*
assembled in the court of Caiaphas, the High Priest, and were *4*
discussing together how they might get hold of Jesus by some
trick and kill him. But they kept saying, "It must not be during *5*
the festival or there might be a riot."

Back in Bethany, while Jesus was in the house of Simon the *6*
leper, a woman came to him with an alabaster flask of most expen- *7*
sive perfume, and poured it on his head as he was at table. The *8*
disciples were indignant when they saw this, and said, "What is
the point of such wicked waste? Couldn't this perfume have been *9*
sold for a lot of money which could be given to the poor?" Jesus *10*
knew what they were saying and spoke to them, "Why must you
make this woman feel uncomfortable? She has done a beautiful
thing for me. You have the poor with you always, but you will *11*
not always have me. When she poured this perfume on my body, *12*
she was preparing it for my burial. I assure you that wherever the *13*
gospel is preached throughout the whole world, this deed of hers
will also be recounted, as her memorial to me."

The betrayal is arranged

14 **After this,** one of the twelve, Judas Iscariot by name,
15 approached the chief priests. "What will you give me," he said to
them, "if I hand him over to you?" They settled with him for
16 thirty silver coins, and from then on he looked for a convenient
opportunity to betray Jesus.

The last supper

17 On the first day of unleavened bread the disciples came to
Jesus with the question, "Where do you want us to make our
preparations for you to eat the Passover?"
18 "Go into the city," Jesus replied, "to a certain man there and
say to him, 'The Master says, "My time is near. I am going to keep
19 the Passover with my disciples at your house." ' " The disciples
20 did as Jesus had instructed them and prepared the Passover. Then
21 late in the evening he took his place at table with the twelve and
during the meal he said, "I tell you plainly that one of you is
22 going to betray me." They were deeply distressed at this and each
began to say to him in turn, "Surely, Lord, I am not the one?"
23 And his answer was, "The man who has dipped his hand into the
24 dish with me is the man who will betray me. It is true that the
Son of Man will follow the road foretold by the scriptures, but
alas for the man through whom he is betrayed! It would be better
25 for that man if he had never been born." And Judas, who actually
betrayed him, said, "Master, am I the one?"
"As you say!" replied Jesus.
26 In the middle of the meal Jesus took a loaf and after blessing
it he broke it into pieces and gave it to the disciples. "Take and
27 eat this," he said, "it is my body." Then he took a cup and, after
thanking God, he gave it to them with the words, "Drink this,
28 all of you, for it is my blood, the blood of the new agreement
29 shed to set many free from their sins. I tell you I will drink no
more wine until I drink it fresh with you in my Father's king-
30 dom." Then they sang a hymn together and went out to the
31 Mount of Olives. There Jesus said to them, "Tonight every one
of you will lose his faith in me. For the scripture says, 'I will smite
the shepherd, and the sheep of the flock shall be scattered abroad.'
32 But after I have risen I shall go before you into Galilee!"
33 At this Peter exclaimed, "Even if everyone should lose his faith
in you, I never will!"

"I tell you, Peter," replied Jesus, "that tonight, before the cock 34
crows, you will disown me three times."

"Even if it means dying with you I will never disown you," 35
said Peter. And all the disciples made the same protest.

The prayer in Gethsemane

Then Jesus came with the disciples to a place called Geth- 36
semane and said to them, "Sit down here while I go over there
and pray." Then he took with him Peter and the two sons of 37
Zebedee and began to be in terrible distress and misery. "My 38
heart is nearly breaking," he told them, "stay here and keep watch
with me." Then he walked on a little way and fell on his face 39
and prayed, "My Father, if it is possible let this cup pass from me
—yet it must not be what I want, but what you want."

Then he came back to the disciples and found them fast asleep. 40
He spoke to Peter, "Couldn't you three keep awake with me for
a single hour? Watch and pray, all of you, that you may not have 41
to face temptation. Your spirit is willing, but human nature is
weak."

Then he went away a second time and prayed, "My Father, if 42
it is not possible for this cup to pass from me without my drinking
it, then your will must be done."

And he came and found them asleep again, for they could not 43
keep their eyes open. So he left them and went away again and 44
prayed for the third time using the same words as before. Then 45
he came back to his disciples and spoke to them, "Are you still
going to sleep and take your ease? In a moment you will see the
Son of Man betrayed into the hands of evil men. Wake up, let 46
us be going! Look, here comes my betrayer!"

The betrayal

And while the words were still on his lips Judas, one of the 47
twelve, appeared with a great crowd armed with swords and
staves, sent by the chief priests and Jewish elders. (The traitor 48
himself had given them a sign, "The one I kiss will be the man.
Get him!")

Without any hesitation he walked up to Jesus. "Greetings, 49
Master!" he cried and kissed him affectionately. "Judas, my 50
friend," replied Jesus, "why are you here?"

Then the others came up, seized hold of Jesus and held him.

51 Suddenly one of Jesus' disciples drew his sword, slashed at the
52 High Priest's servant and cut off his ear. At this Jesus said to him,
"Put your sword back into its proper place. All those who take
53 the sword die by the sword. Do you imagine that I could not
appeal to my Father, and he would at once send more than
54 twelve legions of angels to defend me? But then, how would
the scriptures be fulfilled which say that all this must take
place?"

55 And then Jesus spoke to the crowds around him: "So you've
come out with your swords and staves to capture me like a
bandit, have you? Day after day I sat teaching in the Temple and
56 you never laid a finger on me. But all this is happening as the
prophets said it would." And at this point all the disciples deserted
him and made their escape.

Jesus before the High Priest

57 The men who had seized Jesus took him off to Caiaphas the
High Priest in whose house the scribes and elders were assem-
58 bled. Peter followed him at a safe distance right up to the High
Priest's courtyard. Then he went inside and sat down with the
servants and waited to see the end.

59 Meanwhile the chief priests and the whole council did all they
could to find false evidence against Jesus to get him condemned
60 to death. They failed completely. Even after a number of perjurers came forward they still failed. In the end two of these stood
61 up and said, "This man said, 'I can pull down the Temple of God
62 and rebuild it in three days.'" Then the High Priest rose to his
feet and addressed Jesus, "Have you no answer? What about the
63 evidence of these men against you?" But Jesus was silent. Then
the High Priest said to him, "I command you by the living God,
64 to tell us on your oath if you are Christ, the Son of God." Jesus
said to him, "I am. Yes, and I tell you that in the future you will
see the Son of Man sitting at the right hand of power and coming
on the clouds of Heaven."

65 At this the High Priest tore his robes and cried, "That was
blasphemy! Where is the need for further witnesses? Look, you've
66 heard the blasphemy—what's your verdict now?" And they
replied, "He deserves to die."

67 Then they spat in his face and knocked him about, and some
68 slapped him, crying, "Prophesy, you Christ, who was that who
hit you?"

Peter disowns his master

All this time Peter was sitting outside in the courtyard, and a **69** maidservant came up to him and said, "Weren't you with Jesus, the man from Galilee?" But he denied it before them all, saying, **70** "I don't know what you're talking about." Then when he had **71** gone out into the porch, another maid caught sight of him and said to those who were there, "This man was with Jesus of Nazareth." And again he denied it with an oath—"I don't know **72** the man!" A few minutes later those who were standing about **73** came up to Peter and said to him, "You certainly are one of them, you know; it's obvious from your accent." At that he began to **74** curse and swear—"I tell you I don't know the man!" Immediately the cock crew, and the words of Jesus came back into Peter's **75** mind—"Before the cock crows you will disown me three times." And he went outside and wept bitterly.

CHAPTER 27

WHEN the morning came, all the chief priests and elders of the **1** people met in council to decide how they could get Jesus executed. Then they marched him off with his hands tied, and handed him **2** over to Pilate the governor.

The remorse of Judas

Then Judas, who had betrayed him, saw that he was con- **3** demned and in his remorse returned the thirty silver coins to the chief priests and elders, with the words, "I was wrong—I have **4** betrayed an innocent man to death."

"And what has that got to do with us?" they replied. "That's your affair."

And Judas flung down the silver in the Temple and went out- **5** side and hanged himself. But the chief priests picked up the money **6** and said, "It is not legal to put this into the Temple treasury. It is, after all, blood-money." So, after a further consultation, **7** they purchased with it the Potter's Field to be a burial-ground for foreigners, which is why it is called "the Field of Blood" **8** to this day. And so the words of Jeremiah the prophet came true: **9**

And they took the thirty pieces of silver, the price of him

10 that was priced, whom certain of the children of Israel did price; and they gave them for the potter's field, as the Lord appointed me.

Jesus before Pilate

11 Meanwhile Jesus stood in front of the governor, who asked him, "Well, you—*are* you the King of the Jews?"

"Yes, I am," replied Jesus.

12 But while the chief priests and elders were making their
13 accusations, he made no reply at all. So Pilate said to him, "Can
14 you not hear the evidence they're bringing against you?" And to the governor's amazement, Jesus did not answer a single one of their accusations.

15 Now it was the custom at festival-time for the governor to
16 release any prisoner whom the people chose. And it happened
17 that at this time they had a notorious prisoner called Barabbas. So when they assembled to make their usual request, Pilate said to them, "Which one do you want me to set free, Barabbas or Jesus
18 called Christ?" For he knew very well that the latter had been
19 handed over to him through sheer malice. And indeed while he was actually sitting on the Bench his wife sent a message to him —"Don't have anything to do with that good man! I went
20 through agonies dreaming about him last night!" But the chief priests and elders persuaded the mob to ask for Barabbas and
21 demand Jesus' execution. Then the governor spoke to them, "Which of these two are you asking me to release?"

"Barabbas!" they cried.

22 "Then what am I to do with Jesus who is called Christ?" asked Pilate.

23 "Have him crucified!" they all cried. At this Pilate said, "Why, what is his crime?" But their voices rose to a roar, "Have him
24 crucified!" When Pilate realised that nothing more could be done but that there would soon be a riot, he took a bowl of water and washed his hands before the crowd, saying, "I take no responsibility for the death of this man. You must see to that yourselves."
25 To this the whole crowd replied, "Let his blood be on us and on
26 our children!" Whereupon Pilate released Barabbas for them, but he had Jesus flogged and handed over for crucifixion.

27 Then the governor's soldiers took Jesus into the governor's
28 palace and collected the whole guard around him. There they
29 stripped him and put a scarlet cloak upon him. They twisted some

60

thorn-twigs into a crown and put it on his head and put a stick into his right hand. They bowed low before him and jeered at him with the words, "Hail, your majesty, king of the Jews!" Then they spat on him, took the stick and hit him on the head **30** with it. And when they had finished their fun, they stripped the **31** cloak off again, put his own clothes upon him and led him off for crucifixion. On their way out of the city they met a man called **32** Simon, a native of Cyrene in Africa, and they compelled him to carry Jesus' cross.

The crucifixion

Then when they came to a place called Golgotha (which means **33** Skull Hill) they offered him a drink of wine mixed with some **34** bitter drug, but when he had tasted it he refused to drink. And **35** when they had nailed him to the cross they shared out his clothes by drawing lots.

Then they sat down to keep guard over him. And over his head **36, 37** they put a placard with the charge against him:

THIS IS JESUS, THE KING OF THE JEWS

Now two bandits were crucified with Jesus at the same time, **38** one on either side of him. The passers-by nodded their heads **39** knowingly and called out to him in mockery, "Hi, you who could **40** pull down the Temple and build it up again in three days— why don't you save yourself? If you are the Son of God, step down from the cross!" The chief priests also joined the scribes and **41** elders in jeering at him, saying, "He saved others, but he can't **42** save himself! If this is the king of Israel, why doesn't he come down from the cross now, and we will believe him! He trusted in **43** God . . . let God rescue him if He will have anything to do with him! For he said, 'I am God's son'." Even the bandits who were **44** crucified with him hurled abuse at him.

Then from midday until three o'clock darkness spread over the **45** whole countryside, and then Jesus cried with a loud voice, "My **46** God, my God, why did you forsake me?" Some of those who **47** were standing there heard these words which Jesus spoke in Aramaic (*Eli, Eli lama sabachthani?*), and said, "This man is calling for Elijah!" And one of them ran off and fetched a sponge, **48** soaked it in vinegar and put it on a long stick and held it up for him to drink. But the others said, "Let him alone! Let's see if **49** Elijah will come and save him." But Jesus gave one more great **50** cry, and died.

51 And the sanctuary curtain in the Temple was torn in two from
52 top to bottom. The ground shook, rocks split and graves were
opened. (A number of bodies of holy men who were asleep in
53 death rose again. They left their graves after Jesus' resurrection
54 and entered the holy city and appeared to many people.) When
the centurion and his company who were keeping guard over
Jesus saw the earthquake and all that was happening they were
terrified. "Indeed he *was* a son of God!" they said.

55 There were many women at the scene watching from a distance. They had followed Jesus from Galilee to minister to his
56 needs. Among them was Mary of Magdala, Mary the mother of
James and Joseph, and the mother of Zebedee's sons.

Jesus is buried and the tomb is guarded

57 That evening, Joseph, a wealthy man from Arimathaea, who
58 was himself a disciple of Jesus, went to Pilate and asked for the
body of Jesus, and Pilate gave orders for the body to be handed
59, 60 over to him. So Joseph took it, wrapped it in clean linen and
placed it in his own new tomb which had been hewn in the rock.
Then he rolled a large stone across the doorway of the tomb
61 and went away. But Mary from Magdala and the other Mary
remained there, sitting in front of the tomb.

62 Next day, which was the day after the Preparation, the chief
63 priests and the Pharisees went in a body to Pilate and said, "Sir,
we have remembered that while this impostor was alive, he said,
64 'After three days I shall rise again.' Will you give the order then
to have the grave closely guarded until the third day, so that there
can be no chance of his disciples' coming and stealing the body
and telling people that he has risen from the dead? We should
then be faced with a worse fraud than the first one."

65 "You have a guard," Pilate told them. "Go and make it as safe
66 as you think necessary." And they went and made the grave
secure, putting a seal on the stone and leaving the soldiers on
guard.

CHAPTER 28

The first Lord's day: Jesus rises

1 WHEN the Sabbath was over, just as the first day of the week
was dawning, Mary from Magdala and the other Mary went to

look at the tomb. At that moment there was a great earthquake, 2
for an angel of the Lord came down from Heaven, went forward
and rolled back the stone, and took his seat upon it. His appear- 3
ance was dazzling like lightning and his clothes were white as
snow. The guards shook with terror at the sight of him and col- 4
lapsed like dead men. But the angel spoke to the women, "Do 5
not be afraid. I know that you are looking for Jesus who was
crucified. He is not here—he is risen, just as he said he would. 6
Come and look at the place where he was lying. Then go quickly 7
and tell his disciples that he has risen from the dead. And, listen,
he goes before you into Galilee! You will see him there! Now I
have told you my message." Then the women went away quickly 8
from the tomb, their hearts filled with awe and great joy, and ran
to give the news to his disciples. But quite suddenly, Jesus stood 9
before them in their path, and said, "Peace be with you!" And
they went forward to meet him and, clasping his feet, worshipped
him. Then Jesus said to them, "Do not be afraid. Go now and tell 10
my brothers to go into Galilee and they shall see me there."

And while they were on their way, some of the sentries went 11
into the city and reported to the chief priests everything that had
happened. They got together with the elders, and after con- 12
sultation gave the soldiers a considerable sum of money and told 13
them, "Your story must be that his disciples came after dark, and
stole him away while you were asleep. If by any chance this 14
reaches the governor's ears, we will put it right with him and see
that you do not suffer for it." So they took the money and obeyed 15
their instructions. The story was spread and is current among the
Jews to this day.

Jesus gives his final commission

But the eleven went to the hill-side in Galilee where Jesus had 16
arranged to meet them, and when they had seen him they wor- 17
shipped him, though some of them were doubtful. But Jesus came 18
and spoke these words to them, "All power in Heaven and on
earth has been given to me. You, then, are to go and make 19
disciples of all the nations and baptise them in the name of the
Father and of the Son and of the Holy Spirit. Teach them to 20
observe all that I have commanded you and, remember, I am
with you always, even to the end of the world."

The Gospel of Mark

It is generally agreed that Mark's Gospel is the earliest. It probably appeared in 65, soon after the Great Fire of Rome which devastated a great part of the city in the winter of 64–65. The Christians were made the scapegoats of this disaster by the Emperor Nero, and it is quite probable that there is a definite connection between the appearance of this first-written Gospel and the monstrously false accusations which were being made against Christians. The original papyrus roll is traditionally supposed to have borne the title—"The Gospel of Jesus Christ the Son of God."

The author is generally thought to have been John Mark, a native of Jerusalem. The house of his mother Mary became one of the meeting places of the early Christians (Acts 12, 12). It has been suggested that perhaps John Mark is the mysterious young man who escaped from the soldiers' hands on the night of Jesus' arrest (Mark 14, 51). He is also linked with the early growth of the Church, working with Paul, Barnabas and Peter.

Eusebius, the fourth-century historian, quotes Papias (who wrote about 140) as saying that Mark was the "interpreter of Peter", and this seems to have been generally accepted by the early Church.

We may therefore reasonably assume that Mark, drawing on what Peter had told him personally, and being himself convinced of the Divinity of Christ, wrote down this Gospel, probably at Rome, with non-Jewish readers in mind. We notice, for instance, that he hardly quotes at all from the Old Testament, that he explains particular Jewish customs and that he translates any Aramaic expression by its Greek equivalent.

His style has no literary polish but it has the forceful vitality of the man who believes what he writes, and it is not without certain vivid flashes of realism. He draws with strong lines the portrait of a man who was thoroughly human but also unmistakably the Son of God.

The manuscript of Mark ends abruptly at 16, 8, and nearly all scholars regard the subsequent verses as a later addition.

CHAPTER 1

How it began

THE Gospel of Jesus Christ, the Son of God, begins with the **1**
fulfilment of this prophecy of Isaiah— **2**

    Behold, I send my messenger before thy face,
    Who shall prepare thy way;
    The voice of one crying in the wilderness, **3**
    Make ye ready the way of the Lord,
    Make his paths straight.

For John came and began to baptise men in the desert, pro- **4**
claiming baptism as the mark of a complete change of heart and
of the forgiveness of sins. All the people of the Judaean country- **5**
side and everyone in Jerusalem went out to him in the desert and
received his baptism in the river Jordan, publicly confessing their
sins.

John himself was dressed in camel-hair, with a leather belt **6**
round his waist, and he lived on locusts and wild honey. The **7**
burden of his preaching was, "There is someone coming after me
who is stronger than I—indeed I am not good enough to kneel
down and undo his shoes. I have baptised you with water, but **8**
he will baptise you with the Holy Spirit."

The arrival of Jesus

It was in those days that Jesus arrived from the Galilean village **9**
of Nazareth and was baptised by John in the Jordan. All at once, **10**
as he came up out of the water, he saw the heavens split open, and
the Spirit coming down upon him like a dove. A voice came out **11**
of Heaven, saying,

"You are my dearly-beloved Son, in whom I am well pleased!"

Then the Spirit sent him out at once into the desert, and there **12, 13**
he remained for forty days while Satan tempted him. During this
time no one was with him but wild animals, and only the angels
were there to care for him.

Jesus begins to preach the gospel, and to call men to follow him

It was after John's arrest that Jesus came into Galilee, pro- **14**
claiming the gospel of God, saying, **15**

"The time has come at last—the kingdom of God has arrived. You must change your hearts and minds and believe the good news."

16 As he walked along the shore of the Lake of Galilee, he saw two fishermen, Simon and his brother Andrew, casting their nets into the water.

17 "Come and follow me, and I will teach you to catch men!" he cried.

18 At once they dropped their nets, and followed him.

19 Then he went a little further along the shore and saw James the son of Zebedee, aboard a boat with his brother John, overhauling

20 their nets. At once he called them, and they left their father Zebedee in the boat with the hired men, and went off after him.

Jesus begins healing the sick

21 They arrived at Capernaum, and on the Sabbath day Jesus
22 walked straight into the synagogue and began teaching. They were amazed at his way of teaching, for he taught with the ring
23 of authority—quite unlike the scribes. All at once, a man in the grip of an evil spirit appeared in the synagogue shouting out,

24 "What have you got to do with us, Jesus from Nazareth? Have you come to kill us? I know who you are—you're God's holy one!"

25 But Jesus cut him short and spoke sharply,
"Hold your tongue and get out of him!"

26 At this the evil spirit convulsed the man, let out a loud scream
27 and left him. Everyone present was so astounded that people kept saying to each other,
"What on earth has happened? This new teaching has authority behind it. Why, he even gives his orders to evil spirits and they obey him!"

28 And his reputation spread like wild-fire through the whole Galilean district.

29 Then he got up and went straight from the synagogue to the house of Simon and Andrew, accompanied by James and John.
30 Simon's mother-in-law was in bed with a high fever, and they
31 lost no time in telling Jesus about her. He went up to her, took her hand and helped her to her feet. The fever left her, and she began to see to their needs.

32 Late that evening, after sunset, they kept bringing to him all
33 who were sick or troubled by evil spirits. The whole population

of the town gathered round the doorway. And he healed great **34**
numbers of people who were suffering from various forms of disease. In many cases he expelled evil spirits; but he would not
allow them to say a word, for they knew perfectly well who he was.

He retires for private prayer

Then, in the early morning, while it was still dark, Jesus got **35**
up, left the house and went off to a deserted place, and there he
prayed. Simon and his companions went in search of him, and **36, 37**
when they found him, they said,
  "Everyone is looking for you."
  "Then we will go somewhere else, to the neighbouring towns," **38**
he replied, "so that I may give my message there too—that is why
I have come."
  So he continued preaching in their synagogues and expelling **39**
evil spirits throughout the whole of Galilee.

Jesus cures leprosy

Then a leper came to Jesus, knelt in front of him and appealed **40**
to him,
  "If you want to, you can make me clean."
  Jesus was filled with pity for him, and stretched out his hand **41**
and placed it on the leper, saying,
  "Of course I want to—*be clean!*"
  At once the leprosy left him and he was quite clean. Jesus sent **42, 43**
him away there and then with the strict injunction,
  "Mind you say nothing at all to anybody. Go straight off and **44**
show yourself to the priest, and make the offerings for your
cleansing which Moses prescribed, as public proof of your
recovery."
  But he went off and began to talk a great deal about it in public, **45**
spreading his story far and wide. Consequently, it became impossible for Jesus to show his face in the towns and he had to stay
outside in lonely places. Yet the people still came to him from all
quarters.

CHAPTER 2

Faith at Capernaum

1 WHEN he re-entered Capernaum some days later, a rumour
2 spread that he was in somebody's house. Such a large crowd collected that while he was giving them his message it was impossible
3 even to get near the doorway. Meanwhile, a group of people
arrived to see him, bringing with them a paralytic whom four of
4 them were carrying. And when they found it was impossible to
get near him because of the crowd, they removed the tiles from
the roof over Jesus' head and let down the paralytic's bed through
5 the opening. And when Jesus saw their faith, he said to the man
on the bed,

"My son, your sins are forgiven."

6 But some of the scribes were sitting there silently asking themselves,

7 "Why does this man talk such blasphemy? Who can possibly
forgive sins but God?"

8 Jesus realised instantly what they were thinking, and said to
them,

9 "Why must you argue like this in your minds? Which do you
suppose is easier—to say to a paralysed man, 'Your sins are for-
10 given', or 'Get up, pick up your bed and walk'? But to prove to
you that the Son of Man has full authority to forgive sins on earth,
11 I say to you,"—and here he spoke to the paralytic—"Get up,
pick up your bed and go home."

12 At once the man sprang to his feet, picked up his bed and
walked off in full view of them all. Everyone was amazed, praised
God and said,

"We have never seen anything like this before."

13 Then Jesus went out again by the lake-side and the whole
crowd came to him, and he continued to teach them.

Jesus now calls "a sinner" to follow him

14 As Jesus went on his way, he saw Levi the son of Alphaeus
sitting at his desk in the tax-office, and he said to him,

"Follow me!"

15 Levi got up and followed him. Later, when Jesus was sitting at
dinner in Levi's house, a large number of tax-collectors and dis-

reputable folk came in and joined him and his disciples. For there were many such people among his followers. When the scribes 16 and Pharisees saw him eating in the company of tax-collectors and outsiders, they remarked to his disciples,

"Why does he eat with tax-collectors and sinners?"

When Jesus heard this, he said to them, 17

"It is not the fit and flourishing who need the doctor, but those who are ill. I did not come to invite the 'righteous', but the 'sinners'."

The question of fasting

The disciples of John and those of the Pharisees were fasting. 18 They came and said to Jesus,

"Why do those who follow John or the Pharisees keep fasts but your disciples do nothing of the kind?"

Jesus told them, 19

"Can you expect wedding-guests to fast in the bridegroom's presence? Fasting is out of the question as long as they have the bridegroom with them. But the day will come when the bride- 20 groom will be taken away from them—that will be the time for them to fast.

"Nobody," he continued, "sews a patch of unshrunken cloth 21 on to an old coat. If he does, the new patch tears away from the old and the hole is worse than ever. And nobody puts new wine 22 into old wineskins. If he does, the new wine bursts the skins, the wine is spilt and the skins are ruined. No, new wine must go into new wineskins."

Jesus rebukes the sabbatarians

One day he happened to be going through the cornfields on 23 the Sabbath day. And his disciples, as they made their way along, began to pick the ears of corn. The Pharisees said to him, 24

"Look at that! Why should they do what is forbidden on the Sabbath day?"

Then he spoke to them. 25

"Have you never read what David did, when he and his companions were hungry? Haven't you read how he went into 26 the house of God when Abiathar was High Priest, and ate the presentation loaves, which nobody is allowed to eat, except the priests—and gave some of the bread to his companions? The 27

28 Sabbath," he continued, "was made for man's sake; man was not made for the sake of the Sabbath. That is why the Son of Man is master even of the Sabbath."

CHAPTER 3

1 On another occasion when he went into the synagogue, there
2 was a man there whose hand was shrivelled, and they were watching Jesus closely to see whether he would heal him on the Sabbath
3 day, so that they might bring a charge against him. Jesus said to the man with the shrivelled hand,

"Stand up and come out here in front!"

4 Then he said to them,

"Is it right to do good on the Sabbath day, or to do harm? Is it right to save life or to kill?"

5 There was a dead silence. Then Jesus, deeply hurt as he sensed their inhumanity, looked round in anger at the faces surrounding him, and said to the man,

"Stretch out your hand!"

And he stretched it out, and the hand was restored as sound as
6 the other one. The Pharisees walked straight out and discussed with Herod's party how they could have Jesus put out of the way.

Jesus' enormous popularity

7 Jesus now retired to the lake-side with his disciples. A huge crowd of people followed him, not only from Galilee, but from
8 Judaea, Jerusalem and Idumaea, some from the district beyond the Jordan and from the neighbourhood of Tyre and Sidon. This vast crowd came to him because they had heard about the sort of
9 things he was doing. So Jesus told his disciples to have a small boat kept in readiness for him, in case the people should crowd him too
10 closely. For he healed so many people that all those who were in
11 pain kept pressing forward to touch him with their hands. Evil spirits, as soon as they saw him, acknowledged his authority and screamed,

"You are the Son of God!"

12 But he warned them repeatedly that they must not make him known.

70

Jesus chooses the twelve apostles

Later he went up on to the hill-side and summoned the men 13
whom he wanted, and they went up to him. He appointed a band 14
of twelve to be his companions, whom he could send out to
preach, with power to drive out evil spirits. These were the 15
twelve he appointed:

Peter (which was the new name he gave Simon), James the son 16,17
of Zebedee, and John his brother. (He gave them the name of
Boanerges, which means the "Thunderers".) Andrew, Philip, 18
Bartholomew, Matthew, Thomas, James the son of Alphaeus,
Thaddaeus, Simon the Patriot, and Judas Iscariot, who betrayed 19
him.

Jesus exposes an absurd accusation

Then he went indoors, but again such a crowd collected that 20
it was impossible for them even to eat a meal. When his relatives 21
heard of this, they set out to take charge of him, for people were
saying, "He must be mad!"

The scribes who had come down from Jerusalem were saying 22
that he was possessed by Beelzebub, and that he drove out devils
because he was in league with the prince of devils. So Jesus called 23
them to him and spoke to them in a parable—

"How can Satan be the one who drives out Satan? If a kingdom 24
is divided against itself, then that kingdom cannot last, and if a 25
household is divided against itself, it cannot last either. And if 26
Satan leads a rebellion against Satan—his days are certainly
numbered. No one can break into a strong man's house and steal 27
his property, without first tying up the strong man hand and
foot. But if he did that, he could ransack the whole house.

"Believe me, all men's sins can be forgiven and all their blas- 28
phemies. But there can never be any forgiveness for blasphemy 29
against the Holy Spirit. That is an eternal sin."

He said this because they were saying, "He is in the power of 30
an evil spirit."

The new relationships in the kingdom

Then his mother and his brothers arrived. They stood outside 31
the house and sent a message asking him to come out to them.
There was a crowd sitting round him when the message was 32

brought telling him, "Your mother and your brothers are outside looking for you."

33 Jesus replied, "And who are really my mother and my brothers?"

34 And he looked round at the faces of those sitting in a circle about him.

35 "Look!" he said, "my mother and my brothers are here. Anyone who does the will of God is brother and sister and mother to me."

CHAPTER 4

The story of the sower

1 THEN once again he began to teach them by the lake-side. A bigger crowd than ever collected around him so that he got into the little boat on the lake and sat down, while the crowd covered 2 the ground right up to the water's edge. He taught them a great deal in parables, and in the course of his teaching he said,

3,4 "Listen! A man once went out to sow his seed and as he sowed, some seed fell by the roadside and the birds came and gobbled it 5 up. Some of the seed fell among the rocks where there was not much soil, and sprang up very quickly because there was no 6 depth of earth. But when the sun rose it was scorched, and 7 because it had no root, it withered away. And some of the seed fell among thorn-bushes and the thorns grew up and choked the 8 life out of it, and it bore no crop. And there was some seed which fell on good soil, and when it grew, produced a crop which yielded thirty or sixty or even a hundred times as much as the seed."

9 Then he added,

"Every man who has ears should use them!"

10 Then when they were by themselves, his close followers and 11 the twelve asked him about the parables, and he told them.

"The secret of the kingdom of God has been given to you. But to those who do not know the secret, everything remains in 12 parables, so that,

seeing they may see, and not perceive;
and hearing they may hear, and not understand;
lest haply they should turn again, and it should be forgiven them."

13 Then he continued,

72

"Do you really not understand this parable? Then how are you going to understand all the other parables? The man who sows, **14** sows the message. As for those who are by the roadside where the **15** message is sown, as soon as they hear it Satan comes at once and takes away what has been sown in their minds. Similarly, the **16** seed sown among the rocks represents those who hear the message without hesitation and accept it joyfully. But they have no real **17** roots and do not last—when trouble or persecution arises because of the message, they give up their faith at once. Then there are **18** the seeds which were sown among thorn-bushes. These are the people who hear the message, but the worries of this world **19** and the false glamour of riches and all sorts of other ambitions creep in and choke the life out of what they have heard, and it produces no crop in their lives. As for the seed sown on good soil, **20** this means the men who hear the message and accept it and do produce a crop—thirty, sixty, even a hundred times as much as they received."

Truth is meant to be used

Then he said to them, **21**

"Is a lamp brought into the room to be put under a bucket or underneath the bed? Surely its place is on the lamp-stand! There **22** is nothing hidden which is not meant to be made perfectly plain one day, and there are no secrets which are not meant one day to be common knowledge. If a man has ears he should use them! **23**

"Be careful how you listen," he said to them. "Whatever **24** measure you use will be used towards you, and even more than that. For the man who has something will receive more. As for **25** the man who has nothing, even his nothing will be taken away."

Jesus gives pictures of the kingdom's growth

Then he said, **26**

"The kingdom of God is like a man scattering seed on the ground and then going to bed each night and getting up every **27** morning, while the seed sprouts and grows up, though he has no idea how it happens. The earth produces a crop without any **28** help from anyone: first a blade, then the ear of corn, then the full-grown grain in the ear. And as soon as the crop is ready, he sends **29** his reapers in without delay, for the harvest-time has come."

Then he continued, **30**

"What can we say the kingdom of God is like? How shall we
31 put it in a parable? It is like a tiny grain of mustard-seed which,
32 when it is sown, is smaller than any seed that is ever sown. But
after it is sown in the earth, it grows up and becomes bigger than
any other plant. It shoots out great branches so that birds can
come and nest in its shelter."

33 So he taught them his message with many parables such as their
34 minds could take in. He did not speak to them at all without
using parables, although in private he explained everything to his
disciples.

Jesus shows himself master of natural forces

35 On the evening of that day, he said to them,
"Let us cross over to the other side of the lake."

36 So they sent the crowd home and took him with them in the
little boat in which he had been sitting, accompanied by other
37 small craft. Then came a violent squall of wind which drove the
38 waves aboard the boat until it was almost swamped. Jesus was in
the stern asleep on the cushion. They awoke him with the words,
"Master, don't you care that we're drowning?"

39 And he woke up, rebuked the wind, and said to the waves,
"Hush now! Be still!"

The wind dropped and everything was very still.

40 "Why are you so frightened? What has happened to your
faith?" he asked them.

41 But sheer awe swept over them, and they kept saying to each
other,

"Who ever can he be?—even the wind and the waves do what
he tells them!"

CHAPTER 5

Jesus meets a violent lunatic

1 So they arrived on the other side of the lake in the country of
2 the Gerasenes. As Jesus was getting out of the boat, a man in the
grip of an evil spirit rushed out to meet him from among the
3 tombs where he was living. It was no longer possible for any
4 human being to restrain him even with a chain. Indeed he had
frequently been secured with fetters and lengths of chain, but he
had simply snapped the chains and broken the fetters in pieces. No

one could do anything with him. All through the night as well as 5
in the day-time he screamed among the tombs and on the hill-side,
and cut himself with stones. Now, as soon as he saw Jesus in the 6
distance, he ran and knelt before him, yelling at the top of his 7
voice,

"What have you got to do with me, Jesus, Son of the most
high God? For God's sake, don't torture me!"

For Jesus had already said, "Come out of this man, you evil 8
spirit!"

Then he asked him, 9

"What is your name?"

"My name is legion," he replied, "for there are many of us."

Then he begged and prayed him not to send "them" out of the 10
country.

A large herd of pigs was grazing there on the hill-side, and the 11,12
evil spirits implored him, "Send us over to the pigs and we'll get
into them!"

So Jesus allowed them to do this, and they came out of the 13
man, and made off and went into the pigs. The whole herd of
about two thousand stampeded down the cliff into the lake and
was drowned. The swineherds took to their heels and spread their 14
story in the city and all over the countryside. Then the people
came to see what had happened. As they approached Jesus, they 15
saw the man who had been devil-possessed sitting there properly
clothed and perfectly sane—the same man who had been possessed by "legion"—and they were really frightened. Those who 16
had seen the incident told them what had happened to the devil-
possessed man and about the disaster to the pigs. Then they began 17
to implore Jesus to leave their district. As he was embarking on 18
the small boat, the man who had been possessed begged that he
might go with him. But Jesus would not allow this. 19

"Go home to your own people," he told him, "and tell them
what the Lord has done for you, and how kind he has been to
you!"

So the man went off and began to spread throughout the Ten 20
Towns the story of what Jesus had done for him. And they were
all simply amazed.

Faith is followed by healing

When Jesus had crossed again in the boat to the other side of 21
the lake, a great crowd collected around him as he stood on the

22 shore. Then came a man called Jairus, one of the synagogue presi-
23 dents. And when he saw Jesus, he knelt before him, pleading
    desperately for his help.

"My little girl is dying," he said. "Will you come and put your
hands on her—then she will get better and live."

24 Jesus went off with him, followed by a large crowd jostling
25 at his elbow. Among them was a woman who had had a haemor-
26 rhage for twelve years and who had gone through a great deal
    at the hands of many doctors, spending all her money in the pro-
    cess. She had derived no benefit from them but, on the contrary,
27 was getting worse. This woman had heard about Jesus and came
    up behind him under cover of the crowd, and touched his cloak,
28 "For if I can only touch his clothes," she kept saying, "I shall
    be all right."

29 The haemorrhage stopped immediately, and she knew in her-
30 self that she was cured of her trouble. At once Jesus knew in-
    tuitively that power had gone out of him, and he turned round
    in the middle of the crowd and said,

"Who touched my clothes?"

31 His disciples replied,

"You can see this crowd jostling you. How can you ask, 'Who
touched me?'"

32 But he looked all round at their faces to see who had done so.
33 Then the woman, scared and shaking all over because she knew
    that she was the one to whom this thing had happened, came and
34 flung herself before him and told him the whole story. But he
    said to her,

"Daughter, it is your faith that has healed you. Go home in
peace, and be free from your trouble."

35 While he was still speaking, messengers arrived from the
    synagogue president's house, saying,

"Your daughter is dead—there is no need to bother the master
any further."

36 But when Jesus heard this, he said,

"Now don't be afraid, just go on believing!"

37 Then he allowed no one to follow him except Peter and James
38 and John, James's brother. They arrived at the president's house
39 and Jesus noticed the hubbub and all the weeping and wailing, and
    as he went in, he said to the people in the house,

"Why are you making such a noise with your crying? The
child is not dead; she is fast asleep."

40 They greeted this with a scornful laugh. But Jesus turned them

all out, and taking only the father and mother and his own companions with him, went into the room where the child was. Then **41** he took the little girl's hand and said to her in Aramaic,

"Little girl, I tell you to get up!"

At once she jumped to her feet and walked round the room, for **42** she was twelve years old. This sight sent the others nearly out of their minds with joy. But Jesus gave them strict instructions not to **43** let anyone know what had happened—and ordered food to be given to the little girl.

CHAPTER 6

The "prophet without honour"

THEN he left that district and came into his own native town, **1** followed by his disciples. When the Sabbath day came, he began **2** to teach in the synagogue. The congregation were astonished and remarked,

"Where does he get all this? What is this wisdom that he has been given—and what about these marvellous things that he can do? He's only the carpenter, Mary's son, the brother of James, **3** Joses, Judas and Simon; and his sisters are living here with us!"

And they were deeply offended with him. But Jesus said to **4** them,

"No prophet goes unhonoured—except in his native town or with his own relations or in his own home!"

And he could do nothing miraculous there apart from laying **5** his hands on a few sick people and healing them; their lack of **6** faith astonished him.

The twelve are sent out to preach the gospel

Then he made his way round the villages, continuing his teaching. He summoned the twelve, and began to send them out in **7** twos, giving them power over evil spirits. He instructed them to **8** take nothing for the road except a staff—no satchel, no bread and no money in their pockets. They were to wear sandals and not to **9** take more than one coat. And he told them, **10**

"Wherever you are, when you go into a house, stay there until you leave that place. And wherever people will not welcome you **11** or listen to what you have to say, leave them and shake the dust off your feet as a protest against them!"

12 So they went out and preached that men should change their
13 whole outlook. They expelled many evil spirits and anointed many sick people with oil and healed them.

Herod's guilty conscience

14 All this came to the ears of king Herod, for Jesus' reputation was spreading, and people were saying that John the Baptist had risen from the dead, and that was why he was showing such
15 miraculous powers. Others maintained that he was Elijah, and others that he was one of the prophets of the old days come back
16 again. But when Herod heard of all this, he said, "It must be John whom I beheaded, risen from the dead!"
17 For Herod himself had sent and arrested John and had him bound in prison, all on account of Herodias, wife of his brother
18 Philip. He had married her, though John used to say to Herod, "It is not right for you to possess your own brother's wife."
19 Herodias herself was furious with him for this and wanted to have
20 him executed, but she could not do it, for Herod had a deep respect for John, knowing that he was a just and holy man, and protected him. He used to listen to him and be profoundly disturbed, and yet he enjoyed hearing him.
21 Then a good opportunity came, for Herod gave a birthday party for his courtiers and army commanders and for the leading
22 people in Galilee. Herodias' daughter came in and danced, to the great delight of Herod and his guests. The king said to the girl, "Ask me anything you like and I will give it to you!"
23 And he swore to her, "I will give you whatever you ask me, up to half of my kingdom!"
24 And she went out and spoke to her mother, "What shall I ask for?" And she said, "The head of John the Baptist!"
25 The girl rushed back to the king's presence, and made her request. "I want you to give me, this minute, the head of John the Baptist on a dish!" she said.
26 Herod was aghast, but because of his oath and the presence of
27 his guests, he did not like to refuse her. So he sent one of the palace guardsmen straightaway to bring him John's head. He
28 went off and beheaded him in the prison, brought back his head

78

on the dish, and gave it to the girl who handed it to her mother.
When his disciples heard what had happened, they came and took 29
away the body and put it in a tomb.

The apostles return: the huge crowds make rest impossible

The apostles returned to Jesus and reported to him every detail 30
of what they had done and taught.

"Now come along to some quiet place by yourselves, and rest 31
for a little while," said Jesus, for there were people coming and
going incessantly so that they had not even time for meals. They 32
went off in the boat to a quiet place by themselves, but a great 33
many saw them go and recognised them, and people from all
the towns hurried around the shore on foot to forestall them.
When Jesus disembarked he saw the large crowd and his heart 34
was touched with pity for them because they seemed to him like
sheep without a shepherd. And he settled down to teach them
about many things. As the day wore on, his disciples came to him 35
and said,

"We are right in the wilds here and it is getting late. Let them 36
go now, so that they can buy themselves something to eat from
the farms and villages around here."

But Jesus replied, 37
"You give them something to eat!"

"You mean we're to go and spend ten pounds on bread? Is
that how you want us to feed them?"

"What bread have you got?" asked Jesus. "Go and have a 38
look."

And when they had found out, they told him,
"We have five loaves and two fish."

Jesus miraculously feeds five thousand people

Then Jesus directed the people to sit down in parties on the 39
fresh grass. And they threw themselves down in groups of fifty 40
and a hundred. Then Jesus took the five loaves and the two fish, 41
and looking up to Heaven, thanked God, broke the loaves and
gave them to the disciples to distribute to the people. And he
divided the two fish among them all. Everybody ate and was 42
satisfied. Afterwards they collected twelve baskets full of pieces 43
of bread and fish that were left over. There were five thousand 44
men who ate the loaves.

Jesus' mastery over natural law

45 Directly after this, Jesus made his disciples get aboard the boat and go on ahead to Bethsaida on the other side of the lake, while
46 he himself sent the crowds home. And when he had sent them
47 all on their way, he went off to the hill-side to pray. When it grew late, the boat was in the middle of the lake, and he was by himself
48 on land. He saw them straining at the oars, for the wind was dead against them. And in the small hours he went towards them, walking on the waters of the lake, intending to come alongside
49 them. But when they saw him walking on the water, they thought
50 he was a ghost, and screamed out. For they all saw him and they were absolutely terrified. But Jesus at once spoke quietly to them, "It's all right, it is I myself; don't be afraid!"
51 And he climbed aboard the boat with them, and the wind
52 dropped. But they were scared out of their wits. They had not had the sense to learn the lesson of the loaves. Even that miracle had not opened their eyes to see who he was.
53 And when they had crossed over to the other side of the lake,
54 they landed at Gennesaret and tied up there. As soon as they came
55 ashore, the people recognised Jesus and rushed all over the countryside and began to carry the sick around on their beds to
56 wherever they heard that he was. Wherever he went, in villages or towns or farms, they laid down their sick right in the road-way and begged him that they might "just touch the edge of his cloak". And all those who touched him were healed.

CHAPTER 7

Jesus exposes the danger of man-made traditions

1 AND now Jesus was approached by the Pharisees and some of
2 the scribes who had come from Jerusalem. They had noticed that his disciples ate their meals with "common" hands—meaning
3 that they had not gone through a ceremonial washing. (The Pharisees, and indeed all the Jews, will never eat unless they have washed their hands in a particular way, following a traditional
4 rule. And they will not eat anything bought in the market until they have first performed their "sprinkling". And there are many other things which they consider important, concerned with the
5 washing of cups, jugs and basins.) So the Pharisees and the scribes put this question to Jesus,

"Why do your disciples refuse to follow the ancient tradition, and eat their bread with 'common' hands?"

Jesus replied,   *6*

"You hypocrites, Isaiah described you beautifully when he wrote—

This people honoureth me with their lips,
But their heart is far from me.
But in vain do they worship me,   *7*
Teaching as doctrines the precepts of men.

You are so busy holding on to the traditions of men that you *8*
let go the commandment of God!"

Then he went on,   *9*

"It is wonderful to see how you can set aside the commandment of God to preserve your own tradition! For Moses said, 'Honour *10* thy father and thy mother' and 'He that speaketh evil of father or mother, let him die the death.' But you say, 'if a man says to *11* his father or his mother, Korban—meaning, I have given God whatever duty I owed to you', then he need not lift a finger any *12* longer for his father or mother, so making the word of God *13* invalid for the sake of the tradition which you hold. And this is typical of much of what you do."

Then he called the crowd close to him again, and spoke to them, *14*

"Listen to me now, all of you, and understand this. There is *15* nothing outside a man which can enter into him and make him 'common'. It is the things which come out of a man that make him 'common'!"

Later, when he had gone indoors away from the crowd, his *17* disciples asked him about this parable.

"Oh, are you as dull as they are?" he said. "Can't you see that *18* anything that goes into a man from outside cannot make him 'common' or unclean? You see, it doesn't go into his heart, but *19* into his stomach, and passes out of the body altogether, so that all food is clean enough. But," he went on, "whatever comes out of *20* a man, that is what makes a man 'common' or unclean. For it is *21* from inside, from men's hearts and minds, that evil thoughts arise —lust, theft, murder, adultery, greed, wickedness, deceit, sensu- *22* ality, envy, slander, arrogance and folly! All these evil things *23* come from inside a man and make him unclean!"

The faith of a gentile is rewarded

Then he got up and left that place and went off to the *24*

neighbourhood of Tyre. There he went into a house and wanted
no one to know where he was. But it proved impossible to remain
25 hidden. For no sooner had he got there, than a woman who had
heard about him, and who had a daughter possessed by an evil
26 spirit, arrived and prostrated herself before him. She was a Greek,
a Syrophoenician by birth, and she asked him to drive the evil
27 spirit out of her daughter. Jesus said to her,

"You must let the children have all they want first. It is not
right, you know, to take the children's food and throw it to the
dogs."

28 But she replied,

"Yes, Lord, I know, but even the dogs under the table eat
what the children leave."

29 "If you can answer like that," Jesus said to her, "you can go
home! The evil spirit has left your daughter."

30 And she went back to her home and found the child lying
quietly on her bed, and the evil spirit gone.

Jesus restores speech and hearing

31 Once more Jesus left the neighbourhood of Tyre and passed
through Sidon towards the Lake of Galilee, and crossed the Ten
32 Towns territory. They brought to him a man who was deaf and
unable to speak intelligibly, and they implored him to put his
33 hand upon him. Jesus took him away from the crowd by himself.
He put his fingers in the man's ears and touched his tongue with
34 his own saliva. Then, looking up to Heaven, he gave a deep sigh
and said to him in Aramaic,

"Open!"

35 And his ears were opened and immediately whatever had tied
36 his tongue came loose and he spoke quite plainly. Jesus gave
instructions that they should tell no one about this happening,
but the more he told them, the more they broadcast the news.
37 People were absolutely amazed, and kept saying,

"How wonderfully he has done everything! He even makes
the deaf hear and the dumb speak."

CHAPTER 8

He again feeds the people miraculously

1 ABOUT this time it happened again that a large crowd collected and
had nothing to eat. Jesus called the disciples over to him and said,

"My heart goes out to this crowd; they have been with me three days now and they have no food left. If I send them off home without anything, they will collapse on the way—and some of them have come from a distance." **2** **3**

His disciples replied, **4**

"Where could anyone find the food to feed them here in this deserted spot?"

"How many loaves have you got?" Jesus asked them. **5**

"Seven," they replied.

So Jesus told the crowd to settle themselves on the ground. **6** Then he took the seven loaves into his hands, and with a prayer of thanksgiving broke them, and gave them to the disciples to distribute to the people; and this they did. They had a few small **7** fish as well, and after blessing them, Jesus told the disciples to give these also to the people. They ate and they were satisfied. More- **8** over, they picked up seven baskets full of pieces left over. The **9** people numbered about four thousand. Jesus sent them home, and **10** then he boarded the boat at once with his disciples and went on to the district of Dalmanutha.

Jesus refuses to give a sign

Now the Pharisees came out and began an argument with him, **11** wanting a sign from Heaven. Jesus gave a deep sigh, and then said, **12** "What makes this generation want a sign? I can tell you this, they will certainly not be given one!"

Then he left them and got aboard the boat again, and crossed **13** the lake.

The disciples had forgotten to take any food and had only one **14** loaf with them in the boat. Jesus spoke seriously to them, "Keep **15** your eyes open! Be on your guard against the 'yeast' of the Pharisees and the 'yeast' of Herod!" And this sent them into an **16** earnest consultation among themselves because they had brought no bread. Jesus knew it and said to them, **17**

"Why all this discussion about bringing no bread? Don't you understand or grasp what I say even yet? Are you like the people who 'having eyes, do not see, and having ears, do not hear'? Have **18** you forgotten—when I broke five loaves for five thousand people, **19** how many baskets full of pieces did you pick up?"

"Twelve," they replied.

"And when there were seven loaves for four thousand people, **20** how many baskets of pieces did you pick up?"

"Seven," they said.

21 "And does that still mean nothing to you?" he said.

Jesus restores sight

22 So they arrived at Bethsaida where a blind man was brought to
23 him, with the earnest request that he should touch him. Jesus
took the blind man's hand and led him outside the village. Then
he moistened his eyes with saliva and putting his hands on him,
asked,

"Can you see at all?"

24 The man looked up and said,

"I can see people. They look like trees—only they are walking
about."

25 Then Jesus put his hands on his eyes once more and his sight
came into focus, and he recovered and saw everything sharp and
26 clear. And Jesus sent him off to his own house with the words,

"Don't even go into the village."

Jesus' question: Peter's inspired answer

27 Jesus then went away with his disciples to the villages of
Caesarea Philippi. On the way he asked them,

"Who are men saying that I am?"

28 "John the Baptist," they answered. "But others say that you are
Elijah or, some say, one of the prophets."

29 Then he asked them,

"But what about you—who do you say that I am?"

"You are Christ!" answered Peter.

30 Then Jesus impressed it upon them that they must not mention
this to anyone.

Jesus speaks of the future and of the cost of discipleship

31 And he began to teach them that it was inevitable that the
Son of Man should go through much suffering and be utterly
repudiated by the elders and chief priests and scribes, and be
32 killed, and after three days rise again. He told them all this quite
bluntly.

This made Peter draw him on one side and take him to task
33 about what he had said. But Jesus turned and faced his disciples
and rebuked Peter.

"Out of my way, Satan!" he said. "Peter, you are not looking at things from God's point of view, but from man's!"

Then he called his disciples and the people around him, and **34** said to them,

"If anyone wants to follow in my footsteps, he must give up all right to himself, take up his cross and follow me. The man **35** who tries to save his life will lose it; it is the man who loses his life for my sake and the gospel's who will save it. What good **36** can it do a man to gain the whole world at the price of his own soul? What can a man offer to buy back his soul once he has lost **37** it? If anyone is ashamed of me and my words in this unfaithful **38** and sinful generation, the Son of Man will be ashamed of him when he comes in the Father's glory with the holy angels around him."

CHAPTER 9

Jesus foretells his glory

THEN he added,   **1**

"Believe me, there are some of you standing here who will know nothing of death until you have seen the kingdom of God coming in its power!"

Six days later, Jesus took Peter and James and John with him **2** and led them high up on a hill-side where they were entirely alone. His whole appearance changed before their eyes, while his **3** clothes became white, dazzling white—whiter than any earthly bleaching could make them. Elijah and Moses appeared to the **4** disciples and stood there in conversation with Jesus. Peter burst **5** out to Jesus,

"Master, it is wonderful for us to be here! Shall we put up three shelters—one for you, one for Moses and one for Elijah?"

He really did not know what to say, for they were very fright- **6** ened. Then came a cloud which overshadowed them and a voice **7** spoke out of the cloud,

"This is my dearly-loved Son. Listen to him!"

Then, quite suddenly they looked all round them and saw **8** nobody at all with them but Jesus. And as they came down the **9** hill-side, he warned them not to tell anybody what they had seen till "the Son of Man should have risen again from the dead". They treasured this remark and tried to puzzle out among them- **10** selves what "rising from the dead" could mean. Then they asked **11** him this question,

85

"Why do the scribes say that Elijah must come before Christ?"

12 "It is quite true," he told them, "that Elijah does come first, and begins the restitution of all things. But what does the scripture say about the Son of Man? This: that he must go through

13 much suffering and be treated with contempt! I tell you that not only has Elijah come already but they have done to him exactly what they wanted—just as the scripture says of him."

Jesus heals an epileptic boy

14 Then as they rejoined the other disciples, they saw that they were surrounded by a large crowd and that some of the scribes

15 were arguing with them. As soon as the people saw Jesus, they ran forward excitedly to welcome him.

16 "What is the trouble?" Jesus asked them.

17 A man from the crowd answered,

"Master, I brought my son to you because he has a dumb

18 spirit. Wherever he is, it gets hold of him, throws him down on the ground and there he foams at the mouth and grinds his teeth. It's simply wearing him out. I did speak to your disciples to get them to drive it out, but they hadn't the power to do it."

19 Jesus answered them,

"Oh, what a faithless people you are! How long must I be with you, how long must I put up with you? Bring him here to me."

20 So they brought the boy to him, and as soon as the spirit saw Jesus, it convulsed the boy, who fell to the ground and writhed there, foaming at the mouth.

21 "How long has he been like this?" Jesus asked the father.

22 "Ever since he was a child," he replied. "Again and again it has thrown him into the fire or into water to finish him off. But if you can do anything, please take pity on us and help us."

23 "If you can do anything!" retorted Jesus. "Everything is possible to the man who believes."

24 "I do believe," the boy's father burst out. "Help me to believe more!"

25 When Jesus noticed that a crowd was rapidly gathering, he spoke sharply to the evil spirit, with the words,

"I command you, deaf and dumb spirit, come out of this boy, and never go into him again!"

26 The spirit gave a loud scream and after a dreadful convulsion left him. The boy lay there like a corpse, so that most of the bystanders said, "He is dead."

But Jesus grasped his hands and lifted him up, and then he 27
stood on his own feet. When he had gone home, Jesus' disciples 28
asked him privately,

"Why were we unable to drive it out?"

"Nothing can drive out this kind of thing except prayer," 29
replied Jesus.

Jesus privately warns his disciples of his own death

Then they left that district and went straight through Galilee. 30
Jesus kept this journey secret for he was teaching his disciples that 31
the Son of Man would be betrayed into the power of men, that
they would kill him and that three days after his death he would
rise again. But they were completely mystified by this saying, 32
and were afraid to question him about it.

Jesus defines the new "greatness"

So they came to Capernaum. And when they were indoors he 33
asked them,

"What were you discussing as we came along?"

They were silent, for on the way they had been arguing about 34
who should be the greatest. Jesus sat down and called the twelve, 35
and said to them,

"If any man wants to be first, he must be last and servant of all."

Then he took a little child and stood him in front of them all, 36
and putting his arms round him, said to them,

"Anyone who welcomes one little child like this for my sake is 37
welcoming me. And the man who welcomes me is welcoming not
only me but the one who sent me!"

Then John said to him, 38

"Master, we saw somebody driving out evil spirits in your
name, and we stopped him, for he is not one who follows us."

But Jesus replied, 39

"You must not stop him. No one who exerts such power in my
name would readily say anything against me. For the man who 40
is not against us is on our side. In fact, I assure you that the man 41
who gives you a mere drink of water in my name, because you
are followers of mine, will most certainly be rewarded. And I tell 42
you too, that the man who disturbs the faith of one of the
humblest of those who believe in me would be better off if he
were thrown into the sea with a great mill-stone hung round his
neck!

Entering the kingdom may mean painful sacrifice

43   "Indeed, if it is your own hand that spoils your faith, you must cut it off. It is better for you to enter life maimed than to keep
45 both your hands and go to the rubbish-heap. If your foot spoils your faith, you must cut it off. It is better for you to enter life on one foot than to keep both your feet and be thrown on to the
47 rubbish-heap. And if your eye leads you astray, pluck it out. It is better for you to go one-eyed into the kingdom of God than to
48 keep both eyes and be thrown on to the rubbish-heap, where
49 decay never stops and the fire never goes out. For everyone will
50 be salted with fire. Salt is a very good thing; but if it should lose its saltiness, what can you do to restore its flavour? You must have salt in yourselves, and live at peace with each other."

CHAPTER 10

The divine purpose in marriage

1   THEN he got up and left Galilee and went off to the borders of Judaea and beyond the Jordan. Again great crowds assembled to meet him, and again, according to his custom, he taught them.
2 Then some Pharisees arrived to ask him this test-question.

"Is it right for a man to divorce his wife?"

3   Jesus replied by asking them,

"What has Moses commanded you to do?"

4   "Moses allows men to write a divorce-notice and then to dismiss her," they said.

5   "Moses gave you that commandment," returned Jesus,
6 "because you know so little of the meaning of love. But from the beginning of the creation, God made them male and female. 'For
7 this cause shall a man leave his father and mother, and shall cleave
8 to his wife; and the twain shall become one flesh.' So that in body
9 they are no longer two people but one. That is why man must never separate what God has joined together."

10   On reaching the house, his disciples questioned him again about this matter.

11   "Any man who divorces his wife and marries another woman,"
12 he told them, "commits adultery against his wife. And if she herself divorces her husband and marries someone else, she commits adultery."

He welcomes small children

Then some people came to him bringing little children for him   *13*
to touch. The disciples tried to discourage them. When Jesus saw   *14*
this, he was indignant and told them,

"You must let little children come to me—never stop them!
For the kingdom of God belongs to such as these. Indeed, I assure   *15*
you that the man who does not accept the kingdom of God like
a little child will never enter it."

Then he took the children in his arms and laid his hands on   *16*
them and blessed them.

Jesus shows the danger of riches

As he began to take the road again, a man came running up and   *17*
fell at his feet, and asked him,

"Good Master, tell me, please, what must I do to be sure of
eternal life?"

"I wonder why you call me good," returned Jesus. "No one is   *18*
good—only God. You know the commandments, 'Do no murder,   *19*
Do not commit adultery, Do not steal, Do not bear false witness,
Do not cheat, Honour thy father and mother'."

"Master," he replied, "I have carefully kept all these since I   *20*
was quite young."

Jesus looked steadily at him, and his heart warmed towards him.   *21*
Then he said,

"There is one thing you still want. Go and sell everything you
have, give the money away to the poor—you will have riches in
Heaven. And then come back and follow me."

At these words his face fell and he went away in deep distress,   *22*
for he was very rich. Then Jesus looked round at them all, and   *23*
said to his disciples,

"How difficult it is for those who have great possessions to enter
the kingdom of God!"

The disciples were staggered at these words, but Jesus con-   *24*
tinued,

"Children, you don't know how hard it can be to get into the
kingdom of Heaven. Why, a camel could more easily squeeze   *25*
through the eye of a needle than a rich man get into the kingdom
of God."

At this their astonishment knew no bounds, and they said to   *26*
each other,

"Then who can possibly be saved?"

27 Jesus looked straight at them and said,

"Humanly speaking it is impossible, but not with God. Everything is possible with God."

28 Then Peter burst out,

"But look, we have left everything and followed you!"

29 "I promise you," returned Jesus, "nobody leaves home or brothers or sisters or mother or father or children or property

30 for my sake and the gospel's without getting back a hundred times over, now in this present life, homes and brothers and sisters, mothers and children and land—though not without

31 persecution—and in the next world eternal life. But many who are first now will then be last, and the last now will then be first."

The last journey to Jerusalem begins

32 They were now on their way going up to Jerusalem and Jesus walked on ahead. The disciples were dismayed at this, and those who followed were afraid. Then once more he took the twelve aside and began to tell them what was going to happen to him.

33 "We are now going up to Jerusalem," he said, "as you can see. And the Son of Man will be betrayed into the power of the chief priests and scribes. They are going to condemn him to death and

34 hand him over to pagans who will jeer at him and spit at him and flog him and kill him. But after three days he will rise again."

An ill-timed request

35 Then Zebedee's two sons James and John approached him, saying,

"Master, we want you to grant us a special request."

36 "What do you want me to do for you?" answered Jesus.

37 "Give us permission to sit one on each side of you in the glory of your kingdom!"

38 "You don't know what you are asking," Jesus said to them. "Can you drink the cup I have to drink? Can you go through the baptism I have to bear?"

39 "Yes, we can," they replied.

Then Jesus told them,

"You will indeed drink the cup I am drinking, and you will

40 undergo the baptism which I have to bear! But as for sitting on either side of me, that is not for me to give—such places belong to those for whom they are intended."

When the other ten heard about this, they began to be highly **41**
indignant with James and John; so Jesus called them all to him, **42**
and said,

"You know that the so-called rulers in the heathen world lord
it over them, and their great men have absolute power. But it **43**
must not be so among you. No, whoever among you wants to be
great must become the servant of you all, and if he wants to be **44**
first among you he must be the slave of all men! For the Son **45**
of Man himself has not come to be served but to serve, and to give
his life to set many others free."

Then they came to Jericho, and as he was leaving it accom- **46**
panied by his disciples and a large crowd, Bartimaeus (that is,
the son of Timaeus), a blind beggar, was sitting in his usual place
by the side of the road. When he heard that it was Jesus of **47**
Nazareth he began to call out,

"Jesus, Son of David, have pity on me!"

Many of the people told him sharply to keep quiet, but he **48**
shouted all the more,

"Son of David, have pity on me!"

Jesus stood quite still and said, **49**

"Call him here."

So they called the blind man, saying,

"It's all right now, get up, he's calling you!"

At this he threw off his coat, jumped to his feet and came to **50**
Jesus.

"What do you want me to do for you?" he asked him. **51**

"Oh, Master, let me see again!"

"Go on your way then," returned Jesus, "your faith has healed **52**
you."

And he recovered his sight at once and followed Jesus along the
road.

CHAPTER 11

Jesus arranges for his entry into the city

WHEN they were approaching Jerusalem and had come to **1**
Bethphage and Bethany on the slopes of the Mount of Olives, he
sent off two of his disciples with these instructions, **2**

"Go into the village just ahead of you and as soon as you enter
it you will find a tethered colt on which no one has yet ridden.
Untie it, and bring it here. If anybody asks you, 'Why are you **3**

doing this?', just say, 'The Lord needs it, and will send it back immediately.'"

4 So they went off and found the colt tethered by a doorway
5 outside in the open street, and they untied it. Some of the by-
6 standers did say, "What are you doing, untying this colt?", but they made the reply Jesus told them to make, and the men raised
7 no objection. So they brought the colt to Jesus, threw their coats on its back, and he took his seat upon it.

8 Many of the people spread out their coats in his path as he rode along, and others put down straw which they had cut from the
9 fields. The whole crowd, both those who were in front and those who were behind Jesus, shouted,

"God save him!—God bless the one who comes in the name of
10 the Lord! God bless the coming kingdom of our father David! God save him from on high!"

11 Jesus entered Jerusalem and went into the Temple and looked round on all that was going on. And then, since it was already late in the day, he went out to Bethany with the twelve.

12 On the following day, when they had left Bethany, Jesus felt
13 hungry. He noticed a fig-tree in the distance covered with leaves, and he walked up to it to see if he could find any fruit on it. But when he got to it, he could find nothing but leaves, for it was not
14 yet time for the figs. Then Jesus spoke to the tree,

"May nobody ever eat fruit from you!"

And the disciples heard him say it.

15 Then they came into Jerusalem and Jesus went into the Temple and began to drive out those who were buying and selling there. He over-turned the tables of the money-changers and the benches
16 of the dove-sellers, and he would not allow people to carry their
17 water-pots through the Temple. And he taught them and said,

"Doesn't the scripture say, 'My house shall be called a house of prayer for all nations'? But you have turned it into a thieves' kitchen!"

18 The chief priests and scribes heard him say this and tried to find a way of getting rid of him. But they were in fact afraid of him,
19 for his teaching had captured the imagination of the people. And every evening he left the city.

Jesus talks of faith, prayer and forgiveness

20 One morning as they were walking along, they noticed that the

fig-tree had withered away to the roots. Peter remembered it, and **21**
said,

"Master, look, the fig-tree that you cursed is all shrivelled up!"

"Have faith in God," replied Jesus to them. "I tell you that if **22, 23**
anyone should say to this hill, 'Get up and throw yourself into
the sea', and without any doubt in his heart believe that what he
says will happen, then it *will* happen! That is why I tell you, **24**
whatever you pray about and ask for, believe that you have
received it and it will be yours. And whenever you stand praying, **25**
you must forgive anything that you are holding against anyone
else, and your Heavenly Father will forgive you *your* sins."

Jesus' authority is directly challenged

So they came once more to Jerusalem, and while Jesus was **27**
walking in the Temple, the chief priests, elders and scribes
approached him, and asked, **28**

"What authority have you for what you're doing? And who
gave you permission to do these things?"

"I am going to ask you a question," replied Jesus, "and if you **29**
answer me, I will tell you what authority I have for what I do.
The baptism of John, now—did it come from Heaven or was it **30**
purely human? Tell me that."

At this they argued with each other, "If we say from Heaven, **31**
he will say, 'then why didn't you believe in him?' but if we say **32**
it was purely human, well . . ." For they were frightened of the
people, since all of them believed that John was a real prophet.
So they answered Jesus, **33**

"We do not know."

"Then I cannot tell you by what authority I do these things,"
returned Jesus.

CHAPTER 12

Jesus tells a story, with a pointed application

THEN he began to talk to them in parables. **1**

"A man once planted a vineyard," he said, "fenced it round,
dug out the hole for the wine-press and built a watch-tower.
Then he let it out to some farm-workers and went abroad. At the **2**
end of the season he sent a servant to the tenants to receive his
share of the vintage. But they got hold of him, knocked him about **3**

4 and sent him off empty-handed. The owner tried again. He sent
another servant to them, but this one they knocked on the head
5 and generally insulted. Once again he sent them another servant,
but him they murdered. He sent many others and some they beat
6 up and some they murdered. He had one man left—his own son
who was very dear to him. He sent him last of all to the tenants,
7 saying to himself, 'They will surely respect my own son.' But
they said to each other, 'This fellow is the future owner—come
8 on, let's kill him, and the property will be ours! So they got hold
of him and murdered him, and threw his body out of the vine-
9 yard. What do you suppose the owner of the vineyard is going to
do? He will come and destroy the men who were working his
10 vineyard and will hand it over to others. Have you never read this
scripture—

> The stone which the builders rejected,
> The same was made the head of the corner;
11 > This was from the Lord,
> And it is marvellous in our eyes?"

12 Then they tried to get their hands on him, for they
knew perfectly well that he had aimed this parable at them—
but they were afraid of the people. So they left him and went
away.

A test question

13 Later they sent some of the Pharisees and some of the Herod-
14 party to trap him in an argument. They came up and said to
him,

"Master, we know that you are an honest man and that you are
not swayed by men's opinion of you. Obviously you don't care
for human approval but teach the way of God with the strictest
15 regard for truth—is it right to pay tribute to Caesar or not: are we
to pay or not to pay?"

But Jesus saw through their hypocrisy and said to them,

"Why try this trick on me? Bring me a coin and let me look at
it."

16 So they brought one to him.

"Whose face is this?" asked Jesus, "and whose name is in the
inscription?"

17 "Caesar's," they replied. And Jesus said,

"Then give to Caesar what belongs to Caesar, and to God what
belongs to God!"—a reply which staggered them.

Jesus reveals the ignorance of the Sadducees

Then some of the Sadducees (a party which maintains that there **18** is no resurrection) approached him, and put this question to him, "Master, Moses instructed us that if a man's brother dies **19** leaving a widow but no child, then the man should marry the woman and raise children for his brother. Now there were seven **20** brothers, and the first one married and died without leaving issue. Then the second one married the widow and died leaving no **21** issue behind him. The same thing happened with the third, and indeed the whole seven died without leaving any child behind **22** them. Finally the woman herself died. Now in this 'resurrection', **23** when men rise up again, whose wife is she going to be—for she was the wife of all seven of them?"

Jesus replied, "Does not this show where you go wrong—and **24** how you fail to understand both the scriptures and the power of God? When people rise from the dead they neither marry nor **25** are they given in marriage; they live like the angels in Heaven. But as for this matter of the dead being raised, have you never **26** read in the book of Moses, in the passage about the bush, how God spoke to him in these words, 'I am the God of Abraham and the God of Isaac and the God of Jacob'? God is not God of the **27** dead but of living men! That is where you make your great mistake!"

The most important commandments

Then one of the scribes approached him. He had been listening **28** to the discussion, and noticing how well Jesus had answered them, he put this question to him,

"What are we to consider the greatest commandment of all?"

"The first and most important one is this," Jesus replied— **29** " 'Hear, O Israel: The Lord our God, the Lord is one: and thou **30** shalt love the Lord thy God with all thy heart, and with all thy soul, and with all thy mind, and with all thy strength.' The second **31** is this, 'Thou shalt love thy neighbour as thyself.' No other commandment is greater than these."

"I am well answered," replied the scribe. "You are absolutely **32** right when you say that there is one God and no other God exists but him; and to love him with the whole of our hearts, the whole **33** of our intelligence and the whole of our energy, and to love our neighbours as ourselves is infinitely more important than all these burnt-offerings and sacrifices."

34   Then Jesus, noting the thoughtfulness of his reply, said to him, "You are not far from the kingdom of God!"

    After this nobody felt like asking him any more questions.

Jesus criticises the scribes' teaching and behaviour

35   Later, while Jesus was teaching in the Temple, he remarked,

36   "How can the scribes make out that Christ is David's *son*, for David himself, inspired by the Holy Spirit, said,

> The Lord said unto my *Lord*,
>
> Sit thou on my right hand,
>
> Till I make thine enemies the footstool of thy feet.

37 David is himself calling Christ 'Lord'—where do they get the idea that he is his son?"

38   The vast crowd heard this with great delight, and Jesus continued in his teaching,

    "Be on your guard against these scribes who love to walk about in long robes and to be greeted respectfully in public and

39 to have the front seats in the synagogue and the best places at

40 dinner-parties! These are the men who grow fat on widow's property and cover up what they are doing by making lengthy prayers. They are only adding to their own punishment!"

41   Then Jesus sat down opposite the Temple almsbox and watched the people putting their money into it. A great many rich people

42 put in large sums. Then a poor widow came up and dropped

43 in two little coins, worth together about a halfpenny. Jesus called his disciples to his side and said to them,

    "Believe me, this poor widow has put in more than all the

44 others. For they have all put in what they can easily afford, but she in her poverty who needs so much, has given away everything, her whole living!"

CHAPTER 13

Jesus prophesies the ruin of the Temple

1   THEN as Jesus was leaving the Temple, one of his disciples said to him,

    "Look, Master, what wonderful stonework, what a size these buildings are!"

2   Jesus replied,

    "You see these great buildings? Not a single stone will be left standing on another; every one will be thrown down!"

Then while he was sitting on the slope of the Mount of Olives **3**
facing the Temple, Peter, James, John and Andrew said to him
privately,

"Tell us, when will these things happen? What sign will there **4**
be that all these things are going to be accomplished?"

So Jesus began to tell them: **5**

"Be very careful that no one deceives you. Many are going to **6**
come in my name and say, 'I am he', and will lead many astray.
When you hear of wars and rumours of wars, don't be alarmed. **7**
Such things are bound to happen, but the end is not yet. Nation **8**
will take up arms against nation and kingdom against kingdom.
There will be earthquakes in different places and terrible famines.
But this is only the beginning of 'the pains'. You yourselves must **9**
keep your wits about you, for men will hand you over to their
councils, and will beat you in their synagogues. You will have to
stand in front of rulers and kings for my sake to bear your witness
to them—for before the end comes the gospel must be pro- **10**
claimed to all nations. But when they are taking you off to **11**
trial, do not worry beforehand about what you are going to
say—simply say the words you are given when the time
comes. For it is not really you who will speak, but the Holy
Spirit.

Jesus foretells utter misery

"A brother is going to betray his own brother to death, and a **12**
father his own child. Children will stand up against their parents
and condemn them to death. There will come a time when the **13**
whole world will hate you because you are known as my followers.
Yet the man who holds out to the end will be saved.

"But when you see 'the abomination of desolation' standing **14**
where it ought not—(let the reader take note of this)—then those
who are in Judaea must fly to the hills! The man on his house-top **15**
must not go down nor go into his house to fetch anything out of
it, and the man in the field must not turn back to fetch his coat. **16**
Alas for the women who are pregnant at that time, and alas for **17**
those with babies at their breasts! Pray God that it may not be **18**
winter when that time comes, for there will be such utter misery **19**
in those days as has never been from the creation until now—and
never will be again. Indeed, if the Lord did not shorten those days, **20**
no human being would survive. But for the sake of the people
whom he has chosen he has shortened those days.

He warns against false christs, and commands vigilance

21   "If anyone tells you at that time, 'Look, here is Christ', or
22 'Look, there he is', don't believe it! For false christs and false
    prophets will arise and will perform signs and wonders, to deceive,
23 if it be possible, even the men of God's choice. You must keep
    your eyes open! I am giving you this warning before it happens.
24   "But when that misery is past, the light of the sun will be
25 darkened and the moon will not give her light; stars will be
    falling from the sky and the powers of heaven will rock on their
26 foundations. Then men shall see the Son of Man coming in the
27 clouds with great power and glory. And then shall he send out his
    angels to summon his chosen together from every quarter, from
28 furthest earth to highest heaven. Let the fig-tree illustrate this for
    you: when its branches grow tender and produce leaves, you
29 know that summer is near. So when you see these things happen-
30 ing, you may know that he is near, at your very doors! I tell you
    that this generation will not have passed until all these things
31 have come true. Earth and sky will pass away, but what I have
32 told you will never pass away! But no one knows the day or the
    hour of this happening, not even the angels in Heaven, no, not
33 even the Son—only the Father. Keep your eyes open, keep on the
34 alert, for you do not know when the time will be. It is as if a man
    who is travelling abroad had left his house and handed it over to
    be managed by his servants. He has given each one his work to do
    and has ordered the doorkeeper to be on the look-out for his
35 return. Just so must you keep a look-out, for you do not know
    when the master of the house will come—it might be late evening,
36 or midnight, or cock-crow, or early morning—otherwise he might
37 come unexpectedly and find you sound asleep. What I am saying
    to you I am saying to all; keep on the alert!"

CHAPTER 14

An act of love

1 IN two days' time the festival of the Passover and of un-
    leavened bread was due. Consequently, the chief priests and the
    scribes were trying to think of some trick by which they could
    get Jesus into their power and have him executed.
2   "But it must not be during the festival," they said, "or there
    will be a riot."

Jesus himself was now in Bethany in the house of Simon the *3*
leper. As he was sitting at table, a woman approached him with
an alabaster flask of very costly spikenard perfume. She broke the
neck of the flask and poured the perfume on Jesus' head. Some of *4*
those present were highly indignant and muttered,

"What is the point of such wicked waste of perfume? It could *5*
have been sold for over thirty pounds and the money could have
been given to the poor." And there was a murmur of resentment
against her. But Jesus said, *6*

"Let her alone, why must you make her feel uncomfortable?
She has done a beautiful thing for me. You have the poor with *7*
you always and you can do good to them whenever you like, but
you will not always have me. She has done all she could—for she *8*
has anointed my body in preparation for burial. I assure you that *9*
wherever the gospel is preached throughout the whole world, this
deed of hers will also be recounted, as her memorial to me."

Judas volunteers to betray Jesus

Then Judas Iscariot, who was one of the twelve, went off to the *10*
chief priests to betray Jesus to them. And when they heard what *11*
he had to say, they were delighted and undertook to pay him for
it. So he looked out for a convenient opportunity to betray him.

The Passover-supper prepared

On the first day of unleavened bread, the day when the Passover *12*
was sacrificed, Jesus' disciples said,

"Where do you want us to go and make the preparations for
you to eat the Passover?"

Jesus sent off two of them with these instructions, *13*

"Go into the town and you will meet a man carrying a pitcher
of water. Follow him and say to the owner of the house to which *14*
he goes, 'The master says, where is the room for me to eat the
Passover with my disciples?' And he will show you a large up- *15*
stairs room all ready with the furnishings that we need. That is
the place where you are to make our preparations."

So the disciples set off and went into the town, found every- *16*
thing as he had told them, and prepared for the Passover.

The last supper together: the mysterious bread and wine

Late in the evening he arrived with the twelve. And while they *17,18*
were sitting there, right in the middle of the meal, Jesus remarked,

"Believe me, one of you is going to betray me—someone who is now having his supper with me."

19   This shocked and distressed them and one after another they began to say to him,

"Surely, I'm not the one?"

20   "It is one of the twelve," Jesus told them, "a man who is
21   dipping his hand into the dish with me. It is true that the Son of Man will follow the road foretold by the scriptures, but alas for the man through whom he is betrayed! It would be better for that man if he had never been born."

22   And while they were still eating Jesus took a loaf, blessed it and broke it and gave it to them, with the words,

"Take this, it is my body."

23   Then he took a cup, and after thanking God, he gave it to them,
24   and they all drank from it, and he said to them,

"This is my blood which is shed for many in the new agree-
25   ment. I tell you truly I will drink no more wine until the day comes when I drink it fresh in the kingdom of God!"

26   Then they sang a hymn and went out to the Mount of Olives.
27   "Every one of you will lose your faith in me," Jesus told them, "as the scripture says:

I will smite the shepherd,

And the sheep shall be scattered abroad.

28   Yet after I have risen, I shall go before you into Galilee!"

Peter's bold words—and Jesus' reply

29   Then Peter said to him,

"Even if everyone should lose his faith, I never will."

30   "Believe me, Peter," returned Jesus, "this very night before the cock crows twice, you will disown me three times."

31   But Peter protested violently,

"Even if it means dying with you, I will never disown you!"

And they all made the same protest.

The last desperate prayer in Gethsemane

32   Then they arrived at a place called Gethsemane, and Jesus said to his disciples,

"Sit down here while I pray."

33   He took with him Peter, James and John, and began to be horror-stricken and desperately depressed.

"My heart is nearly breaking," he told them. "Stay here and *34* keep watch for me."

Then he walked forward a little way and flung himself on the *35* ground, praying that, if it were possible, he might not have to face the ordeal.

"Dear Father," he said, "all things are possible to you. Please— *36* let me not have to drink this cup! Yet it is not what I want but what you want."

Then he came and found them fast asleep. He spoke to Peter, *37* "Are you asleep, Simon? Couldn't you manage to watch for a single hour? Watch and pray, all of you, that you may not have *38* to face temptation. Your spirit is willing, but human nature is weak."

Then he went away again and prayed in the same words, and *39, 40* once more he came and found them asleep. They could not keep their eyes open and they did not know what to say for themselves. When he came back for the third time, he said, *41*

"Are you still going to sleep and take your ease? All right— the moment has come; now you are going to see the Son of Man betrayed into the hands of evil men! Get up, let us be going! *42* Look, here comes my betrayer!"

Judas betrays Jesus

And indeed, while the words were still on his lips, Judas, one of *43* the twelve, arrived with a mob armed with swords and staves, sent by the chief priests and scribes and elders. The betrayer had *44* given them a sign; he had said, "The one I kiss will be the man. Get hold of him and you can take him away without any trouble." So he walked straight up to Jesus, cried, "Master!" and kissed him *45* affectionately. And so they got hold of him and held him. Some- *46, 47* body present drew his sword and struck at the High Priest's servant, slashing off his ear. Then Jesus spoke to them, *48*

"So you've come out with your swords and staves to capture me like a bandit, have you? Day after day I was with you in the *49* Temple, teaching, and you never laid a finger on me. But the scriptures must be fulfilled."

Then all the disciples deserted him and made their escape. *50* There happened to be a young man among Jesus' followers who *51* wore nothing but a linen shirt. They seized him, but he left the *52* shirt in their hands and took to his heels stark naked.

Jesus before the High Priest

So they marched Jesus away to the High Priest in whose *53*

presence all the chief priests and elders and scribes had assembled.
54 (Peter followed him at a safe distance, right up to the High Priest's
courtyard. There he sat in the firelight with the servants, keeping
55 himself warm.) Meanwhile, the chief priests and the whole
council were trying to find some evidence against Jesus which
would warrant the death penalty. But they failed completely.
56 There were plenty of people ready to give false testimony against
57 him, but their evidence was contradictory. Then some more
perjurers stood up and said,
58 "We heard him say, 'I will destroy this Temple that was built
by human hands and in three days I will build another made
without human aid.'"
59, 60 But even so their evidence conflicted. So the High Priest himself got up and took the centre of the floor.

"Have you no answer to make?" he asked Jesus. "What about
all this evidence against you?"
61 But Jesus remained silent and offered no reply. Again the High
Priest asked him,

"Are you Christ, Son of the blessed one?"
62 And Jesus said,

"I am! Yes, you will all see the Son of Man sitting at the right
hand of power, coming in the clouds of heaven."
63 Then the High Priest tore his robes and cried,
64 "Why do we still need witnesses? You heard the blasphemy;
what is your opinion now?"
65 And their verdict was that he deserved to die. Then some of
them began to spit at him. They blindfolded him and then slapped
him, saying,

"Now prophesy who hit you!"
Even the servants who took him away slapped his face.

Peter, in fear, disowns his master

66 In the meantime, while Peter was in the courtyard below, one
67 of the High Priest's maids came and saw him warming himself.
She looked closely at him, and said,

"You were with the Nazarene too—with Jesus!"
68 But he denied it, saying,

"I don't understand. I don't know what you're talking about."
And he walked out into the gateway, and a cock crew.
69 Again the maid who had noticed him began to say to the men
standing there,

"This man is one of them!"

But he denied it again. A few minutes later the bystanders them- 70
selves said to Peter,

"You certainly are one of them. Why, you're a Galilean!"

But he started to curse and swear, 71

"I tell you I don't know the man you're talking about!"

Immediately the cock crew for the second time, and back into 72
Peter's mind came the words of Jesus, "Before the cock crows
twice, you will disown me three times."

And he broke down and wept.

CHAPTER 15

Jesus before Pilate

THE moment daylight came the chief priests called together a 1
meeting of elders, scribes and members of the whole council,
bound Jesus and took him off and handed him over to Pilate.
Pilate asked him straight out, 2

"Well, you—*are* you the king of the Jews?"

"Yes, I am," he replied.

The chief priests brought many accusations. So Pilate ques- 3, 4
tioned him again,

"Have you nothing to say? Listen to all their accusations!"

But Jesus made no further answer—to Pilate's astonishment. 5

Now it was Pilate's custom at festival-time to release a prisoner 6
—anyone they asked for. There was in the prison at the time, with 7
some other rioters who had committed murder in a recent out-
break, a man called Barabbas. The crowd surged forward and 8
began to demand that Pilate should do what he usually did for
them. So he spoke to them, 9

"Do you want me to set free the king of the Jews for you?"

For he knew perfectly well that the chief priests had handed 10
Jesus over to him through sheer malice. But the chief priests 11
worked upon the crowd to get them to demand Barabbas' release
instead. So Pilate addressed them once more, 12

"Then what am I to do with the man whom you call the king
of the Jews?"

They shouted back, 13

"Crucify him!"

But Pilate replied, 14

"Why, what crime has he committed?"

But their voices rose to a roar,
"Crucify him!"

15 And as Pilate wanted to satisfy the crowd, he set Barabbas free for them, and after having Jesus flogged handed him over to be crucified.

16 Then the soldiers marched him away inside the courtyard of the governor's residence and called their whole company together.
17 They dressed Jesus in a purple robe, and twisting some thorn-
18 twigs into a crown, they put it on his head. Then they began to greet him,

"Hail, your majesty—king of the Jews!"

19 They hit him on the head with a stick and spat at him, and then
20 bowed low before him on bended knee. And when they had finished their fun with him, they took off the purple cloak and dressed him again in his own clothes. Then they led him outside
21 to crucify him. They compelled Simon, a native of Cyrene in Africa (the father of Alexander and Rufus), who was on his way from the fields at the time, to carry Jesus' cross.

The crucifixion

22 They took him to a place called Golgotha (which means Skull
23 Hill) and they offered him some drugged wine, but he would not
24 take it. Then they crucified him, and shared out his garments,
25 drawing lots to see what each of them would get. It was about nine o'clock in the morning when they nailed him to the cross.
26 Over his head the placard of his crime read, "THE KING OF
27 THE JEWS." They also crucified two bandits at the same time,
29 one on each side of him. And the passers-by jeered at him, shaking their heads in mockery, saying,

"Hi, you! You could destroy the Temple and build it up again
30 in three days, why not come down from the cross and save yourself?"

31 The chief priests also made fun of him among themselves and the scribes, and said,

32 "He saved others, he cannot save himself. If only this Christ, the king of Israel, would come down now from the cross, we should see it and believe!"

And even the men who were crucified with him hurled abuse at him.

33 At midday darkness spread over the whole countryside and
34 lasted until three o'clock in the afternoon, and at three o'clock Jesus cried out in a loud voice,

"My God, my God, why did you forsake me?"

Some of the bystanders heard these words which Jesus spoke in 35 Aramaic (*Eloi, Eloi, lama sabachthani?*), and said,

"Listen, he's calling for Elijah!"

One man ran off and soaked a sponge in vinegar, put it on a 36 stick, and held it up for Jesus to drink, calling out,

"Let him alone! Let's see if Elijah will come and take him down!"

But Jesus let out a great cry, and died. The curtain of the 37, 38 Temple sanctuary was split in two from the top to the bottom. And when the centurion who stood in front of Jesus saw how he 39 died, he said,

"This man was certainly a son of God!"

There were some women there looking on from a distance, 40 among them Mary of Magdala, Mary the mother of the younger James and Joses, and Salome. These were the women who used 41 to follow Jesus as he went about in Galilee and look after him. And there were many other women there who had come up to Jerusalem with them.

The body of Jesus is reverently laid in a tomb

When the evening came, because it was the day of preparation, 42 that is the day before the Sabbath, Joseph from Arimathaea, a 43 distinguished member of the council, who was himself prepared to accept the kingdom of God, went boldly into Pilate's presence and asked for the body of Jesus. Pilate was surprised that he 44 should be dead already and he sent for the centurion and asked whether he had been dead long. On hearing the centurion's report, 45 he gave Joseph the body of Jesus. So Joseph brought a linen 46 winding-sheet, took Jesus down and wrapped him in it, and then put him in a tomb which had been hewn out of the solid rock, rolling a stone over the entrance to it. Mary of Magdala and Mary 47 the mother of Joses were looking on and saw where he was laid.

CHAPTER 16

Early on the first Lord's day: the women are amazed

WHEN the Sabbath was over, Mary of Magdala, Mary the 1 mother of James, and Salome bought spices so that they could go and anoint him. And very early in the morning on the first day 2 of the week, they came to the tomb, just as the sun was rising.

3   "Who is going to roll the stone back from the doorway of the tomb?" they asked each other.

4   And then as they looked closer, they saw that the stone, which
5 was a very large one, had been rolled back. So they went into the tomb and saw a young man in a white robe sitting on the right-
6 hand side, and they were simply astonished. But he said to them, "There is no need to be astonished. You are looking for Jesus of Nazareth who was crucified. He has risen; he is not here. Look,
7 here is the place where they laid him. But now go and tell his disciples, and Peter, that he will be in Galilee before you. You will see him there just as he told you."

8   And they got out of the tomb and ran away from it. They were trembling with excitement. They did not dare to breathe a word to anyone.

An ancient appendix

9   When Jesus rose early on that first day of the week, he appeared first of all to Mary of Magdala, from whom he had driven out
10 seven evil spirits. And she went and reported this to his sorrowing
11 and weeping followers. They heard her say that he was alive and that she had seen him, but they did not believe it.

12   Later, he appeared in a different form to two of them who were
13 out walking, as they were on their way to the country. These two came back and told the others, but they did not believe them
14 either. Still later he appeared to the eleven themselves as they were sitting at table and reproached them for their lack of faith, and reluctance to believe those who had seen him after he had risen.
15 Then he said to them,

"You must go out to the whole world and proclaim the gospel
16 to every creature. He who believes it and is baptised will be
17 saved, but he who disbelieves it will be condemned. These signs will follow those who do believe: they will drive out evil spirits
18 in my name; they will speak with new tongues; they will pick up snakes, and if they drink anything poisonous it will do them no harm; they will lay their hands upon the sick and they will recover."

Jesus, his mission accomplished, returns to Heaven

19   After these words to them, the Lord Jesus was taken up into
20 Heaven and was enthroned at the right hand of God. They went out and preached everywhere. The Lord worked with them, confirming their message by the signs that followed.

The Gospel of Luke

The author of this Gospel is beyond reasonable doubt Luke, "the beloved physician", companion and fellow-worker of Paul. This work is, of course, only the first of his "two volumes", the second being what we know as The Acts of the Apostles. It is generally recognised that he was not a Jew and that he was a doctor by profession.

This Gospel is thought by many to be the most beautiful of the four, both because of its style and of the imaginative sympathy with which Luke paints the portrait of his Master. There is a persistent legend that he was an artist, and while this is a matter of uncertainty, we owe him a definite enrichment and enlargement of the story of Jesus which gives the impression of an artist's sensitivity.

On his own admission Luke has carefully compared and edited existing narratives, but it would seem that he had access to a good deal of additional material, and we can reasonably guess at some of the sources from which he drew it. He would almost certainly know Mark's Gospel; he would be able to draw from the mysterious "Q", which scholars believe to have existed, although there is no trace of it; and he had his own reminiscences and material collected in Caesarea (Acts 24, 27).

Though it is impossible to state accurately how the work was composed, a great many scholars think that there was a first version possibly written during his travels with Paul, and that later material —the birth stories and the preface, for example—was incorporated later. Luke, like Mark, is writing primarily for the non-Jewish reader. A Gentile centurion, for example, is singled out as having more faith than Jesus had found in Israel; more than once, Samaritans, who were anathema to the Jews, are singled out for praise. Jesus' ancestry is traced back, not to Abraham the father of the Jewish race, but to Adam the father of all mankind.

None of the other evangelists shows so clearly the love and sympathy of Jesus for the sinner, the outcast and the unfortunate. And there is a reverence for women as the story unfolds, which shows the writer, through his understanding of his Master, far ahead of his time. Many scholars nowadays would place the writings of Luke's Gospel and of The Acts of the Apostles soon after Paul's death and before the Fall of Jerusalem, i.e. between 65 and 70. The graphic, but always careful and accurate, style conveys a strong impression of veracity.

CHAPTER 1

Prefatory Note

DEAR THEOPHILUS,

1 Many people have already written an account of the events
2 which have happened among us, basing their work on the evidence
of those who, we know, were eye-witnesses as well as teachers
3 of the message. I have therefore decided, since I have traced the
course of these happenings carefully from the beginning, to set them
4 down for you myself in their proper order, so that you may have
reliable information about the matters in which you have already
had instruction.

A vision comes to an old priest of God

5 The story begins in the days when Herod was king of Judaea
with a priest called Zacharias (who belonged to the Abijah section
of the priesthood), whose wife Elisabeth was, like him, a descend-
6 ant of Aaron. They were both truly religious people, blamelessly
7 observing all God's commandments and requirements. They were
childless through Elisabeth's infertility, and both of them were
8 getting on in years. One day, while Zacharias was performing his
9 priestly functions (it was the turn of his division to be on duty), it
10 fell to him to go into the sanctuary and burn the incense. The
crowded congregation outside was praying at the actual time of
11 the incense-burning, when an angel of the Lord appeared on the
12 right side of the incense-altar. When Zacharias saw him, he was
13 terribly agitated and a sense of awe swept over him. But the angel
spoke to him,

"Do not be afraid, Zacharias; your prayers have been heard.
Elisabeth your wife will bear you a son, and you are to call him
14 John. This will be joy and delight to you and many more will be
15 glad because he is born. He will be one of God's great men; he
will touch neither wine nor strong drink and he will be filled with
16 the Holy Spirit from the moment of his birth. He will turn many
17 of Israel's children to the Lord their God. He will go out before
God in the spirit and power of Elijah—to reconcile fathers and
children, and bring back the disobedient to the wisdom of good
men—and he will make a people fully ready for their Lord."
18 But Zacharias replied to the angel,

"How can I know that this is true? I am an old man myself and my wife is getting on in years ..."

"I am Gabriel," the angel answered. "I stand in the presence of God, and I have been sent to speak to you and tell you this good news. Because you do not believe what I have said, you shall live in silence, and you shall be unable to speak a word until the day that it happens. But be sure that everything that I have told you will come true at the proper time." 19 20

Meanwhile, the people were waiting for Zacharias, wondering why he stayed so long in the sanctuary. But when he came out and was unable to speak a word to them—for although he kept making signs, not a sound came from his lips—they realised that he had seen a vision in the Temple. Later, when his days of duty were over, he went back home, and soon afterwards his wife Elisabeth became pregnant and kept herself secluded for five months. 21 22 23 24

"How good the Lord is to me," she would say, "now that he has taken away the shame that I have suffered." 25

A vision comes to a young woman in Nazareth

Then, six months after Zacharias' vision, the angel Gabriel was sent from God to a Galilean town, Nazareth by name, to a young woman who was engaged to a man called Joseph (a descendant of David). The girl's name was Mary. The angel entered her room and said, 26 27 28

"Greetings to you, Mary. O favoured one!—the Lord be with you!"

Mary was deeply perturbed at these words and wondered what such a greeting could possibly mean. But the angel said to her, 29 30

"Do not be afraid, Mary; God loves you dearly. You are going to be the mother of a son, and you will call him Jesus. He will be great and will be known as the Son of the most high. The Lord God will give him the throne of his forefather, David, and he will be king over the people of Jacob for ever. His reign shall never end." 31 32 33

Then Mary spoke to the angel, 34

"How can this be," she said, "I am not married!"

But the angel made this reply to her— 35

"The Holy Spirit will come upon you, the power of the most high will overshadow you. Your child will therefore be called holy—the Son of God. Your cousin Elisabeth has also conceived 36

a son, old as she is. Indeed, this is the sixth month for her, a
37 woman who was called barren. For no promise of God can fail
to be fulfilled."

38 "I belong to the Lord, body and soul," replied Mary, "let it
happen as you say." And at this the angel left her.

39 With little delay Mary got ready and hurried off to the hill-
40 side town in Judaea where Zacharias and Elisabeth lived. She went
41 into their house and greeted her cousin. When Elisabeth heard her
greeting, the unborn child stirred inside her and she herself was
42 filled with the Holy Spirit, and cried out,

"Blessed are you among women, and blessed is your child!
43 What an honour it is to have the mother of my Lord come to see
44 me! Why, as soon as your greeting reached my ears, the child
45 within me jumped for joy! Oh, how happy is the woman who
believes in God, for he does make his promises to her come true."

46 Then Mary said, "My heart is overflowing with praise of my
47, 48 Lord, my soul is full of joy in God my Saviour. For he has
deigned to notice me, his humble servant and, after this, all the
people who ever shall be will call me the happiest of women!
49 The one who can do all things has done great things for me—oh,
50 holy is his Name! Truly, his mercy rests on those who fear him
51 in every generation. He has shown the strength of his arm, he
52 has swept away the high and mighty. He has set kings down from
53 their thrones and lifted up the humble. He has satisfied the hungry
54 with good things and sent the rich away with empty hands. Yes,
55 he has helped Israel, his child: he has remembered the mercy that
he promised to our forefathers, to Abraham and his sons for
evermore!"

The old woman's son, John, is born

56 So Mary stayed with Elisabeth about three months, and then
57 went back to her own home. Then came the time for Elisabeth's
58 child to be born, and she gave birth to a son. Her neighbours and
relations heard of the great mercy the Lord had shown her and
shared her joy.

59 When the eighth day came, they were going to circumcise the
60 child and call him Zacharias, after his father, but his mother said,
"Oh, no! He must be called John."

61, 62 "But none of your relations is called John," they replied. And
they made signs to his father to see what name he wanted the
63 child to have. He beckoned for a writing-tablet and wrote the

words, "His name is John", which greatly surprised everybody.
Then his power of speech suddenly came back, and his first words   64
were to thank God. The neighbours were awe-struck at this, and   65
all these incidents were reported in the hill-country of Judaea.
People turned the whole matter over in their hearts, and said,   66
"What is this child's future going to be?" For the Lord's
blessing was plainly upon him.

Then Zacharias, his father, filled with the Holy Spirit and   67
speaking like a prophet, said,

"Blessings on the Lord, the God of Israel, because he has   68
turned his face towards his people and has set them free! And he   69
has raised up for us a standard of salvation in his servant David's
house! Long, long ago, through the words of his holy prophets,   70
he promised to do this for us, so that we should be safe from our   71
enemies and secure from all who hate us. So does he continue the   72
mercy he showed to our forefathers. So does he remember the
holy agreement he made with them and the oath which he swore   73
to our father Abraham, to make us this gift: that we should be   74
saved from the hands of our enemies, and in his presence should
serve him unafraid in holiness and righteousness all our lives   75

"And you, little child, will be called the prophet of the most   76
high, for you will go before the Lord to prepare the way for his
coming. It will be for you to give his people knowledge of their   77
salvation through the forgiveness of their sins. Because the heart   78
of our God is full of mercy towards us, the first light of Heaven
shall come to visit us—to shine on those who lie in darkness and   79
under the shadow of death, and to guide our feet into the path of
peace."

The little child grew up and became strong in spirit. He lived   80
in lonely places until the day came for him to show himself to
Israel.

CHAPTER 2

The census brings Mary and Joseph to Bethlehem

At that time a proclamation was made by Caesar Augustus that   1
all the inhabited world should be registered. This was the first   2
census, undertaken while Cyrenius was governor of Syria; and   3
everybody went to the town of his birth to be registered. Joseph   4
went up from the town of Nazareth in Galilee to David's town,
Bethlehem, in Judaea, because he was a direct descendant of

5 David, to be registered with his future wife, Mary, now in the
6 later stages of her pregnancy. So it happened that it was while they
7 were there in Bethlehem that she came to the end of her time. She
gave birth to her first child, a son. And as there was no place for
them inside the inn, she wrapped him up and laid him in a manger.

A vision comes to shepherds on the hill-side

8 There were some shepherds living in the same part of the
country, keeping guard throughout the night over their flock in
9 the open fields. Suddenly an angel of the Lord stood by their side,
the splendour of the Lord blazed around them, and they were
10 terror-stricken. But the angel said to them,
"Do not be afraid! Listen, I bring you glorious news of great
11 joy which is for all the people. This very day, in David's town, a
12 Saviour has been born for you. He is Christ, the Lord. Let this
prove it to you: you will find a baby, wrapped up and lying in a
manger."
13 And in a flash there appeared with the angel a vast host of the
armies of Heaven, praising God, saying,
14 "Glory to God in the highest Heaven! Peace upon earth among
men of goodwill!"
15 When the angels left them and went back into Heaven, the
shepherds said to each other,
"Now let us go straight to Bethlehem and see this thing which
the Lord has made known to us."
16 So they came as fast as they could and they found Mary and
17 Joseph—and the baby lying in the manger. And when they had
seen this sight, they told everybody what had been said to them
18 about the little child. And those who heard them were amazed at
19 what the shepherds said. But Mary treasured all these things and
20 turned them over in her mind. The shepherds went back to work,
glorifying and praising God for everything that they had heard
and seen, which had happened just as they had been told.

Mary and Joseph bring their newly-born son to the Temple

21 At the end of the eight days, the time came for circumcising the
child and he was called Jesus, the name given to him by the angel
before his conception.
22 When the "purification" time, stipulated by the Law of Moses,
was completed, they brought Jesus to Jerusalem to present him to
23 the Lord. This was to fulfil a requirement of the Law—

"Every male that openeth the womb shall be called holy to the Lord."

They also offered the sacrifice prescribed by the Law— 24
    "A pair of turtle doves, or two young pigeons."

In Jerusalem was a man by the name of Simeon. He was an 25 upright man, devoted to the service of God, living in expectation of the "salvation of Israel". His heart was open to the Holy Spirit, and it had been revealed to him that he would not die before he 26 saw the Lord's Christ. He had been led by the Spirit to go into the 27 Temple, and when Jesus' parents brought the child in to have done to him what the Law required, he took him up in his arms, 28 blessed God and said—

"At last, Lord, you can dismiss your servant in peace, as you 29 promised! For with my own eyes I have seen your salvation which 30,31 you have made ready for every people—a light to show truth to 32 the gentiles and bring glory to your people Israel."

The child's father and mother were still amazed at what was 33 said about him, when Simeon gave them his blessing. He said to 34 Mary, the child's mother,

"This child is destined to make many fall and many rise in Israel and to set up a standard which many will attack—for he 35 will expose the secret thoughts of many hearts. And for you . . . your very soul will be pierced by a sword."

There was also present, Anna, the daughter of Phanuel of the 36 tribe of Asher, who was a prophetess. She was a very old woman, having had seven years' married life and was now a widow of 37 eighty-four. She spent her whole life in the Temple and worshipped God night and day with fastings and prayers. She came 38 up at this very moment, praised God and spoke about Jesus to all those in Jerusalem who were expecting redemption.

When they had completed all the requirements of the Law of 39 the Lord, they returned to Galilee, to their own town of Nazareth. The child grew up and became strong and full of wisdom. And 40 God's blessing was upon him.

Twelve years later: the boy Jesus goes with his parents to Jerusalem

Every year at the Passover festival, Jesus' parents used to go to 41 Jerusalem. When he was twelve years old they went up to the 42 city as usual for the festival. When it was over they started back 43 home, but the boy Jesus stayed behind in Jerusalem, without his parents' knowledge. They went a day's journey assuming that he 44

45 was somewhere in their company, and then they began to look
46 for him among their relations and acquaintances. They failed to
find him, however, and turned back to the city, looking for him
47 as they went. Three days later, they found him—in the Temple,
sitting among the teachers, listening to them and asking them
48 questions. All those who heard him were astonished at his powers
of comprehension and at the answers that he gave. When Joseph
and Mary saw him, they could hardly believe their eyes, and his
mother said to him,

"Why have you treated us like this, my son? Here have your
father and I been very worried, looking for you everywhere!"

49 And Jesus replied,

"But why were you looking for me? Did you not know that
I must be in my Father's house?"

50, 51 But they did not understand his reply. Then he went home with
them to Nazareth and was obedient to them. And his mother
52 treasured all these things in her heart. And as Jesus continued to
grow in body and mind, he grew also in the love of God and of
those who knew him.

CHAPTER 3

Several years later: John prepares the way of Christ

1 IN the fifteenth year of the reign of the Emperor Tiberius (a
year when Pontius Pilate was governor of Judaea, Herod tetrarch
of Galilee, Philip, his brother, tetrarch of the territory of Ituraea
2 and Trachonitis, and Lysanias tetrarch of Abilene, while Annas
and Caiaphas were the High Priests), the word of God came to
3 John, the son of Zacharias, while he was in the desert. He went
into the whole country round about the Jordan proclaiming
baptism as a mark of a complete change of heart and of the for-
4 giveness of sins, as the book of the prophet Isaiah says—

 The voice of one crying in the wilderness,
 Make ye ready the way of the Lord,
 Make his paths straight.
5 Every valley shall be filled,
 And every mountain and hill shall be brought low:
 And the crooked shall become straight,
 And the rough ways smooth:
6 And all flesh shall see the salvation of God.
7 So John used to say to the crowds who came out to be baptised
by him,

"Who warned you, you serpent's brood, to escape from the wrath to come? See that you do something to show that your 8 hearts are really changed! Don't start thinking that you can say to yourselves, 'We are Abraham's children', for I tell you that God could produce children of Abraham out of these stones! The axe already lies at the root of the tree, and the tree that fails 9 to produce good fruit is cut down and thrown into the fire."

Then the crowds would ask him, "Then what shall we do?" 10

And his answer was, "The man who has two shirts must share 11 with the man who has none, and the man who has food must do the same."

Some of the tax-collectors also came to him to be baptised and 12 they asked him,

"Master, what are we to do?"

"You must not demand more than you are entitled to," he 13 replied.

And the soldiers asked him, "And what are we to do?" 14

"Don't bully people, don't bring false charges, and be content with your pay," he replied.

The people were in a great state of expectation and were in- 15 wardly discussing whether John could possibly be Christ. But 16 John answered them all in these words,

"It is true that I baptise you with water, but the one who follows me is stronger than I am—indeed I am not fit to undo his shoe-laces—he will baptise you with the fire of the Holy Spirit. He will come all ready to separate the wheat from the chaff, and 17 to clear the rubbish from his threshing-floor. The wheat he will gather into his barn and the chaff he will burn with a fire that cannot be put out."

These and many other things John said to the people as he 18 exhorted them and announced the good news. But the tetrarch 19 Herod, who had been condemned by John in the affair of Herodias, his brother's wife, as well as for the other evil things that he had done, crowned his misdeeds by putting John in prison. 20

Jesus is himself baptised

When all the people had been baptised, and Jesus was praying 21 after his own baptism, Heaven opened and the Holy Spirit came 22 down upon him in the bodily form of a dove. Then there came a voice from Heaven, saying,

"You are my dearly-loved Son, in whom I am well pleased."

23   Jesus himself was about thirty years old at this time when he began his work.

The ancestry of Jesus traced to Adam

People assumed that Jesus was the son of Joseph, who was the
24   son of Heli, who was the son of Matthat, who was the son of Levi, who was the son of Melchi, who was the son of Jannai, who
25   was the son of Joseph, who was the son of Mattathias, who was the son of Amos, who was the son of Nahum, who was the son
26   of Esli, who was the son of Naggai, who was the son of Maath, who was the son of Mattathias, who was the son of Semein, who
27   was the son of Josech, who was the son of Joda, who was the son of Joanan, who was the son of Rhesa, who was the son of Zerubbabel, who was the son of Shealtiel, who was the son of
28   Neri, who was the son of Melchi, who was the son of Addi, who was the son of Cosam, who was the son of Elmadam, who was
29   the son of Er, who was the son of Jesus, who was the son of Eliezer, who was the son of Jorim, who was the son of Matthat,
30   who was the son of Levi, who was the son of Symeon, who was the son of Judas, who was the son of Joseph, who was the son of
31   Jonam, who was the son of Eliakim, who was the son of Melea, who was the son of Menna, who was the son of Mattatha, who
32   was the son of Nathan, who was the son of David, who was the son of Jesse, who was the son of Obed, who was the son of Boaz,
33   who was the son of Salmon, who was the son of Nahshon, who was the son of Amminadab, who was the son of Arni, who was the son of Hezron, who was the son of Perez, who was the son
34   of Judah, who was the son of Jacob, who was the son of Isaac, who was the son of Abraham, who was the son of Terah, who
35   was the son of Nahor, who was the son of Serug, who was the son of Reu, who was the son of Peleg, who was the son of Eber,
36   who was the son of Shelah, who was the son of Cainan, who was the son of Arphaxad, who was the son of Shem, who was
37   the son of Noah, who was the son of Lamech, who was the son of Methuselah, who was the son of Enoch, who was the son of Jared, who was the son of Mahalaleel, who was the son of Cainan,
38   who was the son of Enos, who was the son of Seth, who was the son of Adam, who was the son of God.

CHAPTER 4

Jesus faces temptation

JESUS returned from the Jordan full of the Holy Spirit and he 1
was led by the Spirit to spend forty days in the desert, where he 2
was tempted by the devil. He ate nothing during that time and
afterwards he felt very hungry.

"If you really are the Son of God," the devil said to him, "tell 3
this stone to turn into a loaf."

Jesus answered, 4

"The scripture says, 'Man shall not live by bread alone.'"

Then the devil took him up and showed him all the kingdoms 5
of mankind in a sudden vision, and said to him, 6

"I will give you all this power and magnificence, for it belongs
to me and I can give it to anyone I please. It shall all be yours if 7
you will fall down and worship me."

To this Jesus replied, 8

"It is written, 'Thou shalt worship the Lord thy God and him
only shalt thou serve'."

Then the devil took him to Jerusalem and set him on the highest 9
ledge of the Temple.

"If you really are the Son of God," he said, "throw yourself
down from here, for the scripture says, 'He shall give his angels 10
charge concerning thee, to guard thee', and 'On their hands they 11
shall bear thee up, lest haply thou dash thy foot against a stone.'"

To which Jesus replied, 12

"It is also said, 'Thou shalt not tempt the Lord thy God.'"

And when he had exhausted every kind of temptation, the devil 13
withdrew until his next opportunity.

Jesus begins his ministry in Galilee

And now Jesus returned to Galilee in the power of the Spirit, 14
and news of him spread through all the surrounding district. He 15
taught in their synagogues, to everyone's great admiration.

Then he came to Nazareth where he had been brought up and, 16
according to his custom, went to the synagogue on the Sabbath
day. He stood up to read the scriptures and the book of the 17
prophet Isaiah was handed to him. He opened the book and found
the place where these words are written—

18   The Spirit of the Lord is upon me,
      Because he anointed me to preach good tidings to the poor:
      He hath sent me to proclaim release to the captives,
      And recovering of sight to the blind,
      To set at liberty them that are bruised,
19   To proclaim the acceptable year of the Lord.
20 Then he shut the book, handed it back to the attendant and
   resumed his seat. Every eye in the synagogue was fixed upon him
21 and he began to tell them, "This very day this scripture has been
   fulfilled, while you have been listening to it!"
22   Everybody noticed what he said and was amazed at the
   beautiful words that came from his lips, and they kept saying,
      "Isn't this Joseph's son?"
23   So he said to them,
      "I expect you will quote this proverb to me, 'Cure yourself,
   doctor!' Let us see you do in your own country all that we have
24 heard that you did in Capernaum!" Then he added, "I assure you
25 that no prophet is ever welcomed in his own country. I tell you
   the plain fact that in Elijah's time, when the heavens were shut
   up for three and a half years and there was a great famine through
26 the whole country, there were plenty of widows in Israel, but
   Elijah was not sent to any of them. But he *was* sent to Sarepta, to
27 a widow in the country of Sidon. In the time of Elisha the
   prophet, there were a great many lepers in Israel, but not one of
   them was healed—only Naaman, the Syrian."
28   But when they heard this, everyone in the synagogue was
29 furiously angry. They sprang to their feet and drove him right
   out of the town, taking him to the brow of the hill on which it
30 was built, intending to hurl him down bodily. But he walked
   straight through the whole crowd and went on his way.

Jesus heals in Capernaum

31   So he came down to Capernaum, a town in Galilee, and taught
32 them on the Sabbath day. They were astonished at his teaching,
   for his words had the ring of authority.
33   There was a man in the synagogue under the influence of some
34 evil spirit and he yelled at the top of his voice, "Hi! What have
   you got to do with us, Jesus, you Nazarene—have you come to
   kill us? I know who you are all right, you're God's holy one!"
35   Jesus cut him short and spoke sharply,
      "Be quiet! Get out of him!"

And after throwing the man down in front of them, the devil did come out of him without hurting him in the slightest. At this *36* everybody present was amazed and they kept saying to each other,

"What sort of words are these? He speaks to these evil spirits with authority and power and out they come."

And his reputation spread over the whole surrounding district. *37*

When Jesus got up and left the synagogue he went into Simon's *38* house. Simon's mother-in-law was suffering from a high fever, and they asked Jesus about her. He stood over her as she lay in *39* bed, brought the fever under control and it left her. At once she got up and began to see to their needs.

Then, as the sun was setting, all those who had friends suffering *40* from every kind of disease brought them to Jesus and he laid his hands on each one of them separately and healed them. Evil spirits *41* came out of many of these people, shouting, "You are the Son of God!"

But he spoke sharply to them and would not allow them to say any more, for they knew perfectly well that he was Christ.

Jesus attempts to be alone—in vain

At daybreak, he went off to a deserted place, but the crowds *42* tried to find him and when they did discover him, tried to prevent him from leaving them. But he told them, "I must tell the good *43* news of the kingdom of God to other towns as well—that is my mission."

And he continued proclaiming his message in the synagogues *44* of Judaea.

CHAPTER 5

Simon, James and John become Jesus' followers

ONE day the people were crowding closely round Jesus to hear *1* God's message, as he stood on the shore of Lake Gennesaret. Jesus noticed two boats drawn up on the beach, for the fishermen *2* had left them there while they were cleaning their nets. He went *3* aboard one of the boats, which belonged to Simon, and asked him to push out a little from the shore. Then he sat down and continued his teaching of the crowds from the boat.

When he had finished speaking, he said to Simon, "Push out *4* now into deep water and let down your nets for a catch."

5   Simon replied, "Master! We've worked all night and never caught a thing, but if you say so, I'll let the nets down."

6   And when they had done this, they caught an enormous shoal
7   of fish—so big that the nets began to tear. So they signalled to their friends in the other boat to come and help them. They came
8   and filled both the boats to sinking point. When Simon Peter saw this, he fell on his knees before Jesus and said,

"Keep away from me, Lord, for I'm only a sinful man!"

9, 10   For he and his companions (including Zebedee's sons, James and John, Simon's partners) were staggered at the haul of fish that they had made.

Jesus said to Simon, "Don't be afraid, Simon. From now on your catch will be *men*."

11   So they brought the boats ashore, left everything and followed him.

Jesus cures leprosy

12   While he was in one of the towns, Jesus came upon a man who was a mass of leprosy. When he saw Jesus, he prostrated himself before him and begged,

"If you want to, Lord, you can make me clean."

13   Jesus stretched out his hand, placed it on the leper, saying, "Certainly I want to. Be clean!"

14   Immediately the leprosy left him and Jesus warned him not to tell anybody, but to go and show himself to the priest and to make the offerings for his recovery that Moses prescribed, as evidence to the authorities.

15   Yet the news about him spread all the more, and enormous crowds collected to hear Jesus and to be healed of their diseases.
16   But he slipped quietly away to deserted places for prayer.

Jesus cures a paralytic in soul and body

17   One day while Jesus was teaching, some Pharisees and experts in the Law were sitting near him. They had come out of every village in Galilee and Judaea as well as from Jerusalem. God's
18   power to heal people was with him. Soon some men arrived carrying a paralytic on a small bed and they kept trying to carry
19   him in to put him down in front of Jesus. When they failed to find a way of getting him in because of the dense crowd, they went up on to the top of the house and let him down, bed and all,

through the tiles, into the middle of the crowd in front of Jesus. When Jesus saw their faith, he said to the man,   20

"My friend, your sins are forgiven."

The scribes and the Pharisees began to argue about this, saying,   21
"Who is this man who talks blasphemy? Who can forgive sins? Only God can do that."

Jesus realised what was going on in their minds and spoke   22
straight to them.

"Why must you argue like this in your minds? Which do you   23
suppose is easier—to say, 'Your sins are forgiven' or to say, 'Get up and walk'? But to make you realise that the Son of Man has   24
full authority on earth to forgive sins—I tell *you*," he said to the man who was paralysed, "get up, pick up your bed and go home!"

Instantly the man sprang to his feet before their eyes, picked   25
up the bedding on which he used to lie, and went off home, praising God. Sheer amazement gripped every man present, and   26
they praised God and said in awed voices, "We have seen incredible things today."

Jesus calls Levi to be his disciple

Later on, Jesus went out and looked straight at a tax-collector   27
called Levi, as he sat at his office desk.

"Follow me," he said to him.

And he got to his feet at once, left everything behind and   28
followed him.

Then Levi gave a big reception for Jesus in his own house, and   29
there was a great crowd of tax-collectors and others at table with them. The Pharisees and their companions the scribes kept   30
muttering indignantly about this to Jesus' disciples, saying,

"Why do you have your meals with tax-collectors and sinners?"
Jesus answered them,   31
"It is not the healthy who need the doctor, but those who are ill. I have not come to invite the 'righteous' but the 'sinners'—to   32
change their ways."

Jesus hints at who he is

Then people said to him,   33
"Why is it that John's disciples are always fasting and praying, just like the Pharisees' disciples, but yours both eat and drink?"

34   Jesus answered,
      "Can you expect wedding-guests to fast while they have the
35   bridegroom with them? The day will come when they will lose
      the bridegroom; that will be the time for them to fast!"
36   Then he gave them this illustration.
      "Nobody tears a piece from a new coat to patch up an old one.
      If he does, he ruins the new one and the new piece does not
      match the old.
37   "Nobody puts new wine into old wineskins. If he does, the
      new wine will burst the skins—the wine will be spilt and the skins
38, 39 ruined. No, new wine must be put into new wineskins. Of
      course, nobody who has been drinking old wine will want the
      new at once. He is sure to say, 'The old is a good sound wine.' "

CHAPTER 6

Jesus speaks of the Sabbath—

1   ONE Sabbath day, as Jesus happened to be passing through the
     cornfields, his disciples began picking the ears of corn, rubbing
2   them in their hands, and eating them. Some of the Pharisees
     remarked,
     "Why are you doing what the Law forbids men to do on the
     Sabbath day?"
3   Jesus answered them and said,
     "Have you never read what David and his companions did
4   when they were hungry? How he went into the house of God,
     took the presentation loaves, ate some bread himself and gave
     some to his companions, even though the Law does not permit
     anyone except the priests to eat it?"
5   Then he added, "The Son of Man is master even of the
     Sabbath."

—and provokes violent antagonism

6   On another Sabbath day when he went into a synagogue to
     teach, there was a man there whose right hand was wasted away.
7   The scribes and the Pharisees were watching Jesus closely to see
     whether he would heal on the Sabbath day, which would, of
8   course, give them grounds for an accusation. But he knew exactly
     what was going on in their minds, and said to the man with the
     wasted hand,

"Stand up and come out in front."

And he got up and stood there. Then Jesus said to them, 9

"I am going to ask you a question. Does the Law command us to do good on Sabbath days or do harm—to save life or destroy it?"

He looked round, meeting all their eyes, and said to the man, 10 "Now stretch out your hand."

He did so, and his hand was restored as sound as the other one. But they were filled with insane fury and kept discussing with 11 each other what they could do to Jesus.

After a night of prayer Jesus selects the twelve

It was in those days that he went up the hill-side to pray, and 12 spent the whole night in prayer to God. When daylight came, he 13 summoned his disciples to him and out of them he chose twelve whom he called apostles. They were—

Simon (whom he called Peter), 14
Andrew, his brother,
James,
John,
Philip,
Bartholomew,
Matthew, 15
Thomas,
James, the son of Alphaeus,
Simon, called the patriot,
Judas, the son of James, and 16
Judas Iscariot, who later betrayed him.

Then he came down with them and stood on a level piece of 17 ground, surrounded by a large crowd of his disciples and a great number of people from all parts of Judaea and Jerusalem and the coastal district of Tyre and Sidon, who had come to hear him and to be healed of their diseases. (And even those who were 18 troubled with evil spirits were cured.) The whole crowd were 19 trying to touch him with their hands, for power was going out from him and he was healing them all.

Jesus declares who is happy and who is to be pitied, and defines a new attitude towards life

Then Jesus looked steadily at his disciples and said, 20

123

"How happy are you who own nothing, for the kingdom of God is yours!

21 "How happy are you who are hungry now, for you will be satisfied!

"How happy are you who weep now, for you are going to laugh!

22 "How happy you are when men hate you and turn you out of their company; when they slander you and detest all that you

23 stand for because you are loyal to the Son of Man. Be glad when that happens and jump for joy—your reward in Heaven is magnificent. For that is exactly how their fathers treated the prophets.

24 "But how miserable for you who are rich, for you have had all your comforts!

25 "How miserable for you who have all you want, for you are going to be hungry!

"How miserable for you who are laughing now, for you will know sorrow and tears!

26 "How miserable for you when everybody says nice things about you, for that is exactly how their fathers treated the false prophets.

27 "But I say to all of you who will listen to me: love your enemies,

28 do good to those who hate you, bless those who curse you, and pray for those who treat you badly.

29 "As for the man who hits you on one cheek, offer him the other one as well! And if a man is taking away your coat, do not

30 stop him from taking your shirt as well. Give to everyone who asks you, and when a man has taken what belongs to you, don't demand it back.

31, 32 "Treat men exactly as you would like them to treat you. If you love only those who love you, what credit is that to you? Even

33 sinners love those who love them! And if you do good only to those who do good to you, what credit is that to you? Even

34 sinners do that. And if you lend only to those from whom you hope to get your money back, what credit is that to you? Even

35 sinners lend to sinners and expect to get their money back. No, you are to love your *enemies* and do good and lend without hope of return. Your reward will be wonderful and you will be sons of the most high. For he is kind to the ungrateful and the wicked!

36 "You must be merciful, as your Father in Heaven is merciful.

37 Don't judge other people and you will not be judged yourselves. Don't condemn and you will not be condemned. Make allowances

38 for others and people will make allowances for you. Give and

men will give to you—yes, good measure, pressed down, shaken together and running over will they pour into your lap. For whatever measure you use with other people, they will use in their dealings with you."

The need for thorough-going sincerity

Then he gave them an illustration— 39
"Can one blind man be guide to another blind man? Surely they will both fall into the ditch together. A disciple is not above 40 his teacher, but when he is fully trained he will be like his teacher.

"Why do you look at the speck of sawdust in your brother's 41 eye and fail to notice the plank in your own? How can you say 42 to your brother, 'Let me take the speck out of your eye' when you cannot see the plank in your own? You fraud, take the plank out of your own eye first and then you can see clearly enough to remove your brother's speck.

"It is impossible for a good tree to produce bad fruit—as 43 impossible as it is for a bad tree to produce good fruit. Do not 44 men know what a tree is by its fruit? You cannot pick figs from briars, or gather a bunch of grapes from a blackberry bush! A 45 good man produces good things from the good stored up in his heart, and a bad man produces evil things from his own stores of evil. For a man's words will always express what has been treasured in his heart.

"And what is the point of calling me, 'Lord, Lord', without 46 doing what I tell you to do? Let me show you what the man who 47 comes to me, hears what I have to say, and puts it into practice, is really like. He is like a man building a house, who dug down to 48 rock-bottom and laid the foundation of his house upon it. Then when the flood came and the flood-water swept down upon that house, it could not shift it because it was properly built. But the 49 man who hears me and does nothing about it is like a man who built his house with its foundation upon soft earth. When the flood-water swept down upon it, it collapsed and the whole house crashed down in ruins."

CHAPTER 7

A Roman centurion's extraordinary faith in Jesus

1 WHEN Jesus had finished these talks to the people, he came to
2 Capernaum, where it happened that there was a man very
seriously ill and in fact at the point of death. He was the slave of a
3 centurion who thought very highly of him. When the centurion
heard about Jesus, he sent some Jewish elders to him with the
4 request that he would come and save his servant's life. When they
came to Jesus, they urged him strongly to grant this request,
saying that the centurion deserved to have this done for him.
5 "He loves our nation and has built us a synagogue out of his own
pocket," they said.

6 So Jesus went with them, but as he approached the house, the
centurion sent some of his personal friends with the message,

"Don't trouble yourself, sir! I'm not important enough for you
7 to come into my house—I didn't think I was fit to come to you
in person. Just give the order, please, and my servant will recover.
8 I am used to working under orders, and I have soldiers under me.
I can say to one, 'Go', and he goes, or I can say to another, 'Come
here', and he comes; or I can say to my slave, 'Do this job', and he
does it."

9 These words amazed Jesus and he turned to the crowd who
were following behind him, and said,

"I have never found faith like this anywhere, even in Israel!"
10 Then those who had been sent by the centurion returned to the
house and found the slave perfectly well.

Jesus brings a dead youth back to life

11 Not long afterwards, Jesus went into a town called Nain,
12 accompanied by his disciples and a large crowd. As they approached the city gate, it happened that some people were carrying out a dead man, the only son of his widowed mother. The
13 usual crowd of fellow-townsmen was with her. When the Lord
saw her, his heart went out to her and he said,

"Don't cry."

14 Then he walked up and put his hand on the bier while the
bearers stood still. Then he said,

"Young man, *wake up!*"

And the dead man sat up and began to talk, and Jesus handed   15
him to his mother. Everybody present was awe-struck and they   16
praised God, saying,

"A great prophet has arisen among us and God has turned his
face towards his people."

And this report of him spread through the whole of Judaea and   17
the surrounding countryside.

Jesus sends John a personal message

John's disciples reported all these happenings to him. Then he   18, 19
summoned two of them and sent them to the Lord with this
message,

"Are you the one who was to come, or are we to look for
someone else?"

When the men came to Jesus, they said,   20

"John the Baptist has sent us to you with this message, 'Are you
the one who was to come, or are we to look for someone else?'"

At that very time Jesus was healing many people of their dis-   21
eases and ailments and evil spirits, and he restored sight to many
who were blind. Then he answered them,   22

"Go and tell John what you have seen and heard. The blind are
recovering their sight, cripples are walking again, lepers being
healed, the deaf hearing, dead men are being brought to life again,
and the good news is being given to those in need. And happy is   23
the man who never loses his faith in me."

Jesus emphasises the greatness of John—and the greater importance of the kingdom of God

When these messengers had gone back, Jesus began to talk to   24
the crowd about John.

"What did you go out into the desert to look at? Was it a
reed waving in the breeze? Well, *what* was it you went out to see?   25
A man dressed in fine clothes? But the men who wear fine clothes
live luxuriously in palaces. But what *did* you really go to see? A   26
prophet? Yes, I tell you, a prophet and far more than a prophet!
This is the man of whom the scripture says,   27

Behold, I send my messenger before thy face,
Who shall prepare thy way before thee.
Believe me, no one greater than John has ever been born, and yet   28
a humble member of the kingdom of God is greater than he.

29 "All the people, yes, even the tax-collectors, when they heard
30 John, acknowledged God and were baptised by his baptism. But
the Pharisees and the experts in the Law frustrated God's purpose
for them, for they refused John's baptism.

31 "What can I say that the men of this generation are like—what
32 sort of men are they? They are like children sitting in the market-
place and calling out to each other, 'We played at weddings for
you, but you wouldn't dance, and we played at funerals for you,
33 and you wouldn't cry!' For John the Baptist came in the strictest
34 austerity and you say he is crazy. Then the Son of Man came,
enjoying life, and you say, 'Look, a drunkard and a glutton, a
35 bosom-friend of the tax-collector and the outsider!' Ah, well,
wisdom's reputation is entirely in the hands of her children!"

Jesus contrasts unloving righteousness with loving penitence

36 Then one of the Pharisees asked Jesus to a meal with him.
When Jesus came into the house, he took his place at the table
37 and a woman, known in the town as a bad woman, found out that
38 Jesus was there and brought an alabaster flask of perfume and
stood behind him crying, letting her tears fall on his feet and then
drying them with her hair. Then she kissed them and anointed
39 them with the perfume. When the Pharisee who had invited him
saw this, he said to himself, "If this man were really a prophet,
he would know who this woman is and what sort of a person is
touching him. He would have realised that she is a bad woman."
40 Then Jesus spoke to him,

"Simon, there is something I want to say to you."

"Very well, Master," he returned, "say it."

41 "Once upon a time, there were two men in debt to the same
money-lender. One owed him fifty pounds and the other five.
42 And since they were unable to pay, he generously cancelled both
of their debts. Now, which one of them do you suppose will love
him more?"

43 "Well," returned Simon, "I suppose it will be the one who has
been more generously treated."

44 "Exactly," replied Jesus, and then turning to the woman, he
said to Simon,

"You can see this woman? I came into your house but you
provided no water to wash my feet. But she has washed my feet
45 with her tears and dried them with her hair. There was no warmth
in your greeting, but she, from the moment I came in, has not

stopped covering my feet with kisses. You gave me no oil for   *46*
my head, but she has put perfume on my feet. That is why I tell   *47*
you, Simon, that her sins, many as they are, are forgiven; for she
has shown me so much love. But the man who has little to be
forgiven has only a little love to give."

Then he said to her,   *48*
"Your sins are forgiven."

And the men at table with him began to say to themselves,   *49*
"And who is this man, who even forgives sins?"

But Jesus said to the woman,   *50*
"It is your faith that has saved you. Go in peace."

CHAPTER 8

Not long after this incident, Jesus went through every town and   *1*
village preaching and telling the people the good news of the
kingdom of God. He was accompanied by the twelve and some   *2*
women who had been cured of evil spirits and illnesses—Mary,
known as "the woman from Magdala" (who had once been
possessed by seven evil spirits), Joanna the wife of Chuza, Herod's   *3'*
agent, Susanna, and many others who used to look after his
comfort from their own resources.

Jesus' parable of the mixed reception given to the truth

When a large crowd had collected and people were coming to   *4*
him from one town after another, he spoke to them and gave them
this parable:

"A sower went out to sow his seed, and while he was sowing,   *5*
some of the seed fell by the roadside and was trodden down and
the birds gobbled it up. Some fell on the rock, and when it   *6*
sprouted it withered for lack of moisture. Some fell among thorn-   *7*
bushes which grew up with the seeds and choked the life out of
them. But some seed fell on good soil and grew and produced a   *8*
crop—a hundred times what had been sown."

And when he had said this, he called out,
"Let the man who has ears to hear use them!"

Then his disciples asked him the meaning of the parable. To   *9,10*
which Jesus replied,

"You have been given the chance to understand the secrets of
the kingdom of God, but the others are given parables so that

they may go through life with their eyes open and see nothing, and with their ears open, and understand nothing of what they hear.

11 "This is what the parable means. The seed is the message of
12 God. The seed sown by the roadside represents those who hear the message, and then the devil comes and takes it away from
13 their hearts so that they cannot believe it and be saved. That sown on the rock represents those who accept the message with great delight when they hear it, but have no real root. They believe for a little while but when the time of temptation comes,
14 they lose faith. And the seed sown among the thorns represents the people who hear the message and go on their way, and with the worries and riches and pleasures of living, the life is choked
15 out of them, and in the end they produce nothing. But the seed sown on good soil means the men who hear the message and accept it with a good and honest heart, and go on steadily producing a good crop.

Truth is not a secret to be hidden but a gift to be used

16 "Nobody lights a lamp and covers it with a basin or puts it under the bed. No, a man puts his lamp on a lamp-stand so that
17 those who come in can see the light. For there is nothing hidden now which will not become perfectly plain and there are no
18 secrets now which will not become as clear as daylight. So take care how you listen—more will be given to the man who has something already, but the man who has nothing will lose even what he thinks he has."

19 Then his mother and his brothers arrived to see him, but could
20 not get near him because of the crowd. So a message was passed to him,

"Your mother and your brothers are standing outside wanting to see you."

21 To which he replied,

"My mother and my brothers ? That means those who listen to God's message and obey it."

Jesus' mastery of wind and water

22 It happened on one of these days that he embarked on a boat with his disciples and said to them,

"Let us cross over to the other side of the lake."

130

So they set sail, and when they were under way he dropped off **23** to sleep. Then a squall of wind swept down upon the lake and they were in grave danger of being swamped. Coming forward, **24** they woke him up, saying,

"Master, master, we're drowning!"

Then he got up and reprimanded the wind and the stormy waters, and they died down, and everything was still. Then he **25** said to them,

"What has happened to your faith?"

But they were frightened and bewildered and kept saying to each other,

"Who ever can this be? He gives orders even to the winds and waters and *they obey him.*"

Jesus encounters and heals a dangerous lunatic

They sailed on to the country of the Gerasenes which is on the **26** opposite side of the lake to Galilee. And as Jesus disembarked, a **27** man from the town who was possessed by evil spirits met him. He had worn no clothes for a long time and did not live inside a house, but among the tombs. When he saw Jesus, he let out a **28** howl and fell down in front of him, yelling,

"What have you got to do with me, you Jesus, Son of the most high God? Please, please, don't torment me."

For Jesus was commanding the evil spirit to come out of the **29** man. Again and again the evil spirit had taken control of him, and though he was bound with chains and fetters and closely watched, he would snap his bonds and go off into the desert with the devil at his heels. Then Jesus asked him, **30**

"What is your name?"

"Legion!" he replied. For many evil spirits had gone into him, and were now begging Jesus not to order them off to the bottom- **31** less pit. It happened that there was a large herd of pigs feeding **32** on the hill-side, so they implored him to allow them to go into the pigs, and he let them go. And when the evil spirits came out **33** of the man and went into the pigs, the whole herd rushed down the cliff into the lake and were drowned. When the swineherds **34** saw what had happened, they took to their heels, pouring out the story to the people in the town and countryside. These people **35** came out to see what had happened, and approached Jesus. They found the man, whom the evil spirits had left, sitting down at Jesus' feet, properly clothed and quite sane. That frightened them.

36 Those who had seen it told the others how the man with the evil
37 spirits had been cured. And the whole crowd of people from the
district surrounding the Gerasenes' country begged Jesus to go
away from them, for they were thoroughly frightened. Then he
38 re-embarked on the boat and turned back. The man who had had
the evil spirits kept begging to go with Jesus, but he sent him
away with the words,

39 "Go back home and tell them all what wonderful things God
has done for you."

So the man went away and told the marvellous story of what
Jesus had done for him, all over the town.

40 On Jesus' return, the crowd welcomed him back, for they had
all been looking for him.

Jesus heals in response to faith

41 Then up came Jairus (who was president of the synagogue),
42 and fell at Jesus' feet, begging him to come into his house, for his
daughter, an only child about twelve years old, was dying.

43 But as he went, the crowds nearly suffocated him. Among them
was a woman, who had had a haemorrhage for twelve years and
44 who had derived no benefit from anybody's treatment. She came
up behind Jesus and touched the edge of his cloak, with the result
that her haemorrhage stopped at once.

45 "Who was that who touched me?" said Jesus.

And when everybody denied it, Peter remonstrated,

"Master, the crowds are all round you and are pressing you on
all sides. . . ."

46 But Jesus said,

"Somebody touched me, for I felt that power went out from
me."

47 When the woman realised that she had not escaped notice she
came forward trembling, and fell at his feet and admitted before
everybody why she had had to touch him, and how she had been
instantaneously cured.

48 "Daughter," said Jesus, "It is your faith that has healed you—
go in peace."

49 While he was still speaking, somebody came from the synagogue
president's house to say,

"Your daughter is dead—there is no need to trouble the master
any further."

50 But when Jesus heard this, he said to him,

132

"Now don't be afraid, go on believing and she will be all right."

Then when he came to the house, he would not allow anyone 51 to go in with him except Peter, John and James, and the child's parents. All those already there were weeping and wailing over 52 her, but he said,

"Stop crying! She is not dead, she is fast asleep."

This drew a scornful laugh from them, for they were quite 53 certain that she had died. But he turned them all out, took the little 54 girl's hand and called out to her,

"Wake up, my child!"

And her spirit came back and she got to her feet at once, and 55 Jesus ordered food to be given to her. Her parents were nearly out 56 of their minds with joy, but Jesus told them not to tell anyone what had happened.

CHAPTER 9

Jesus commissions the twelve to preach and heal

THEN he called the twelve together and gave them power and 1 authority over all evil spirits and the ability to heal disease. He 2 sent them out to preach the kingdom of God and to heal the sick, with these words, 3

"Take nothing for your journey—neither a stick nor a purse nor food nor money, nor even extra clothes! When you come 4 to stay at a house, remain there until you go on your way again. And where they will not welcome you, leave that town, and shake 5 the dust off your feet as a protest against them!"

So they set out, and went from village to village preaching the 6 gospel and healing people everywhere.

Herod's uneasy conscience after his execution of John

All these things came to the ears of Herod the tetrarch and 7 caused him acute anxiety, because some people were saying that John had risen from the dead, some maintaining that the prophet 8 Elijah had appeared, and others that one of the old-time prophets had come back.

"I beheaded John," said Herod. "Who can this be that I hear 9 all these things about?"

And he tried to find a way of seeing Jesus.

The twelve return and tell their story

10   Then the apostles returned, and when they had made their report to Jesus of what they had done, he took them with him privately and retired into a town called Bethsaida.

Jesus welcomes the crowds, teaches, heals and feeds them

11   But the crowds observed this and followed him. And he welcomed them and talked to them about the kingdom of God, and
12   cured those who were in need of healing. As the day drew to its close the twelve came to him and said,

"Please dismiss the crowd now so that they can go to the villages and country round about and find some food and shelter, for we're quite in the wilds here."

13   "You give them something to eat!" returned Jesus.

"But we've nothing here," they replied, "except five loaves and two fish, unless you want us to go and buy food for all this
14   crowd?" (There were approximately five thousand men there.)

Then Jesus said to the disciples,

"Get them to sit down in groups of about fifty."

15,16   This they did, making them all sit down. Then he took the five loaves and the two fish and looked up to Heaven, blessed them, broke them into pieces and passed them to his disciples to serve
17   to the crowd. Everybody ate and was satisfied. Afterwards they collected twelve baskets full of broken pieces which were left over.

Jesus asks a question and receives Peter's momentous answer

18   Then came this incident. While Jesus was praying by himself, having only the disciples near him, he asked them this question:

"Who are the crowd saying that I am?"

19   "Some say that you are John the Baptist," they replied. "Others that you are Elijah, and others think that one of the old-time prophets has come to life again."

20   Then he said,

"And who do you say that I am?"

"*God's Christ!*" said Peter.

Jesus foretells his own suffering: the paradox of
losing life to find it

21   But Jesus expressly told them not to say a word to anybody,

at the same time warning them of the inevitability of the Son 22
of Man's great suffering, of his repudiation by the elders, chief
priests and scribes, and of his death and of being raised to life
again on the third day. Then he spoke to them all. 23

"If anyone wants to follow in my footsteps, he must give up
all right to himself, carry his cross every day and keep close behind
me. For the man who wants to save his life will lose it, but the 24
man who loses his life for my sake will save it. For what is the 25
use of a man gaining the whole world if he loses or forfeits his
own soul? If anyone is ashamed of me and my words, the Son of 26
Man will be ashamed of him, when he comes in his glory and
the glory of the Father and the holy angels. I tell you the simple 27
truth—there are men standing here today who will not taste
death until they have seen the kingdom of God!"

Peter, John and James are allowed to see the glory of Jesus

About eight days after these sayings, Jesus took Peter, James 28
and John and went off with them to the hill-side to pray. And 29
then, while he was praying, the whole appearance of his face
changed and his clothes became white and dazzling. And two men 30
were talking with Jesus. They were Moses and Elijah—revealed 31
in heavenly splendour, and their talk was about the way he must
take and the end he must fulfil in Jerusalem. But Peter and his 32
companions had been overcome by sleep and it was as they
struggled into wakefulness that they saw the glory of Jesus and
the two men standing with him. Just as they were parting from 33
him, Peter said to Jesus,

"Master, it is wonderful for us to be here! Let us put up three
shelters—one for you, one for Moses and one for Elijah." But he
did not know what he was saying. While he was still talking, a 34
cloud overshadowed them and awe swept over them as it en-
veloped them. A voice came out of the cloud, saying, 35

"This is my Son, my chosen! Listen to him!"

And while the voice was speaking, they found there was no one 36
there at all but Jesus. The disciples were reduced to silence, and
in those days never breathed a word to anyone of what they had
seen.

Jesus heals an epileptic boy

Then on the following day, as they came down the hill-side, a 37
great crowd met him. Suddenly a man from the crowd shouted out, 38

"Master, please come and look at my son! He's my only child,
39 and without any warning some spirit gets hold of him and he
calls out suddenly. Then it convulses him until he foams at the
mouth, and only after a fearful struggle does it go away and leave
40 him bruised all over. I begged your disciples to get rid of it, but
they couldn't."

41 "You really are an unbelieving and difficult people," replied
Jesus. "How long must I be with you, how long must I put up
with you? Bring him here to me."

42 But even while the boy was on his way, the spirit hurled him
to the ground in a dreadful convulsion. Then Jesus reprimanded
the evil spirit, healed the lad and handed him back to his father.
43 And everybody present was amazed at this demonstration of the
power of God.

The realism of Jesus in the midst of enthusiasm

And while everybody was full of wonder at all the things they
saw him do, Jesus was saying to the disciples,

44 "Store up in your minds what I tell you nowadays, for the Son
of Man is going to be handed over to the power of men."

45 But they made no sense of this saying—something made it
impossible for them to understand it, and they were afraid to ask
him what he meant.

Jesus and "greatness"

46 Then an argument arose among them as to who should be the
47 greatest. But Jesus, knowing what they were arguing about, took
48 a little child and made him stand by his side. And then he said to
them,

"Anyone who accepts a little child in my name is really accepting me, and the man who accepts me is really accepting the one
who sent me. It is the humblest among you all who is really the
greatest."

49 Then John broke in,

"Master, we saw a man driving out evil spirits in your name,
but we stopped him, for he is not one of us who follow you."

50 But Jesus told him,

"You must not stop him. The man who is not against you is
on your side."

He sets off for Jerusalem to meet inevitable death

Now as the days before he should be taken back into Heaven 51
were running out, he resolved to go to Jerusalem, and sent 52
messengers in front of him. They set out and entered a Samaritan
village to make preparations for him. But the people there refused 53
to welcome him because he was obviously intending to go to
Jerusalem. When the disciples James and John saw this, they said, 54

"Master, do you want us to call down fire from heaven and
burn them all up?"

But Jesus turned and reproved them, and they all went on to 55, 56
another village.

As the little company made its way along the road, a man said 57
to him,

"I'm going to follow you wherever you go."

And Jesus replied, 58

"Foxes have earths, birds have nests, but the Son of Man has
nowhere that he can call his own."

But he said to another man, 59

"Follow me."

And he replied,

"Let me go and bury my father first."

But Jesus told him, 60

"Leave the dead to bury their own dead. You must come away
and preach the kingdom of God."

Another man said to him, 61

"I am going to follow you, Lord, but first let me bid farewell
to my people at home."

But Jesus told him, 62

"Anyone who puts his hand to the plough and then looks
behind him is useless for the kingdom of God."

CHAPTER 10

Jesus now despatches thirty-five couples to preach and heal the sick

LATER on the Lord commissioned seventy other disciples and 1
sent them off in twos as advance-parties into every town and
district where he intended to go.

"There is a great harvest," he told them, "but only a few are 2
working in it—which means you must pray to the Lord of the
harvest that he will send out more reapers.

3 "Now go on your way. I am sending you out like lambs among
4 wolves. Don't carry a purse or a bag or a pair of shoes, and don't
stop to pass the time of day with anyone you meet on the road.
5 When you go into a house, say first of all, 'Peace be to this house-
6 hold!' If there is a lover of peace there, he will accept your words
7 of blessing, and if not, they will come back to you. Stay in the
same house and eat and drink whatever they put before you—a
workman deserves his wages. But don't move from one house to
another.

8 "Whatever town you go into and the people welcome you, eat
9 the meals they give you and heal the people who are ill there.
10 Tell them, 'The kingdom of God is very near to you now.' But
whenever you come into a town and they will not welcome you,
11 you must go into the streets and say, 'We brush off even the
dust of your town from our feet as a protest against you. But it
12 is still true that the kingdom of God has arrived!' I assure
you that it will be better for Sodom in 'that day' than for that
town.

13 "Alas for you, Chorazin, and alas for you, Bethsaida! For if
Tyre and Sidon had seen the demonstrations of God's power that
you have seen, they would have repented long ago and sat in
14 sackcloth and ashes. It will be better for Tyre and Sidon in the
15 judgment than for you! As for you, Capernaum, are you on your
way up to heaven? I tell you you will go hurtling down among
the dead!"

Then he added to the seventy,

16 "Whoever listens to you is listening to me, and the man who
has no use for you has no use for me either. And the man who has
no use for me has no use for the one who sent me!"

*Jesus tells the returned missioners not to be enthusiastic
over mere power*

17 Later the seventy came back full of joy.

"Lord," they said, "even evil spirits obey us when we use your
name!"

18 "Yes," returned Jesus, "I was watching and saw Satan fall from
19 heaven like a flash of lightning! It is true that I have given you the
power to tread on snakes and scorpions and to overcome all the
enemy's power—there is nothing at all that can do you any harm.
20 Yet it is not your power over evil spirits which should give such
joy, but the fact that your names are written in Heaven."

Jesus prays aloud to his Father

At that moment Jesus himself was inspired with joy, and **21** exclaimed,

"O Father, Lord of Heaven and earth, I thank you for hiding these things from the clever and intelligent and for showing them to mere children! Yes, I thank you, Father, that this was your will." Then he went on,

"Everything has been put in my hands by my Father; and **22** nobody knows who the Son really is except the Father. Nobody knows who the Father really is except the Son—and the man to whom the Son chooses to reveal him!"

Then he turned to his disciples and said to them quietly, **23**

"How fortunate you are to see what you are seeing! I tell you **24** that many prophets and kings have wanted to see what you are seeing but they never saw it, and to hear what you are hearing but they never heard it."

Jesus shows the relevance of the Law to actual living

Then one of the experts in the Law stood up to test him and **25** said,

"Master, what must I do to be sure of eternal life?"

"What does the Law say and what has your reading taught **26** you?" said Jesus.

"The Law says, 'Thou shalt love the Lord thy God with all thy **27** heart and with all thy soul and with all thy strength and with all thy mind—and thy neighbour as thyself'," he replied.

"Quite right," said Jesus. "Do that and you will live." **28**

But the man, wanting to justify himself, continued, **29**

"But who is my 'neighbour'?"

And Jesus gave him the following reply: **30**

"A man was once on his way down from Jerusalem to Jericho. He fell into the hands of bandits who stripped off his clothes, beat him up, and left him half dead. It so happened that a priest **31** was going down that road, and when he saw him, he passed by on the other side. A Levite also came on the scene and when he **32** saw him, he too passed by on the other side. But then a Samaritan **33** traveller came along to the place where the man was lying, and at the sight of him he was touched with pity. He went across to **34** him and bandaged his wounds, pouring on oil and wine. Then he put him on his own mule, brought him to an inn and did

35 what he could for him. Next day he took out two silver coins and
gave them to the inn-keeper with the words, 'Look after him,
will you? I will pay you back whatever more you spend, when I
36 come through here on my return.' Which of these three seems to
you to have been a neighbour to the bandits' victim?"

37   "The man who gave him practical sympathy," he replied.
"Then you go and give the same," returned Jesus.

Yet emphasises the need for quiet listening to his words

38   As they continued their journey, Jesus came to a village and a
39 woman called Martha welcomed him to her house. She had a
sister by the name of Mary who settled down at the Lord's feet
40 and was listening to what he said. But Martha was very worried
about her elaborate preparations and she burst in, saying,

"Lord, don't you *mind* that my sister has left me to do everything by myself? Tell her to get up and help me!"
41   But the Lord answered her,

"Martha, my dear, you are worried and bothered about pro-
42 viding so many things. Only a few things are really needed, perhaps only one. Mary has chosen the best part and you must not
tear it away from her!"

CHAPTER 11

Jesus gives a model prayer

1   ONE day it happened that Jesus was praying in a certain place,
and after he had finished, one of his disciples said,

"Lord, teach us how to pray, as John used to teach his
disciples."
2   "When you pray," returned Jesus, "you should say, 'Father,
3 may your name be honoured—may your kingdom come! Give
4 us each day the bread we need, and forgive us our sins, for we
forgive anyone who owes anything to us; and keep us clear of
temptation.' "

The willingness of the Father to answer prayer

5   Then he added,

"If any of you has a friend, and goes to him in the middle of
6 the night and says, 'Lend me three loaves, my dear fellow, for a

friend of mine has just arrived after a journey and I have no food
to put in front of him'; and then he answers from inside the   7
house, 'Don't bother me with your troubles. The front door is
locked and my children and I have gone to bed. I simply cannot
get up now and give you anything!' Yet, I tell you, that even if   8
he won't get up and give him what he wants simply because he
is his friend, yet if he persists, he will rouse himself and give him
everything he needs. And so I tell you, ask and it will be given   9
you, search and you will find, knock and the door will be opened
to you. The one who asks will always receive; the one who is   10
searching will always find, and the door is opened to the man who
knocks. Some of you are fathers, and if your son asks you for   11
some fish, would you give him a snake instead, or if he asks you   12
for an egg, would you make him a present of a scorpion? So, if   13
you, for all your evil, know how to give good things to your
children, how much more likely is it that your Heavenly Father
will give the Holy Spirit to those who ask him!"

Jesus shows the absurdity of "his being in league with the devil"

Another time, Jesus was expelling an evil spirit which was   14
preventing a man from speaking, and as soon as the evil spirit
left him, the dumb man found his speech, to the amazement of
the crowds.

But some of them said,   15
"He expels these spirits because he is in league with Beelzebub,
the chief of the evil spirits."

Others among them, to test him, tried to get a sign from Heaven   16
out of him. But he knew what they were thinking and told them,   17
"Any kingdom divided against itself is doomed and a dis-
united household will collapse. And if Satan disagrees with Satan, 18
how does his kingdom continue?—for I know you are saying that
I expel evil spirits because I am in league with Beelzebub. But if I 19
do expel devils because I am an ally of Beelzebub, who is your
own sons' ally when they do the same thing? They can settle that
question for you. But if it is by the finger of God that I am   20
expelling evil spirits, 'then the kingdom of God has swept over you
unawares'!

"When a strong man armed to the teeth guards his own house,   21
his property is in peace. But when a stronger man comes and   22
conquers him, he removes all the arms on which he pinned his
faith and divides the spoil among his friends.

23 "Anyone who is not with me is against me, and the man who does not gather with me is really scattering.

The danger of a spiritual vacuum in a man's soul

24 "When the evil spirit comes out of a man, it wanders through waterless places looking for rest, and when it fails to find any, it
25 says, 'I will go back to my house from which I came.' When it
26 arrives, it finds it cleaned and all in order. Then it goes and collects seven other spirits more evil than itself to keep it company, and they all go in and make themselves at home. The last state of that man is worse than the first."

Jesus brings sentimentality down to earth

27 And while he was still saying this, a woman in the crowd called out and said,
    "Oh, what a blessing for a woman to have brought you into the world and nursed you!"
28 But Jesus replied,
    "Yes, but a far greater blessing to hear the word of God and obey it."

His scathing judgment on his contemporary generation

29 Then as the people crowded closely around him, he continued,
    "This is an evil generation! It looks for a sign and it will be
30 given no sign except that of Jonah. Just as Jonah was a sign to the people of Nineveh, so will the Son of Man be a sign to this
31 generation. When the judgment comes, the Queen of the South will rise up with the men of this generation and she will condemn them. For she came from the ends of the earth to listen to the wisdom of Solomon, and there is more than the wisdom of
32 Solomon with you now! The men of Nineveh will stand up at the judgment with this generation and will condemn it. For they did repent when Jonah preached to them, and there is something more than Jonah's preaching with you now!

The need for complete sincerity

33 "No one takes a lamp and puts it in a cupboard or under a bucket, but on a lamp-stand, so that those who come in can see
34 the light. The lamp of your body is your eye. When your eye is

sound, your whole body is full of light, but when your eye is
evil, your whole body is full of darkness. So be very careful that   35
your light never becomes darkness. For if your whole body is full   36
of light, with no part of it in shadow, it will all be radiant—it will
be like having a bright lamp to give you light."

While he was talking, a Pharisee invited him to dinner. So he   37
went into his house and sat down at table. The Pharisee noticed   38
with some surprise that he did not wash before the meal. But   39
the Lord said to him,

"You Pharisees are fond of cleaning the outside of your cups
and dishes, but inside yourselves you are full of greed and wickedness! Have you no sense? Don't you realise that the one who made   40
the outside is the maker of the inside as well? If you would only   41
make the inside clean by doing good to others, the outside things
become clean as a matter of course! But alas for you Pharisees, for   42
you pay out your tithe of mint and rue and every little herb, and
lose sight of the justice and the love of God. Yet these are the
things you ought to have been concerned with—it need not mean
leaving the lesser duties undone. Yes, alas for you Pharisees,   43
who love the front seats in the synagogues and having men bow
down to you in public! Alas for you, for you are like unmarked   44
graves—men walk over your corruption without ever knowing it is
there."

Jesus denounces the learned for obscuring the truth

Then one of the experts in the Law said to him,   45
"Master, when you say things like this, you are insulting us as
well."
And he returned,
"Yes, and I do blame you experts in the Law! For you pile up   46
back-breaking burdens for men to bear, but you yourselves will
not raise a finger to lift them. Alas for you, for you build memorial   47
tombs for the prophets—the very men whom your fathers
murdered. You show clearly enough how you approve your   48
fathers' actions. They did the actual killing and you put up a
memorial to it. That is why the wisdom of God has said, 'I will   49
send them prophets and apostles; some they will kill and some
they will persecute!' So that the blood of all the prophets shed   50
from the foundation of the earth, from Abel to Zachariah who   51
died between the altar and the sanctuary, shall be charged to this
generation!

52 "Alas for you experts in the Law, for you have taken away the key of knowledge. You have never gone in yourselves and you have hindered everyone else who was at the door!"

53 And when he left the house, the scribes and the Pharisees began to regard him with bitter animosity and tried to draw him out
54 on a great many subjects, waiting to pounce on some incriminating remark.

CHAPTER 12

1 MEANWHILE, the crowds had gathered in thousands, so that they were actually treading on each other's toes, and Jesus, speaking primarily to his disciples, said,

"Be on your guard against yeast—I mean the yeast of the
2 Pharisees, which is sheer pretence. For there is nothing covered up which is not going to be exposed, nor anything private which
3 is not going to be made public. Whatever you may say in the dark will be heard in daylight, and whatever you whisper within four walls will be shouted from the house-tops.

Man need only fear God

4 "I tell you, as friends of mine, that you need not be afraid of those who can kill the body, but afterwards cannot do anything
5 more. I will show you the only one you need to fear—the one who, after he has killed, has the power to throw you into destruc-
6 tion! Yes, I tell you, it is right to stand in awe of him. The market-price of five sparrows is two farthings, isn't it? Yet not one of
7 them is forgotten in God's sight. Why, the very hairs of your heads are all numbered! Don't be afraid, then; you are worth
8 more than a great many sparrows! I tell you that every man who publicly acknowledges me, I, the Son of Man, will acknowledge
9 in the presence of the angels of God. But the man who publicly disowns me will find himself disowned before the angels of God!

10 "Anyone who speaks against the Son of Man will be forgiven, but there is no forgiveness for the man who speaks evil against the
11 Holy Spirit. And when they bring you before the synagogues and magistrates and authorities, don't worry as to what defence you
12 are going to put up or what words you are going to use. For the Holy Spirit will tell you at the time what is the right thing for you to say."

Jesus gives a warning about the love of material security

Then someone out of the crowd said to him,   13
"Master, tell my brother to share his legacy with me."
But Jesus replied,   14
"My dear man, who appointed me a judge or arbitrator in your
affairs?"
And then, turning to the disciples, he said to them,   15
"Notice that, and be on your guard against covetousness in any
shape or form. For a man's real life in no way depends upon the
number of his possessions."
Then he gave them a parable in these words,   16
"Once upon a time a rich man's farmland produced heavy
crops. So he said to himself, 'What shall I do, for I have no room   17
to store this harvest of mine?' Then he said, 'I know what I'll do.   18
I'll pull down my barns and build bigger ones where I can store
all my grain and my goods and I can say to my soul, Soul, you   19
have plenty of good things stored up there for years to come.
Relax! Eat, drink and have a good time!' But God said to him,   20
'You fool, this very night you will be asked for *your soul*! Then,
who is going to possess all that you have prepared?' That is what   21
happens to the man who hoards things for himself and is not rich
where God is concerned."
And then he added to the disciples,   22
"That is why I tell you, don't worry about life, wondering
what you are going to eat. And stop bothering about what clothes
you will need. Life is much more important than food, and the   23
body more important than clothes. Think of the ravens. They   24
neither sow nor reap, and they have neither store nor barn, but
God feeds them. And how much more valuable do you think you
are than birds? Can any of you make himself an inch taller how-   25
ever much he worries about it? And if you can't manage a little   26
thing like this, why do you worry about anything else? Think of   27
the wild flowers, and how they neither work nor weave. Yet I
tell you that Solomon in all his glory was never arrayed like one
of these. If God so clothes the grass, which flowers in the field   28
today and is burnt in the stove tomorrow, is he not much more
likely to clothe you, you little-faiths? You must not set your heart   29
on what you eat or drink, nor must you live in a state of anxiety.
The whole heathen world is busy about getting food and drink,   30
and your Father knows well enough that you need such things.
No, set your heart on his kingdom, and your food and drink will   31

32 come as a matter of course. Don't be afraid, you tiny flock! Your
33 Father plans to give you the kingdom. Sell your possessions and
give the money away. Get yourselves purses that never grow old,
inexhaustible treasure in Heaven, where no thief can ever reach
34 it, or moth ruin it. For wherever your treasure is, you may be
certain that your heart will be there too!

Jesus' disciples must be on the alert

35, 36 "You must be ready dressed and have your lamps alight, like
men who wait to welcome their lord and master on his return
from the wedding-feast, so that when he comes and knocks at the
37 door, they may open it for him at once. Happy are the servants
whom their lord finds on the alert when he arrives. I assure you
that he will then take off his outer clothes, make them sit down
38 to dinner, and come and wait on them. And if he should come
just after midnight or in the very early morning, and find them
39 still on the alert, their happiness is assured. But be certain of this,
that if the householder had known the time when the burglar
40 would come, he would not have let his house be broken into. So
you must be on the alert, for the Son of Man is coming at a time
when you may not expect him."

41 Then Peter said to him,
"Lord, do you mean this parable for us or for everybody?"

42 But the Lord continued,
"Well, who will be the faithful, sensible steward whom his
master will put in charge of his household to give them their
43 supplies at the proper time? Happy is the servant if his master
44 finds him so doing when he returns. I tell you he will promote
45 him to look after all his property. But suppose the servant says to
himself, 'My master takes his time about returning', and then
begins to beat the men and women servants and to eat and drink
46 and get drunk, that servant's lord and master will return suddenly
and unexpectedly, and he will punish him severely and send him
47 to share the penalty of the unfaithful. The slave who knows his
master's plan but does not get ready or act upon it will be severely
48 punished, but the servant who did not know the plan, though he
has done wrong, will be let off lightly. Much will be expected
from the one who has been given much, and the more a man is
trusted, the more people will expect of him.

49 "It is fire that I have come to bring upon the earth—how I
50 could wish it were already ablaze! There is a baptism that I must
undergo and how strained I am until it is over!

146

Jesus declares that his coming is bound to bring division

"Do you think I have come to bring peace on the earth? No, *51*
I tell you, not peace, but division! For from now on, there will be *52*
five people divided against each other in one house, three against
two, and two against three. It is going to be father against son, and *53*
son against father, and mother against daughter, and daughter
against mother; mother-in-law against her daughter-in-law, and
daughter-in-law against mother-in-law!"

Intelligence should be used not only about the weather but about the
times in which men live

Then he said to the crowds, *54*
"When you see a cloud rising in the west, you say at once that
it is going to rain, and so it does. And when you feel the south *55*
wind blowing, you say that it is going to be hot, and so it is.
You frauds! You know how to interpret the look of the earth and *56*
the sky. Why can't you interpret the meaning of the times in
which you live?

"And why can't you decide for yourselves what is right? For *57, 58*
instance, when you are going before the magistrate with your
opponent, do your best to come to terms with him while you
have the chance, or he may rush you off to the judge, and the
judge hand you over to the police-officer, and the police-officer
throw you into prison. I tell you you will never get out again *59*
until you have paid your last farthing."

CHAPTER 13

Jesus is asked about the supposed significance of disasters

It was just at this moment that some people came up to tell *1*
him the story of the Galileans whose blood Pilate had mixed with
that of their own sacrifices. Jesus made this reply to them: *2*
"Are you thinking that these Galileans were worse sinners than
any other men of Galilee because this happened to them? I assure *3*
you that is not so. You will all die just as miserable a death unless
your hearts are changed! You remember those eighteen people *4*
who were killed at Siloam when the tower collapsed upon them?
Are you imagining that they were worse offenders than any of
the other people who lived in Jerusalem? I assure you they were *5*

not. You will all die as tragically unless your whole outlook is changed!"

And hints at God's patience with the Jewish nation

6   Then he gave them this parable:

    "Once upon a time a man had a fig-tree growing in his garden,
7 and when he came to look for the figs, he found none at all. So he said to his gardener, 'Look, I have come expecting fruit on this fig-tree for three years running and never found any. Better cut
8 it down. Why should it use up valuable space?' And the gardener replied, 'Master, don't touch it this year till I have had a chance
9 to dig round it and give it a bit of manure. Then, if it bears after that, it will be all right. But if it doesn't, then you can cut it down.'"

Jesus reduces the sabbatarians to silence

10   It happened that he was teaching in one of the synagogues on
11 the Sabbath day. In the congregation was a woman who for eighteen years had been ill from some psychological cause; she was bent double and was quite unable to straighten herself up.
12 When Jesus noticed her, he called her and said,

    "You are set free from your illness!"

13   And he put his hands upon her, and at once she stood upright
14 and praised God. But the president of the synagogue, in his annoyance at Jesus' healing on the Sabbath, announced to the congregation,

    "There are six days in which men may work. Come on one of them and be healed, and not on the Sabbath day!"

15   But the Lord answered him, saying,

    "You hypocrites, every single one of you unties his ox or his ass from the stall on the Sabbath day and leads him away to
16 water! This woman, a daughter of Abraham, whom you all know Satan has kept bound for eighteen years—surely she should be released from such bonds on the Sabbath day!"

17   These words reduced his opponents to shame, but the crowd was thrilled at all the glorious things he did.

18   Then he went on,

    "What is the kingdom of God like? What illustration can I use
19 to make it plain to you? It is like a grain of mustard-seed which a man took and dropped in his own garden. It grew and became a tree and the birds came and nested in its branches."

Then again he said, *20*
"What can I say the kingdom of God is like? It is like the yeast *21*
which a woman took and covered up in three measures of flour
until the whole lot had risen."

The kingdom is not entered by drifting but by decision

So he went on his way through towns and villages, teaching *22*
as he went and making his way towards Jerusalem. Someone *23*
remarked,
"Lord, are only a few men to be saved?"
And Jesus told them,
"You must do your utmost to get in through the narrow door, *24*
for many, I assure you, will try to do so and will not succeed, once *25*
the master of the house has got up and shut the door. Then you
may find yourselves standing outside and knocking at the door
crying, 'Lord, please open the door for us.' He will reply to you,
'I don't know who you are or where you come from.' 'But . . .' *26*
you will protest, 'we have had meals with you, and you taught in
our streets!' Yet he will say to you, 'I tell you I do not know where *27*
you have come from. Be off, you scoundrels!' At that time there *28*
will be tears and bitter regret—to see Abraham and Isaac and
Jacob and all the prophets inside the kingdom of God, and you
yourselves excluded, outside! Yes, and people will come from the *29*
east and the west, and from the north and the south, and take their
seats in the kingdom of God. There are some at the back now *30*
who will be in front then, and there are some in front now who
will then be far behind."

The Pharisees warn Jesus of Herod; he replies

Just then some Pharisees arrived to tell him, *31*
"You must get right away from here, for Herod intends to kill
you."
"Go and tell that fox," returned Jesus, "today and tomorrow *32*
I am expelling evil spirits and continuing my work of healing,
and on the third day my work will be finished. But I must journey *33*
on today, tomorrow, and the next day, for it would never do for
a prophet to meet his death outside Jerusalem!
"O Jerusalem, Jerusalem, you murder the prophets and stone *34*
the messengers that are sent to you! How often have I longed to
gather your children round me like a bird gathering her brood

35 together under her wings, but you would never have it. Now, all that is left is yourselves, and your house. For I tell you that you will never see me again till the day when you cry, 'Blessed is he who comes in the name of the Lord!' "

CHAPTER 14

Strict sabbatarianism is again rebuked

1 ONE Sabbath day he went into the house of one of the leading Pharisees for a meal, and they were all watching him closely.

2, 3 Right in front of him was a man afflicted with dropsy. So Jesus spoke to the scribes and Pharisees and said,

"Well, is it right to heal on the Sabbath day or not?"

4 But there was no reply. So Jesus took the man and healed him
5 and let him go. Then he said to them,

"If an ass or a cow belonging to one of you fell into a well, wouldn't you rescue him without the slightest hesitation even though it were the Sabbath?"

6 And this again left them quite unable to reply.

A lesson in humility

7 Then he gave a little word of advice to the guests when he noticed how they were choosing the best seats.

8 "When you are invited to a wedding reception, don't sit down in the best seat. It might happen that a more distinguished man
9 than you has also been invited. Then your host might say, 'I am afraid you must give up your seat for this man.' And then, with considerable embarrassment, you will have to sit in the humblest
10 place. No, when you are invited, go and take your seat in an inconspicuous place, so that when your host comes in he may say to you, 'Come on, my dear fellow, we have a much better seat than this for you.' That is the way to be important in the eyes of
11 all your fellow-guests! For everyone who makes himself important will become insignificant, while the man who makes himself insignificant will find himself important."

12 Then, addressing his host, Jesus said,

"When you give a luncheon or a dinner party, don't invite your friends or your brothers or relations or wealthy neighbours, for the chances are they will invite you back, and you will be fully
13 repaid. No, when you give a party, invite the poor, the lame, the

crippled and the blind. That way lies real happiness for you. They **14** have no means of repaying you, but you will be repaid when good men are rewarded—at the resurrection."

Then, one of the guests, hearing these remarks of Jesus, said, **15** "What happiness for a man to eat a meal in the kingdom of God!"

Men who are "too busy" for the kingdom of God

But Jesus said to him, **16**

"Once upon a time, a man planned a big dinner party and invited a great many people. At dinner-time, he sent his servant **17** out to tell those who were invited, 'Please come, everything is ready now.' But they all, as one man, began to make their excuses. **18** The first one said to him, 'I have bought some land. I must go and look at it. Please excuse me.' Another one said, 'I have bought five **19** yoke of oxen and am on my way to try them out. Please convey my apologies.' And another one said, 'I have just got married and **20** I am sure you will understand I cannot come.' So the servant **21** returned and reported all this to his master. The master of the house was extremely annoyed and said to his servant, 'Hurry out now into the streets and alleys of the town, and bring here the poor and crippled and blind and lame.' Then the servant said, 'I **22** have done what you told me, sir, and there are still empty places.' Then the master replied, 'Now go out to the roads and **23** hedgerows and make them come inside, so that my house may be full. For I tell you that not one of the men I invited shall have a **24** taste of my dinner.' "

Now as Jesus proceeded on his journey, great crowds accom- **25** panied him, and he turned and spoke to them,

"If anyone comes to me without 'hating' his father and mother **26** and wife and children and brothers and sisters, and even his own life, he cannot be a disciple of mine. The man who will **27** not take up his cross and follow in my footsteps cannot be my disciple.

"If any of you wanted to build a tower, wouldn't he first sit **28** down and work out the cost of it, to see if he can afford to finish it? Otherwise, when he has laid the foundation and found himself **29** unable to complete the building, everyone who sees it will begin to jeer at him, saying, 'This is the man who started to build a **30** tower but couldn't finish it!' Or, suppose there is a king who is **31** going to war with another king, doesn't he sit down first and

consider whether he can engage the twenty thousand of the other
32 king with his own ten thousand? And if he decides he can't, then,
while the other king is still a long way off, he sends messengers to
33 him to ask for conditions of peace. So it is with you; only the man
who says goodbye to all his possessions can be my disciple.

34 "Salt is a very good thing, but if salt loses its flavour, what can
35 you use to restore it? It is no good for the ground and no good as
manure. People just throw it away. Every man who has ears
should use them!"

CHAPTER 15

Jesus speaks of the love of God for "the lost"

1 Now all the tax-collectors and "outsiders" were crowding
2 around to hear what he had to say. The Pharisees and the scribes
complained of this, remarking,
"This man accepts sinners and even eats his meals with them."
3 So Jesus spoke to them, using this parable:
4 "Wouldn't any man among you who owned a hundred sheep,
and lost one of them, leave the ninety-nine to themselves in the
5 open, and go after the one which is lost until he finds it? And
when he has found it, he will put it on his shoulders with great
6 joy, and as soon as he gets home, he will call his friends and
neighbours together. 'Come and celebrate with me,' he will say,
7 'for I have found that sheep of mine which was lost.' I tell you
that it is the same in Heaven—there is more joy over one sinner
whose heart is changed than over ninety-nine righteous people
who have no need for repentance.
8 "Or if there is a woman who has ten silver coins, if she should
lose one, won't she take a lamp and sweep and search the house
9 from top to bottom until she finds it? And when she has found it,
she calls her friends and neighbours together. 'Come and celebrate
10 with me,' she says, 'for I have found that coin I lost.' I tell you, it
is the same in Heaven—there is rejoicing among the angels of
God over one sinner whose heart is changed."
11 Then he continued,
12 "Once there was a man who had two sons. The younger one
said to his father, 'Father, give me my share of the property that
will come to me.' So he divided up his property between the two
13 of them. Before very long, the younger son collected all his
belongings and went off to a foreign land, where he squandered

his wealth in the wildest extravagance. And when he had run *14* through all his money, a terrible famine arose in that country, and he began to feel the pinch. Then he went and hired himself out to *15* one of the citizens of that country who sent him out into the fields to feed the pigs. He got to the point of longing to stuff himself *16* with the food the pigs were eating, and not a soul gave him anything. Then he came to his senses and cried aloud, 'Why, dozens *17* of my father's hired men have got more food than they can eat and here am I dying of hunger! I will get up and go back to my *18* father, and I will say to him, "Father, I have done wrong in the sight of Heaven and in your eyes. I don't deserve to be called your *19* son any more. Please take me on as one of your hired men." ' So he got up and went to his father. But while he was still some *20* distance off, his father saw him and his heart went out to him, and he ran and fell on his neck and kissed him. But his son said, *21* 'Father, I have done wrong in the sight of Heaven and in your eyes. I don't deserve to be called your son any more. . . .' 'Hurry!' *22* called out his father to the servants, 'fetch the best clothes and put them on him! Put a ring on his finger and shoes on his feet, and *23* get that calf we've fattened and kill it, and we will have a feast and a celebration! For this is my son—I thought he was dead, and *24* he's alive again. I thought I had lost him, and he's found!' And they began to get the festivities going.

"But his elder son was out in the fields, and as he came near the *25* house, he heard music and dancing. So he called one of the *26* servants across to him and enquired what was the meaning of it all. 'Your brother has arrived, and your father has killed the calf *27* we fattened because he has got him home again safe and sound,' was the reply. But he was furious and refused to go inside the *28* house. So his father came outside and called him. Then he burst *29* out, 'Look, how many years have I slaved for you and never disobeyed a single order of yours, and yet you have never given me so much as a young goat, so that I could give my friends a dinner? But when that son of yours arrives, who has spent all your *30* money on prostitutes, for *him* you kill the calf we've fattened!' But the father replied, 'My dear son, you have been with me *31* all the time and everything I have is yours. But we *had* to cele- *32* brate and show our joy. For this is your brother; I thought he was dead—and he's alive. I thought he was lost—and he is found!' "

CHAPTER 16

A clever rogue, and the right use of money

1 THEN there is this story he told his disciples:

"Once there was a rich man whose agent was reported to him
2 to be mismanaging his property. So he summoned him and said,
'What's this that I hear about you? Give me an account of your
stewardship—you're not fit to manage my household any longer.'
3 At this the agent said to himself, 'What am I going to do now that
my employer is taking away the stewardship from me? I am not
4 strong enough to dig and I can't sink to begging. Ah, I know
what I'll do so that when I lose my position people will welcome
5 me into their homes!' So he sent for each one of his master's
debtors. 'How much do you owe my master?' he said to the first.
6 'A hundred barrels of oil,' he replied. 'Here,' replied the agent,
7 'take your bill, sit down, hurry up and write in fifty.' Then he said
to another, 'And what's the size of your debt?' 'A thousand bushels
of wheat,' he replied. 'Take your bill,' said the agent, 'and write
8 in eight hundred.' Now the master praised this rascally steward
because he had been so careful for his own future. For the children
of this world are considerably more shrewd in dealing with their
9 contemporaries than the children of light. Now my advice to you
is to use 'money', tainted as it is, to make yourselves friends, so
that when it comes to an end, they may welcome you into eternal
habitations.

10 "The man who is faithful in the little things will be faithful
in the big things, and the man who cheats in the little things
11 will cheat in the big things too. So that if you are not fit to be
trusted to deal with the wicked wealth of this world, who will
12 trust you with the true riches? And if you are not trustworthy
with someone else's property, who will give you property of your
13 own? No servant can serve two masters. He is bound to hate one
and love the other, or give his loyalty to one and despise the other.
You cannot serve God and the power of money at the same time."

14 Now the Pharisees, who were very fond of money, heard all
15 this with a sneer. But he said to them,

"You are the people who advertise your goodness before men,
but God knows your hearts. Remember, there are things men
consider perfectly splendid which are detestable in the sight of
God!

Jesus states that the kingdom of God has superseded "the Law and the Prophets"

"The Law and the Prophets were in force until John's day. 16
From then on the good news of the kingdom of God has been
proclaimed and men are forcing their way into it.

"Yet it would be easier for Heaven and earth to disappear than 17
for a single point of the Law to become a dead letter.

"Any man who divorces his wife and marries another woman 18
commits adultery. And so does any man who marries the woman
who was divorced from her husband.

Jesus shows the fearful consequence of social injustice

"There was once a rich man who used to dress in purple and 19
fine linen and lead a life of daily luxury. And there was a poor 20
man called Lazarus who was put down at his gate. He was
covered with sores. He used to long to be fed with the scraps from 21
the rich man's table. Yes, and the dogs used to come and lick his
sores. Well, it happened that the poor man died, and was carried 22
by the angels into Abraham's bosom. The rich man also died and
was buried. And from among the dead he looked up and saw 23
Abraham a long way away, and Lazarus in his arms. 'Father 24
Abraham!' he cried out, 'please pity me. Send Lazarus to dip the
tip of his finger in water and cool my tongue, for I am in agony
in these flames.' But Abraham replied, 'Remember, my son, that 25
you used to have the good things in your lifetime, while Lazarus
suffered the bad. Now he is being comforted here, while you are
in agony. And besides this, a great chasm has been set between 26
you and us, so that those who want to go to you from this side
cannot do so, and people cannot come to us from your side.' At 27
this he said, 'Then I beg you, father, to send him to my father's
house for I have five brothers. He could warn them about all this 28
and prevent their coming to this place of torture.' But Abraham 29
said, 'They have Moses and the Prophets: they can listen to them.'
'Ah no, father Abraham,' he said, 'if only someone were to go 30
to them from the dead, they would change completely.' But 31
Abraham told him, 'If they will not listen to Moses and the
Prophets, they would not be convinced even if somebody were
to rise from the dead.' "

CHAPTER 17

Jesus warns his disciples about spoiling the spirit of the new kingdom

1 THEN Jesus said to his disciples,
"It is inevitable that there should be pitfalls, but alas for the
2 man who is responsible for them! It would be better for that man
to have a mill-stone hung round his neck and be thrown into the
3 sea, than that he should trip up one of these little ones. So be
careful how you live. If your brother offends you, take him to
4 task about it, and if he is sorry, forgive him. Yes, if he wrongs you
seven times in one day and turns to you and says, 'I am sorry'
seven times, you must forgive him."
5 And the apostles said to the Lord,
"Give us more faith."
6 And he replied,
"If your faith were as big as a grain of mustard-seed, you could
say to this fig-tree, 'Pull yourself up by the roots and plant yourself in the sea', and it would do what you said!

Work in the kingdom must be taken as a matter of course

7 "If any of you has a servant ploughing or looking after the
sheep, are you likely to say to him when he comes in from the
8 fields, 'Come straight in and sit down to your meal'? Aren't you
more likely to say, 'Get my supper ready: change your coat,
and wait while I eat and drink: and then, when I've finished, you
9 can have your meal'? Do you feel particularly grateful to your
10 servant for doing what you tell him? I don't think so. It is the
same with yourselves—when you have done everything that you
are told to do, you can say, 'We are not much good as servants,
for we have only done what we ought to do.' "

Jesus heals ten men of leprosy: only one shows his gratitude

11 In the course of his journey to Jerusalem, Jesus crossed the
12 boundary between Samaria and Galilee, and as he was approaching a village, ten lepers met him. They kept their distance but
13 shouted out,
"Jesus, Master, have pity on us!"

When Jesus saw them, he said, 14
"Go and show yourselves to the priests."

And it happened that as they went on their way they were cured. One of their number, when he saw that he was cured, 15 turned round and praised God at the top of his voice, and then 16 fell on his face before Jesus and thanked him. This man was a Samaritan. And at this Jesus remarked, 17

"Weren't there ten men healed? Where are the other nine? Is 18 nobody going to turn and praise God for what has been done, except this stranger?"

And he said to the man, 19

"Stand up now, and go on your way. It is your faith that has made you well."

Jesus tells the Pharisees that the kingdom is here and now

Later, he was asked by the Pharisees when the kingdom of 20 God was coming, and he gave them this reply:

"The kingdom of God never comes by watching for it. Men 21 cannot say, 'Look, here it is', or 'there it is', for the kingdom of God is inside you."

Jesus tells his disciples about the future

Then he said to the disciples, 22

"The time will come when you will long to see again a single day of the Son of Man, but you will not see it. People will say to 23 you, 'Look, there he is', or 'Look, here he is.' Stay where you are and don't go off looking for him! For the day of the Son of Man 24 will be like lightning flashing from one end of the sky to the other. But before that happens, he must go through much suffer- 25 ing and be utterly rejected by this generation. In the time of the 26 coming of the Son of Man, life will be as it was in the days of Noah. People ate and drank, married and were given in marriage, 27 right up to the day when Noah entered the ark—and then came the flood and destroyed them all. It will be just the same as it was 28 in the days of Lot. People ate and drank, bought and sold, planted and built, but on the day that Lot left Sodom, it rained fire and 29 brimstone from heaven, and destroyed them all. That is how it 30 will be on the day when the Son of Man is revealed. When that 31 day comes, the man who is on the roof of his house, with his goods inside it, must not come down to get them. And the man

32 out in the fields must not turn back for anything. Remember
33 what happened to Lot's wife. Whoever tries to preserve his life
will lose it, and the man who is prepared to lose his life will
34 preserve it. I tell you, that night there will be two men in one
35 bed; one man will be taken and the other will be left. Two
women will be turning the grinding-mill together; one will be
taken and the other left."

37 "But where, Lord?" they asked him.

"Wherever there is a dead body, there the vultures will
flock," he replied.

CHAPTER 18

Jesus urges his disciples to persist in prayer

1 THEN he gave them an illustration to show that they must
always pray and never lose heart.

2 "Once upon a time," he said, "there was a magistrate in a town
who had neither fear of God nor respect for his fellow-men.
3 There was a widow in the town who kept coming to him, saying,
4 'Please protect me from the man who is trying to ruin me.' And
for a long time he refused. But later he said to himself, 'Although
5 I don't fear God and have no respect for men, yet this woman
is such a nuisance that I shall give judgment in her favour, or
else her continual visits will be the death of me!' "

6 Then the Lord said,

7 "Notice how this dishonest magistrate behaved. Do you suppose God, patient as he is, will not see justice done for his chosen,
8 who appeal to him day and night? I assure you he will not delay
in seeing justice done. Yet, when the Son of Man comes, will he
find men on earth who believe in him?"

Jesus tells a story against the self-righteous

9 Then he gave this illustration to certain people who were
confident of their own goodness and looked down on others:

10 "Two men went up to the Temple to pray, one was a Pharisee,
11 the other was a tax-collector. The Pharisee stood and prayed like
this with himself, 'O God, I do thank thee that I am not like the
rest of mankind, greedy, dishonest, impure, or even like that tax-
12 collector over there. I fast twice every week; I give away a tenth-
13 part of all my income.' But the tax-collector stood in a distant

corner, scarcely daring to look up to Heaven, and with a gesture of despair, said, 'God, have mercy on a sinner like me.' I assure you that he was the man who went home justified in God's sight, rather than the other one. For everyone who sets himself up as somebody will become a nobody, and the man who makes himself nobody will become somebody." *14*

Jesus welcomes babies

Then people began to bring babies to him so that he could put his hands on them. But when the disciples noticed it, they frowned on them. But Jesus called them to him, and said, *15* *16*

"You must let little children come to me, and you must never prevent their coming. The kingdom of Heaven belongs to little children like these. I tell you, the man who will not accept the kingdom of God like a little child will never get into it at all." *17*

Jesus and riches

Then one of the Jewish rulers put this question to him, *18*

"Master, I know that you are good; tell me, please, what must I do to be sure of eternal life?"

"I wonder why you call me good?" returned Jesus. "No one is good—only the one God. You know the commandments— *19* *20*

"Thou shalt not commit adultery.

"Thou shalt not commit murder.

"Thou shalt not steal.

"Thou shalt not bear false witness.

"Honour thy father and thy mother."

"All these," he replied, "I have carefully kept since I was quite young." *21*

And when Jesus heard that, he said to him, *22*

"There is still one thing you have missed. Sell everything you possess and give the money away to the poor, and you will have riches in Heaven. Then come and follow me."

But when he heard this, he was greatly distressed for he was very rich. *23*

And when Jesus saw how his face fell, he remarked, *24*

"How difficult it is for those who have great possessions to enter the kingdom of God! A camel could squeeze through the eye of a needle more easily than a rich man could get into the kingdom of God." *25*

26 Those who heard Jesus say this, exclaimed,
"Then who can possibly be saved?"
27 Jesus replied,
"What men find impossible is perfectly possible with God."
28 "Well," rejoined Peter, "we have left all that we ever had and followed you."
29 And Jesus told them,
"Believe me, nobody has left his home or wife, or brothers or
30 parents or children for the sake of the kingdom of God, without receiving very much more in this present life—and eternal life in the world to come."

Jesus foretells his death and resurrection

31 Then Jesus took the twelve on one side and spoke to them,
"Listen to me. We are now going up to Jerusalem and everything that has been written by the prophets about the Son of Man
32 will come true. For he will be handed over to the heathen, and
33 he is going to be jeered at and insulted and spat upon, and then they will flog him and kill him. But he will rise again on the third day."
34 But they did not understand any of this. His words were quite obscure to them and they had no idea of what he meant.

On the way to Jericho he heals a blind beggar

35 Then, as he was approaching Jericho, it happened that there
36 was a blind man sitting by the roadside, begging. He heard the
37 crowd passing and enquired what it was all about. And they told
38 him, "Jesus the man from Nazareth is going past you." So he shouted out,
"Jesus, Son of David, have pity on me!"
39 Those who were in front tried to hush his cries. But that made him call out all the more,
"Son of David, have pity on me!"
40 So Jesus stood quite still and ordered the man to be brought to him. And when he was quite close, he said to him,
41 "What do you want me to do for you?"
"Lord, make me see again," he cried.
42 "You can see again! Your faith has cured you," returned Jesus.
43 And his sight was restored at once, and he followed Jesus, praising God. All the people who saw it thanked God too.

CHAPTER 19

The chief tax-collector is converted to faith in Jesus

THEN he went into Jericho and was making his way through it. 1
And here we find a wealthy man called Zacchaeus, a chief collector 2
of taxes, wanting to see what sort of person Jesus was. But the 3
crowd prevented him from doing so, for he was very short. So 4
he ran ahead and climbed up into a sycamore tree to get a view of
Jesus as he was heading that way. When Jesus reached the spot, he 5
looked up and saw the man and said,

"Zacchaeus, hurry up and come down. I must be your guest
today."

So Zacchaeus hurriedly climbed down and gladly welcomed 6
him. But the bystanders muttered their disapproval, saying, 7

"Now he has gone to stay with a real sinner."

But Zacchaeus himself stopped and said to the Lord, 8

"Look, sir, I will give half my property to the poor. And if I
have swindled anybody out of anything I will pay him back four
times as much."

Jesus said to him, 9

"Salvation has come to this house today! Zacchaeus is a descendant of Abraham, and it was the lost that the Son of Man came 10
to seek—and to save."

*Life requires courage, and is hard on those who
dare not use their gifts*

Then as the crowd still listened attentively, Jesus went on to 11
give them this parable. For the fact that he was nearing Jerusalem
made them imagine that the kingdom of God was on the point of
appearing.

"Once upon a time a man of good family went abroad to accept 12
a kingdom and then return. He summoned ten of his servants and 13
gave them each ten pounds, with the words, 'Use this money to
trade with until I come back.' But the citizens detested him and 14
they sent a delegation after him, to say, 'We will not have this
man to be our king.' Then later, when he had received his king- 15
dom, he returned and gave orders for the servants to whom he
had given the money to be called to him, so that he could find out
what profit they had made. The first came into his presence, and 16

said, 'Sire, your ten pounds have made a hundred pounds more.'
17 'Splendid, my good fellow,' he said, 'since you have proved trustworthy over this small amount, I am going to put you in
18 charge of ten towns.' The second came in and said, 'Sire, your
19 ten pounds have made fifty pounds.' And he said to him, 'Good,
20 you're appointed governor of five towns.' When the last came, he said, 'Sire, here are your ten pounds, which I have been keeping
21 wrapped up in a handkerchief. I have been scared—I know you're a hard man, getting something for nothing and reaping where
22 you never sowed.' To which he replied, 'You scoundrel, your own words condemn you! You knew perfectly well, did you, that I am a hard man who gets something for nothing and reaps where
23 he never sowed? Then why didn't you put my money into the bank, and then when I returned I could have had it back with
24 interest?' Then he said to those who were standing by, 'Take away his ten pounds and give it to the fellow who has a hundred.'
25 "'But, sire, he has a hundred pounds already,' they said to
26 him. 'Yes,' he replied, 'and I tell you that the man who has something will get more given to him. But as for the man who has
27 nothing, even his "nothing" will be taken away. And as for these enemies of mine who objected to my being their king, bring them here and execute them in my presence.'"
28 After these words, Jesus walked on ahead of them on his way to Jerusalem.

Jesus arranges his own entrance into Jerusalem

29 Then as he was approaching Bethphage and Bethany, near the hill called the Mount of Olives, he sent off two of his disciples,
30 telling them,
"Go into the village just ahead of you, and there you will find a colt tied, on which no one has ever yet ridden. Untie it and bring
31 it here. And if anybody asks you, 'Why are you untying it?' just say, 'The Lord needs it.'"
32 So the messengers went off and found things just as he had told
33 them. In fact, as they were untying the colt, the owners did say,
34 "Why are you untying it?" and they replied, "The Lord needs
35 it." So they brought it to Jesus and, throwing their cloaks upon
36 it, mounted Jesus on its back. Then as he rode along, people
37 spread out their coats in the roadway. And as he approached the city, where the road slopes down from the Mount of Olives, the whole crowd of his disciples joyfully shouted praises to God for all the marvellous things that they had seen him do.

"God bless the king who comes in the name of the Lord!" they **38**
cried. "There is peace in Heaven and glory on high!"

There were some Pharisees in the crowd who said to Jesus, **39**
"Master, restrain your disciples!"

To which he replied, **40**

"I tell you that if they kept quiet, the very stones in the road
would burst out cheering!"

The sight of the city moves him to tears

And as he came still nearer to the city, he caught sight of it and **41**
wept over it, saying, **42**

"Ah, if you only knew, even at this eleventh hour, on what
your peace depends—but you cannot see it. The time is coming **43**
when your enemies will encircle you with ramparts, surrounding
you and hemming you in on every side. And they will hurl you **44**
and all your children to the ground—yes, they will not leave you
one stone standing upon another—all because you did not know
when God Himself was visiting you!"

Then he went into the Temple, and proceeded to throw out **45**
the traders there.

"It is written," he told them, " 'My house shall be a house of **46**
prayer', but you have turned it into a thieves' kitchen!"

Jesus teaches daily in the Temple

Then day after day he was teaching inside the Temple. The **47**
chief priests, the scribes and the national leaders were all the time
trying to get rid of him, but they could not find any way to do it **48**
since all the people hung upon his words.

CHAPTER 20

THEN one day as he was teaching the people in the Temple, and **1**
preaching the gospel to them, the chief priests, the scribes and
elders confronted him in a body and asked him this direct **2**
question,

"Tell us by whose authority you act as you do—who gave you
such authority?"

"I have a question for you, too," replied Jesus. "John's baptism, **3, 4**
now—tell me, did it come from Heaven or was it purely human?"

163

5 At this they began arguing with each other, saying,
"If we say, 'from Heaven,' he will say to us, 'Then why didn't
6 you believe in him?' but if we say it was purely human, this mob
will stone us to death, for they are convinced that John was a
7 prophet." So they replied that they did not know where it came
from.
8 "Then," returned Jesus, "neither will I tell you by what
authority I do what I am doing."

He tells the people a pointed story

9 Then he turned to the people and told them this parable:
"There was once a man who planted a vineyard, let it out to
10 farm-workers, and went abroad for some time. Then, when the
season arrived, he sent a servant to the farm-workers so that they
could give him the proceeds of the vineyard. But the farm-
11 workers beat him up and sent him back empty-handed. So he
sent another servant, and they beat him up as well, manhandling
12 him disgracefully, and sent him back empty-handed. Then he
sent a third servant, but after wounding him severely they threw
13 him out. Then the owner of the vineyard said, 'What shall I do
now? I will send them my son who is so dear to me. Perhaps they
14 will respect *him*.' But when the farm-workers saw him, they
talked the matter over with each other and said, 'This man is the
heir—come on, let's kill him, and we shall get everything that he
15 would have had!' And they threw him outside the vineyard and
killed him. What then do you suppose the owner will do to them?
16 He will come and destroy the men who were working his property,
and hand it over to others."
When they heard this, they said,
"God forbid!"
17 But he looked them straight in the eyes and said,
"Then what is the meaning of this scripture—
The stone which the builders rejected,
The same was made the head of the corner?
18 The man who falls on that stone will be broken, and the man on
whom it falls will be crushed to powder."

The authorities resort to trickery

19 The scribes and chief priests longed to get their hands on him
at that moment, but they were afraid of the people. They knew

well enough that his parable referred to them. They watched him, 20
however, and sent some spies into the crowd, pretending that they
were honest men, to fasten on something that he might say which
could be used to hand him over to the authority and power of the
governor.

These men asked him, 21

"Master, we know that what you say and teach is right, and
that you teach the way of God truly without fear or favour. Now, 22
is it right for us to pay taxes to Caesar or not?"

But Jesus saw through their cunning and said to them, 23

"Show me one of the coins. Whose face is this, and whose name 24
is in the inscription?"

"Caesar's," they said.

"Then give to Caesar," he replied, "what belongs to Caesar, 25
and to God what belongs to God."

So his reply gave them no sort of handle that they could use 26
against him publicly. And in fact they were so taken aback by his
answer that they had nothing more to say.

Jesus exposes the ignorance of the Sadducees

Then up came some of the Sadducees (who deny that there is 27
any resurrection) and they asked him,

"Master, Moses told us in the scripture, 'If a man's brother 28
should die without any children, he should marry the widow and
raise up a family for his brother.' Now, there were once seven 29
brothers. The first got married and died childless, and the second 30
and the third married the woman, and in fact all the seven married 31
her and died without leaving any children. Lastly, the woman her- 32
self died. Now in this 'resurrection' whose wife is she of these 33
seven men, for she belonged to all of them?"

"People in this world," Jesus replied, "marry and are given in 34
marriage. But those who are considered worthy of reaching that 35
world, which means rising from the dead, neither marry nor are
they given in marriage. They cannot die any more but live like 36
the angels; for being children of the resurrection, they are the sons
of God. But that the dead are raised, even Moses showed to be 37
true in the story of the bush, when he calls the Lord the God of
Abraham, the God of Isaac and the God of Jacob. For God is not 38
God of the dead, but of the living. For all men are alive to
him."

To this some of the scribes replied, 39

"Master, that was a good answer."

40 And indeed nobody had the courage to ask him any more
41 questions. But Jesus went on to say,
42 "How can they say that Christ is David's *son*? For David himself says in the book of psalms—

The Lord said unto my *Lord*,
Sit thou on my right hand,
43 Till I make thine enemies the footstool of thy feet.
44 David is plainly calling him 'Lord'. How then can he be his *son*?"

Jesus warns his disciples against religious pretentiousness

45 Then while everybody was listening, Jesus remarked to his disciples,
46 "Be on your guard against the scribes, who enjoy walking round in long robes and love having men bow to them in public, getting front seats in the synagogue, and the best places at dinner
47 parties—while all the time they are battening on widows' property and covering it up with long prayers. These men are only heading for deeper damnation."

CHAPTER 21

1 THEN he looked up and saw the rich people dropping their gifts
2 into the treasury, and he noticed a poor widow drop in two
3 coppers, and he commented,
"I assure you that this poor widow has put in more than all of
4 them, for they have all put in what they can easily spare, but she in her poverty has given away her whole living."

Jesus foretells the destruction of the Temple

5 Then when some of them were talking about the Temple and pointing out the beauty of its lovely stonework and the various ornaments that people had given, he said,
6 "Yes, you can gaze on all this today, but the time is coming when not a single stone will be left upon another, without being thrown down."
7 So they asked him,
"Master, when will this happen, and what sign will there be that these things are going to take place?"

"Be careful that you are not deceived," he replied. "There will 8
be many coming in my name, saying 'I am he' and 'The time is
very near now.' Never follow men like that. And when you hear 9
about wars and disturbances, don't be alarmed. These things must
indeed happen first, but the end will not come immediately."

And prophesies world-wide suffering

Then he continued, 10
"Nation will rise up against nation, and kingdom against
kingdom; there will be great earthquakes and famines and plagues 11
in this place or that. There will be dreadful sights, and great signs
from heaven. But before all this happens, men will arrest you and 12
persecute you, handing you over to synagogue or prison, or
bringing you before kings and governors, for my name's sake.
This will be your chance to witness for me. So make up your 13,14
minds not to think out your defence beforehand. I will give you 15
such eloquence and wisdom that none of your opponents will be
able to resist or contradict it. But you will be betrayed, even by 16
parents and brothers and kinsfolk and friends, and there will be
some of you who will be killed and you will be hated everywhere 17
for my name's sake. Yet, not a hair of your head will perish. Hold 18,19
on, and you will win your souls!

"But when you see Jerusalem surrounded by armed forces, then 20
you will know that the time of her devastation has arrived. Then 21
is the time for those who are in Judaea to fly to the hills. And those
who are in the city itself must get out of it, and those who are
already in the country must not try to get into the city. For these 22
are the days of vengeance, when all that the scriptures have said
will come true. Alas for those who are pregnant and those who 23
have tiny babies in those days! For there will be bitter misery in
the land and great anger against this people. They will die by the 24
sword. They will be taken off as prisoners into all nations.
Jerusalem will be trampled under foot by the heathen until the
heathen's day is over. There will be signs in the sun and moon 25
and stars, and on the earth there will be dismay among the nations
and bewilderment at the roar of the surging sea. Men's courage 26
will fail completely as they realise what is threatening the world,
for the very powers of heaven will be shaken. Then men will 27
see the Son of Man coming in a cloud with great power and
splendour! But when these things begin to happen, look up, hold 28
your heads high, for you will soon be free."

Vigilance is essential

29 Then he gave them a parable.

30 "Look at a fig-tree, or indeed any tree, when it begins to burst its buds, and you realise without anybody telling you that summer

31 is nearly here. So, when you see these things happening, you can

32 be equally sure that the kingdom of God has nearly come. Believe me, this generation will not disappear until all this has taken place.

33 Earth and heaven will pass away, but my words will never pass away.

34 "Be on your guard—see to it that your minds are never clouded by dissipation or drunkenness or the worries of this life, or else

35 that day may catch you like the springing of a trap—for it will come upon every inhabitant of the whole earth.

36 "You must be vigilant at all times, praying that you may be strong enough to come safely through all that is going to happen, and stand in the presence of the Son of Man."

37 And every day he went on teaching in the Temple, and every evening he went off and spent the night on the hill which is called

38 the Mount of Olives. And the people used to come early in the morning to listen to him in the Temple.

CHAPTER 22

Judas Iscariot becomes the tool of the authorities

1 Now as the feast of unleavened bread, called the Passover, was

2 approaching, fear of the people made the chief priests and scribes

3 try desperately to find a way of getting rid of Jesus. Then a diabolical plan came into the mind of Judas Iscariot, who was one

4 of the twelve. He went and discussed with the chief priests and

5 officers a method of getting Jesus into their hands. They were

6 delighted and arranged to pay him for it. He agreed, and began to look for a suitable opportunity for betrayal when there was no crowd present.

Jesus makes arrangements for his last Passover with his disciples

7 Then the day of unleavened bread arrived, on which the

8 Passover lamb had to be sacrificed, and Jesus sent off Peter and John with the words, "Go and make all the preparations for us to eat the Passover."

"Where would you like us to do this?" they asked. 9

And he replied, 10

"Listen, just as you're going into the city a man carrying a jug of water will meet you. Follow him to the house he is making for. Then say to the owner of the house, 'The master has this message 11 for you—which is the room where my disciples and I may eat the Passover?' And he will take you upstairs and show you a 12 large room furnished for our needs. Make all the preparations there."

So they went off and found everything exactly as he had told 13 them it would be, and they made the Passover preparations.

Then, when the time came, he took his seat at table with the 14 apostles, and spoke to them, 15

"With all my heart I have longed to eat this Passover with you before the time comes for me to suffer. Believe me, I shall not 16 eat the Passover again until all that it means is fulfilled in the kingdom of God."

Then taking a cup from them, he thanked God and said, 17

"Take this and share it amongst yourselves, for I tell you that 18 I shall drink no more wine until the kingdom of God comes."

The mysterious words which were remembered later

Then he took a loaf and after thanking God he broke it and 19 gave it to them, with these words,

"This is my body which is given for you: do this in remembrance of me."

So too, he gave them a cup after supper with the words, 20

"This cup is the new agreement made in my own blood which is shed for you. Yet the hand of the man who is betraying me lies 21 with mine at this moment on the table. The Son of Man goes on 22 his appointed way: yet alas for the man by whom he is betrayed!"

Jesus again teaches humility

And at this they began to debate among themselves as to which 23 of them would do this thing.

And then a dispute arose among them as to who should be 24 considered the most important.

But Jesus said to them, 25

"Among the heathen it is their kings who lord it over them, and their rulers are given the title of 'benefactors'. But it must not 26

be so with you! *Your* greatest man must become like a junior and
27 your leader must be a servant. Who is the greater, the man who
sits down to dinner or the man who serves him? Obviously, the
man who sits down to dinner—yet *I* am the one who is the
28 servant among you. But you are the men who have stood by me
29 in all that I have gone through, and as surely as my Father has
30 given me my kingdom, so I give you the right to eat and drink
at my table in that kingdom. Yes, you will sit on thrones and rule
the twelve tribes of Israel!

The personal warning to Simon

31 "Oh, Simon, Simon, do you know that Satan has asked to have
32 you all to sift like wheat?—but I have prayed for *you* that you
may not lose your faith. Yes, when you have turned back to me,
you must strengthen these brothers of yours."
33 Peter said to him,
"Lord, I am ready to go to prison, or even to die with you!"
34 "I tell you, Peter," returned Jesus, "before the cock crows today
you will deny three times that you know me!"

Jesus tells his disciples that the crisis has arrived

35 Then he continued to them all,
"That time when I sent you out without any purse or wallet or
shoes—did you find you needed anything?"
"No, not a thing," they replied.
36 "But now," Jesus continued, "if you have a purse or wallet,
take it with you, and if you have no sword, sell your coat and buy
37 one! For I tell you that this scripture must be fulfilled in me—
And he was reckoned with transgressors.
So comes the end of what they wrote about me."
38 Then the disciples said,
"Lord, look, here are two swords."
And Jesus returned,
"That is enough."
39 Then he went out of the city and up on to the Mount of Olives,
as he had often done before, with the disciples following him.
40 And when he reached his usual place, he said to them,
"Pray that you may not have to face temptation!"
41 Then he went off by himself, about a stone's throw away, and
42 falling on his knees, prayed in these words—

"Father, if you are willing, take this cup away from me—but it is not my will, but yours, that must be done."

And an angel from Heaven appeared, strengthening him. He *43, 44* was in agony and prayed even more intensely so that his sweat was like great drops of blood falling to the ground. Then he got *45* to his feet from his prayer and walking back to the disciples, he found them sleeping through sheer grief.

"Why are you sleeping?" he said to them. "You must get up *46* and go on praying that you may not have to face temptation."

The mob arrives and Judas betrays

While he was still speaking a crowd of people arrived, led by *47* the man called Judas, one of the twelve. He stepped up to Jesus to kiss him.

"Judas, would you betray the Son of Man with a kiss?" said *48* Jesus to him.

And the disciples, seeing what was going to happen, cried, *49* "Lord, shall we use our swords?"

And one of them did slash at the High Priest's servant, cutting *50* off his right ear. But Jesus retorted, *51* "That will do!"

And he touched his ear and healed him. Then he spoke to the *52* chief priests, Temple officers and elders who were there to arrest him,

"So you have come out with your swords and staves as if I were a bandit. Day after day I was with you in the Temple and *53* you never laid a finger on me—but this is your hour and the power of darkness is yours!"

Jesus is arrested: Peter follows but denies his master three times

Then they arrested him and marched him off to the High *54* Priest's house. Peter followed at a distance, and sat down among *55* some people who had lighted a fire in the middle of the courtyard and were sitting round it. A maid-servant saw him sitting *56* there in the firelight, peered into his face and said,

"This man was with him too."

But he denied it and said, *57* "I don't know him, girl!"

A few minutes later someone else noticed Peter, and said, *58* "You're one of these men too."

171

But Peter said,

"Man, I am not!"

59 Then about an hour later someone else insisted,

"I am convinced this fellow was with him. Why, he is a Galilean!"

60 "Man," returned Peter, "I don't know what you're talking about."

And immediately, while he was still speaking, the cock crew.

61 The Lord turned his head and looked straight at Peter, and into his mind flashed the words that the Lord had said to him . . . "You will disown me three times before the cock crows today."

62 And he went outside and wept bitterly.

63 Then the men who held Jesus made a great game of knocking
64 him about. And they blindfolded him and asked him,

"Now, prophet, guess who hit you that time!"

65 And that was only the beginning of the way they insulted him.

In the early morning Jesus is formally interrogated

66 Then when daylight came, the assembly of the elders of the people, which included both chief priests and scribes, met and marched him off to their own council. There they asked him,

67 "If you really are Christ, tell us!"

68 "If I tell you, you will never believe me, and if I ask you a
69 question, you will not answer me. But from now on the Son of Man will take his seat at the right hand of almighty God."

70 Then they all said,

"So you are the Son of God then?"

"You are right; I am," Jesus told them.

71 Then they said,

"Why do we need to call any more witnesses, for we ourselves have heard this thing from his own lips?"

CHAPTER 23

Jesus is taken before Pilate and Herod

1, 2 THEN they rose up in a body and took him off to Pilate, and began their accusation in these words,

"Here is this man whom we have found corrupting our people, and telling them that it is wrong to pay taxes to Caesar, claiming that he himself is Christ, a king."

But Pilate addressed his question to Jesus,   3
"Are you the king of the Jews?"
"Yes, I am," he replied.
Then Pilate spoke to the chief priests and the crowd,   4
"I find nothing criminal about this man."
But they pressed their charge, saying,   5
"He's a trouble-maker among the people. He teaches through
the whole of Judaea, all the way from Galilee to this place."

When Pilate heard this, he enquired whether the man were a   6
Galilean, and when he discovered that he came under Herod's   7
jurisdiction, he passed him on to Herod who happened to be in
Jerusalem at that time. When Herod saw Jesus, he was delighted,   8
for he had been wanting to see him for a long time. He had
heard a lot about Jesus and was hoping to see him perform a
miracle. He questioned him very thoroughly, but Jesus gave him   9
absolutely no reply, though the chief priests and scribes stood   10
there making the most violent accusations. So Herod joined his   11
own soldiers in scoffing and jeering at Jesus. Finally, they dressed
him up in a gorgeous cloak, and sent him back to Pilate. On that   12
day Herod and Pilate became firm friends, though previously they
had been at daggers drawn.

Pilate declares Jesus' innocence

Then Pilate summoned the chief priests, the officials and the   13
people and addressed them in these words,   14
"You have brought this man to me as a mischief-maker among
the people, and I want you all to realise that, after examining him
in your presence, I have found nothing criminal about him, in
spite of all your accusations. And neither has Herod, for he has   15
sent him back to us. Obviously, then, he has done nothing to
deserve the death penalty. I propose, therefore, to teach him a   16
sharp lesson and let him go."
But they all yelled as one man,   18
"Take this man away! We want Barabbas set free!"
(Barabbas was a man who had been put in prison for causing a   19
riot in the city and for murder.) But Pilate wanted to set Jesus   20
free and he called out to them again, but they shouted back at   21
him,
"Crucify, crucify him!"
Then he spoke to them, for the third time,   22
"What is his crime, then? I have found nothing in him that

deserves execution; I am going to teach him his lesson and let him go."

23 But they shouted him down, yelling their demand that he should be crucified.

24 Their shouting won the day, and Pilate pronounced the official
25 decision that their request should be granted. He released the man for whom they asked, the man who had been imprisoned for rioting and murder, and surrendered Jesus to their demands.

26 And as they were marching him away, they caught hold of Simon, a native of Cyrene in Africa, who was on his way home from the fields, and put the cross on his back for him to carry behind Jesus.

On the way to the cross

27 A huge crowd of people followed him, including women who
28 wrung their hands and wept for him. But Jesus turned to them and said,

‘"Women of Jerusalem, do not shed your tears for me, but for
29 yourselves and for your children! For the days are coming when men will say, 'Lucky are the women who are childless—the bodies which have never borne, and the breasts which have never
30 given nourishment.' Then men will begin to say to the mountains,
31 'Fall upon us!' and will say to the hills, 'Cover us up!' For if this is what men do when the wood is green, what will they do when it is seasoned?"

Jesus is crucified with two criminals

32, 33 Two criminals were also led out with him for execution, and when they came to the place called The Skull, they crucified him
34 with the criminals, one on either side of him. But Jesus himself was saying,

"Father, forgive them; they do not know what they are doing."
Then they shared out his clothes by casting lots.

35 The people stood and stared while their rulers continued to scoff, saying, "He saved other people, let's see him save himself, if he is really God's Christ—his chosen!"

36 The soldiers also mocked him by coming up and presenting
37 sour wine to him, saying,
38 "If you are the king of the Jews, why not save yourself?" For there was a placard over his head which read,

THIS IS THE KING OF THE JEWS.

One of the criminals hanging there covered him with abuse, 39
and said,

"Aren't you Christ? Why don't you save yourself—and us?"

But the other one checked him with the words, 40

"Aren't you afraid of God even when you're getting the same
punishment as he is? And it's fair enough for us, for we've only 41
got what we deserve, but this man never did anything wrong in
his life."

Then he said, 42

"Jesus, remember me when you come into your kingdom."

And Jesus answered, 43

"I tell you truly, this very day you will be with me in paradise."

The darkness, and the death of Jesus

It was now about midday, but darkness came over the whole 44
countryside until three in the afternoon, for there was an eclipse 45
of the sun. The veil in the Temple sanctuary was split in two. 46
Then Jesus gave a great cry and said,

"Father, I commend my spirit into your hands."

And with these words, he died.

When the centurion saw what had happened, he exclaimed 47
reverently,

"That was indeed a good man!"

And the whole crowd who had collected for the spectacle, when 48
they saw what had happened, went home in deep distress. And 49
those who had known him, as well as the women who had
followed him from Galilee, remained standing at a distance and
saw all this happen.

Joseph from Arimathaea lays the body of Jesus in a tomb

Now there was a man called Joseph, a member of the Jewish 50
council. He was a good and just man, and had neither agreed 51
with their plan nor voted for their decision. He came from the
Jewish city of Arimathaea and was awaiting the kingdom of God.
He went to Pilate and asked for Jesus' body. He took it down and 52, 53
wrapped it in linen and placed it in a rock-hewn tomb which had
not been used before.

It was now the day of the preparation and the Sabbath was 54
beginning to dawn, so the women who had accompanied Jesus 55

56 from Galilee followed Joseph, noted the tomb and the position of the body, and then went home to prepare spices and perfumes. On the Sabbath they rested, in obedience to the commandment.

CHAPTER 24

The first day of the week: the empty tomb

1 BUT at the first signs of dawn on the first day of the week, they went to the tomb, taking with them the aromatic spices they had

2 prepared. They discovered that the stone had been rolled away

3 from the tomb, but on going inside, the body of the Lord Jesus

4 was not to be found. While they were still puzzling over this, two

5 men suddenly stood at their elbow, dressed in dazzling light. The women were terribly frightened, and turned their eyes away and looked at the ground. But the two men spoke to them,

6 "Why do you look for the living among the dead? He is not here: he has risen! Remember what he said to you, while he was

7 still in Galilee—that the Son of Man must be betrayed into the hands of sinful men, and must be crucified, and must rise again on the third day."

8, 9 Then they did remember what he had said, and they turned their backs on the tomb and went and told all this to the eleven and the others who were with them.

10 It was Mary of Magdala, Joanna, Mary, the mother of James,

11 and their companions who made this report to the apostles. But it struck them as sheer imagination, and they did not believe the

12 women. Only Peter got up and ran to the tomb. He stooped down and saw the linen clothes lying there all by themselves, and he went home wondering at what had happened.

The walk to Emmaus

13 Then on the same day we find two of them going off to

14 Emmaus, a village about seven miles from Jerusalem. As they went they were deep in conversation about everything that had

15 happened. While they were absorbed in their serious talk and discussion, Jesus himself approached and walked along with them,

16, 17 but something prevented them from recognising him. Then he spoke to them,

"What is all this discussion that you are having on your walk?"

They stopped, their faces drawn with misery, and the one called 18
Cleopas replied,

"You must be the only stranger in Jerusalem who hasn't heard
all the things that have happened there recently!"

"What things?" asked Jesus. 19

"Oh, all about Jesus, from Nazareth. There was a man—a
prophet strong in what he did and what he said, in God's eyes as
well as the people's. Haven't you heard how our chief priests and 20
rulers handed him over for execution, and had him crucified? But 21
we were hoping he was the one who was to come and set Israel
free. . . .

"Yes, and as if that were not enough, it's getting on for three
days since all this happened; and some of our womenfolk have 22
disturbed us profoundly. For they went to the tomb at dawn, and 23
then when they couldn't find his body they said that they had
had a vision of angels who said that he was alive. Some of our 24
people went straight off to the tomb and found things just as the
women had described them—but they didn't see *him*!"

Then he himself spoke to them, 25

"Aren't you failing to understand, and slow to believe in all
that the prophets have said? Was it not inevitable that Christ 26
should suffer like that and so find his glory?"

Then, beginning with Moses and all the prophets, he explained 27
to them everything in the scriptures that referred to himself.

They were by now approaching the village to which they were 28
going. He gave the impression that he meant to go on further,
but they stopped him with the words, 29

"Do stay with us. It is nearly evening and soon the day will be
over."

So he went indoors to stay with them. Then it happened! While 30
he was sitting at table with them he took the loaf, gave thanks,
broke it and passed it to them. Their eyes opened wide and they 31
knew him! But he vanished from their sight. Then they said to 32
each other,

"Weren't our hearts glowing while he was with us on the road,
and when he made the scriptures so plain to us?"

And they got to their feet without delay and turned back to 33
Jerusalem. There they found the eleven and their friends all
together, full of the news— 34

"The Lord is really risen—he has appeared to Simon now!"

Then they told the story of their walk, and how they recognised 35
him when he broke the loaf.

Jesus suddenly appears to the disciples

36 And while they were still talking about these things, Jesus himself stood among them and said,

"Peace be to you all!"

37 But they shrank back in terror for they thought they were seeing a ghost.

38 "Why are you so worried?" said Jesus, "and why do doubts
39 arise in your minds? Look at my hands and my feet—it is really I
40 myself! Feel me and see; ghosts have no flesh or bones as you can see that I have."

41 But while they still could not believe it through sheer joy and were quite bewildered, Jesus said to them,

"Have you anything here to eat?"

42 They gave him a piece of broiled fish and part of a honeycomb,
43,44 which he took and ate before their eyes. Then he said,

"Here and now are fulfilled the words that I told you when I was with you: that everything written about me in the Law of Moses and in the prophets and psalms must come true."

45 Then he opened their minds so that they could understand the
46 scriptures, and added,

"That is how it was written, and that is why it was inevitable that Christ should suffer, and rise from the dead on the third day.
47 So must the change of heart which leads to the forgiveness of sins be proclaimed in his name to all nations, beginning at Jerusalem.

Jesus commissions them with the new message

48,49 "You are eye-witnesses of these things. Now I hand over to you the command of my Father. Stay in the city, then, until you are clothed with power from on high."

50 Then he led them outside as far as Bethany, where he blessed
51 them with uplifted hands. While he was in the act of blessing them
52 he was parted from them and was carried up to Heaven. They worshipped him, and turned back to Jerusalem with great joy,
53 and spent their days in the Temple, praising and blessing God.

The Gospel of John

It is quite plain that in this Gospel we are breathing a very different atmosphere from that of Matthew, Mark and Luke. The story itself shows great differences, almost the whole of the "action" taking place in Jerusalem; while a large amount of both the teaching and the healing ministries described by Mark, for example, find no place in "John" at all. There is also the remarkable difference that in this Gospel Jesus is recognised as the Messiah in the very first chapter by John, Andrew and Philip. Consequently John's version lacks the note of mounting tension which is very strong in the other three. The discourses of Jesus differ remarkably from those in the other three Gospels, where they consist for the most part of parables or short memorable rules of the way in which life is meant to be lived. In John's Gospel the discourses are long and different in style; they deal almost entirely with the great themes of life, light, love, truth and Christ's relationship with the Father. There are many similes and metaphors but no parables at all.

Naturally, this and many other sharp differences have given rise to an enormous amount of study and research. There is a vast body of literature commenting on the situation, and offering widely different explanations. To mention but one basic problem: in view of the difference of style between this and the other three Gospels, are we to suppose that Jesus spoke in different styles on different occasions, or are we to suppose that John is re-writing in his own style of Greek what Jesus spoke in Aramaic? The subject is obviously much too large to be more than introduced here, and the reader in search of further information is referred to the work of scholars writing particularly about St. John's Gospel.

Whether this Gospel was written as a conscious supplement (or even a deliberate corrective) to the other three, we simply do not know. But the majority of Christian scholars, for all their disagreements, would not deny the enormous spiritual value of this document. It seems probable that the author knew Jesus personally, and although modern scholarship is mostly against considering him to be the apostle John, there can be no doubt that the author had close spiritual acquaintance with Christ, and had reflected long and deeply on the nature of the divine Word. Here he gives to the world the results of *his thoughts, prayers and meditations about the life which is the light of men.*

Modern scholarship has gradually set the probable date of the Gospel earlier and earlier, and it is now fairly generally agreed that it was written at Ephesus between 90 and 110.

CHAPTER 1

Prologue

1 AT the beginning God expressed himself. That personal expres-
2 sion, that word, was with God, and was God, and he existed with
3 God from the beginning. All creation took place through him,
4 and none took place without him. In him appeared life and this
5 life was the light of mankind. The light still shines in the darkness
and the darkness has never put it out.

The gospel's beginning on earth

6, 7 A man called John was sent by God as a witness to the light,
so that any man who heard his testimony might believe in the
8 light. This man was not himself the light: he was sent simply as
a personal witness to that light.
9 That was the true light which shines upon every man as he
10 comes into the world. He came into the world—the world he had
11 created—and the world failed to recognise him. He came into his
12 own creation, and his own people would not accept him. Yet
wherever men did accept him he gave them the power to become
13 sons of God. These were the men who truly believed in him, and
their birth depended not on the course of nature nor on any impulse or plan of man, but on God.
14 So the word of God became a human being and lived among
us. We saw his splendour (the splendour as of a father's only son),
15 full of grace and truth. And it was about him that John stood up
and testified, exclaiming: "Here is the one I was speaking about
when I said that although he would come after me he would
always be in front of me; for he existed before I was born!"
16 Indeed, every one of us has shared in his riches—there is a grace
17 in our lives because of his grace. For while the Law was given by
18 Moses, love and truth came through Jesus Christ. It is true that no
one has ever seen God at any time. Yet the divine and only Son, who
lives in the closest intimacy with the Father, has made him known.

John's witness

This then is the testimony of John, when the Jews sent priests 19
and Levites to ask him who he was. He admitted with complete 20
candour, "I am not Christ."

So they asked him, "Who are you then? Are you Elijah?" 21
"No, I am not," he replied.

"Are you the Prophet?"

"No," he replied.

"Well, then," they asked again, "who are you? We want to 22
give an answer to the people who sent us. What would you call
yourself?"

"I am a voice shouting in the desert, 'Make straight the way of 23
the Lord!' as Isaiah the prophet said."

Now some of the Pharisees had been sent to John, and they 24, 25
questioned him, "What is the reason, then, for your baptising
people if you are not Christ and not Elijah and not the Prophet?"

To which John returned, "I do baptise—with water. But some- 26
where among you stands a man you do not know. He comes after 27
me, it is true, but I am not fit to undo his shoes!" (All this hap- 28
pened in the Bethany on the far side of the Jordan where the
baptisms of John took place.)

On the following day, John saw Jesus coming towards him and 29
said, "Look, there is the lamb of God who will take away the
sin of the world! This is the man I meant when I said 'A man 30
comes after me who is always in front of me, for he existed before
I was born!' It is true I have not known him, yet it was to make 31
him known to the people of Israel that I came and baptised people
with water."

Then John gave this testimony, "I have seen the Spirit come 32
down like a dove from Heaven and rest upon him. Indeed, it is 33
true that I did not recognise him by myself, but he who sent me
to baptise with water told me this: 'The one on whom you will
see the Spirit coming down and resting is the man who baptises
with the Holy Spirit!' Now I have seen this happen and I declare 34
publicly before you all that he is the Son of God!"

Men begin to follow Jesus

On the following day John was again standing with two of his 35
disciples. He looked straight at Jesus as he walked along and said, 36
"There is the lamb of God!" The two disciples heard what he 37

38 said and followed Jesus. Then Jesus turned round and when he saw them following him, spoke to them. "What do you want?" he said.

"Master, where are you staying?" they replied.

39 "Come and see," returned Jesus.

So they went and saw where he was staying and remained with him the rest of that day. (It was then about four o'clock in the
40 afternoon.) One of the two men who had heard what John said
41 and had followed Jesus was Andrew, Simon Peter's brother. He went straight off and found his own brother, Simon, and told him, "We have found the Messiah!" (meaning, of course, Christ).
42 And he brought him to Jesus.

Jesus looked steadily at him and said, "You are Simon, the son of John. From now on your name is Cephas"—(that is, Peter, meaning "a rock").

43 The following day Jesus decided to go into Galilee. He found
44 Philip and said to him, "Follow me!" Philip was a man from Beth-
45 saida, the town that Andrew and Peter came from. Now Philip found Nathanael and told him, "We have discovered the man whom Moses wrote about in the Law and about whom the Prophets wrote too. He is Jesus, the son of Joseph and comes from Nazareth."

46 "Can anything good come out of Nazareth?" retorted Nathanael.

"You come and see," replied Philip.

47 Jesus saw Nathanael coming towards him and remarked, "Now here is a true man of Israel; there is no deceit in him!"

48 "How can you know me?" returned Nathanael.

"When you were underneath that fig-tree," replied Jesus, "before Philip called you, I saw you."

49 At which Nathanael exclaimed, "Master, you are the Son of God, you are the king of Israel!"

50 "Do you believe in me," replied Jesus, "because I said I had seen you underneath that fig-tree? You are going to see something
51 greater than that! Believe me," he added, "I tell you all that you will see Heaven wide open and God's angels ascending and descending around the Son of Man!"

CHAPTER 2

The Son of God and a village wedding

Two days later there was a wedding in the Galilean village of 1
Cana. Jesus' mother was there and he and his disciples were in- 2
vited to the festivities. Then it happened that the supply of wine 3
gave out, and Jesus' mother told him, "They have no more wine."

"Is that your concern, or mine?" replied Jesus. "My time has 4
not come yet."

So his mother said to the servants, "Mind you do whatever he 5
tells you."

In the room six very large stone water-jars stood on the floor 6
(actually for the Jewish ceremonial cleansing), each holding about
twenty gallons. Jesus gave instructions for these jars to be filled 7
with water, and the servants filled them to the brim. Then he 8
said to them, "Now draw some out and take it to the master of
ceremonies", which they did. When this man tasted the water, 9
which had now become wine, without knowing where it came
from (though naturally the servants who had drawn the water
knew), he called out to the bridegroom and said to him, "Every- 10
body I know puts his good wine on first and then when men have
had plenty to drink, he brings out the poor stuff. But you have
kept back your good wine till now!" Jesus gave this, the first of 11
his signs, at Cana in Galilee. He demonstrated his power and his
disciples believed in him.

Jesus in the Temple

After this incident, Jesus, accompanied by his mother, his 12
brothers and his disciples, went down to Capernaum and stayed
there a few days. The Jewish Passover was approaching and Jesus 13
made the journey up to Jerusalem. In the Temple he discovered 14
cattle and sheep dealers and pigeon-sellers, as well as money-
changers sitting at their tables. So he made a rough whip out of 15
rope and drove the whole lot of them, sheep and cattle as well,
out of the Temple. He sent the coins of the money-changers
flying and turned their tables upside down. Then he said to the 16
pigeon-dealers, "Take those things out of here. Don't you dare
turn my Father's house into a market!" His disciples remembered 17
the scripture—
The zeal of thine house shall eat me up.

18 As a result of this, the Jews said to him, "What sign can you give us to justify what you are doing?"

19 "Destroy this temple," Jesus retorted, "and I will rebuild it in three days!"

20 To which the Jews replied, "This Temple took forty-six years to build, and are you going to rebuild it in three days?"

21 He was, in fact, speaking about the temple of his own body,
22 and when he was raised from the dead the disciples remembered what he had said to them and that made them believe both the scripture and what Jesus had said.

23 While he was in Jerusalem at Passover-time, during the festivi-
24 ties many believed in him as they saw the signs that he gave. But Jesus, on his side, did not trust himself to them—for he knew them
25 all. He did not need anyone to tell him what people were like: he understood human nature.

CHAPTER 3

Jesus and a religious leader

1, 2 ONE night Nicodemus, a leading Jew and a Pharisee, came to see Jesus.

"Master," he began, "we realise that you are a teacher who has come from God. Obviously no one could show the signs that you show unless God were with him."

3 "Believe me," returned Jesus, "a man cannot even see the kingdom of God without being born again."

4 "And how can a man who's getting old possibly be born?" replied Nicodemus. "How can he go back into his mother's womb and be born a second time?"

5 "I assure you," said Jesus, "that unless a man is born from
6 water and from spirit he cannot enter the kingdom of God. Flesh
7 gives birth to flesh and spirit gives birth to spirit: you must not be
8 surprised that I told you that all of you must be born again. The wind blows where it likes, you can hear the sound of it but you have no idea where it comes from and where it goes. Nor can you tell how a man is born by the wind of the Spirit."

9 "How on earth can things like this happen?" replied Nicodemus.

10 "So you are a teacher of Israel," said Jesus, "and you do not
11 recognise such things? I assure you that we are talking about something we really know and we are witnessing to something we

have actually observed, yet men like you will not accept our evidence. Yet if I have spoken to you about things which happen 12 on this earth and you will not believe me, what chance is there that you will believe me if I tell you about what happens in Heaven? No one has ever been up to Heaven except the Son of Man who 13 came down from Heaven. The Son of Man must be lifted above 14 the heads of men—as Moses lifted up that serpent in the desert— so that any man who believes in him may have eternal life. For 15,16 God loved the world so much that he gave his only Son, so that everyone who believes in him should not be lost, but should have eternal life. You must understand that God has not sent his Son 17 into the world to pass sentence upon it, but to save it—through him. Any man who believes in him is not judged at all. It is the 18 one who will not believe who stands already condemned, because he will not believe in the character of God's only Son. This *is* 19 the judgment—that light has entered the world and men have preferred darkness to light because their deeds are evil. Anybody 20 who does wrong hates the light and keeps away from it, for fear his deeds may be exposed. But anybody who is living by the 21 truth will come to the light to make it plain that all he has done has been done through God."

Jesus and John again

After this Jesus went into the country of Judaea with his 22 disciples and stayed there with them while the work of baptism was being carried on. John, too, was in Aenon near Salim, 23 baptising people because there was plenty of water in that district and they were still coming to him for baptism. (John, of course, 24 had not yet been put in prison.)

This led to a question arising between John's disciples and one 25 of the Jews about the whole matter of being cleansed. They approached John and said to him, "Master, look, the man who was with you on the other side of the Jordan, the one you testified to, is now baptising and everybody is coming to him!"

"A man can receive nothing at all," replied John, "unless it is 27 given him from Heaven. You yourselves can witness that I said, 28 'I am not Christ but I have been sent as his forerunner.' It is the 29 bridegroom who possesses the bride, yet the bridegroom's friend who merely stands and listens to him can be overjoyed to hear the bridegroom's voice. That is why my happiness is now complete. He must grow greater and greater and I less and less. 30

31 "The one who comes from above is naturally above everybody. The one who arises from the earth belongs to the earth and speaks from the earth. The one who comes from Heaven is above all 32 others and he bears witness to what he has seen and heard—yet 33 no one is accepting his testimony. Yet if a man does accept it, he 34 is acknowledging the fact that God is true. For the one whom God sent speaks the authentic words of God—and there can be no 35 measuring of the Spirit given to *him*! The Father loves the Son 36 and has put everything into his hand. The man who believes in the Son has eternal life. The man who refuses to believe in the Son will not see life; he lives under the anger of God."

CHAPTER 4

Jesus meets a Samaritan woman

1 Now, when the Lord found that the Pharisees had heard that "Jesus is making and baptising more disciples than John"— 2 although, in fact, it was not Jesus who did the baptising but his 3, 4 disciples—he left Judaea and went off again to Galilee, which 5 meant his passing through Samaria. There he came to a little town called Sychar, which is near the historic plot of land that Jacob 6 gave to his son, Joseph, and "Jacob's Spring" was there. Jesus, tired with the journey, sat down beside it, just as he was. The time 7 was about midday. Presently, a Samaritan woman arrived to draw some water.

8 "Please give me a drink," Jesus said to her, for his disciples had 9 gone away to the town to buy food. The Samaritan woman said to him, "How can you, a Jew, ask for a drink from me, a woman of Samaria?" (For Jews have no dealings with Samaritans.)

10 "If you knew what God can give," Jesus replied, "and if you knew who it is that said to you, 'Give me a drink', I think you would have asked him, and he would have given you living water!"

11 "Sir," said the woman, "you have nothing to draw water with 12 and this well is deep—where can you get your living water? Are you a greater man than our ancestor, Jacob, who gave us this well, and drank here himself with his family, and his cattle?"

13 Jesus said to her, "Everyone who drinks this water will be 14 thirsty again. But whoever drinks the water I will give him will never be thirsty again. For my gift will become a spring in the man himself, welling up into eternal life."

The woman said, "Sir, give me this water, so that I may stop 15
being thirsty—and not have to come here to draw water any
more!"

"Go and call your husband and then come back here," said 16
Jesus to her.

"I haven't got a husband!" the woman answered. 17

"You are quite right in saying, 'I haven't got a husband',"
replied Jesus, "for you have had five husbands and the man you 18
have now is not your husband at all. Yes, you spoke the simple
truth when you said that."

"Sir," said the woman again, "I can see that you are a prophet! 19
Now our ancestors worshipped on this hill-side, but you Jews 20
say that Jerusalem is the place where men ought to worship——"

"Believe me," returned Jesus, "the time is coming when wor- 21
shipping the Father will not be a matter of 'on this hill-side' or
'in Jerusalem'. Nowadays you are worshipping with your eyes 22
shut. We Jews are worshipping with our eyes open, for the salvation of mankind is to come from our race. Yet the time is coming, 23
yes, and has already come, when true worshippers will worship the
Father in spirit and in reality. Indeed, the Father looks for men
who will worship him like that. God is Spirit, and those who 24
worship him can only worship in spirit and in reality."

"Of course I know that Messiah is coming," returned the 25
woman, "you know, the one who is called Christ. When he
comes he will make everything plain to us."

"I am Christ speaking to you now," said Jesus. 26

At this point his disciples arrived, and were very surprised to 27
find him talking to a woman, but none of them asked, "What do
you want?" or "What are you talking to her about?" So the 28
woman left her water-pot behind and went into the town and
began to say to the people, "Come out and see the man who 29
told me everything I've ever done! Can this be 'Christ'?" So they 30
left the town and started to come to Jesus.

Meanwhile the disciples were begging him, "Master, do eat 31
something."

To which Jesus replied, "I have food to eat that you know 32
nothing about."

This, of course, made the disciples ask each other, "Do you 33
think anyone has brought him any food?"

Jesus said to them, "My food is doing the will of him who sent 34
me and finishing the work he has given me. Don't you say, 'Four 35
months more and then comes the harvest'? But I tell you to open

your eyes and look at the fields—they are gleaming white, all
36 ready for the harvest! The reaper is already being rewarded and
getting in a harvest for eternal life, so that both sower and reaper
37 may be glad together. For in this harvest the old saying comes
38 true, 'One man sows and another reaps.' I have sent you to reap
a harvest for which you never laboured; other men have worked
hard and you have reaped the result of their labours."

39 Many of the Samaritans who came out of that town believed
in him through the woman's testimony—"He told me everything
40 I've ever done." And when they arrived they begged him to stay
41 with them. He did stay there two days and far more believed in
42 him because of what he himself said. As they told the woman,
"We don't believe any longer now because of what you said.
We have heard him with our own ears. We know now that this
must be the man who will save the world!"

Jesus, in Cana again, heals in response to faith

43 After the two days were over, Jesus left and went away to
44 Galilee. (For Jesus himself testified that a prophet enjoys no
45 honour in his own country.) And on his arrival the people received
him with open arms. For they had seen all that he had done in
Jerusalem during the festival, since they had themselves been
46 present. So Jesus came again to Cana in Galilee, the place where
he had made the water into wine. At Capernaum there was an
47 official whose son was very ill. When he heard that Jesus had left
Judaea and had arrived in Galilee, he went off to see him and
begged him to come down and heal his son, who was by this
time at the point of death.

48 Jesus said to him, "I suppose you will never believe unless you
see signs and wonders!"

49 "Sir," returned the official, "please come down before my boy
dies!"

50 "You can go home," returned Jesus, "your son is alive and
well."

And the man believed what Jesus had said to him and went on
his way.

51 On the journey back his servants met him with the report:
52 "Your son is alive and well." So he asked them at what time he
had begun to recover, and they replied: "The fever left him
53 yesterday at one o'clock in the afternoon." Then the father knew
that this must have happened at the very moment when Jesus had

said to him, "Your son is alive and well." And he and his whole household believed in Jesus. This, then, was the second sign that Jesus gave on his return from Judaea to Galilee. 54

CHAPTER 5

Jesus heals in Jerusalem

SOME time later came one of the Jewish feast-days and Jesus 1 went up to Jerusalem. There is in Jerusalem near the sheep-gate 2 a pool surrounded by five arches, which has the Hebrew name of Bethzatha. Under these arches a great many sick people were in 3 the habit of lying; some of them were blind, some lame, and some had withered limbs. (They used to wait there for the "moving of the water", for at certain times an angel used to come 4 down into the pool and disturb the water, and then the first person who stepped into the water after the disturbance would be healed of whatever he was suffering from.) One particular 5 man had been there ill for thirty-eight years. When Jesus saw 6 him lying there on his back—knowing that he had been like that for a long time, he said to him, "Do you want to get well again?"

"Sir," replied the sick man, "I just haven't got anybody to put 7 me into the pool when the water is all stirred up. While I'm trying to get there somebody else gets down into it first."

"Get up," said Jesus, "pick up your bed and walk!" 8

At once the man recovered, picked up his bed and walked. 9

This happened on a Sabbath day, which made the Jews keep 10 on telling the man who had been healed, "It's the Sabbath, you know; it's not right for you to carry your bed."

"The man who made me well," he replied, "was the one who 11 told me, 'Pick up your bed and walk.' "

Then they asked him, "And who is the man who told you to 12 do that?"

But the one who had been healed had no idea who it was, for 13 Jesus had slipped away in the dense crowd. Later Jesus found him 14 in the Temple and said to him, "Look: you are a fit man now. Do not sin again or something worse might happen to you!"

Then the man went off and informed the Jews that the one who 15 had made him well was Jesus. It was because Jesus did such things 16 on the Sabbath day that the Jews persecuted him. But Jesus' 17 answer to them was this, "My Father is still at work and therefore I work as well."

18   This remark made the Jews all the more determined to kill him, because not only did he break the Sabbath but he referred to God as his own Father, so putting himself on equal terms with God.

Jesus makes his tremendous claim

19   Jesus said to them, "I assure you that the Son can do nothing of his own accord, but only what he sees the Father doing. What
20 the Son does is always modelled on what the Father does, for the Father loves the Son and shows him everything that he does himself. Yes, and he will show him even greater things than these to
21 fill you with wonder. For just as the Father raises the dead and makes them live, so does the Son give life to any man he chooses.
22 The Father is no man's judge: he has put judgment entirely into
23 the Son's hands, so that all men may honour the Son equally with the Father. The man who does not honour the Son does not
24 honour the Father who sent him. I solemnly assure you that the man who hears what I have to say and believes in the one who has sent me has eternal life. He does not have to face judgment; he
25 has already passed from death into life. Yes, I assure you that a time is coming, in fact has already come, when the dead will hear the voice of the Son of God and when they have heard it they will
26 live! For just as the Father has life in himself, so by the Father's
27 gift, the Son also has life in himself. And he has given him author-
28 ity to judge because he is Son of Man. No, do not be surprised —the time is coming when all those who are dead and buried
29 will hear his voice and out they will come—those who have done right will rise again to life, but those who have done wrong will rise to face judgment!

30   "By myself I can do nothing. As I hear, I judge, and my judg-ment is true because I do not live to please myself but to do the
31 will of the Father who sent me. You may say that I am bearing witness about myself, that therefore what I say about myself has
32 no value, but I would remind you that there is one who witnesses about me and I know that his witness about me is absolutely true.
33, 34 You sent to John, and he testified to the truth. Not that it is man's testimony that I accept—I only tell you this to help you to be
35 saved. John certainly was a lamp that burned and shone, and for
36 a time you were willing to enjoy the light that he gave. But I have a higher testimony than John's. The work that the Father gave me to complete, yes, these very actions which I do are my witness
37 that the Father has sent me. This is how the Father who has sent me has given his own personal testimony to me.

"Now you have never at any time heard what he says or seen what he is like. Nor do you really believe his word in your hearts, *38* for you refuse to believe the man whom he has sent. You pore *39* over the scriptures for you imagine that you will find eternal life in them. And all the time they give their testimony to me! But you *40* are not willing to come to me to have real life! Men's approval *41* or disapproval means nothing to me, but I can tell that you have *42* none of the love of God in your hearts. I have come in the name *43* of my Father and you will not accept me. Yet if another man comes simply in his own name, you will accept him. How on *44* earth can you believe while you are for ever looking for each other's approval and not for the glory that comes from the one God? There is no need for you to think that I have come to accuse *45* you before the Father. You already have an accuser—Moses, in whom you put all your confidence! For if you really believed *46* Moses, you would be bound to believe me; for it was about me that he wrote. But if you do not believe what he wrote, how can *47* you believe what I say"?

CHAPTER 6

Jesus shows his power over material things

AFTER this, Jesus crossed the Lake of Galilee (or Tiberias), and *1, 2* a great crowd followed him because they had seen the signs which he gave in his dealings with the sick. But Jesus went up the hill- *3* side and sat down there with his disciples. The Passover, the *4* Jewish festival, was near. So Jesus, raising his eyes and seeing a *5* great crowd on their way towards him, said to Philip, "Where can we buy food for these people to eat?" (He said this to test *6* Philip, for he himself knew what he was going to do.)

"Ten pounds' worth of bread would not be enough for them," *7* Philip replied, "even if they had only a little each."

Then Andrew, Simon Peter's brother, another disciple, put in, *8* "There is a boy here who has five small barley loaves and a couple *9* of fish, but what's the good of that for such a crowd?"

Then Jesus said, "Get the people to sit down." *10*

There was plenty of grass there, and the men, some five thousand of them, sat down. Then Jesus took the loaves, gave *11* thanks for them and distributed them to the people sitting on the grass, and he distributed the fish in the same way, giving them as much as they wanted. When they had eaten enough, Jesus said *12* to his disciples, "Collect the pieces that are left over so that nothing is wasted."

13 So they did as he suggested and filled twelve baskets with the broken pieces of the five barley loaves, which were left over after
14 the people had eaten! When the men saw this sign of Jesus' power, they kept saying, "This certainly is the Prophet who was to come into the world!"

15 Then Jesus, realising that they were going to carry him off and make him their king, retired once more to the hill-side quite alone.
16, 17 In the evening, his disciples went down to the lake, embarked on the boat and made their way across the lake to Capernaum. Darkness had already fallen and Jesus had not returned to them.
18, 19 A strong wind sprang up and the water grew very rough. When they had rowed about three or four miles, they saw Jesus walking on the water and coming towards the boat, and they were terrified.
20 But he spoke to them, "Don't be afraid: it is I myself."
21 So they gladly took him aboard, and at once the boat reached the shore they were making for.

Jesus teaches about the true bread

22 The following day, the crowd, who had remained on the other side of the lake, noticed that only the one boat had been there, and that Jesus had not embarked on it with his disciples, but that they
23 had in fact gone off by themselves. Some other small boats from Tiberias had landed quite near the place where they had eaten
24 the food and the Lord had given thanks. When the crowd realised that neither Jesus nor the disciples were there any longer, they themselves got into the boats and went off to Capernaum to look
25 for Jesus. When they had found him on the other side of the lake, they said to him, "Master, when did you come here?"

26 "Believe me," replied Jesus, "you are looking for me now not because you saw my signs but because you ate that food and had
27 all you wanted. You should not work for the food which does not last but for the food which lasts on into eternal life. This is the food the Son of Man will give you, and he is the one who bears the stamp of God the Father."

28 This made them ask him, "What must we do to carry out the work of God?"

29 "The work of God for you," replied Jesus, "is to believe in the one whom he has sent to you."

30 Then they asked him, "Then what sign can you give us that

will make us believe in you? What work are you doing? Our *31*
forefathers ate manna in the desert just as the scripture says,
> He gave them bread out of Heaven to eat."

To which Jesus replied, "Yes, but what matters is not that *32*
Moses *gave you* bread from Heaven but that my Father is *giving*
you the true bread from Heaven. For the bread of God which *33*
comes down from Heaven gives life to the world."

This made them say to him, "Lord, please give us this bread, *34*
always!"

Then Jesus said to them, "I myself am the bread of life. The *35*
man who comes to me will never be hungry and the man who
believes in me will never again be thirsty. Yet I have told you that *36*
you have seen me and do not believe. Everything that my Father *37*
gives me will come to me and I will never refuse anyone who
comes to me. For I have come down from Heaven, not to do what *38*
I want, but to do the will of him who sent me. The will of him who *39*
sent me is that I should not lose anything of what he has given
me, but should raise it up when the last day comes. And this is *40*
the will of the one who sent me, that everyone who sees the Son
and trusts him should have eternal life, and I will raise him up
when the last day comes."

At this, the Jews began grumbling at him because he said, "I am *41*
the bread which came down from Heaven", remarking "Is not *42*
this Jesus, the son of Joseph, whose parents we know? How can
he say that 'I have come down from Heaven'?"

So Jesus answered them, "Do not grumble among yourselves. *43*
Nobody comes to me unless he is drawn to me by the Father who *44*
sent me, and I will raise him up when the last day comes. In the *45*
Prophets it is written—
> 'And they shall all be taught of God,'
and this means that everybody who has heard the Father's voice
and learned from him will come to me. Not that anyone has ever *46*
seen the Father except the one who comes from God—he has seen
the Father. I assure you that the man who trusts in him has eternal *47*
life already. I myself am the bread of life. Your forefathers ate *48,49*
manna in the desert, *and they died*. This is bread that comes down *50*
from Heaven, so that a man may eat it and not die. I myself *51*
am the living bread which came down from Heaven, and if
anyone eats this bread he will live for ever. The bread which I
will give is my body and I shall give it for the life of the world."

This led to a fierce argument among the Jews, some of them *52*
saying, "How can this man give us his body to eat?"

53 So Jesus said to them, "Unless you do eat the body of the Son
54 of Man and drink his blood, you are not really living at all. The
    man who eats my flesh and drinks my blood has eternal life and
55 I will raise him up when the last day comes. For my body is real
56 food and my blood is real drink. The man who eats my body and
57 drinks my blood shares my life and I share his. Just as the living
    Father sent me and I am alive because of the Father, so the man
58 who lives on me will live because of me. *This* is the bread which
    came down from Heaven! It is not like the manna which your
    forefathers used to eat, *and died*. The man who eats this bread will
    live for ever."

59 Jesus said all these things while teaching in the synagogue at
60 Capernaum. Many of his disciples heard him say these things, and
    commented, "This is hard teaching indeed; who could accept that?"

61 Then Jesus, knowing intuitively that his disciples were com-
    plaining about what he had just said, went on, "Is this too much
62 for you? Then what would happen if you were to see the Son of
63 Man going up to the place where he was before? It is the Spirit
    which gives life. The flesh will not help you. The things which I
64 have told you are spiritual and are life. But some of you will not
    believe me."

    For Jesus knew from the beginning which of his followers did
65 not trust him and who was the man who would betray him. Then
    he added, "This is why I said to you, 'No one can come to me
    unless my Father puts it into his heart to come.' "

66 As a consequence of this, many of his disciples withdrew and
67 no longer followed him. So Jesus said to the twelve, "And are
    you too wanting to go away?"

68 "Lord," answered Simon Peter, "who else should we go to?
69 Your words have the ring of eternal life! And we believe and are
    convinced that you are the holy one of God."

70 Jesus replied, "Did I not choose you twelve—and one of you
    has the devil in his heart?"

71 He was speaking of Judas, the son of Simon Iscariot, one of
    the twelve, who was planning to betray him.

CHAPTER 7

Jesus delays his arrival at the festival

1 AFTER this, Jesus moved about in Galilee but decided not to do
2 so in Judaea since the Jews were planning to take his life. A Jewish

festival, "The feast of the tabernacles", was approaching and his **3**
brothers said to him, "You ought to leave here and go to Judaea
so that your disciples can see what you are doing, for nobody **4**
works in secret if he wants to be known publicly. If you are
going to do things like this, let the world see what you are doing."
For not even his brothers had any faith in him. Jesus replied by **5, 6**
saying, "It is not yet the right time for me, but any time is right
for you. You see, it is impossible for you to arouse the world's **7**
hatred, but I provoke hatred because I show the world how evil
its deeds really are. No, you go up to the festival; I shall not go **8**
up now, for it is not yet time for me to go." And after these **9**
remarks he remained where he was in Galilee.

Later, after his brothers had gone up to the festival, he went **10**
up himself, not openly but as though he did not want to be seen.
Consequently, the Jews kept looking for him at the festival and **11**
asking "Where is that man?" And there was an undercurrent of **12**
discussion about him among the crowds. Some would say, "He
is a good man", others maintained that he was not, but that he
was "misleading the people". Nobody, however, spoke openly **13**
about him for fear of the Jews.

Jesus openly declares his authority

But at the very height of the festival, Jesus went up to the **14**
Temple and began teaching. The Jews were amazed and remarked, **15**
"How does this man know all this—he has never been taught?"

Jesus replied to them, "My teaching is not really mine but **16**
comes from the one who sent me. If anyone wants to do God's **17**
will, he will know whether my teaching is from God or whether
I merely speak on my own authority. A man who speaks on his **18**
own authority has an eye for his own reputation. But the man who
is considering the glory of God who sent him is a true man.
There can be no dishonesty about him.

"Did not Moses give you the Law? Yet not a single one of you **19**
obeys the Law. Why are you trying to kill me?"

The crowd answered, "You must be mad! Who is trying to **20**
kill you?"

Jesus answered them, "I have done one thing and you are all **21**
amazed at it. Moses gave you circumcision (not that it came from **22**
Moses originally but from your forefathers), and you will circumcise a man even on the Sabbath. If a man receives the cutting **23**
of circumcision on the Sabbath to avoid breaking the Law of

195

24 Moses, why should you be angry with me because I have made a man's body perfectly whole on the Sabbath? You must not judge by the appearance of things but by the reality!"

25 Some of the people of Jerusalem, hearing him talk like this,
26 were saying, "Isn't this the man whom they are trying to kill? It's amazing—he talks quite openly and they haven't a word to say to him. Surely our rulers haven't decided that this really is Christ!
27 But then, we know this man and where he comes from—when Christ comes, no one will know where he comes from."

Jesus makes more unique claims

28 Then Jesus, in the middle of his teaching, called out in the Temple, "So you know me and know where I have come from? But I have not come of my own accord; I am sent by one who is
29 true and you do not know him! I do know him, because I come from him and he has sent me here."

30 Then they attempted to arrest him, but actually no one laid
31 a finger on him because the right moment had not yet come. Many of the crowd believed in him and kept on saying, "When Christ comes, is he going to show greater signs than this man?"

32 The Pharisees heard the crowd whispering these things about him, and they and the chief priests sent officers to arrest him.
33 Then Jesus said, "I shall be with you only a little while longer and
34 then I am going to him who sent me. You will look for me then but you will never find me. You cannot come where I shall be."

35 This made the Jews say to each other, "Where is he going to hide himself so that we cannot find him? Surely he's not going
36 to our refugees among the Greeks to teach Greeks? What does he mean when he says, 'You will look for me and you will never find me' and 'You cannot come where I shall be'?"

37 Then, on the last day, the climax of the festival, Jesus stood up and cried out, "If any man is thirsty, he can come to me and drink!
38 The man who believes in me, as the scripture said, will have
39 rivers of living water flowing from his inmost heart." (Here he was speaking about the Spirit which those who believe in him would receive. The Holy Spirit had not yet been given because
40 Jesus had not yet been glorified.) When they heard these words, some of the people were saying, "This really is the Prophet."
41 Others said, "This is Christ!" But some said, "And does Christ
42 come from Galilee? Don't the scriptures say that Christ will be

descended from David, and will come from Bethlehem, the village where David lived?"

So the people were in two minds about him—some of them 43, 44 wanted to arrest him, but so far no one laid hands on him.

Then the officers returned to the Pharisees and chief priests, 45 who said to them, "Why haven't you brought him?"

"No man ever spoke like that!" they replied. 46

"Has he pulled the wool over your eyes, too?" retorted the 47 Pharisees. "Have any of the authorities or any of the Pharisees 48 believed in him? But this crowd, who know nothing about the 49 Law, is damned anyway!"

One of their number, Nicodemus (the one who had previously 50 been to see Jesus), remarked to them, "But surely our Law does 51 not condemn the accused without hearing what he has to say, and finding out what he has done?"

"Are you a Galilean, too?" they answered him. "Look where 52 you will—you won't find that any prophet comes out of Galilee!"

So they broke up their meeting and went home, while Jesus 53 went off to the Mount of Olives.* 8:1

CHAPTER 8

Jesus deflates the rigorists

EARLY next morning he returned to the Temple and the entire 2 crowd came to him. So he sat down and began to teach them. But the scribes and Pharisees brought in to him a woman who had 3 been caught in adultery. They made her stand in front, and then 4 said to him, "Now, master, this woman has been caught in adultery, in the very act. According to the Law, Moses com- 5 manded us to stone such women to death. Now, what do you say about her?"

They said this to test him, so that they might have some good 6 grounds for an accusation. But Jesus stooped down and began to write with his finger in the dust on the ground. But as they 7 persisted in their questioning, he straightened himself up and said to them, "Let the one among you who has never sinned throw the first stone at her." Then he stooped down again and con- 8 tinued writing with his finger on the ground. And when they 9 heard what he said, they were convicted by their own consciences

* See note 4, page 552.

197

and went out, one by one, beginning with the eldest until they had all gone.

10   Jesus was left alone, with the woman still standing where they had put her. So he stood up and said to her, "Where are they all —did no one condemn you?"

11   And she said, "No one, sir."

"Neither do I condemn you," said Jesus to her. "Go home and do not sin again."

Jesus' bold claims—about himself—and his Father

12   Later, Jesus spoke to the people again and said, "I am the light of the world. The man who follows me will never walk in the dark but will live his life in the light."

13   This made the Pharisees say to him, "You are testifying to yourself—your evidence is not valid."

14   Jesus answered, "Even if I am testifying to myself, my evidence is valid, for I know where I have come from and I know where I am going. But as for you, you have no idea where I come from

15 or where I am going. You are judging by human standards, but

16 I am not judging anyone. Yet if I should judge, my decision would be just, for I am not alone—the Father who sent me is with

17 me. In your Law, it is stated that the witness of two persons is

18 valid. I am one testifying to myself and the second witness to me is the Father who sent me."

19   "And where is this father of yours?" they replied.

"You do not know my Father," returned Jesus, "any more than you know me: if you had known me, you would have known him."

20   Jesus made these statements while he was teaching in the Temple treasury. Yet no one arrested him, for his time had not yet come.

21   Later, Jesus spoke to them again and said, "I am going away and you will try to find me, but you will die in your sins. You cannot come where I am going."

22   This made the Jews say, "Is he going to kill himself, then? Is *that* why he says, 'You cannot come where I am going'?"

23   "The difference between us," Jesus said to them, "is that you come from below and I am from above. You belong to this world

24 but I do not. That is why I told you you will die in your sins. For unless you believe that I am who I am, you will die in your sins."

25   Then they said, "*Who are you?*"

"I am what I have told you I was from the beginning," replied

Jesus. "There is much in you that I could speak about and con- **26**
demn. But he who sent me is true and I am only speaking to
this world what I myself have heard from him."

They did not realise that he was talking to them about the **27**
Father. So Jesus resumed, "When you have lifted up the Son of **28**
Man, then you will realise that I am who I say I am, and that I
do nothing on my own authority but speak simply as my Father
has taught me. The one who sent me is with me now: the Father **29**
has never left me alone for I always do what pleases him." And **30**
even while he said these words, many people believed in him.

Jesus speaks of personal freedom

So Jesus said to the Jews who believed in him, "If you are **31**
faithful to what I have said, you are truly my disciples. And you **32**
will know the truth and the truth will set you free!"

"But we are descendants of Abraham," they replied, "and we **33**
have never in our lives been any man's slaves. How can you say
to us, 'You will be set free'?"

Jesus returned, "Believe me when I tell you that every man who **34**
commits sin is a slave. For a slave is no permanent part of a house- **35**
hold, but a son is. If the Son, then, sets you free, you are really **36**
free! I know that you are descended from Abraham, but some of **37**
you are looking for a way to kill me because you can't bear my
words. I am telling you what I have seen in the presence of my **38**
Father, and you are doing what you have seen in the presence of
your father."

"Our father is Abraham!" they retorted. **39**

"If you were the children of Abraham, you would do the sort
of things Abraham did. But in fact, at this moment, you are **40**
looking for a way to kill me, simply because I am a man who has
told you the truth that I have heard from God. Abraham would
never have done that. No, you are doing your father's work." **41**

"We are not illegitimate!" they retorted. "We have one Father
—God."

"If God were really your Father," replied Jesus, "you would **42**
have loved me. For I came from God; and I am here. I did not
come of my own accord—he sent me, and I am here. Why do **43**
you not understand my words? It is because you cannot hear
what I am really saying. Your father is the devil, and what you **44**
are wanting to do is what your father longs to do. He always was
a murderer, and has never dealt with the truth, since the truth

will have nothing to do with him. Whenever he tells a lie, he
45 speaks in character, for he is a liar and the father of lies. And it
46 is because I speak the truth that you will not believe me. Which
of you can prove me guilty of sin? If I am speaking the truth,
47 why is it that you do not believe me? The man who is born of God
can hear the words of God and the reason why you cannot hear
the words of God is simply this, that you are not the sons of God."

48 "How right we are," retorted the Jews, "in calling you a
Samaritan, and mad at that!"

49 "No," replied Jesus, "I am not mad. I am honouring my
50 Father and you are trying to dishonour me. But I am not concerned with my own glory: there is one whose concern it is, and
51 he is the true judge. Believe me when I tell you that if anybody
accepts my words, he will never see death at all."

52 "Now we know that you're mad," replied the Jews. "Why,
Abraham died and the prophets, too, and yet you say, 'If a man
53 accepts my words, he will never experience death!' Are you greater
than our father, Abraham? He died, and so did the prophets—
who are you making yourself out to be?"

54 "If I were trying to glorify myself," returned Jesus, "such glory
would be worthless. But it is my Father who glorifies me, the
55 very one whom you say is your God—though you have never
known him. But I know him, and if I said I did not know him,
I should be as much a liar as you are! But I do know him and I am
56 faithful to what he says. As for your father, Abraham, his great
joy was that he would see my coming. Now he has seen it and he
is overjoyed."

57 "Look," said the Jews to him, "you are not fifty yet—and has
Abraham seen you?"

58 "I tell you in solemn truth," returned Jesus, "before there was
an Abraham, I AM!"

59 At this, they picked up stones to hurl at him, but Jesus disappeared and made his way out of the Temple.

CHAPTER 9

Jesus and blindness, physical and spiritual

1 LATER, as Jesus walked along he saw a man who had been blind
from birth.

2 "Master, whose sin caused this man's blindness," asked the
disciples, "his own or his parents'?"

"He was not born blind because of his own sin or that of his *3* parents," returned Jesus, "but to show the power of God at work in him. We must carry on the work of him who sent me while *4* the daylight lasts. Night is coming, when no one can work. I *5* am the world's light as long as I am in it."

Having said this, he spat on the ground and made a sort of clay *6* with the saliva. This he applied to the man's eyes and said, "Go *7* and wash in the pool of Siloam." (Siloam means "one who has been sent".) So the man went off and washed and came home with his sight restored.

His neighbours and the people who had often seen him before *8* as a beggar remarked, "Isn't this the man who used to sit and beg?"

"Yes, that's the one," said some. *9*

Others said, "No, but he's very like him."

But he himself said, "I'm the man all right!"

"Then how was your blindness cured?" they asked. *10*

"The man called Jesus made some clay and smeared it on my *11* eyes," he replied, "and then he said, 'Go to Siloam and wash.' So off I went and washed—and that's how I got my sight!"

"Where is he now?" they asked. *12*

"I don't know," he returned.

So they brought the man who had once been blind before the *13* Pharisees. (It should be noted that Jesus made the clay and *14* restored his sight on a Sabbath day.) The Pharisees asked the *15* question all over again as to how he had become able to see.

"He put clay on my eyes; I washed it off; now I can see— that's all," he replied.

Some of the Pharisees commented, "This man cannot be from *16* God since he does not observe the Sabbath."

"But how can a sinner give such wonderful signs as these?" others demurred. And they were in two minds about him. Finally, they asked the blind man again, "And what do *you* say *17* about him? You're the one whose sight was restored."

"I believe he is a prophet," he replied.

The Jews did not really believe that the man had been blind and *18* then had become able to see, until they had summoned his parents and asked them, "Is this your son who you say was born blind? *19* How does it happen that he can now see?"

"We know that this is our son, and we know that he was born *20* blind," returned his parents, "but how he can see now, or who *21* made him able to see, we have no idea. Why don't you ask him? He is a grown-up man; he can speak for himself."

22   His parents said this because they were afraid of the Jews who had already agreed that anybody who admitted that Christ had
23 done this thing should be excommunicated. It was this fear which made his parents say, "Ask him, he is a grown-up man."

24   So, once again they summoned the man who had been born blind and said to him, "You should give God the glory for what has happened to you. We know that this man is a sinner."

25   "Whether he is a sinner or not, I couldn't tell, but one thing I am sure of," the man replied, "I used to be blind, now I can see!"

26   "But what did he *do* to you—how did he make you see?" they continued.

27   "I've told you before," he replied. "Weren't you listening? Why do you want to hear it all over again? Are you wanting to be his disciples too?"

28   At this, they turned on him furiously.

"You're the one who is his disciple! We are disciples of Moses.
29 We know that God spoke to Moses, but as for this man, we don't even know where he came from."

30   "Now here's the extraordinary thing," he retorted, "you don't know where he came from and yet he gave me the gift of sight.
31 Everybody knows that God does not listen to sinners. It is the man who has a proper respect for God and does what God wants
32 him to do—he's the one God listens to. Why, since the world began, nobody's ever heard of a man who was born blind being
33 given his sight. If this man did not come from God, he couldn't do such a thing!"

34   "You misbegotten wretch!" they flung back at him. "Are you trying to teach *us*?" And they threw him out.

35   Jesus heard that they had expelled him and when he had found him, he said, "Do you believe in the Son of Man?"

36   "And who is he, sir?" the man replied. "Tell me, so that I can believe in him."

37   "You have seen him," replied Jesus. "It is the one who is talking to you now."

38   "Lord, I do believe," he said, and worshipped him.

39   Then Jesus said, "My coming into this world is itself a judgment—those who cannot see have their eyes opened and those who think they can see become blind."

40   Some of the Pharisees near him overheard this and said, "So we're blind, too, are we?"

41   "If you were blind," returned Jesus, "nobody could blame you, but, as you insist 'We can see', your guilt remains."

CHAPTER 10

Jesus declares himself the true shepherd of men

THEN Jesus said, "Believe me when I tell you that anyone who *1* does not enter the sheepfold through the door, but climbs in by some other way, is a thief and a rogue. It is the shepherd of the *2* flock who goes in by the door. It is to him the door-keeper opens *3* the door and it is his voice that the sheep recognise. He calls his own sheep by name and leads them out of the fold, and when he *4* has driven all his own flock outside, he goes in front of them himself, and the sheep follow him because they know his voice. They *5* will never follow a stranger—indeed, they will run away from him, for they do not recognise strange voices."

Jesus gave them this illustration but they did not grasp the *6* point of what he was saying to them. So Jesus said to them once *7* more, "I do assure you that I myself am the door for the sheep. All who have gone before me are like thieves and rogues, but the *8* sheep did not listen to them. I am the door. If a man goes in *9* through me, he will be safe and sound; he can come in and out and find his food. The thief comes with the sole intention of steal- *10* ing and killing and destroying, but I came to bring them life, and far more life than before. I am the good shepherd. The good *11* shepherd will give his life for the sake of his sheep. But the hired *12* man, who is not the shepherd, and does not own the sheep, will see the wolf coming, desert the sheep and run away. And the wolf will attack the flock and send them flying. The hired man runs *13* away because he is only a hired man and has no interest in the sheep. I am the good shepherd, and I know those that are *14* mine and my sheep know me, just as the Father knows me and *15* I know the Father. And I am giving my life for the sake of the sheep.

"And I have other sheep who do not belong to this fold. I *16* must lead these also, and they will hear my voice. So there will be one flock and one shepherd. This is the reason why the Father *17* loves me—that I lay down my life, and I lay it down to take it up again! No one is taking it from me, but I lay it down of my *18* own free will. I have the power to lay it down and I have the power to take it up again. This is an order that I have received from my Father."

Jesus plainly declares who he is

19 Once again, the Jews were in two minds about him because of
20 these words, many of them remarking, "The devil's in him and
he's insane. Why do you listen to him?"

21 But others were saying, "This is not the sort of thing a devil-
possessed man would say! Can a devil make a blind man see?"

22 Then came the dedication festival at Jerusalem. It was winter-
23 time and Jesus was walking about inside the Temple in Solomon's
24 cloisters. So the Jews closed in on him and said, "How much
longer are you going to keep us in suspense? If you really are
Christ, tell us so straight out!"

25 "I have told you," replied Jesus, "and you do not believe it.
What I have done in my Father's name is sufficient to prove my
26, 27 claim, but you do not believe because you are not my sheep. My
sheep recognise my voice and I know who they are. They follow
28 me and I give them eternal life. They will never die and no one
29 can snatch them out of my hand. My Father, who has given them
to me, is greater than all. And no one can tear anything out of
30 the Father's hand. I and the Father are One."

31 Again the Jews reached for stones to stone him to death, but
32 Jesus answered them, "I have shown you many good things from
the Father—for which of these do you intend to stone me?"

33 "We're not going to stone you for any good things," replied
the Jews, "but for blasphemy: because you, who are only a man,
are making yourself out to be God."

34 "Is it not written in your own Law," replied Jesus, " 'I have
35 said ye are gods'? And if he called those men 'gods' to whom the
36 word of God came (and the scripture cannot be broken), can you
say to the one whom the Father has consecrated and sent into the
world, 'You are blaspheming' because I said, 'I am the Son of
37 God'? If I fail to do what my Father does, then do not believe
38 me. But if I do, even though you have no faith in me personally,
then believe in the things that I do. Then you may come to know
and realise that the Father is in me and I am in the Father."

39 And again they tried to arrest him, but he moved out of their
reach.

40 Then Jesus went off again across the Jordan to the place where
41 John had first baptised and there he stayed. A great many people
came to him, and said, "John never gave us any sign but all that
he said about this man was true."

42 And in that place many believed in him.

CHAPTER 11

Jesus shows his power over death

Now there was a man by the name of Lazarus who became **1**
seriously ill. He lived in Bethany, the village where Mary and her
sister Martha lived. (Lazarus was the brother of the Mary who **2**
poured perfume upon the Lord and wiped his feet with her hair.)
So the sisters sent word to Jesus: "Lord, your friend is very ill." **3**

When Jesus received the message, he said, "This illness is not **4**
meant to end in death; it is going to bring glory to God—for it
will show the glory of the Son of God."

Now Jesus loved Martha and her sister and Lazarus. So when **5, 6**
he heard of Lazarus' illness he stayed where he was two days
longer. Only then did he say to the disciples, "Let us go back into **7**
Judaea."

"Master!" returned the disciples, "only a few days ago, the **8**
Jews were trying to stone you to death—are you going there
again?"

"There are twelve hours of daylight every day, are there not?" **9**
replied Jesus. "If a man walks in the daytime, he does not stumble,
for he has the daylight to see by. But if he walks at night he **10**
stumbles, because he cannot see where he is going."

Jesus spoke these words; then after a pause he said to them, **11**
"Our friend Lazarus has fallen asleep, but I am going to wake
him up."

At this, his disciples said, "Lord, if he has fallen asleep, he will **12**
be all right."

Actually Jesus had spoken about his death, but they thought **13**
that he was speaking about falling into natural sleep. This made **14**
Jesus tell them quite plainly, "Lazarus has died, and I am glad **15**
that I was not there—for your sakes, that you may learn to
believe. And now, let us go to him."

Thomas (known as the twin) then said to his fellow-disciples, **16**
"Come on, then, let us all go and die with him!"

When Jesus arrived, he found that Lazarus had already been in **17**
the grave four days. Now Bethany is quite near Jerusalem, rather **18**
less than two miles away, and a good many of the Jews had come **19**
out to see Martha and Mary to offer them sympathy over their
brother's death. When Martha heard that Jesus was on his way, **20**
she went out and met him, while Mary stayed in the house.

21   "If only you had been here, Lord," said Martha, "my brother
22 would never have died. And I know that, even now, God will give
you whatever you ask from him."

23   "Your brother will rise again," Jesus replied to her.

24   "I know," said Martha, "that he will rise again in the resurrection at the last day."

25   "I myself am the resurrection and the life," Jesus told her.
26 "The man who believes in me will live even though he dies, and
anyone who is alive and believes in me will never die at all. Can
you believe that?"

27   "Yes, Lord," replied Martha. "I do believe that you are Christ,
28 the Son of God, the one who was to come into the world." Saying this she went away and called Mary her sister, whispering,
29 "The master's here and is asking for you." When Mary heard this
30 she sprang to her feet and went to him. Now Jesus had not yet
arrived at the village itself, but was still where Martha had met
31 him. So when the Jews who had been condoling with Mary in
the house saw her get up quickly and go out, they followed her,
imagining that she was going to the grave to weep there.

32   When Mary met Jesus, she looked at him, and then fell down
at his feet. "If only you had been here, Lord," she said, "my
brother would never have died."

33   When Jesus saw Mary weep and noticed the tears of the Jews
who came with her, he was deeply moved and visibly distressed.

34   "Where have you put him?" he asked.

35   "Lord, come and see," they replied, and at this Jesus himself
wept.

36, 37   "Look how much he loved him!" remarked the Jews, though
some of them asked, "Could he not have kept this man from
dying if he could open that blind man's eyes?"

38   Jesus was again deeply moved at these words, and went on to
the grave. It was a cave, and a stone lay in front of it.

39   "Take away the stone," said Jesus.
   "But Lord," said Martha, the dead man's sister, "he has been
dead four days. By this time he will be decaying. . . ."

40   "Did I not tell you," replied Jesus, "that if you believed, you
would see the wonder of what God can do?"

41   Then they took the stone away and Jesus raised his eyes and
42 said, "Father, I thank you that you have heard me. I know that
you always hear me, but I have said this for the sake of these
people standing here so that they may believe that you have
sent me."

And when he had said this, he called out in a loud voice, 43
"Lazarus, come out!"

And the dead man came out, his hands and feet bound with 44
grave-clothes and his face muffled with a handkerchief.

"Now unbind him," Jesus told them, "and let him go home."

Jesus' miracle leads to deadly hostility

After this many of the Jews who had accompanied Mary and 45
observed what Jesus did, believed in him. But some of them went 46
off to the Pharisees and told them what Jesus had done. Conse- 47
quently, the Pharisees and chief priests summoned the council
and said, "What can we do? This man obviously shows many
remarkable signs. If we let him go on doing this sort of thing we 48
shall have everybody believing in him. Then we shall have the
Romans coming and that will be the end of our holy place and
our very existence as a nation!"

But one of them, Caiaphas, who was High Priest that year, 49
addressed the meeting: "You plainly don't understand what is
involved here. You do not realise that it would be a good thing 50
for us if one man should die for the sake of the people—instead of
the whole nation being destroyed." (He did not make this remark 51
on his own initiative but, since he was High Priest that year, he
was in fact inspired to say that Jesus was going to die for the
nation's sake—and in fact not for that nation only, but to bring 52
together into one family all the children of God scattered throughout the world.) From that day then, they planned to kill him. As 53, 54
a consequence Jesus made no further public appearance among the
Jews but went away to the countryside on the edge of the desert,
and stayed with his disciples in a town called Ephraim. The Jewish 55
Passover was approaching and many people went up from the
country to Jerusalem before the actual Passover, to go through a
ceremonial cleansing. They were looking for Jesus there and kept 56
saying to one another as they stood in the Temple, "What do
you think? Surely he won't come to the festival?"

It should be understood that the chief priests and the Pharisees 57
had issued an order that anyone who knew of Jesus' whereabouts
should tell them, so that they could arrest him.

CHAPTER 12

An act of love as the end approaches

1 Six days before the Passover, Jesus came to Bethany, the village
2 of Lazarus whom he had raised from the dead. They gave a
supper for him there, and Martha waited on the party while
3 Lazarus took his place at table with Jesus. Then Mary took a whole
pound of very expensive perfume and anointed Jesus' feet and
then wiped them with her hair. The entire house was filled with
4 the fragrance of the perfume. But one of his disciples, Judas
Iscariot (the man who was going to betray Jesus), burst out,
5 "Why on earth wasn't this perfume sold? It's worth thirty
pounds, which could have been given to the poor!"
6 He said this, not because he cared about the poor, but because
he was dishonest, and when he was in charge of the purse used
to help himself from the contents.
7 But Jesus replied to this outburst, "Let her alone, let her keep
8 this for the day of my burial. You have the poor with you always
—you will not always have me!"
9 The large crowd of Jews discovered that he was there and came
to the scene—not only because of Jesus but to catch sight of
10 Lazarus, the man whom he had raised from the dead. Then the
11 chief priests planned to kill Lazarus as well, because he was the
reason for many of the Jews' going away and putting their faith
in Jesus.

Jesus experiences a temporary triumph

12 The next day, the great crowd who had come to the festival
13 heard that Jesus was coming into Jerusalem, and went out to meet
him with palm branches in their hands, shouting, "God save
him! God bless the man who comes in the name of the Lord,
God bless the king of Israel!"
14 For Jesus had found a young ass and was seated upon it, just
as the scripture foretold—
15 Fear not, daughter of Zion: behold, thy king cometh, sitting
on an ass's colt.
16 (The disciples did not realise the significance of what was happening at the time, but when Jesus was glorified, then they recollected that these things had been written about him and that they had carried them out for him.)

208

The people who had been with him, when he had summoned **17**
Lazarus from the grave and raised him from the dead, were
continually talking about him. This accounts for the crowd who **18**
went out to meet him, for they had heard that he had given this
sign. Seeing all this, the Pharisees remarked to one another, "You **19**
see?—There's nothing one can do! The whole world is running
after him."

Among those who had come up to worship at the festival were **20**
some Greeks. They approached Philip (whose home town was **21**
Bethsaida in Galilee) with the request, "Sir, we want to see Jesus."

Philip went and told Andrew, and Andrew went with Philip **22**
and told Jesus.

Jesus told them, "The time has come for the Son of Man to be **23**
glorified. I tell you truly that unless a grain of wheat falls into the **24**
earth and dies, it remains a single grain·of wheat; but if it dies, it
brings a good harvest. The man who loves his own life will **25**
destroy it, and the man who hates his life in this world will
preserve it for eternal life. If a man wants to enter my service, he **26**
must follow my way; and where I am, my servant will also be.
And my Father will honour every man who enters my service.

"Now comes my hour of heart-break, and what can I say, **27**
'Father, save me from this hour'? No, it was for this very purpose
that I came to this hour. 'Father, honour your own name!' " **28**

At this there came a voice from Heaven, "I have honoured it
and I will honour it again!"

When the crowd of bystanders heard this, they said it thun- **29**
dered, but some of them said, "An angel spoke to him."

Then Jesus said, "That voice came for your sake, not for mine. **30**
Now is the time for the judgment of this world to begin, and **31**
now will the spirit that rules this world be driven out. As for me, **32**
if I am lifted up from the earth, I will draw all men to myself."
(He said this to show the kind of death he was going to die.) **33**

Then the crowd said, "We have heard from the Law that Christ **34**
lives for ever. How can you say that the Son of Man must be
'lifted up'? Who is this Son of Man?"

At this, Jesus said to them, "You have the light with you only **35**
a little while longer. Go on while the light is good, before the
darkness comes down upon you. For the man who walks in the
dark has no idea where he is going. You must believe in the light **36**
while you have the light, that you may become the sons of light."

Jesus said all these things, and then went away, out of their
sight. But though he had given so many signs, yet they did not **37**

38 believe in him, so that the prophecy of Isaiah was fulfilled, when
he said,

> Lord, who hath believed our report?
> And to whom hath the arm of the Lord been revealed?

39 Thus, they could not believe, for Isaiah said again—
40

> He hath blinded their eyes, and he hardened their heart:
> Lest they should see with their eyes, and perceive with
> their heart,
> And should turn,
> And I should heal them.

41 Isaiah said these things because he saw the glory of Christ, and
42 spoke about him. Nevertheless, many even of the authorities did
believe in him. But they would not admit it for fear of the
43 Pharisees, in case they should be excommunicated. They were
more concerned to have the approval of men than to have the
approval of God.

44 But later, Jesus cried aloud, "Every man who believes in me,
45 is believing in the one who sent me; and every man who sees
46 me is seeing the one who sent me. I have come into the world as
light, so that no one who believes in me need remain in the dark.
47 Yet, if anyone hears my sayings and does not keep them, I do not
judge him—for I did not come to judge the world but to save it.
48 Every man who rejects me and will not accept my sayings has a
judge—at the last day, the very words that I have spoken will be
49 his judge. For I have not spoken on my own authority: the Father
who sent me has commanded me what to say and what to speak.
50 And I know that what he commands means eternal life. All that
I say I speak only in accordance with what the Father has told
me."

CHAPTER 13

Jesus teaches his disciples humility

1 BEFORE the festival of the Passover began, Jesus realised that the
time had come for him to leave this world and return to the
Father. He had loved those who were his own in this world and
2 he loved them to the end. By supper-time, the devil had already
put the thought of betraying Jesus into the mind of Judas Iscariot,
3 Simon's son. Jesus, with the full knowledge that the Father had
put everything into his hands and that he had come from God
4 and was going to God, rose from the supper-table, took off his

outer clothes, picked up a towel and fastened it round his waist. Then he poured water into the basin and began to wash the dis- 5 ciples' feet and to dry them with the towel around his waist.

So he came to Simon Peter, who said to him, "Lord, are you 6 going to wash my feet?"

"You do not realise now what I am doing," replied Jesus, "but 7 later on you will understand."

Then Peter said to him, "You must never wash my feet!" 8

"Unless you let me wash you, Peter," replied Jesus, "you can- not share my lot."

"Then," returned Simon Peter, "please—not just my feet but 9 my hands and my face as well!"

"The man who has bathed," returned Jesus, "only needs to 10 wash his feet to be clean all over. And you are clean—though not all of you."

(For Jesus knew his betrayer and that is why he said, "though 11 not all of you".)

When Jesus had washed their feet and put on his clothes, he sat 12 down again and spoke to them, "Do you realise what I have just done to you? You call me 'teacher' and 'Lord' and you are quite 13 right, for I am your teacher and your Lord. But if I, your teacher 14 and Lord, have washed your feet, you must be ready to wash one another's feet. I have given you this as an example so that you 15 may do as I have done. Believe me, the servant is not greater 16 than his master and the messenger is not greater than the man who sent him. Once you have realised these things, you will find 17 your happiness in doing them.

Jesus foretells his betrayal

"I am not speaking about all of you—I know the men I have 18 chosen. But let this scripture be fulfilled—

He that eateth my bread lifted up his heel against me.

From now onwards, I shall tell you about things before they 19 happen, so that when they do happen, you may believe that I am the one I claim to be. I tell you truly that anyone who accepts 20 my messenger will be accepting me, and anyone who accepts me will be accepting the one who sent me."

After Jesus had said this, he was clearly in anguish of soul, and 21 he added solemnly,

"I tell you plainly, one of you is going to betray me."

At this the disciples stared at each other, completely mystified 22

23 as to whom he could mean. And it happened that one of them,
24 whom Jesus loved, was sitting very close to him. So Simon Peter nodded to this man and said, "Tell us who he means."

25 He simply leaned forward on Jesus' shoulder, and asked, "Lord, who is it?"

26 And Jesus answered, "It is the one I am going to give this piece of bread to, after I have dipped it in the dish."

Then he took a piece of bread, dipped it in the dish and gave
27 it to Simon's son, Judas Iscariot. After he had taken the piece of bread, Satan entered his heart. Then Jesus said to him, "Be quick about your business!"

28 No one else at table knew what he meant in telling him this.
29 Indeed, some of them thought that, since Judas had charge of the purse, Jesus was telling him to buy what they needed for the
30 festival, or that he should give something to the poor. So Judas took the piece of bread and went out quickly—into the night.

31 When he had gone, Jesus spoke, "Now comes the glory of the
32 Son of Man, and the glory of God in him! If God is glorified through him then God will glorify the Son of Man—and that
33 without delay. Oh, my children, I am with you such a short time! You will look for me and I have to tell you as I told the
34 Jews, 'Where I am going, you cannot follow.' Now I am giving you a new command—love one another. Just as I have loved you,
35 so you must love one another. This is how all men will know that you are my disciples, because you have such love for one another."

36 Simon Peter said to him, "Lord, where are you going?"

"I am going," replied Jesus, "where you cannot follow me now, though you will follow me later."

37 "Lord, why can't I follow you now?" said Peter. "I would lay down my life for you!"

38 "Would you lay down your life for me?" replied Jesus. "Believe me, you will disown me three times before the cock crows!"

CHAPTER 14

Jesus reveals spiritual truths

1 "You must not let yourselves be distressed—you must hold on
2 to your faith in God and to your faith in me. There are many rooms in my Father's House. If there were not, should I have told
3 you that I am going away to prepare a place for you? It is true

that I am going away to prepare a place for you, but it is just as true that I am coming again to welcome you into my own home, so that you may be where I am. You know where I am going 4 and you know the road I am going to take."

"Lord," Thomas remonstrated, "we do not know where you're 5 going, and how can we know what road you're going to take?"

"I myself am the road," replied Jesus, "and the truth and the 6 life. No one approaches the Father except through me. If you had 7 known who I am, you would have known my Father. From now on, you do know him and you have seen him."

Jesus explains his relationship with the Father

Then Philip said to him, "Show us the Father, Lord, and we 8 shall be satisfied."

"Have I been such a long time with you," returned Jesus, 9 "without your really knowing me, Philip? The man who has seen me has seen the Father. How can you say, 'Show us the Father'? Do you not believe that I am in the Father and the Father is in 10 me? The very words I say to you are not my own. It is the Father who lives in me who carries out his work through me. Do you 11 believe me when I say that I am in the Father and the Father is in me? But if you cannot, then believe me because of what you see me do. I assure you that the man who believes in me will do 12 the same things that I have done, yes, and he will do even greater things than these, for I am going away to the Father. Whatever 13 you ask the Father in my name, I will do—that the Son may bring glory to the Father. And if you ask me anything in my 14 name, I will grant it.

Jesus promises the Spirit

"If you really love me, you will keep the commandments I 15 have given you and I shall ask the Father to give you someone 16 else to stand by you, to be with you always. I mean the Spirit of 17 truth, whom the world cannot accept, for it can neither see nor recognise that Spirit. But you recognise him, for he is with you now and will be in your hearts. I am not going to leave you alone 18 in the world—I am coming to you. In a very little while, the 19 world will see me no more but you will see me, because I am really alive and you will be alive too. When that day comes, you 20 will realise that I am in my Father, that you are in me, and I am in you.

21   "Every man who knows my commandments and obeys them is the man who really loves me, and every man who really loves me will himself be loved by my Father, and I too will love him and make myself known to him."

22   Then Judas (not Iscariot) said, "Lord, how is it that you are going to make yourself known to us but not to the world?"

23   And to this Jesus replied, "When a man loves me, he follows my teaching. Then my Father will love him, and we will come
24 to that man and make our home within him. The man who does not really love me will not follow my teaching. Indeed, what you are hearing from me now is not really my saying, but comes from the Father who sent me.

25, 26   "I have said all this while I am still with you. But the one who is coming to stand by you, the Holy Spirit whom the Father will send in my name, will be your teacher and will bring to your minds all that I have said to you.

27   "I leave behind with you—peace; I give you my own peace and my gift is nothing like the peace of this world. You must not
28 be distressed and you must not be daunted. You have heard me say, 'I am going away and I am coming back to you.' If you really loved me, you would be glad because I am going to my Father,
29 for my Father is greater than I. And I have told you of it now, before it happens, so that when it does happen, your faith in me
30 will not be shaken. I shall not be able to talk much longer to you, for the spirit that rules this world is coming very close. He has no
31 hold over me, but I go on my way to show the world that I love the Father and do what he sent me to do. . . . Get up now! Let us leave this place.

CHAPTER 15

Jesus teaches union with himself

1, 2   "I AM the real vine, my Father is the vine-dresser. He removes any of my branches which are not bearing fruit and he prunes
3 every branch that does bear fruit to increase its yield. Now, you
4 have already been pruned by my words. You must go on growing in me and I will grow in you. For just as the branch cannot bear any fruit unless it shares the life of the vine, so you can produce
5 nothing unless you go on growing in me. I am the vine itself, you are the branches. It is the man who shares my life and whose life I share who proves fruitful. For the plain fact is that apart from

me you can do nothing at all. The man who does not share my **6**
life is like a branch that is broken off and withers away. He becomes just like the dry sticks that men pick up and use for fire-
wood. But if you live your life in me, and my words live in your **7**
hearts, you can ask for whatever you like and it will come true
for you. This is how my Father will be glorified—in your **8**
becoming fruitful and being my disciples.

"I have loved you just as the Father has loved me. You must **9**
go on living in my love. If you keep my commandments you **10**
will live in my love just as I have kept my Father's commandments and live in his love. I have told you this so that you can **11**
share my joy, and that your happiness may be complete. This is **12**
my commandment: that you love each other as I have loved you.
There is no greater love than this—that a man should lay down **13**
his life for his friends. You are my friends if you do what I tell **14**
you to do. I shall not call you servants any longer, for a servant **15**
does not share his master's confidence. No, I call you friends, now,
because I have told you everything that I have heard from the
Father.

"It is not that you have chosen me; but it is I who have chosen **16**
you. I have appointed you to go and bear fruit that will be lasting;
so that whatever you ask the Father in my name, he will give it
to you.

Jesus speaks of the world's hatred

"This I command you, love one another! If the world hates **17, 18**
you, you know that it hated me first. If you belonged to the **19**
world, the world would love its own. But because you do not
belong to the world and I have chosen you out of it, the world
will hate you. Do you remember what I said to you, 'The servant **20**
is not greater than his master'? If they have persecuted me, they
will persecute you as well, but if they have followed my teaching,
they will also follow yours. They will do all these things to you **21**
as my disciples because they do not know the one who sent me.
If I had not come and spoken to them, they would not have been **22**
guilty of sin, but now they have no excuse for their sin. The man **23**
who hates me, hates my Father as well. If I had not done among **24**
them things that no other man has ever done, they would not
have been guilty of sin, but as it is they have seen and they have
hated both me and my Father. Yet this only fulfils what is written **25**
in their Law—
They hated me without a cause.

26 But when the helper comes, that is, the Spirit of truth, who comes from the Father and whom I myself will send to you from the

27 Father, he will speak plainly about me. And you yourselves will also speak plainly about me for you have been with me from the first.

CHAPTER 16

Jesus speaks of the future without his bodily presence

1 "I AM telling you this now so that your faith in me may not be

2 shaken. They will excommunicate you from their synagogues. Yes, the time is coming when a man who kills you will think he

3 is thereby serving God! They will act like this because they have

4 never had any true knowledge of the Father or of me, but I have told you all this so that when the time comes for it to happen you may remember that I told you about it. I have not spoken like

5 this to you before, because I have been with you; but now the time has come for me to go away to the one who sent me. None

6 of you asks me, 'Where are you going?' That is because you are

7 so distressed at what I have told you. Yet I am telling you the simple truth when I assure you that it is a good thing for you that I should go away. For if I did not go away, the divine helper would not come to you. But if I go, then I will send him to you.

8 When he comes, he will convince the world of the meaning of

9 sin, of true goodness and of judgment. He will expose their sin

10 because they do not believe in me; he will reveal true goodness for I am going away to the Father and you will see me no longer;

11 and he will show them the meaning of judgment, for the spirit which rules this world will have been judged.

12 "I have much more to tell you but you cannot bear it now.

13 Yet when that one I have spoken to you about comes—the Spirit of truth—he will guide you into everything that is true. For he will not be speaking of his own accord but exactly as he hears,

14 and he will inform you about what is to come. He will bring glory to me for he will draw on my truth and reveal it to you.

15 Whatever the Father possesses is also mine; that is why I tell you that he will draw on my truth and will show it to you.

The disciples are puzzled: Jesus explains

16 "In a little while you will not see me any longer, and again, in a little while you will see me."

At this some of his disciples remarked to each other, "What is 17
this that he tells us now, 'A little while and you will not see me,
and again, in a little while you will see me' and 'for I am going
away to the Father'? What is this 'little while' that he talks about?" 18
they were saying. "We simply do not know what he means!"

Jesus knew that they wanted to ask him what he meant, so he 19
said to them, "Are you trying to find out from each other what I
meant when I said, 'In a little while you will not see me, and
again, in a little while you will see me'? I tell you truly that you 20
are going to be both sad and sorry while the world is glad. Yes,
you will be deeply distressed, but your pain will turn into joy.
When a woman gives birth to a child, she certainly knows pain 21
when her time comes. Yet as soon as she has given birth to the
child, she no longer remembers her agony for joy that a man has
been born into the world. Now you are going through pain, but 22
I shall see you again and your hearts will thrill with joy—the joy
that no one can take away from you—and on that day you will 23
not ask me any questions.

"I assure you that whatever you ask the Father he will give
you in my name. Up to now you have asked nothing in my name; 24
ask now, and you will receive, that your joy may be overflowing.

Jesus speaks further of the future

"I have been speaking to you in parables—but the time is 25
coming to give up parables and tell you plainly about the Father.
When that time comes, you will make your requests to him in 26
my name, for I need make no promise to plead to the Father for
you, for the Father himself loves you, because you have loved 27
me and have believed that I came from God. Yes, I did come 28
from the Father and I came into the world. Now I leave the
world behind and return to the Father."

"Now you are speaking plainly," cried the disciples, "and are 29
not using parables. Now we know that everything is known to 30
you—no more questions are needed. This makes us sure that you
did come from God."

"So you believe in me now?" replied Jesus. "The time is 31, 32
coming, indeed, it has already come, when you will be scattered,
every one of you going home and leaving me alone. Yet I am not
really alone, for the Father is with me. I have told you all this so 33
that you may find your peace in me. You will find trouble in the
world—but, never lose heart, I have conquered the world!"

CHAPTER 17

Jesus' prayer for his disciples—present and future

1 WHEN Jesus had said these words, he raised his eyes to Heaven and said, "Father, the hour has come. Glorify your Son now so 2 that he may bring glory to you, for you have given him authority over all men to give eternal life to all that you have given to him. 3 And this is eternal life, to know you, the only true God, and him whom you have sent—Jesus Christ.

4 "I have brought you honour upon earth, I have completed the 5 task which you gave me to do. Now, Father, honour me in your own presence with the glory that I knew with you before the 6 world was made. I have shown your self to the men whom you gave me from the world. They were your men and you gave 7 them to me, and they have accepted your word. Now they realise 8 that all that you have given me comes from you—and that every message that you gave me I have given them. They have accepted it all and have come to know in their hearts that I did come from you—they are convinced that you sent me.

9 "I am praying to you for them: I am not praying for the world 10 but for the men whom you gave me, for they are yours—everything that is mine is yours and yours mine—and they have done 11 me honour. Now I am no longer in the world, but they are in the world and I am returning to you. Holy Father, keep the men you gave me by your power that they may be one, as we are one. 12 As long as I was with them, I kept them by the power that you gave me; I guarded them, and not one of them was destroyed, except the son of destruction—that the scripture might come true.

13 "And now I come to you and I say these things in the world 14 that these men may find my joy completed in themselves. I have given them your word, and the world has hated them, for they 15 are no more sons of the world than I am. I am not praying that you will take them out of the world but that you will keep them 16 from the evil one. They are no more the sons of the world than 17 I am—make them holy by the truth; for your word is the truth. 18, 19 I have sent them to the world just as you sent me to the world and I consecrate myself for their sakes that they may be made holy by the truth.

20 "I am not praying only for these men but for all those who will 21 believe in me through their message, that they may all be one.

Just as you, Father, live in me and I live in you, I am asking that
they may live in us, that the world may believe that you did
send me. I have given them the honour that you gave me, that 22
they may be one, as we are one—I in them and you in me, that 23
they may grow complete into one, so that the world may realise
that you sent me and have loved them as you loved me. Father, 24
I want those whom you have given me to be with me where I
am; I want them to see that glory which you have made mine—
for you loved me before the world began. Father of goodness and 25
truth, the world has not known you, but I have known you and
these men now know that you have sent me. I have made your
self known to them and I will continue to do so that the love 26
which you have had for me may be in their hearts—and that I
may be there also."

CHAPTER 18

Jesus is arrested in the garden

WHEN Jesus had spoken these words, he went out with his 1
disciples across the Cedron valley to a place where there was a
garden, and they went into it together. Judas who betrayed him 2
knew the place, for Jesus often met his disciples there. So Judas 3
fetched the guard and the officers which the chief priests and
Pharisees had provided for him, and came to the place with
torches and lanterns and weapons. Jesus, fully realising all that 4
was going to happen to him, went forward and said to them,
"Who are you looking for?"

"Jesus of Nazareth," they answered. 5

"I am the man," said Jesus. (Judas who was betraying him was
standing there with the others.)

When he said to them, "I am the man", they retreated and fell 6
to the ground. So Jesus asked them again, "Who are you looking 7
for?"

And again they said, "Jesus of Nazareth."

"I have told you that I am the man," replied Jesus. "If I am 8
the man you are looking for, let these others go." (Thus fulfilling 9
his previous words, "I have not lost one of those whom you gave
me.")

At this, Simon Peter, who had a sword, drew it and slashed at 10
the High Priest's servant, cutting off his right ear. (The servant's
name was Malchus.) But Jesus said to Peter, "Put your sword 11

back into its sheath. Am I not to drink the cup the Father has given me?"

Peter follows Jesus, only to deny him

12 Then the guard, with their captain and the Jewish officers, took
13 hold of Jesus and tied his hands together, and led him off to
Annas first, for he was father-in-law to Caiaphas, who was High
14 Priest that year. Caiaphas was the man who advised the Jews,
"that it would be a good thing that one man should die for the
15 sake of the people". Behind Jesus followed Simon Peter, and one
other disciple who was known personally to the High Priest. He
16 went in with Jesus into the High Priest's courtyard, but Peter was
left standing at the door outside. So this other disciple, who was
acquainted with the High Priest, went out and spoke to the door-
17 keeper, and brought Peter inside. The young woman at the door
remarked to Peter, "Are you one of this man's disciples, too?"

"No, I am not," retorted Peter.

18 In the courtyard, the servants and officers stood around a charcoal fire which they had made, for it was cold. They were warming
themselves, and Peter stood there with them, keeping himself
warm.

19 Meanwhile the High Priest interrogated Jesus about his disciples and about his own teaching.

20 "I have always spoken quite openly to the world," replied
Jesus. "I have always taught in the synagogue or in the Temple
where all Jews meet together, and I have said nothing in secret.
21 Why do you question me? Why not question those who have
heard me about what I said to them? Obviously they are the ones
who know what I actually said."

22 As he said this, one of those present, an officer, slapped Jesus
with his open hand, remarking, "Is that the way for you to
answer the High Priest?"

23 "If I have said anything wrong," Jesus said to him, "you must
give evidence about it, but if what I said was true, why do you
strike me?"

24 Then Annas sent him, with his hands still tied, to the High
Priest Caiaphas.

Peter's denial

25 In the meantime Simon Peter was still standing, keeping himself warm. Some of them said to him, "Surely you too are one of
his disciples, aren't you?"

And he denied it and said, "No, I am not."

Then one of the High Priest's servants, a relation of the man 26
whose ear Peter had cut off, remarked, "Didn't I see you in the
garden with him?"

And again Peter denied it. And immediately the cock crew. 27

Jesus is taken before the Roman authority

Then they led Jesus from Caiaphas' presence into the palace. 28
It was now early morning and the Jews themselves did not go
into the palace, for fear that they would be contaminated and
would not be able to eat the Passover. So Pilate walked out to 29
them and said, "What is the charge that you are bringing against
this man?"

"If he were not an evil-doer, we should not have handed him 30
over to you," they replied.

To which Pilate retorted, "Then take him yourselves and judge 31
him according to your law."

"We are not allowed to put a man to death," replied the Jews
(thus fulfilling Christ's prophecy of the method of his own death). 32

So Pilate went back into the Palace and called Jesus to him. 33
"Are you the king of the Jews?" he asked.

"Are you asking this of your own accord," replied Jesus, "or 34
have other people spoken to you about me?"

"Do you think *I* am a Jew?" replied Pilate. "It's your people 35
and your chief priests who handed you over to me. What have you
done, anyway?"

"My kingdom is not founded in this world—if it were, my 36
servants would have fought to prevent my being handed over to
the Jews. But in fact my kingdom is not founded on all this!"

"So you are a king, are you?" returned Pilate. 37

"Indeed I am a king," Jesus replied; "the reason for my birth
and the reason for my coming into the world is to witness to the
truth. Every man who loves truth recognises my voice."

To which Pilate retorted, "What is 'truth'?" and went straight 38
out again to the Jews and said:

"I find nothing criminal about him at all. But I have an 39
arrangement with you to set one prisoner free at Passover time.
Do you wish me then to set free for you the 'king of the Jews'?"

At this, they shouted out again, "No, not this man, but 40
Barabbas!"

Barabbas was a bandit.

CHAPTER 19

Pilate's vain efforts to save Jesus

1, 2 THEN Pilate took Jesus and had him flogged, and the soldiers twisted thorn-twigs into a crown and put it on his head, threw
3 a purple robe around him and kept coming into his presence, saying, "Hail, king of the Jews!" And then they slapped him with their open hands.

4 Then Pilate went outside again and said to them, "Look, I bring him out before you here, to show that I find nothing criminal about him at all."

5 And at this Jesus came outside too, wearing the thorn crown and the purple robe.

"Look," said Pilate, "here's the man!"

6 The sight of him made the chief priests and Jewish officials shout at the top of their voices, "Crucify! Crucify!"

"You take him and crucify him," retorted Pilate. "He's no criminal as far as I can see!"

7 The Jews answered him, "We have a Law, and according to that Law, he must die, for he made himself out to be Son of God!"

8 When Pilate heard them say this, he became much more un-
9 easy, and returned to the palace again and spoke to Jesus, "Where *do* you come from?"

10 But Jesus gave him no reply. So Pilate said to him, "Won't you speak to me? Don't you realise that I have the power to set you free, and I have the power to have you crucified?"

11 "You have no power at all against me," replied Jesus, "except what was given to you from above. And for that reason the one who handed me over to you is even more guilty than you are."

12 From that moment, Pilate tried hard to set him free but the Jews were shouting, "If you set this man free, you are no friend of Caesar! Anyone who makes himself out to be a king is anti-Caesar!"

13 When Pilate heard this, he led Jesus outside and sat down upon the Judgment-seat in the place called the Pavement (in Hebrew,
14 Gabbatha). It was the preparation day of the Passover and it was now getting on towards midday. Pilate now said to the Jews, "Look, here's your king!"

15 At which they yelled, "Take him away, take him away, crucify him!"

"Am I to crucify your king?" Pilate asked them.

"Caesar is our king and no one else," replied the chief priests. And at this Pilate handed Jesus over to them for crucifixion.   *16*

The crucifixion

So they took Jesus and he went out carrying the cross himself,   *17* to a place called Skull Hill (in Hebrew, Golgotha). There they   *18* crucified him, and two others, one on either side of him with Jesus in the middle. Pilate had a placard written out and put on the   *19* cross, reading, JESUS OF NAZARETH, THE KING OF THE JEWS. This placard was read by many of the Jews because   *20* the place where Jesus was crucified was quite near Jerusalem, and it was written in Hebrew as well as in Latin and Greek. So the   *21* chief priests said to Pilate, "You should not write 'The King of the Jews', but 'This man said, I am King of the Jews.'"

To which Pilate retorted, "Indeed? What I have written, I have   *22* written."

When the soldiers had crucified Jesus, they divided his clothes   *23* between them, taking a quarter-share each. There remained his shirt, which was seamless—woven in one piece from the top to the bottom. So they said to each other, "Don't let us tear it; let's   *24* draw lots and see who gets it."

This happened to fulfil the scripture which says—

They parted my garments among them,
And upon my vesture did they cast lots.

Jesus provides for his mother from the cross

While the soldiers were doing this, Jesus' mother was standing   *25* near the cross with her sister, and with them Mary, the wife of Clopas, and Mary of Magdala. Jesus saw his mother and the   *26* disciple whom he loved standing by her side, and said to her, "Look, there is your son!" And then he said to the disciple, "And   *27* there is your mother!"

And from that time the disciple took Mary into his own home.

After this, Jesus realising that everything was now completed,   *28* said (fulfilling the saying of scripture), "I am thirsty."

There was a bowl of sour wine standing there. So they soaked   *29* a sponge in the wine, put it on a spear, and pushed it up towards his mouth. When Jesus had taken it, he cried, "It is finished!" his   *30* head fell forward, and he died.

The body of Jesus is removed

31 As it was the day of preparation for the Passover, the Jews wanted to avoid the bodies being left on the crosses over the Sabbath (for that was a particularly important Sabbath), and they requested Pilate to have the men's legs broken and the bodies
32 removed. So the soldiers went and broke the legs of the first man
33 and of the other who was crucified with Jesus. But when they came to him, they saw that he was dead already and they did
34 not break his legs. But one of the soldiers pierced his side with a
35 spear, and at once there was an outrush of blood and water. And the man who saw this is our witness: his evidence is true. (He is certain that he is speaking the truth, so that you may believe as
36 well.) For this happened to fulfil the scripture,

A bone of him shall not be broken.

37 And again another scripture says—

They shall look on him whom they pierced.

38 After it was all over, Joseph (who came from Arimathaea and was a disciple of Jesus, though secretly for fear of the Jews) requested Pilate that he might take away Jesus' body, and Pilate gave him permission. So he came and took his body down.
39 Nicodemus also, the man who had come to him at the beginning by night, arrived bringing a mixture of myrrh and aloes, weigh-
40 ing about a hundred pounds. So they took his body and wound it round with linen strips with the spices, according to the Jewish
41 custom of preparing a body for burial. In the place where he was crucified, there was a garden containing a new tomb in which
42 nobody had yet been laid. Because it was the preparation day and because the tomb was conveniently near, they laid Jesus in this tomb.

CHAPTER 20

The first day of the week: the risen Lord

1 BUT on the first day of the week, Mary of Magdala arrived at the tomb, very early in the morning, while it was still dark, and
2 noticed that the stone had been taken away from the tomb. At this she ran, found Simon Peter and the other disciple whom Jesus loved, and told them, "They have taken the Lord out of the tomb and we don't know where they have put him."
3 Peter and the other disciple set off at once for the tomb, the
4 two of them running together. The other disciple ran faster than

Peter and was the first to arrive at the tomb. He stooped and **5**
looked inside and noticed the linen cloths lying there but did not
go in himself. Hard on his heels came Simon Peter and went **6**
straight into the tomb. He noticed that the linen cloths were
lying there, and that the handkerchief, which had been round **7**
Jesus' head, was not lying with the linen cloths but was rolled
up by itself, a little way apart. Then the other disciple, who was **8**
the first to arrive at the tomb, came inside as well, saw what
had happened and believed. (They did not yet understand the **9**
scripture which said that he must rise from the dead.) So the disci- **10**
ples went back again to their homes.

But Mary stood just outside the tomb, and she was crying. And **11**
as she cried, she looked into the tomb and saw two angels in white **12**
who sat, one at the head and the other at the foot of the place
where the body of Jesus had lain.

The angels spoke to her, "Why are you crying?" they asked. **13**

"Because they have taken away my Lord, and I don't know
where they have put him!" she said.

Then she turned and noticed Jesus standing there, without **14**
realising that it was Jesus.

"Why are you crying?" said Jesus to her. "Who are you **15**
looking for?"

She, supposing that he was the gardener, said, "Oh, sir, if you
have carried him away, please tell me where you have put him
and I will take him away."

Jesus said to her, "Mary!" **16**

At this she turned right round and said to him, in Hebrew,
"Master!"

"No!" said Jesus, "do not hold me now. I have not yet gone **17**
up to the Father. Go and tell my brothers that I am going up to
my Father and your Father, to my God and your God."

And Mary of Magdala went off to the disciples, with the news, **18**
"I have seen the Lord!", and she told them what he had said to
her.

In the evening of that first day of the week, the disciples had **19**
met together with the doors locked for fear of the Jews. Jesus
came and stood right in the middle of them and said, "Peace be
with you!"

Then he showed them his hands and his side, and when they **20**
saw the Lord the disciples were overjoyed.

Jesus said to them again, "Yes, peace be with you! Just as the **21**
Father sent me, so I am now going to send you."

22
23 And then he breathed upon them and said, "Receive holy spirit.* If you forgive any men's sins, they are forgiven, and if you hold them unforgiven, they are unforgiven."

The risen Jesus and Thomas

24
25 But one of the twelve, Thomas (called the Twin), was not with them when Jesus came. The other disciples kept on telling him, "We have seen the Lord", but he replied, "Unless I see in his own hands the mark of the nails, and put my finger where the nails were, and put my hand into his side, I will never believe!"

26 Just over a week later, the disciples were indoors again and Thomas was with them. The doors were shut, but Jesus came and stood in the middle of them and said, "Peace be with you!"

27 Then he said to Thomas, "Put your finger here—look, here are my hands. Take your hand and put it in my side. You must not doubt, but believe."

28 "My Lord and my God!" cried Thomas.

29 "Is it because you have seen me that you believe?" Jesus said to him. "Happy are those who have never seen me and yet have believed!"

30
31 Jesus gave a great many other signs in the presence of his disciples which are not recorded in this book. But these have been written so that you may believe that Jesus is Christ, the Son of God, and that in that faith you may have life as his disciples.

CHAPTER 21

The risen Jesus and Peter

1
2 LATER on, Jesus showed himself again to his disciples on the shore of Lake Tiberias, and he did it in this way. Simon Peter, Thomas (called the Twin), Nathanael from Cana of Galilee, the

3 sons of Zebedee and two other disciples were together, when Simon Peter said,

"I'm going fishing."

"All right," they replied, "we'll go with you."

So they went out and got into the boat and during the night
4 caught nothing at all. But just as dawn began to break, Jesus stood

* Lit. "receive holy spirit". Historically the Holy Spirit was not given until Pentecost.

there on the beach, although the disciples had no idea that it was Jesus.

"Have you caught anything, lads?" Jesus called out to them. 5
"No," they replied.

"Throw the net on the right side of the boat," said Jesus, "and 6
you'll have a catch."

So they threw out the net and found that they were now not strong enough to pull it in because it was so full of fish! At this, 7
the disciple that Jesus loved said to Peter, "It is the Lord!"

Hearing this, Peter slipped on his clothes, for he had been naked, and plunged into the sea. The other disciples followed in 8
the boat, for they were only about a hundred yards from the shore, dragging in the net full of fish. When they had landed, 9
they saw that a charcoal fire was burning, with a fish placed on it, and some bread. Jesus said to them, "Bring me some of the fish 10
you've just caught."

So Simon Peter got into the boat and hauled the net ashore full 11
of large fish, one hundred and fifty-three altogether. But in spite of the large number the net was not torn.

Then Jesus said to them, "Come and have your breakfast." 12

None of the disciples dared to ask him who he was; they knew it was the Lord.

Jesus went and took the bread and gave it to them and gave 13
them all fish as well. This is already the third time that Jesus 14
showed himself to his disciples after his resurrection from the dead.

When they had finished breakfast Jesus said to Simon Peter, 15
"Simon, son of John, do you love me more than these others?"

"Yes, Lord," he replied, "you know that I am your friend."

"Then feed my lambs," returned Jesus. Then he said for the 16
second time,

"Simon, son of John, do you love me?"

"Yes, Lord," returned Peter. "You know that I am ·your friend."

"Then care for my sheep," replied Jesus. Then for the third 17
time, Jesus spoke to him and said,

"Simon, son of John, *are* you my friend?"

Peter was deeply hurt because Jesus' third question to him was "Are you my friend?", and he said, "Lord, you know everything. You know that I am your friend!"

"Then feed my sheep," Jesus said to him. "I tell you truly, 18
Peter, that when you were younger, you used to dress yourself

and go where you liked, but when you are an old man, you are going to stretch out your hands and someone else will dress you and take you where you do not want to go."

19 (He said this to show the kind of death by which Peter was going to honour God.)

Then Jesus said to him, "You must follow me."

20 Then Peter turned round and noticed the disciple whom Jesus loved following behind them. (He was the one who had his head on Jesus' shoulder at supper and had asked, "Lord, who is the
21 one who is going to betray you?") So he said, "Yes, Lord, but what about him?"

22 "If it is my wish," returned Jesus, "for him to stay until I come, is that your business, Peter? You must follow me."

23 This gave rise to the saying among the brothers that this disciple would not die. Yet, of course, Jesus did not say, "He will not die", but simply, "If it is my wish for him to stay until I come, is that your business?"

All the above was written by an eye-witness

24 Now it is this same disciple who is hereby giving his testimony to these things and has written them down. We know that his
25 witness is reliable. Of course, there are many other things which Jesus did, and I suppose that if each one were written down in detail, there would not be room in the whole world for all the books that would have to be written.

PALESTINE
in the time of Christ

Sidon

ABILENE

S Y R I A

Tyre

Cæsarea
Philippi

ITURÆA

TRACHONITIS

Chorazin
Capernaum
Bethsaida

G A L I L E E

Magdala
LAKE
OF
GALILEE
(Gennesareth)
Gergesa

Cana
Tiberias

Nazareth

Dalmanutha
Gadara

Nain

DECAPOLIS
(TEN TOWNS)

Aenon

SAMARIA

Sychar

R. Jordan

P E R Æ A

Arimathæa

J U D Æ A

Jericho
Rama
Bethphage
Bethany

Emmaus

Jerusalem

Bethlehem

I D U M Æ A

DEAD
SEA

Miles

0   10   20   30   40

THE YOUNG CHURCH IN ACTION

The Acts of the Apostles

The above, which is the conventional title of this remarkable book, is something of a mistranslation. The Greek title, Praxeis Apostolōn, *has no definite articles and could be translated more accurately "Acts of Apostles", or, quite fairly, "Some Acts of Some Apostles". The author, who is unquestionably Luke, makes no attempt to give an exhaustive history of the early days of the Church—much as we may wish he had done so—but he does record with vividness and accuracy some* actions *of some* Apostles.

The book is characterised by the same easy-flowing Greek as the third Gospel, its vocabulary containing some fifty words common to these two works, but not found elsewhere in the New Testament. As in his Gospel Luke shows the same deep interest in women, the same sympathy for the sick and poor, and the same concern for the Gentiles. There is also the same doctor's precision in the use of medical language.

Luke's sources of information were probably first-class. The deacon Philip was still living at Caesarea during the two years of Paul's captivity at Rome with which this book closes, and Luke would have been able to obtain much early information from him. There would also be many still living who were present on the day of Pentecost and who would have supplied information about those early days. In the latter part of the book Luke is obviously making use of his own personal diaries. The first person plural is used quite naturally (16, 10–17; 20, 5 to 21, 18; 27, 1 to 28, 16) and the narrative gains in dramatic power through the reader's sudden realisation that the author was actually present at the time. Indeed, Luke's close association with Paul, an association which meant sharing a good deal of the latter's dangers and fatigues, is not the least of Luke's qualifications as an author of a book such as this. It is rash to surmise, but humanly speaking, the Gospel for all men might easily have been confined to Jews and Gentile proselytes if it had not been for the vision, courage and tenacity of Paul.

The period covered by this book is roughly from 30 to 63, i.e. from the Ascension of Christ to Paul's imprisonment at Rome. It is a fascinating guess, though no more than a guess, that Luke intended to write a third work, for the present book ends on a triumphant but rather unfinished note. Possibly Luke was never able to complete the story, possibly the work never got beyond the notes of events which he almost certainly took, possibly the work is irretrievably lost. Or, of course, the existence of such a work may be a wild guess with no foundation at all. Nevertheless readers of this book may feel, as I do, not only a hunger for more, but a sense that the author had not fully finished the history he set out to write.

Luke is a careful historian and his geographical as well as his historical accuracy should be noted. He has a sound knowledge of Roman government and procedure. Although it cannot be proved, there is at least a likelihood that he was a Greek-speaking Gentile, converted under the ministry of Paul and Barnabas at Antioch.

It is most difficult to assign a date to this work. Some incline to the belief that it was written shortly after the closing date mentioned in the book, which would put it as early as 65. Others are convinced that it was written after the fall of Jerusalem (70), and others again that Luke must have had access to Josephus' "Jewish Antiquities", which did not appear till 94. I myself am inclined to place the date not very long after Paul's two-year imprisonment, possibly in 65 or 66.

CHAPTER 1

Introduction

MY DEAR THEOPHILUS,   *1*
In my first book I gave you some account of all that Jesus began to do and teach until the time of his ascension. Before he ascended   *2*
he gave his instructions, through the Holy Spirit, to the special messengers of his choice. For after his suffering he showed himself   *3*
alive to them in many convincing ways, and appeared to them repeatedly over a period of forty days talking with them about the affairs of the kingdom of God.

Jesus' parting words before his ascension

On one occasion, while he was eating a meal with them, he   *4*
emphasised that they were not to leave Jerusalem, but to wait for the Father's promise.

"You have already heard me speak about this," he said, "for   *5*

John used to baptise with water, but before many days are passed you will be baptised with the Holy Spirit."

6   This naturally brought them all together, and they asked him, "Lord, is this the time when you are going to restore the kingdom to Israel?"

7   To this he replied,

"You cannot know times and dates which have been fixed by 8 the Father's sole authority. But you are to be given power when the Holy Spirit has come to you. You will be witnesses to me, not only in Jerusalem, not only throughout Judaea, not only in Samaria, but to the very ends of the earth!"

9   When he had said these words he was lifted up before their 10 eyes till a cloud hid him from their sight. While they were still gazing up into the sky as he went, suddenly two men dressed in 11 white stood beside them and said,

"Men of Galilee, why are you standing here looking up into the sky? This very Jesus who has been taken up from you into Heaven will come back in just the same way as you have seen him go."

12   At this they returned to Jerusalem from the Mount of Olives 13 which is near the city, only a sabbath day's journey away. On entering Jerusalem they went straight to the upstairs room where they had been staying. There were Peter, John, James, Andrew, Philip, Thomas, Bartholomew, Matthew, James the son of 14 Alphaeus, Simon the Patriot, and Judas the son of James. By common consent all these men, together with the women who had followed Jesus, Mary his mother, as well as his brothers, devoted themselves to prayer.

Judas' place is filled

15   It was during this period that Peter stood up among the brothers —there were about a hundred and twenty present at the time— and said,

16   "My brothers, the prophecy of scripture given through the Holy Spirit by the lips of David concerning Judas was bound to come true. He was the man who acted as guide to those who 17 arrested Jesus, though he was one of our number and he had a share in this ministry of ours."

18   (This man had bought a piece of land with the proceeds of his 19 infamy, but his body swelled up and his intestines burst. This fact became well known to all the residents of Jerusalem so that the

piece of land came to be called in their language Akeldama, which means "the field of blood".)

"Now it is written in the book of psalms of such a man: 20
Let his habitation be made desolate,
And let no man dwell therein:
and
His office let another take.

"It becomes necessary then that whoever joins us must be some-   21
one who has been in our company during the whole time that
the Lord Jesus lived his life with us, from the beginning when   22
John baptised him until the day when he was taken up from us.
This man must be an eye-witness with us to the resurrection of
Jesus."

Two men were put forward, Joseph called Barsabas who was   23
also called Justus, and Matthias. Then they prayed,   24

"Thou Lord, who knowest the hearts of all men, show us which
of these two thou hast chosen to accept that ministry of an apostle   25
which Judas forfeited to go where he belonged."

Then they drew lots for these men, and the lot fell to Matthias,   26
and thereafter he was considered equally an apostle with the
eleven.

CHAPTER 2

The first Pentecost for the young Church

THEN when the actual day of Pentecost came they were all   1
assembled together. Suddenly there was a sound from heaven like   2
the rushing of a violent wind, and it filled the whole house where
they were seated. Before their eyes appeared tongues like flames,   3
which separated off and settled above the head of each one of
them. They were all filled with the Holy Spirit and began to   4
speak in different languages as the Spirit gave them power to
proclaim his message.

The Church's first impact on devout Jews

Now there were staying in Jerusalem Jews of deep faith from   5
every nation of the world. When they heard this sound a crowd   6
quickly collected and were completely bewildered because each
one of them heard these men speaking in his own language. They   7
were absolutely amazed and said in their astonishment,

"Listen, surely all these speakers are Galileans ? Then how does   8

233

it happen that every single one of us can hear the particular
9   language he has known from a child? There are Parthians, Medes
and Elamites; there are men whose homes are in Mesopotamia,
10   in Judaea and Cappadocia, Pontus, Asia, Phrygia, Pamphylia,
Egypt, and the parts of Africa near Cyrene, as well as visitors from
11   Rome! There are Jews and proselytes, men from Crete and men
from Arabia, yet we can all hear these men speaking of the
magnificence of God in our native language."

12   Everyone was utterly amazed and did not know what to make
of it. Indeed they kept saying to each other,
    "What on earth can this mean?"

13   But there were others who laughed mockingly and said,
    "These fellows have drunk too much new wine!"

Peter explains the fulfilment of God's promise

14   Then Peter, with the eleven standing by him, raised his voice
and addressed them:
    "Fellow-Jews, and all who are living now in Jerusalem, listen
carefully to what I say while I explain to you what has happened!
15   These men are not drunk as you suppose—it is after all only nine
16   o'clock in the morning of this great feast day. No, this is something
which was predicted by the prophet Joel,

17   And it shall be in the last days, saith God,
     I will pour forth of my Spirit upon all flesh:
     And your sons and your daughters shall prophesy,
     And your young men shall see visions,
     And your old men shall dream dreams:
18   Yea and on my servants and on my handmaidens in those
       days
     Will I pour forth of my Spirit; and they shall prophesy.
19   And I will shew wonders in the heaven above,
     And signs on the earth beneath;
     Blood, and fire, and vapour of smoke:
20   The sun shall be turned into darkness,
     And the moon into blood,
     Before the day of the Lord come,
     That great and notable day:
21   And it shall be, that whosoever shall call on the name of the
      Lord shall be saved.
22   "Men of Israel, I beg you to listen to my words. Jesus of Nazareth was a man proved to you by God himself through the works

234

of power, the miracles and the signs which God showed through
him here amongst you—as you very well know. This man, who 23
was put into your power by the predetermined plan and foreknowledge of God, you nailed up and murdered, and you used
for your purpose men without the Law! But God would not 24
allow the bitter pains of death to touch him. He raised him to life
again—and indeed there was nothing by which death could hold
such a man. When David speaks about him he says, 25

> I beheld the Lord always before my face;
> For he is on my right hand, that I should not be moved;
> Therefore my heart was glad, and my tongue rejoiced; 26
> Moreover my flesh also shall dwell in hope:
> Because thou wilt not leave my soul in Hades, 27
> Neither wilt thou give thy holy one to see corruption.
> Thou madest known unto me the ways of life; 28
> Thou shalt make me full of gladness with thy countenance.

"Men and brother-Jews, I can surely speak freely to you about 29
the patriarch David. There is no doubt that he died and was
buried, and his grave is here among us to this day. But while he 30
was alive he was a prophet. He knew that God had given him a
most solemn promise that he would place one of his descendants
upon his throne. He foresaw the resurrection of Christ, and it 31
is this of which he is speaking. Christ was not deserted in death
and his body was never destroyed. 'Christ is the man Jesus, whom 32
God raised up—a fact of which all of us are eye-witnesses!' He has 33
been raised to the right hand of God; he has received from the
Father and poured out upon us the promised Holy Spirit—*that* is
what you now see and hear! David never ascended to Heaven, but 34
he certainly said,

> The Lord said unto my *Lord*,
> Sit thou on my right hand,
> Till I make thine enemies the footstool of thy feet. 35

"Now therefore the whole nation of Israel must know beyond 36
the shadow of a doubt that this Jesus, whom you crucified, God
has declared to be both Lord and Christ."

The reaction to Peter's speech

When they heard this they were cut to the quick, and they cried 37
to Peter and the other apostles,

"Men and fellow-Jews, what shall we do now?"

Peter told them, 38

"You must repent and every one of you must be baptised in the name of Jesus Christ, so that you may have your sins forgiven
39 and receive the gift of the Holy Spirit. For this great promise is for you and your children—yes, and for all who are far away, for as many as the Lord our God shall call to himself!"

40 Peter said much more than this as he gave his testimony and implored them, saying,

"Save yourselves from this perverted generation!"

The first large-scale conversion

41 Then those who welcomed his message were baptised, and on that day alone about three thousand souls were added to the
42 number of disciples. They continued steadily learning the teaching of the apostles, and joined in their fellowship, in the breaking of bread, and in prayer.

43 Everyone felt a deep sense of awe, while many miracles and
44 signs took place through the apostles. All the believers shared
45 everything in common; they sold their possessions and goods and divided the proceeds among the fellowship according to individual
46 need. Day after day they met by common consent in the Temple; they broke bread together in their homes, sharing meals with
47 simple joy. They praised God continually and all the people respected them. Every day the Lord added to their number those who were finding salvation.

CHAPTER 3

A public miracle and its explanation

1 ONE afternoon Peter and John were on their way to the Temple
2 for the three o'clock hour of prayer. A man who had been lame from birth was being carried along in the crowd, for it was the daily practice to put him down at what was known as the Beautiful Gate of the Temple, so that he could beg from the people as
3 they went in. As this man saw Peter and John just about to enter
4 he asked them to give him something. Peter looked intently at the man and so did John. Then Peter said,

"Look straight at us!"

5 The man looked at them expectantly, hoping that they would give him something.

6 "If you are expecting silver or gold," Peter said to him, "I

have neither, but what I have I will certainly give you. In the name of Jesus Christ of Nazareth, *walk!*"

Then he took him by the right hand and helped him up. At 7 once his feet and ankle bones were strengthened, and he positively 8 jumped to his feet, stood, and then walked. Then he went with them into the Temple, where he walked about, leaping and thanking God. Everyone noticed him as he walked and praised God 9 and recognised him as the same beggar who used to sit at the 10 Beautiful Gate, and they were all overcome with wonder and sheer astonishment at what had happened to him. Then while 11 the man himself still clung to Peter and John all the people in their excitement ran together and crowded round them in Solomon's Porch. When Peter saw this he spoke to the crowd. 12

"Men of Israel, why are you so surprised at this, and why are you staring at us as though we had made this man walk through some power or piety of our own? It is the God of Abraham and 13 Isaac and Jacob, the God of our fathers, who has done this thing to honour his servant Jesus—the man whom you betrayed and denied in the presence of Pilate, even when he had decided to let him go. But you disowned the holy and righteous one, and 14 begged to be granted instead a man who was a murderer! You 15 killed the prince of life, but God raised him from the dead—a fact of which we are eye-witnesses. It is the name of this same 16 Jesus, it is faith in that name, which has cured this man whom you see and recognise. Yes, it was faith in Christ which gave this man perfect health and strength in full view of you all.

Peter explains ancient prophecy

"Now of course I know, my brothers, that you had no idea 17 what you were doing any more than your leaders had. But God 18 had foretold through all his prophets that his Christ must suffer and this was how his words came true. Now you must repent 19 and turn to God so that your sins may be wiped out, that time after time your souls may know the refreshment that comes from the presence of God. Then he will send you Jesus, your long- 20 heralded Christ, although for the time he must remain in Heaven 21 until that universal restoration of which God spoke in ancient times through all his holy prophets. For Moses said, 22

A prophet shall the Lord God raise up unto you from among your brethren, like unto me; to him shall ye hearken in all things whatsoever he shall speak unto you. And it shall be 23 that every soul, which shall not hearken to that prophet, shall be utterly destroyed from among the people.

24 Indeed, all the prophets from Samuel onwards who have spoken
25 at all have foretold these days. You are the sons of the prophets and heirs of the agreement which God made with our fathers when he said to Abraham, 'Through your children shall all the
26 families of the earth be blessed.' It was to you first that God sent his servant after he had raised him up, to bring you great blessing by turning every one of you away from his evil ways."

CHAPTER 4

The first clash with Jewish authorities

1 WHILE they were still talking to the people the priests, the captain of the Temple guard and the Sadducees moved towards
2 them, thoroughly incensed that they should be teaching the people and should assure them that the resurrection of the dead
3 had been proved through the rising of Jesus. So they arrested them and, since it was now evening, kept them in custody until
4 the next day. Nevertheless, many of those who had heard what they said believed, and the number of men alone rose to about five thousand.

Peter's boldness at formal questioning

5 Next day the leading members of the council, the elders and
6 scribes, met in Jerusalem with Annas the High Priest, Caiaphas,
7 John, Alexander, and the whole of the High Priest's family. They had the apostles brought in to stand before them and they asked them formally,

"By what power and in whose name have you done this thing?"

8 At this Peter, filled with the Holy Spirit, spoke to them,
9 "Leaders of the people and elders, if we are being called in question today over the matter of a kindness done to a helpless
10 man and as to how he was healed, it is high time that all of you and the whole people of Israel knew that it was done in the name of Jesus Christ of Nazareth! He is the one whom you crucified but whom God raised from the dead, and it is by his power that
11 this man at our side stands in your presence perfectly well. He is the 'stone which you builders rejected, which has now become

the head of the corner'. In no one else can salvation be found. For **12** in all the world no other name has been given to men but this, and it is by this name that we must be saved!"

The embarrassment of the authorities

When they saw the complete assurance of Peter and John, who **13** were obviously uneducated and untrained men, they were staggered. They recognised them as men who had been with Jesus, yet since they could see the man who had been cured standing **14** beside them, they could find no effective reply. All they could **15** do was to order them out of the Sanhedrin and hold a conference among themselves.

"What are we going to do with these men?" they said to each **16** other. "It is evident to everyone living in Jerusalem that an extraordinary miracle has taken place through them, and that is something we cannot deny. Nevertheless, to prevent such a thing **17** spreading further among the people, let us warn them that if they say anything more to anyone in this name it will be at their peril."

So they called them in and ordered them bluntly not to speak **18** or teach a single further word about the name of Jesus. But **19** Peter and John gave them this reply:

"Whether it is right in the eyes of God for us to listen to what you say rather than to what he says, you must decide; for we can- **20** not help speaking about what we have actually seen and heard!"

After further threats they let them go. They could not think **21** of any way of punishing them because of the attitude of the people. Everybody was thanking God for what had happened— that this miracle of healing had taken place in a man who was **22** more than forty years old.

The united prayer of the young Church—

After their release the apostles went back to their friends and **23** reported to them what the chief priests and elders had said to them. When they heard it they raised their voices to God in **24** united prayer and said,

"Almighty Lord, thou art the one who hast made the heaven and the earth, the sea and all that is in them. It was thou who didst **25** speak by the Holy Spirit through the lips of our forefather David thy servant in the words:

Why did the gentiles rage,
And the peoples imagine vain things?
26 The kings of the earth set themselves in array,
And the rulers were gathered together,
Against the Lord, and against his anointed:
27 For indeed in this city the rulers have gathered together against thy holy servant, Jesus, thine anointed—yes, Herod and Pontius Pilate, the gentiles and the peoples of Israel have gathered together
28 to carry out what thine hand and will had planned to happen.
29 And now, O Lord, observe their threats and give thy servants
30 courage to speak thy word fearlessly, while thou dost stretch out thine hand to heal, and cause signs and wonders to be performed in the name of thy holy servant Jesus."
31 When they had prayed their meeting-place was shaken; they were all filled with the Holy Spirit and spoke the Word of God fearlessly.

—and their close fellowship

32 Among the large number who had become believers there was complete agreement of heart and soul. Not one of them claimed any of his possessions as his own but everything was common
33 property. The apostles continued to give their witness to the resurrection of the Lord Jesus with great force, and a wonderful
34 spirit of generosity pervaded the whole fellowship. Indeed, there was not a single person in need among them. For those who owned land or property would sell them and bring the proceeds of the
35 sales and place them at the apostles' feet. They would distribute to each one according to his need.

Generosity and covetousness

36 It was at this time that Barnabas (the name, meaning son of comfort, given by the apostles to Joseph, a Levite from Cyprus)
37 sold his farm and put the proceeds at the apostles' disposal.

CHAPTER 5

1 BUT there was a man named Ananias who, with his wife Sapphira,
2 had sold a piece of property, but with her full knowledge, reserved

part of the price for himself. He brought the remainder to put at
the apostles' disposal. But Peter said to him,   3
  "Ananias, why has Satan so filled your mind that you could
cheat the Holy Spirit and keep back for yourself part of the price
of the land? Before the land was sold it was yours, and after the   4
sale the disposal of the price you received was entirely in your
hands, wasn't it? Then whatever made you think of such a thing
as this? You have not lied to men, but to God!"
  As soon as Ananias heard these words he collapsed and died.   5
All who were within earshot were appalled at this incident. The   6
young men got to their feet and after wrapping up his body
carried him out and buried him.
  About three hours later it happened that his wife came in not   7
knowing what had taken place. Peter spoke directly to her,   8
  "Tell me, did you sell your land for so much?"
  "Yes," she replied, "that was it."
  Then Peter said to her,   9
  "How could you two have agreed to put the Spirit of the
Lord to such a test? Listen, you can hear the footsteps of the men
who have just buried your husband coming back through the
door, and they will carry you out as well!"
  Immediately she collapsed at Peter's feet and died. When the 10
young men came into the room they found her a dead woman,
and they carried her out and buried her by the side of her husband.
At this happening a deep sense of awe swept over the whole   11
Church and indeed over all those who heard about it.

The young Church takes its stand in the Temple—

  By common consent they all used to meet now in Solomon's   12
Porch. But as far as the others were concerned no one dared to   13
associate with them, even though their general popularity was
very great. Yet more and more believers in the Lord joined them, 14
both men and women in really large numbers.

—and miraculous power radiates from it

  *Many signs and wonders were now happening among the   (12)
people through the apostles' ministry. In consequence people   15
would bring out their sick into the streets and lay them down on

  * Transposing the first part of v. 12 to the beginning of v. 15,
which makes better sense.

16 stretchers or beds, so that as Peter came by at least his shadow might fall upon some of them. In addition a large crowd collected from the cities round about Jerusalem, bringing with them their sick and all those who were suffering from evil spirits. And they were all cured.

Furious opposition reduced to impotence

17 All this roused the High Priest and his allies the Sadducean
18 party, and in a fury of jealousy they had the apostles arrested and
19 put into the common jail. But during the night an angel of the Lord opened the prison doors and led them out, saying,

20 "Go and stand and speak in the Temple. Tell the people all about this new life!"

21 After receiving these instructions they entered the Temple about daybreak, and began to teach. When the High Priest arrived he and his supporters summoned the Sanhedrin and indeed the whole senate of the people of Israel. Then he sent to the jail to
22 have the apostles brought in. But when the officers arrived at the
23 prison they could not find them there. They came back and reported,

"We found the prison securely locked and the guard standing on duty at the doors, but when we opened up we found no one inside."

24 When the captain of the Temple guard and the chief priests heard this report they were completely mystified at the apostles' disappearance and wondered what further developments there
25 would be. However, someone arrived and reported to them,

"Why, the men you put in jail are standing in the Temple teaching the people!"

26 Then the captain went out with his men and fetched them. They dared not use any violence however, for the people might
27 have stoned them. So they brought them in and made them stand before the Sanhedrin. The High Priest called for an explanation.

28 "We gave you the strictest possible orders," he said to them, "not to give any teaching in this name. And look what has happened—you have filled Jerusalem with your teaching, and what is more you are determined to fasten the guilt of that man's death upon us!"

The apostles speak the unpalatable truth

29 Then Peter and the apostles answered him,

"It is our duty to obey the orders of God rather than the orders

of men. It was the God of our fathers who raised up Jesus, whom *30*
you murdered by hanging him on a cross of wood. God has *31*
raised this man to his own right hand as prince and saviour, to
bring repentance and the forgiveness of sins to Israel. What is *32*
more, we are witnesses to these matters, and so is the Holy Spirit
which God gives to those who obey his commands."

Calm counsel temporarily prevails

When the members of the council heard these words they were *33*
so furious that they wanted to kill them. But one man stood up *34*
in the assembly, a Pharisee by the name of Gamaliel, a teacher of
the Law who was held in great respect by the people, and gave
orders for the apostles to be taken outside for a few minutes.
Then he addressed the assembly: *35*

"Men of Israel, be very careful of what action you intend to
take against these men! Remember that some time ago a man *36*
called Theudas made himself conspicuous by claiming to be someone or other, and he had a following of four hundred men. He
was killed, all his followers were dispersed, and the movement
came to nothing. Then later, in the days of the census, that man *37*
Judas from Galilee appeared and enticed many of the people to
follow him. But he too died and his whole following melted
away. My advice to you now therefore is to let these men alone; *38*
leave them to themselves. For if this teaching or movement is
merely human it will collapse of its own accord. But if it should *39*
be from God you cannot defeat them, and you might actually
find yourselves to be fighting against God!"

They accepted his advice and called in the apostles. They had *40*
them beaten and after commanding them not to speak in the name
of Jesus they let them go. So the apostles went out from the *41*
presence of the Sanhedrin full of joy that they had been considered
worthy to bear humiliation for the sake of the name. Then day *42*
after day in the Temple and in people's houses they continued to
teach unceasingly and to proclaim the good news of Jesus Christ.

CHAPTER 6

The first deacons are chosen

ABOUT this time, when the number of disciples was continually *1*
increasing, the Greeks complained that in the daily distribution of

food the Hebrew widows were being given preferential treatment.
2 The twelve summoned the whole body of the disciples together, and said,

3 "It is not right that we should have to neglect preaching the Word of God in order to look after the accounts. You, our brothers, must look round and pick out from your number seven men of good reputation who are both practical and spiritually-
4 minded and we will put them in charge of this matter. Then we shall devote ourselves whole-heartedly to prayer and the ministry of the Word."

5 This brief speech met with unanimous approval and they chose Stephen, a man full of faith and the Holy Spirit, Philip, Prochorus, Nicanor, Timon, Parmenas, and Nicolas of Antioch who had
6 previously been a convert to the Jewish faith. They brought these men before the apostles, and they, after prayer, laid their hands upon them.

7 So the Word of God gained more and more ground. The number of disciples in Jerusalem very greatly increased, while a considerable proportion of the priesthood accepted the faith.

The attack on the new deacon, Stephen

8 Stephen, full of grace and spiritual power, continued to per-
9 form miracles and remarkable signs among the people. However, members of a Jewish synagogue known as the Libertines, together with some from the synagogues of Cyrene and Alexandria, as well as some men from Cilicia and Asia, tried debating with Stephen,
10 but found themselves quite unable to stand up against either his
11 practical wisdom or the spiritual force with which he spoke. In desperation they bribed men to allege, "We have heard this man making blasphemous statements against Moses and against God."
12 At the same time they worked upon the feelings of the people, the elders and the scribes. Then they suddenly confronted Stephen,
13 seized him and marched him off before the Sanhedrin. There they brought forward false witnesses to say, "This man's speeches are
14 one long attack against this holy place and the Law. We have heard him say that Jesus of Nazareth will destroy this place and
15 change the customs which Moses handed down to us." All who sat there in the Sanhedrin looked intently at Stephen, and as they looked his face appeared to them like the face of an angel.

244

CHAPTER 7

Stephen makes his defence from Israel's history:

i. THE TIME OF ABRAHAM

THEN the High Priest said,   *1*
"Is this statement true?"
And Stephen answered,   *2*
"My brothers and my fathers, listen to me. Our glorious God appeared to our forefather Abraham while he was in Mesopotamia before he ever came to live in Haran, and said to him, 'Get *3* thee out of thy land and from thy kindred, and come into a land which I shall shew thee.' That was how he came to leave the land *4* of the Chaldeans and settle in Haran. And it was from there after his father's death that God moved him into this very land where you are living today. Yet God gave him no part of it as an inheri- *5* tance, not a foot that he could call his own, and yet promised that it should eventually belong to him and his descendants—even though at the time he had no descendant at all. And this is the *6* way in which God spoke to him: he told him that his descendants should live as strangers in a foreign land where they would become slaves and be ill-treated for four hundred years, 'And the nation *7* to which they shall be in bondage will I judge, said God: and after that shall they come forth, and serve me in this place.'

"Further, he gave him the agreement of circumcision, so that *8* when Abraham became the father of Isaac he circumcised him on the eighth day.

Stephen's defence:

ii. THE PATRIARCHS

"Isaac became the father of Jacob, and Jacob the father of the twelve patriarchs. Then the patriarchs in their jealousy of Joseph *9* sold him as a slave into Egypt. But God was with him and saved *10* him from all his troubles and gave him favour and wisdom in the eyes of Pharaoh the king of Egypt. Pharaoh made him governor of Egypt and put him in charge of his own entire household.

"Then came the famine over all the land of Egypt and Canaan *11* which caused great suffering, and our forefathers could find no

12 food. But when Jacob heard that there was corn in Egypt he
sent our forefathers out of their own country for the first time.
13 It was on their second visit that Joseph was recognised by his
14 brothers, and his ancestry became plain to Pharaoh. Then Joseph
sent and invited to come and live with him his father and all his
15 kinsmen, seventy-five people in all. So Jacob came down to
16 Egypt and both he and our fathers ended their days there. After
their death they were carried back into Shechem and laid in the
tomb which Abraham had bought with silver from the sons of
Hamor in Shechem.

17 "But as the time drew near for the fulfilment of the promise
which God had made to Abraham, our people grew more and
18 more numerous in Egypt. Finally another king came to the
19 Egyptian throne who knew nothing of Joseph. This man cleverly
victimised our race. He treated our forefathers abominably, forcing them to expose their infant children so that the race should
die out.

Stephen's defence:

iii. GOD'S PROVIDENCE AND MOSES

20 "It was at this very time that Moses was born. He was a child
of remarkable beauty, and for three months he was brought up
21 in his father's house, and then when the time came for him to
be abandoned Pharaoh's daughter adopted him and brought him
22 up as her own son. So Moses was trained in all the wisdom of the
Egyptians, and became not only an excellent speaker but a man
of action as well.

Moses' first abortive attempt at rescue

23 "Now when he was turned forty the thought came into his
mind that he should go and visit his own brothers, the sons of
24 Israel. He saw one of them being unjustly treated, went to the
rescue and paid rough justice for the man who had been ill-
25 treated by striking down the Egyptian. He fully imagined that
his brothers would understand that God was using him to rescue
26 them. But they did not understand. Indeed, on the very next day
he came upon two of them who were quarrelling and urged them
to make peace, saying, 'Men, you are brothers. What good can
27 come from your injuring each other?' But the man who was

wronging his neighbour pushed Moses aside, saying, 'Who made you a ruler and judge over us? Do you want to kill me as you [28] killed that Egyptian yesterday?' At that retort Moses fled and [29] lived as an exile in the land of Midian, where he became the father of two sons.

Moses hears the voice of God

"It was forty years later in the desert of Mount Sinai that an [30] angel appeared to him in the flames of a burning bush, and the [31] sight filled Moses with wonder. As he approached to look at it more closely the voice of the Lord spoke to him, saying, 'I am the [32] God of thy fathers, the God of Abraham, and the God of Isaac, and the God of Jacob.' Then Moses trembled and was afraid to look any more. But the Lord spoke to him and said, 'Loose the [33] shoes from thy feet: for the place whereon thou standest is holy ground. I have surely seen the affliction of my people which is in [34] Egypt, and have heard their groaning, and I am come down to deliver them: and now come, I will send thee into Egypt.'

But Israel rejects Moses

"So this same Moses whom they had rejected in the words, [35] 'Who appointed you a ruler and judge?' God sent to be both ruler and deliverer with the help of the angel who had appeared to him in the bush. This is the man who showed wonders and signs [36] in Egypt and in the Red Sea, the man who led them out of Egypt and was their leader in the desert for forty years. He was Moses, [37] the man who said to the sons of Israel, 'A prophet shall God raise up unto you from among your brethren, like unto me.' In that [38] church in the desert this was the man who was the mediator between the angel who used to talk with him on Mount Sinai and our fathers. This was the man who received words, living words, which were to be given to you; and this was the man to whom our [39] forefathers turned a deaf ear! They disregarded him, and in their hearts hankered after Egypt. They said to Aaron, 'Make us gods [40] to go before us. For as for this Moses who led us out of Egypt, we do not know what has become of him.' In those days they even [41] made a calf, and offered sacrifices to their idol. They rejoiced in the work of their own hands. So God turned away from them and [42] left them to worship the Host of Heaven, as it is written in the book of the prophets,

> Did ye offer unto me slain beasts and sacrifices
> Forty years in the wilderness, O house of Israel?
43 And ye took up the tabernacle of Moloch,
> And the star of the god Rephan,
> The figures which ye made to worship them:
> And I will carry you away beyond Babylon.

God's privileges to Israel

44 "There in the desert our forefather possessed the Tabernacle of witness made according to the pattern which Moses saw when
45 God instructed him to build it. This Tabernacle was handed down to our forefathers, and they brought it here when the gentiles were defeated under Joshua, for God drove them out as our an-
46 cestors advanced. Here it stayed until the time of David. David won the approval of God and prayed that he might find a habi-
47 tation for the God of Jacob, even though it was not he but Solo-
48 mon who actually built a house for him. Yet of course the most high does not live in man-made houses. As the prophet says,
49 > The heaven is my throne,
> And the earth the footstool of my feet:
> What manner of house will ye build me? saith the Lord:
> Or what is the place of my rest?
50 > Did not my hand make all these things?

Yet Israel is blind and disobedient

51 "You obstinate people, heathen in your thinking, heathen in the way you are listening to me now! It is always the same—you never fail to resist the Holy Spirit! Just as your fathers did
52 so are you doing now. Can you name a single prophet whom your fathers did not persecute? They killed the men who long ago foretold the coming of the just one, and now in our own day
53 you have become his betrayers and his murderers. You are the men who have received the Law of God miraculously, by the hand of angels, and you are the men who have disobeyed it!"

The truth arouses murderous fury

54 These words stung them to fury and they ground their teeth
55 at him in rage. Stephen, filled through all his being with the Holy Spirit, looked steadily up into Heaven. He saw the glory of God, and Jesus himself standing at his right hand.

"Look!" he exclaimed, "the heavens are opened and I can see *56*
the Son of Man standing at God's right hand!"

At this they put their fingers in their ears. Yelling with fury, as *57*
one man they made a rush at him and hustled him out of the city *58*
and stoned him. The witnesses* of the execution flung their
clothes at the feet of a young man by the name of Saul.

So they stoned Stephen while he called upon God, and said, *59*
"Jesus, Lord, receive my spirit!"

Then, on his knees, he cried in ringing tones, *60*
"Lord, forgive them for this sin."

And with these words he fell into the sleep of death, while *8:1a*
Saul gave silent assent to his execution.

CHAPTER 8

Widespread persecution follows Stephen's death

ON that very day a great storm of persecution burst upon the *1b*
Church in Jerusalem. All Church members except the apostles
were scattered over the countryside of Judaea and Samaria. While *2*
reverent men buried Stephen and mourned deeply over him, Saul *3*
harassed the Church bitterly. He would go from house to house,
drag out both men and women and have them committed to
prison. Those who were dispersed by this action went throughout *4*
the country, preaching the good news of the message as they
went. Philip, for instance, went down to the city of Samaria and *5*
preached Christ to the people there. His words met with a ready *6*
and sympathetic response from the large crowds who listened to
him and saw the miracles which he performed. With loud cries *7*
evil spirits came out of those who had been possessed by them;
and many paralysed and lame people were cured. As a result there *8*
was great rejoicing in that city.

A magician believes in Christ

But there was a man named Simon in the city who had been *9*
practising magic for some time and mystifying the people of
Samaria. He pretended that he was somebody great and everyone *10*
from the lowest to the highest was fascinated by him. Indeed,
they used to say, "This man must be that great power of God."
He had influenced them for a long time, astounding them by his *11*

* In Jewish Law the "witnesses" were also the executioners.

12 magical practices. But when they had come to believe Philip as
he proclaimed to them the good news of the kingdom of God
and of the name of Jesus Christ, men and women alike were
13 baptised. Even Simon himself became a believer and after his
baptism attached himself closely to Philip. As he saw the signs
and remarkable demonstrations of power which took place, he
lived in a state of constant wonder.

God confirms Samaria's acceptance of the gospel

14 When the apostles in Jerusalem heard that Samaria had accepted the Word of God, they sent Peter and John down to them.
15 When these two had arrived they prayed for the Samaritans that
16 they might receive the Holy Spirit for as yet he had not fallen
upon any of them. They were living simply as men and women
17 who had been baptised in the name of the Lord Jesus. So then and
there they laid their hands on them and they received the Holy
Spirit.

Simon's monstrous suggestion is sternly rebuked

18 When Simon saw how the Spirit was given through the apostles'
19 laying their hands upon people he offered them money with the
words,
"Give me this power too, so that if I were to put my hands
on anyone he could receive the Holy Spirit."
20 But Peter said to him,
"To hell with you and your money!* How dare you think you
21 could buy the gift of God! You can have no share or place in this
22 ministry, for your heart is not honest before God. All you can do
now is to repent of this wickedness of yours and pray earnestly to
23 God that the evil intention of your heart may be forgiven. For
I can see inside you, and I see a man bitter with jealousy and
bound with his own sin!"
24 To this Simon answered,
"Please pray to the Lord for me that none of these things that
you have spoken about may come upon me!"
25 When Peter and John had given their clear witness and spoken
the Word of the Lord, they returned to Jerusalem, preaching the
good news to many Samaritan villages as they went.

* These words are exactly what the Greek means. It is a pity that
their real meaning is obscured by modern slang usage.

Philip is given an unique opportunity

But an angel of the Lord said to Philip,   26
"Get up and go south down the road which runs from Jerusalem to Gaza, out in the desert."

Philip arose and began his journey. At this very moment an   27
Ethiopian eunuch, a minister and in fact the treasurer to Candace,
queen of the Ethiopians, was on his way home after coming to
Jerusalem to worship. He was sitting in his carriage reading the   28
prophet Isaiah. The Spirit said to Philip,   29
"Approach this carriage, and keep close to it."

Then as Philip ran forward he heard the man reading the   30
prophet Isaiah, and he said,

"Do you understand what you are reading?"

And he replied,   31

"How can I unless I have someone to guide me?"

And he invited Philip to get up and sit by his side. The passage   32
of scripture he was reading was this:

> He was led as a sheep to the slaughter;
> And as a lamb before his shearer is dumb,
> So he openeth not his mouth:
> In his humiliation his judgment was taken away: 33
> His generation who shall declare?
> For his life is taken from the earth.

The eunuch turned to Philip and said,   34

"Tell me, I beg you, about whom is the prophet saying this—is
he speaking about himself or about someone else?"

Then Philip began, and using this scripture as a starting point,   35
he told the eunuch the good news about Jesus. As they proceeded   36
along the road they came to some water, and the eunuch said,

"Look, here is some water; is there any reason why I should not
be baptised now?"

And he gave orders for the carriage to stop. Then both of them   38
went down to the water and Philip baptised the eunuch. When   39
they came up out of the water the Spirit of the Lord took Philip
away suddenly and the eunuch saw no more of him, but proceeded on his journey with a heart full of joy. Philip found himself   40
at Azotus and as he passed through the countryside he went on
telling the good news in all the cities until he came to Caesarea.

CHAPTER 9

The crisis for Saul

1 BUT Saul, still breathing murderous threats against the disciples
2 of the Lord, went to the High Priest and begged him for letters
to the synagogues in Damascus, so that if he should find there
any followers of the Way, whether men or women, he could bring
them back to Jerusalem as prisoners.

3 But on his journey, as he neared Damascus, a light from Heaven
4 suddenly blazed around him, and he fell to the ground. Then he
heard a voice speaking to him,

"Saul, Saul, why are you persecuting me?"

5 "Who are you, Lord?" he asked.

6 "I am Jesus whom you are persecuting," was the reply. "But
now stand up and go into the city and there you will be told what
you must do."

7 His companions on the journey stood there speechless, for they
8 had heard the voice but could see no one. Saul got up from the
ground, but when he opened his eyes he could see nothing. So
9 they took him by the hand and led him into Damascus. There he
remained sightless for three days, and during that time he had
nothing either to eat or drink.

God's preparation for the converted Saul

10 Now in Damascus there was a disciple by the name of Ananias.
The Lord spoke to this man in a dream, calling him by his name.

"I am here, Lord," he replied.

11 Then the Lord said to him,

"Get up and go down to the street called Straight and enquire
at the house of Judas for a man named Saul from Tarsus. At this
12 moment he is praying and he sees in his mind's eye a man by the
name of Ananias coming into the house, and placing his hands
upon him to restore his sight."

13 But Ananias replied,

"Lord, I have heard on all hands about this man and how much
14 harm he has done to your holy people in Jerusalem! Why even
now he holds powers from the chief priests to arrest all who call
upon your name."

15 But the Lord said to him,

252

"Go on your way, for this man is my chosen instrument to bear my name before the gentiles and their kings, as well as to the sons of Israel. Indeed, I myself will show him what he must suffer for 16 the sake of my name."

Then Ananias set out and went to the house, and there he laid 17 his hands upon Saul, and said,

"Saul, brother, the Lord has sent me—Jesus who appeared to you on your journey here—so that you may recover your sight and be filled with the Holy Spirit."

Immediately something like scales fell from Saul's eyes, and 18 he could see again. He got to his feet and was baptised. Then he 19 took some food and regained his strength.

Saul's conversion astounds the disciples

Saul stayed with the disciples in Damascus for some time. Without delay he proclaimed Jesus in the synagogues declaring 20 that he is the Son of God. All his hearers were staggered and kept 21 saying,

"Isn't this the man who so bitterly persecuted those who called on the name in Jerusalem, and came down here with the sole object of taking back all such people as prisoners before the chief priests?"

But Saul went on from strength to strength, reducing to con- 22 fusion the Jews who lived at Damascus by proving beyond doubt that this man is Christ.

The long revenge on the "renegade" begins

After some time the Jews made a plot to kill Saul, but news of 23, 24 this came to his ears. Although in their murderous scheme the Jews watched the gates day and night for him, Saul's disciples took 25 him one night and let him down through an opening in the wall by lowering him in a basket.

At Jerusalem Saul is suspect: Barnabas conciliates

When Saul reached Jerusalem he tried to join the disciples. 26 But they were all afraid of him, finding it impossible to believe that he was a disciple. Barnabas, however, took him by the hand 27 and introduced him to the apostles, and explained to them how he had seen the Lord on his journey, and how the Lord had spoken to

28
29

30

him. He further explained how Saul had spoken in Damascus with
the utmost boldness in the name of Jesus. After that Saul joined
with them in all their activities in Jerusalem, preaching fearlessly
in the name of the Lord. He used to talk and argue with the Greek-
speaking Jews, but they made several attempts on his life. When
the brothers realised this they took him down to Caesarea and
sent him off to Tarsus.

A time of peace

31
The whole Church throughout Judaea, Galilee and Samaria
now enjoyed a period of peace. It became established and as it
went forward in reverence for the Lord and in the strengthening
presence of the Holy Spirit, continued to grow in numbers.

Peter heals at Lydda

32

33
34

Now it happened that Peter, in the course of travelling about
among them all, came down to God's people living at Lydda.
There he found a man called Æneas who had been bed-ridden
for eight years through paralysis. Peter said to him,
"Æneas, Jesus Christ heals you! Get up and make your bed."

35
He got to his feet at once. And all those who lived in Lydda and
Sharon saw him and turned to the Lord.

And again at Joppa

36

37
38

Then there was a woman in Joppa, a disciple called Tabitha,
whose name in Greek was Dorcas (meaning Gazelle). She was
a woman whose whole life was full of good and kindly actions,
but in those days she became seriously ill and died. So when they
had washed her body they laid her in an upper room. Now Lydda
is quite near Joppa, and when the disciples heard that Peter was in
Lydda, they sent two men to him and begged him,
"Please come to us without delay."

39
Peter got up and went back with them, and when he arrived
in Joppa they took him to the room upstairs. All the widows stood
around him with tears in their eyes, holding out for him to see
the dresses and cloaks which Dorcas used to make for them while

40
she was with them. But Peter put them all outside the room and
knelt down and prayed. Then he turned to the body and said,
"Tabitha, get up!"
She opened her eyes, and as soon as she saw Peter she sat up.

He took her by the hand, helped her to her feet, and then called 41
out to the believers and widows and presented her to them alive.
This became known throughout the whole of Joppa and many 42
believed in the Lord. Peter himself remained there for some time,
staying with a tanner called Simon.

CHAPTER 10

God speaks to a good-living gentile

THERE was a man in Caesarea by the name of Cornelius, a 1
centurion in what was called the Italian regiment. He was a 2
deeply religious man who reverenced God, as did all his household. He made many charitable gifts to the people and was a real
man of prayer. About three o'clock one afternoon he saw perfectly 3
clearly in a dream an angel of God coming into his room,
approaching him, and saying,

"Cornelius!"

He stared at the angel in terror, and said, 4

"What is it, Lord?"

The angel replied,

"Your prayers and your deeds of charity have gone up to
Heaven and are remembered before God. Now send men to Joppa 5
for a man called Simon, who is also known as Peter. He is staying 6
as a guest with another Simon, a tanner, whose house is down by
the sea."

When the angel who had spoken to him had gone, Cornelius 7
called out for two of his house-servants and a devout soldier, who
was one of his personal attendants. He told them the whole story 8
and then sent them off to Joppa.

Peter's startling vision

Next day, while these men were still on their journey and 9
approaching the city, Peter went up about mid-day on to the flat
roof of the house to pray. He became very hungry and longed 10
for something to eat. But while the meal was being prepared he
fell into a trance and saw the heavens open and something like a 11
great sheet descending upon the earth, let down by its four
corners. In it were all kinds of animals, reptiles and birds. Then 12, 13
came a voice which said to him,

"Get up, Peter, kill and eat!"

14 But Peter said,

"Never, Lord! For not once in all my life have I ever eaten anything common or unclean."

15 Then the voice spoke to him a second time,

"You must not call what God has cleansed common."

16 This happened three times, and then the thing was gone, taken back into heaven.

The meaning of the vision becomes apparent

17 While Peter was still puzzling about the meaning of the vision which he had just seen, the men sent by Cornelius had arrived asking for the house of Simon. They were in fact standing at the

18 very doorway of the house calling out to enquire if Simon,

19 surnamed Peter, were lodging there. Peter was still thinking deeply about the vision when the Spirit said to him,

20 "Three men are here looking for you. Get up and go downstairs. Go with them without any misgiving, for I myself have sent them."

21 So Peter went down to the men and said,

"I am the man you are looking for; what brings you here?"

22 They replied,

"Cornelius the centurion, a good-living and God-fearing man, whose character can be vouched for by the whole Jewish people, was commanded by a holy angel to send for you to come to his house, and to listen to your message."

23 Then Peter invited them in and entertained them.

Peter, obeying the Spirit, disobeys Jewish law

On the next day he got up and set out with them, accompanied

24 by some of the brothers from Joppa, arriving at Caesarea on the day after that. Cornelius was expecting them and had invited

25 together all his relations and intimate friends. As Peter entered the house Cornelius met him by falling on his knees before him

26 and worshipping him. But Peter roused him with the words,

"Stand up, I am a human being too!"

27 Then Peter went right into the house in deep conversation with Cornelius and found that a large number of people had assembled.

28 Then he spoke to them,

"You all know that it is forbidden for a man who is a Jew to associate with, or even visit, a man of another nation. But God

256

has shown me plainly that no man must be called 'common' or 'unclean'. That is why I came here when I was sent for without raising any objection. Now I want to know what made you send for me."   *29*

Then Cornelius replied,   *30*

"Three days ago, about this time, I was observing the afternoon hour of prayer in my house, when suddenly a man in shining clothes stood before me and said, 'Cornelius, your prayer *31* has been heard and your charitable gifts have been remembered before God. Now you must send to Joppa and invite here a man *32* called Simon whose surname is Peter. He is staying in the house of a tanner by the name of Simon, down by the sea.' So I sent to *33* you without delay and you have been most kind in coming. Now we are all here in the presence of God to listen to everything that the Lord has commanded you to say."

Peter's momentous discovery

Then Peter began to speak,   *34*

"In solemn truth I can see now that God is no respecter of persons, but that in every nation the man who reverences him and *35* does what is right is acceptable to him! He has sent his message *36* to the sons of Israel by giving us the good news of peace through Jesus Christ—he is the Lord of us all. You must know the story *37* of Jesus of Nazareth—why, it has spread through the whole of Judaea, beginning from Galilee after the baptism that John proclaimed. You must have heard how God anointed him with the *38* power of the Holy Spirit, of how he went about doing good and healing all who suffered from the devil's power—because God was with him. Now we are eye-witnesses of everything that he *39* did, both in the Judaean country and in Jerusalem itself, and yet they murdered him by hanging him on a cross. But on the third *40* day God raised that same Jesus and let him be clearly seen, not *41* indeed by the whole people, but by witnesses whom God had previously chosen. We are those witnesses, we who ate and drank with him after he had risen from the dead! Moreover, we are the *42* men whom he commanded to preach to the people and bear fearless witness to the fact that he is the one appointed by God to be the judge of both the living and the dead. It is to *43* him that all the prophets bear witness, that every man who believes in him may receive forgiveness of sins through his name."

The Holy Spirit confirms Peter's action

44 While Peter was still speaking these words the Holy Spirit
45 fell upon all who were listening to his message. The Jewish
believers who had come with Peter were absolutely amazed that
the gift of the Holy Spirit was being poured out on gentiles also;
46 for they heard them speaking in foreign tongues and glorifying
God.

Then Peter exclaimed,

47 "Could anyone refuse water or object to these men being
baptised—men who have received the Holy Spirit just as we did
ourselves?"
48 And he gave orders for them to be baptised in the name of
Jesus Christ. Afterwards they asked him to stay with them for
some days.

CHAPTER 11

The Church's disquiet at Peter's action

1 Now the apostles and the brothers who were in Judaea heard
2 that the gentiles also had received God's message. So when Peter
next visited Jerusalem the circumcision-party were full of criti-
3 cism, saying to him, "You actually went in and shared a meal
with uncircumcised men!"

Peter's explanation

4 But Peter began to explain how the situation had actually arisen.
5 "I was in the city of Joppa praying," he said, "and while completely unconscious of my surroundings I saw a vision—something like a great sheet coming down towards me, let down from
6 heaven by its four corners. It came right down to me and when I
looked at it closely I saw animals and wild beasts, reptiles and
7 birds. Then I heard a voice say to me, 'Get up, Peter, kill and eat.'
8 But I said, 'Never, Lord, for nothing common or unclean has ever
9 passed my lips.' But the voice from Heaven spoke a second time
and said, 'You must not call what God has cleansed common.'
10 This happened three times, and then the whole thing was drawn
11 up again into heaven. The extraordinary thing is that at that very
moment three men arrived at the house where we were staying,
12 sent to me personally from Caesarea. The Spirit told me to go with

258

these men without any misgiving. And these six of our brothers accompanied me and we went into the man's house. He told us **13** how he had seen the angel standing in his house, saying, 'Send to Joppa and bring Simon, surnamed Peter. He will give you a **14** message which will save both you and your whole household.' While I was beginning to tell them this message the Holy Spirit **15** fell upon them just as on us at the beginning. There came into my **16** mind the words of our Lord when he said, 'John indeed baptised with water, but you will be baptised with the Holy Spirit.' If then **17** God gave to them exactly the same gift as he gave to us when we believed on the Lord Jesus Christ, who was I to think that I could hinder the working of God?"

The flexibility of the young Church

When they heard this they had no further objection to raise. **18** And they praised God, saying,

"Then obviously God has given to the gentiles as well the gift of repentance which leads to life."

Persecution has spread the gospel

Now those who had been dispersed by the persecution which **19** arose over Stephen travelled as far as Phoenicia, Cyprus and Antioch, giving the message as they went to Jews only. How- **20** ever, among their number were natives of Cyprus and Cyrene, and these men, on their arrival at Antioch, proclaimed their message to the Greeks as well, telling them the good news of the Lord Jesus. The hand of the Lord was with them, and a great **21** number believed and turned to the Lord. News of these things **22** came to the ears of the Church in Jerusalem and they sent Barnabas to Antioch. When he arrived and saw this working of God's **23** grace, he was delighted. He urged them all to be resolute in their faithfulness to the Lord, for he was a good man, full of the Holy **24** Spirit and of faith. So it happened that a considerable number of people became followers of the Lord.

Believers are called "Christians" for the first time

Then Barnabas went to Tarsus to find Saul. When he found **25, 26** him he brought him up to Antioch. Then for a whole year they met together with the Church and taught a large crowd. It was in Antioch that the disciples were first given the name of "Christians".

The young Church and famine relief

27   During this period some prophets came down from Jerusalem
28 to Antioch. One of them by the name of Agabus stood up and foretold by the Spirit that there was to be a great famine throughout the world. (This actually happened in the days of Claudius.)
29 The disciples determined to send relief to the brothers in Judaea,
30 each contributing as he was able. This they did, sending their contribution to the elders there personally through Barnabas and Saul.

CHAPTER 12

Herod kills James and imprisons Peter

1   It was at this time that King Herod laid violent hands on some
2 of the Church members. James, John's brother, he executed with
3 the sword, and when he found this action pleased the Jews he went on to arrest Peter as well. It was during the days of unleavened
4 bread that he actually made the arrest. He put Peter in prison with no less than four squads of soldiers to guard him, intending to
5 bring him out to the people after the Passover. So Peter was closely guarded in the prison, while the Church prayed to God earnestly on his behalf.

Peter's miraculous rescue

6   On the very night that Herod was planning to bring him out, Peter was asleep between two soldiers, chained with double chains, while guards maintained a strict watch in the doorway of the
7 prison. Suddenly an angel of the Lord appeared, and light shone in the cell. He tapped Peter on the side and woke him up, saying,
8 "Get up quickly." His chains fell away from his hands and the angel said to him, "Fasten your belt and put on your sandals." And he did so. Then the angel continued, "Wrap your cloak
9 round you and follow me." So Peter followed him out, not knowing whether what the angel was doing were real—indeed he felt he
10 must be taking part in a vision. So they passed right through the first and second guard-points and came to the iron gate that led

Miles

0   100   200   300

EUXINE SEA

Antioch PISIDIA
Iconium
Lystra
LYCAONIA
Attalia Perga Derbe
SEA OF PAMPHYLIA
Antioch
Seleucia
CYPRUS Salamis
Paphos

MEDITERRANEAN SEA

N

PAUL'S
JOURNEY
№ 1

out into the city. This opened for them of its own accord, and they went out and had passed along one street when the angel
11 suddenly vanished from Peter's sight. Then Peter came to himself and said aloud, "Now I know for certain that the Lord has sent his angel to rescue me from the power of Herod and from all
12 that the Jewish people are expecting." As the truth broke upon him he went to the house of Mary, the mother of John surnamed
13 Mark, where many were gathered together in prayer. As he knocked at the door a young maid called Rhoda came to answer
14 it, but on recognising Peter's voice failed to open the door from sheer joy. Instead she ran inside and reported that Peter was
15 standing on the doorstep. At this they said to her,

"You must be mad!"

But she insisted that it was true. Then they said,

"Then it is his angel."

16 But Peter continued to stand there knocking on the door, and when they opened it and recognised him they were simply
17 amazed. Peter, however, made a gesture to them to stop talking while he explained to them how the Lord had brought him out of prison. Then he said,

"Go and tell James and the other brothers what has happened."

After this he left them and went on to another place.

Peter's escape infuriates Herod

18 But when morning came there was a great commotion among
19 the soldiers as to what could have happened to Peter. When Herod had had a search put out for him without success, he cross-examined the guards and then ordered their execution. Then he left Judaea and went down to Caesarea and stayed there.

But Herod dies a terrible death

20 Now Herod was very angry with the people of Tyre and Sidon. They approached him in a body and after winning over Blastus the king's chamberlain, they begged him for peace. They were forced to do this because their country's food supply was depend-
21 ent on the king's dominions. So on an appointed day Herod put on his royal robes, took his seat on the public throne and made a
22 speech to them. At this the people kept shouting, "This is a god
23 speaking, not a mere man!" Immediately an angel of the Lord struck him down because he did not give God the glory. And in fearful internal agony he died.

The message continues to spread

But the Word of the Lord continued to gain ground and in- 24
crease its influence. Barnabas and Saul returned from Jerusalem 25
when they had completed their mission there, bringing with them
John whose surname was Mark.

CHAPTER 13

Saul and Barnabas are called to a special task

Now there were in the Church at Antioch both prophets and 1
teachers—Barnabas, for example, Simeon surnamed Niger,
Lucius the Cyrenian, Manaen the foster-brother of the governor
Herod, and Saul. While they were worshipping the Lord and 2
fasting, the Holy Spirit spoke to them, saying,

"Set Barnabas and Saul apart for me for a task to which I have
called them."

At this, after further fasting and prayer, they laid their hands 3
on them and set them free for this work. So these two, sent at the 4
Holy Spirit's command, went down to Seleucia and from there
they sailed off to Cyprus.* On their arrival at Salamis they began 5
to proclaim God's message in the Jewish synagogues, having John
as their assistant. As they made their way through the island as far 6
as Paphos they came across a man named Bar-Jesus, a Jew who
was both a false prophet and a magician. This man was attached 7
to Sergius Paulus, the proconsul, who was himself a man of
intelligence. He sent for Barnabas and Saul as he was anxious to
hear God's message. But Elymas the magician (for that is the 8
translation of his name), opposed them, doing his best to dissuade
the proconsul from accepting the faith. Then Saul (who is also 9
called Paul), filled with the Holy Spirit, eyed him closely and said, 10

"You son of the devil, you enemy of all true goodness, you
monster of trickery and evil, is it not high time you gave up
trying to pervert the truth of the Lord? Now listen, the Lord 11
himself will touch you, for some time you will not see the light
of the sun—you will be blind!"

Immediately a mist and then an utter blackness came over his
eyes, and he went round trying to find someone to lead him by
the hand. When the proconsul saw what had happened he 12
believed, for he was shaken to the core at the Lord's teaching.

* See page 261.

Saul (now Paul) comes to Antioch in Pisidia

13   Then Paul and his companions set sail from Paphos and went to Perga in Pamphylia. There John left them and turned back to
14 Jerusalem, but they continued their journey through Perga to the Antioch in Pisidia. They went to the synagogue on the Sabbath
15 day and took their seats. After the reading of the Law and Prophets, the leaders of the synagogue sent to them with a message,

    "Men and brothers, if you have any message of encouragement for the people, by all means speak."

Paul shows the Jews where their history leads

16   So Paul stood up, and motioning with his hand, began:
17   "Men of Israel and all of you who fear God, listen to me. The God of this people Israel chose our fathers and prospered the people while they were exiles in the land of Egypt. Then he
18 lifted up his arm and led them out of that land. Yes, and he bore
19 with them for forty years in the desert. He destroyed seven nations in the land of Canaan before he gave them that land as their
20 inheritance for some four hundred and fifty years. After that he
21 gave them judges until the time of the prophet Samuel. Then when they begged for a king God gave them Saul the son of Kish, a man of the tribe of Benjamin, to be their king for forty
22 years. After he had deposed him he raised David to the throne, a man of whom God himself bore testimony in the words, 'I have found David, the son of Jesse, a man after my own heart, who shall
23 do all my will.' From the descendants of this man, according to his
24 promise, God has brought Jesus to Israel to be their saviour. John came before him to prepare his way preaching the baptism of
25 repentance for all the people of Israel. Indeed, as John reached the end of his time he said these words: 'What do you think I am? I am not he. But know this, someone comes after me whose shoe-lace I am not fit to untie!'

Now the message is urgent and contemporary

26   "Men and brothers, sons of the race of Abraham, and all among you who fear God, it is to us that this message of salvation
27 has now been sent! For the people of Jerusalem and their rulers refused to recognise him and to understand the voice of the

prophets which are read every Sabbath day—even though in condemning him they fulfilled these very prophecies! For though they   28
found no cause for putting him to death, they begged Pilate to
have him executed. And when they had completed everything   29
that was written about him, they took him down from the cross
and laid him in a tomb. But God raised him from the dead. For 30, 31
many days he was seen by those who had come up from Galilee
to Jerusalem with him, and these men are now his witnesses to
the people. And as for us we tell you the good news that the   32
promise made to our forefathers has come true—that, in raising up   33
Jesus, God has fulfilled it for us their children. This is endorsed in
the second psalm: 'Thou art my son, this day have I begotten
thee.' And as for the fact of God's raising him from the dead, never   34
to return to corruption, he has spoken in these words: 'I will give
you the sure mercies of David.' And then going further he says in   35
another psalm, 'Thou shalt not suffer thine holy one to see corruption.' For David, remember, after he had served God's purpose   36
in his own generation fell asleep and was laid with his ancestors.
He did in fact 'see corruption', but this man whom God raised   37
never saw corruption! It is therefore imperative, men and   38
brothers, that every one of you should realise that forgiveness of
sins is proclaimed to you through this man. And through faith in   39
him a man is absolved from all those things from which the Law of
Moses could never set him free. Take care then that this saying   40
of the prophets should never apply to you:

Behold, ye despisers, and wonder, and perish;   41
For I work a work in your days,
A work which ye shall in no wise believe, if one declare it unto
you."

Paul succeeds in arousing deep interest—

As they were going out the people kept on asking them to say   42
all this again on the following Sabbath. After the meeting of the   43
synagogue broke up many of the Jews and devout proselytes
followed Paul and Barnabas who spoke personally to them and
urged them to put their trust in the grace of God.

—but a week later he meets bitter opposition

On the next Sabbath almost the entire population of the city   44
assembled to hear the message of God, but when the Jews saw the   45
crowds they were filled with jealousy and contradicted what Paul

46 was saying, covering him with abuse. At this Paul and Barnabas did not mince their words but said,

"We felt it our duty to speak the message of God to you first, but since you spurn it and evidently do not think yourselves fit for
47 eternal life, watch us now as we turn to the gentiles! Indeed the Lord has commanded us to do so in the words:

I have set thee for a light of the gentiles,

That thou shouldest be for salvation unto the uttermost part of the earth."

48 When the gentiles heard this they were delighted and thanked God for his message. All those who were destined for eternal life
49 believed, and the Word of the Lord spread over the whole
50 country. But the Jews worked upon the feelings of religious and respectable women and some of the leading citizens, and succeeded in starting a persecution against Paul and Barnabas, and
51 expelled them from the district. But they on their part simply shook off the dust from their feet in protest and went on to Icon-
52 ium. And the disciples continued to be full of joy and the Holy Spirit.

CHAPTER 14

Jewish behaviour repeats itself

1 MUCH the same thing happened at Iconium. On their arrival they went to the Jewish synagogue and spoke with such conviction that a very large number of both Jews and Greeks
2 believed. But the unbelieving Jews stirred up the feelings of the
3 gentiles and poisoned their minds against the brothers. So they remained there for a long time and spoke fearlessly for the Lord, who made it plain that they were proclaiming the Word of his
4 grace, by allowing them to perform signs and miracles. But the great mass of the people of the city were divided in their opinions, some taking the side of the Jews, and some that of the apostles.
5 But when a hostile movement arose from both gentiles and Jews in
6 collaboration with the authorities to insult and stone them, they got to know about it, fled to the Lycaonian cities of Lystra and
7 Derbe, and the surrounding countryside—and from there they continued to proclaim the gospel.

A miracle in a completely pagan city

8 Now it happened one day at Lystra that a man was sitting who

had no power in his feet. He had in fact been lame from birth and
had never been able to walk. He was listening to Paul as he spoke, *9*
and Paul, looking him straight in the eye and seeing that he had
the faith to be made well, said in a loud voice, *10*

"Stand straight up on your feet!"

And he sprang to his feet and walked. When the crowd saw *11*
what Paul had done they shouted in the Lycaonian language,

"The gods have come down to us in human form!"

They began to call Barnabas Jupiter, and Paul Mercury, since *12*
he was the chief speaker. What is more, the high priest of Jupiter *13*
whose temple was at the gateway of the city, brought garlanded
oxen to the gates and wanted to offer sacrifice with the people.
But when the apostles, Barnabas and Paul, heard of their intention *14*
they tore their clothes and rushed into the crowd, crying at the
top of their voices,

"Men, men, why are you doing these things? We are only *15*
human beings with feelings just like yours! We are here to tell
you good news—that you should turn from these meaningless
things to the living God! He is the one who made heaven and
earth, the sea and all that is in them. In generations gone by he *16*
allowed all nations to go on in their own ways—not that he left *17*
men without evidence of himself. For he has shown kindnesses to
you; he has sent you rain from heaven and fruitful seasons, giving
you food and happiness to your hearts' content."

Yet even with these words they only just succeeded in re- *18*
straining the crowd from making sacrifices to them.

Paul is dogged by his Jewish enemies

Then some Jews arrived from Antioch and Iconium and after *19*
turning the minds of the people against Paul they stoned him and
dragged him out of the city thinking he was dead. But while the *20*
disciples were gathered in a circle round him, Paul got up and
walked back to the city. And the very next day he went out with
Barnabas to Derbe, and when they had preached the gospel to *21*
that city and made many disciples, they turned back to Lystra,
Iconium and Antioch. They put fresh heart into the disciples *22*
there, urging them to stand firm in the faith, and reminding them
that it is "through many tribulations that we must enter into the
kingdom of God". They appointed elders for them in each *23*
Church, and with prayer and fasting commended these men to the
Lord in whom they had believed. They then crossed Pisidia and *24*

25 arrived in Pamphylia. They proclaimed their message in Perga and
26 then went down to Attalia. From there they sailed back to Antioch
(in Syria) where they had first been commended to the grace of
27 God for the task which they had now completed. When they
arrived there they called the Church together and reported to them
how greatly God had worked with them and how he had opened
28 the door of faith for the gentiles. And here at Antioch they spent a
considerable time with the disciples.

CHAPTER 15

The opposition from reactionaries

1 THEN some men came down from Judaea and began to teach
the brothers, saying, "unless you are circumcised according to the
2 custom of Moses you cannot be saved". Naturally this caused a
serious upset among them and much earnest discussion followed
with Paul and Barnabas. Finally it was agreed that Paul and
Barnabas should go up to Jerusalem with some of their own
people to confer with the apostles and elders about the whole
question.
3 The Church sent them off on their journey and as they went
through Phoenicia and Samaria they told the story of the con-
version of the gentiles, and all the brothers were overjoyed to
4 hear about it. On their arrival at Jerusalem they were welcomed
by the Church, by the apostles and elders, and they reported how
5 greatly God had worked with them. But some members of the
Pharisees' party who had become believers stood up and declared
that it was absolutely essential that these men be told that they
must be circumcised and observe the Law of Moses.

Peter declares that God is doing something new

6, 7 The apostles and elders met to consider this matter. After an
exhaustive enquiry Peter stood up and addressed them in these
words:
"Men and brothers, you know that from the earliest days God
chose me as the one from whose lips the gentiles should hear the
8 Word and should believe it. Moreover, God who knows men's
9 inmost thoughts has plainly shown that this is so, for when he
had cleansed their hearts through their faith he gavē the Holy
10 Spirit to the gentiles exactly as he did to us. Why then must you

PAUL'S JOURNEY Nº 2

Miles
0 100 200 300

ITALY

ADRIATIC SEA

MACEDONIA
Amphipolis
Neapolis
Thessalonica
Philippi
Berœa
SAMOTHRACE
Apollonia

GREECE
Athens
Corinth
Cenchrea

BITHYNIA

MYSIA
Troas

PHRYGIA
Ephesus

GALATIA
Iconium
Derbe
Lystra

CILICIA
Antioch

CYPRUS

SYRIA

PHOENICIA
Caesarea
Samaria
Jerusalem

MEDITERRANEAN SEA

CRETE

N

now strain the patience of God by trying to put on the shoulders of these disciples a burden which neither our fathers nor we were
11 able to bear? Surely the fact is that it is by the grace of the Lord Jesus that we are saved by faith, just as they are!"

12 These words produced absolute silence, and they listened to Barnabas and Paul while they gave a detailed account of the signs and wonders which God had worked through them among the gentiles.

James expresses the feeling of the meeting

13 Silence again followed their words and then James made this reply:

14 "Men and brothers, listen to me. Symeon has shown how in the first place God chose a people from among the nations who
15 should bear his name. This is in full agreement with what the prophets wrote, as in this scripture:

16 After these things I will return,
And I will build again the tabernacle of David, which is fallen;
And I will build again the ruins thereof,
And I will set it up:
17 That the residue of men may seek after the Lord,
And all the gentiles, upon whom my name is called,
18 Saith the Lord who maketh these things known from the beginning of the world.

19 "I am firmly of the opinion that we should not put any additional obstacles before any gentiles who are turning towards
20 God. Instead, I think we should write to them telling them to avoid anything polluted by idols, sexual immorality, eating the
21 meat of strangled animals, or tasting blood. For after all, for many generations now Moses has had his preachers in every city and has been read aloud in the synagogues every Sabbath day."

The Church's deputation: the message to gentile Christians

22 Then the apostles, the elders and the whole Church agreed to choose representatives and send them to Antioch with Paul and Barnabas. Their names were Judas, surnamed Barsabas, and Silas,
23 both leading men of the brotherhood. They carried with them a letter bearing this message: "The apostles and elders who are your brothers send their greetings to the brothers who are gentiles in

Antioch, Syria and Cilicia. Since we have heard that some of our 24
number have caused you deep distress and have unsettled your
minds by giving you a message which certainly did not originate
from us, we are unanimously agreed to send you chosen repre- 25
sentatives with our well-loved Barnabas and Paul—men who have 26
risked their lives for the name of our Lord Jesus Christ. So we 27
have sent you Judas and Silas who will give you the same message
personally by word of mouth. For it has seemed right to the 28
Holy Spirit and to us to lay no further burden upon you except
what is absolutely essential, namely, that you avoid what has 29
been sacrificed to idols, tasting blood, eating the meat of what has
been strangled and sexual immorality. Keep yourselves clear of
these things and you will make good progress. Farewell."

The message is received with delight

So this party, sent off by the Church, went down to Antioch 30
and after gathering the congregation together, they handed
over the letter to them. And they, when they read it, were 31
delighted with the encouragement it gave them. Judas and Silas 32
were themselves both inspired preachers and greatly encouraged
and strengthened the brothers by many talks to them. Then, 33
after spending some time there, the brothers sent them back in
peace to those who had commissioned them. Paul and Barnabas 35
however stayed on in Antioch teaching and preaching the gospel
of the Word of the Lord in company with many others.

Paul and Barnabas flatly disagree, but the work prospers

Some days later Paul spoke to Barnabas, 36
"Now let us go back and visit the brothers in every city where
we have proclaimed the Word of the Lord to see how they are."

Barnabas wanted to take John, surnamed Mark, as their com- 37
panion. But Paul strongly disapproved of taking with them a man 38
who had deserted them in Pamphylia and was not prepared to go
on with them in their work. There was a sharp clash of opinion, 39
so much so that they went their separate ways, Barnabas taking
Mark and sailing to Cyprus, while Paul* chose Silas and set out 40
on his journey, commended to the grace of the Lord by the
brothers as he did so. He travelled through Syria and Cilicia and 41
strengthened the churches.

* See page 269.

CHAPTER 16

Paul chooses Timothy as companion

1 He also went to Derbe and Lystra. At Lystra there was a disciple by the name of Timothy whose mother was a Jewish Christian,
2 though his father was a Greek. Timothy was held in high regard
3 by the brothers at Lystra and Iconium, and Paul wanted to take him on as his companion. Everybody knew that his father was a Greek, and Paul therefore had him circumcised because of the
4 attitude of the Jews in these places. As they went on their way through the cities they passed on to them for their observance the decisions which had been reached by the apostles and elders
5 in Jerusalem. Consequently the churches grew stronger and stronger in the faith and their numbers increased daily.

Paul and Silas find their journey divinely directed

6 They made their way through Phrygia and Galatia, but the Holy Spirit prevented them from speaking God's message in Asia.
7 When they came to Mysia they tried to enter Bithynia, but again
8 the Spirit of Jesus would not allow them. So they passed by Mysia
9 and came down to Troas, where one night Paul had a vision of a Macedonian man standing and appealing to him in the words:
10 "Come over to Macedonia and help us!" As soon as Paul had seen this vision we made every effort to get on to Macedonia, convinced that God had called us to give them the good news.

The gospel comes to Europe: a business-woman is converted

11 So we set sail from Troas and ran a straight course to Samo-
12 thrace, and on the following day to Neapolis. From there we went to Philippi, a Roman garrison-town and the chief city in
13 that part of Macedonia. We spent some days in Philippi and on the Sabbath day we went out of the city gate to the riverside, where we supposed there was a place for prayer. There we sat
14 down and spoke to the women who had assembled. One of our hearers was a woman named Lydia. (She came from Thyatira and was a dealer in purple-dyed cloth.) She was already a believer
15 in God, and he opened her heart to accept Paul's words. When she and her household had been baptised, she appealed to us, saying,

272

"If you are satisfied that I am a true believer in the Lord, then come down to my house and stay there."

And she insisted on our doing so.

Conflict with evil spirits and evil men

One day while we were going to the place of prayer we were **16** met by a young girl who had a spirit of clairvoyance and brought her owners a good deal of profit by foretelling the future. She **17** would follow Paul and the rest of us, crying out, "These men are servants of the most high God, and they are telling you the way of salvation." She continued this behaviour for many days, and **18** then Paul, in a burst of irritation, turned round and spoke to the spirit in her.

"I command you in the name of Jesus Christ to come out of her!"

And it came out immediately. But when the girl's owners saw **19** that their hope of making money out of her had disappeared, they seized Paul and Silas and dragged them before the authorities in the market-square. There they brought them before the chief **20** magistrates, and said,

"These men are Jews and are causing a great disturbance in our city. They are proclaiming customs which it is illegal for us as **21** Roman citizens to accept or practise."

At this the crowd joined in the attack, and the magistrates had **22** them stripped and ordered them to be beaten with rods. Then, **23** after giving them a severe beating, they threw them into prison, instructing the jailer to keep them safe. On receiving such strict **24** orders, he hustled them into the inner jail and fastened their feet securely in the stocks.

The midnight deliverance: the jailer becomes a Christian

But about midnight Paul and Silas were praying and singing **25** hymns to God while the other prisoners were listening to them. Suddenly there was a great earthquake, big enough to shake the **26** foundations of the prison. Immediately all the doors flew open and everyone's chains were unfastened. When the jailer woke and **27** saw that the doors of the prison had been opened he drew his sword and was on the point of killing himself, for he imagined that all the prisoners had escaped. But Paul called out to him at **28** the top of his voice,

"Don't hurt yourself—we are all here!"

29 Then the jailer called for lights, rushed in, and trembling all
30 over, fell at the feet of Paul and Silas. He led them outside, and said,

"Sirs, what must I do to be saved?"

31 And they replied,

"Believe in the Lord Jesus and then you will be saved, you and your household."

32 Then they told him and all the members of his household the
33 message of God. There and then in the middle of the night he took them aside and washed their wounds and he himself and all
34 his family were baptised without delay. Then he took them into his house and offered them food, he and his whole household overjoyed at finding faith in God.

Paul, in a strong position, makes the authorities apologise

35 When morning came, the magistrates sent their constables with
36 the message, "Let those men go." The jailer reported this message to Paul, saying,

"The magistrates have sent to have you released. So now you can leave this place and go on your way in peace."

37 But Paul said to the constables,

"They beat us publicly without any kind of trial; they threw us into prison despite the fact that we are Roman citizens. And now do they want to get rid of us in this underhand way? Oh no, let them come and take us out themselves!"

38 The constables reported this to the magistrates, who were thoroughly alarmed when they heard that they were Romans.
39 So they came in person and apologised to them, and after taking
40 them outside the prison, requested them to leave the city. But on leaving the prison Paul and Silas went to Lydia's house, and when they had seen the brothers and given them fresh courage, they took their leave.

CHAPTER 17

Bitter opposition at Thessalonica—

1 NEXT they journeyed through Amphipolis and Apollonia and arrived at Thessalonica. Here there was a synagogue of the Jews
2 which Paul entered, following his usual custom. On three Sabbath

days he argued with them from the scriptures, explaining and 3
quoting passages to prove the necessity for the death of Christ and
his rising again from the dead. "This Jesus whom I am proclaiming to you," he concluded, "is God's Christ!" Some of them were 4
convinced and threw in their lot with Paul and Silas, and they
were joined by a great many believing Greeks and a considerable
number of influential women. But the Jews, in a fury of jealousy, 5
got hold of some of the unprincipled loungers of the market-
place, gathered a crowd together and set the city in an uproar.
Then they attacked Jason's house in an attempt to bring Paul and
Silas out before the people. When they could not find them they 6
hustled Jason and some of the brothers before the civic authorities,
shouting, "These are the men who have turned the world upside
down and have now come here, and Jason has taken them into his 7
house. What is more, all these men act against the decrees of
Caesar, saying that there is another king called Jesus!" By these 8
words the Jews succeeded in alarming both the people and the
authorities, and they only released Jason and the others after 9
binding them over to keep the peace.

—followed by encouragement at Berœa

Without delay the brothers despatched Paul and Silas off to 10
Berœa that night. On their arrival there they went to the Jewish
synagogue. The Jews proved more generous-minded than those 11
in Thessalonica, for they accepted the message most eagerly and
studied the scriptures every day to see if what they were now
being told were true. Many of them became believers, as did a 12
number of Greek women of social standing and quite a number
of men. But when the Jews at Thessalonica found out that God's 13
message had been proclaimed by Paul at Berœa as well, they came
there too to cause trouble and spread alarm among the people.
The brothers at Berœa then sent Paul off at once to make his way 14
to the sea-coast, but Silas and Timothy remained there. The men 15
who accompanied Paul took him as far as Athens and returned
with instructions for Silas and Timothy to rejoin Paul as soon as
possible.

Paul is irritated by the idols of Athens

Paul had some days to wait at Athens for Silas and Timothy 16
to arrive, and while he was there his soul was exasperated beyond

17 endurance at the sight of a city so completely idolatrous. He felt compelled to discuss the matter with the Jews in the synagogue as well as with God-fearing gentiles, and he even argued daily in
18 the open market-place with the passers-by. While he was speaking there some Epicurean and Stoic philosophers came across him, and some of them remarked,

"What is this cock-sparrow trying to say?"

Others said,

"He seems to be trying to proclaim some more gods to us, and outlandish ones at that!"

For Paul was actually proclaiming "Jesus" and "the resur-
19 rection". So they got hold of him and conducted him to their council, the Areopagus. There they asked him,
20 "May we know what this new teaching of yours really is? You talk of matters which sound strange to our ears, and we should
21 like to know what they mean." (For all the Athenians, and even foreign visitors to Athens, had an obsession for any novelty and would spend their whole time talking about or listening to anything new.)

Paul's speech to the "gentlemen of Athens"

22 So Paul got to his feet in the middle of their council, and began, "Gentlemen of Athens, my own eyes tell me that you are in all
23 respects an extremely religious people. For as I made my way here and looked at your shrines I noticed one altar on which were inscribed the words, TO GOD THE UNKNOWN. It is this God whom you are worshipping in ignorance that I am here to
24 proclaim to you! God who made the world and all that is in it, being Lord of both Heaven and earth, does not live in temples
25 made by human hands, nor is he ministered to by human hands, as though he had need of anything—seeing that he is the one
26 who gives to all men life and breath and everything else. From one forefather he has created every race of men to live over the face of the whole earth. He has determined the times of their
27 existence and the limits of their habitation, so that they might search for God, in the hope that they might feel for him and find
28 him—yes, even though he is not far from any one of us. Indeed, it is in him that we live and move and have our being. Some of your own poets have endorsed this in the words, 'For we are
29 indeed his children'. If then we are the children of God, we ought not to imagine God in terms of gold or silver or stone, contrived

by human art or imagination. Now while it is true that God has 30
overlooked the days of ignorance he now commands all men
everywhere to repent. For he has fixed a day on which he will 31
judge the whole world in justice by the standard of a man whom
he has appointed. That this is so he has guaranteed to all men by
raising this man from the dead."

But when his audience heard Paul talk about the resurrection 32
from the dead some of them laughed outright, but others said,

"We should like to hear you speak again on this subject."

So with this mixed reception Paul retired from their assembly. 33
Yet some did in fact join him and accept the faith, including 34
Dionysius a member of the Areopagus, a woman by the name of
Damaris, and some others as well.

CHAPTER 18

At Corinth Paul is yet again rejected by the Jews

BEFORE long Paul left Athens and went on to Corinth where he 1, 2
found a Jew called Aquila, a native of Pontus. This man had
recently come from Italy with his wife Priscilla, because Claudius
had issued a decree that all Jews should leave Rome. He went to
see them in their house and because they practised the same trade 3
as himself he stayed with them. They all worked together, for
their trade was tent-making. Every Sabbath Paul used to speak in 4
the synagogue trying to persuade both Jews and Greeks. By the 5
time Silas and Timothy arrived from Macedonia Paul was completely absorbed in preaching the message, showing the Jews as
clearly as he could that Jesus is Christ. However, when they 6
turned against him and abused him he shook his garments at
them, and said,

"Your blood be on your own heads! From now on I go with
a perfectly clear conscience to the gentiles."

Then he left them and went to the house of a man called Titius 7
Justus, a man who reverenced God and whose house was next
door to the synagogue. Crispus, the leader of the synagogue, 8
became a believer in the Lord, with all his household, and many
of the Corinthians who heard the message believed and were
baptised. Then one night the Lord spoke to Paul in a vision, 9

"Do not be afraid, but go on speaking and let no one silence
you, for I myself am with you and no man shall lift a finger to 10
harm you. There are many in this city who belong to me."

277

11   So Paul settled down there for eighteen months and taught
them God's message.

Paul's enemies fail to impress the governor

12   Then, while Gallio was governor of Achaia, the Jews banded
13   together to attack Paul, and took him to court, saying,
"This man is perverting men's minds to make them worship
God in a way that is contrary to the Law."
14   Paul was all ready to speak, but before he could utter a word
Gallio said to the Jews,
"Listen, Jews! If this were a matter of some crime or wrong-
15   doing I might reasonably be expected to put up with you. But
since it is a question which concerns a word and names and your
own Law, you must attend to it yourselves. I flatly refuse to be
judge in these matters."
16, 17 And he had them ejected from the court. Then they got hold
of Sosthenes, the synagogue-leader, and beat him in front of the
court-house. But Gallio remained completely unmoved.

Paul returns, and reports to Jerusalem and Antioch

18   Paul stayed for some time after this incident and then took
leave of the brothers and sailed for Syria, taking Priscilla and
Aquila with him. At Cenchrea he had his hair cut short, for he
19   had taken a solemn vow. They all arrived at Ephesus and there
Paul left Aquila and Priscilla, but he himself went into the syna-
20   gogue and debated with the Jews. When they asked him to stay
21   longer he refused, bidding them farewell with the words, "If it
is God's will I will come back to you again." Then he set sail from
22   Ephesus and went down to Caesarea. Here he disembarked and
after paying his respects to the Church in Jerusalem, he went
23   down to Antioch. He spent some time there before he left and
proceeded to visit systematically throughout Galatia and Phrygia,
putting new heart into all the disciples as he went.

Apollos speaks powerfully at Ephesus and Corinth

24   Now a Jew called Apollos, a native of Alexandria and a gifted
25   speaker, well-versed in the scriptures, arrived at Ephesus. He had
been instructed in the way of the Lord, and he spoke with burning zeal, teaching the facts about Jesus faithfully even though he

only knew the baptism of John. This man began to speak with 26 great boldness in the synagogue. But when Priscilla and Aquila heard him they took him aside and explained the Way of God to him more accurately. Then as he wanted to cross into Achaia, the 27 brothers gave him every encouragement and wrote a letter to the disciples there, asking them to make him welcome. On his arrival he proved a source of great strength to those who had believed through grace, for by his powerful arguments he publicly refuted 28 the Jews, quoting from the scriptures to prove that Jesus is Christ.

CHAPTER 19

Ephesus has its own Pentecost

WHILE Apollos was in Corinth* Paul journeyed through the 1 upper parts of the country and arrived at Ephesus. There he discovered some disciples, and he asked them, 2

"Did you receive the Holy Spirit when you believed?"

"No," they replied, "we have never even heard that there is a Holy Spirit."

"Well then, how were you baptised?" asked Paul. 3

"We were baptised with John's baptism," they replied.

"John's baptism was a baptism to show a change of heart," 4 Paul explained, "but he always told the people that they must believe in the one who should come after him, that is, in Jesus."

When these men heard this they were baptised in the name of 5 the Lord Jesus, and then, when Paul had laid his hands on them, 6 the Holy Spirit came upon them and they began to speak with tongues and the inspiration of prophets. (There were about twelve 7 of them in all.)

Paul's two-year ministry at Ephesus

Then Paul made his way into the synagogue there and for three 8 months he spoke with the utmost confidence, using both argument and persuasion as he talked of the kingdom of God. But 9 when some of them hardened in their attitude towards the message and refused to believe it, and, what is more, spoke offensively about the Way in public, Paul left them, and withdrew his disciples, and held daily discussions in the lecture-hall of Tyrannus.

* See page 281.

10 He continued this practice for two years, so that all who lived in
11 Asia, both Greeks and Jews, could hear the Lord's message. God
gave most unusual demonstrations of power through Paul's hands,
12 so much so that people took to the sick any handkerchiefs or
small-clothes which had been in contact with his body, and they
were cured of their diseases and their evil spirits left them.

The violence of evil and the power of the "name"

13 But there were some itinerant Jewish exorcists who attempted
to invoke the name of the Lord Jesus when dealing with those
who had evil spirits. They would say, "I command you in the
14 name of Jesus whom Paul preaches." Seven brothers, sons of a
chief priest called Sceva, were engaged in this practice on one
15 occasion, when the evil spirit answered, "Jesus I know, and I am
16 acquainted with Paul, but who on earth are you?" And the man
in whom the evil spirit was living sprang at them and overpowered them all with such violence that they rushed out of that
17 house wounded, with their clothes torn off their backs. This incident became known to all the Jews and Greeks who were living
in Ephesus, and a great sense of awe came over them all, while
18 the name of the Lord Jesus became highly respected. Many of
those who had professed their faith began openly to admit their
19 former practices. A number of those who had previously practised magic collected their books and burned them publicly.
(They estimated the value of these books and found it to be no
20 less than five thousand pounds.) In this way the Word of the
Lord continued to grow irresistibly in power and influence.

Paul speaks of his plans

21 After these events Paul set his heart on going to Jerusalem by
way of Macedonia and Achaia, remarking,
"After I have been there I must see Rome as well."
22 Then he despatched to Macedonia two of his assistants,
Timothy and Erastus, while he himself stayed for a while in Asia.

The silversmiths' riot at Ephesus

23 Now it happened about this time that a great commotion arose
24 concerning the Way. A man by the name of Demetrius, a silver-
smith who made silver shrines for Diana, provided considerable

PAUL'S
JOURNEY
Nº3

25 business for his craftsmen. He gathered these men together with workers in similar trades, and spoke to them,

"Men," he said, "you all realise how our prosperity depends on
26 this particular work. If you use your eyes and ears you also know that not only in Ephesus but practically throughout Asia this man Paul has succeeded in changing the minds of a great number of people by telling them that gods made by human hands are
27 not gods at all. Now the danger is not only that this trade of ours might fall into disrepute, but also that the temple of the great goddess Diana herself might come to be lightly regarded. There is a further danger, that her actual majesty might be degraded, she whom the whole of Asia, and indeed the whole world, worships!"

28 When they heard this they were furiously angry, and shouted, "Great is Diana of the Ephesians!"

29 Soon the whole city was in an uproar, and on a common impulse the people rushed into the theatre dragging with them Gaius and Aristarchus, two Macedonians who were Paul's travel-
30 ling companions. Paul himself wanted to go in among the crowd,
31 but the disciples would not allow him. Moreover, some high-ranking officials who were Paul's friends sent to him begging him
32 not to risk himself in the theatre. Meanwhile some were shouting one thing and some another, and the whole assembly was at sixes and sevens, for most of them had no idea why they had come
33 together at all. A man called Alexander whom the Jews put forward was pushed into the forefront of the crowd, and there, after making a gesture with his hand, he tried to make a speech of
34 defence to the people. But as soon as they realised that he was a Jew they shouted as one man for about two hours, "Great is Diana of the Ephesians!"

Public authority intervenes

35 But when the town clerk had finally quietened the crowd, he said,

"Gentlemen of Ephesus, who in the world could be ignorant of the fact that our city of Ephesus is temple-guardian of the great Diana and of the image which fell down from Jupiter himself?
36 These are undeniable facts and it is your plain duty to remain calm
37 and do nothing which you might afterwards regret. For you have brought these men forward, though they are neither plunderers of the temple, nor have they uttered any blasphemy against our
38 goddess. If Demetrius and his fellow-craftsmen have a charge to

bring against anyone, well, the courts are open and there are magistrates; let them take legal action. But if you require anything beyond that then it must be resolved in the regular assembly. For all of us are in danger of being charged with rioting over today's events particularly as we have no real excuse to offer for this commotion." **39 40**

And with these words he dismissed the assembly. **41**

CHAPTER 20

Paul departs on his second journey to Europe

*AFTER this disturbance had died down, Paul sent for the disciples and after speaking encouragingly said good-bye to them, and went on his way to Macedonia. As he made his journey through these districts he spoke many heartening words to the people and then went on to Greece, where he stayed for three months. Then when he was on the point of setting sail for Syria the Jews made a further plot against him and he decided to make his way back through Macedonia. His companions on the journey were Sopater a Berœan, the son of Pyrrhus, two Thessalonians, Aristarchus and Secundus, Gaius from Derbe, Timothy, and two Asians, Tychicus and Trophimus. This party proceeded to Troas to await us there, while we sailed from Philippi after the days of unleavened bread, and joined them five days later at Troas, where we spent a week. **1 2 3 4 5 6**

Paul's enthusiasm leads to an accident

On the first day of the week, when we were assembled for the breaking of bread, Paul, since he intended to leave on the following day, began to speak to them and prolonged his address until almost midnight. There were a great many lamps burning in the upper room where we met, and a young man called Eutychus who was sitting on the window-sill fell fast asleep as Paul's address became longer and longer. Finally, completely overcome by sleep, he fell to the ground from the third storey and was picked up as dead. But Paul went down, bent over him and holding him gently in his arms, said, **7 8 9 10**

"Don't be alarmed; he is still alive."

Then he went upstairs again and, when he had broken bread and eaten, continued a long earnest talk with them until daybreak, **11**

* See page 281.

12 and so finally departed. As for the boy, they took him home alive, feeling immeasurably relieved.

We sail to Miletus

13 Meanwhile we had gone aboard the ship and sailed on ahead for Assos, intending to pick up Paul there, for that was the arrangement he had made, since he himself had planned to go
14 overland. When he met us on our arrival at Assos we took him
15 aboard and went on to Mitylene. We sailed from there and arrived off the coast of Chios the next day. On the day following we crossed to Samos, and the day after that we reached Miletus.
16 For Paul had decided to sail past Ephesus with the idea of spending as little time as possible in Asia. He hoped, if it should prove possible, to reach Jerusalem in time for the day of Pentecost.

Paul's moving farewell message to the elders of Ephesus

17 At Miletus he sent to Ephesus to summon the elders of the
18 Church. On their arrival he addressed them in these words:
    "I am sure you know how I have lived among you ever since
19 I first set foot in Asia. You know how I have served the Lord most humbly and what tears I have shed over the trials that have
20 come to me through the plots of the Jews. You know I have never shrunk from telling you anything that was for your good, nor
21 from teaching you in public or in your own homes. On the contrary I have most emphatically urged upon both Jews and Greeks
22 repentance towards God and faith in our Lord Jesus. And now here I am, compelled by the Spirit to go to Jerusalem. I do not
23 know what may happen to me there, except that the Holy Spirit warns me that imprisonment and persecution await me in every
24 city that I visit. But frankly I do not consider my own life valuable to me so long as I can finish my course and complete the ministry which the Lord Jesus has given me in declaring the
25 good news of the grace of God. Now I know well enough that not one of you among whom I have moved as I preached the
26 kingdom of God will ever see my face again. That is why I must tell you solemnly today that my conscience is clear as far as any
27 of you is concerned, for I have never shrunk from declaring to
28 you the complete will of God. Now be on your guard for yourselves and for every flock of which the Holy Spirit has made you guardians—you are to be shepherds to the Church of God, which

he won at the cost of his own blood. I know that after my depar- 29
ture savage wolves will come in among you without mercy for
the flock. Yes, and even from among you men will arise speaking 30
perversions of the truth, trying to draw away the disciples and
make them followers of themselves. This is why I tell you to 31
keep on the alert, remembering that for three years I never failed
night and day to warn every one of you, even with tears in my
eyes. Now I commend you to the Lord and to the message of his 32
grace which can build you up and give you your place among all
those who are consecrated to God. I have never coveted any- 33
body's gold or silver or clothing. You know well enough that 34
these hands of mine have provided for my own needs and for
those of my companions. In everything I have shown you that 35
by such hard work we must help the weak and must remember
the words of the Lord Jesus when he said, 'To give is happier
than to receive'."

With these words he knelt down with them all and prayed. 36
All of them were in tears, and throwing their arms round Paul's 37
neck they kissed him affectionately. What saddened them most 38
of all was his saying that they would never see his face again. And
they went with him down to the ship.

CHAPTER 21

The brothers at Tyre warn Paul not to go to Jerusalem

WHEN we had finally said farewell to them we set sail, running 1
a straight course to Cos, and the next day we went to Rhodes
and from there to Patara. Here we found a ship bound for 2
Phoenicia, and we went aboard her and set sail. After sighting 3
Cyprus and leaving it on our left we sailed to Syria and put in at
Tyre, since that was where the ship was to discharge her cargo.
We sought out the disciples there and stayed with them for a 4
week. They felt led by the Spirit again and again to warn Paul
not to go up to Jerusalem. But when our time was up we left 5
them and continued our journey. They all came out to see us off,
bringing their wives and children with them, accompanying us
till we were outside the city. Then kneeling down on the beach
we prayed and said good-bye to each other. Then we went 6
aboard the ship, while the disciples went back home. We sailed 7
away from Tyre and arrived at Ptolemais. We greeted the
brothers there and stayed with them for just one day. On the 8

following day we left and proceeded to Caesarea and there we went to stay at the house of Philip the evangelist, one of the seven

9 deacons. He had four unmarried daughters, all of whom spoke by

10 the Spirit of God. During our stay there of several days a prophet

11 by the name of Agabus came down from Judaea. When he came to see us he took Paul's girdle and used it to tie his own hands and feet together, saying, "The Holy Spirit says this: the man to whom this girdle belongs will be bound like this by the Jews in Jerusalem and handed over to the gentiles!"

We all warn Paul, but he is immovable

12 When we heard him say this, we and the people there begged

13 Paul not to go up to Jerusalem. Then Paul answered us,

"What do you mean by unnerving me with all your tears? I am perfectly prepared not only to be bound but to die in Jerusalem for the sake of the name of the Lord Jesus."

14 Since he could not be dissuaded all we could do was to say, "May the Lord's will be done," and hold our tongues.

Paul is warmly welcomed at first

15 After this we made our preparations and went up to Jerusalem.

16 Some of the disciples from Caesarea accompanied us and they brought us to the house of Mnason, a native of Cyprus and one

17 of the earliest disciples, with whom we were going to stay. On our arrival at Jerusalem the brothers gave us a very warm

18 welcome. On the following day Paul went with us to visit James,

19 and all the elders were present. When he had greeted them he gave them a detailed account of all that God had done among

20 the gentiles through his ministry, and they, on hearing this account, glorified God. Then they said to him,

"You know, brother, how many thousands there are among the Jews who have become believers, and that every one of these

21 is a staunch upholder of the Law. They have been told about you—that you teach all Jews who live among the gentiles to disregard the Law of Moses, and tell them not to circumcise their

22 children nor observe the old customs. What will happen now, for

23 they are simply bound to hear that you have arrived? Now why not follow this suggestion of ours? We have four men here under

24 a vow. Suppose you join them and be purified with them, pay their expenses so that they may have their hair cut short, and then

everyone will know there is no truth in the stories about you, but that you yourself observe the Law. As for those gentiles who 25 have believed, we have sent them a letter with our decision that they should abstain from what has been offered to idols, from blood and from what has been strangled, and from sexual immorality."

But his enemies attempt to murder him

So Paul joined the four men and on the following day, after 26 being purified with them, went into the Temple to give notice of the time when the period of purification would be finished and an offering would be made on behalf of each one of them. The 27 seven days were almost over when the Jews from Asia caught sight of Paul in the Temple. They stirred up the whole crowd and seized him, shouting, "Men of Israel, help! This is the man who is 28 teaching everybody everywhere to despise our people, our Law and this place. Why, he has even brought Greeks into the Temple and he has defiled this holy place!" For they had previously seen 29 Trophimus the Ephesian with Paul in the city and they had concluded that Paul had brought him into the Temple. The whole 30 city was stirred by this speech and a mob collected who seized Paul and dragged him outside the Temple, and the doors were slammed behind him.

Paul is rescued by Roman soldiers

They were trying to kill him when a report reached the ears of 31 the colonel of the regiment that the whole of Jerusalem was in an uproar. Without a moment's delay he took soldiers and centur- 32 ions and ran down to them. When they saw the colonel and the soldiers they stopped beating Paul. The colonel came up to Paul 33 and arrested him and ordered him to be bound with two chains. Then he enquired who the man was and what he had been doing. Some of the crowd shouted one thing and some another, and 34 since he could not be certain of the facts because of the shouting that was going on, the colonel ordered him to be brought to the barracks. When Paul got to the steps he was actually carried by 35 the soldiers because of the violence of the mob. For the mass of 36 the people followed, shouting, "Kill him!" Just as they were 37 going to take him into the barracks Paul asked the colonel,

"May I say something to you?"

38 "So you know Greek, do you?" the colonel replied. "Aren't you that Egyptian who not long ago raised a riot and led those four thousand assassins into the desert?"

39 "I am a Jew," replied Paul. "I am a man of Tarsus, a citizen of that not insignificant city. I ask you to let me speak to the people."

Paul attempts to defend himself

40 On being given permission Paul stood on the steps and made a gesture with his hand to the people. There was a deep hush as he began to speak to them in Hebrew.

CHAPTER 22

1 "My brothers and my fathers, listen to what I have to say in my own defence."

2 As soon as they heard him addressing them in Hebrew the silence became intense.

3 "I myself am a Jew," Paul went on. "I was born in Tarsus in Cilicia, but I was brought up here in the city, I received my training at the feet of Gamaliel, and I was schooled in the strictest observance of our fathers' Law. I was as much on fire with zeal

4 for God as you all are today. I am also the man who persecuted this way to the death, arresting both men and women and throw-

5 ing them into prison, as the High Priest and the whole council can readily testify. Indeed, it was after receiving letters from them to their brothers in Damascus that I was on my way to that city, intending to arrest any followers of the way I could find there

6 and bring them back to Jerusalem for punishment. Then this happened to me. As I was on my journey and getting near to Damascus, about midday a great light from Heaven suddenly

7 blazed around me. I fell to the ground, and I heard a voice saying

8 to me, 'Saul, Saul, why are you persecuting me?' I replied, 'Who are you, Lord?' He said to me, 'I am Jesus of Nazareth whom you

9 are persecuting.' My companions naturally saw the light, but they

10 did not hear the voice of the one who was talking to me. 'What am I to do, Lord?' I asked. And the Lord told me, 'Get up and go to Damascus and there you will be told of all that has been

11 determined for you to do.' I was blinded by the brightness of that light and my companions had to take me by the hand as we

went on to Damascus. There, there was a man called Ananias, a 12
reverent observer of the Law and a man highly respected by all
the Jews who lived there. He came to visit me and as he stood by 13
my side said, 'Saul, brother, you may see again!' At once I regained my sight and looked up at him. 'The God of our fathers,' 14
he went on, 'has chosen you to know his will, to see the righteous
one, to hear words from his own lips, so that you may become his 15
witness before all men of what you have seen and heard. And now 16
what are you waiting for? Get up and be baptised! Be clean from
your sins as you call on his name.'

Paul claims that God sent him to the gentiles

"Then it happened that after my return to Jerusalem, while I 17
was at prayer in the Temple, unconscious of everything else, I saw 18
him, and he said to me, 'Make haste and leave Jerusalem at once,
for they will not accept your testimony about me.' And I said, 19
'But, Lord, they know how I have been through all the synagogues imprisoning and beating all those who believe in you.
They know also that when the blood of your martyr Stephen was 20
shed I stood by, giving my approval—why, I was even holding in
my arms the outer garments of those who killed him.' But he 21
said to me, 'Go, for I will send you far away to the gentiles'."

The consequence of Paul's speech

They had listened to him until he said this, but now they 22
raised a great shout,
"Kill him, and rid the earth of such a man! He is not fit to
live!"
As they were yelling and ripping their clothes and hurling dust 23
into the air, the colonel gave orders to bring Paul into the 24
barracks and directed that he should be examined by scourging, so
that he might discover the reason for such an uproar against him.
But when they had strapped him up, Paul spoke to the centurion 25
standing by,
"Is it legal for you to flog a man who is a Roman citizen, and
untried at that?"
On hearing this the centurion went in to the colonel and 26
reported to him, saying,
"Do you realise what you were about to do? This man is a
Roman citizen!"

27   Then the colonel himself came up to Paul, and said,
"Tell me, are you a Roman citizen?"
And he said,
"Yes."

28   Whereupon the colonel replied,
"It cost me a good deal to get my citizenship."
"Ah," replied Paul, "but I was born a citizen."

29   Then those who had been about to examine him left hurriedly,
while even the colonel himself was alarmed at discovering that
Paul was a Roman and that he had had him bound.

Roman fair-mindedness

30   Next day the colonel, determined to get to the bottom of
Paul's accusation by the Jews, released him and ordered the
assembly of the chief priests and the whole Sanhedrin. Then he
took Paul down and placed him in front of them.

CHAPTER 23

Paul again attempts defence

1   PAUL looked steadily at the Sanhedrin and spoke to them,
"Men and brothers, I have lived my life with a perfectly clear
2 conscience before God up to the present day——" Then Ananias
the High Priest ordered those who were standing near to strike
3 him on the mouth. At this Paul said to him,
"God will strike you, you white-washed wall! How dare you
sit there judging me by the Law and give orders for me to be
struck, which is clean contrary to the Law?"
4   Those who stood by said,
"Do you mean to insult God's High Priest?"
5   But Paul said,
"My brothers, I did not know that he was the High Priest, for
it is written:
Thou shalt not speak evil of a ruler of thy people."

Paul seizes his opportunity

6   Then Paul, realising that part of the council were Sadducees
and the other part Pharisees, raised his voice and said to them,

"I am a Pharisee, the son of Pharisees. It is for my hope in the resurrection of the dead that I am on trial!"

At these words an immediate tension arose between the Pharisees and the Sadducees, and the meeting was divided. For the Sadducees claim that there is no resurrection and that there is neither angel nor spirit, while the Pharisees believe in all three. A great uproar ensued and some of the scribes of the Pharisees' party jumped to their feet and protested violently. 7 8 9

"We find nothing wrong with this man! Suppose some angel or spirit has really spoken to him?"

As the tension mounted the colonel began to fear that Paul would be torn to pieces between them. He therefore ordered his soldiers to come down and rescue him from them and bring him back to the barracks. 10

God's direct encouragement to Paul

That night the Lord stood by Paul, and said, 11
"Take heart!—for as you have witnessed boldly for me in Jerusalem so you must give your witness for me in Rome."

Paul's acute danger

Early in the morning the Jews made a conspiracy and bound themselves by a solemn oath that they would neither eat nor drink until they had killed Paul. Over forty of them were involved in this plot, and they approached the chief priests and elders, and said, 12 13 14

"We have bound ourselves by a solemn oath to let nothing pass our lips until we have killed Paul. Now you and the council must make it plain to the colonel that you want him to bring Paul down to you, suggesting that you want to examine his case more closely. We shall be standing by ready to kill him before he gets here." 15

Leakage of information leads to Paul's protection

However, Paul's nephew got wind of this plot and he came and found his way into the barracks and told Paul about it. Paul called one of the centurions and said, 16 17
"Take this young man to the colonel for he has something to report to him."

18 So the centurion took him and brought him into the colonel's presence, and said,

"The prisoner Paul called me and requested that this young man should be brought to you as he has something to say to you."

19 The colonel took his hand, and drew him aside (where they could not be overheard), and asked,

"What have you got to tell me?"

20 And he replied,

"The Jews have agreed to ask you to bring Paul down to the Sanhedrin tomorrow as though they were going to enquire more 21 carefully into his case. But I beg you not to let them persuade you. For more than forty of them are waiting for him—they have sworn a solemn oath that they will neither eat nor drink until they have killed him. They are all ready at this moment—all they want is for you to give the order."

22 At this the colonel dismissed the young man with the caution, "Don't let a soul know that you have given me this information."

23 Then he summoned two of his centurions, and said,

"Get two hundred men ready to proceed to Caesarea, with seventy horsemen and two hundred spearmen, by nine o'clock 24 tonight." (Mounts were also to be provided to carry Paul safely to Felix the governor.)

The Roman view of Paul's position

25 He further wrote a letter to Felix of which this is a copy:

26 "Claudius Lysias sends greeting to his excellency the governor Felix.

27 "This man had been seized by the Jews and was on the point of being murdered by them when I arrived with my troops and rescued him, since I had discovered that he was a Roman citizen. 28 Wishing to find out what the accusation was that they were making against him, I had him brought down to their Sanhedrin. 29 There I discovered he was being accused over questions of their laws, and that there was no charge against him which deserved 30 either death or imprisonment. Now, however, that I have received private information of a plot against his life, I have sent him to you without delay. At the same time I have notified his accusers that they must make their charges against him in your presence."

Paul is taken into protective custody

The soldiers, acting on their orders, took Paul and, riding **31** through that night, brought him down to Antipatris. Next day **32** they returned to the barracks, leaving the horsemen to accompany him further. They went into Caesarea and after delivering the **33** letter to the governor, they handed Paul over to him. When the **34** governor had read the letter he asked Paul what province he came from, and on learning that he came from Cilicia, he said, **35** "I will hear your case as soon as your accusers arrive."

Then he ordered him to be kept under guard in Herod's palace.

CHAPTER 24

The "professional" puts the case against Paul

FIVE days later Ananias the High Priest came down himself **1** with some of the elders and a barrister by the name of Tertullus. They presented their case against Paul before the governor, and **2** when Paul had been summoned, Tertullus began the prosecution in these words:

"We owe it to you personally, your excellency, that we enjoy lasting peace, and we know that it is due to your foresight that the nation enjoys improved conditions of living. At all times, and **3** indeed everywhere, we acknowledge these things with the deepest gratitude. However—for I must not detain you too long—I beg **4** you to give us a brief hearing with your customary kindness. The **5** simple fact is that we have found this man a pestilential disturber of the peace among the Jews all over the world. He is a ringleader of the Nazareth sect, and he was on the point of desecrating **6** the Temple when we overcame him. But you yourself will soon **8** discover from the man himself all the facts about which we are accusing him."

Paul is given the chance to defend himself

While Tertullus was speaking the Jews kept joining in, asserting **9** that these were the facts. Then Paul, at a nod from the governor, **10** made his reply:

"I am well aware that you have been governor of this nation for many years, and I can therefore make my defence with every confidence. You can easily verify the fact that it is not more than **11**

12 twelve days ago that I went up to worship at Jerusalem. I was
never found either arguing with anyone in the Temple or gather-
13 ing a crowd, either in the synagogues or in the open air. These
men are quite unable to prove the charges they are now making
14 against me. I will freely admit to you, however, that I do worship
the God of our fathers according to the Way which they call a
heresy, although in fact I believe in the scriptural authority of both
15 the Law and the Prophets. I have the same hope in God which
they themselves hold, that there is to be a resurrection of both
16 good men and bad. With this hope before me I do my utmost to
live my whole life with a clear conscience before God and man.

Paul has nothing to hide

17 "It was in fact after several years' absence from Jerusalem that
I came back to make charitable gifts to my own nation and to
18 make my offerings. It was in the middle of these duties that they
found me, a man purified in the Temple. There was no mob and
19 there was no disturbance until these Jews from Asia came, who
should in my opinion have come before you and made their
20 accusation, if they had anything against me. Or else, let these men
themselves speak out now and say what crime they found me
21 guilty of when I stood before the Sanhedrin—unless it was that
one sentence that I shouted as I stood among them. All I said was
this, 'It is about the resurrection of the dead that I am on trial
before you this day'."

Felix defers decision

22 Then Felix, who was better acquainted with the Way than most
people, adjourned the case and said,
"As soon as Colonel Lysias arrives I will give you my decision."
23 Then he gave orders to the centurion to keep Paul in custody,
but to grant him reasonable liberty and allow any of his personal
friends to look after his needs.

Felix plays for safety—and hopes for personal gain

24 Some days later Felix arrived with his wife Drusilla, herself a
Jewess, and sent for Paul, and heard what he had to say about
25 faith in Christ Jesus. But while Paul was talking about goodness,
self-control and the judgment that is to come, Felix became
alarmed, and said,

"You may go for the present. When I find a convenient moment I will send for you again."

At the same time he nursed a secret hope that Paul would pay 26
him money—which is why Paul was frequently summoned to come and talk with him. However, when two full years had 27
passed, Felix was succeeded by Porcius Festus and, as he wanted to remain in favour with the Jews, he left Paul still a prisoner.

CHAPTER 25

Felix's successor begins his duties with vigour—

THREE days after Festus had taken over his province he went up 1
from Caesarea to Jerusalem. The chief priests and elders of the 2
Jews informed him of the case against Paul and begged him as a 3
special favour to have Paul sent to Jerusalem. They themselves had already made a plot to kill him on the way. But Festus replied 4
that Paul was in custody in Caesarea, and that he himself was going there shortly.

"What you must do," he told them, "is to provide some compe- 5
tent men of your own to go down with me and if there is anything wrong with the man they can present their charges against him."

Festus spent not more than eight or ten days among them at 6
Jerusalem and then went down to Caesarea. On the day after his arrival he took his seat on the bench and ordered Paul to be brought in. As soon as he arrived the Jews from Jerusalem stood 7
up on all sides of him, bringing forward many serious accusations which they were quite unable to substantiate. Paul, in his defence, 8
maintained,

"I have committed no offence in any way against the Jewish Law, or against the Temple or against Caesar."

—but is afraid of antagonising the Jews

But Festus, wishing to gain the goodwill of the Jews, spoke 9
direct to Paul,

"Are you prepared to go up to Jerusalem and stand your trial over these matters in my presence there?"

But Paul replied, 10

"I am standing in Caesar's court and that is where I should be judged. I have done the Jews no harm, as you very well know. It comes to this: if I were a criminal and had committed some 11 crime which deserved the death penalty, I should not try to evade sentence of death. But as in fact there is no truth in the accusations these men have made, I am not prepared to be used as a means of gaining their favour—— *I appeal to Caesar!*"

12 Then Festus, after a conference with his advisers, replied to Paul,
"You have appealed to Caesar—then to Caesar you shall go!"

Festus outlines Paul's case to Agrippa

13 Some days later King Agrippa and Bernice arrived at Caesarea
14 on a state visit to Festus. They prolonged their stay for some days, and this gave Festus an opportunity of laying Paul's case before the king.
"I have a man here," he said, "who was left a prisoner by Felix.
15 When I was in Jerusalem the chief priests and Jewish elders made
16 allegations against him and demanded his conviction! I told them that the Romans were not in the habit of giving anybody up to please anyone, until the accused had had the chance of facing his accusers personally and been given the opportunity of defending
17 himself on the charges made against him. Since these Jews came back here with me, I wasted no time but on the very next day I took my seat on the bench and ordered the man to be brought in.
18 But when his accusers got up to speak they did not charge him
19 with any such crimes as I had anticipated. Their differences with him were about their own religion and concerning a certain
20 Jesus who had died, but whom Paul claimed to be still alive. I did not feel qualified to investigate such matters and so I asked the man if he were willing to go to Jerusalem and stand his trial over
21 these matters there. But when he appealed to have his case reserved for the decision of the emperor himself, I ordered him to be kept in custody until such time as I could send him to Caesar."
22 Then Agrippa said to Festus,
"I have been wanting to hear this man myself."
"Then you shall hear him tomorrow," replied Festus.

Festus formally explains the difficulty of Paul's case

23 When the next day came, Agrippa and Bernice proceeded to the audience chamber with great pomp and ceremony, with an escort of military officers and prominent townsmen. Festus
24 ordered Paul to be brought in and then he spoke:

"King Agrippa and all of you who are present, you see here the man about whom the whole Jewish people both at Jerusalem and in this city have petitioned me. They din it into my ears that he ought not to live any longer, but I for my part discovered 25 nothing that he has done which deserves the death penalty. And since he has appealed to Caesar, I have decided to send him to Rome. Frankly, I have nothing specific to write to the emperor 26 about him, and I have therefore brought him forward before you all, and especially before you, King Agrippa, so that from your examination of him there may emerge some charge which I may put in writing. For it seems ridiculous to me to send a prisoner 27 before the emperor without indicating the charges against him."

CHAPTER 26

THEN Agrippa said to Paul, *1*
"You have our permission to speak for yourself."

Paul repeats his story on a state occasion

So Paul, with that characteristic gesture of the hand, began his defence:

"King Agrippa, in answering all the charges that the Jews have *2* made against me, I must say how fortunate I consider myself to be in making my defence before you personally today. For I know *3* that you are thoroughly familiar with all the customs and disputes that exist among the Jews. I therefore ask you to listen to me patiently.

"The fact that I lived from my youth upwards among my own *4* people in Jerusalem is well known to all Jews. They have known *5* all the time, and could witness to the fact if they wished, that I lived as a Pharisee according to the strictest sect of our religion. Even today I stand here on trial because of a hope that I hold in a *6* promise that God made to our forefathers—a promise for which *7* our twelve tribes serve God zealously day and night, hoping to see it fulfilled. It is about this hope, your majesty, that I am being accused by Jews! Why does it seem incredible to you all that God *8* should raise the dead? I once thought it my duty to oppose with *9* the utmost vigour the name of Jesus of Nazareth. Yes, that is what *10* I did in Jerusalem, and I had many of God's people imprisoned on

the authority of the chief priests, and when they were on trial for
11   their lives I gave my vote against them. Many and many a time
in all the synagogues I had them punished and I used to try and
force them to deny their Lord. I was mad with fury against them,
12   and I hounded them to distant cities. Once, your majesty, on my
way to Damascus on this business, armed with the full authority
13   and commission of the chief priests, at midday I saw a light from
Heaven, far brighter than the sun, blazing about me and my
14   fellow-travellers. We all fell to the ground and I heard a voice
saying to me in Hebrew, 'Saul, Saul, why are you persecuting
me? It is not easy for you to kick against your own conscience.'
15   'Who are you, Lord?' I said. And the Lord said to me, 'I am Jesus
16   whom you are persecuting. Now get up and stand on your feet
for I have shown myself to you for a reason—you are chosen to
be my servant and a witness of what you have seen of me today,
17   and of other visions of myself which I will give you. I will keep
you safe both from your own people and from the gentiles to
18   whom I now send you. I send you to open their eyes, to turn
them from darkness to light, from the power of Satan to God
himself, so that they may know forgiveness of their sins and take
their place with all those who are made holy by their faith in me.'
19   After that, King Agrippa, I could not disobey the heavenly vision.
20   But both in Damascus and in Jerusalem, through the whole of
Judaea, and to the gentiles, I preached that men should repent and
21   turn to God and live lives to prove their change of heart. This is
22   why the Jews seized me in the Temple and tried to kill me. To
this day I have received help from God himself, and I stand here as
a witness to high and low, adding nothing to what the prophets
23   and Moses foretold should take place, that is, that Christ should
suffer, that he should be the first to rise from the dead, and so
proclaim the message of light both to our people and to the
gentiles!"

Festus concludes that Paul's enthusiasm is insanity

24   While he was thus defending himself Festus burst out,
"You are raving, Paul! All your learning has driven you mad!"
25   But Paul replied,
"I am not mad, your excellency. I speak nothing but the sober
26   truth. The king knows of these matters, and I can speak freely
before him. I cannot believe that any of these matters has escaped
27   his notice, for it has been no hole-and-corner business. King

Agrippa, do you believe the prophets? But I know that you believe them."

"Much more of this, Paul," returned Agrippa, "and you will 28 be making me a Christian!"

"Ah," returned Paul, "whether it means 'much more' or 'only 29 a little', I would to God that both you and all who can hear me this day might stand where I stand—but without these chains!"

The Roman officials consider Paul innocent

Then the king rose to his feet and so did the governor and 30 Bernice and those sitting with them, and when they had retired 31 from the assembly they discussed the matter among themselves and agreed, "This man is doing nothing to deserve either death or imprisonment."

Agrippa remarked to Festus, 32

"He might easily have been discharged if he had not appealed to Caesar."

CHAPTER 27

The last journey begins

As soon as it was decided that we should sail away to Italy, 1 Paul and some other prisoners were put in charge of a centurion named Julius, of the emperor's own regiment.* We embarked on 2 a ship hailing from Adramyttium, bound for the Asian ports, and set sail. Among our company was Aristarchus, a Macedonian from Thessalonica. On the following day we put in at Sidon, where 3 Julius treated Paul most considerately by allowing him to visit his friends and accept their hospitality. From Sidon we put to sea 4 again and sailed to leeward of Cyprus, since the wind was against us. Then, when we had crossed the gulf that lies off the coasts of 5 Cilicia and Pamphylia, we arrived at Myra in Lycia. There the 6 centurion found an Alexandrian ship bound for Italy and put us aboard her. For several days we beat slowly up to windward and 7 only just succeeded in arriving off Cnidus. Then, since the wind was still blowing against us, we sailed under the lee of Crete, and rounded Cape Salmone. Coasting along with difficulty we came 8 to a place called Fair Havens, near which is the city of Lasea. We 9 had by now lost a great deal of time and sailing had already become dangerous as it was so late in the year.

* See page 301.

Paul's warning is disregarded

10 So Paul warned them, and said,

"Men, I can see that this voyage is likely to result in damage and considerable loss—not only to ship and cargo, but even of our own lives as well."

11 But Julius paid more attention to the helmsman and the captain
12 than to Paul's words of warning. Moreover, since the harbour is unsuitable for a ship to winter in, the majority were in favour of setting sail again in the hope of reaching Phoenix and wintering there. Phoenix is a harbour in Crete, facing south-west and north-
13 west. So, when a moderate breeze sprang up, thinking they had obtained just what they wanted, they weighed anchor, and coasted
14 along, hugging the shores of Crete. But before long a terrific gale, which they called a north-easter, swept down upon us from the
15 land. The ship was caught by it and since she could not be brought
16 up into the wind we had to let her fall off and run before it. Then, running under the lee of a small island called Clauda, we managed
17 with some difficulty to secure the ship's boat. After hoisting it aboard they used cables to brace the ship. To add to the difficulties they were afraid all the time of drifting on to the Syrtis banks, so
18 they shortened sail and lay to, drifting. The next day, as we were still at the mercy of the violent storm, they began to throw cargo
19 overboard. On the third day with their own hands they threw
20 the ship's tackle over the side. Then, when for many days there was no glimpse of sun or stars and we were still in the grip of the gale, all hope of our being saved was given up.

Paul's practical courage and faith

21 Nobody had eaten for some time, when Paul came forward among the men and said,

"Men, you should have listened to me and not set sail from
22 Crete and suffered this damage and loss. However, now I beg you to keep up your spirits for no one's life is going to be lost, though
23 we shall lose the ship. I know this because last night, the angel of
24 God to whom I belong, and whom I serve, stood by me and said, 'Have no fear, Paul! You must stand before Caesar. And God, as a mark of his favour towards you, has granted you the lives of those
25 who are sailing with you.' Take courage then, men, for I believe God, and I am certain that everything will happen exactly as I
26 have been told. But we shall have to run the ship ashore on some island."

PAUL'S JOURNEY TO ROME

At last we near land

27 On the fourteenth night of the storm, as we were drifting in the Adriatic, about midnight the sailors sensed that we were nearing
28 land. Indeed, when they sounded they found twenty fathoms, and then after sailing on only a little way they sounded again and
29 found fifteen. So, for fear that we might be hurled on the rocks, they threw out four anchors from the stern and prayed for day-
30 light. The sailors wanted to desert the ship and they got as far as letting a boat down into the sea, pretending that they were going
31 to run out anchors from the bow. But Paul said to the centurion and the soldiers,

"Unless these men stay aboard the ship there is no hope of your being saved."

32 At this the soldiers cut the ropes of the boat and let her fall away.

Paul's sturdy commonsense

33 Then while everyone waited for the day to break Paul urged them to take some food, saying,

"For a fortnight now you've had no food—you haven't had a
34 bite while you've been on watch. Now take some food, I beg of you—you need it for your own well-being, for not a hair of any-one's head will be lost."

35 When he had said this he took some bread and, after thanking
36 God before them all, he broke it and began to eat. This raised
37 everybody's spirits and they began to take food themselves. There were about two hundred and seventy-six of us all told aboard that
38 ship. When they had eaten enough they lightened the ship by throwing the grain over the side.

Land at last—but we lose the ship

39 When daylight came no one recognised the land. But they made out a bay with a sandy shore where they planned to beach
40 the ship if they could. So they cut away the anchors and left them in the sea, and at the same time cut the ropes which held the steering-oars. Then they hoisted the foresail to catch the wind
41 and made for the beach. But they struck a shoal and the ship ran aground. The bow stuck fast, while the stern began to break up
42 under the strain. The soldiers' plan had been to kill the prisoners

in case any of them should try to swim to shore and escape. But   43
the centurion, in his desire to save Paul, put a stop to this, and
gave orders that all those who could swim should jump overboard
first and get to land, while the rest should follow, some on planks   44
and others on the wreckage of the ship. So it came true that
everyone reached the shore in safety.

CHAPTER 28

A small incident establishes Paul's reputation

AFTER our escape we discovered that the island was called   1
Melita. The natives treated us with uncommon kindness. Because   2
of the driving rain and cold they lit a fire and made us all welcome.
Then when Paul had collected a large bundle of sticks and was   3
about to put it on the fire, a viper driven out by the heat fastened
itself on his hand. When the natives saw the creature hanging   4
from his hand they said to each other, "This man is obviously a
murderer. He has escaped from the sea but justice will not let him
live." But Paul shook off the viper into the fire without suffering   5
any ill effect. Naturally they expected him to swell up or suddenly   6
fall down dead, but after waiting a long time and seeing nothing
untoward happen to him, they changed their minds and kept
saying that he was a god.

Paul's acts of healing: the islanders' gratitude

In that part of the island were estates belonging to the governor,   7
whose name was Publius. This man welcomed us and entertained
us most kindly for three days. Now it happened that Publius'   8
father was lying ill with fever and dysentery. Paul visited him and
after prayer laid his hands on him and healed him. After that all   9
the other sick people on the island came forward and were cured.
Consequently they loaded us with presents, and when the time   10
came for us to sail they provided us with everything we needed.

Spring returns and we resume our journey

It was no less than three months later that we set sail in an   11
Alexandrian ship which had wintered in the island, a ship that
had the heavenly twins as her figurehead. We put in at Syracuse   12
and stayed there three days, and from there we tacked round to   13

14 Rhegium. A day later the south wind sprang up and we sailed to Puteoli, reaching it in only two days. There we found some of the brothers and they begged us to stay a week with them, and so we finally came to Rome.

A Christian welcome awaits us in the capital

15 The brothers there had heard about us and came out from the city to meet us, as far as the Market of Appius and the Three Taverns. When Paul saw them he thanked God and his spirits 16 rose. When we reached Rome Paul was given permission to live alone with the soldier who was guarding him.

Paul explains himself frankly to the Jews in Rome

17 Three days later Paul invited the leading Jews to meet him, and when they arrived he spoke to them,

"Men and brothers, although I have done nothing against our people or the customs of our forefathers, I was handed over to 18 the Romans as a prisoner in Jerusalem. They examined me and were prepared to release me, since they found me guilty of nothing 19 deserving the death penalty. But the attacks of the Jews there forced me to appeal to Caesar—not that I had any charge to make 20 against my own nation. But it is because of this accusation of the Jews that I have asked to see you and talk matters over with you. In actual fact it is on account of the hope of Israel that I am here in chains."

21 But they replied,

"We have received no letters about you from Judaea, nor have any of the brothers who have arrived here said anything, officially 22 or unofficially, against you. We want to hear you state your views, although as far as this sect is concerned we do know that serious objections have been raised to it everywhere."

Paul's earnest and prolonged effort to win his own people for Christ

23 When they had arranged a day for him they came to his lodging in great numbers. From morning till evening he explained the kingdom of God to them, giving his personal testimony, trying to persuade them about Jesus from the Law of Moses and the 24 Prophets. As a result several of them were won over by his words, 25 but others would not believe. When they could not reach any

agreement among themselves and began to go away, Paul added
as a parting shot, "How rightly did the Holy Spirit speak to your
forefathers through the prophet Isaiah when he said,   26

> Go thou unto this people, and say,
> By hearing ye shall hear, and shall in no wise understand;
> And seeing ye shall see, and shall in no wise perceive:
> For this people's heart is waxed gross,   27
> And their ears are dull of hearing,
> And their eyes they have closed;
> Lest haply they should perceive with their eyes,
> And hear with their ears,
> And understand with their heart,
> And should turn again,
> And I should heal them.

"Let it be plainly understood then that this salvation of our God   28
has been sent to the gentiles, and they at least will listen to it!"

The last glimpse of Paul . . .

So Paul stayed for two full years in his own rented apartment   30
welcoming all who came to see him. He proclaimed to them all   31
the kingdom of God and gave them the teaching of the Lord
Jesus Christ with the utmost freedom and without hindrance from
anyone.

THE WORLD
OF THE
YOUNG CHURCH

307

LETTERS TO YOUNG CHURCHES

(THE EPISTLES)

The Letter to the Christians at Rome

AUTHOR. *Paul, probably written from Corinth (Acts 20, 3).*

DATE. *About 57.*

DESTINATION. *The Christians at Rome. No one knows how the church at Rome was founded, though it is perfectly possible that some Romans present on the day of Pentecost in Jerusalem (Acts 2, 10) carried back with them the Christian faith. The Roman Catholic tradition that Peter founded the Church in Rome is without reliable evidence.*

Paul is evidently writing to both converted Jews and converted pagans, which is what one would expect to find in the metropolitan city of the Roman Empire.

THEME. *This letter, with the possible exception of the "Letter to Jewish Christians", is the only one that appears to be written deliberately as a religious treatise and not merely in the ordinary way of correspondence. It is possible that Paul, naturally impressed that he was writing to the heart of the Empire, would take extra pains to "polish" this exposition of the faith.*

The theme is almost entirely that of God's "salvation" and needs a little explanation to the modern mind.

To Paul, brought up under the rigid Jewish Law, God was pre-eminently the God of Righteousness, i.e. moral perfection. In these days when the majority of people assume God to be a vague easy-going Benevolence it is difficult to appreciate the force of Paul's problem, or the wonder of its solution.

If we are prepared to grant the absolute moral perfection of God, eternally aflame with positive goodness, truth and beauty, we can perhaps understand that any form of sin or evil cannot approach God without instant dissolution. This is as inevitable as, for example, the destruction of certain germs by the light of the sun.

How then, asks Paul, can man who has failed and, moreover, sinned deliberately, ever approach God or hope to share in his timeless existence?

The Law offers the first method. If men will themselves fully

*obey the law of God they will be free from moral taint and able to
approach God in safety. Unhappily, as Paul points out at some
length, men have signally failed to keep either the Law revealed
to the Jews or the universal moral law of human conscience. If
they have broken all the laws or only a few they have all failed
and are all guilty. They can, moreover, do nothing to remove their
guilt. The Law which ought to be a finger-post to God becomes to
them nothing but a warning-notice. This is the crux of Paul's
problem.*

*The heart of the Gospel is that God himself meets this frightful
deadlock by a personal visit to this world. God, as Jesus Christ,
became representative man, and as such deliberately accepted the
eventual consequence of evil, namely, suffering and death. Any
man therefore who sincerely entrusts his life to Christ can now be
accepted by God by virtue of God's personal act of atonement.
Salvation, i.e. being safe from the horrible long-term consequences
of sin and safe in the presence of God's utter holiness, now becomes
a matter of "believing" and not "achieving".*

*The theme is worked out in this letter, with a parenthetical
passage about God's chosen people, the Jews, and is closely followed
by advice as to the sort of life that the "justified" and "saved" man
should now live.*

The letter closes with personal news and greetings.

CHAPTER 1

THIS letter comes to you from Paul, a servant of Jesus Christ, 1
called as a messenger and appointed for the service of that gospel
of God which was long ago promised by the prophets in the holy 2
scriptures.

The gospel is centred in God's Son, a descendant of David by 3
human genealogy and patently marked out as the Son of God by 4
the power of that Spirit of holiness which raised him to life again
from the dead. He is our Lord, Jesus Christ, from whom we 5
received grace and our commission in his name to forward
obedience to the faith in all nations. And of this great number 6
you at Rome are also called to belong to him.

To you all then, loved of God and called to be Christ's men 7
and women, grace and peace from God the Father and from the
Lord Jesus Christ.

A personal message

8 I must begin by telling you how I thank God through Jesus Christ for you all, since the news of your faith has become known

9 everywhere. Before God, whom I serve with my spirit in the gospel of his Son, I assure you that you are always in my prayers.

10 I am constantly asking him that he will somehow make it possible

11 for me now, at long last, to come to Rome. I am longing to see

12 you: I want to bring you some spiritual strength, and that will mean that I shall be strengthened by you, each of us helped by the other's faith.

13 Then I should like you to know, my brothers, that I have long intended to come to you (but something has always prevented me), for I should like to see some results among you, as I have

14 among other gentiles. I feel myself under a sort of universal obligation, I owe something to all men, from cultured Greek to

15 ignorant savage. That is why I want, as far as my ability will carry

16 me, to preach the gospel to you who live in Rome as well. For I am not ashamed of the gospel. I see it as the very power of God working for the salvation of everyone who believes it, both Jew

17 and Greek. I see in it God's plan for imparting righteousness to men, a process begun and continued by their faith. For, as the scripture says:

The righteous shall live by faith.

The righteousness of God and the sin of man

18 Now the holy anger of God is disclosed from Heaven against the godlessness and evil of those men who render truth dumb

19 and inoperative by their wickedness. It is not that they do not know the truth about God; indeed he has made it quite plain to

20 them. For since the beginning of the world the invisible attributes of God, e.g. his eternal power and divinity, have been plainly discernible through things which he has made and which are commonly seen and known, thus leaving these men without a rag

21 of excuse. They knew all the time that there is a God, yet they refused to acknowledge him as such, or to thank him for what he is or does. Thus they became fatuous in their argumentations,

22 and plunged their silly minds still further into the dark. Behind a

23 façade of "wisdom" they became just fools, fools who would exchange the glory of the immortal God for an imitation image of

24 a mortal man, or of creatures that run or fly or crawl. They gave

up God: and therefore God gave them up—to be the playthings of their own foul desires in dishonouring their own bodies.

The fearful consequence of deliberate atheism

These men deliberately forfeited the truth of God and accepted 25 a lie, paying homage and giving service to the creature instead of to the Creator, who alone is worthy to be worshipped for ever and ever, amen. God therefore handed them over to disgraceful 26 passions. Their women exchanged the normal practices of sexual intercourse for something which is abnormal and unnatural. Similarly the men, turning from natural intercourse with women, 27 were swept into lustful passions for one another. Men with men performed these shameful horrors, receiving, of course, in their own personalities the consequences of sexual perversity.

Moreover, since they considered themselves too high and 28 mighty to acknowledge God, he allowed them to become the slaves of their degenerate minds, and to perform unmentionable deeds. They became filled with wickedness, rottenness, greed and 29 malice; their minds became steeped in envy, murder, quarrelsomeness, deceitfulness and spite. They became whisperers-behind-doors, stabbers-in-the-back, God-haters; they overflowed 30 with insolent pride and boastfulness, and their minds teemed with diabolical invention. They scoffed at duty to parents, they mocked 31 at learning, recognised no obligations of honour, lost all natural affection, and had no use for mercy. More than this—being well 32 aware of God's pronouncement that all who do these things deserve to die, they not only continued their own practices, but did not hesitate to give their thorough approval to others who did the same.

CHAPTER 2

Yet we cannot judge them, for we also are sinners: God is the only judge

Now if you feel inclined to set yourself up as a judge of those 1 who sin, let me assure you, whoever you are, that you are in no position to do so. For at whatever point you condemn others you automatically condemn yourself, since you, the judge, commit the same sins. God's judgment, we know, is utterly impartial in 2 its action against such evil-doers. What makes you think that you, 3 who so readily judge the sins of others, can consider yourself

4 beyond the judgment of God? Are you, perhaps, misinterpreting God's generosity and patient mercy towards you as weakness on his part? Don't you realise that God's kindness is meant to lead
5 you to repentance? Or are you by your obstinate refusal to repent simply storing up for yourself an experience of the wrath of God in the day when, in his holy anger against evil, he shows his hand in righteous judgment?

6 There is no doubt at all that he will "render to every man
7 according to his works", and that means eternal life to those who, in patiently doing good, aim at the unseen (but real) glory and
8 honour of the eternal world. It also means anger and wrath for those who rebel against God's plan of life, and refuse to obey his rules, and who, in so doing, make themselves the very servants of
9 evil. Yes, it means bitter pain and a fearful undoing for every human soul who works on the side of evil, for the Jew first and
10 then the Greek. But, let me repeat, there is glory and honour and peace for every worker on the side of good, for the Jew first and
11 then the Greek. For there is no preferential treatment with God.

God's judgment is absolutely just

12 All who have sinned without knowledge of the Law will die without reference to the Law; and all who have sinned knowing
13 the Law shall be judged according to the Law. It is not familiarity with the Law that justifies a man in the sight of God, but obedience to it.
14 When the gentiles, who have no knowledge of the Law, act in accordance with it by the light of nature, they show that they
15 have a law in themselves, for they demonstrate the effect of a law operating in their own hearts. Their own consciences endorse the existence of such a law, for there is something which condemns or excuses their actions.
16 We may be sure that all this will be taken into account in the day of true judgment, when God will judge men's secret lives by Christ Jesus, as my gospel plainly states.

You Jews are privileged—do you live up to your privileges?

17 Now you, my reader, who bear the name of Jew, take your stand upon the Law, and are, so to speak, proud of your God.
18 You know his plan, and are able through your knowledge of the
19 Law truly to appreciate moral values. You can, therefore, con-

fidently look upon yourself as a guide to those who do not know
the way, and as a light to those who are groping in the dark.
You can instruct those who have no spiritual wisdom: you can   20
teach those who, spiritually speaking, are only just out of the
cradle. You have a certain grasp of the basis of true knowledge.
You have without doubt very great advantages. But, prepared   21
as you are to instruct others, do you ever teach yourself anything?
You preach against stealing, for example, but are you sure of
your own honesty? You denounce the practice of adultery, but   22
are you sure of your own purity? You loathe idolatry, but *how
honest are you towards the property of heathen temples?* Everyone   23
knows how proud you are of the Law, but that means a propor-
tionate dishonour to God when men know that you break it!
Don't you know that the very name of God is cursed among the   24
gentiles because of the behaviour of Jews? There is, you know, a
verse of scripture to that effect.

Being a true "Jew" is an inward not an outward matter

That most intimate sign of belonging to God that we call cir-   25
cumcision does indeed mean something if you keep the Law.
But if you flout the Law you are to all intents and purposes uncir-
cumcising yourself! Conversely, if an uncircumcised man keep   26
the Law's commandments, does he not thereby "circumcise"
himself? Moreover, is it not plain to you that those who are   27
physically uncircumcised, and yet keep the Law, are a continual
judgment upon you who, for all your circumcision and knowledge of the Law, break it?

I have come to the conclusion that a true Jew is not the man   28
who is merely a Jew outwardly, and real circumcision is not just
a matter of the body. The true Jew is one who belongs to God in   29
heart, a man whose circumcision is not just an outward physical
affair but is a God-made sign upon the heart and soul, and results
in a life lived not for the approval of man, but for the approval of
God.

CHAPTER 3

Jews are privileged, but even they have failed

Is there any advantage then in being one of the chosen people?   1
Does circumcision mean anything? Yes, of course, a great deal in   2
every way. You have only to think of one thing to begin with—

3 it was the Jews to whom God's messages were entrusted. Some of them were undoubtedly faithless, but what then? Can you imagine that their faithlessness could disturb the faithfulness of

4 God? Of course not! Let us think of God as true, even if every living man be proved a liar. Remember the scripture?

> That thou mightest be justified in thy words,
> And mightest prevail when thou comest into judgment.

5 But if our wickedness advertises the goodness of God, do we feel that God is being unfair to punish us in return? (I'm using a

6 human tit-for-tat argument.) Not a bit of it! What sort of a

7 person would God be then to judge the world? It is like saying that if my lying throws into sharp relief the truth of God and, so to speak, enhances his reputation, then why should he repay me

8 by judging me a sinner? Similarly, why not do evil that good may be, by contrast, all the more conspicuous and valuable? (As a matter of fact, I am reported as urging this very thing, by some slanderously and others quite seriously! But, of course, such an argument is quite properly condemned.)

9 Are we Jews then a march ahead of other men? By no means. For I have shown above that all men from Jews to Greeks are

10 under the condemnation of sin. The scriptures endorse this fact plainly enough.

> There is none righteous, no, not one.

11
> There is none that understandeth,
> There is none that seeketh after God;

12
> They have all turned aside, they are together become
>   unprofitable;
> There is none that doeth good, no, not so much as one:

13
> Their throat is an open sepulchre;
> With their tongues they have used deceit;
> The poison of asps is under their lips:

14
> Whose mouth is full of cursing and bitterness:

15
> Their feet are swift to shed blood;

16
> Destruction and misery are in their ways:

17
> And the way of peace have they not known;

18
> There is no fear of God before their eyes.

19 We know what the message of the Law is, to those who live under it—that every excuse may die on the lips of him who makes it and no living man may think himself beyond the judgment of

20 God. No man can justify himself before God by a perfect performance of the Law's demands—indeed it is the straight-edge of the Law that shows us how crooked we are.

God's new plan—righteousness by faith, not through the Law

But now we are seeing the righteousness of God declared quite   21
apart from the Law (though amply testified to by both Law and
Prophets)—it is a righteousness imparted to, and operating in, all   22
who have faith in Jesus Christ. (For there is no distinction to be
made anywhere: everyone has sinned, everyone falls short of the   23
beauty of God's plan.) Under this divine system a man who   24
has faith is now freely acquitted in the eyes of God by his generous
dealing in the redemptive act of Christ Jesus. God has appointed   25
him as the means of propitiation, a propitiation accomplished by
the shedding of his blood, to be received and made effective in
ourselves by faith. God has done this to demonstrate his righteousness both by the wiping out of the sins of the past (the time when
he withheld his hand), and by showing in the present time that he   26
is a just God and that he justifies every man who has faith in Jesus
Christ.

Faith, not pride of achievement

What happens now to human pride of achievement? There is   27
no more room for it. Why, because failure to keep the Law has
killed it? Not at all, but because the whole matter is now on a
different plane—believing instead of achieving. We see now that   28
a man is justified before God by the fact of his faith in God's
appointed Saviour and not by what he has managed to achieve
under the Law.

And God is God of both Jews and gentiles, let us be quite clear   29
about that! The one God is ready to justify the circumcised by   30
faith and the uncircumcised by faith also.

Are we then undermining the Law by this insistence on faith?   31
Not a bit of it! We put the Law in its proper place.

CHAPTER 4

Let us go back and consider our father Abraham

Now how does all this affect the position of our ancestor   1
Abraham? Well, if justification were by achievement he could   2
quite fairly be proud of what he achieved—but not, I am sure,
proud before God. For what does the scripture say about him?   3

And Abraham believed God, and it was reckoned unto him for righteousness.

4 Now if a man *works* his wages are not counted as a gift but as
5 a fair reward. But if a man, irrespective of his work, has faith in him who justifies the sinful, then that man's *faith* is counted as
6 righteousness, and that is the gift of God. This is the happy state of the man whom God accounts righteous, apart from his achieve-
7 ments, as David expresses it:

Blessed are they whose iniquities are forgiven
And whose sins are covered.

8 Blessed is the man to whom the Lord will not reckon sin.

It is a matter of faith, not circumcision

9 Now the question, an important one, arises: is this happiness for the circumcised only, or for the uncircumcised as well?

Note this carefully. We began by saying that Abraham's faith
10 was counted unto him for righteousness. When this happened, was he a circumcised man? He was not, he was still uncircum-
11 cised. It was *afterwards* that the sign of circumcision was given to him, as a seal upon that righteousness which God was accounting to him *as yet an uncircumcised man!* God's purpose here is twofold. First, that Abraham might be the spiritual father of all who since that time, despite their uncircumcision, show the faith that is
12 counted as righteousness. Then, secondly, that he might be the circumcised father of all those who are not only circumcised, but are living by the same sort of faith which he himself had before he was circumcised.

The promise, from the beginning, was made to faith

13 The ancient promise made to Abraham and his descendants, that they should eventually possess the world, was given not because of any achievements made through obedience to the Law, but because of the righteousness which had its root in faith.
14 For if, after all, they who pin their faith to keeping the Law were to inherit God's world, it would make nonsense of faith in God himself, and destroy the whole point of the promise.
15 For we have already noted that the Law can produce no promise, only the threat of wrath to come. And, indeed, if there were no Law the question of sin would not arise.

The whole thing, then, is a matter of faith on man's part and   *16*
generosity on God's. He gives the security of his own promise
to all men who can be called "children of Abraham", i.e. both
those who have lived in faith by the Law, and those who have
exhibited a faith like that of Abraham. To whichever group
we belong, Abraham is in a real sense our father, as the scripture   *17*
says:

A father of many nations have I made thee.

This faith is valid because of the existence of God himself,
who can make the dead live, and speak his Word to those who
are yet unborn.

Abraham was a shining example of faith

Abraham, when hope was dead within him, went on hoping   *18*
in faith, believing that he would become "the father of many
nations". He relied on the word of God which definitely referred
to "thy seed". With undaunted faith he looked at the facts—his   *19*
own impotence (he was practically a hundred years old at the
time) and his wife Sarah's apparent barrenness. Yet he refused to   *20*
allow any distrust of a definite pronouncement of God to make
him waver. He drew strength from his faith, and, while giving
the glory to God, remained absolutely convinced that God was   *21*
able to implement his own promise. This was the "faith" which   *22*
was counted unto him for righteousness.

Now this counting of faith for righteousness was not recorded   *23*
simply for Abraham's credit, but as a divine principle which   *24*
should apply to us as well. Faith is to be reckoned as righteousness
to us also, who believe in him who raised from the dead Jesus our
Lord, who was delivered to death for our sins and raised again to   *25*
secure our justification.

CHAPTER 5

Faith means the certainty of God's love, now and hereafter

SINCE then it is by faith that we are justified, let us grasp the   *1*
fact that we *have* peace with God through our Lord Jesus Christ.
Through him we have confidently entered into this new relation-   *2*
ship of grace, and here we take our stand, in happy certainty of
the glorious things he has for us in the future.

This doesn't mean, of course, that we have only a hope of   *3*

future joys—we can be full of joy here and now even in our
trials and troubles. Taken in the right spirit these very things will
4 give us patient endurance; this in turn will develop a mature
5 character, and a character of this sort produces a steady hope, a
hope that will never disappoint us. Already we have some
experience of the love of God flooding through our hearts by the
6 Holy Spirit given to us. And we can see that it was while we were
7 powerless to help ourselves that Christ died for sinful men. In
human experience it is a rare thing for one man to give his life
for another, even if the latter be a good man, though there have
8 been a few who have had the courage to do it. Yet the proof of
God's amazing love is this: that it was *while we were sinners* that
9 Christ died for us. Moreover, if he did that for us while we were
sinners, now that we are men justified by the shedding of his
10 blood, what reason have we to fear the wrath of God? If, while
we were his enemies, Christ reconciled us to God by *dying for us*,
surely now that we are reconciled we may be perfectly certain of
11 our salvation through his *living in us*. Nor, I am sure, is this a
matter of bare salvation—we may hold our heads high in the
light of God's love because of the reconciliation which Christ has
made.

A brief résumé—the consequence of sin and the gift of God

12 This, then, is what has happened. Sin made its entry into the
world through one man, and through sin, death. The entail of
sin and death passed on to the whole human race, and no one
could break it for no one was himself free from sin.
13 Sin, you see, was in the world long before the Law, though I
suppose, technically speaking, it was not "sin" where there was
14 no law to define it. Nevertheless death, the complement of sin,
held sway over mankind from Adam to Moses, even over those
whose sin was quite unlike Adam's.
Adam, the first man, corresponds in some degree to the man
15 who has to come. But the gift of God through Christ is a very
different matter from the "account rendered" through the sin of
Adam. For while as a result of one man's sin death by natural
consequence became the common lot of men, it was by the
generosity of God, the free giving of the grace of the one man
Jesus Christ, that the love of God overflowed for the benefit of
all men.
16 Nor is the effect of God's gift the same as the effect of that one

318

man's sin. For in the one case one man's sin brought its inevitable judgment, and the result was condemnation. But, in the other, countless men's sins are met with the free gift of grace, and the result is justification before God.

For if one man's offence meant that men should be slaves to 17 death all their lives, it is a far greater thing that through another man, Jesus Christ, men by their acceptance of his more than sufficient grace and righteousness, should live all their lives like kings!

We see, then, that as one act of sin exposed the whole race of 18 men to God's judgment and condemnation, so one act of perfect righteousness presents all men freely acquitted in the sight of God. One man's disobedience placed all men under the threat of con- 19 demnation, but one man's obedience has the power to present all men righteous before God.

Grace is a bigger thing than the Law

Now we find that the Law keeps slipping into the picture to 20 point the vast extent of sin. Yet, though sin is shown to be wide and deep, thank God his grace is wider and deeper still! The whole 21 outlook changes—sin used to be the master of men and in the end handed them over to death: now grace is the ruling factor, with righteousness as its purpose and its end the bringing of men to the eternal life of God through Jesus Christ our Lord.

CHAPTER 6

Righteousness by faith, in practice

Now what is our response to be? Shall we sin to our heart's 1 content and see how far we can exploit the grace of God? What 2 a ghastly thought! We, who have died to sin—how could we live in sin a moment longer? Have you forgotten that all of us 3 who were baptised into Jesus Christ were, by that very action, sharing in his death? We were dead and buried with him in 4 baptism, so that just as he was raised from the dead by that splendid revelation of the Father's power so we too might rise to life on a new plane altogether. If we have, as it were, shared his death, 5 let us rise and live our new lives with him! Let us never forget 6 that our old selves died with him on the cross that the tyranny of sin over us might be broken—for a dead man can safely be 7

8 said to be immune to the power of sin. And if we were dead men
   with him we can believe that we shall also be men newly alive
9 with him. We can be sure that the risen Christ never dies again—
10 death's power to touch him is finished. He died, because of sin,
11 once: he lives for God for ever. In the same way look upon yourselves as dead to the appeal and power of sin but alive and sensitive
   to the call of God through Jesus Christ our Lord.

12   Do not, then, allow sin to establish any power over your mortal
13 bodies in making you give way to your lusts. Nor hand over your
   organs to be, as it were, weapons of evil for the devil's purposes.
   But, like men rescued from certain death, put yourselves in God's
14 hands as weapons of good for his own purposes. For sin is not
   meant to be your master—you are no longer living under the
   Law, but under grace.

The new service completely ousts the old

15   Now, what shall we do? Shall we go on sinning because we
   have no Law to condemn us any more, but are living under
16 grace? Never! Just think what it would mean. You *belong* to the
   power which you choose to obey, whether you choose sin, whose
   reward is death, or God, obedience to whom means the reward
17 of righteousness. Thank God that you, who were at one time
   the servants of sin, honestly responded to the impact of Christ's
18 teaching when you came under its influence. Then, released from
19 the service of sin, you entered the service of righteousness. (I use
   an everyday illustration because human nature grasps truth more
   readily that way.) In the past you voluntarily gave your bodies to
   the service of vice and wickedness—for the purpose of becoming
   wicked. So, now, give yourselves to the service of righteousness
20 —for the purpose of becoming really good. For when you were
21 employed by sin you owed no duty to righteousness. Yet what
   sort of a harvest did you reap from those things that today you
   blush to remember? In the long run those things mean one thing
   only—death.

22   But now that you are employed by God, you owe no duty to
   sin, and you reap the fruit of being made righteous, while at the
   end of the road there is life for evermore.

23   Sin *pays* its servants: the wage is death. But God *gives* to those
   who serve him: his free gift is eternal life through Jesus Christ
   our Lord.

CHAPTER 7
How to be free from the Law

You know very well, my brothers (for I am speaking to those **1**
well acquainted with the subject), that the Law can only exercise
authority over a man so long as he is alive. A married woman, for **2**
example, is bound by law to her husband so long as he is alive.
But if he dies, then his legal claim over her disappears. This **3**
means that, if she should give herself to another man while her
husband is alive, she incurs the stigma of adultery. But if, after
her husband's death, she does exactly the same thing, no one
could call her an adulteress, for the legal hold over her has been
dissolved by her husband's death.

There is, I think, a fair analogy here. The death of Christ on **4**
the cross has made you "dead" to the claims of the Law, and
you are free to give yourselves in marriage, so to speak, to
another, the one who was raised from the dead, that you may
be productive for God.

While we were "in the flesh" the Law stimulated our sinful **5**
passions and so worked in our nature that we became productive
—for death! But now that we stand clear of the Law, the claims **6**
which existed are dissolved by our "death", and we are free to
serve God not in the old obedience to the letter of the Law, but in
a new way, in the Spirit.

Sin and the Law

It now begins to look as if sin and the Law were very much the **7**
same thing—can this be a fact? Of course it cannot. But it must
in fairness be admitted that I should never have had sin brought
home to me but for the Law. For example, I should never have
felt guilty of the sin of coveting if I had not heard the Law
saying "Thou shalt not covet". But the sin in me, finding in the **8**
commandment an opportunity to express itself, stimulated all my
covetous desires. For sin, in the absence of the Law, has no chance
to function technically as "sin". As long, then, as I was without **9**
the Law I was, spiritually speaking, alive. But when the commandment arrived, sin sprang to life and I "died". The com- **10**
mandment, which was meant to be a direction to life, I found was
a sentence to death. The commandment gave sin an opportunity, **11**
and without my realising what was happening, it "killed" me.

The Law is itself good

12 It can scarcely be doubted that in reality the Law itself is holy,
13 and the commandment is holy, fair and good. Can it be that something that is intrinsically good could mean death to me? No, what happened was this. Sin, at the touch of the Law, was forced to express itself as sin, and *that* meant death for me. The contact of the Law showed the sinful nature of sin.

But it cannot make men good

14 After all, the Law itself is really concerned with the spiritual—
15 it is I who am carnal, and have sold my soul to sin. In practice, what happens? My own behaviour baffles me. For I find myself not doing what I really want to do but doing what I really loathe.
16 Yet surely if I do things that I really don't want to do, I am admit-
17 ting that I really agree with the Law. But it cannot be said that "I" am doing them at all—it must be sin that has made its home
18 in my nature. (And indeed, I know from experience that the carnal side of my being can scarcely be called the home of good!) I often find that I have the will to do good, but not the power.
19 That is, I don't accomplish the good I set out to do, and the evil
20 I don't really want to do I find I am always doing. Yet if I do things that I don't really want to do then it is not, I repeat, "I" who do them, but the sin which has made its home within me.
21 When I come up against the Law I want to do good, but in
22 practice I do evil. My conscious mind whole-heartedly endorses the Law, yet I observe an entirely different principle at work in
23 my nature. This is in continual conflict with my conscious attitude, and makes me an unwilling prisoner to the law of sin and death. In my mind I am God's willing servant, but in my own
24 nature I am bound fast, as I say, to the law of sin and death. It is an agonising situation, and who on earth can set me free from
25 the clutches of my own sinful nature? I thank God there *is* a way out through Jesus Christ our Lord.

CHAPTER 8

The way out—new life in Christ

1 No condemnation now hangs over the head of those who are
2 "in" Christ Jesus. For the new spiritual principle of life "in" Christ Jesus lifts me out of the old vicious circle of sin and death.

The Law never succeeded in producing righteousness—the *3*
failure was always the weakness of human nature. But God has
met this by sending his own Son Jesus Christ to live in that
human nature which causes the trouble. And, *while Christ was
actually taking upon himself the sins of men, God condemned that
sinful nature.* So that we are able to meet the Law's requirements, *4*
so long as we are living no longer by the dictates of our sinful
nature, but in obedience to the promptings of the Spirit. The *5*
carnal attitude sees no further than natural things. But the spiritual
attitude reaches out after the things of the spirit. The former *6*
attitude means, bluntly, death: the latter means life and inward
peace. And this is only to be expected, for the carnal attitude is *7*
inevitably opposed to the purpose of God, and neither can nor
will follow his laws for living. Men who hold this attitude cannot *8*
possibly please God.

What the presence of Christ within means

But you are not carnal but spiritual if the Spirit of God finds a *9*
home within you. You cannot, indeed, be a Christian at all
unless you have something of his Spirit in you. Now if Christ *10*
does live within you his presence means that your sinful nature
is dead, but your spirit becomes alive because of the righteousness
he brings with him. I said that our nature is "dead" in the presence *11*
of Christ, and so it is, because of its sin. Nevertheless once the
Spirit of him who raised Christ Jesus from the dead lives within
you he will, by that same Spirit, bring to your whole being new
strength and vitality.

So then, my brothers, you can see that we have no particular *12*
reason to feel grateful to our sensual nature, or to live life on the
level of the instincts. Indeed that way of living leads to certain *13*
spiritual death. But if on the other hand you cut the nerve of your
instinctive actions by obeying the Spirit, you are on the way to
real living.

Christ is within—follow the lead of his Spirit

All who follow the leading of God's Spirit are God's own sons. *14*
Nor are you meant to relapse into the old slavish attitude of fear *15*
—you have been adopted into the very family circle of God and
you can say with a full heart, "Father, my Father". The Spirit *16*
himself endorses our inward conviction that we really are the

17 children of God. Think what that means. If we are his children
we share his treasures, and all that Christ claims as his will belong
to all of us as well! Yes, if we share in his sufferings we shall certainly share in his glory.

Present distress is temporary and negligible

18 In my opinion whatever we may have to go through now is
less than nothing compared with the magnificent future God has
19 planned for us. The whole creation is on tiptoe to see the wonder-
20 ful sight of the sons of God coming into their own. The world of
creation cannot as yet see reality, not because it chooses to be
blind, but because in God's purpose it has been so limited—yet
21 it has been given hope. And the hope is that in the end the whole
of created life will be rescued from the tyranny of change and
decay, and have its share in that magnificent liberty which can
only belong to the children of God!
22 It is plain to anyone with eyes to see that at the present time
23 all created life groans in a sort of universal travail. And it is plain,
too, that we who have a foretaste of the Spirit are in a state of
painful tension, while we wait for that redemption of our bodies
which will mean that at last we have realised our full sonship in
24 him. We were saved by this hope, but in our moments of
impatience let us remember that hope always means waiting for
25 something that we do not yet possess. But if we hope for something
we cannot see, then we must settle down to wait for it in patience.

This is not mere theory—the Spirit helps us to find it true

26 The Spirit of God not only maintains this hope within us, but
helps us in our present limitations. For example, we do not know
how to pray worthily as sons of God, but his Spirit within us is
actually praying for us in those agonising longings which never
27 find words. And God who knows the heart's secrets understands,
of course, the Spirit's intention as he prays for those who love
God.
28 Moreover we know that to those who love God, who are called
according to his plan, everything that happens fits into a pattern
29 for good. God, in his foreknowledge, chose them to bear the
family likeness of his Son, that he might be the eldest of a family
30 of many brothers. He chose them long ago; when the time came
he called them, he made them righteous in his sight, and then
lifted them to the splendour of life as his own sons.

We hold, in Christ, an impregnable position

In face of all this, what is there left to say? If God is for us, 31
who can be against us? He who did not grudge his own Son but 32
gave him up for us all—can we not trust such a God to give us, with
him, everything else that we can need?

Who would dare to accuse us, whom God has chosen? The 33
judge himself has declared us free from sin. Who is in a position 34
to condemn? Only Christ, and Christ died for us, Christ rose for
us, Christ reigns in power for us, Christ prays for us!

Who can separate us from the love of Christ? Can trouble, 35
pain or persecution? Can lack of clothes and food, danger to life
and limb, the threat of force of arms? Indeed some of us know 36
the truth of that ancient text:

For thy sake we are killed all the day long;
We were accounted as sheep for the slaughter.

No, in all these things we win an overwhelming victory through 37
him who has proved his love for us.

I have become absolutely convinced that neither death nor life, 38
neither messenger of Heaven nor monarch of earth, neither what
happens today nor what may happen tomorrow, neither a power 39
from on high nor a power from below, nor anything else in God's
whole world has any power to separate us from the love of God in
Christ Jesus our Lord!

CHAPTER 9

The fly in the ointment—the infidelity of my own race

BEFORE Christ and my own conscience in the Holy Spirit I assure 1
you that I am speaking the plain truth when I say that there is 2
something that makes me feel very depressed, like a pain that
never leaves me. It is the condition of my brothers and fellow- 3
Israelites, and I have actually reached the pitch of wishing myself
cut off from Christ if it meant that they could be won for God.

Just think what the Israelites have had given to them. The 4
privilege of being adopted as sons of God, the experience of seeing something of the glory of God, the receiving of the agreements made with God, the gift of the Law, true ways of worship,
God's own promises—all these are theirs. The patriarchs are 5
theirs, and so too, as far as human descent goes, is Christ himself,
Christ who is God over all, blessed for ever.

God's purpose is not utterly defeated by this infidelity

6   Now this does not mean that God's word to Israel has failed. For you cannot count all "Israelites" as the true Israel of God.
7   Nor can all Abraham's descendants be considered truly children of Abraham. The promise was that "in Isaac shall thy children
8   be called". That means that it is not the natural descendants who automatically inherit the promise, but, on the contrary, that the children of the promise (i.e. the sons of God) are to be considered
9   truly Abraham's children. For it was a promise when God said: "About this time I will come and Sarah shall have a son." (Everybody, remember, thought it quite impossible for Sarah to
10 have a child.) And then, again, a word of promise came to Rebecca, at the time when she was pregnant with two children by the one
11 man, Isaac our forefather. It came before the children were born or had done anything good or bad, plainly showing that God's act of choice has nothing to do with achievements, good or bad,
12 but is entirely a matter of his will. The promise was:

The elder shall serve the younger.

13 And we get a later endorsement of this divine choice in the words:

Jacob I loved, but Esau I hated.

We must not jump to conclusions about God

14 Now do we conclude that God is monstrously unfair? Never!
15 God said long ago to Moses:

I will have mercy on whom I have mercy, and I will have compassion on whom I have compassion.

16 It is obviously not a question of human will or human effort, but
17 of divine mercy. The scripture says to Pharaoh:

For this very purpose did I raise thee up, that I might show in thee my power, and that my name might be published abroad in all the earth.

18 It seems plain, then, that God chooses on whom he will have mercy, and whom he will harden in their sin.
19 Of course I can almost hear your retort: "If this is so, and God's will is irresistible, why does God blame men for what they do?"
20 But the question really is this: "Who are you, a man, to make any such reply to God?" When a craftsman makes anything he doesn't expect it to turn round and say, "Why did you make me like
21 this?" The potter, for instance, is always assumed to have complete control over the clay, making with one part of the lump a

lovely vase, and with another a pipe for sewage. Can we not 22
assume that God has the same control over human clay? May it
not be that God, though he must sooner or later expose his wrath
against sin and show his controlling hand, has yet most patiently
endured the presence in his world of things that cry out to be
destroyed? Can we not see, in this, his purpose in demonstrating 23
the boundless resources of his glory upon those whom he considers fit to receive his mercy, and whom he long ago planned to
raise to glorious life? And by these chosen people I mean you and 24
me, whom he has called out from both Jews and gentiles. He 25
says in Hosea:

I will call that my people, which was not my people;
And her beloved, which was not beloved.
And it shall be, that in the place where it was said unto them, 26
Ye are not my people,
There shall they be called sons of the living God.
And Isaiah, speaking about Israel, proclaims: 27
If the number of the children of Israel be as the sand of the
sea, it is the remnant that shall be saved:
For the Lord will execute his word upon the earth, finishing it 28
and cutting it short.
And previously, Isaiah said: 29
Except the Lord of Sabaoth had left us a seed,
We had become as Sodom and had been made like unto
Gomorrah.

At present the gentiles have gone further than the Jews

Now, how far have we got? That the gentiles who never had 30
the Law's standard of righteousness to guide them, have attained
righteousness, righteousness-by-faith. But Israel, following the 31
Law of righteousness, failed to reach the goal of righteousness.
And why? Because their minds were fixed on what they achieved 32
instead of on what they believed. They tripped over that very
stone the scripture mentions: 33
Behold, I lay in Zion a stone of stumbling and a rock of
offence:
And he that believeth on him shall not be put to shame.

327

CHAPTER 10

How Israel has missed the way

1 My brothers, from the bottom of my heart I long and pray to
2 God that Israel may be saved! I know from experience what a
passion for God they have, but alas, it is not a passion based on
3 knowledge. They do not know God's righteousness, and all the
time they are going about trying to prove their own righteous-
4 ness they have the wrong attitude to receive his. For Christ means
the end of the struggle for righteousness-by-the-Law for everyone who believes in him.

5 Moses writes of righteousness-by-the-Law when he says that
the man who perfectly obeys the Law shall find life in it. But
6 righteousness-by-faith says something like this:
"You need not say in your heart, 'Who could go up to Heaven
7 to bring Christ down to us, or who could descend into the depths
8 to bring him up from the dead?' For the secret is very near you,
in *your own heart*, in *your own mouth*!" It is the secret of faith,
9 which is the burden of our preaching, and it says, in effect, "If
you openly admit by *your own mouth* that Jesus Christ is the Lord,
and if you believe in *your own heart* that God raised him from the
10 dead, you will be saved." For it is believing *in the heart* that makes
a man righteous before God, and it is stating his belief by *his own*
11 *mouth* that confirms his salvation. And the scripture says: "Who-
12 soever believes in him shall not be disappointed." And that
"whosoever" means anyone, without distinction between Jew
or Greek. For all have the same Lord, whose boundless resources
13 are available to all who turn to him in faith. For:
Whosoever shall call upon the name of the Lord shall be
saved.

Can we offer the excuse of ignorance on Israel's behalf?

14 Now how can they call on one in whom they have never
believed? How can they believe in one of whom they have
never heard? And how can they hear unless someone proclaims
15 him? And who will go to tell them unless he is sent? As the
scripture puts it:
How beautiful are the feet of them that bring glad tidings of
good things!

Yet all who have heard have not responded to the gospel. **16**
Isaiah asks, you remember,
> Lord, who hath believed our report?

(Belief, you see, can only come from hearing the message, and **17**
the message is the word of Christ.)

But when I ask myself: "Did they never hear?" I have to **18**
answer that they *have* heard, for
> Their sound went out into all the earth,
> And their words unto the ends of the world.

Then I say to myself: "Did Israel not know?" And my answer **19**
must be that they did. For Moses says:
> I will provoke you to jealousy with that which is no nation,
> With a nation void of understanding will I anger you.

And Isaiah, more daring still, puts these words into the mouth of **20**
God:
> I was found of them that sought me not.
> I became manifest unto them that asked not of me.

And then, speaking of Israel: **21**
> All the day long did I spread out my hands unto a disobedient
> and gainsaying people.

CHAPTER 11

Israel's failure—yet remember the faithful few

THIS leads naturally to the question, "Has God then totally **1**
repudiated his people?" Certainly not! I myself, for one, am an
Israelite, a descendant of Abraham and of the tribe of Benjamin. It is unthinkable that God should have repudiated his own **2**
people, the people whose destiny he himself appointed. Don't you
remember what the scripture says in the story of Elijah? How
he pleaded with God on Israel's behalf:
> Lord, they have killed thy prophets **3**
> They have digged down thine altars:
> And I am left alone, and they seek my life.

And do you remember God's reply? **4**
> I have left for myself seven thousand men
> Who have not bowed the knee to Baal.

In just the same way, there is at the present time a minority, **5**
chosen by the grace of God. And if it is a matter of the grace of **6**
God, it cannot be a question of their actions especially deserving
God's favour, for that would make grace meaningless.

7   What conclusion do we reach now? That Israel did not, on the whole, obtain the object of his striving, but a chosen few "got there", while the remainder became more and more insensitive

8   to the righteousness of God. This is borne out by the scripture:

God gave them a spirit of stupor,
Eyes that they should not see,
And ears that they should not hear,
Unto this very day.

9   And David says of them:

Let their table be made a snare, and a trap,
And a stumbling-block, and a recompense unto them:

10   Let their eyes be darkened, that they may not see,
And bow thou down their back alway.

In the providence of God disaster has been turned to good account

11   Now I ask myself, "Was this fall of theirs an utter disaster?" It was not! For through their failure the benefit of salvation has passed to the gentiles, with the result that Israel is made to see and

12   feel what it has missed. For if their failure has so enriched the world, and their defection proved such a benefit to the gentiles, think what tremendous advantages their fulfilling of God's plan could mean!

13   Now a word to you who are gentiles. I should like you to know that I make as much as I can of my ministry as "God's

14   messenger to the gentiles" so as to make my kinsfolk jealous and

15   thus save some of them. For if their exclusion from the pale of salvation has meant the reconciliation of the rest of mankind to God, what would their inclusion mean? It would be nothing less

16   than life from the dead! If the flour is consecrated to God so is the whole loaf, and if the roots of a tree are dedicated to God every branch will belong to him also.

A word of warning

17   But if some of the branches of the tree have been broken off, while you, like shoots of wild-olive, have been grafted in, and

18   share like a natural branch the rich nourishment of the root, don't let yourself feel superior to those former branches. (If you feel inclined that way, remind yourself that you do not support the

19   root, the root supports you.) You may make the natural retort, "But the branches were broken off to make room for my graft-

ing!" It wasn't quite like that. They lost their position because 20
they failed to believe; you only maintain yours because you do
believe. The situation does not call for conceit but for a certain
wholesome fear. If God removed the natural branches for a good 21
reason, take care that you don't give him the same reason for
removing you. You must try to appreciate both the kindness and 22
the strict justice of God. Those who fell experienced his justice,
while you are experiencing his kindness, and will continue to do
so as long as you do not abuse that kindness. Otherwise you too
will be cut off from the tree. And as for the fallen branches, 23
unless they are obstinate in their unbelief, they will be grafted in
again. Such a restoration is by no means beyond the power of
God. And, in any case, if you who were, so to speak, cuttings 24
from a wild-olive, were grafted in, is it not a far simpler matter
for the natural branches to be grafted back into the parent stem?

God still has a plan for Israel

Now I don't want you, my brothers, to start imagining things, 25
and I must therefore share with you my knowledge of God's
secret plan. It is this, that the partial insensibility which has come
to Israel is only to last until the full number of the gentiles has
been called in. Once this has happened, all Israel will be saved, 26
as the scripture says:

> There shall come out of Zion the deliverer;
> He shall turn away ungodliness from Jacob:
> And this is my covenant unto them, 27
> When I shall take away their sins.

As far as the gospel goes, they are at present God's enemies— 28
which is to your advantage. But as far as God's purpose in
choosing is concerned, they are still beloved for their fathers'
sakes. For once they are made, God does not withdraw his gifts 29
or his calling.

The whole scheme looks topsy-turvy, until we see the amazing wisdom of God!

Just as in the past you were disobedient to God but have found 30
that mercy which might have been theirs but for their disobedience, so they, who at the present moment are disobedient, 31
will eventually share the mercy which has been extended to you.
God has all men penned together in the prison of disobedience, 32
that he may have mercy upon them all.

33 Frankly, I stand amazed at the unfathomable complexity of God's wisdom and God's knowledge. How could man ever understand his reasons for action, or explain his methods of working?

34 For:

Who hath known the mind of the Lord?
Or who hath been his counsellor?

35 Or who hath first given to him, and it shall be recompensed unto him again?

36 For of him, and through him, and unto him, are all things.
To him be the glory for ever, amen.

CHAPTER 12

We have seen God's mercy and wisdom: how shall we respond?

1 WITH eyes wide open to the mercies of God, I beg you, my brothers, as an act of intelligent worship, to give him your bodies, as a living sacrifice, consecrated to him and acceptable by him.

2 Don't let the world around you squeeze you into its own mould, but let God re-mould your minds from within, so that you may prove in practice that the plan of God for you is good, meets all his demands and moves towards the goal of true maturity.

3 As your spiritual teacher I give this piece of advice to each one of you. Don't cherish exaggerated ideas of yourself or your importance, but try to have a sane estimate of your capabilities

4 by the light of the faith that God has given to you all. For just as you have many members in one physical body and those

5 members differ in their functions, so we, though many in number, compose one body in Christ and are all members of one another.

6 Through the grace of God we have different gifts. If our gift is

7 preaching, let us preach to the limit of our vision. If it is serving others let us concentrate on our service; if it is teaching let us give

8 all we have to our teaching; and if our gift be the stimulating of the faith of others let us set ourselves to it. Let the man who is called to give, give freely; let the man who wields authority think of his responsibility; and let the man who feels sympathy for his fellows act cheerfully.

Let us have real Christian behaviour

9 Let us have no imitation Christian love. Let us have a genuine

10 break with evil and a real devotion to good. Let us have real

332

warm affection for one another as between brothers, and a
willingness to let the other man have the credit. Let us not allow *11*
slackness to spoil our work and let us keep the fires of the spirit
burning, as we do our work for the Lord. Base your happiness on *12*
your hope in Christ. When trials come endure them patiently;
steadfastly maintain the habit of prayer. Give freely to fellow- *13*
Christians in want, never grudging a meal or a bed to those who
need them. And as for those who try to make your life a misery, *14*
bless them. Don't curse, bless. Share the happiness of those who *15*
are happy, and the sorrow of those who are sad. Live in harmony *16*
with each other. Don't become snobbish but take a real interest
in ordinary people. Don't become set in your own opinions.
Don't pay back a bad turn by a bad turn, to *anyone*. See that your *17*
public behaviour is above criticism. As far as your responsibility *18*
goes, live at peace with everyone. Never take vengeance into your *19*
own hands, my dear friends: stand back and let God punish if he
will. For it is written:

Vengeance belongeth unto me: I will recompense.

And these are God's words:

If thine enemy hunger, feed him; *20*

If he thirst, give him to drink:

For in so doing thou shalt heap coals of fire upon his head.

Don't allow yourself to be overpowered by evil. Take the offensive *21*
—overpower evil with good!

CHAPTER 13

The Christian and the civil law

EVERY Christian ought to obey the civil authorities, for all *1*
legitimate authority is derived from God's authority, and the
existing authority is appointed under God. To oppose authority *2*
then is to oppose God, and such opposition is bound to be
punished.

The honest citizen has no need to fear the keepers of law and *3*
order, but the dishonest man will always be nervous of them. If
you want to avoid this anxiety just lead a law-abiding life, and
all that can come your way is a word of approval. The officer is *4*
God's servant for your protection. But if you are leading a wicked
life you have reason to be alarmed. The "power of the law"
which is vested in every legitimate officer, is no empty phrase.

He is, in fact, divinely appointed to inflict God's punishment upon evil-doers.

5 You should, therefore, obey the authorities, not simply because
6 it is the safest, but because it is the right thing to do. It is right, too, for you to pay taxes for the civil authorities are appointed by God for the good purposes of public order and well-being.
7 Give everyone his legitimate due, whether it be rates, or taxes, or reverence, or respect!

To love others is the highest conduct

8 Keep out of debt altogether, except that perpetual debt of love which we owe one another. The man who loves his neighbour
9 has obeyed the whole Law in regard to his neighbour. For the commandments, "Thou shalt not commit adultery", "Thou shalt not kill", "Thou shalt not steal", "Thou shalt not covet" and all other commandments are summed up in this one saying: "Thou
10 shalt love thy neighbour as thyself." Love hurts nobody: therefore love is the answer to the Law's commands.

Wake up and live!

11 Why all this stress on behaviour? Because, as I think you have realised, the present time is of the highest importance—it is time to wake up to reality. Every day brings God's salvation nearer.
12 The night is nearly over, the day has almost dawned. Let us therefore fling away the things that men do in the dark, let us
13 arm ourselves for the fight of the day! Let us live cleanly, as in the daylight, not in the "delights" of getting drunk or playing
14 with sex, nor yet in quarrelling or jealousies. Let us be Christ's men from head to foot, and give no chances to the flesh to have its fling.

CHAPTER 14

Don't criticise each other's convictions

1 WELCOME a man whose faith is weak, but not with the idea of
2 arguing over his scruples. One man believes that he may eat anything, another man, without this strong conviction, is a
3 vegetarian. The meat-eater should not despise the vegetarian, nor should the vegetarian condemn the meat-eater—they should re-

flect that God has accepted them both. After all, who are you to **4**
criticise the servant of somebody else, especially when that somebody else is God? It is to his own master that he gives, or fails
to give, satisfactory service. And don't doubt that satisfaction,
for God is well able to transform men into servants who are
satisfactory.

People are different—make allowances

Again, one man thinks some days of more importance than **5**
others. Another man considers them all alike. Let every one be
definite in his own convictions. If a man specially observes one **6**
particular day, he does so "to the Lord". The man who eats, eats
"to the Lord", for he thanks God for the food. The man who fasts
also does it "to the Lord", for he thanks God for the benefits of
fasting. The truth is that we neither live nor die as self-contained **7**
units. At every turn life links us to the Lord, and when we die we **8**
come face to face with him. In life or death we are in the hands of
the Lord. Christ lived and died that he might be the Lord in both **9**
life and death.

Why, then, criticise your brother's actions, why try to make **10**
him look small? We shall all be judged one day, not by each
other's standards or even by our own, but by the judgment of God. **11**
It is written:

As I live, saith the Lord, to me every knee shall bow,
And every tongue shall confess to God.

It is to God alone that we have to answer for our actions. **12**

This should be our attitude

Let us therefore stop turning critical eyes on one another. If **13**
we must be critical, let us be critical of our own conduct and see
that we do nothing to make a brother stumble or fall.

I am convinced, and I say this as in the presence of the Lord **14**
Christ, that nothing is intrinsically unholy. But none the less it
is unholy to the man who thinks it is. If your habit of unrestricted **15**
diet seriously upsets your brother, you are no longer living in love
towards him. And surely you wouldn't let food mean ruin to a
man for whom Christ died. You mustn't let something that is all **16**
right for you look like an evil practice to somebody else. After **17**
all, the kingdom of Heaven is not a matter of whether you get
what you like to eat and drink, but of righteousness and peace

18 and joy in the Holy Spirit. If you put these things first in serving
19 Christ you will please God and are not likely to offend men. So
let us concentrate on the things which make for harmony, and
20 on the growth of one another's character. Surely we shouldn't
wish to undo God's work for the sake of a plate of meat!

I freely admit that all food is, in itself, harmless, but it can be
21 harmful to the man who eats it with a guilty conscience. We
should be willing to be both vegetarians and teetotallers if by
doing otherwise we should impede a brother's progress in the
22 faith. Your personal convictions are a matter of faith between
yourself and God, and you are happy if you have no qualms about
23 what you allow yourself to eat. Yet if a man eats meat with an
uneasy conscience about it, you may be sure he is wrong to do so.
For his action does not spring from his faith, and when we act
apart from our faith we sin.

CHAPTER 15

Christian behaviour to one another

1 WE who have strong faith ought to shoulder the burden of the
doubts and qualms of others and not just to go our own sweet
2 way. Our actions should mean the good of others—should help
3 them to build up their characters. For even Christ did not choose
his own pleasure, but as it is written:

The reproaches of them that reproached thee fell upon me.
4 For all those words which were written long ago are meant
to teach us today; that when we read in the scriptures of the endurance of men and of all the help that God gave them in those
days, we may be encouraged to go on hoping in our own time.
5 May the God who inspires men to endure, and gives them a
Father's care, give you a mind united towards one another be-
6 cause of your common loyalty to Jesus Christ. And then, as one
man, you will sing from the heart the praises of God the Father
7 of our Lord Jesus Christ. So open your hearts to one another as
Christ has opened his heart to you, and God will be glorified.

A reminder—Christ the universal saviour

8 Christ was made a servant of the Jews to prove God's trust-
worthiness, since he personally implemented the promises made
9 long ago to the fathers, and also that the gentiles might bring
glory to God for his mercy to them. It is written:

336

Therefore will I give praise unto thee among the gentiles
And sing unto thy name.
And again: *10*
Rejoice, ye gentiles, with his people.
And yet again: *11*
Praise the Lord, all ye gentiles;
And let all the peoples praise him.
And then Isaiah says: *12*
There shall be the root of Jesse,
And he that ariseth to rule over the gentiles:
On him shall the gentiles hope.
May the God of hope fill *you* with joy and peace in your faith,   *13*
that by the power of the Holy Spirit, your whole life and outlook
may be radiant with hope.

What I have tried to do

For myself I feel certain that you, my brothers, have real   *14*
Christian character and experience, and that you are capable of
keeping each other on the right road. Nevertheless I have written   *15*
to you with a certain frankness, to refresh your minds with truths
that you already know, by virtue of my commission as minister   *16*
of Christ Jesus to the gentiles in the service of the gospel of God.
For my constant endeavour is to present the gentiles to God as an
offering which he can accept, because they are sanctified by the
Holy Spirit. And I think I have something to be proud of (through   *17*
Christ, of course) in my work for God. I am not competent to   *18*
speak of the work Christ has done through others, but I do know
that through me he has secured the obedience of gentiles in word
and deed, working by sign and miracle and all the power of the   *19*
Holy Spirit. I have fully preached the gospel from Jerusalem and
the surrounding country as far as Illyricum. My constant ambition   *20*
has been to preach the gospel where the name of Christ was previously unknown, and to avoid as far as possible building on
another man's foundation, so that: *21*
They shall see, to whom no tidings of him came,
And they who have not heard shall understand.

My future plans

Perhaps this will explain why I have so frequently been pre-   *22*
vented from coming to see you. But now, since my work in   *23*

these places no longer needs my presence, and since for many
24 years I have had a great desire to see you, I hope to visit you on
my way to Spain. I hope also that you will speed me on my
25 journey, after I have had the satisfaction of seeing you all. At the
moment my next call is to Jerusalem, to look after the welfare
26 of the Christians there. The churches in Macedonia and Achaia,
you see, have thought it a good thing to make a contribution to-
27 wards the poor Christians in Jerusalem. They have thought it a
good thing to make this gesture and yet, really, they received "a
good thing" from their first! For if the gentiles have had a share
in the Jews' spiritual "good things" it is only fair that they should
look after the Jews as far as the good things of this world are
concerned.

28 When I have completed this task, then, and turned their gesture
into a good deed done, I shall come to you *en route* for Spain.
29 I feel sure that in this long-looked-for visit I shall bring with me
the full blessing of Christ.

30 Now, my brothers, I am going to ask you, for the sake of our
Lord Jesus Christ and for the love we bear each other in the Spirit,
31 to stand behind me in earnest prayer to God on my behalf—that
I may not fall into the hands of the unbelievers in Judaea, and
that the Jerusalem Christians may receive the gift I am taking to
32 them in the spirit in which it was made. Then I shall come to you,
in the purpose of God, with a happy heart, and may even enjoy
with you a little holiday.

33 The God of peace be with you all, amen.

CHAPTER 16

Personal greetings and messages

1 I WANT this letter to introduce to you Phoebe, our sister, a
2 deaconess of the Church at Cenchrea. Please give her a Christian
welcome, and any assistance with her work that she may need.
She has herself been of great assistance to many, not excluding
myself.

3 Shake hands for me with Prisca and Aquila. They have not
4 only worked with me for Christ Jesus, but have risked their necks
to save my life. Not only I, but all the gentile churches, owe them
5 a great debt. Give my love to the church that meets in their house.
Shake the hand of dear Epaenetus, Achaia's first man to be
6 won for Christ, and of course greet Mary who has worked so

338

hard for you. A handshake too, for Andronicus and Junias my 7
kinsmen and fellow-prisoners; they are outstanding men among
the messengers and were Christians before I was.

Another warm greeting for Ampliatus, dear Christian that he 8
is, and also for Urbanus, who has worked with me, and dear old 9
Stachys, too.

More greetings from me, please, to: 10
Apelles, the man who has proved his faith,
The household of Aristobulus,
Herodion, my kinsman, 11
Narcissus' household, who are Christians.

Remember me to Tryphena and Tryphosa, who work so hard 12
for the Lord, and to my dear Persis who has also done great work
for him.

Shake the hand of Rufus for me—that splendid Christian, and 13
greet his mother, who has been a mother to me too. Greetings 14
to Asyncritus, Phlegon, Hermes, Patrobas, Hermas and their
Christian group: also to Philologus and Julia, Nereus and his 15
sister, and Olympas and the Christians who are with them.

Give each other a hearty handshake all round for my sake. The 16
greetings of all the churches I am in touch with come to you with
this letter.

A final warning

And now I implore you, my brothers, to keep a watchful eye 17
on those who cause trouble and make difficulties among you, in
plain opposition to the teaching you have been given, and steer
clear of them. Such men do not really serve our Lord Christ at all 18
but are utterly self-centred. Yet with their plausible and attractive
arguments they deceive those who are too simple-hearted to see
through them.

Your loyalty to the principles of the gospel is known every- 19
where, and that gives me great joy. I want to see you experts in
good, and not even beginners in evil. It will not be long before 20
the God of peace will crush Satan under your feet. May the grace
of our Lord Jesus Christ be with you.

Timothy, who works with me, sends his greetings, and so do 21
Lucius and Jason and Sosipater my fellow-countrymen. (Paul has 22
just told me that I, Tertius, who have been taking down this
epistle from his dictation, may send you my Christian greetings
too.) Gaius, my host (and the host as a matter of fact of the whole 23

church here), sends you his greetings. Erastus, our town clerk, and Quartus, another Christian brother, send greetings too.

25 Now to him who is able to set you on your feet as his own sons—according to my gospel, according to the preaching of Jesus Christ himself, and in accordance with the disclosing of that
26 secret purpose which, after long ages of silence, has now been made known (in full agreement with the writings of the prophets long ago), by the command of the everlasting God to all the gentiles, that they might turn to him in the obedience of faith—
27 to him, I say, the only God who is wise, be glory for ever through Jesus Christ, amen!

PAUL.

The First Letter to the Christians at Corinth

AUTHOR. *Paul, writing from Ephesus, where he stayed for more than two years. He had evidently written at least one previous letter to the church at Corinth.*

DATE. *About 56.*

DESTINATION. *The Christian church at Corinth, which was then the largest town in Greece. Acts 18 gives some account of the beginnings of the church there. It is worth remembering that Corinth was a most important seaport, a garrison town, and a strategic road-junction. It was the capital of the Roman province of Achaia. It would have been full of a cosmopolitan crowd, and even in those days was a byword for immorality, idolatry and loose-living of all kinds.*

THEME. *The beginning of the letter is an impassioned indictment of the "party-spirit", which can have no place in a church where all men belong to Christ. Paul then proceeds to deal sternly with a particularly revolting case of sexual immorality, which the Corinthian Christians appear to treat with complacency. The litigiousness of the Corinthian church is next censured. Paul's somewhat ascetic views on marriage follow, and modern readers need to remind themselves of the shameless sexual promiscuity existing in Corinth, against which Paul is obviously violently reacting.*

Butcher's meat in a city like Corinth had often been exposed

340

*before heathen idols before being offered for sale. This meant a
practical difficulty for Christians and Paul advises upon it.*

*He then lays down some rules about public worship, particularly
on the reverent conduct of what we now call the Holy Communion.*

*The question of the diversity of the gifts of God's Spirit is
dealt with patiently and logically, and then follows the famous
passage about the highest gift of all—Christian love.*

*Then comes the almost equally famous passage on the
"resurrection of the body", by no means irrelevant to modern
ears.*

*The matter of the Jerusalem Sick and Poor Fund and some
interesting personal messages close the letter.*

CHAPTER 1

PAUL, commissioned by the will of God as a messenger of Christ   1
Jesus, and Sosthenes, a Christian brother, to the church of God   2
at Corinth—to those whom Christ Jesus has made holy, who are
called to be God's men and women, to all true believers in Jesus
Christ, their Lord and ours—grace and peace be to you from God   3
the Father and the Lord, Jesus Christ!

I am thankful for your faith

I am always thankful to God for what the gift of his grace in   4
Christ Jesus has meant to you—how, as the Christian message   5
has become established among you, he has enriched your whole   6
lives, from the words on your lips to the understanding in your
hearts. And you have been eager to receive his gifts during this   7
time of waiting for his final appearance. He will keep you stead-   8
fast in the faith to the end, so that when his day comes you need
fear no condemnation. God is utterly dependable, and it is he who   9
has called you into fellowship with his Son Jesus Christ, our Lord.

But I am anxious over your "divisions"

Now I do beg you, my brothers, by all that our Lord Jesus   10
Christ means to you, to speak with one voice, and not allow yourselves to be split up into parties. All together you should be
achieving a unity in thought and judgment. For I know, from what
some of Chloe's people have told me, that you are each making   11

12 different claims—"I am one of Paul's men," says one; "I am one
of Apollos'," says another; or "I am one of Cephas'"; while
someone else says, "I owe my faith to Christ alone."

Do consider how serious these divisions are !

13 What *are* you saying ? Is there more than one Christ ? Was it
Paul who died on the cross for you ? Were you baptised in the
14 name of Paul ? It makes me thankful that I didn't actually baptise
15 any of you (except Crispus and Gaius), or perhaps someone would
16 be saying I did it in my own name. (Oh yes, I did baptise
17 Stephanas' family, but I can't remember anyone else.) For Christ
did not send me to see how many I could baptise, but to proclaim
the gospel. And I have not done this by the persuasiveness of clever
18 words, for I have no desire to rob the cross of its power. The
preaching of the cross is, I know, nonsense to those who are involved in this dying world, but to us who are being saved from
that death it is nothing less than the power of God.

The cross shows that God's wisdom is not man's wisdom by any means

19 It is written:
I will destroy the wisdom of the wise,
And the prudence of the prudent will I reject.
20 For consider, what have the philosopher, the writer and the critic
of this world to show for all their wisdom ? Has not God made
21 the wisdom of this world look foolish ? For it was after the world
in its wisdom had failed to know God, that he in his wisdom chose
to save all who would believe by the "simple-mindedness" of
22 the gospel message. For the Jews ask for miraculous proofs and
23 the Greeks an intellectual panacea, but all we preach is Christ
crucified—a stumbling-block to the Jews and sheer nonsense to
24 the gentiles, but for those who are called, whether Jews or Greeks,
25 Christ the power of God and the wisdom of God. And this is
really only natural, for God's "foolishness" is wiser than men, and
his "weakness" is stronger than men.

Nor are God's values the same as man's

26 For look at your own calling as Christians, my brothers. You
don't see among you many of the wise (according to this world's
judgment) nor many of the ruling class, nor many from the

noblest families. But God has chosen what the world calls foolish 27
to shame the wise; he has chosen what the world calls weak to
shame the strong. He has chosen things of little strength and small 28
repute, yes and even things which have no real existence to ex-
plode the pretensions of the things that are—that no man may 29
boast in the presence of God. Yet from this same God you have 30
received your standing in Jesus Christ, and he has become for
us the true wisdom, a matter, in practice, of being made righteous
and holy, in fact, of being redeemed. And this makes us see the 31
truth of the scripture:

He that glorieth, let him glory in the Lord.

CHAPTER 2

I came to you in God's strength not my own

IN the same way, my brothers, when I came to proclaim to you 1
God's secret purpose, I did not come equipped with any brilliance
of speech or intellect. You may as well know now that it was 2
my secret determination to concentrate entirely on Jesus Christ
himself and the fact of his death upon the cross. As a matter of 3
fact, in myself I was feeling far from strong; I was nervous and
rather shaky. What I said and preached had none of the attrac- 4
tiveness of the clever mind, but it was a demonstration of the
power of the Spirit! Plainly God's purpose was that your faith 5
should rest not upon man's cleverness but upon the power of God.

*There is, of course, a real wisdom, which God allows us
to share with him*

We do, of course, speak "wisdom" among those who are 6
spiritually mature, but it is not what is called wisdom by this
world, nor by the powers-that-be, who soon will be only the
powers that have been. The wisdom we speak of is that mysterious 7
secret wisdom of God which he planned before the creation for
our glory today. None of the powers of this world have known 8
this wisdom—if they had they would never have crucified the
Lord of glory! But, as it is written: 9

Things which eye saw not, and ear heard not,
And which entered not into the heart of man,
Whatsoever things God prepared for them that love him.

But God has, through the Spirit, let us share his secret. For 10

nothing is hidden from the Spirit, not even the deep wisdom of
11 God. For who could really understand a man's inmost thoughts
except the spirit of the man himself? How much less could anyone understand the thoughts of God except the very Spirit of
12 God? And the marvellous thing is this, that we now receive not the
spirit of the world but the Spirit of God himself, so that we can
actually understand something of God's generosity towards us.

This wisdom is only understood by the spiritual

13   It is these things that we talk about, not using the expressions
of the human intellect but those which the Holy Spirit teaches us,
explaining spiritual things to those who are spiritual.
14   But the unspiritual man simply cannot accept the matters which
the Spirit deals with—they just don't make sense to him, for, after
15 all, you must be spiritual to see spiritual things. The spiritual man,
on the other hand, has an insight into the meaning of everything,
though his insight may baffle the man of the world. This is
because the former is sharing in God's wisdom, and
16   Who hath known the mind of the Lord,
            That he should instruct him?
      Incredible as it may sound, we who are spiritual have the very
thoughts of Christ!

CHAPTER 3

But I cannot yet call you spiritual

1   I, MY brothers, was unable to talk to you as spiritual men: I
had to talk to you as unspiritual, as yet babies in the Christian
2 life. And my practice has been to feed you, as it were, with
"milk" and not with "meat". You were unable to digest "meat"
3 in those days, and I don't believe you can do it now. For you are
still unspiritual; all the time that there is jealousy and squabbling
among you you show that you are—you are living just like men
4 of the world. While one of you says, "I am one of Paul's converts"
and another says, "I am one of Apollos' ", are you not plainly
unspiritual?
5   After all, who is Paul? Who is Apollos? No more than servants
through whom you came to believe as the Lord gave each man
6 his opportunity. I may have done the planting and Apollos the
7 watering, but it was God who made the seed grow! The planter

344

and the waterer are nothing compared with him who gives life
to the seed. Planter and waterer are alike insignificant, though each **8**
shall be rewarded according to his particular work.

We work on God's foundation

In this work, we work with God, and that means that you are **9**
a field under God's cultivation, or, if you like, a house being built
to his plan. I, like a master-builder who knows his job, by the grace **10**
God has given me, lay the foundation; someone else builds upon
it. I only say this, let the builder be careful how he builds! The **11**
foundation is laid already, and no one can lay another, for it is
Jesus Christ himself. But any man who builds on the foundation **12**
using as his material gold, silver, precious stones, wood, hay or
stubble, must know that each man's work will one day be shown **13**
for what it is. The day will show it plainly enough, for the day
will arise in a blaze of fire, and that fire will prove the nature of
each man's work. If the work that the man has built upon the **14**
foundation will stand this test, he will be rewarded. But if a **15**
man's work be destroyed under the test, he loses it all. He personally will be safe, though rather like a man rescued from a
fire.

Make no mistake: you are God's holy building

Don't you realise that you yourselves are the temple of God, **16**
and that God's Spirit lives in you? God will destroy anyone who **17**
defiles his temple, for his temple is holy—*and that is exactly what
you are*!

Let no one be under any illusion over this. If any man among **18**
you thinks himself one of the world's clever ones, let him discard
his cleverness that he may learn to be truly wise. For this world's **19**
cleverness is stupidity to God. It is written:

> He that taketh the wise in their craftiness.

And again: **20**

> The Lord knoweth the reasonings of the wise, that they are
> vain.

So let no one boast of men. Everything belongs to you! Paul, **21 22**
Apollos or Cephas; the world, life, death, the present or the
future, everything is yours! For you belong to Christ, and Christ **23**
belongs to God!

CHAPTER 4

Trust us, but make no hasty judgments

1 You should look upon us as ministers of Christ, as trustees of
2 the secrets of God. And it is a prime requisite in a trustee that he
3 should prove worthy of his trust. But, as a matter of fact, it
matters very little to me what you, or any man, thinks of me—
4 I don't even value my opinion of myself. For I might be quite
ignorant of any fault in myself—but that doesn't justify me before
God. My only true judge is the Lord.
5 The moral of this is that we should make no hasty or premature
judgments. When the Lord comes he will bring into the light of
day all that at present is hidden in darkness, and he will expose
the secret motives of men's hearts. Then shall God himself give
each man his share of praise.

Having your favourite teacher is not only silly but wrong

6 I have used myself and Apollos above as an illustration, so that
you might learn from what I have said about us not to assess man
above his value in God's sight, and may thus avoid the friction that
7 comes from exalting one teacher against another. For who makes
you different from somebody else, and what have you got that was
not given to you? And if anything has been given to you, why
boast of it as if it were something you had achieved yourself?

Think sometimes of what your happiness has cost us!

8 Oh, I know you are rich and flourishing! You've been living
like kings, haven't you, while we've been away? I would to God
you were really kings in God's sight so that we might reign with
you!
9 I sometimes think that God means us, the messengers, to appear
last in the procession of mankind, like the men who are to die
in the arena. For indeed we are made a public spectacle before the
10 angels of Heaven and the eyes of men. We are looked upon as
fools, for Christ's sake, but you are wise in the Christian faith.
We are considered weak, but you have become strong: you have
11 found honour, we little but contempt. Up to this very hour we
are hungry and thirsty, ill-clad, knocked about and practically

homeless. We still have to work for our living by manual labour. *12*
Men curse us, but we return a blessing: they make our lives
miserable but we take it patiently. They ruin our reputations but *13*
we go on trying to win them for God. We are the world's rubbish,
the scum of the earth, yes, up to this very day.

A personal plea

I don't write these things merely to make you feel uncom- *14*
fortable, but that you may realise facts, as my dear children. After *15*
all, you may have ten thousand teachers in the Christian faith,
but you cannot have many fathers! For in Christ Jesus I am your
spiritual father through the gospel; that is why I implore you to *16*
follow the footsteps of me your father. I have sent Timothy to *17*
you to help you in this. For he himself is my much-loved and
faithful son in the Lord, and he will remind you of those ways of
living in Christ which I teach in every church to which I go.

Some of you have apparently grown conceited enough to think *18*
that I should not visit you. But please God it will not be long before *19*
I do come to you in person. Then I shall be able to see what power,
apart from their words, these pretentious ones among you really
possess. For the kingdom of God is not a matter of a spate of *20*
words but of the power of Christian living.

Now it's up to you to choose! Shall I come to you ready to *21*
chastise you, or in love and gentleness?

CHAPTER 5

A horrible sin and a stern remedy

IT is actually reported that there is sexual immorality among *1*
you, and immorality of a kind that even pagans condemn—a
man has apparently taken his father's wife! Are you still proud *2*
of your church? Shouldn't you be overwhelmed with sorrow
and shame? The man who has done such a thing should certainly
be expelled from your fellowship!

I know I am not with you physically but I am with you in *3*
spirit, and I assure you as solemnly as if I were actually present
before your assembly that I have already pronounced judgment
in the name of the Lord Jesus on the man who has done this thing, *4*
and I do this with full divine authority. My judgment is this: *5*
that the man should be left to the mercy of Satan so that while

his body will experience the destructive powers of sin his spirit may yet be saved in the day of the Lord Jesus.

6 Your pride in your church is lamentably out of place. Don't you know how a little yeast can permeate the whole lump?

7 Clear out every bit of the old yeast that you may be new unleavened bread! We Christians have had a Passover lamb sacrificed

8 for us—none other than Christ himself! So let us "keep the feast" with no trace of the yeast of the old life, nor the yeast of vice and wickedness, but with the unleavened bread of unadulterated truth!

9 In my previous letter I said, "Don't mix with the immoral."

10 I didn't mean, of course, that you were to have no contact at all with the immoral of this world, nor with any cheats or thieves or idolaters—for that would mean going out of the world

11 altogether! But in this letter I tell you not to associate with any professing Christian who is known to be an impure man or a swindler, an idolater, a man with a foul tongue, a drunkard or a thief. My instruction is: "Don't even eat with such a man."

12 Those outside the church it is not my business to judge. But surely

13 it is your business to judge those who are inside the church—God alone can judge those who are outside. It is your plain duty to expel from your church this wicked man!

CHAPTER 6

Don't go to law in pagan courts

1 WHEN any of you has a grievance against another, aren't you ashamed to bring the matter to be settled before a pagan court

2 instead of before the church? Don't you know that Christians will one day judge the world? And if you are to judge the world do you consider yourselves incapable of settling such infinitely

3 smaller matters? Don't you also know that we shall judge the very angels themselves—how much more then matters of this

4 world only! In any case, if you find you have to judge matters of this world, why choose as judges those who count for nothing

5 in the church? I say this deliberately to rouse your sense of shame. Are you really unable to find among your number one man with enough sense to decide a dispute between one and another of you,

6 or must one brother resort to law against another and that before

7 those who have no faith in Christ! It is surely obvious that something must be seriously wrong in your church for you to be

having lawsuits at all. Why not *let* yourself be wronged or cheated? For when you go to law against your brother you yourself do $\quad$ 8 him wrong, for you cheat him of Christian love and forgiveness.

Have you forgotten that the kingdom of God will never belong $\quad$ 9 to the wicked? Don't be under any illusion—neither the impure, the idolater or the adulterer; neither the effeminate, the pervert or the thief; neither the swindler, the drunkard, the foul-mouthed $\quad$ 10 or the rapacious shall have any share in the kingdom of God. *And such men, remember, were some of you!* But you have cleansed $\quad$ 11 yourselves from all that, you have been made whole in spirit, you have been justified in the name of the Lord Jesus and in the Spirit of our God.

Christian liberty does not mean moral licence

As a Christian I *may* do anything, but that does not mean that $\quad$ 12 everything is good for me. I may do everything, but I must not be a slave of anything. Food was meant for the stomach and the $\quad$ 13 stomach for food; but God has no permanent purpose for either. But you cannot say that our physical body was made for sexual promiscuity; it was made for God, and God is the answer to our deepest longings. The God who raised the Lord from the dead $\quad$ 14 will also raise us mortal men by his power. Have you realised $\quad$ 15 the almost incredible fact that your bodies are integral parts of Christ himself? Am I then to take parts of Christ and join them to a prostitute? Never! Don't you realise that when a man joins $\quad$ 16 himself to a prostitute he makes with her a physical unity? For, God says, "the two shall be one flesh". On the other hand the man $\quad$ 17 who joins himself to the Lord is one with him in spirit.

Avoid sexual looseness like the plague! Every other sin that a $\quad$ 18 man commits is done outside his own body, but this is an offence against his own body. Have you forgotten that your body is the $\quad$ 19 temple of the Holy Spirit, who lives in you and is God's gift to you, and that you are not the owner of your own body? You have been bought, and at what a price! Therefore bring glory to God in your $\quad$ 20 body.

CHAPTER 7

The question of marriage in present circumstances

Now let me deal with the questions raised in your letter. $\quad$ *1*
It is a good principle for a man to have no physical contact with

2 women. Nevertheless, because casual liaisons are so prevalent, let every man have his own wife and every woman her own husband.
3 The husband should give his wife what is due to her as his wife,
4 and the wife should be as fair to her husband. The wife has no longer full rights over her own person, but shares them with her husband. In the same way the husband shares his personal rights
5 with his wife. Do not cheat each other of normal sexual intercourse, unless of course you both decide to abstain temporarily to make special opportunity for fasting and prayer. But afterwards you should resume relations as before, or you will expose yourselves to the obvious temptation of the devil.

6 I give the advice above more as a concession than as a command.
7 I wish that all men were like myself, but I realise that everyone has his own particular gift from God, some one thing and some
8 another. Yet to those who are unmarried or widowed, I say definitely that it is a good thing to remain unattached, as I am.
9 But if they find they have not the gift of self-control in such matters, by all means let them get married. I think it is far better for them to be married than to be tortured by unsatisfied desire.
10 To those who are already married my command, or rather, the Lord's command, is that the wife should not leave her husband.
11 But if she is separated from him she should either remain unattached or else be reconciled to her husband. A husband is not, in similar circumstances, to divorce his wife.

Advice over marriage between Christian and pagan

12 To other people my advice (though this is not a divine command) is this. For a brother who has a non-Christian wife who
13 is willing to live with him he should not divorce her. A wife in
14 a similar position should not divorce her husband. For the unbelieving husband is, in a sense, consecrated by being joined to the person of his wife; the unbelieving wife is similarly "consecrated" by the Christian brother she has married. If this were not so then your children would bear the stains of paganism, whereas they are actually consecrated to God.
15 But if the unbelieving partner decides to separate, then let there be a separation. The Christian partner need not consider himself bound in such cases. Yet God has called us to live in peace,
16 and after all how can you, who are a wife, know whether you will be able to save your husband or not? And the same applies to you who are a husband.

350

I merely add to the above that each man should live his life with 17
the gifts that God has given him and in the condition in which
God has called him. This is the rule I lay down in all the churches.

For example, if a man was circumcised when God called him 18
he should not attempt to remove the signs of his circumcision. If
on the other hand he was uncircumcised he should not become
circumcised. Being circumcised or not being circumcised, what 19
do they matter? The great thing is to obey the orders of God.
Everyone should stick to the calling in which he heard the call 20
of God. Were you a slave when you heard the call? Don't let 21
that worry you, though if you find an opportunity to become free
you had better take it. But a slave who is called to life in Christ 22
is set free in the eyes of the Lord. And a man who was free
when God called him becomes a slave—to Christ himself! You 23
have been redeemed, at tremendous cost; don't therefore sell yourselves as slaves to men! My brothers, let every one of us continue 24
to live his life with God in the state in which he was when he
was called.

In present circumstances it is really better not to marry

Now as far as young unmarried women are concerned, I must 25
confess that I have no direct commands from the Lord. Nevertheless, I give you my considered opinion as of one who is, I think,
to be trusted after all his experience of God's mercy.

My opinion is this, that amid all the difficulties of the present 26
time you would do best to remain just as you are. Are you 27
married? Well, don't try to be separated. Are you unattached?
Then don't try to get married. But if you, a man, should marry, 28
don't think that you have done anything sinful. And the same
applies to a young woman. Yet I do believe that those who take
this step are bound to find the married state an extra burden in
these critical days, and I should like you to be as unencumbered
as possible. All our futures are so foreshortened, indeed, that those 29
who have wives should live, so to speak, as though they had none!
There is no time to indulge in sorrow, no time for enjoying our 30
joys; those who buy have no time to enjoy their possessions, and 31
indeed their every contact with the world must be as light as
possible, for the present scheme of things is rapidly passing away.
That is why I should like you to be as free from worldly entangle- 32
ments as possible. The unmarried man is free to concern himself
with the Lord's affairs, and how he may please him. But the 33
married man is sure to be concerned also with matters of this

world, that he may please his wife—his interests are divided.

34 You find the same difference in the case of the unmarried and the married woman. The unmarried concerns herself with the Lord's affairs, and her aim in life is to make herself holy, in body and in spirit. But the married woman must concern herself with the things of this world, and her aim will be to please her husband.

35 I tell you these things to help you; I am not putting difficulties in your path but setting before you an ideal, so that your service of God may be as far as possible free from worldly distractions.

But marriage is not wrong

36 But if any man feels he is not behaving honourably towards the woman he loves, especially as she is beginning to lose her first youth and the emotional strain is considerable, let him do what his heart tells him to do—let them be married, there is no sin in

37 that. Yet for the man of steadfast purpose who is able to bear the strain and has his own desires well under control, if he decides not to marry the young woman, he too will be doing the right thing.

38 Both of them are right, one in marrying and the other in refraining from marriage, but the latter has chosen the better of two right courses.

39 A woman is bound to her husband while he is alive, but if he dies she is free to marry whom she likes—but let her be guided

40 by the Lord. In my opinion she would be happier to remain as she is, unmarried. And I think I am here expressing not only my opinion, but the will of the Spirit as well.

CHAPTER 8

A practical problem: shall we be guided by superior knowledge or love ?

1 Now to deal with the matter of meat which has been sacrificed to idols. It is easy to think that we "know" over problems like this, but we should remember that while knowledge may make a man look big, it is only love that can make him grow to his full

2 stature. For whatever a man may know, he still has a lot to learn,

3 but if he loves God, he is opening his whole life to the Spirit of God.

4 In this matter, then, of eating meat which has been offered to idols, knowledge tells us that no idol has any real existence, and

5 that there is no God but one. For though there are so-called gods

both in heaven and earth, gods and lords galore in fact, to us **6**
there is only one God, the Father, from whom everything comes,
and for whom we live. And there is one Lord, Jesus Christ, by
whom everything exists, and by whom we ourselves are alive.
But this knowledge of ours is not shared by all men. For some, **7**
who until now have been used to idols, eat the meat as meat
really sacrificed to a god, and their delicate conscience is thereby
injured. Now our acceptance by God is not a matter of meat. If **8**
we eat it, that does not make us better men, nor are we the worse
if we do not eat it. You must be careful that your freedom to eat **9**
meat does not in any way hinder anyone whose faith is not as
robust as yours. For suppose you with your knowledge of God **10**
should be observed eating meat in an idol's temple, are you not
encouraging the man with a delicate conscience to do the same?
Surely you would not want your superior knowledge to bring **11**
spiritual disaster to a weaker brother for whom Christ died? And **12**
when you sin like this and damage the weak consciences of your
brethren you really sin against Christ. This makes me determined **13**
that, if there is any possibility of meat injuring my brother, I
will have none of it as long as I live, for fear I might do him harm.

CHAPTER 9

A word of personal defence to my critics

Is there any doubt that I am a genuine messenger, any doubt **1**
that I am a free man? Have I not seen Jesus our Lord with my
own eyes? Are not you yourselves samples of my work for the
Lord? Even if other people should refuse to recognise my divine **2**
commission, yet to you at any rate I shall always be a true messenger, for you are a living proof of God's call to me. This is my **3**
real ground of defence to those who cross-examine me.

Aren't we allowed to eat and drink? May we not travel with a **4, 5**
Christian wife like the other messengers, like other Christian
brothers, and like Cephas? Are Barnabas and I the only ones **6**
not allowed to leave their ordinary work to give time to the
ministry?

Even a preacher of the gospel has some rights!

Just think for a moment. Does any soldier ever go to war at **7**
his own expense? Does any man plant a vineyard and have no
share in its fruits? Does the shepherd who tends the flock never

8 taste the milk? This is, I know, an argument from everyday life,
9 but it is a principle endorsed by the Law. For is it not written in the Law of Moses:

Thou shalt not muzzle the ox when he treadeth out the corn?

10 Now does this imply merely God's care for oxen, or does it include his care for us too? Surely we are included! You might even say that the words were written for us. For both the ploughman as he ploughs, and the thresher as he threshes should have
11 some hope of an ultimate share in the harvest. If we have sown for you the seed of spiritual things need you be greatly perturbed
12 because we reap some of your material things? And if there are others with the right to have these things from you, have not we an even greater right? Yet we have never exercised this right and have put up with all sorts of things, so that we might not hinder the spread of the gospel.

I am entitled to a reward, yet I have not taken it

13 Are you ignorant of the fact that those who minister sacred things take part of the sacred food of the Temple for their own use, and those who attend the altar have their share of what is
14 placed on the altar? On the same principle the Lord has ordered that those who proclaim the gospel should receive their livelihood from those who accept the gospel.
15 But I have never used any of these privileges, nor am I writing now to suggest that I should be given them. Indeed I would rather die than have anyone make this boast of mine an empty one!

My reward is to make the gospel free to all men

16 For I take no special pride in the fact that I preach the gospel. I feel compelled to do so; I should be utterly miserable if I failed
17 to preach it. If I do this work because I choose to do so then I am entitled to a reward. But if it is no choice of mine, but a sacred
18 responsibility put upon me, what can I expect in the way of reward? This, that when I preach the gospel, I can make it absolutely free of charge, and need not claim what is my rightful due as a
19 preacher. For though I am no man's slave, yet I have made myself
20 everyone's slave, that I might win more men to Christ. To the Jews I was a Jew that I might win the Jews. To those who were under the Law I put myself in the position of being under the Law (although in fact I stand free of it), that I might win those

who are under the Law. To those who had no Law I myself became **21**
like a man without the Law (even though in fact I cannot be a
lawless man for I am bound by the law of Christ), so that I might
win the men who have no Law. To the weak I became a weak man, **22**
that I might win the weak. I have, in short, been all things to all
sorts of men that by every possible means I might win some to
God. I do all this for the sake of the gospel; I want to play my **23**
part in it properly.

To preach the gospel faithfully is my set purpose

Do you remember how, on a racing-track, every competitor **24**
runs, but only one wins the prize? Well, you ought to run with
your minds fixed on winning the prize! Every competitor in **25**
athletic events goes into serious training. Athletes will take tremendous pains—for a fading crown of leaves. But our contest
is for an eternal crown that will never fade.

I run the race then with determination. I am no shadow-boxer, **26**
I really fight! I am my body's sternest master, for fear that when **27**
I have preached to others I should myself be disqualified.

CHAPTER 10

Spiritual experience does not guarantee infallibility

FOR I should like to remind you, my brothers, that our an- **1**
cestors all had the experience of being guided by the cloud in the
desert and of crossing the sea dry-shod. They were all, so to speak, **2**
"baptised" into Moses by these experiences. They all shared the **3**
same spiritual food and drank the same spiritual drink (for they **4**
drank from the spiritual rock which followed them, and that rock
was Christ). Yet in spite of all these wonderful experiences many **5**
of them failed to please God, and left their bones in the desert.
Now in these events our ancestors stand as examples to us, warning **6**
us not to crave after evil things as they did. Nor are you to worship **7**
false gods as they did. The scripture says—

The people sat down to eat and drink, and rose up to play.
Neither should we give way to sexual immorality as did some of **8**
them, for we read that twenty-three thousand fell in a single day!
Nor should we dare to exploit the goodness of God as some of **9**
them did, and fell victims to poisonous snakes. Nor yet must you **10**

355

curse the lot that God has appointed to you as they did, and met their end at the hand of the angel of death.

11 Now these things which happened to our ancestors are illustrations of the way in which God works, and they were written down to be a warning to us who are the heirs of the ages which have gone before us.

12 So let the man who feels sure of his standing today be careful that he does not fall tomorrow.

God still governs human experience

13 No temptation has come your way that is too hard for flesh and blood to bear. But God can be trusted not to allow you to suffer any temptation beyond your powers of endurance. He will see to it that every temptation has a way out, so that it will never be impossible for you to bear it.

We have great spiritual privileges: let us live up to them

14 The lesson we must learn, my brothers, is at all costs to avoid
15 worshipping a false god. I am speaking to you as intelligent men: think over what I am saying.

16 The cup of blessing which we bless, is it not a very sharing in the blood of Christ? When we break the bread do we not actually
17 share in the body of Christ? The very fact that we all share one
18 bread makes us all one body. Look at the Jews of our own day. Isn't there a fellowship between all those who eat the altar sacrifices?

19 Now am I implying that a false god really exists, or that sacri-
20 fices made to any god have some value? Not at all! I say emphatically that gentile sacrifices are made to evil spiritual powers and not to God at all. I don't want you to have any fellowship
21 with such powers. You cannot drink both the cup of the Lord and the cup of devils. You cannot be a guest at the Lord's table and at
22 the table of devils. Are we trying to arouse the wrath of God? Have we forgotten how completely we are in his hands?

The Christian's guiding principle is love not knowledge

23 As I have said before, the Christian position is this: I may do anything, but everything is not useful. Yes, I may do anything,
24 but everything is not constructive. Let no man, then, set his own

advantage as his objective, but rather the good of his neighbour.

You should eat whatever is sold in the meat-market without 25
asking any of the questions of an over-scrupulous conscience. The 26
whole earth and all that is in it belongs to the Lord.

If a pagan asks you to dinner and you want to go, feel free 27
to eat whatever is set before you, without asking any questions
through conscientious scruples. But if your host should say straight 28
out, "This meat has been offered to an idol", then don't eat it,
for his sake—I mean for the sake of conscience, not yours but 29
his.

Now why should my freedom to eat be at the mercy of someone else's conscience? Or why should any evil be said of me when 30
I have eaten meat with thankfulness, and have thanked God for
it? Because, whatever you do, eating or drinking or anything else, 31
everything should be done to bring glory to God.

Do nothing that might make men stumble, whether they are 32
Jews or Greeks or members of the Church of God. I myself try 33
to adapt myself to all men without considering my own advantage
but *their* advantage, that if possible they may be saved.

CHAPTER 11

Copy me, my brothers, as I copy Christ himself. 1

The reasons that lie behind some of the traditions

I must give you credit for remembering what I taught you and 2
adhering to the traditions I passed on to you. But I want you to 3
know that Christ is the head of every individual man, just as a
man is the "head" of the woman and God is the head of Christ.
If a man prays or preaches with his head covered, he is dishonour- 4
ing his own head. But in the case of a woman, if she prays or 5
preaches with her head uncovered it is just as much a disgrace as
if she had had it closely shaved. For if a woman does not cover her 6
head she might just as well have her hair cropped. And if to be
cropped or closely shaven is a sign of disgrace to women (as it is
with many peoples), then that is all the more reason for her to
cover her head. A man ought not to cover his head, for he repre- 7
sents the very person and glory of God, while the woman reflects

8 the person and glory of the man. For man does not exist because
9 woman exists, but vice versa. Man was not created originally for
10 the sake of woman, but woman was created for the sake of man.
For this reason a woman ought to bear on her head an outward
sign of man's authority for all the angels to see.

11 Of course, in the sight of God neither "man" nor "woman"
12 has any separate existence. For if woman was made originally for
man, no man is now born except by a woman, and both man and
13 woman, like everything else, owe their existence to God. But use
your own judgment, do you think it right and proper for a woman
14 to pray to God bare-headed? Isn't there a natural principle here,
15 that makes us feel that long hair is disgraceful to a man, but of
glorious beauty to a woman? We feel this because the long hair
16 is the cover provided by nature for the woman's head. But if
anyone wants to be argumentative about it, I can only say that
we and the churches of God generally hold this ruling on the
matter.

I must mention serious faults in your Church

17 But in giving you the following rules, I cannot commend your
conduct, for it seems that your church meetings do you more
18 harm than good! For first, when you meet for worship I hear that
you split up into small groups, and I think there must be truth in
19 what I hear. For there must be cliques among you or your favour-
20 ite leaders would not be so conspicuous. It follows, then, that
when you are assembled in one place you do not eat the *Lord's* sup-
21 per. For everyone tries to grab his food before anyone else, with
the result that one goes hungry and another has too much to drink!
22 Haven't you houses of your own to have your meals in, or are you
making a convenience of the church of God and causing acute
embarrassment to those who have no other home?

Am I to commend this sort of conduct? Most certainly not!

To partake of the Lord's supper is a supremely serious thing

23 The teaching I gave you was given me personally by the
Lord himself, and it was this: the Lord Jesus, in the same night
24 in which he was betrayed, took bread and when he had given
thanks he broke it and said, "Take, eat, this is my body which is
25 being broken for you. Do this in remembrance of me." Similarly,
when supper was ended, he took the cup saying, "This cup is the

new agreement in my blood: do this, whenever you drink it, in remembrance of me."

This can only mean that whenever you eat this bread or drink 26 of this cup, you are proclaiming that the Lord has died for you, and you will do that until he comes again. So that, whoever eats 27 the bread or drinks the cup of the Lord without proper reverence is sinning against the body and blood of the Lord.

No, a man should thoroughly examine himself, and only then 28 should he eat the bread or drink of the cup. He that eats and drinks 29 carelessly is eating and drinking a judgment on himself, for he is blind to the presence of the Lord's body.

Careless communion means spiritual weakness: let us take due care

It is this careless participation which is the reason for the many 30 feeble and sickly Christians in your church, and the explanation of the fact that many of you are spiritually asleep.

If we were closely to examine ourselves beforehand, we should 31 avoid the judgment of God. But when God does judge us, he 32 disciplines us as his own sons, that we may not be involved in the general condemnation of the world.

Now, my brothers, when you come together to eat this bread, 33 wait your proper turn. If a man is really hungry let him satisfy his 34 appetite at home. Don't let your communions be God's judgment upon you!

The other matters I will settle in person, when I come.

CHAPTER 12

The Holy Spirit inspires men's faith and imparts spiritual gifts

Now I want to give you some further information in some 1 spiritual matters. You have not forgotten that you were gentiles, 2 following dumb idols just as your impulses led you. Now I want 3 you to understand, as Christians, that no one speaking by the Spirit of God could call Jesus accursed, and no one could say that he is the Lord, except by the Holy Spirit.

Men have different gifts, but it is the same Spirit who gives 4 them. There are different ways of serving God, but it is the same 5 Lord who is served. God works through different men in different 6 ways, but it is the same God who achieves his purposes through

7 them all. Each man is given his gift by the Spirit that he may use
it for the common good.

8 One man's gift by the Spirit is to speak with wisdom, another's
9 to speak with knowledge. The same Spirit gives to another man
10 faith, to another the ability to heal, to another the power to do
great deeds. The same Spirit gives to another man the gift of
preaching the word of God, to another the ability to discriminate
in spiritual matters, to another speech in different tongues and to
11 yet another the power to interpret the tongues. Behind all these
gifts is the operation of the same Spirit, who distributes to each
individual man, as he wills.

The human body is an example of organic unity

12 As the human body, which has many parts, is a unity, and those
parts, despite their multiplicity, constitute one single body, so it
13 is with Christ. For we were all baptised by the Spirit into one
body, whether we were Jews, Greeks, slaves or free men, and we
have all had experience of the same Spirit.

14, 15 Now the body is not one member but many. If the foot should
say, "Because I am not a hand I don't belong to the body," does
16 that alter the fact that the foot *is* a part of the body? Or if the ear
should say, "Because I am not an eye I don't belong to the body,"
17 does that mean that the ear really is no part of the body? After all,
if the body were all one eye, for example, where would be the
sense of hearing? Or if it were all one ear, where would be the
18 sense of smell? But God has arranged all the parts in the one body
19 according to his design. For if everything were concentrated in
20 one part, how could there be a body at all? The fact is there are
21 many parts, but only one body. So that the eye cannot say to the
hand, "I don't need you!" nor, again, can the head say to the feet,
22 "I don't need you!" On the contrary, those parts of the body
which have no obvious function are the more essential to health:
23 and to those parts of the body which seem to us to be less deserving of notice we have to allow the highest honour of function.
The parts which do not look beautiful have a deeper beauty in
24 the work they do, while the parts which look beautiful may not
be at all essential to life! But God has harmonised the whole body
by giving importance of function to the parts which lack apparent
25 importance, that the body should work together as a whole with
all the members in sympathetic relationship with one another.
26 So it happens that if one member suffers all the other members

suffer with it, and if one member is honoured all the members share a common joy.

Now you are together the body of Christ, and individually you 27 are members of him. And in his Church God has appointed first 28 some to be his messengers, secondly, some to be preachers of power, thirdly teachers. After them he has appointed workers of spiritual power, men with the gift of healing, helpers, organisers and those with the gift of speaking in "tongues".

As we look at the body of Christ do we find all are his mes- 29 sengers, all are preachers, or all teachers? Do we find all wielders of spiritual power, all able to heal, all able to speak with tongues, 30 or all able to interpret the tongues? No, we find God's distribution of gifts is on the same principles of harmony that he has shown in the human body.

You should set your hearts on the best spiritual gifts, but I will 31 show you a way which surpasses them all.

CHAPTER 13

Christian love—the highest and best gift

If I speak with the eloquence of men and of angels, but have no 1 love, I become no more than blaring brass or crashing cymbal. If I have the gift of foretelling the future and hold in my mind not 2 only all human knowledge but the very secrets of God, and if I also have that absolute faith which can move mountains, but have no love, I amount to nothing at all. If I dispose of all that I 3 possess, yes, even if I give my own body to be burned, but have no love, I achieve precisely nothing.

This love of which I speak is slow to lose patience—it looks for 4 a way of being constructive. It is not possessive: it is neither anxious to impress nor does it cherish inflated ideas of its own importance.

Love has good manners and does not pursue selfish advantage. 5 It is not touchy. It does not keep account of evil or gloat over the 6 wickedness of other people. On the contrary, it is glad with all good men when truth prevails.

Love knows no limit to its endurance, no end to its trust, no 7 fading of its hope; it can outlast anything. It is, in fact, the one 8 thing that still stands when all else has fallen.

All gifts except love will be superseded one day

For if there are prophecies they will be fulfilled and done with, if there are "tongues" the need for them will disappear, if there
9 is knowledge it will be swallowed up in truth. For our knowledge
10 is always incomplete and our prophecy is always incomplete, and when the complete comes, that is the end of the incomplete.

11 When I was a little child I talked and felt and thought like a little child. Now that I am a man my childish speech and feeling and thought have no further significance for me.

12 At present we are men looking at puzzling reflections in a mirror. The time will come when we shall see reality whole and face to face! At present all I know is a little fraction of the truth, but the time will come when I shall know it as fully as God now knows me!

13 In this life we have three great lasting qualities—faith, hope and love. But the greatest of them is love.

CHAPTER 14

"Tongues" are not the greatest gift

1 FOLLOW, then, the way of love, while you set your heart on the gifts of the Spirit. The highest gift you can wish for is to be able
2 to speak the messages of God. The man who speaks in a "tongue" addresses not men (for no one understands a word he says) but
3 God: and only in his spirit is he speaking spiritual secrets. But he who preaches the word of God is using his speech for the building up of the faith of one man, the encouragement of another or the
4 consolation of another. The speaker in a "tongue" builds up his own soul, but the preacher builds up the Church of God.

5 I should indeed like you all to speak with "tongues", but I would much rather that you all preached the word of God. For the preacher of the word does a greater work than the speaker with "tongues", unless of course the latter interprets his words for the benefit of the Church.

Unless "tongues" are interpreted do they help the Church?

6 For suppose I came to you, my brothers, speaking with "tongues", what good could I do you unless I could give you some revelation of truth, some knowledge in spiritual things,

some message from God, or some teaching about the Christian life?

Even in the case of inanimate objects which are capable of making sound, such as a flute or harp, if their notes all sound alike, who can tell what tune is being played? Unless the bugle-note is clear who will be called to arms? So, in your case, unless you make intelligible sounds with your "tongue" how can anyone know what you are talking about? You might just as well be addressing an empty room! 7 8 9

There are in the world a great variety of spoken sounds and each has a distinct meaning. But if the sounds of the speaker's voice mean nothing to me I am a foreigner to him, and he is a foreigner to me. 10 11

So, with yourselves, since you are so eager to possess spiritual gifts, concentrate your ambition upon receiving those which make for the real growth of your church. And that means if one of your number speaks with a "tongue", he should pray that he may be able to interpret what he says. 12 13

If I pray in a "tongue" my spirit is praying but my mind is inactive. I am therefore determined to pray with my spirit *and* my mind, and if I sing I will sing with both spirit and mind. Otherwise, if you are blessing God with your spirit, how can those who are ungifted say amen to your thanksgiving, since they do not know what you are talking about? You may be thanking God splendidly, but it doesn't help the other man at all. I thank God that I have a greater gift of "tongues" than any of you, yet when I am in church I would rather speak five words with my mind (which might teach something to other people) than ten thousand words in a "tongue" which nobody understands. 14 15 16 17 18 19

You must use your minds in this matter of tongues

My brothers, don't be like excitable children but use your intelligence! By all means be innocent as babes as far as evil is concerned, but where your minds are concerned be full-grown men! In the Law it is written: 20 21

> By men of strange tongues and by the lips of strangers will I speak unto this people: and not even thus will they hear me, saith the Lord.

That means that tongues are a sign of God's power, not for those who are unbelievers but to those who already believe.* 22

* See note 5, page 552.

23 Preaching the word of God, on the other hand, is a sign of God's power to those who do not believe rather than to believers. So that, if at a full church meeting you are all speaking with tongues and men come in who are both uninstructed and without faith,

24 will they not say that you are insane? But if you are preaching God's word and such a man should come in to your meeting, he is convicted and challenged by your united speaking of the truth.

25 His secrets are exposed and he will fall on his knees acknowledging God and saying that God is truly among you!

Some practical regulations for the exercise of spiritual gifts

26 Well then, my brothers, whenever you meet let everyone be ready to contribute a psalm, a piece of teaching, a spiritual truth, or a "tongue" with an interpreter. Everything should be done to make your church strong in the faith.

27 If the question of speaking with a "tongue" arises, confine the speaking to two or three at the most and have someone to interpret

28 what is said. If you have no interpreter then let the speaker with a "tongue" keep silent in the church and speak only to himself and

29 God. Don't have more than two or three preachers either, while

30 the others think over what has been said. But should a message of truth come to one who is seated, then the original speaker

31 should stop talking. For in this way you can all have opportunity to give a message, one after the other, and everyone will learn

32 something and everyone will have his faith stimulated. The spirit

33 of a true preacher is under that preacher's control, for God is not a God of disorder but of harmony, as is plain in all the churches.

The speaking of women in church is forbidden

34 Let women be silent in church; they are not to be allowed to speak. They must submit to this regulation, as the Law itself in-

35 structs. If they have questions to ask they must ask their husbands at home, for there is something indecorous about a woman's speaking in church.

You must accept the rules I have given by authority

36 Do I see you questioning my instructions? Are you beginning to imagine that the Word of God originated in your church, or

37 that you have a monopoly of God's truth? If any of your number

think himself a true preacher and a spiritually-minded man, let him recognise that what I have written is by divine command! As for those who don't know it, well, we must just leave them in **38** ignorance.

In conclusion then, my brothers, set your heart on preaching **39** the word of God, while not forbidding the use of "tongues". Let **40** everything be done decently and in order.

CHAPTER 15

A reminder of the gospel message: the resurrection is an integral part of our faith

Now, my brothers, I want to speak about the gospel which I **1** have previously preached to you, which you accepted, in which you are at present standing, and by which, if you remain faithful **2** to the message I gave you, your salvation is being worked out— unless, of course, your faith had no meaning behind it at all.

For I passed on to you,—as among the first to hear it, the **3** message I had myself received—that Christ died for our sins, as the scriptures said he would; that he was buried and rose again on **4** the third day, again as the scriptures foretold. He was seen by **5** Cephas, then by the twelve, and subsequently he was seen simul- **6** taneously by over five hundred Christians, of whom the majority are still alive, though some have since died. He was then seen by **7** James, then by all the messengers. And last of all, as if to one born **8** abnormally late, he appeared to me! I am the least of the mes- **9** sengers, and indeed I do not deserve that title at all, because I persecuted the Church of God. But what I am now I am by the **10** grace of God. The grace he gave me has not proved a barren gift. I have worked harder than any of the others—and yet it was not I but this same grace of God within me. In any event, whoever has **11** done the work, whether I or they, this has been the message and this has been the foundation of your faith.

If the resurrection is the heart of the gospel how can any Christian deny life after death?

Now if the rising of Christ from the dead is the very heart of **12** our message, how can some of you deny that there is any resur- rection? For if there is no such thing as the resurrection of the **13** dead, then Christ was never raised. And if Christ was not raised **14**

then neither our preaching nor your faith has any meaning at all.
15 Further it would mean that we are lying in our witness for God,
for we have given our solemn testimony that he did raise up
Christ—and that is utterly false if it should be true that the dead
16 do not, in fact, rise again! For if the dead do not rise neither did
17 Christ rise, and if Christ did not rise your faith is futile and your
18 sins have never been forgiven. Moreover those who have died
19 believing in Christ are utterly dead and gone. Truly, if our hope
in Christ were limited to this life only we should, of all mankind,
be the most to be pitied!

But Christianity rests on a fact—Christ did rise

20 But the glorious fact is that Christ *did* rise from the dead: he
has become the very first to rise of all who sleep the sleep of
21 death. As death entered the world through a man, so has rising
22 from the dead come to us through a man! As members of a sinful
race all men die; as members of the Christ of God all men shall
23 be raised to life, each in his proper order, with Christ the very
first and after him all who belong to him when he comes.

24 Then, and not till then, comes the end when Christ, having
abolished all other rule, authority and power, hands over the
25 kingdom to God the Father. Christ's reign will and must con-
26 tinue until every enemy has been conquered. The last enemy of
27 all to be destroyed is death itself. The scripture says:

He hath put all things in subjection under his feet.

But in the term "all things" it is quite obvious that God, who
brings them all under subjection to Christ, is himself excepted.
28 Nevertheless, when everything created has been made obedient
to God, then shall the Son acknowledge himself subject to God
the Father, who gave the Son power over all things. Thus, in the
end, shall God be wholly and absolutely God.

To refuse to believe in the resurrection is both foolish and wicked

29 Further, you should consider this, that if there is to be no resurrection what is the point of some of you being baptised for the
30 dead by proxy? Why should you be baptised for *dead bodies*? And
31 why should I live a life of such hourly danger? I assure you, by
the certainty of Jesus Christ that we possess, that I face death
32 every day of my life! And if, to use the popular expression, I have

366

"fought with wild beasts" here in Ephesus, what is the good of an ordeal like that if there is no life after this one? Let us rather eat, drink and be merry, for tomorrow we die!

Don't let yourselves be deceived. Talking about things that are 33
not true is bound to be reflected in practical conduct. Come back 34
to your senses, and don't dabble in sinful doubts. Remember that there are men who have plenty to say but have no knowledge of God. You should be ashamed that I have to write like this at all!

Parallels in nature help us to grasp the truths of the resurrection

But perhaps someone will ask, "How is the resurrection 35
achieved? With what sort of body do the dead arrive?" Now that 36
is talking without using your minds! In your own experience you know that a seed does not germinate without itself "dying". When you sow a seed you do not sow the "body" that will 37
eventually be produced, but bare grain, of wheat, for example, or one of the other seeds. God gives the seed a "body" according to 38
his laws—a different "body" to each kind of seed.

Then again, even in this world, all flesh is not identical. There 39
is a difference in the flesh of human beings, animals, fish and birds.

There are bodies which exist in this world, and bodies which 40
exist in the heavens. These bodies are not, as it were, in competition; the splendour of an earthly body is quite a different thing from the splendour of a heavenly body. The sun, the moon and 41
the stars all have their own particular splendour, while among the stars themselves there are different kinds of splendour.

There are illustrations here of the raising of the dead. The body 42
is "sown" in corruption; it is raised beyond the reach of corruption. It is "sown" in dishonour; it is raised in splendour. It is sown 43
in weakness; it is raised in power. It is sown a natural body; it is 44
raised a spiritual body. As there is a natural body so will there be a spiritual body.

It is written, moreover, that: 45
    The first man Adam became a living soul.
So the last Adam is a life-giving Spirit. But we should notice that 46
the order is "natural" first and then "spiritual". The first man 47
came out of the earth, a material creature. The second man came from Heaven and was the Lord himself. For the life of this world 48
men are made like the material man; but for the life that is to come they are made like the one from Heaven. So that just as we 49
have been made like the material pattern, so we shall be made like

50 the Heavenly pattern. For I assure you, my brothers, it is utterly impossible for flesh and blood to possess the kingdom of God. The transitory could never possess the everlasting.

The dead and the living will be fitted for immortality

51 Listen, and I will tell you a secret. We shall not all die, but
52 suddenly, in the twinkling of an eye, every one of us will be changed as the trumpet sounds! The trumpet will sound and the dead shall be raised beyond the reach of corruption, and we who
53 are still alive shall suddenly be utterly changed. For this perishable nature of ours must be wrapped in imperishability, these bodies
54 which are mortal must be wrapped in immortality. So when the perishable is lost in the imperishable, the mortal lost in the immortal, this saying will come true:
Death is swallowed up in victory.
55 For where now, O death, is your power to hurt us ? Where now,
56 O grave, is the victory you hoped to win ? It is sin which gives
57 death its sting, and it is the Law which gives sin its strength. All thanks to God, then, who gives us the victory over these things through our Lord Jesus Christ!
58 And so, brothers of mine, stand firm! Let nothing move you as you busy yourselves in the Lord's work. Be sure that nothing you do for him is ever lost or ever wasted.

CHAPTER 16

The matter of the fund: my own immediate plans

1 Now as far as the fund for Christians in need is concerned, I should like you to follow the same rule that I gave to the Galatian church.
2 On the first day of the week let everyone put so much by him, according to his financial prosperity, so that there will be no need
3 for collections when I come. Then, on my arrival, I will send whomever you approve to take your gift, with my recommenda-
4 tion, to Jerusalem. If it seems right for me to go as well, we will
5 make up a party together. I shall come to you after my intended
6 journey through Macedonia and I may stay with you awhile or even spend the winter with you. Then you can see me on my way
7 —wherever it is that I go next. I don't wish to see you now, for it would merely be in passing, and I hope to spend some time with

you, if it is the Lord's will. I shall stay here in Ephesus until the 8
feast of Pentecost, for there is a great opportunity of doing useful 9
work, and there are many people against me.

News of Timothy and Apollos

If Timothy comes to you, put him at his ease. He is as genuine 10
a worker for the Lord as I am, and there is therefore no reason to 11
look down on him. Send him on his way in peace, for I am
expecting him to come to me here with the other Christian
brothers. As for our brother Apollos I pressed him strongly to go 12
to you with the rest, but it was definitely not God's will for him
to do so then. However, he will come to you as soon as an
opportunity occurs.

A little sermon in a nutshell!

Be on your guard, stand firm in the faith, live like men, be 13
strong! Let everything that you do be done in love. 14

A request, and final greetings

You remember the household of Stephanas, the first men of 15
Achaia to be won for Christ? Well, they have made up their
minds to devote their lives to looking after Christian brothers. I 16
do beg you to recognise them as Christ's ministers, and to extend
your recognition to all their helpers and workers.

I am very glad that Stephanas, Fortunatus and Achaicus have 17
arrived. They have made up for my not seeing you. They are a 18
tonic to me and to you. You should appreciate having men like
that!

Greetings from the churches of Asia. Aquila and Prisca send 19
you their warmest Christian greetings and so does the church that
meets in their house. All the Christians here send greetings. I 20
should like you to shake hands all round as a sign of Christian
love.

Here is my own greeting, written by me, Paul. If any man does 21,22
not love the Lord, let him be accursed; may the Lord soon come!

The grace of the Lord Jesus be with you and my love be with 23,24
you all in Christ Jesus.

PAUL.

The Second Letter to the Christians at Corinth

AUTHOR. *Paul, writing in Macedonia, probably as soon as Titus had arrived back from Corinth, bringing news of the reception of the "first letter". (Some think that Paul had paid a hurried personal visit to Corinth between the writing of these two letters.)*

DATE. *Possibly 57.*

DESTINATION. *The church at Corinth, as in the "first letter".*

THEME. *There is a good deal of Paul's personal circumstances, feelings, activities, and attitude to his own ministry in this highly interesting letter. The Corinthian church appears to have disciplined the guilty member referred to in the first letter, and Paul recommends his restoration to the fellowship of the church.*

Again in this letter Paul has to defend his own divine commission as messenger, and even has to threaten strong action against his traducers in a personal visit.

Throughout this letter the reader cannot help feeling how "human" was Paul, and how genuine in his concern for the young and struggling churches under his care.

NOTE. *Many scholars believe that this letter contains parts of other "lost" letters in the passages: 6, 14 to 7, 1, and chapters X–XIII, which seem out of key with the rest. The first-named passage may form part of the letter referred to by Paul in I Corinthians 5, 9.*

CHAPTER 1

1 THIS letter comes to you from Paul, God's messenger for Christ Jesus by the will of God, and from brother Timothy, and is addressed to the church of God in Corinth and all Christians throughout Achaia.

2 May grace and peace come to you from God our Father and from the Lord Jesus Christ.

God's encouragements are adequate for all life's troubles

Thank God, the Father of our Lord Jesus Christ, that he is our 3
Father and the source of all mercy and comfort. For he gives us 4
comfort in our trials so that we in turn may be able to give the
same sort of strong sympathy to others in theirs. Indeed, experi- 5
ence shows that the more we share Christ's suffering the more we
are able to give of his encouragement. This means that if we 6
experience trouble we can pass on to you comfort and spiritual
help; for if we ourselves have been comforted we know how to
encourage you to endure patiently the same sort of troubles that
we have ourselves endured. We are quite confident that if you 7
have to suffer troubles as we have done, then, like us, you will find
the comfort and encouragement of God.

Man's extremity is God's opportunity

We should like you, our brothers, to know something of what 8
we went through in Asia. At that time we were completely
overwhelmed, the burden was more than we could bear, in fact
we told ourselves that this was the end. Yet we believe now 9
that we had this experience of coming to the end of our tether
that we might learn to trust, not in ourselves, but in God who can
raise the dead. It was God who preserved us from imminent 10
death, and it is he who still preserves us. Further, we trust him to
keep us safe in the future, and here you can join in and help by 11
praying for us, so that the good that is done to us in answer to
many prayers will mean eventually that many will thank God for
our preservation.

Our dealings with you have always been straightforward

Now it is a matter of pride to us—endorsed by our conscience 12
—that our activities in this world, particularly our dealings with
you, have been absolutely above-board and sincere before God.
They have not been marked by any worldly wisdom, but by the
grace of God. Our letters to you have no double meaning—they 13
mean just what you understand them to mean when you read
them. I hope you will always understand these letters, as I believe 14
some of you have understood me, and realise that you can be as
honestly proud of us as we shall be of you on the day of the Lord
Jesus.

Change of plan does not necessarily mean fickleness of heart

15 Trusting you, and believing that you trusted us, our original plan was to pay you a visit first, and give you a double "treat".
16 We meant to come here to Macedonia after first visiting you, and then to visit you again on leaving here. You could thus have
17 helped us on our way towards Judaea. Because we had to change this plan, does it mean that we are fickle? Do you think I plan with
18 my tongue in my cheek, saying "yes" and meaning "no"? We solemnly assure you that as certainly as God is faithful so we have
19 never given you a message meaning "yes" and "no". Jesus Christ, the Son of God, whom Silvanus, Timothy and I have preached to you, is himself no doubtful quantity, he is the divine "yes".
20 Every promise of God finds its affirmative in him, and through
21 him can be said the final amen, to the glory of God. We owe our position in Christ to this God of positive promise: it is he who has
22 consecrated us to this special work, he who has given us the living guarantee of the Spirit in our hearts. Are we then the men to say one thing and mean another?

I have never wanted to hurt you

23 No, I declare before God that it was to avoid hurting you that
24 I did not come to Corinth. We are not trying to dominate you and your faith—your faith is firm enough—but we can work with you to increase your joy.

CHAPTER 2

1 AND I made up my mind that I would not pay you another painful
2 visit. For what point is there in my depressing the very people
3 who can give me such joy? The real purpose of my previous letter was in fact to save myself from being saddened by those whom I
4 might reasonably expect to bring me joy. I have such confidence in you that my joy depends on all of you! I wrote to you in deep distress and out of a most unhappy heart (I don't mind telling you I shed tears over that letter), not, believe me, to cause you pain, but to show you how deep is my care for your welfare.

A word of explanation

5 There was a reason for my stern words; this is my advice now. If the behaviour of a certain person has caused distress, it does not

mean so much that he has injured me, but that to some extent (I do not wish to exaggerate), he has injured all of you. But now 6 I think that the punishment you have inflicted on him has been sufficient. Now is the time to offer him forgiveness and comfort, 7 for it is possible for a man in his position to be completely over-whelmed by remorse. I ask you to show him plainly now that 8 you love him. My previous letter was something of a test—I 9 wanted to make sure that you would follow my orders implicitly. If you will forgive a certain person, rest assured that I forgive him 10 too. Insofar as I had anything personally to forgive, I do forgive him, as before Christ. We don't want Satan to win any victory 11 here, and well we know his methods!

And a further confidence

Well, when I came to Troas to preach the gospel of Christ, 12 although there was an obvious God-given opportunity, I must 13 confess I was on edge the whole time because there was no sign of brother Titus. So I said good-bye and went from there to Macedonia. Thanks be to God who leads us, wherever we are, 14 on Christ's triumphant way and makes our knowledge of him spread throughout the world like a lovely perfume! We Christians 15 have the unmistakable "scent" of Christ, discernible alike to those who are being saved and to those who are heading for death. To 16 the latter it seems like the deathly smell of doom, to the former it has the refreshing fragrance of life itself.

Who could think himself adequate for a responsibility like this? Only the man who refuses to join that large class which traffics 17 in the Word of God—the man who speaks, as we do, in the name of God, under the eyes of God, as Christ's chosen minister.

CHAPTER 3

You yourselves are the proof of our ministry

Is this going to be more self-advertisement in your eyes? Do 1 we need, as some apparently do, to exchange testimonials before we can be friends? You yourselves are our testimonial, written in 2 our hearts and yet open for anyone to inspect and read. You are 3 an open letter about Christ which we ourselves have written, not with pen and ink but with the Spirit of the living God. Our message has been engraved not in stone, but in living men and women.

4 We dare to say such things because of the confidence we have
5 in God through Christ. Not that we are in any way confident of our own resources—our ability comes from God. It is he who
6 makes us competent administrators of the new agreement, and we deal not in the letter but in the Spirit. The letter of the Law leads to the death of the soul; the Spirit of God alone can give life to the soul.

The splendour of our ministry outshines that of Moses

7 The administration of the Law which was engraved in stone (and which led in fact to spiritual death) was so magnificent that the Israelites were unable to look unflinchingly at Moses' face, for
8 it was alight with heavenly splendour. Now if the old administration held such heavenly, even though transitory, splendour, can we not see what a much more glorious thing is the new adminis-
9 tration of the Spirit of life? If to administer a system which is to end in condemning men was a splendid task, how infinitely more splendid is it to administer a system which ends in making men
10 good! And while it is true that the former temporary glory has been completely eclipsed by the latter, we do well to remember
11 that it is eclipsed simply because the present permanent plan is such a very much more glorious thing than the old.

Our ministry is an open and splendid thing

12 With this hope in our hearts we are quite frank and open in
13 our ministry. We are not like Moses, who veiled his face to
14 prevent the Israelites from seeing its fading glory. But it was their minds really which were blinded, for even today when the old agreement is read to them there is still a veil over their minds—
15 though the veil has actually been lifted by Christ. Yes, alas, even to this day there is still a veil over their hearts when the writings of
16 Moses are read. Yet if they "turned to the Lord" the veil would
17 disappear. For the Lord to whom they could turn is the Spirit of the new agreement, and wherever the Spirit of the Lord is, men's souls are set free.

18 But all of us who are Christians have no veils on our faces, but reflect like mirrors the glory of the Lord. We are transfigured in ever-increasing splendour into his own image, and the trans-formation comes from the Lord who is the Spirit.

374

CHAPTER 4

Ours is a straightforward ministry bringing light into darkness

THIS is the ministry which God in his mercy has given us and *1*
nothing can daunt us. We use no hocus-pocus, no clever tricks, no *2*
dishonest manipulation of the Word of God. We speak the plain
truth and so commend ourselves to every man's conscience in the
sight of God. If our gospel is "veiled", the veil must be in the *3*
minds of those who are spiritually dying. The spirit of this world *4*
has blinded the minds of those who do not believe, and prevents
the light of the glorious gospel of Christ, the image of God, from
shining on them. For it is Christ Jesus as Lord whom we preach, *5*
not ourselves; we are your servants for Jesus' sake. God, who first *6*
ordered light to shine in darkness, has flooded our hearts with his
light. We now can enlighten men only because we can give them
knowledge of the glory of God, as we see it in the face of Jesus
Christ.

We experience death—we give life, by the power of God

This priceless treasure we hold, so to speak, in a common *7*
earthenware jar—to show that the splendid power of it belongs to
God and not to us. We are handicapped on all sides, but we are *8*
never frustrated; we are puzzled, but never in despair. We are *9*
persecuted, but we never have to stand it alone: we may be
knocked down but we are never knocked out! Every day we *10*
experience something of the death of Jesus, so that we may also
know the power of the life of Jesus in these bodies of ours. Yes, *11*
we who are living are always being exposed to death for Jesus'
sake, so that the life of Jesus may be plainly seen in our mortal
lives. We are always facing death, but this means that you know *12*
more and more of life. Our faith is like that mentioned in the *13*
scripture:
I believed and therefore did I speak.
For we too speak because we believe, and we know for certain *14*
that he who raised the Lord Jesus from death shall also raise us
with Jesus. We shall all stand together before him.

We live a transitory life with our eyes on the life eternal

We wish you could see how all this is working out for your *15*

benefit, and how the more grace God gives, the more thanks-
16 giving will redound to his glory. This is the reason why we never
collapse. The outward man does indeed suffer wear and tear, but
17 every day the inward man receives fresh strength. These little
troubles (which are really so transitory) are winning for us a
permanent, glorious and solid reward out of all proportion to our
18 pain. For we are looking all the time not at the visible things but
at the invisible. The visible things are transitory: it is the invisible
things that are really permanent.

CHAPTER 5

1 WE know, for instance, that if our earthly dwelling were taken
down, like a tent, we have a permanent house in Heaven, made,
2 not by man, but by God. In this present frame we sigh with deep
3 longing for the heavenly house, for we do not want to face utter
nakedness when death destroys our present dwelling—these bodies
4 of ours. So long as we are clothed in this temporary dwelling we
have a painful longing, not because we want just to get rid of these
"clothes" but because we want to know the full cover of the
permanent house that will be ours. We want our transitory life
to be absorbed into the life that is eternal.

Death can have no terrors, for it means being with God

5 Now the power that has planned this experience for us is God,
6 and he has given us his Spirit as a guarantee of its truth. This
makes us confident, whatever happens. We realise that being "at
home" in the body means that to some extent we are "away"
7 from the Lord, for we have to live by trusting him without seeing
8 him. We are so sure of this that we would really rather be "away"
from the body and be "at home" with the Lord.
9 It is our aim, therefore, to please him, whether we are "at
10 home" or "away". For every one of us will have to stand without
pretence before Christ our judge, and we shall be rewarded for
what we did when we lived in our bodies, whether it was good
or bad.

Our ministry is based on solemn convictions

11 All our persuading of men, then, is with this solemn fear of God
in our minds. What we are is utterly plain to God—and I hope

to your consciences as well. (No, we are not recommending our- 12
selves to you again, but we can give you grounds for legitimate
pride in us—if that is what you need to meet those who are so
proud of the outward rather than the inward qualification). If we 13
are "mad" it is for God's glory; if we are perfectly sane it is
for your benefit. At any rate there has been no selfish motive. 14
The very spring of our actions is the love of Christ. We look at it
like this: if one died for all men, then, in a sense, they all died, and 15
his purpose in dying for them is that their lives should now be
no longer lived for themselves but for him who died and rose
again for them. This means that our knowledge of men can no 16
longer be based on their outward lives (indeed, even though we
knew Christ as a man we do not know him like that any longer).
For if a man is in Christ he becomes a new person altogether— 17
the past is finished and gone, everything has become fresh and
new. All this is God's doing, for he has reconciled us to himself 18
through Jesus Christ; and he has made us agents of the reconciliation. God was in Christ personally reconciling the world to him- 19
self—not counting their sins against them—and has commissioned
us with the message of reconciliation. We are now Christ's 20
ambassadors, as though God were appealing direct to you through
us. As his personal representatives we say, "Make your peace with
God." For God caused Christ, who himself knew nothing of sin, 21
actually to *be* sin for our sakes, so that in Christ we might be
made good with the goodness of God.

CHAPTER 6

The hard but glorious life of God's ministers

As co-operators with God himself we beg you, then, not to 1
fail to use the grace of God. For God's word is— 2
> At an acceptable time I hearkened unto thee,
> And in a day of salvation did I succour thee.

Now *is* the "acceptable time", and this very day *is* the
"day of salvation".

As far as we are concerned we do not wish to stand in any- 3
one's way, nor do we wish to bring discredit on the ministry God
has given us. Indeed we want to prove ourselves genuine ministers 4
of God whatever we have to go through—patient endurance of
troubles or even disasters, being flogged or imprisoned; being 5
mobbed, having to work like slaves, having to go without food

6   or sleep. All this we want to meet with sincerity, with insight and
    patience; by sheer kindness and the Holy Spirit; with genuine
7   love, speaking the plain truth, and living by the power of God.
8   Our sole defence, our only weapon, is a life of integrity, whether
    we meet honour or dishonour, praise or blame. Called "impostors"
9   we must be true, called "nobodies" we must be in the public eye.
    Never far from death, yet here we are alive, always "going
10 through it" yet never "going under". We know sorrow, yet
    our joy is inextinguishable. We have "nothing to bless ourselves
    with" yet we bless many others with true riches. We are penniless,
    and yet in reality we have everything worth having.

We have used utter frankness, won't you do the same?

11 Oh, our dear friends in Corinth, we are hiding nothing from
12 you and our hearts are absolutely open to you. Any stiffness
    between us must be on your side, for we assure you there is none
13 on ours. Do reward me (I talk to you as though you were my own
    children) with the same complete candour!

We must warn you against entanglement with pagans

14 Don't link up with unbelievers and try to work with them.
    What common interest can there be between goodness and evil?
15 How can light and darkness share life together? How can there be
    harmony between Christ and the devil? What can a believer have
16 in common with an unbeliever? What common ground can
    idols hold with the temple of God? For we, remember, are our-
    selves living temples of the living God, as God has said:
        I will dwell in them and walk in them:
        And I will be their God, and they shall be my people.
17 Wherefore
        Come ye out from among them and be ye separate, saith the
            Lord,
        And touch no unclean thing;
        And I will receive you,
18   And will be to you a Father,
        And ye shall be to me sons and daughters,
        Saith the Lord Almighty.

CHAPTER 7

WITH these promises ringing in our ears, dear friends, let us keep *1*
clear of anything that smirches body or soul. Let us prove our
reverence for God by consecrating ourselves to him completely.

Does "that letter" still rankle? Hear my explanation

Do make room in your hearts again for us! Not one of you has *2*
ever been wronged or ruined or cheated by us. I don't say this to *3*
condemn your attitude, but simply because, as I said before,
whether we live or die you live in our hearts. To your face I talk *4*
to you with utter frankness; behind your back I talk about you
with deepest pride. Whatever troubles I have gone through, the
thought of you has filled me with comfort and deep happiness.

For even when we arrived in Macedonia we had a wretched *5*
time with trouble all round us—wrangling outside and anxiety
within. Not but what God, who cheers the depressed, gave us the *6*
comfort of the arrival of Titus. And it wasn't merely his coming *7*
that cheered us, but the comfort you had given him, for he could
tell us of your eagerness to help, your deep sympathy and keen
interest on my behalf. All that made me doubly glad to see him.
For although my letter had hurt you I don't regret it now (as I *8*
did, I must confess, at one time). I can see that the letter did upset
you, though only for a time, and now I am glad I sent it, not *9*
because I want to hurt you but because it made you grieve for
things that were wrong. In other words, the result was to make
you sorry as God would have had you sorry, and not merely to
make you offended by what we said. The sorrow which God *10*
uses means a change of heart and leads to salvation—it is the world's
sorrow that is such a deadly thing. You can look back now and *11*
see how the hand of God was in that sorrow. Look how seriously
it made you think, how eager it made you to prove your inno-
cence, how indignant it made you and, in some cases, how afraid!
Look how it made you long for my presence, how it stirred up
your keenness for the faith, how ready it made you to punish the
offender! Yes, that letter cleared the air for you as nothing else
would have done.

Now I did not write that letter really for the sake of the man *12*
who sinned, or even for the sake of the one who was sinned

against, but to let you see for yourselves, in the sight of God, how
13 deeply you really do care for us. That is why we now feel so
deeply comforted, and our sense of joy was greatly enhanced by
14 the satisfaction that your attitude had obviously given Titus. You
see, I had told him of my pride in you, and you have not let me
down. I have always spoken the truth *to* you, and this proves that
15 my proud words *about* you were true as well. Titus himself has a
much greater love for you, now that he has seen for himself the
obedience you gave him, and the respect and reverence with
16 which you treated him. I am profoundly glad to have my confidence in you so fully proved.

CHAPTER 8

*The Macedonian churches have given magnificently: will you not
do so too?*

1 Now, my brothers, we must tell you about the grace that God
2 has given to the Macedonian churches. Somehow, in most difficult
circumstances, their joy and the fact of being down to their last
penny themselves, produced a magnificent concern for other
3 people. I can guarantee that they were willing to give to the limit
of their means, yes and beyond their means, without the slightest
4 urging from me or anyone else. In fact they simply begged us to
accept their gifts and so let them share the honours of supporting
5 their brothers in Christ. Nor was their gift, as I must confess I had
expected, a mere cash payment. Instead they made a complete
dedication of themselves first to the Lord and then to us, as God's
appointed ministers.

6 Now this has made us ask Titus, who has already done so much
among you, to complete his task by arranging for you too to
7 share in this work of generosity. Already you are well to the fore
in every good quality—you have faith, you can express that faith
in words; you have knowledge, enthusiasm and your love for us.
8 Could you not add generosity to your virtues? I don't want you
to read this as an order. It is only my suggestion, prompted by what
I have seen in others of eagerness to help, and here is a way to prove
9 the reality of your love. Do you remember the generosity of Jesus
Christ, the Lord of us all? He was rich beyond our telling, yet he
became poor for your sakes so that his poverty might make you
rich.

I merely suggest that you finish your original generous gesture

Here is my opinion in the matter. I think it would be a good 10
thing for you, who were the first a year ago to think of helping,
as well as the first to give, to carry through what you then
intended to do. Finish it, then, as well as you can, and show that 11
you can complete what you set out to do with as much efficiency
as you showed readiness to begin. After all, the important thing 12
is to be willing to give as much as we can—that is what God
accepts, and no one is asked to give what he has not got. Of 13
course, I don't mean that others should be relieved to an extent
that leaves you in distress. It is a matter of share and share alike. 14
At present your plenty should supply their need, and then at some
future date their plenty may supply your need. In that way we
share with each other, as the scripture says, 15
<blockquote>
He that gathered much had nothing over,
And he that gathered little had no lack.
</blockquote>

Titus is bringing you this letter personally

Thank God Titus feels the same deep concern for you as we do! 16
He accepts the suggestion outlined above, and in his enthusiasm 17
comes to you personally at his own request. We are sending with 18
him that brother whose services to the gospel are universally
praised in the churches. He has been unanimously chosen to travel 19
with us in this work of administering the gifts of others. It is a task
that brings glory to God and demonstrates also the willingness of
us Christians to help each other. Naturally we want to avoid the 20
slightest breath of criticism in the distribution of their gifts, and 21
to be absolutely above-board not only in the sight of God but in
the eyes of men.

With these two we are also sending our brother, of whose 22
keenness we have ample proof and whose interest is especially
aroused on this occasion as he has such confidence in you. As for 23
Titus, he is our colleague and partner in your affairs, and both the
brothers are official messengers of the churches and shining examples of their faith. So do let them, and all the churches, see how 24
genuine is your love, and justify all the nice things we have said
about you!

CHAPTER 9

A word in confidence about this gift of yours

1 OF course I know it is really quite superflous for me to be writing to you about this matter of giving to fellow Christians,

2 for I know how willing you are. Indeed I have told the Macedonians with some pride that "Achaia was ready to undertake this service twelve months ago". Your enthusiasm has conse-

3 quently been a stimulus to many of them. I am, however, sending the brothers just to make sure that our pride in you is not un-

4 justified. For, between ourselves, it would never do if some of the Macedonians were to accompany me on my visit to you and find you unprepared for this act of generosity! We (not to speak of you) should be horribly ashamed, just because we had been so

5 proud and confident of you. This is my reason, then, for urging the brothers to visit you before I come myself, so that they can get your promised gift ready in good time. But, having let you into my confidence, I should like it to be a spontaneous gift, and

6 not money squeezed out of you by what I have said. All I will say is that poor sowing means a poor harvest, and generous sowing means a generous harvest.

Giving does not only help the one who receives

7 Let everyone give as his heart tells him, neither grudgingly nor under compulsion, for God loves the man who gives cheer-

8 fully. After all, God can give you everything that you need, so that you may always have sufficient both for yourselves and for

9 giving away to other people. As the scripture says:
    He hath scattered abroad, he hath given to the poor;
    His righteousness abideth for ever.

10 He who gives the seed to the sower and turns that seed into bread to eat, will give you the seed of generosity to sow and, for

11 harvest, the satisfying bread of good deeds done. The more you are enriched by God the more scope will there be for generous giving, and your gifts, administered through us, will mean that

12 many will thank God. For your giving does not end in meeting the wants of your fellow-Christians. It also results in an over-

13 flowing tide of thanksgiving to God. Moreover, your very giving proves the reality of your faith, and that means that men thank

God that you practise the gospel that you profess to believe in, as well as for the actual gifts you make to them and to others. And yet further, men will pray for you and feel drawn to you **14** because you have obviously received a generous measure of the grace of God.

Thank God, then, for his indescribable generosity to you! **15**

CHAPTER 10

We are not merely human agents but God-appointed ministers

Now I am going to appeal to you personally, by the gentleness **1** and sympathy of Christ himself. Yes, I, Paul, the one who is "humble enough in our presence but outspoken when away from us", am begging you to make it unnecessary for me to be out- **2** spoken and stern in your presence. For I am afraid otherwise that I shall have to do some plain speaking to those of you who will persist in reckoning that our activities are on the purely human level. The truth is that, although of course we lead normal human **3** lives, the battle we are fighting is on the spiritual level. The very **4** weapons we use are not those of human warfare but powerful in God's warfare for the destruction of the enemy's strongholds. Our battle is to bring down every deceptive fantasy and every **5** imposing defence that men erect against the true knowledge of God. We even fight to capture every thought until it acknow- ledges the authority of Christ. Once we are sure of your obedience **6** we shall not shrink from dealing with those who refuse to obey.

I really am a Christian, you know !

Do look at things which stare you in the face! So-and-so **7** considers himself to belong to Christ. All right; but let him reflect that we belong to Christ every bit as much as he. You may think **8** that I have boasted unduly of my authority (which the Lord gave me, remember, to build you up not to break you down), but I don't think I have done anything to be ashamed of. Yet I don't **9** want you to think of me merely as the man who writes you terrifying letters. I know my critics say, "His letters are impressive **10** and moving but his actual presence is feeble and his speaking beneath contempt." Let them realise that we can be just as **11** "impressive and moving" in person as they say we are in our letters.

God's appointment means more than self-recommendation

12   Of course we shouldn't dare include ourselves in the same class
as those who write their own testimonials, or even to compare
ourselves with them! All they are doing, of course, is to measure
themselves by their own standards or by comparisons within their
own circle, and that doesn't make for accurate estimation, you
13   may be sure. No, we shall not make any wild claims, but simply
judge ourselves by that line of duty which God has marked out
14   for us, and that line includes our work on your behalf. We do not
exceed our duty when we embrace your interests, for it was our
preaching of the gospel which brought us into contact with you.
15   Our pride is not in matters beyond our proper sphere nor in the
labours of other men. No, our hope is that your growing faith
16   will mean the expansion of our sphere of action, so that before
long we shall be preaching the gospel in districts beyond you,
instead of being proud of work that has already been done in
someone else's province.
17   But,
He that glorieth let him glory in the Lord.
18   It is not self-commendation that matters, it is winning the
approval of God.

CHAPTER 11

Why do you so readily accept the false and reject the true?

1   I WISH you could put up with a little of my foolishness—please
2   try! My jealousy over you is the right sort of jealousy, for in my
eyes you are like a fresh unspoiled girl whom I am presenting as
3   fiancée to your true husband, Christ himself. I am afraid that your
minds may be seduced from a single-hearted devotion to him by
4   the same subtle means that the serpent used towards Eve. For
apparently you cheerfully accept a man who comes to you
preaching a different Jesus from the one we told you about, and
you readily receive a spirit and a gospel quite different from the
5   ones you originally accepted. Yet I cannot believe I am in the least
6   inferior to these extra-special messengers of yours. Perhaps I am
not a polished speaker, but I do know what I am talking about,
and both what I am and what I say is pretty familiar to you.
7   Perhaps I made a mistake in cheapening myself (though I did it to
8   help you) by preaching the gospel without a fee? As a matter of

fact I was only able to do this by "robbing" other churches, for it was what they paid me that made it possible to minister to you free of charge. Even when I was with you and very hard up, I 9 did not bother any of you. It was the brothers who came from Macedonia who brought me all that I needed. Yes, I kept myself from being a burden to you then, and so I intend to do in the future. By the truth of Christ within me, no one shall stop my 10 being proud of this independence through all Achaia!

Does this mean that I do not love you? God knows it doesn't, 11 but I am determined to maintain this boast, so as to cut the ground 12 from under the feet of those who profess to be God's messengers on the same terms as I am. *God's* messengers? They are counter- 13 feits of the real thing, dishonest practitioners, "God's messengers" only by their own appointment. Nor do their tactics surprise me 14 when I consider how Satan himself masquerades as an angel of light. It is only to be expected that his agents shall have the appear- 15 ance of ministers of righteousness—but they will get their deserts one day.

If you like self-commendations, listen to mine!

Once more, let me advise you not to look upon me as a fool. 16 Yet if you do, then listen to what this "fool" has to boast about.

I am not now speaking as the Lord commands me but as a fool 17 who must be "in on" this business of boasting. Since all the others 18 are so proud of themselves, let me do a little boasting as well. From your heights of superior wisdom I am sure you can smile 19 tolerantly on a fool. Oh, you're tolerant all right! You don't 20 mind, do you, if a man takes away your liberty, spends your money, takes advantage of you, puts on airs or even smacks your face? I am almost ashamed to say that I never did brave strong 21 things like that to you. Yet in whatever particular they enjoy such confidence I (speaking as a fool, remember) have just as much confidence.

Are they Hebrews? So am I. 22
Are they Israelites? So am I.
Are they descendants of Abraham? So am I.
Are they ministers of Christ? I have more claim to this title than 23 they. This is a silly game but look at this list:
I have worked harder than any of them.
I have served more prison sentences!
I have been beaten times without number.
I have faced death again and again.

24 I have been beaten the regulation thirty-nine stripes by the Jews five times.

25 I have been beaten with rods three times.
I have been stoned once.
I have been shipwrecked three times.
I have been twenty-four hours in the open sea.

26 In my travels I have been in constant danger from rivers and floods, from bandits, from my own countrymen, and from pagans. I have faced danger in city streets, danger in the desert, danger on

27 the high seas, danger among false Christians. I have known exhaustion, pain, long vigils, hunger and thirst, doing without meals, cold and lack of clothing.

28 Apart from all external trials I have the daily burden of re-
29 sponsibility for all the churches. Do you think anyone is weak without my feeling his weakness? Does anyone have his faith upset without my longing to restore him?

30 Oh, if I am going to boast, let me boast of the things which
31 have shown up my weakness! The God and Father of the Lord Jesus, he who is blessed for ever, knows that I speak the simple truth.

32 In Damascus, the town governor, acting by King Aretas' order,
33 had men out to arrest me. I escaped by climbing through a window and being let down the wall in a basket. That's the sort of dignified exit I can boast about.

CHAPTER 12

I have real grounds for "boasting", but I will only hint at them

1 No, I don't think it's really a good thing for me to boast at all, but I will just mention visions and revelations of the Lord himself.

2 I know a man in Christ who, fourteen years ago, had the experience of being caught up into the third Heaven. I don't know whether it was an actual physical experience, only God knows

3 that. All I know is that this man was caught up into paradise. (I repeat, I do not know whether this was a physical happening or

4 not, God alone knows.) This man heard words that cannot, and

5 indeed must not, be translated into human speech. I am honestly proud of an experience like that, but I have made up my mind not to boast of anything personal, except of what may be called

6 my weaknesses. If I should want to boast I should certainly be no fool to be proud of my experiences, and I should be speaking

nothing but the sober truth. Yet I am not going to do so, for I don't want anyone to think more highly of me than his experience of me and what he hears of me should warrant. So tremendous, *7* however, were the revelations that God gave me that, in order to prevent my becoming absurdly conceited, I was given a physical handicap—one of Satan's angels—to harass me and effectually stop any conceit. Three times I begged the Lord for *8* it to leave me, but his reply has been, "My grace is enough for *9* you: for where there is weakness, my power is shown the more completely." Therefore, I have cheerfully made up my mind to be proud of my weaknesses, because they mean a deeper experience of the power of Christ. I can even enjoy weaknesses, *10* suffering, privations, persecutions and difficulties for Christ's sake. For my very weakness makes me strong in him.

This boasting is silly, but you made it necessary

I have made a fool of myself in this "boasting" business, but *11* you forced me to do it. If only you had had a better opinion of me it would have been quite unnecessary. For I am not really in the least inferior, nobody as I am, to these extra-special messengers. You have had an exhaustive demonstration of the power God *12* gives to a genuine messenger of his in the miracles, signs and works of spiritual power that you saw with your own eyes. What makes *13* you feel so inferior to other churches? Is it because I have not allowed you to support me financially? My humblest apologies for this great wrong!

What can be your grounds for suspicion of me?

Now I am all ready to visit you for the third time, and I am *14* still not going to be a burden to you. It is you I want—not your money. Children don't have to put by their savings for their parents; parents do that for their children. Consequently I will *15* most gladly spend and be spent for your good, even though it means that the more I love you the less you love me.

"All right then," I hear you say, "we agree that he himself had *16* none of our money." But are you thinking that I nevertheless was rogue enough to catch you by some trick? Just think. Did I make *17* any profit out of the messengers I sent you? I asked Titus to go, *18* and sent the brother with him. You don't think Titus made anything out of you, do you? Yet didn't I act in the same spirit as he, and take the same line as he did?

Remember what I really am, and whose authority I have

19 Are you thinking all this time that I am trying to justify myself in your eyes? Actually I am speaking in Christ before God himself, and my only reason for so doing is to help you in your spiritual life.

20 For I must confess that I am afraid that when I come I shall not perhaps find you as I should like to find you, and that you will not find me coming quite as you would like me to come. I am afraid of finding arguments, jealousy, ill-feeling, divided loyalties, slander,

21 whispering, pride and disharmony. When I come, will God make me feel ashamed of you as I stand among you? Shall I have to grieve over many who have sinned already and are not yet sorry for the impurity, the immorality and the lustfulness of which they are guilty?

CHAPTER 13

1 THIS third time I am really coming to you in person. Remember the ancient Law: "In the mouth of two or three witnesses shall

2 every word be established." My previous warning, given on my second visit, still stands and, though absent, I repeat it now as though I were present—my coming will *not* mean leniency for those who had sinned before that visit and those who have sinned

3 since. It will in fact be a proof that I speak by the power of Christ. The Christ you have to deal with is not a weak person outside

4 you, but a tremendous power inside you. He was "weak" enough to be crucified, yes, but he lives now by the power of God. I am weak as he was weak, but I am strong enough to deal with you for I share his life by the power of God.

Why not test yourselves instead of me?

5 You should be looking at yourselves to make sure that you are really Christ's. It is yourselves that you should be testing, not me. You ought to know by this time that Christ is in you, unless you

6 are not real Christians at all. And when you have applied your test, I am confident that you will soon find that I myself am a

7 genuine Christian. I pray God that you may find the right answer to your test, not because I have any need of your approval, but

because I earnestly want you to find the right answer, even if that
should make me no real Christian. For, after all, we can make no 8
progress against the truth; we can only work for the truth.

We are glad to be weak if it means that you are strong. Our 9
ambition for you is true Christian maturity. Hence the tone of 10
this letter, so that when I do come I shall not be obliged to use
that power of severity which God has given me—though even
that is not meant to break you down but to build you up.

Finally, Farewell

Finally, then, my brothers, cheer up! Straighten yourselves 11
out, comfort yourselves, agree with one another and live at peace.
So shall the God of love and peace be ever with you.

A handshake all round, please! All the Christians here send 12, 13
greeting.

The grace of the Lord Jesus Christ, the love of God, and the 14
fellowship that is ours in the Holy Spirit be with you all!

PAUL.

The Letter to the Christians in Galatia

AUTHOR. *Paul probably writing from Corinth, or possibly from
Macedonia just before Titus returned from Corinth.*

DATE. 56 *or* 57.

DESTINATION. *The meaning of "Galatia", to which this letter is
addressed, has aroused some controversy, for it could mean the
ancient district known by that name or the Roman province also
called "Galatia", which included several other districts.*

THEME. *The Galatians appear to have been seduced from their first
faith by teachers who insisted that they must still keep the old
Jewish Law, including the rite of circumcision. In so doing they
impugned Paul's authority, which he feels called upon to justify
in this letter. Paul warns the Galatians that although they are free,
as Christians, from the Law, yet their lives must exhibit the fruits
of the inner law of love implanted by God's Spirit.*

CHAPTER 1

1 I, PAUL, who am appointed and commissioned a messenger not
by man but by Jesus Christ and God the Father (who raised him
2 from the dead), I and all the brothers with me send the churches
3 in Galatia greeting. Grace and peace to you from God the Father
4 and from our Lord Jesus Christ, who according to the will of our
God and Father gave himself for our sins and thereby rescued
5 us from the present evil world-order. To him be glory for ever
and ever!

The gospel is God's truth: men must not dare to pervert it

6 I am amazed that you have so quickly transferred your allegi-
ance from him who called you in the grace of Christ to another
7 "gospel"! Not, of course, that it is or ever could be another
gospel, but there are obviously men who are upsetting your faith
8 with a travesty of the gospel of Christ. Yet I say that if I, or an
angel from Heaven, were to preach to you any other gospel than
9 the one you have heard, may he be damned! You have heard me
say it before and now I put it down in black and white—may
anybody who preaches any other gospel than the one you have
10 already heard be a damned soul! (Does that make you think now
that I am serving man's interests or God's? If I were trying to win
human approval I should never be Christ's servant.)

The gospel was given to me by Christ himself, and not by any human agency, as my story will show

11, 12 The gospel I preach to you is no human invention. No man
gave it to me, no man taught it to me; it came to me as a direct
13 revelation from Jesus Christ. For you have heard of my past career
in the Jewish religion, how I persecuted the Church of God with
14 fanatical zeal and, in fact, did my best to destroy it. I was ahead of
most of my contemporaries in the Jewish religion, and had a
15 greater enthusiasm for the old traditions. But when the time came
for God (who had chosen me from the moment of my birth,
16 and then called me by his grace) to reveal his Son within me so
that I might proclaim him to the non-Jewish world, I did not, as
might have been expected, talk over the matter with any human
17 being. I did not even go to Jerusalem to meet those who were

God's messengers before me—no, I went away to Arabia and later came back to Damascus. It was not until three years later **18** that I went up to Jerusalem to see Cephas, and I only stayed with him just over a fortnight. I did not meet any of the other messen- **19** gers, except James, the Lord's brother.

All this that I am telling you is, I assure you before God, the **20** plain truth. Later, I visited districts in Syria and Cilicia, but I was **21, 22** still personally unknown to the churches of Judaea. All they knew **23** of me, in fact, was the saying: "The man who used to persecute us is now preaching the faith he once tried to destroy." And they **24** thanked God for what had happened to me.

CHAPTER 2

Years later I met church leaders in Jerusalem: no criticism of my gospel was made

FOURTEEN years later, I went up to Jerusalem again, this time **1** with Barnabas, and we took Titus with us. My visit on this **2** occasion was by divine command, and I gave a full exposition of the gospel which I preach among the gentiles. I did this first in private conference with the church leaders, to make sure that what I had done and proposed doing was acceptable to them. Not one of them intimated that Titus, because he was a Greek, **3** ought to be circumcised. In fact, the suggestion would never have **4** arisen but for the presence of some pseudo-Christians, who wormed their way into our meeting to spy on the liberty we enjoy in Christ Jesus, and then attempted to tie us up with rules and regulations. We did not give those men an inch, for the **5** truth of the gospel for you and all gentiles was at stake. And as **6** far as the leaders of the conference were concerned (I neither know nor care what their exact position was: God is not impressed with a man's office), they had nothing to add to my gospel. In fact they recognised that the gospel for the uncircumcised **7** was as much my commission as the gospel for the circum- cised was Peter's. For the God who had done such great work in **8** Peter's ministry for the Jews was plainly doing the same in my ministry for the gentiles. When, therefore, James, Cephas and **9** John (who were the recognised "pillars" of the church there) saw how God had given me his grace, they held out to Barnabas and me the right hand of fellowship, in full agreement that our mission was to the gentiles and theirs to the Jews. The only suggestion **10** they made was that we should not forget the poor—and with this I was, of course, only too ready to agree.

I had once to defend the truth of the gospel even against a church leader

11 Later, however, when Cephas came to Antioch I had to oppose
12 him publicly, for he was then plainly in the wrong. It happened like this. Until the arrival of some of James' companions, he, Peter, was in the habit of eating his meals with the gentiles. After they came, however, he withdrew and ate separately from the
13 gentiles—out of sheer fear of what the Jews might think. The other Jewish Christians carried out a similar piece of deception, and the force of their bad example was so great that even Barnabas
14 was affected by it. But when I saw that this behaviour was a contradiction of the truth of the gospel, I said to Cephas so that everyone could hear, "If you, who are a Jew, do not live like a Jew but like a gentile, why on earth do you try to make gentiles live
15 like Jews?" And then I went on to explain that we, who are Jews
16 by birth and not gentile sinners, know that a man is justified not by performing what the Law commands but by faith in Jesus Christ. We ourselves are justified by our faith and not by our obedience to the Law, for we have recognised that no one can
17 achieve justification by doing the "works of the Law". Now if, as we seek the real truth about justification, we find we are as much sinners as the gentiles, does that mean that Christ makes us
18 sinners? Of course not! But if I attempt to build again the whole structure of justification by the Law then I do, in earnest, make
19 myself a sinner. For under the Law I "died", and now I am dead
20 to the Law's demands so that I may live for God. As far as the Law is concerned I may consider that I died on the cross with Christ. And my present life is not that of the old "I", but the living Christ within me. The bodily life I now live, I live believing in the Son of God, who loved me and sacrificed himself
21 for me. Consequently I refuse to stultify the grace of God by reverting to the Law. For if righteousness were possible under the Law then Christ died for nothing!

CHAPTER 3

What has happened to your life of faith?

O you dear idiots of Galatia, who saw Jesus Christ the crucified   **1**
so plainly, who has been casting a spell over you? I will ask you   **2**
one simple question: did you receive the Spirit by trying to keep
the Law or by believing the message of the gospel? Surely you
can't be so idiotic as to think that a man begins his spiritual life   **3**
in the Spirit and then completes it by reverting to outward observances? Has all your painful experience brought you nowhere? I   **4**
simply cannot believe it of you! Does God, who gives you his   **5**
Spirit and works miracles among you, do these things because you
have obeyed the Law or because you have believed the gospel?
Ask yourselves that.

The futility of trying to be justified by the Law:
the promises to men of faith

You can go right back to Abraham to see the principle of faith   **6**
in God. He, we are told, "believed God and it was counted unto
him for righteousness". Can you not see, then, that all those who   **7**
"believe God" are the real "sons of Abraham"? The scripture,   **8**
foreseeing that God would justify the gentiles "by faith", really
proclaimed the gospel centuries ago in the words spoken to
Abraham, "In thee shall all nations be blessed." All men of faith   **9**
share the blessing of Abraham who "believed God".

Everyone, however, who is involved in trying to keep the   **10**
Law's demands falls under a curse, for it is written:
   Cursed is everyone which continueth not
   In *all things* which are written·in the book of the Law,
   To do them.
It is made still plainer that no one is justified in God's sight by   **11**
obeying the Law, for:
   The righteous shall live by *faith*.
And the Law is not a matter of faith at all but of doing, as, for   **12**
example, in the scripture:
   He that *doeth* them shall live in them.
Now Christ has redeemed us from the curse of the Law's con-   **13**
demnation, by himself becoming a curse for us when he was
crucified. For the scripture is plain:
   Cursed is every one that hangeth on a tree.

14   God's purpose is therefore plain: that the blessing promised to Abraham might reach the gentiles through Christ Jesus, and the promise of the Spirit might become ours by faith.

The Law cannot interfere with the original promise

15   Let me give you an everyday illustration, my brothers. Once a contract has been properly drawn up and signed, it is honoured by both parties, and can neither be disregarded nor modified by a third party.

16   Now the promises were made to Abraham and his seed. (Note in passing that the scripture says not "seeds" but uses the singular 17 "seed", meaning Christ.) I say then that the Law, which came into existence four hundred and thirty years later, cannot render null and void the original "contract" which God had made, and 18 thus rob the promise of its value. For if the receiving of the promised blessing were now made to depend on the Law, that would amount to a cancellation of the original "contract" which God made with Abraham as a promise.

19   Where then lies the point of the Law? It was an addition made to underline the existence and extent of sin until the arrival of the "seed" to whom the promise referred. The Law was inaugurated in the presence of angels and by the hand of a human inter- 20 mediary. The very fact that there was an intermediary is enough to show that this was not the fulfilling of the promise. For the promise of God needs neither angelic witness nor human intermediary but depends on him alone.

21   Is the Law then to be looked upon as a contradiction of the promise? Certainly not, for if there could have been a law which gave men spiritual life then that law would have produced righteousness (which would have been, of course, in full harmony 22 with the purpose of the promise). But, as things are, the scripture has all men "imprisoned" for their sins, because they are found guilty by the Law, that to men in such condition the promise might come to release all who believe in Jesus Christ.

By faith we are rescued from the Law and become sons of God

23   Before the coming of faith we were all imprisoned under the power of the Law, with our only hope of deliverance the faith 24 that was to be shown to us. Or, to change the metaphor, the Law was like a strict governess in charge of us until we went to

the school of Christ and learned to be justified by faith in him. Once we had that faith we were completely free from the gover- 25 ness's authority. For now that you have faith in Christ Jesus you 26 are all sons of God. All of you who were baptised "into" Christ 27 have put on the family likeness of Christ. Gone is the distinction 28 between Jew and Greek, slave and free man, male and female— you are all one in Christ Jesus. And if you belong to Christ, you 29 are true descendants of Abraham, you are true heirs of his promise.

CHAPTER 4

But you must realise that so long as an heir is a child, though 1 he is destined to be master of everything, he is, in practice, no different from a servant. He has to obey a guardian or trustee 2 until the time which his father has chosen for him to receive his inheritance. So is it with us: while we were "children" we lived 3 under the authority of basic moral principles. But when the 4 proper time came God sent his Son, born of a human mother and born under the jurisdiction of the Law, that he might redeem 5 those who were under the authority of the Law and lead us into becoming, by adoption, true sons of God. It is because you really 6 are his sons that God has sent the Spirit of his Son into our hearts to cry "Father, dear Father". You, my brother, are not a 7 servant any longer; through God you are a *son*. And, if you are a son, then you are certainly an heir.

Consider your own progress: do you want to go backwards?

At one time when you had no knowledge of God, you were 8 under the authority of gods who had no real existence. But now 9 that you have come to know God, or rather are known by him, how can you revert to dead and sterile principles and consent to be under their power all over again? Your religion is beginning 10 to be a matter of observing certain days or months or seasons or years. Frankly, you stagger me, you make me wonder if all my 11 efforts over you have been wasted!

I appeal to you by our past friendship, don't be misled

I do beg you to follow me here, my brothers. I am a man like 12 yourselves, and I have nothing against you personally. You know 13

how handicapped I was by illness when I first preached the gospel
14 to you. You didn't shrink from me or let yourselves be revolted
at the disease which was such a trial to you. No, you welcomed
me as though I were an angel of God, or even as though I were
15 Christ Jesus himself! What has happened to that fine spirit of
yours? I guarantee that in those days you would, if you could,
16 have plucked out your eyes and given them to me. Have I now
become your enemy because I continue to tell you the truth?
17 Oh, I know how keen these men are to win you over, but can't
you see that it is for their own ends? They would like to see
you and me separated altogether, and have your zeal all to them-
18 selves. Don't think I'm jealous—it is a grand thing that men
should be keen to win you, whether I'm there or not, provided
19 it is for the truth. Oh, my dear children, I feel the pangs of child-
20 birth all over again till Christ be formed within you, and how I
long to be with you now! Perhaps I could then alter my tone
to suit your mood. As it is, I honestly don't know how to deal
with you.

Let us see what the Law itself has to say

21 Now tell me, you who want to be under the Law, have you
heard what the Law says?
22 It is written that Abraham had two sons, one by the slave and
23 the other by the free woman. The child of the slave was born in
the ordinary course of nature, but the child of the free woman
24 was born in accordance with God's promise. This can be regarded
as an allegory. Here are the two agreements represented by the
two women: the one from Mount Sinai bearing children into
25 slavery, typified by Hagar (Mount Sinai being in Arabia, the land
of the descendants of Ishmael, Hagar's son), and corresponding to
present-day Jerusalem—for the Jews are still, spiritually speaking,
26 "slaves". But the free woman typifies the heavenly Jerusalem,
27 which is the mother of us all, and is spiritually "free". It is
written:

> Rejoice, thou barren that bearest not;
> Break forth and cry, thou that travailest not:
> For more are the children of the desolate
> Than of her which hath the husband.

28 Now we, my brothers, are like Isaac, for we are children born
29 "by promise". But just as in those far-off days the natural son
30 persecuted the "spiritual" son, so it is today. Yet what is the
scriptural instruction?

Cast out the handmaid and her son:
For the son of the handmaid shall not inherit
With the son of the free woman.

So then, my brothers, we are not to look upon ourselves as the **31** sons of the slave woman but of the free, not sons of slavery under the Law but sons of freedom under grace.

CHAPTER 5

Do not lose your freedom by giving in to those who urge circumcision

PLANT your feet firmly therefore within the freedom that Christ **1** has won for us, and do not let yourselves be caught again in the shackles of slavery. Listen! I, Paul, say this to you as solemnly as **2** I can: if you consent to be circumcised then Christ will be of no use to you at all. I will say it again: every man who consents to **3** be circumcised is bound to obey all the rest of the Law! If you **4** try to be justified by the Law you automatically cut yourself off from the power of Christ, you put yourself outside the range of his grace. For it is *by faith* that we await in his Spirit the righteous- **5** ness we hope to see. In Christ Jesus there is no validity in either **6** circumcision or uncircumcision; it is a matter of faith, faith which expresses itself in love.

You were making splendid progress; who put you off the course **7** you had set for the truth? That sort of "persuasion" does not **8** come from the one who is calling you. Alas, it takes only a little **9** leaven to affect the whole lump! I feel confident in the Lord that **10** you will not take any fatal step. But whoever it is who is worrying you will have a serious charge to answer one day.

And as for me, my brothers, if I were still advocating circum- **11** cision (as some apparently allege!), why am I still suffering perse- cution? I suppose if only I would recommend this little rite all the hostility which the preaching of the cross provokes would dis- appear! I wish those who are so eager to cut your bodies would **12** cut themselves off from you altogether!

It is to freedom that you have been called, my brothers. Only **13** be careful that freedom does not become mere opportunity for your lower nature. You should be free to serve each other in love. For after all, the whole Law toward others is summed up by this **14** one command, "Thou shalt love thy neighbour as thyself."

But if freedom means merely that you are free to attack and **15** tear each other to pieces, be careful that it doesn't mean that between you you destroy your fellowship altogether!

The way to live in freedom is by the Spirit

16
17 Here is my advice. Live your whole life in the Spirit and you will not satisfy the desires of your lower nature. For the whole energy of the lower nature is set against the Spirit, while the whole power of the Spirit is contrary to the lower nature. Here is the conflict, and that is why you are not free to do what you

18 want to do. But if you follow the leading of the Spirit, you stand clear of the Law.

19 The activities of the lower nature are obvious. Here is a list:
20 sexual immorality, impurity of mind, sensuality, worship of false gods, witchcraft, hatred, quarrelling, jealousy, bad temper,
21 rivalry, factions, party-spirit, envy, drunkenness, orgies and things like that. I solemnly assure you, as I did before, that those who
22 indulge in such things will never inherit God's kingdom. The Spirit, however, produces in human life fruits such as these: love,
23 joy, peace, patience, kindness, generosity, fidelity, tolerance and self-control—and no law exists against any of them.

24 Those who belong to Christ Jesus have crucified their old
25 nature with all that it loved and lusted for. If our lives are centred
26 in the Spirit, let us be guided by the Spirit. Let us not be ambitious for our own reputations, for that only means making each other jealous.

CHAPTER 6

Some practical wisdom

1 EVEN if a man should be detected in some sin, my brothers, the spiritual ones among you should quietly set him back on the right path, not with any feeling of superiority but being your-
2 selves on guard against temptation. Carry each other's burdens and so live out the law of Christ.

3 If a man thinks he is "somebody", he is deceiving himself, for
4 that very thought proves that he is nobody. Let every man learn to assess properly the value of his own work and he can then be glad when he has done something worth doing without depend-
5 ing on the approval of others. For every man must "shoulder his own pack".

6 The man under Christian instruction should be willing to contribute towards the livelihood of his teacher.

The inevitability of life's harvest

Don't be under any illusion: you cannot make a fool of God! **7**
A man's harvest in life will depend entirely on what he sows. If **8**
he sows for his own lower nature his harvest will be the decay
and death of his own nature. But if he sows for the Spirit he will
reap the harvest of everlasting life by that Spirit. Let us not grow **9**
tired of doing good, for, unless we throw in our hand, the ultimate
harvest is assured. Let us then do good to all men as opportunity **10**
offers, especially to those who belong to the Christian household.

A final appeal, in my own hand-writing

Look at these huge letters I am making in writing these words **11**
to you with my own hand!*

These men who are always urging you to be circumcised— **12**
what are they after? They want to present a pleasing front to the
world and they want to avoid being persecuted for the cross of
Christ. For even those who have been circumcised do not them- **13**
selves keep the Law. But they want you circumcised so that they
may be able to boast about your submission to their ruling. Yet **14**
God forbid that I should boast about anything or anybody except
the cross of our Lord Jesus Christ, which means that the world is a
dead thing to me and I am a dead man to the world. But in **15**
Christ it is not circumcision or uncircumcision that counts but
the power of new birth. To all who live by this principle, to the **16**
true Israel of God, may there be peace and mercy!

Let no one interfere with me after this. I carry on my scarred **17**
body the marks of Jesus.

The grace of our Lord Jesus Christ, my brothers, be with your **18**
spirit.

PAUL.

* According to centuries-old Eastern usage, this could easily
mean, "Note how heavily I have pressed upon the pen in writing
this." Thus it could be translated, "Notice how heavily I have
underlined these words to you."

The Letter to the Christians at Ephesus

(*and in other places*)

AUTHOR. *This letter was almost certainly written by Paul, although some argue from the style that it was drafted by another hand, possibly Timothy's, and then corrected and signed by Paul. It is very widely accepted that the letter was issued by him, during the same period as the letters to Colossae and Philippi and the personal note to Philemon, while he was in prison. Almost certainly his imprisonment while he despatched these letters was at Rome (Acts 28, 30)*

DATE. *About 62*

DESTINATION. *Probably not only Ephesus, for although Paul had spent two years there (Acts 19, 9, 10), there are no personal references. For this and other good reasons it is generally believed that this is a circular letter meant to reach the churches in Asia. Tychicus, who took the letter in person, would probably reach Ephesus first. The letter would then be copied and taken on to the other churches. It is quite possible that the letter to Laodicaea, mentioned in Colossians 4, 16, was this particular letter.*

THEME. *Paul is concerned first to establish in his readers' minds as great and wide and deep a conception of Christ as he can. He points out that he is not only the Saviour of the world, but also the divinely appointed focal point of all activity and all knowledge, whether it is physical, mental or spiritual. Race distinctions cannot matter therefore for those who are "in Christ".*

He follows this by stressing the resultant responsibility of the Christian, and his own proper authority as the messenger commissioned to deliver such news.

Then, as usual, Paul points out the practical outcome of being "members of Christ's body", "new men", "children of God", etc., and begs his readers to see that their lives are lived on a level worthy of the staggering privileges that God has given them.

CHAPTER 1

PAUL, messenger of Christ Jesus by God's will, to all faithful   1
Christians at Ephesus (and other places where this letter is read):
grace and peace be to you from God our Father and the Lord   2
Jesus Christ.

Praise God for what he has done for us Christians!

Praise be to the God and Father of our Lord Jesus Christ for   3
giving us through Christ every possible spiritual benefit as citizens
of Heaven! For consider what he has done—before the foundation   4
of the world he chose us to become, in Christ, his holy and blameless children living within his constant care. He planned, in his   5
purpose of love, that we should be adopted as his own children   6
through Jesus Christ—that we might learn to praise that glorious
generosity of his which has made us welcome in the everlasting   7
love he bears towards the Beloved. It is through him, at the cost
of his own blood, that we are redeemed, freely forgiven through   8
that full and generous grace which has overflowed into our lives
and opened our eyes to the truth. For God has allowed us to   9
know the secret of his plan, and it is this: he purposes in his   10
sovereign will that all human history shall be consummated in
Christ, that everything that exists in Heaven or earth shall find
its perfection and fulfilment in him. And here is the staggering   11
thing—that in all which will one day belong to him we have been
promised a share (since we were long ago destined for this by the
one who achieves his purposes by his sovereign will), so that we,   12
as the first to put our confidence in Christ, may bring praise to his   13
glory! And you too trusted him, when you had heard the message
of truth, the gospel of your salvation. And after you gave
your confidence to him you were, so to speak, stamped with the
promised Holy Spirit as a guarantee of purchase, until the day   14
when God completes the redemption of what he has paid for as
his own; and that will again be to the praise of his glory.

I thank God for you, and pray for you

Since, then, I heard of this faith of yours in the Lord Jesus and   15

the practical way in which you are expressing it towards fellow-
16 Christians, I thank God continually for you and I never give up
17 praying for you; and this is my prayer. That God, the God of our
Lord Jesus Christ and the all-glorious Father, will give you
18 spiritual wisdom and the insight to know more of him: that you
may receive that inner illumination of the spirit which will make
you realise how great is the hope to which he is calling you—the
magnificence and splendour of the inheritance promised to Christ-
19 ians—and how tremendous is the power available to us who
20 believe in God. That power is the same divine energy which was
demonstrated in Christ when he raised him from the dead and
21 gave him the place of supreme honour in Heaven—a place that is
infinitely superior to any conceivable command, authority, power
or control, and which carries with it a name far beyond any name
that could ever be used in this world or the world to come.

22 God has placed everything under the power of Christ and has
23 set him up as head of everything for the Church. For the Church
is his body, and in that body lives fully the one who fills the
whole wide universe.

CHAPTER 2

We were all dead: God gave us life through Christ

1, 2 To you, who were spiritually dead all the time that you drifted
along on the stream of this world's ideas of living, and obeyed its
unseen ruler (who is still operating in those who do not respond
3 to the truth of God), to you Christ has given life! We all lived
like that in the past, and followed the impulses and imaginations
of our evil nature, being in fact under the wrath of God by
nature, like everyone else. But even though we were dead in our
4, 5 sins God, who is rich in mercy, because of the great love he had
for us, gave us life together with Christ—it is, remember, by
6 grace and not by achievement that you are saved—and has lifted
us right out of the old life to take our place with him in Christ
7 Jesus in the Heavens. Thus he shows for all time the tremendous
generosity of the grace and kindness he has expressed towards us
8 in Christ Jesus. It was nothing you could or did achieve—it was
9 God's gift of grace which saved you. No one can pride himself
10 upon earning the love of God. The fact is that what we are we owe
to the hand of God upon us. For we are his workmanship, created
in Christ Jesus to do those good deeds which God planned for us
to do.

You were gentiles: we were Jews. God has made us fellow-Christians

Do not lose sight of the fact that you were born "gentiles", **11**
known by those whose bodies were circumcised as "the uncircumcised". You were without Christ, you were utter strangers **12**
to God's chosen community, Israel, and you had no knowledge of, or right to, the promised agreements. You had nothing
to look forward to and no God to whom you could turn. But **13**
now, through the blood of Christ, you who were once outside
the pale are with us inside the circle of God's love in Christ Jesus.
For Christ is our living peace. He has made a unity of the con- **14**
flicting elements of Jew and gentile by breaking down the barrier
which lay between us. By his sacrifice he removed the hostility of **15**
the Law, with all its commandments and rules, and made in himself out of the two, Jew and gentile, one new man, thus producing
peace. For he reconciled both to God by the sacrifice of one **16**
body on the cross, and by this act made utterly irrelevant the
antagonism between them. Then he came and told both you who **17**
were far from God and us who were near that the war was over.
And it is through him that both of us now can approach the Father **18**
in the one Spirit.

So you are no longer outsiders or aliens, but fellow-citizens **19**
with every other Christian—you belong now to the household of
God. Firmly beneath you is the foundation, God's messengers and **20**
prophets, the actual foundation-stone being Christ Jesus himself.
In him each separate piece of building, properly fitting into its **21**
neighbour, grows together into a temple consecrated to the Lord. **22**
You are all part of this building in which God himself lives by his
Spirit.

CHAPTER 3

God has made me minister to you gentiles

It is in this great cause that I, Paul, have become a prisoner of **1**
Christ Jesus for you gentiles. For you must have heard how God **2**
gave me grace to become your minister, and how he allowed me to **3**
understand his secret by giving me a direct revelation. (What I **4**
have written briefly of this above will explain to you my knowledge of the mystery of Christ.) This secret was hidden to past **5**
generations of mankind, but it has now, by the Spirit, been made
plain to God's consecrated messengers and prophets. It is simply **6**

this: that the gentiles, who were previously excluded from God's agreements, are to be equal heirs with his chosen people, equal members and equal partners in God's promise given by Christ

7 through the gospel. And I was made a minister of that gospel by the grace he gave me, and by the power with which he equipped

8 me. Yes, to me, less than the least of all Christians, has God given this grace, to enable me to proclaim to the gentiles the incalculable

9 riches of Christ, and to make plain to all men the meaning of that divine secret which he who created everything has kept hidden

10 from the creation until now. The purpose is that all the angelic powers should now see the complex wisdom of God's plan being

11 worked out through the Church, in conformity to that timeless

12 purpose which he centred in Christ Jesus, our Lord. It is in this same Jesus, because we have faith in him, that we dare, even with

13 confidence, to approach God. In view of these tremendous issues, I beg you not to lose heart because I am now suffering for my part in bringing you the gospel. Indeed, you should be honoured.

I pray that you may know God's power in practice

14 When I think of the greatness of this great plan I fall on my
15 knees before the Father (from whom all fatherhood, earthly or
16 heavenly, derives its name), and I pray that out of the glorious richness of his resources he will enable you to know the strength
17 of the Spirit's inner re-inforcement—that Christ may actually live in your hearts by your faith. And I pray that you, firmly fixed in
18 love yourselves, may be able to grasp (with all Christians) how
19 wide and deep and long and high is the love of Christ—and to know for yourselves that love so far beyond our comprehension. May you be filled through all your being with God himself!
20 Now to him who by his power within us is able to do infinitely
21 more than we ever dare to ask or imagine—to him be glory in the Church and in Christ Jesus for ever and ever, amen!

CHAPTER 4

Christians should be at one, as God is one

1 As God's prisoner, then, I beg you to live lives worthy of your
2 high calling. Accept life with humility and patience, making
3 allowances for each other because you love each other. Make it your aim to be at one in the Spirit, and you will inevitably be at

peace with one another. You all belong to one body, of which **4** there is one Spirit, just as you all experienced one calling to one hope. There is one Lord, one faith, one baptism, one God, one **5, 6** Father of us all, who is the one over all, the one working through all and the one living in all.

God's gifts vary, but it is the same God who gives

Naturally there are different gifts and functions; individually **7** grace is given to us in different ways out of the rich diversity of Christ's giving. As the scripture says: **8**

When he ascended on high, he led captivity captive,

And gave gifts unto men.

(Note the implication here—to say that Christ "ascended" **9** means that he must previously have "descended", that is from the height of Heaven to the depth of this world. The one who made **10** this descent is identically the same person as he who has now ascended high above the very Heavens—that the whole universe from lowest to highest might know his presence.)

His "gifts unto men" were varied. Some he made his mes- **11** sengers, some prophets, some preachers of the gospel; to some he gave the power to guide and teach his people. His gifts were **12** made that Christians might be properly equipped for their service, that the whole body might be built up until the time comes when, **13** in the unity of common faith and common knowledge of the Son of God, we arrive at real maturity—that measure of development which is meant by "the fulness of Christ".

True maturity means growing up "into" Christ

We are not meant to remain as children at the mercy of every **14** chance wind of teaching and the jockeying of men who are expert in the crafty presentation of lies. But we are meant to hold firmly **15** to the truth in love, and to grow up in every way into Christ, the head. For it is from the head that the whole body, as a har- **16** monious structure knit together by the joints with which it is provided, grows by the proper functioning of individual parts to its full maturity in love.

Have no more to do with the old life! Learn the new

This is my instruction, then, which I give you from the Lord. **17** Do not live any longer as the gentiles live. For they live blindfold **18**

19 in a world of illusion, and are cut off from the life of God through ignorance and insensitiveness. They have stifled their consciences

20 and then surrendered themselves to sensuality, practising any form of impurity which lust can suggest. But you have learned nothing

21 like that from Christ, if you have really heard his voice and under-

22 stood the truth that Jesus has taught you. No, what you learned was to fling off the dirty clothes of the old way of living, which

23 were rotted through and through with lust's illusions, and, with

24 yourselves mentally and spiritually re-made, to put on the clean fresh clothes of the new life which was made by God's design for righteousness and the holiness which is no illusion.

25 Finish, then, with lying and tell your neighbour the truth. For we are not separate units but intimately related to each other in

26 Christ. If you are angry, be sure that it is not out of wounded

27 pride or bad temper. Never go to bed angry—don't give the devil that sort of foothold.

The new life means positive good

28 If you used to be a thief you must not only give up stealing, but you must learn to make an honest living, so that you may be able to give to those in need.

29 Let there be no more foul language, but good words instead— words suitable for the occasion, which God can use to help other

30 people. Never hurt the Holy Spirit. He is, remember, the personal pledge of your eventual full redemption.

31 Let there be no more resentment, no more anger or temper, no more violent self-assertiveness, no more slander and no more

32 malicious remarks. Be kind to each other, be understanding. Be as ready to forgive others as God for Christ's sake has forgiven you.

CHAPTER 5

1 As children copy their fathers you, as God's children, are to

2 copy him. Live your lives in love—the same sort of love which Christ gives us and which he perfectly expressed when he gave

3 himself up for us in sacrifice to God. But as for sexual immorality in all its forms, and the itch to get your hands on what belongs to other people—don't even talk about such things; they are no fit

4 subjects for Christians to talk about. The key-note of your con-

versation should not be nastiness or silliness or flippancy, but a sense of all that we owe to God.

Evil is as utterly different from good as light from darkness

For of this much you can be quite certain: that neither the 5 immoral nor the dirty-minded nor the covetous man (which latter is, in effect, worshipping a false god) has any inheritance in the kingdom of Christ and of God. Don't let anyone fool you on this 6 point, however plausible his argument. It is these very things which bring down the wrath of God upon the disobedient. Have 7 nothing to do with men like that—once you were "darkness" but 8 now you are "light". Live then as children of the light. The light 9 produces in men quite the opposite of sins like these—everything that is wholesome and good and true. Let your lives be living 10 proofs of the things which please God. Steer clear of the activities 11 of darkness; let your lives show by contrast how dreary and futile these things are. (You know the sort of things I mean—to detail 12 their secret doings is really too shameful.) For light is capable of 13 "showing up" everything for what it really is. It is even possible (after all, it happened with you!) for light to turn the thing it shines upon into light also. Thus God speaks through the 14 scriptures:

> Awake thou that sleepest, and arise from the dead,
> And Christ shall shine upon thee.

You know the truth—let your life show it !

Live life, then, with a due sense of responsibility, not as men 15 who do not know the meaning and purpose of life but as *those who do*. Make the best use of your time, despite all the difficulties 16 of these days. Don't be vague but firmly grasp what you know 17 to be the will of the Lord. Don't get your stimulus from wine (for 18 there is always the danger of excessive drinking), but let the Spirit stimulate your souls. Express your joy in singing among your- 19 selves psalms and hymns and spiritual songs, making music in your hearts for the ears of the Lord! Thank God at all times for 20 everything, in the name of our Lord Jesus Christ. And "fit in 21 with" each other, because of your common reverence for Christ.

Christ and the Church the pattern relationship for husband and wife

You wives must learn to adapt yourselves to your husbands, 22

23 as you submit yourselves to the Lord, for the husband is the "head" of the wife in the same way that Christ is head of
24 the Church and saviour of his body. The willing subjection of the Church to Christ should be reproduced in the submission of wives
25 to their husbands. But, remember, this means that the husband must give his wife the same sort of love that Christ gave to the
26 Church, when he sacrificed himself for her. Christ gave himself to make her holy, having cleansed her through the baptism of his
27 Word—to make her an altogether glorious Church in his eyes. She is to be free from spots, wrinkles or any other disfigurement—a Church holy and perfect.
28 Men ought to give their wives the love they naturally have for their own bodies. The love a man gives his wife is the extending
29 of his love for himself to enfold her. Nobody ever hates or neglects his own body; he feeds it and looks after it. And that is what
30 Christ does for his body, the Church. And we are all members of that body.
31 For this cause shall a man leave his father and mother,
And shall cleave to his wife; and the twain shall become one flesh.
32 The marriage relationship is doubtless a great mystery, but I am speaking of something deeper still—the marriage of Christ and his Church.
33 In practice what I have said amounts to this: let every one of you who is a husband love his wife as he loves himself, and let the wife reverence her husband.

CHAPTER 6

Children and parents: servants and masters

1 CHILDREN, the right thing for you to do is to obey your parents
2 as those whom the Lord has set over you. The first commandment to contain a promise was:
Honour thy father and thy mother
3 That it may be well with thee, and that thou mayest live long on the earth.
4 Fathers, don't over-correct your children or make it difficult for them to obey the commandment. Bring them up with Christian teaching in Christian discipline.
5 Slaves, obey your human masters sincerely with a proper sense of respect and responsibility, as service rendered to Christ himself;

not with the idea of currying favour with men, but as the servants **6**
of Christ conscientiously doing what you believe to be the will of **7**
God for you. You may be sure that God will reward a man for **8**
good work, irrespectively of whether the man be slave or free.
And as for you employers, be as conscientious and responsible **9**
towards those who serve you as you expect them to be towards
you, neither misusing the power over others that has been put in
your hands, nor forgetting that you are responsible yourselves to
a heavenly employer who makes no distinction between master
and man.

Be forewarned and forearmed in your spiritual conflict

In conclusion be strong—not in yourselves but in the Lord, in **10**
the power of his boundless resource. Put on God's complete **11**
armour so that you can successfully resist all the devil's methods of
attack. For our fight is not against any physical enemy: it is against **12**
organisations and powers that are spiritual. We are up against the
unseen power that controls this dark world, and spiritual agents
from the very headquarters of evil. Therefore you must wear the **13**
whole armour of God that you may be able to resist evil in its
day of power, and that even when you have fought to a standstill
you may still stand your ground. Take your stand then with truth **14**
as your belt, righteousness your breastplate, the gospel of peace **15**
firmly on your feet, salvation as your helmet and in your hand **17**
the sword of the Spirit, the Word of God. Above all be sure you **16**
take faith as your shield, for it can quench every burning missile
the enemy hurls at you. Pray at all times with every kind of **18**
spiritual prayer, keeping alert and persistent as you pray for all
Christ's men and women. And pray for me, too, that I may be **19**
able to speak freely here to make known the secret of that gospel
for which I am, so to speak, an ambassador in chains. Pray that I **20**
may speak out about it as is my plain and obvious duty.

Tychicus, beloved brother and faithful Christian minister, will **21**
tell you personally what I am doing and how I am getting on. I **22**
am sending him to you bringing this letter for that purpose, so
that you will know exactly how we are and may take fresh heart.

Peace be to all Christian brothers, and love with faith from **23**
God the Father and the Lord Jesus Christ!

Grace be with all those who love our Lord Jesus Christ with **24**
unfailing love.

PAUL.

The Letter to the Christians at Philippi

AUTHOR. *Paul, writing from prison, probably in Rome (Acts 28, 30).*

DATE. *About 62.*

DESTINATION. *The church at Philippi, where Paul had been beaten and imprisoned but had seen his gaoler converted (Acts 16, 25–34). It was also at Philippi that Lydia, a business woman selling purple-dyed cloth, became one of the first Christians.*

THEME. *The first purpose of the letter is to acknowledge a gift sent to Paul in prison by Epaphroditus from the Christians at Philippi. Possibly this letter was delayed by the serious illness of Epaphroditus while with Paul (2, 27) and Paul is evidently by now himself expecting early release from prison (2, 24). Except possibly for the letter to Philemon, this is the most personal example of Paul's correspondence, and he is obviously very fond of the little church at Philippi. It expresses his high hopes for their unity, faithfulness and progress in the faith. It also contains a warning, like that in the letter to the Galatians, against false teachers who wanted to bring these inexperienced Christians under the Jewish Law.*

CHAPTER 1

1
2 PAUL and Timothy, servants of Jesus Christ, to the bishops, deacons and all true Christians at Philippi, grace and peace from God our Father and Jesus Christ the Lord!

I have the most pleasant memories of you all

3 I thank my God for you Christians at Philippi whenever I think
4, 5 of you. My constant prayers for you are a real joy, for they bring back to my mind how we have worked together for the gospel
6 from the earliest days until now. I feel sure that the one who has begun his good work in you will go on developing it until the day of Jesus Christ.
7 It is only natural that I should feel like this about you all—you are very dear to me. For during the time I was in prison as well as when I was out defending and demonstrating the power of

the gospel we shared together the grace of God. God knows how **8**
much I long, with the deepest Christian love and affection, for
your companionship. My prayer for you is that you may have **9**
still more love—a love that is full of knowledge and wise insight.
I want you to be able always to recognise the highest and the best, **10**
and to live sincere and blameless lives until the day of Christ. I
want to see your lives full of true goodness, produced by the **11**
power that Jesus Christ gives you to the praise and glory of God.

My imprisonment has turned out to be no bad thing

Now, concerning myself, I want you to know, my brothers, **12**
that what has happened to me has, in effect, turned out to the
advantage of the gospel. For, first of all, my imprisonment means **13**
a personal witness for Christ before the palace guards, not to
mention others who come and go. Then, it means that most **14**
of our brothers, somehow taking fresh heart in the Lord from
the very fact that I am a prisoner for Christ's sake, have shown
far more courage in boldly proclaiming the Word of God. I know **15**
that some are preaching Christ out of jealousy, in order to annoy
me, but some are preaching him in good faith. These latter are **16**
preaching out of their love for me. For they know that God has
set me here in prison to defend our right to preach the gospel.
The motive of the former is questionable—they preach in a par- **17**
tisan spirit, hoping to make my chains even more galling than
they would otherwise be. But what does it matter? However they **18**
may look at it, the fact remains that Christ *is* being preached,
whether sincerely or not, and that fact makes me very happy. Yes,
and I shall go on being very happy, for I know that what is hap- **19**
pening will be for the good of my own soul, thanks to your prayers
and the resources of the Spirit of Jesus Christ. It all accords with **20**
my own earnest wishes and hopes, which are that I should never
be in any way ashamed, but that now, as always, I should honour
Christ with the utmost boldness by the way I live, whether that
means I am to face death or to go on living. For living to me **21**
means simply "Christ", and if I die I should merely gain more
of him. I realise, of course, that the work which I have started **22**
may make it necessary for me to go on living in this world. I
should find it very hard to make a choice. I am torn in two **23**
directions—on the one hand I long to leave this world and live
with Christ, and that is obviously the best thing for me. Yet, **24**
on the other hand, it is probably more necessary for you that I

25 should stay here on earth. That is why I feel pretty well convinced that I shall not leave this world yet, but shall be able to
stand by you, to help you forward in Christian living and to find
26 increasing joy in your faith. So you can look forward to making
much of me as your minister in Christ when I come to see you
again!

27 But whatever happens, make sure that your everyday life is
worthy of the gospel of Christ. So that whether I do come and
see you, or merely hear about you from a distance, I may know
that you are standing fast in a united spirit, battling with a single
28 mind for the faith of the gospel and not caring two straws for
your enemies. The very fact that they are your enemies is plain
proof that they are lost to God, while the fact that you have such
men as enemies is plain proof that you yourselves are being saved
29 by God. You are given, in this battle, the privilege not merely of
30 believing in Christ but also of suffering for his sake. It is now your
turn to take part in that battle you once saw me engaged in, and
which, in point of fact, I am still fighting.

CHAPTER 2

Above all things be loving, humble, united

1 Now if your experience of Christ's encouragement and love
means anything to you, if you have known something of the
fellowship of his Spirit, and all that it means in kindness and deep
2 sympathy, do make my best hopes for you come true! Live
together in harmony, live together in love, as though you had
3 only one mind and one spirit between you. Never act from
motives of rivalry or personal vanity, but in humility think more
4 of each other than you do of yourselves. None of you should
think only of his own affairs, but should learn to see things from
other people's point of view.

Let Christ be your example of humility

5 Let Christ Jesus be your example as to what your attitude
6 should be. For he, who had always been God by nature, did not
7 cling to his prerogatives as God's equal, but stripped himself of
all privilege by consenting to be a slave by nature and being born
8 as mortal man. And, having become man, he humbled himself
by living a life of utter obedience, even to the extent of dying,

and the death he died was the death of a common criminal. That is 9
why God has now lifted him so high, and has given him the name
beyond all names, so that at the name of Jesus "every knee shall 10
bow", whether in Heaven or earth or under the earth. And that 11
is why, in the end, "every tongue shall confess" that Jesus Christ
is the Lord, to the glory of God the Father.

God is himself at work within you

So then, my dearest friends, as you have always followed my 12
advice—and that not only when I was present to give it—so now
that I am far away be keener than ever to work out the salvation
that God has given you with a proper sense of awe and responsibility. For it is God who is at work within you, giving you the 13
will and the power to achieve his purpose.

Do all you have to do without grumbling or arguing, so that 14, 15
you may be God's children, blameless, sincere and wholesome,
living in a warped and diseased world, and shining there like
lights in a dark place. For you hold in your hands the very word 16
of life. Thus can you give me something to be proud of in the
day of Christ, for I shall know then that I did not spend my
energy in vain. Yes, and if it should happen that my life-blood 17
is, so to speak, poured out upon the sacrifice and offering which
your faith means to God, then I can still be very happy, and I can
share my happiness with you all. I should like to feel that you 18
could be glad about this too, and could share with me the
happiness I speak of.

I am sending Epaphroditus with this letter, and Timothy later

But I hope in the Lord Jesus that it will not be long before I can 19
send Timothy to you, and then I shall be cheered by a first-hand
account of you and your doings. I have nobody else with a 20
genuine interest in your well-being. All the others seem to be 21
wrapped up in their own affairs and do not really care for the
business of Jesus Christ. But you know how Timothy has proved 22
his worth, working with me for the gospel like a son with his
father. I hope to send him to you as soon as I can tell how things 23
will work out for me, but God gives me some hope that it will 24
not be long before I am able to come myself as well. I have con- 25
sidered it desirable, however, to send you Epaphroditus. He has
been to me brother, fellow-worker and comrade-in-arms, as well

26 as being the messenger you set to see to my wants. He has been
home-sick for you, and was worried because he knew that you
27 had heard that he was ill. Indeed he was ill, very dangerously ill,
but God had mercy on him—and incidentally on me as well, so
that I did not have the sorrow of losing him to add to my suffer-
28 ings. I am particularly anxious, therefore, to send him to you so
that when you see him again you may be glad, and to know of
29 your joy will lighten my own sorrows. Welcome him in the
Lord with great joy! You should hold men like him in highest
30 honour, for his loyalty to Christ brought him very near death—
he risked his life to do for me in person what distance prevented
you all from doing.

CHAPTER 3

1 IN conclusion, my brothers, delight yourselves in the Lord! It
doesn't bore me to repeat a piece of advice like this, and if you
follow it you will find it a great safeguard to your souls.

The "circumcision" party are the enemies of your faith and freedom

2 Be on your guard against these curs, these wicked workmen,
3 these would-be mutilators of your bodies! We are, remember,
truly circumcised when we worship God by the Spirit, when we
find our joy in Jesus Christ and put no confidence in what we are
in the flesh.

*I was even more of a Jew than these Jews, yet knowing Christ has
changed my whole life*

4 If it were right to have such confidence, I could certainly have
it, and if any of these men thinks he has grounds for such con-
5 fidence I can assure him I have more. I was born from the people
of Israel, I was circumcised on the eighth day, I was a member of
the tribe of Benjamin. I was in fact a full-blooded Jew. As far as
6 keeping the Law is concerned I was a Pharisee, and you can judge
my enthusiasm for the Jewish faith by my active persecution of
the Church. As far as the Law's righteousness is concerned, I
7 don't think anyone could have found fault with me. Yet every
advantage that I had gained I considered lost for Christ's sake.
8 Yes, and I look upon everything as loss compared with the over-

414

whelming gain of knowing Christ Jesus my Lord. For his sake I did in actual fact suffer the loss of everything, but I considered it useless rubbish compared with being able to win Christ. For now my place is in him, and I am not dependent upon any of the self-achieved righteousness of the Law. God has given me that genuine righteousness which comes from faith in Christ. How changed are my ambitions! Now I long to know Christ and the power shown by his resurrection: now I long to share his sufferings, even to die as he died, so that I may perhaps attain as he did, the resurrection from the dead. Yet, my brothers, I do not consider myself to have "arrived", spiritually, nor do I consider myself already perfect. But I keep going on, grasping ever more firmly that purpose for which Christ Jesus grasped me. My brothers, I do not consider myself to have fully grasped it even now. But I do concentrate on this: I leave the past behind and with hands out-stretched to whatever lies ahead I go straight for the goal—my reward the honour of my high calling by God in Christ Jesus.

My ambition is the true goal of the spiritually adult: make it yours too

All of us who are spiritually adult should set ourselves this sort of ambition, and if at present you cannot see this, yet you will find that this is the attitude which God is leading you to adopt. It is important that we go forward in the light of such truth as we have ourselves attained to.

Let me be your example here, my brothers: let my example be the standard by which you can tell who are the genuine Christians among those about you. For there are many, of whom I have told you before and tell you again now, even with tears, that they are the enemies of the cross of Christ. These men are heading for utter destruction—their god is their own appetite, their pride is in what they should be ashamed of, and this world is the limit of their horizon. But we are citizens of Heaven; our outlook goes beyond this world to the hopeful expectation of the saviour who will come from Heaven, the Lord Jesus Christ. He will change these wretched bodies of ours so that they resemble his own glorious body, by that power of his which makes him the master of everything that is.

CHAPTER 4

1 So, my brothers whom I love and long for, my joy and my crown, do stand firmly in the Lord, and remember how much I love you.

Be united, be joyful, be at peace

2 Euodias and Syntyche, I beg you by name to make up your
3 differences as Christians should! And you, my true fellow-worker, I ask you to help these women. They both worked hard with me for the gospel, as did Clement and all my other fellow-workers whose names are in the book of life.

4 Delight yourselves in the Lord, yes, find your joy in him at all
5 times. Have a reputation for gentleness, and never forget the nearness of your Lord.

6 Don't worry over anything whatever; tell God every detail of
7 your needs in earnest and thankful prayer, and the peace of God, which transcends human understanding, will keep constant guard over your hearts and minds as they rest in Christ Jesus.

8 Here is a last piece of advice. If you believe in goodness and if you value the approval of God, fix your minds on whatever is true and honourable and just and pure and lovely and praise-
9 worthy. Model your conduct on what you have learned from me, on what I have told you and shown you, and you will find that the God of peace will be with you.

The memory of your generosity is an abiding joy to me

10 It has been a great joy to me that after all this time you have shown such interest in my welfare. I don't mean that you had forgotten me, but up till now you had no opportunity of expressing
11 your concern. Nor do I mean that I have been in actual need, for I have learned to be content, whatever the circumstances may be.
12 I know now how to live when things are difficult and I know how to live when things are prosperous. In general and in particular I have learned the secret of facing either plenty or poverty.
13 I am ready for anything through the strength of the one who lives
14 within me. Nevertheless I am not disparaging the way in which
15 you were willing to share my troubles. You Philippians will re-

member that in the early days of the gospel when I left Macedonia, you were the only church who shared with me the fellowship of giving and receiving. Even in Thessalonica you twice sent 16
me help when I was in need. It isn't the value of the gift that I am 17
keen on, it is the reward that will come to you because of these
gifts that you have made.

Now I have everything I want—in fact I am rich. Yes, I am 18
quite content, thanks to your gifts received through Epaphroditus.
Your generosity is like a lovely fragrance, a sacrifice that pleases
the very heart of God. My God will supply all that you need from 19
his glorious resources in Christ Jesus. And may glory be to our 20
God and our Father for ever and ever, amen!

Farewell messages

Greetings to every true Christian, from me and all the brothers 21
here with me. All the Christians here would like to send their best 22
wishes, particularly those who belong to the emperor's household.
The grace of the Lord Jesus Christ be with your spirit. 23

PAUL.

The Letter to the Christians at Colossae

AUTHOR. *Paul, writing probably at the same time as he wrote the letters to Ephesus, Philippi and Philemon while a prisoner in Rome.*

DATE. *About 62.*

DESTINATION. *The church at Colossae, a town in Asia Minor about a hundred miles inland from Ephesus. Paul had never himself been there, and it appears that the church was founded by Epaphras. The latter was apparently imprisoned in Rome after his arrival from Colossae, and this letter was sent back by the hand of Tychicus.*

THEME. *This letter is plainly written to refute the false teaching which was poisoning the church life at Colossae. This false teaching was propagating two errors: first, that the universe contained a number of beings of various degrees of power and importance ranging from man to God, and that Christ was to be thought of as merely one of the superior powers. Paul combats this by his unequivocal declaration that Christ is God's "Son", the first*

417

*principle and the upholding principle of the whole creation. The
second false tendency was the attempt to force on the Colossian
Christians a system of purely arbitrary observances and angel-
worship, coupled with an extreme asceticism. Paul meets this by
pointing out that the Christian's position in God is far beyond the
petty observances of man-made rules. The true asceticism, moreover,
is to abstain from evil passions and evil thoughts, not to cut oneself
off from the normal use of God's good gifts.*

*Although writing to those he had never seen, Paul writes with
obvious love and interest and is sincerely pleased with the genuine
Christianity which has taken root at Colossae.*

CHAPTER 1

1 PAUL, a messenger of Christ Jesus by God's will, and our brother
2 Timothy send this greeting to all faithful Christians at Colossae:
grace and peace be to you from God our Father!

We thank God for you and pray constantly for you

3 I want you to know by this letter that we here are constantly
praying for you, and whenever we do we thank God the Father
4 of our Lord Jesus Christ because you believe in Christ Jesus and
because you are showing true Christian love towards other
5 Christians. We know that you are showing these qualities because
you have grasped the hope reserved for you in Heaven—that hope
which first became yours when the truth was brought to you.
6 It is, of course, part of the gospel itself, which has reached you as
it spreads all over the world. Wherever that gospel goes, it produces Christian character, and develops it, as it has done in your
own case from the time you first heard and realised the truth of
God's grace.
7 You learned these things, we understand, from Epaphras, who
is in the same service as we are. He is a most well-loved minister
8 of Christ, and has your well-being very much at heart. As a
matter of fact, it was from him that we heard about your growth
9 in Christian love, so you will understand that since we heard
about you we have never missed you in our prayers. We are
asking God that you may see things, as it were, from his point of
10 view by being given spiritual insight and understanding. We also

pray that your outward lives, which men see, may bring credit to your master's name, and that you may bring joy to his heart by bearing genuine Christian fruit, and that your knowledge of God may grow yet deeper.

We pray for you to have real Christian experience

As you live this new life, we pray that you will be strengthened 11 from God's boundless resources, so that you will find yourselves able to pass through any experience and endure it with joy. You will even be able to thank God in the midst of pain and dis- 12 tress because you are privileged to share the lot of those who are living in the light. For we must never forget that he rescued us 13 from the power of darkness, and re-established us in the kingdom of his beloved Son. For it is by his Son alone that we have been 14 redeemed and have had our sins forgiven.

Who Christ is, and what he has done

Now Christ is the visible expression of the invisible God. He 15 existed before creation began, for it was through him that every- 16 thing was made, whether spiritual or material, seen or unseen. Through him, and for him, also, were created power and dominion, ownership and authority. In fact, every single thing was created through, and for, him. He is both the first principle 17 and the upholding principle of the whole scheme of creation. And 18 now he is the head of the body which is the Church. Life from nothing began through him, and life from the dead began through him, and he is, therefore, justly called the Lord of all. It was in 19 him that the full nature of God chose to live, and through him 20 God planned to reconcile in his own person, as it were, everything on earth and everything in Heaven by virtue of the sacrifice of the cross.

And you yourselves, who were strangers to God, and, in fact, 21 through the evil things you had done, his spiritual enemies, he has now reconciled through the death of his body on the cross, so that 22 he might welcome you to his presence clean and pure, without blame or reproach. This reconciliation assumes, of course, that 23 you maintain a firm position in the faith, and do not allow yourselves to be shifted away from the hope of the gospel, which you have heard, and which, indeed, the whole world is now having an opportunity of hearing.

My divine commission

24 I myself have been made a minister of this same gospel, and though it is true at this moment that I am suffering on behalf of you who have heard the gospel, yet I am far from sorry about it. Indeed, I am glad, because it gives me a chance to complete in my own sufferings something of the untold pains which Christ suffers
25 on behalf of his body, the Church. For I am a minister of the Church by divine commission, a commission granted to me for your benefit, and for a special purpose: that I might fully declare
26 God's Word—that sacred mystery which up till now has been hidden in every age and every generation, but which is now as
27 clear as daylight to those who love God. They are those to whom God has planned to give a vision of the full wonder and splendour of his secret plan for the nations. And the secret is simply this: Christ *in you*! Yes, Christ *in you* bringing with him the hope of all the glorious things to come.

To preach and teach Christ is everything to us

28 So, naturally, we proclaim Christ! We warn everyone we meet, and we teach everyone we can, all that we know about him, so that, if possible, we may bring every man up to his full maturity
29 in Christ Jesus. This is what I am working at all the time, with all the strength that God gives me.

CHAPTER 2

1 I WISH you could understand how deep is my anxiety for you, and for those at Laodicea, and for all who have never met me.
2 How I long that you may be encouraged, and find out more and more how strong are the bonds of Christian love. How I long for you to grow more certain in your knowledge and more sure in your grasp of God himself. May your spiritual experience become richer as you see more and more fully God's great secret,
3 Christ himself! For it is *in him*, and in him alone, that men will find all the treasures of wisdom and knowledge.

Let me warn you against "intellectuals"

4 I write like this to prevent you from being led astray by some-
5 one or other's attractive arguments. For though I am a long way

420

away from you in body, in spirit I am by your side, watching like a proud father the solid steadfastness of your faith in Christ. Just *6* as you received Christ Jesus the Lord, so go on living in him—in simple faith. Grow out of him as a plant grows out of the soil it is *7* planted in, becoming more and more sure of the faith as you were taught it, and your lives will overflow with joy and thankfulness.

Be careful that nobody spoils your faith through intellec- *8* tualism or high-sounding nonsense. Such stuff is at best founded on men's ideas of the nature of the world and disregards Christ! Yet it is in him that God gives a full and complete expression of *9* himself (within the physical limits that he set himself in Christ). Moreover, your own completeness is only realised in him, who *10* is the authority over all authorities, and the supreme power over all powers.

The old Law can't condemn you now

In Christ, you were circumcised, not by any physical act, but *11* by being set free from the sins of the flesh by virtue of Christ's circumcision. You, so to speak, shared in that, just as in baptism *12* you shared in his death, and in him are sharing the miracle of rising again to new life—and all this because you have faith in the tremendous power of God, who raised Christ from the dead. You, who were spiritually dead because of your sins and your *13* uncircumcision (i.e. the fact that you were outside the Law), God has now made to share in the very life of Christ! He has forgiven you all your sins: Christ has utterly wiped out the damning *14* evidence of broken laws and commandments which always hung over our heads, and has completely annulled it by nailing it over his own head on the cross. And then, having drawn the sting of all *15* the powers ranged against us, he exposed them, shattered, empty and defeated, in his final glorious triumphant act!

It is the spiritual, not the material, attitude which matters

In view of these tremendous facts, don't let anyone worry you *16* by criticising what you eat or drink, or what holy days you ought to observe, or bothering you over new moons or sabbaths. All *17* these things have at most only a symbolical value: the solid fact is Christ. Nor let any man cheat you of your joy in Christ by *18* persuading you to make yourselves "humble" and fall down and worship angels. Such a man, inflated by an unspiritual imagina- tion, is pushing his way into matters he knows nothing about, and *19* in his cleverness forgetting the head. It is from the head alone that the body, by natural channels, is nourished and built up and grows according to God's laws of growth.

20 So if, through your faith in Christ, you are dead to the principles of this world's life, why, as if you were still part and parcel of this world-wide system, do you take the slightest notice of
21 these purely human prohibitions—"Don't touch this," "Don't taste that" and "Don't handle the other"? "This", "that" and "the
22, 23 other" will all pass away after use! I know that these regulations look wise with their self-inspired efforts at worship, their policy of self-humbling, and their studied neglect of the body. But in actual practice they do honour, not to God, but to man's own pride.

CHAPTER 3

Live a new life by the power of the risen Christ

1 IF you are then "risen" with Christ, reach out for the highest
2 gifts of Heaven, where Christ reigns in power. Give your heart to the heavenly things, not to the passing things of earth. For,
3 as far as this world is concerned, you are already dead, and your
4 true life is a hidden one in God, through Christ. One day, Christ, the secret centre of our lives, will show himself openly, and you will all share in that magnificent dénouement.

5 In so far, then, as you have to live upon this earth, consider yourselves dead to worldly contacts: have nothing to do with sexual immorality, dirty-mindedness, uncontrolled passion, evil desire, and the lust for other people's goods, which last, remember,
6 is as serious a sin as idolatry. It is because of these very things that the holy anger of God falls upon those who refuse to obey
7 him. And never forget that you had your part in those dreadful things when you lived that old life.

8 But now, put all these things behind you. No more evil temper or furious rage: no more evil thoughts or words about others, no more evil thoughts or words about God, and no more filthy con-
9 versation. Don't tell each other lies any more, for you have
10 finished with the old man and all he did and have begun life as the new man, who is out to learn what he ought to be, according
11 to the plan of God. In this new man of God's design there is no distinction between Greek and Hebrew, Jew or gentile, foreigner or savage, slave or free man. Christ is all that matters for Christ lives in them all.

The expression of the new life (i)

As, therefore, God's picked representatives of the new   *12*
humanity, purified and beloved of God himself, be merciful in
action, kindly in heart, humble in mind. Accept life, and be most
patient and tolerant with one another, always ready to forgive if   *13*
you have a difference with anyone. Forgive as freely as the Lord
has forgiven you. And, above everything else, be truly loving, for   *14*
love is the golden chain of all the virtues. Let the peace of Christ   *15*
rule in your hearts, remembering that as members of the one
body you are called to live in harmony, and never forget to be
thankful for what God has done for you.

Let Christ's teaching live in your hearts, making you rich in the   *16*
true wisdom. Teach and help one another along the right road
with your psalms and hymns and Christian songs, singing God's
praises with joyful hearts. And whatever work you may have to   *17*
do, do everything in the name of the Lord Jesus, thanking God
the Father through him.

The expression of the new life (ii)

Wives, adapt yourselves to your husbands, that your marriage   *18*
may be a Christian unity. Husbands, be sure you give your wives   *19*
much love and sympathy; don't let bitterness or resentment spoil
your marriage. As for you children, your duty is to obey your   *20*
parents, for at your age this is one of the best things you can do
to show your love for the Lord. Fathers, don't over-correct your   *21*
children, or they will grow up feeling inferior and frustrated.
Slaves, your job is to obey your masters, not with the idea of   *22*
currying favour, but as a sincere expression of your devotion to
the Lord. Whatever you do, put your whole heart and soul into it,   *23*
as into work done for the Lord, and not merely for men—knowing   *24*
that your real reward, a heavenly one, will come from the Lord,
since you are actually employed by the Lord Christ, and not just
by your earthly master.

But the wicked man will be punished for his misdeeds, and   *25*
naturally no distinction will be made between master and man.

CHAPTER 4

REMEMBER, then, you employers, that your responsibility is to be   *1*
fair and just towards those whom you employ, never forgetting
that you yourselves have a heavenly employer.

Some simple, practical advice

2 Always maintain the habit of prayer: be both alert and thankful
3 as you pray. Include us in your prayers, please, that God may open for us a door for the entrance of the gospel. Pray that we may talk freely of the mystery of Christ (for which talking I am
4 at present in chains), and that I may make that mystery plain to men, which I know is my duty.

5 Be wise in your behaviour towards non-Christians, and make
6 the best possible use of your time. Speak pleasantly to them, but never sentimentally, and learn how to give a proper answer to every questioner.

Greetings and farewell

7 Tychicus (a well-loved brother, a faithful minister and a fellow-servant of the Lord) will tell you all about my present circum-
8 stances. This is partly why I am sending him to you. The other reasons are that you may find out how we are all getting on, and
9 that he may put new heart into you. With him is Onesimus, one of your own congregation (well-loved and faithful, too). Between them they will tell you of conditions and activities here.

10 Aristarchus, who is also in prison here, sends greetings, and so does Barnabas' cousin, Mark. I believe I told you before about
11 him; if he comes to you, make him welcome. Jesus Justus is here too. Only these few fellow-Jews are working with me for the kingdom, but what a help they have been!

12 Epaphras, another member of your Church, and a real servant of Christ Jesus, sends his greeting. He works hard for you even here, for he prays constantly and earnestly for you, that you may
13 become mature Christians, and may fulfil God's will for you. From my own observation I can tell you that he has a real passion for your welfare, and for that of the churches at Laodicea and Hierapolis.

14 Luke, our beloved doctor, and Demas send their best wishes.
15 My own greetings to the Christians in Laodicea, and to Nymphas and the congregation who meet in her house.

16 When you have had this letter read in your church, see that the Laodiceans have it read in their church too; and see that you read the letter I have written to them.

17 A brief message to Archippus: God ordained you to your work —see that you don't fail him!

18 My personal greeting to you written by myself.
   Don't forget I'm in prison. Grace be with you.

PAUL.

The First Letter to the Christians in Thessalonica

AUTHOR. *Paul, writing from Corinth.*

DATE. *About 50. The earliest Pauline letter in our possession.*

DESTINATION. *The Christian church in Thessalonica (now Salonika) which was founded by Paul (Acts 17, 1–10). There were evidently many Jews in the town, many of whom were bitterly opposed to the Christian message.*

THEME. *This letter is an encouragement to the young church to stand firm under persecution. It contains a defence of Paul's own position as divinely appointed messenger, in view of the bitter and malicious attacks that were being made upon him. Then follows a plea for sexual purity on the grounds that the sex instinct is part of God's design and is not meant to be despised or exploited.*

The closing section gives some definite teaching about the second coming of Christ, which the Thessalonian Christians were expecting at any moment.

CHAPTER 1

To the church of the Thessalonians, founded on God the Father 1
and the Lord Jesus Christ, grace and peace from Paul, Silvanus
and Timothy.

Your faith cheers us and encourages many others

We are always thankful as we pray for you all, for we never 2, 3
forget that your faith has meant solid achievement, your love
has meant hard work, and the hope that you have in our Lord
Jesus Christ means sheer dogged endurance in the life that you
live before God, the Father of us all.

We know that God not only loves you but has selected you for 4
a special purpose. For we remember how our gospel came to you 5
not as mere words, but as a message with power behind it—the
effectual power, in fact, of the Holy Spirit. You know how we
lived among you. You remember how you set yourselves to 6
copy us, and through us, the Lord himself. You remember how,

425

although accepting the message meant bitter persecution, yet
7 you experienced the joy of the Holy Spirit. You thus became
8 examples to all who believe in Macedonia and Achaia. You have
become a sort of sounding-board from which the Word of the
Lord has rung out, not only in Macedonia and Achaia but everywhere where the story of your faith in God has become known.
9 We find we don't have to tell people about it. They tell *us* the
story of our coming to you: how you turned from idols to serve
10 the true living God, and how your whole lives now look forward
to the coming of his Son from Heaven—the Son Jesus, whom
God raised from the dead, and who personally delivered us from
the judgment which hung over our heads.

CHAPTER 2

The spirit of our visit to you is well known to you all

1 My brothers, you know from your own experience that our
2 visit to you was no failure. We had, as you also know, been
treated abominably at Philippi, and we came on to you only
because God gave us courage. We came to tell you the gospel,
whatever the opposition might be.
3 Our message to you is true, our motives are pure, our conduct
4 is absolutely above board. We speak under the solemn sense of
being entrusted by God with the gospel. We do not aim to
please men, but to please God who knows us through and
5 through. No one could ever say, as again you know, that we
used flattery to conceal greedy motives, and God himself is wit-
6 ness to our honesty. We made no attempt to win honour from
men, either from you or from anybody else, though I suppose
7 as Christ's own messengers we might have done so. Our attitude
among you was one of tenderness, rather like that of a devoted
8 nurse among her babies. Because we loved you, it was a joy to
us to give you not only the gospel of God but our very hearts—
9 so dear did you become to us. Our struggles and hard work, my
brothers, must be still fresh in your minds. Day and night we
worked so that our preaching of the gospel to you might not cost
10 you a penny. You are witnesses, as is God himself, that our life
among you believers was honest, straightforward and above
11 criticism. You will remember how we dealt with each one of you
personally, like a father with his own children, stimulating your
12 faith and courage and giving you instruction. Our only object

was to help you to live lives worthy of the God who has called you to share the splendour of his own kingdom.

And so we are continually thankful that when you heard us **13** preach the Word of God you accepted it, not as a mere human message, but as it really is, God's Word, a power in the lives of you who believe.

You have experienced persecution like your Jewish brothers

For you, my brothers, fell into line with the churches of God **14** which have come into being through Christ Jesus in Judaea. For when you suffered at the hands of your fellow-countrymen you were sharing the experience of the Judaean Christian churches, who suffered persecution by the Jews. It was the Jews **15** who killed their own prophets, the Jews who killed the Lord Jesus, and the Jews who drove out us, his messengers. Their present attitude is in opposition to both God and man. They **16** refused to let us speak to those who were not Jews, to tell them the news of salvation. Alas, I fear they are completing the full tale of their sins and the wrath of God is over their heads.

Absence has indeed made our hearts grow fonder

Since we have been physically separated from you, my **17** brothers (though never for a moment separated in heart), we have longed all the more to see you face to face. Yes, I, Paul, have **18** longed to come and see you more than once—but somehow Satan prevented our coming.

For who could take your place as our hope and joy and pride **19** when Jesus comes? Who but you, as you will stand before him at his coming? Yes, you are indeed our pride and our joy! **20**

CHAPTER 3

AND so at length, when the separation became intolerable, we **1** thought the best plan was for me to stay at Athens alone, while **2** Timothy, our brother and fellow-worker in the gospel of Christ, was sent to strengthen and encourage you in your faith. We **3** did not want any of you to lose heart at the troubles you were going through, but to realise that we Christians must expect such things. Actually we did warn you what to expect, when we were **4** with you, and our words have come true, as you know. You will **5** understand that, when the suspense became unbearable, I sent someone to find out how your faith was standing the strain, and to make sure that the tempter's activities had not destroyed our work.

The good news about you is a tonic to us

6 But now that Timothy has just come straight from you to us —with a glowing account of your faith and love, and definite news that you cherish happy memories of us and long to see us 7 as much as we to see you—how these things have cheered us in 8 all the miseries and troubles we ourselves are going through. To know that you are standing fast in the Lord is indeed a breath of 9 life to us. How can we thank our God enough for all the joy 10 you give us as we serve him, praying earnestly day and night to see you face to face again, and to complete whatever is imperfect in your faith?

This is our prayer for you

11 So may God our Father himself and our Lord Jesus guide 12 our steps to you. May the Lord give you the same increasing and overflowing love for each other and towards all men as we 13 have towards you. May he establish you, holy and blameless in heart and soul, before God, the Father of us all, when our Lord Jesus comes with all who belong to him.

CHAPTER 4
Purity, love and hard work are good rules for life

1 To sum up, my brothers, we beg and pray you by the Lord Jesus, that you continue to learn more and more of the life that 2 pleases God, the sort of life we told you about before. You will remember the instructions we gave you then in the name of the 3 Lord Jesus. God's plan is to make you holy, and that entails first 4 of all a clean cut with sexual immorality. Every one of you should learn to control his body, keeping it pure and treating it with 5 respect, and never regarding it as an instrument for self-gratifica-6 tion, as do pagans with no knowledge of God. You cannot break this rule without in some way cheating your fellow-men. And you must remember that God will punish all who do offend in this matter; and we have warned you how we have seen this work 7 out in our experience of life. The calling of God is not to impurity 8 but to the most thorough purity, and anyone who makes light

of the matter is not making light of a man's ruling but of God's command. It is not for nothing that the Spirit God gives us is called the *Holy* Spirit.

Next, as regards brotherly love, you don't need any written 9 instructions. God himself is teaching you to love each other, and you are already extending your love to all the Macedonians. 10 Yet we urge you to have more and more of this love, and to make it your ambition to have no ambition! Be busy with your 11 own affairs and do your work yourselves. The result will be a 12 reputation for honesty in the world outside and an honourable independence.

God's message regarding those who have died

Now we don't want you, my brothers, to be in any doubt 13 about those who "fall asleep" in death, or to grieve over them like men who have no hope. After all, if we believe that Jesus 14 died and rose again from death, then we can believe that God will just as surely bring with Jesus all who are "asleep" in him. Here 15 we have a definite message from the Lord. It is that those who are still living when he comes will not in any way precede those who have previously fallen asleep. One word of command, one shout 16 from the archangel, one blast from the trumpet of God and the Lord himself will come down from Heaven! Those who have died in Christ will be the first to rise, and then we who are still 17 living on the earth will be swept up with them into the clouds to meet the Lord in the air. And after that we shall be with him for ever. So by all means use this message to encourage one 18 another.

CHAPTER 5

We must keep awake for his sudden coming

But as far as times and seasons go, my brothers, you don't need 1 written instructions. You are well aware that the day of the Lord 2 will come as unexpectedly as a burglary to a householder. When 3 men are saying "Peace and security" catastrophe will sweep down upon them as suddenly and inescapably as birth-pangs to a pregnant woman.

But because you, my brothers, are not living in darkness the 4 day cannot take you completely by surprise. After all, burglary

5 only takes place at night! You are all sons of light, sons of the
6 day, and none of us belongs to darkness or the night. Let us then
never fall into the sleep that stupefies the rest of the world: let
7 us keep awake, with our wits about us. Night is the time for
8 sleep and the time when men get drunk, but we men of the daylight should be alert, with faith and love as our breastplate and
9 the hope of our salvation as our helmet. For God did not choose
us to condemn us, but that we might secure his salvation through
10 Jesus Christ our Lord. He died for us, so that whether we are
11 "awake" or "asleep" we share his life. So go on cheering and
strengthening each other with thoughts like these, as I have no
doubt you have been doing.

Reverence your ministers: regulate the conduct of church members

12 We ask you too, my brothers, to get to know those who work
so hard among you. They are your spiritual leaders to keep you
13 on the right path. Because of this high task of theirs, hold them in
highest honour.
14 Live together in peace, and our instruction to this end is to
reprimand the unruly, encourage the timid, help the weak and
15 be very patient with all men. Be sure that no one repays a bad
turn by a bad turn; good should be your objective always, among
yourselves and in the world at large.
16,17 Be happy in your faith at all times. Never stop praying. Be
18 thankful, whatever the circumstances may be.
If you follow this advice you will be working out the will of
God expressed to you in Christ Jesus.

Final advice and farewell

19,20 Never damp the fire of the Spirit, and never despise what is
21 spoken in the name of the Lord. By all means use your judgment,
22 and hold on to whatever is really good. Steer clear of evil in any form.
23 May the God of peace make you holy through and through.
May you be kept in soul and mind and body in spotless integrity
24 until the coming of our Lord Jesus Christ. He who calls you is
utterly faithful and he will finish what he has set out to do.
25,26 Pray for us, my brothers. Give a handshake all round among
27 the brotherhood. God's command, which I give you now, is that
this letter should be read to all the brothers.
28 The grace of our Lord Jesus Christ be with you all.

PAUL.

The Second Letter to the Christians in Thessalonica

AUTHOR. *Paul, writing from Corinth.*

DATE. *Possibly 51.*

DESTINATION. *The Christian church in Thessalonica.*

THEME. *Since the first letter was written to this church, Paul had evidently heard that the idea of Christ's second coming had become such an obsession with the Thessalonians that some of them had given up working for their living and were thereby bringing the faith into disrepute. He tells them quite plainly that the coming is not to be immediate; and in the meantime it is part of a Christian's duty to work hard and conscientiously.*

CHAPTER 1

To the church of the Thessalonians, founded on God our Father 1
and Jesus Christ the Lord, from Paul, Silvanus and Timothy;
grace to you and peace from God the Father and the Lord Jesus 2
Christ!

Your sufferings are a guarantee of great joy one day

My brothers, nowadays I thank God for you not only in 3
common fairness but as a moral obligation! Your faith has made
such strides, and (without any individual exceptions) your love
towards each other has reached such proportions that we actually 4
boast about you in the churches of God, because you have shown
such endurance and faith in all the trials and persecutions you
have gone through, and in the afflictions you are now enduring.

These qualities show how justly the judgment of God works 5
out in your case. Without doubt he intends to use your suffering
to make you worthy of his kingdom, yet his justice will one day 6
repay trouble to those who have troubled you, and peace to all of 7
us who, like you, have suffered. This judgment will issue eventually in the final dénouement of the personal coming of the Lord

8 Jesus from Heaven with the angels of his power. It will bring full justice in dazzling flame upon those who have refused to know
9 God or to obey the gospel of our Lord Jesus. Their punishment will be eternal exclusion from the radiance of the face of the Lord,
10 and the glorious majesty of his power. But to those whom he has made holy his coming will mean splendour unimaginable. It will be a breath-taking wonder to all who believe—including you, for you have believed the message that we have given you.
11 In view of this great prospect, we pray for you constantly, that God will think you worthy of this calling, and that he will effect in you all his goodness desires to do, and that your faith makes
12 possible. We pray that the name of our Lord Jesus may become more glorious through you, and that you may share something of his glory—all through the grace of our God and the Lord Jesus Christ.

CHAPTER 2

Before Christ's coming there will be certain signs

1 Now we do implore you, by the very certainty of the coming of our
2 Lord Jesus Christ and of our meeting him together, to keep your heads and not be thrown off your balance by any prediction or message or letter purporting to come from us, and saying that the
3 day of the Lord has already come. Don't let anyone deceive you by any means whatsoever. That day will not come before there arises a definite rejection of God and the appearance of the lawless
4 man. He is the product of all that leads to death, and he sets himself up in opposition to every religion. He himself takes his seat in the temple of God, to show that he really claims to be God.
5 I expect you remember now how I talked about this when I
6 was with you. You will probably also remember how I used to talk about a "restraining power" which would operate until the
7 time should come for the emergence of this man. Evil is already insidiously at work but its activities are restricted until what I
8 have called the "restraining power" is removed. When that happens the lawless man will be plainly seen—though the truth of the Lord Jesus spells his doom, and the radiance of the coming
9 of the Lord Jesus will be his utter destruction. The lawless man is produced by the spirit of evil and armed with all the force,
10 wonders and signs that falsehood can devise. To those involved in this dying world he will come with evil's undiluted power to

432

deceive, for they have refused to love the truth which could have saved them. God sends upon them, therefore, the full force of 11 evil's delusion, so that they put their faith in an utter fraud and 12 meet the inevitable judgment of all who have refused to believe the truth and who have made evil their play-fellow.

You, thank God, belong to those who believe the truth

But we can thank God continually for you, brothers, whom the 13 Lord loves. He has chosen you from the beginning to save you, to make you holy by the work of his Spirit and your own belief in the truth. It was his call that you followed when we preached 14 the gospel to you, and he has set before you the prospect of sharing the glory of our Lord Jesus Christ. So stand firm, and 15 hold on! Be loyal to the teachings we passed on to you, whether by word of mouth or in our writings.

May our Lord Jesus Christ and God our Father (who has loved 16 us and given us unending encouragement and unfailing hope by his grace) inspire you with courage and confidence in every good 17 thing you say or do.

CHAPTER 3

We ask your prayers for God's work here

FINALLY, my brothers, do pray for us here. Pray that the Lord's 1 message may go forward unhindered and may bring him glory, as it has done with you. Pray, too, that we may not be embroiled 2 with bigoted and wicked men; for all men, alas, have not faith. Yet the Lord is utterly to be depended upon by all who have faith 3 in him, and he will give you stability and protection against all that is evil. It is he who makes us feel confident about you, that 4 you are acting and will act in accordance with our commands. May the Lord guide your hearts into ever deeper understanding of 5 his love and of the patient suffering of Christ.

Remember our example: everyone should do his fair share of work

One further order we must give you in the name of our Lord 6 Jesus Christ: don't associate with the brother whose life is undisciplined, and who despises the teaching we gave you. You know 7 well that we ourselves are your examples here, and that our lives

8 among you were never undisciplined. We did not eat anyone's food without paying for it. In fact we toiled and laboured night
9 and day to avoid being the slightest expense to any of you. This was not because we had no right to ask our necessities of you, but
10 because we wanted to set you an example. When we were actually with you we gave you this principle to work on: "If a man
11 will not work, he shall not eat." Now we hear that you have some among you living quite undisciplined lives, never doing a
12 stroke of work, and busy only in other people's affairs. Our order to such men, indeed our appeal by the Lord Jesus Christ, is to settle down to work and eat the food they have earned themselves.
13,14 And the rest of you—don't get tired of honest work! If anyone refuses to obey the command given above, mark that man, do
15 not associate with him until he is ashamed of himself. I don't mean, of course, treat him as an enemy, but reprimand him as a brother.

My blessing on you all!

16 Now may the Lord of peace personally give you his peace at all times and in all ways. The Lord be with you all.
17 This is the farewell message of PAUL, written in my own writing—my "mark" on all my letters. This is how I write.
18 The grace of our Lord Jesus Christ be with you all.

The First Letter to Timothy

AUTHOR. *Probably Paul, writing from Rome during a second term of imprisonment which ended in his martyrdom. Many scholars do not accept the Pauline authorship of the two letters to Timothy or the letter to Titus.*

DATE. *About 66, but some hold that it was written by someone other than Paul between the years of 90 and 115.*

DESTINATION. *This is a personal letter to Timothy, son of a Greek father and a Jewish mother. He was converted during Paul's visit to Lystra (Acts 16, 1). He became Paul's special protégé, and, though evidently diffident and nervous in temperament, was his loyal assistant. He accompanied Paul on various missions and has now been left in charge of the church at Ephesus.*

THEME. *Paul reminds Timothy of his responsibility as a minister ordained for the preaching of the Gospel and warns him of the dangers of false teaching. He then gives him some interesting details for the ordering of the life of the church, the choosing of church officers and the administration of charitable funds. The letter closes with an earnest plea to Timothy to remain loyal to the true Gospel.*

CHAPTER 1

PAUL, Jesus Christ's messenger by command of God our saviour and Christ Jesus our hope, to Timothy my true son in the faith: grace, mercy and peace be to you from God the Father and Christ Jesus our Lord. 1 2

A reminder

I am repeating in this letter the advice I gave you just before I went to Macedonia and urged you to stay at Ephesus. I wanted you to do this so that you could order certain persons to stop inventing new doctrines and to leave hoary old myths and interminable genealogies alone. Such things lead men to speculation rather than to the ordered living which results from faith in God. The ultimate aim of the Christian ministry, after all, is to produce the love which springs from a pure heart, a good conscience and a genuine faith. Some seem to have forgotten this and to have lost themselves in endless words. They want a reputation as teachers of the Law, yet they fail to realise the meaning of their own words still less of the subject they are so dogmatic about. We know, of course, that the Law is good in itself and has a legitimate function. Yet we also know that the Law is not really meant for the good man, but for the man who has neither principles nor self-control, for the man who is really wicked, who has neither scruples nor reverence. Yes, the Law is directed against the sort of people who attack their own parents, who kill their fellows, who are sexually uncontrolled or perverted, or who traffic in the bodies of others. It is against liars and perjurers—in fact it is against any and every action which contradicts the wholesome teaching of the glorious gospel which the blessed God has given and entrusted to me. 3 4 5 6 7 8 9 10 11

My debt to Jesus Christ

I am deeply grateful to Christ Jesus our Lord (to whom I owe all 12

435

that I have accomplished) for trusting me enough to appoint me
13 his minister, despite the fact that I had previously blasphemed his
name, persecuted his Church and insulted him. I believe he
was merciful to me because what I did was done in the ignorance
14 of a man without faith. Our Lord poured out his grace upon
15 me, giving me tremendous faith in, and love for, himself. This
statement is completely reliable and should be universally
accepted:—"Christ Jesus entered the world to rescue sinners". I
16 realise that I was the worst of them all, and that because of this
very fact God was particularly merciful to me. It was a kind of
demonstration of the extent of Christ's patience towards the
worst of men, to serve as an example to all who in the future
should trust him for eternal life.
17 So to the king of all the ages, the immortal, invisible, and only
God, be honour and glory for ever and ever, amen!

My personal charge to you

18 Timothy my son, I give you the following charge. (And may
I say, before I give it to you, that it is in full accord with those
prophecies made at your ordination, which sent you out to battle
19 for the right armed only with your faith and a clear conscience.
Some, alas, have laid these simple weapons contemptuously
aside and, as far as their faith is concerned, have run their ships on
20 the rocks. Hymenaeus and Alexander are men of this sort, and as a
matter of fact I had to expel them from the Church to teach them
not to blaspheme.)

CHAPTER 2

1 HERE then is my charge:
First, supplications, prayers, intercessions and thanksgivings
2 should be made on behalf of all men: for kings and rulers in
positions of responsibility, so that our common life may be lived
in peace and quiet, with a proper sense of God and of our respon-
3 sibility to him for what we do with our lives. In the sight of God
4 our saviour this is undoubtedly the right thing to pray for; for
his purpose is that all men should be saved and come to realise
5 the truth. And that is, that there is only one God, and only one
6 intermediary between God and men, the Man Christ Jesus. He

gave himself as a ransom for us all—an act of redemption which happened once, but which stands for all times as a witness to what he is. I was appointed proclaimer and messenger of this great 7 act of his, to teach (incredible as it may sound) the gentile world to believe and know the truth.

My views on men and women in the Church

Therefore, I want the men to pray in all the churches with sin- 8 cerity, without resentment or doubt in their minds. The women 9 should be dressed quietly, and their demeanour should be modest and serious. The adornment of a Christian woman is not a matter of an elaborate coiffure, expensive clothes or valuable jewellery but the living of a good life. A woman should learn quietly and 10,11 humbly. Personally, I don't allow women to teach, nor do I ever 12 put them in positions of authority over men—I believe their role is to be receptive. (My reasons are that man was created before 13 woman. Further, it was Eve and not Adam who was first deceived 14 and fell into sin. Nevertheless I believe that women will come 15 safely through child-birth if they maintain a life of faith, love, holiness and gravity.)

CHAPTER 3

The sort of men to bear office: bishops

IT is quite true to say that a man who sets his heart on holding 1 office has laudable ambition. Well, for the office of a bishop a man 2 must be of blameless reputation, he must be married to one wife only, and be a man of self-control and discretion. He must be a man of disciplined life; he must be hospitable and have the gift of teaching. He must be neither intemperate nor violent, but 3 gentle. He must not be a controversialist nor must he be fond of money-grabbing. He must have proper authority in his own 4 household, and be able to control and command the respect of his children. (For if a man cannot rule in his own house how can he 5 look after the Church of God?) He must not be a beginner in the 6 faith, for fear of his becoming conceited and sharing the devil's downfall. He should, in addition to the above qualifications, have 7 a good reputation with the outside world, in case his good name is attacked and he is caught by the devil that way.

Deacons

8 Deacons, similarly, should be men of serious outlook and sincere conviction. They too should be temperate and not greedy for
9 money. They should hold the mystery of the faith with complete sincerity.
10 Let them serve a period of probation first, and only serve as
11 deacons if they prove satisfactory. Their wives should share their serious outlook, and must be women of discretion and self-
12 control—women who can be trusted. Deacons should be men with only one wife, able to control their children and manage
13 their own households properly. Those who do well as deacons earn for themselves a certain legitimate standing, as well as gaining confidence and freedom in the Christian faith.

The tremendous responsibility of being God's minister

14,15 At the moment of writing I hope to be with you soon, but if there should be any considerable delay then what I have written will show you the sort of character men of God's household ought to have. It is, remember, the Church of the living God,
16 the pillar and the foundation of the truth. No one would deny that this religion of ours is a tremendous mystery, resting as it does on the one who showed himself as a human being, and met, as such, every demand of the Spirit in the sight of the angels. He has been proclaimed among the nations, believed in throughout the world, and received back into the glory of Heaven.

CHAPTER 4

Beware of false teachers: warn your people

1 GOD's Spirit specifically tells us that in later days there will be men who abandon the true faith and allow themselves to be
2 spiritually seduced by teachings of demons, teachings given by men who are lying hypocrites, whose consciences are as dead as
3 seared flesh. These men forbid marriage and command abstinence from foods—good things which, in fact, God intends to be thankfully enjoyed by those who believe in him and know the truth.
4 Everything God made is good, and is meant to be gratefully used, not despised. (The holiness or otherwise of a certain food,

for instance, depends not on its nature but on whether it is eaten
thankfully or not.) It is consecrated by the Word of God and 5
by prayer.

You will be doing your duty as Christ's minister if you remind 6
your church members of these things, and you will show yourself as one who owes his strength to the truth of the faith he has
absorbed and the sound teaching he has followed. But steer clear 7
of all these stupid Godless fictions.

Take time and trouble to keep yourself spiritually fit. Bodily 8
fitness has a certain value, but spiritual fitness is essential both for
this present life and for the life to come. There is no doubt about 9
this at all, and Christians should remember it. It is because we 10
realise the paramount importance of the spiritual that we labour
and struggle. We place our whole confidence in the living God, the
saviour of all men, and particularly of those who believe in him.
These convictions should be the basis of your instruction and 11
teaching.

A little personal advice

Don't let people look down on you because you are young: 12
see that they look up to you because you are an example to them
in your speech and behaviour, in your love and faith and sincerity.
Concentrate until my arrival on your reading and on your preach- 13
ing and teaching. Do not neglect the gift that was given to you in 14
the proclaiming of God's Word when the assembled elders laid
their hands on you. Give your whole attention, all your energies, 15
to these things, so that your progress is plain for all to see. Keep a 16
critical eye both upon your own life and on the teaching you
give, and if you continue to follow the line I have indicated you
will not only save your own soul but the souls of your hearers as
well.

CHAPTER 5

DON'T reprimand a senior member of your church, appeal to 1
him as a father. Treat the young men as brothers, and the older 2
women as mothers. Treat the younger women as sisters, and no
more.

How to deal with widows in the church

3   You should treat with great consideration widows who are
4 really alone in the world. But remember that if a widow has
children or grandchildren it is primarily their duty to show the
genuineness of their religion in their own homes by repaying their
parents for what has been done for them, and God readily accepts
such service.

5   But the widow who is really alone and desolate can only hope
6 in God, and she will pray to him day and night. The widow who
plunges into all the pleasure that the world can give her is killing
her own soul.

7   You should therefore make the following rules for the widows,
to avoid abuses:

8   1. You should make it clear that for a man to refuse to look
after his own relations, especially those actually living in his house,
is a denial of the faith he professes. He is far worse than a man who
makes no profession.

9   2. Widows for your church list should be at least sixty years
10 of age, should have had only one husband and have a well-
founded reputation for having lived a good life. Some such questions as these should be asked:—has she brought up her children
well, has she been hospitable to strangers, has she been willing to
serve fellow-Christians in menial ways, has she relieved those in
distress, has she, in a word, conscientiously done all the good
she can?

11   3. Don't put the younger widows on your list. My experience
is that when their natural desires grow stronger than their
12 spiritual devotion to Christ they want to marry again, thus
13 proving themselves unfaithful to their first loyalty. Moreover,
they get into habits of slackness by being so much in and out of
other people's houses. In fact they easily become worse than lazy,
and degenerate into gossips and busybodies with dangerous
tongues.

14   4. My advice is that the younger widows should, normally,
marry again, bear children and run their own households. They
should certainly not be the means of lowering the reputation of
15 the church, although some, alas, have already played into the
enemy's hands.

16   5. As a general rule it should be taken for granted that any
Christian, man or woman, who has a widow in the family should
do everything possible for her, and not allow her to become the

church's responsibility. The church will then be free to look after those widows who are alone in the world.

You and your elders

Elders with a gift of leadership should be considered worthy of **17** respect, and of adequate salary, particularly if they work hard at their preaching and teaching. Remember the scriptural principle: **18**
> Thou shalt not muzzle the ox when he treadeth out the corn,

and
> The labourer is worthy of his hire.

Take no notice of charges brought against an elder unless they **19** can be substantiated by proper witnesses. If sin is actually proved, **20** then the offenders should be publicly rebuked as a salutary warning to others.

Timothy, I solemnly charge you in the sight of God and Christ **21** Jesus and the holy angels to follow these orders with the strictest impartiality and to have no favourites.

Never be in a hurry to ordain a man, or you may be making **22** yourself responsible for his sins. Be careful that your own life is pure. (By the way, I should advise you to drink wine in modera- **23** tion, instead of water. It will do your stomach good and help you to get over your frequent spells of illness.) Remember that **24** some men's sins are obvious, and are equally obviously bringing them to judgment. The sins of other men are not apparent, but are dogging them, nevertheless, under the surface. Similarly **25** some virtues are plain to see, while others, though not at all conspicuous, will eventually make themselves felt.

CHAPTER 6

The behaviour of slaves in the church

CHRISTIAN slaves should treat their masters with respect, and **1** avoid causing dishonour to the name of God and our teaching. If **2** they have Christian masters they should not despise them because they work for brothers in the faith. Indeed they should serve them all the better because they are thereby benefiting those who have the same faith and love as themselves.

The dangers of false doctrine and the love of money

This is the sort of thing you should teach, and if anyone tries **3**

441

to teach some doctrinal novelty which is not compatible with sound teaching (which we base on Christ's own words and which
4 leads to Christ-like living), then he is a conceited idiot! His mind is a morbid jumble of disputation and argument, things which lead to nothing but jealousy, quarrelling, insults and malicious
5 innuendoes—continual wrangling, in fact, among men of warped minds who have lost their real hold on the truth but hope to
6 make some profit out of the Christian religion. There is a real profit, of course, but it comes only to those who live contentedly
7 as God would have them live. We brought absolutely nothing with us when we entered this world and we can be sure we shall
8 take absolutely nothing with us when we leave it. Surely then, as far as physical things are concerned, it is sufficient for us to keep
9 our bodies fed and clothed. For men who set their hearts on being wealthy expose themselves to temptation. They fall into one of the world's traps, and lay themselves open to all sorts of silly and wicked desires, which are quite capable of utterly ruining and
10 destroying their souls. For loving money leads to all kinds of evil, and some men in the struggle to be rich have lost their faith and caused themselves untold agonies of mind.

Maintain a fearless witness until the last day

11 But you, the man of God, keep clear of such things. Set your heart not on riches, but on goodness, Christ-likeness, faith, love,
12 patience and humility. Fight the worthwhile battle of the faith, keep your grip on that life eternal to which you have been called, and to which you boldly professed your loyalty before many
13 witnesses. I charge you in the sight of God who gives life to all things and Christ Jesus who fearlessly witnessed to the truth
14 before Pontius Pilate, to keep your commission clean and above reproach until the final coming of Christ. This will be, in his own
15 time, the final dénouement of God, who is the blessed controller of all things, the king over all kings and the master of all masters,
16 the only source of immortality, the one who lives in unapproachable light, the one whom no mortal eye has ever seen or ever can see. To him be acknowledged all honour and power for ever, amen!

Have a word for the rich

17 Tell those who are rich in this present world not to be contemptuous of others, and not to rest the weight of their confidence

on the transitory power of wealth but on the living God, who generously gives us everything for our enjoyment. Tell them to do good, to be rich in kindly actions, to be ready to give to others and to sympathise with those in distress. Their security should be invested in the life to come, so that they may be sure of holding a share in the life which is permanent. 18 19

My final appeal

O Timothy, guard most carefully your divine commission. Avoid the Godless mixture of contradictory notions which is falsely known as "knowledge"—some have followed it *and lost their faith*. 20 21

Grace be with you.

PAUL.

The Second Letter to Timothy

AUTHOR. *Paul, almost certainly writing from Rome, where he is awaiting sentence of death. (But see note on I Timothy.)*

DATE. *About* 67.

DESTINATION. *Timothy, still at Ephesus.*

THEME. *This second letter also aims at stimulating Timothy's faith and courage, and renews its plea for faithfulness to sound teaching and loyalty to what he, Timothy, knows to be true.*

The personal requests which end this letter are peculiarly touching since we realise that Paul knew that it was only a question of time before he was executed.

CHAPTER 1

PAUL, messenger by God's appointment in the promised life of Christ Jesus, to Timothy, my own dearly loved son: grace, mercy and peace be to you from God the Father and Christ Jesus, our Lord. 1 2

I thank God for your faith: guard it well

I thank the God of my forefathers, whom I serve with a clear 3

443

conscience, as I remember you constantly in my prayers. Every
4 day and every night I have been longing to see you, for I can't
forget how moved you were when I left you, and to have you with
me again would be the greatest possible joy. I often think of that
5 genuine faith of yours—a faith that first appeared in your grand-
mother Lois, then in Eunice your mother, and is now, I am con-
6 vinced, in you as well. Because of this faith, I now remind you to
stir up that inner fire which God gave you at your ordination
7 through my hands. For God has not given us a spirit of fear, but
a spirit of power and love and a sound mind. So never be ashamed
8 of bearing witness to our Lord, nor of me, his prisoner. Accept,
as I do, all the hardship that faithfulness to the gospel entails in
9 the strength that God gives you. For he has rescued us from all
that is really evil and called us to a life of holiness—not because
of any of our achievements but for his own purpose. Before time
10 began he planned to give us in Christ Jesus the grace to achieve
this purpose, but it is only since our saviour Christ Jesus has been
revealed that the method has become apparent. For Christ has
completely abolished death, and has now, through the gospel,
11 opened to us men the shining possibilities of the life that is eternal.
It is this gospel that I am commissioned to proclaim; it is of this
12 gospel that I am appointed both messenger and teacher, and it is
for this gospel that I am now suffering these things. Yet I am not
in the least ashamed. For I know the one in whom I have placed
my confidence, and I am perfectly certain that the work he has
committed to me is safe in his hands until that day.

13 So keep my words in your mind as the pattern of sound teach-
14 ing, given to you in the faith and love of Christ Jesus. Take the
greatest care of the good things which were entrusted to you by
the Holy Spirit who lives within us.

Deserters—and a friend

15 You will know, I expect, that all those who are in Asia have
16 turned against me, Phygelus and Hermogenes among them. But
may the Lord have mercy on the household of Onesiphorus.
Many times did that man put fresh heart into me, and he was not
17 in the least ashamed of my being a prisoner in chains. Indeed,
when he was in Rome he went to a great deal of trouble to find
18 me—may the Lord grant he finds his mercy in that day!—and
you well know in how many ways he helped me at Ephesus as well.

CHAPTER 2

Above all things be faithful

So, my son, be strong in the grace that Christ Jesus gives. 1
Everything that you have heard me teach in public you should 2
in turn entrust to reliable men, who will be able to pass it on to
others.

Put up with your share of hardship as a loyal soldier in Christ's 3
army. Remember: 1. That no soldier on active service gets him- 4
self entangled in business, or he will not please his commanding
officer. 2. A man who enters an athletic contest wins no prize 5
unless he keeps the rules laid down. 3. Only the man who works 6
on the land has the right to the first share of its produce. Consider 7
these three illustrations of mine and the Lord will help you to
understand all that I mean.

Remember always, as the centre of everything, Jesus Christ, a 8
descendant of David, yet raised by God from the dead according to my gospel. For preaching this I am having to endure being 9
chained in prison as if I were some sort of a criminal. But they
cannot chain the Word of God, and I can endure all these things 10
for the sake of those whom God is calling, so that they too may
receive the salvation of Christ Jesus, and its complement of glory
after the world of time. I rely on this saying: *If we died with him* 11
we shall also live with him: if we suffer we shall also reign with him. 12
If we deny him he will also deny us: yet if we are faithless he always 13
remains faithful. He cannot deny his own nature.

Hold fast to the true: avoid dangerous error

Remind your people of things like this, and tell them as before 14
God not to fight wordy battles, which help no one and may
undermine the faith of those who hear them.

For yourself, concentrate on winning God's approval, on being 15
a workman with nothing to be ashamed of, and who knows how
to use the word of truth to the best advantage. But steer clear of 16
these unchristian babblings, which in practice lead further and
further away from Christian living. For their teachings are as 17
dangerous as blood-poisoning to the body, and spread like sepsis
from a wound. Hymenaeus and Philetus are responsible for this
sort of thing, and they are men who are palpable traitors to the 18

truth, for they say that the resurrection has already occurred and, of course, badly upset some people's faith.

19 God's solid foundation still stands, however, with this double inscription: *The Lord knows those who belong to him*, and *Let every true Christian have no dealings with evil*.

20 In any big household there are naturally not only gold and silver vessels but wooden and earthenware ones as well. Some are
21 used for the highest purposes and some for the lowest. If a man keeps himself clean from the contaminations of evil he will be a vessel used for honourable purposes, clean and serviceable for the use of the master of the household, all ready, in fact, for any good purpose.

Be positively good—and patient

22 Turn your back on the turbulent desires of youth and give your positive attention to goodness, faith, love and peace in company
23 with all those who approach God in sincerity. But have nothing to do with silly and ill-informed controversies which lead inevit-
24 ably, as you know, to strife. And the Lord's servant must not be a man of strife: he must be kind to all, ready and able to teach: he
25 must have patience and the ability gently to correct those who oppose his message. He must always bear in mind the possibility that God will give them a different outlook, and that they may
26 come to know the truth. They may come to their senses and be rescued from the snare of the devil by the servant of the Lord and set to work for God's purposes.

CHAPTER 3

A warning of what to expect

1 BUT you must realise that in the last days the times will be full
2 of danger. Men will become utterly self-centred, greedy for money, full of big words. They will be proud and contemptuous, without any regard for what their parents taught them. They will
3 be utterly lacking in gratitude, purity and normal human affections. They will be men of unscrupulous speech and have no control of themselves. They will be passionate and unprincipled,
4 treacherous, self-willed and conceited, loving all the time what
5 gives them pleasure instead of loving God. They will maintain a façade of "religion", but their conduct will deny its validity. You must keep clear of people like this.

From their number come those creatures who worm their way 6
into people's houses, and find easy prey in silly women with an
exaggerated sense of sin and morbid cravings—who are always 7
learning and yet never able to grasp the truth. These men are as 8
much enemies to the truth as Jannes and Jambres were to Moses.
Their minds are distorted, and they are traitors to the faith. But 9
in the long run they won't get very far. Their folly will become as
obvious to everybody as did that of Moses' opponents.

Your knowledge of the truth should be your safeguard

But you, Timothy, have known intimately both what I have 10
taught and how I have lived. My purpose and my faith are no
secrets to you. You saw my endurance and love and patience as I
met all those persecutions and difficulties at Antioch, Iconium and 11
Lystra. And you know how the Lord brought me safely through
them all. Persecution is inevitable for those who are determined 12
to live really Christian lives, while wicked and deceitful men will 13
go from bad to worse, deluding others and deluding themselves.

Yet you must go on steadily in those things that you have 14
learned and which you know are true. Remember from what
sort of people your knowledge has come, and how from early 15
childhood your mind has been familiar with the holy scriptures,
which can open the mind to the salvation which comes through
believing in Christ Jesus. All scripture is inspired by God and is 16
useful for teaching the faith and correcting error, for re-setting
the direction of a man's life and training him in good living. The 17
scriptures are the comprehensive equipment of the man of God,
and fit him fully for all branches of his work.

CHAPTER 4

My time is nearly over: you must carry on

I SOLEMNLY charge you, Timothy, in the presence of God and of 1
Christ Jesus who will judge the living and the dead, by his appearing and his kingdom, to preach the Word of God. Never lose your 2
sense of urgency, in season or out of season. Prove, correct, and
encourage, using the utmost patience in your teaching. For the 3
time is coming when men will not tolerate wholesome teaching.
They will want something to tickle their own fancies, and they will
collect teachers who will pander to their own desires. They will 4

no longer listen to the truth, but will wander off after man-made fictions.

5   For yourself, stand fast in all that you are doing, meeting whatever suffering this may involve. Go on steadily preaching the gospel and carry out to the full the commission that God gave you.

6   As for me, I feel that the last drops of my life are being poured
7 out for God. The time for my departure has arrived. The glorious fight that God gave me I have fought, the course that I was set I
8 have finished, and I have kept the faith. The future for me holds the crown of righteousness which God, the true judge, will give to me in that day—and not, of course, only to me but to all those who have loved what they have seen of him.

Personal messages

9, 10   Do your best to come to me as soon as you can. Demas, loving this present world, I fear, has left me and gone to Thessalonica. Crescens has gone to Galatia, and Titus is away in Dalmatia.
11 Only Luke is with me now.

    When you come, pick up Mark and bring him with you. I can
12 certainly find a job for him here. (I had to send Tychicus off to
13 Ephesus.) And please bring with you the cloak I left with Carpus
14 at Troas, and the books, especially the manuscripts. Alexander the coppersmith did me a great deal of harm—the Lord will reward
15 him for what he did—and I should be very careful of him if I were you. He has been an obstinate opponent of our teaching.

16   The first time I had to defend myself no one was on my side
17 —they all deserted me, God forgive them! Yet the Lord himself stood by me and gave me the strength to proclaim the message clearly and fully, so that the gentiles could hear it, and I was
18 rescued "from the lion's mouth". I am sure the Lord will rescue me from every evil plot, and will keep me safe until I reach his heavenly kingdom. Glory be to him for ever and ever, amen!

Closing greetings

19   Give my love to Prisca and Aquila and Onesiphorus and his
20 family. Erastus is still staying on at Corinth, and Trophimus I had to leave sick at Miletus.

21   Do your best to get here before the winter. Eubulus, Pudens,
22 Linus, Claudia and all here send their greetings to you. The Lord be with your spirit. Grace be with you.

PAUL.

The Letter to Titus

AUTHOR. *Paul wrote this letter towards the end of his life, possibly from Rome at roughly the same time as the second letter to Timothy, if it is true that he was released from his first imprisonment mentioned in Acts 28, 30, and was imprisoned again later.*

DATE. *About 66.*

DESTINATION. *This is a letter of guidance and instruction to Titus, a pagan convert, and plainly now a man whom Paul completely trusts. He is believed by some to have been Luke's brother. He apparently helped Paul to found a church in Crete, where he now receives this letter.*

THEME. *This letter contains directions as to the type of church officer Titus should appoint in Crete, and the sort of Christian character he should try to develop in the Cretan church.*

CHAPTER 1

PAUL, a servant of God and messenger of Jesus Christ in the faith 1
God gives to his chosen, in the knowledge of the truth that comes
from a God-fearing life, and in the hope of the everlasting life 2
which God, who cannot lie, promised before the beginning of
time—(at the right moment he made his Word known in the 3
declaration which has been entrusted to me by his command)
to Titus, my true son in our common faith, be grace, mercy and 4
peace from God the Father and the Lord Jesus Christ our saviour.

Men who are appointed to the ministry must be of the highest character

I left you in Crete to set right matters which needed attention, 5
and gave you instructions to appoint elders in every city. They 6
were to be men of unquestioned integrity with only one wife,
and with children brought up as Christians and not likely to be
accused of loose living or law-breaking. To exercise spiritual 7
oversight a man must be of unimpeachable virtue, for he is God's
agent in the affairs of his household. He must not be aggressive
or hot-tempered or over-fond of wine; nor must he be violent

449

8   or greedy for financial gain. On the contrary, he must be hospitable, a genuine lover of what is good, a man who is discreet,
9   fair-minded, holy and self-controlled: a man who takes his stand on the orthodox faith, so that he can by sound teaching both stimulate faith and confute opposition.

Be on your guard against counterfeit Christians

10   For there are many, especially among the Jews, who will not recognise authority, who talk nonsense and yet in so doing have
11   managed to deceive men's minds. They must be silenced, for they upset the faith of whole households, teaching what they have no
12   business to teach for the sake of what they can get. One of them, yes, one of their prophets, has said: "Men of Crete are always
13   liars, evil and beastly, lazy and greedy." There is truth in this testimonial of theirs! Don't hesitate to reprimand them sharply,
14   for you want them to be sound and healthy Christians, with a proper contempt for Jewish fairy tales and orders issued by men
15   who have forsaken the path of truth. Everything is wholesome to those who are themselves wholesome. But nothing is wholesome to those who are themselves unwholesome and who have no faith in God—their very minds and consciences are diseased.
16   They profess to know God, but their actual behaviour denies their profession, for they are obviously vile and rebellious and when it comes to doing any real good they are palpable frauds.

CHAPTER 2

Good character should follow good teaching

1   Now you must tell them the sort of character which should spring
2   from sound teaching. The old men should be temperate, serious, wise—spiritually healthy through their faith and love and
3   patience. Similarly the old women should be reverent in their behaviour, should not make unfounded complaints and should not be over-fond of wine. They should be examples of the good
4   life, so that the younger women may learn to love their husbands
5   and their children, to be sensible and chaste, home-lovers, kind-hearted and willing to adapt themselves to their husbands—a good
6   advertisement for the Christian faith. The young men, too, you
7   should urge to take life seriously, letting your own life stand as a pattern of good living. In all your teaching show the strictest

regard for truth, and show that you appreciate the seriousness of the matters you are dealing with. Your speech should be un- 8 affected and logical, so that your opponent may feel ashamed at finding nothing in which to pick holes.

The duty of slaves—and of us all

Slaves should be told that it is their duty as Christians to obey 9 their masters and to give them satisfactory service in every way. They are not to "answer back" or to be light-fingered, but they 10 are to show themselves utterly trustworthy, a living testimonial to the teaching of God our saviour. For the grace of God, which 11 can save every man, has now become known, and it teaches us 12 to have no more to do with godlessness or the desires of this world but to live, here and now, responsible, honourable and God-fearing lives. And while we live this life we hope and wait 13 for the glorious dénouement of the great God and of Jesus Christ our saviour. For he gave himself for us, that he might rescue us 14 from all our evil ways and make for himself a people of his own, clean and pure, with our hearts set upon living a life that is good.

Tell men of these things, Titus. Urge them to action, using a 15 reprimand where necessary with all the authority of God's minister—and as such let no one treat you with contempt.

CHAPTER 3

Instructions for the Christians of Crete

REMIND your people to recognise the power of those who rule 1 and bear authority. They must obey the laws of the state and be prepared to render whatever good service they can. They are not 2 to speak evil of any man, they must not be argumentative but gentle, showing themselves agreeable to everybody. For we our- 3 selves have known what it is to be ignorant, disobedient and deceived, the slaves of various desires and pleasant feelings, while our lives were spent in malice and jealousy—we were hateful and we hated each other. But when the kindness of God our saviour 4 and his love towards man appeared, he saved us in his mercy—not 5 by virtue of any moral achievements of ours, but by the cleansing power of a new birth and the moral renewal of the Holy Spirit, 6 which he gave us so generously through Jesus Christ our Saviour.

7 The result is that we are acquitted by his grace, and can look
8 forward to inheriting life for evermore. This is solid truth: I want
you to speak about these matters with absolute certainty, so that
those who have believed in God may concentrate upon a life of
goodness.

9 Subjects like this are always good and useful but mind you
steer clear of stupid arguments, genealogies, controversies and
10 quarrels over the Law. They settle nothing and lead nowhere. If
a man is still argumentative after the second warning you should
11 reject him. You can be sure that he has a moral twist, and he
knows it.

Final messages

12 As soon as I send Artemas to you (or perhaps it will be
Tychicus), do your best to come to me at Nicopolis, for I have
13 made up my mind to spend the winter there. See that Zenas the
lawyer and Apollos have what they require and give them a good
14 send-off. And our people should learn to earn what they require
by leading an honest life and so be self-supporting.

15 All those here with me send you greetings. Please give our
greetings to all who love us in the faith. Grace be with you all.

                                                        PAUL.

The Letter to Philemon

AUTHOR. *Paul, who wrote this letter when in prison at the same time
as those to Ephesus, Colossae and Philippi, probably in Rome.*

DATE. *About 62.*

DESTINATION. *This is a personal letter to Philemon, a rich leading
member of the church at Colossae.*

THEME. *Here we have a charming intimate letter written by Paul to a
dear friend. Philemon's slave Onesimus (which means "useful"
and explains the untranslatable pun in verse 11 !), had run away
from him and come under Paul's influence in Rome. He not only
became a Christian but became very dear to Paul. They both
realise, however, that he must return to his master and Paul sends
him back with this "covering" letter.*

PAUL, a prisoner for the sake of Jesus Christ, and brother Timothy   *1*
to Philemon our much-loved fellow-worker, Apphia our sister   *2*
and Archippus who is with us in the fight; to the church that
meets in your house—grace and peace be to you from God our   *3*
Father and from the Lord Jesus Christ.

A personal appeal

I always thank God for you, Philemon, in my constant prayers   *4*
for you all, for I have heard how you love and trust both the   *5*
Lord Jesus himself and those who believe in him. And I pray   *6*
that those who share your faith may also share your knowledge
of all the good things that believing in Christ Jesus can mean to
us. It is your love, my brother, that gives us such comfort and   *7*
happiness, for it cheers the hearts of your fellow-Christians. And   *8*
although I could rely on my authority in Christ and dare to *order*
you to do what I consider right, I am not doing that. No, I am   *9*
appealing to that love of yours, a simple personal appeal from
Paul the old man, in prison for Jesus Christ's sake. I am appealing   *10*
for my child. Yes, I have become a father though I have been
under lock and key, and the child's name is—Onesimus! Oh, I   *11*
know you have found him pretty useless in the past but he is
going to be useful now, to both of us. I am sending him back to   *12*
you: *will you receive him as my son, part of me?* I should have dearly   *13*
loved to have kept him with me: he could have done what you
would have done—looked after me here in prison for the gospel's
sake. But I would do nothing without consulting you first, for if   *14*
you have a favour to give me, let it be spontaneous and not
forced from you by circumstances!

It occurs to me that there has been a purpose in your losing   *15*
him. You lost him, a slave for a time; now you are having him
back for good, not merely as a slave, but as a brother-Christian.   *16*
He is already especially loved by me—how much more will you
be able to love him, both as a man and as a fellow-Christian!
You and I have so much in common, haven't we? Then do   *17*
welcome him as you would welcome me. If you feel he has   *18*
wronged or cheated you put it down to my account. I've written   *19*
this with my own hand: I, Paul, hereby promise to repay you.
(Of course I'm not stressing the fact that you might be said to
owe me your very soul!) Now do grant me this favour, my   *20*
brother—such an act of love will do my old heart good. As I   *21*

send you this letter I know you'll do what I ask—I believe, in fact, you'll do more.

22 Will you do something else? Get the guest-room ready for *me*, for I have great hopes that through your prayers I myself will be returned to you as well!

23, 24 Epaphras, here in prison with me, sends his greetings: so do Mark, Aristarchus, Demas and Luke, all fellow-workers for God.

25 The grace of our Lord Jesus Christ be with your spirit, amen.

PAUL.

The Letter to Jewish Christians

(THE EPISTLE TO THE HEBREWS)

AUTHOR. *Although the Authorised Version calls this letter "the Epistle of Paul the Apostle to the Hebrews" it is almost universally agreed that he did not write it. The style is very unlike Paul's, and every other letter of his is plainly stated to be by him. Various fascinating speculations have been made as to its authorship, including the names of Barnabas, Luke, Silas, Apollos and Priscilla.*

DATE. *Probably before the fall of Jerusalem. Possibly 67.*

DESTINATION. *Christian Jews probably living in some large town. Rome is favoured by some scholars.*

THEME. *The general idea of this letter is to demonstrate that Jesus amply fulfils all the highest conceptions of the Jewish religion, and is infinitely superior to any predecessors. Christian Jews must realise that Christ has fulfilled and surpassed all their old ideas, and they must not therefore relapse into the old Jewish religion. Because the new agreement was established by God's visiting the earth in person, it is infinitely more important than the old agreement of the Law. There is, therefore, for those who belong to Christ far greater privilege in knowing God, but far greater responsibility in serving him loyally.*

CHAPTER 1

GOD, who gave to our forefathers many different glimpses of the **1** truth in the words of the prophets, has now, at the end of the **2** present age, given us the truth in the Son. Through the Son God made the whole universe, and to the Son he has ordained that all creation shall ultimately belong. This Son, radiance of **3** the glory of God, flawless expression of the nature of God, himself the upholding principle of all that is, effected in person the reconciliation between God and man and then took his seat at the right hand of the majesty on high—thus proving himself, by **4** the more glorious name that he has won, far greater than all the angels of God.

Scripture endorses this superiority

For to which of the angels did he ever say such words as these: **5**
> Thou art my Son,
> This day have I begotten thee?

Or, again:
> I will be to him a Father,
> And he shall be to me a Son?

Further, when he brings his first-born into this world of men, **6** he says:
> Let all the angels of God worship him.

This is what he says of the angels: **7**
> Who maketh his angels winds
> And his ministers a flame of fire.

But when he speaks of the Son, he says: **8**
> Thy throne, O God, is for ever and ever;
> And the sceptre of uprightness is the sceptre of thy kingdom.
> Thou hast loved righteousness and hated iniquity; **9**
> Therefore God, thy God, hath anointed thee
> With the oil of gladness above thy fellows.

He also says: **10**
> Thou, *Lord*, in the beginning hast laid the foundation of the earth,
> And the heavens are the work of thy hands:
> They shall perish, but thou continuest: **11**
> And they all shall wax old as doth a garment;

12   And as a mantle shalt thou roll them up,
      As a garment, and they shall be changed:
      But thou art the same,
      And thy years shall not fail.
13 But does he ever say this of any of the angels:
      Sit thou on my right hand,
      Till I make thine enemies the footstool of thy feet?
14 Surely the angels are no more than spirits in the service of God,
    commissioned to serve the heirs of God's salvation.

CHAPTER 2

The angels had authority in past ages: today the Son is the authority

1   WE ought, therefore, to pay the greatest attention to the truth
    that we have heard and not allow ourselves to drift away from it.
2   For if the message given through angels proved authentic, so that
    defiance of it and disobedience to it received appropriate re-
3   tribution, how shall we escape if we refuse to pay proper atten-
    tion to the salvation which is offered us today? For this salvation
    came first through the words of the Lord himself: it was con-
4   firmed for our hearing by men who had heard him speak, and
    God moreover has plainly endorsed their witness by signs and
    miracles, by all kinds of spiritual power, and by gifts of the Holy
    Spirit, distributed according to his Will.

5   For though in past ages God did grant authority to angels, yet
    he did not put the future world of men under their control, and
    it is this world that we are now talking about.
6   But someone has said:
      What is man, that thou art mindful of him?
      Or the son of man, that thou visitest him?
7   Thou madest him a little lower than the angels;
      Thou crownedst him with glory and honour,
      And didst set him over the works of thy hands;
8   Thou didst put all things in subjection under his feet.
    Notice that the writer puts "all things" under the sovereignty
    of man: he left nothing outside his control. But we do not yet see
    "all things" under his control.

Christ became man, not angel, to save mankind

9   What we actually see is Jesus, after being made temporarily

inferior to the angels (and so subject to pain and death), in order that he should, by God's grace, taste death for every man, now crowned with glory and honour. It was right and proper that in **10** bringing many sons to glory, God (from whom and by whom everything exists) should make the leader of their salvation a perfect leader through the fact that he suffered. For the one **11** who makes men holy and the men who are made holy share a common humanity. So that he is not ashamed to call them his brothers, for he says: **12**

I will declare thy name unto my brethren,
In the midst of the congregation will I sing thy praise.

And again, speaking as a man, he says: **13**

I will put my trust in him.

And, one more instance, in these words:

Behold, I and the children which God hath given me. . . .

Since, then, "the children" have a common physical nature as **14** human beings, he also became a human being, so that by going through death as a man he might destroy him who had the power of death, that is, the devil; and might also set free those who lived **15** their whole lives a prey to the fear of death. It is plain that for **16** this purpose he did not become an angel; he became a *man*, in actual fact a descendant of Abraham. It was imperative that he **17** should be made like his brothers in every respect, if he were to become a High Priest both compassionate and faithful in the things of God, and at the same time able to make atonement for the sins of the people. For by virtue of his own suffering under **18** temptation he is able to help those who are exposed to temptation.

CHAPTER 3

Moses was a faithful servant: Christ a faithful son

So then, my brothers in holiness who share the highest of all **1** callings, I want you to think of Jesus the messenger and High Priest of the faith we hold. See him as faithful to the charge **2** God gave him, and compare him with Moses who also faithfully discharged his duty in the household of God. For this man has **3** been considered worthy of greater honour than Moses, just as the builder of a house may be truly said to have more honour than the house itself. Every house is built by someone, but **4** the builder of everything is God himself. Moses was certainly **5** faithful in all his duties in God's household, but he was faithful

6 as a servant and his work was only a foreshadowing of the truth that would be known later. But Christ was faithful as a son in the household of his own Father. And we are members of this household if we maintain our trust and joyful hope steadfast to the end.

Let us be on our guard that unbelief does not creep in

7 We ought to take note of these words in which the Holy Spirit says:

Today if ye shall hear his voice,

8 Harden not your hearts, as in the provocation,

Like as in the day of the temptation in the wilderness,

9 Wherewith your fathers tempted me by proving me,

And saw my works forty years.

10 Wherefore I was displeased with this generation,

And said, they do alway err in their heart:

But they did not know my ways;

11 As I sware in my wrath,

They shall not enter into my rest.

12 You should therefore be most careful, my brothers, that there should not be in any of you that wickedness of heart which refuses

13 to trust, and deserts the cause of the living God. Help each other to stand firm in the faith every day, while it is still called "today", and beware that none of you becomes deaf and blind to God

14 through the delusive glamour of sin. For we continue to share in all that Christ has for us so long as we steadily maintain until the

15 end the trust with which we began. These words are still being said for our ears to hear:

Today if ye shall hear his voice,

Harden not your hearts, as in the provocation.

16 For who was it who heard the Word of God and yet provoked his indignation? Was it not all who were rescued from slavery in

17 Egypt under the leadership of Moses? And who was it with whom God was displeased for forty long years? Was it not those who, after all their hearing of God's Word, fell into sin, and left their

18 bones in the desert? And to whom did God swear that they should never enter into his rest? Was it not these very men who refused to trust him?

19 Yes, it is all too plain that it was refusal to trust God that prevented these men from entering his rest.

CHAPTER 4

Men failed in the past to find God's rest: let us not fail!

Now since the same promise of rest is offered to us today, let *1*
us be continually on our guard that none of us even looks like
failing to attain it. For we too have had a gospel preached to us, *2*
as those men had. Yet the message proclaimed to them did them
no good, because they only heard and did not believe as well.
It is only as a result of our faith and trust that we experience that *3*
rest. For he said:

As I sware in my wrath,
They shall not enter into my rest:

not because the rest was not prepared—it had been ready since
the work of creation was completed, as he says elsewhere in the *4*
scriptures, speaking of the seventh day of creation,

And God rested on the seventh day from all his works.

In the passage above he says, "They shall not enter into my rest." *5*
It is clear that some were intended to experience this rest and, since *6*
the previous hearers of the message failed to attain to it because
they would not believe God, he proclaims a further opportunity *7*
when he says through David, many years later, "today", just as
he had said "today" before.

Today if ye shall hear his voice,
Harden not your hearts.

For if Joshua had given them the rest, we should not find *8*
God saying, at a much later date, "today". There still exists, *9*
therefore, a full and complete rest for the people of God. And *10*
he who experiences his rest is resting from his own work as
fully as God from his.

Let us then be eager to know this rest for ourselves, and *11*
let us beware that no one misses it through falling into the same
kind of unbelief as those we have mentioned. For the Word that *12*
God speaks is alive and active; it cuts more keenly than any two-
edged sword: it strikes through to the place where soul and spirit
meet, to the innermost intimacies of a man's being: it exposes the
very thoughts and motives of a man's heart. No creature has any *13*
cover from the sight of God; everything lies naked and exposed
before the eyes of him with whom we have to do.

For our help and comfort—Jesus the great High Priest

14 Seeing that we have a great High Priest who has entered the inmost Heaven, Jesus the Son of God, let us hold firmly to our
15 faith. For we have no superhuman High Priest to whom our weaknesses are unintelligible—he himself has shared fully in all our experience of temptation, except that he never sinned.
16 Let us therefore approach the throne of grace with fullest confidence, that we may receive mercy for our failures and grace to help in the hour of need.

CHAPTER 5

A High Priest must be duly qualified and divinely appointed

1 NOTE that when a man is chosen as High Priest he is appointed on men's behalf as their representative in the things of God—he offers gifts to God and makes the necessary sacrifices for sins on
2 behalf of his fellow-men. He must be able to deal sympathetically with the ignorant and foolish because he realises that he is him-
3 self prone to human weakness. This naturally means that the offering which he makes for sin is made on his own personal behalf as well as on behalf of those whom he represents.
4 Note also that nobody chooses for himself the honour of being a High Priest, but he is called by God to the work, as was Aaron, the first High Priest in ancient times.
5 Thus we see that the Christ did not choose for himself the glory of being High Priest, but he was honoured by the one who said:

Thou art my Son,
This day have I begotten thee.

6 And he says in another passage:

Thou art a priest for ever
After the order of Melchizedek.

Christ, the perfect High Priest, was the perfect Son

7 Christ, in the days when he was a man on earth, appealed to the one who could save him from death in desperate prayer and the agony of tears. His prayers were heard; he was freed from his
8 shrinking from death but, Son though he was, he had to prove
9 the meaning of obedience through all that he suffered. Then, when he had been proved the perfect Son, he became the source of

eternal salvation to all who should obey him, being designated **10**
by God himself as High Priest "after the order of Melchizedek".

There is much food for thought here—but only for the mature Christian

There is a great deal that we should like to say about this high **11**
priesthood, but it is not easy to explain to you since you seem so
slow to grasp spiritual truth. At a time when you should be **12**
teaching others, you need teachers yourselves to repeat to you the
ABC of God's revelation to men. You have become people who
need a milk diet and cannot face solid food! For anyone who **13**
continues to live on "milk" is obviously immature—he simply
has not grown up. "Solid food" is only for the adult, that is, for **14**
the man who has developed by experience his power to discriminate between what is good and bad for him.

CHAPTER 6

Can we not leave spiritual babyhood behind—and go on to maturity?

Let us leave behind the elementary teaching about Christ and **1**
go forward to adult understanding. Let us not lay over and over
again the foundation truths—repentance from the deeds which led
to death, believing in God, baptism and laying-on of hands, belief **2**
in the life to come and the final judgment. No, if God allows, let **3**
us go on.

Going back to the foundations will not help those who have deliberately turned away from God

When you find men who have been enlightened, who have **4**
experienced salvation and received the Holy Spirit, who have **5**
known the wholesome nourishment of the Word of God and
touched the spiritual resources of the eternal world and who then **6**
fall away, it proves impossible to make them repent as they did
at first. For they are re-crucifying the Son of God in their own
souls, and by their conduct exposing him to shame and contempt.
Ground which absorbs the rain that is constantly falling upon it **7**
and produces plants which are useful to those who cultivate it, is
ground which has the blessing of God. But ground which pro- **8**
duces nothing but thorns and thistles is of no value and is bound

sooner or later to be condemned—the only thing to do is to burn it clean.

We want you to make God's promise real through your faith, hope and patience

9 But although we give these words of warning we feel sure that you, whom we love, are capable of better things and will enjoy
10 the full experience of salvation. God is not unfair: he will not lose sight of all that you have done nor of the loving labour which you have shown for his sake in looking after fellow-Christians
11 (as you are still doing). It is our earnest wish that every one of you should show a similar keenness in fully grasping the hope
12 that is within you, until the end. We do not want any of you to grow slack, but to follow the example of those who through sheer patient faith came to possess the promises.

13 When God made his promise to Abraham he swore by himself,
14 for there was no one greater by whom he could swear, and he said:

Surely blessing I will bless thee
And multiplying I will multiply thee.

15 And then Abraham, after patient endurance, found the promise true.
16 Among men it is customary to swear by something greater than themselves. And if a statement is confirmed by an oath, that is
17 the end of all quibbling. So in this matter, God, wishing to show beyond doubt that his plan was unchangeable, confirmed it with
18 an oath. So that by two utterly immutable things, the word of God and the oath of God, who cannot lie, we who are refugees from this dying world might have a source of strength, and might
19 grasp the hope that he holds out to us. This hope we hold as the utterly reliable anchor for our souls, fixed in the innermost shrine
20 of Heaven, where Jesus has already entered on our behalf, having become, as we have seen, "High Priest for ever after the order of Melchizedek".

CHAPTER 7

The mysterious Melchizedek: his superiority to Abraham and the Levites

1 Now this Melchizedek was, we know, king of Salem and priest of God most high. He met Abraham when the latter was return-

ing from the defeat of the kings, and blessed him. Abraham gave 2
him a tribute of a tenth part of all the spoils of battle.

(Melchizedek means "king of righteousness," and his other title
is "king of peace" (for Salem means peace). He had no father or 3
mother and no family tree. He was not born nor did he die, but,
being like the Son of God, is a perpetual priest.)

Now notice the greatness of this man. Even Abraham the 4
patriarch pays him a tribute of a tenth part of the spoils. Further, 5
we know that, according to the Law, the descendants of Levi who
accept the office of priest have the right to demand a "tenth"
from the people, that is from their brothers, despite the fact that
the latter are descendants of Abraham. But here we have one who 6
is quite independent of Levitic ancestry taking a "tenth" from
Abraham, and giving a blessing to Abraham, the holder of God's
promises! And no one can deny that the receiver of a blessing is 7
inferior to the one who gives it. Again, in the one case it is mortal 8
men who receive the "tenths", and in the other it is one who, we
are assured, is alive. One might say that even Levi, the proper 9
receiver of "tenths", has paid his tenth to this man, for in a sense 10
he already existed in the body of his father Abraham when
Melchizedek met him.

*The revival of the Melchizedek priesthood means that the Levitical
priesthood is superseded*

We may go further. If it be possible to bring men to spiritual 11
maturity through the Levitical priestly system (for that is the
system under which the people were given the Law), why does
the necessity arise for another priest to make his appearance *after
the order of Melchizedek*, instead of following the normal priestly
calling of Aaron? For if there is a transference of priestly powers, 12
there will necessarily follow an alteration of the Law regarding
priesthood. He who is described as our High Priest belongs to 13
another tribe, no member of which had ever attended the altar!
For it is a matter of history that our Lord was a descendant of 14
Judah, and Moses made no mention of priesthood in connection
with that tribe.

How fundamental is this change becomes all the more apparent 15
when we see this other priest appearing according to the Melchizedek pattern, and deriving his priesthood not by virtue of a 16
command imposed from outside, but from the power of indestructible life within. For the witness to him, as we have seen, is: 17

Thou art a priest for ever
After the order of Melchizedek.

18   Quite plainly, then, there is a definite cancellation of the previous commandment because of its ineffectiveness and uselessness
19 —the Law was incapable of bringing anyone to real maturity—followed by the introduction of a better hope, through which we approach our God.

The High Priesthood of Christ rests upon the oath of God

20   This means a "better" hope for us because Jesus has become
21 our priest by the oath of God. Other men have been priests without any sworn guarantee, but Jesus has the oath of him that said of him:

The Lord sware and will not repent himself,
Thou art a priest for ever.

22 And he is, by virtue of this fact, himself the living guarantee of
23 a "better" agreement. Human High Priests have always been changing, for death made a permanent appointment impossible.
24 But Christ, because he lives for ever, possesses a priesthood that
25 needs no successor. This means that he can save fully and completely those who approach God through him, for he is always living to intercede on their behalf.

Christ the perfect High Priest, who meets our need

26   Here is the High Priest we need. A man who is holy, faultless, unstained, beyond the very reach of sin and lifted above the very
27 Heavens. There is no need for him, like the High Priests we know, to offer up daily sacrifices, first for his own sins and then for the people's. He made one sacrifice, once for all, when he offered up himself.
28   The Law makes for its High Priests men of human weakness. But the word of the oath, which came after the Law, makes for High Priest the Son, who is perfect for ever!

CHAPTER 8

Christ our High Priest in Heaven is High Priest of a new agreement

1 Now to sum up—we have an ideal High Priest such as has been described above. He has taken his seat on the right hand of the
2 heavenly majesty. He is the minister of the sanctuary and of the real tabernacle—that is the one which the Lord has set up and not

464

man. Every High Priest is appointed to offer gifts and make **3**
sacrifices. It follows, therefore, that in these holy places this man
has something that he is offering.

Now if he were still living on earth he would not be a priest at **4**
all, for there are already priests offering the gifts prescribed by
the Law. These men are serving what is only a pattern or repro- **5**
duction of things that exist in Heaven. (Moses, you will remember,
when he was going to construct the tabernacle, was cautioned by
God in these words:

>   See that thou make all things
>   According to the pattern that was showed thee in the mount.)

But Christ has been given a far higher ministry for he mediates a **6**
higher agreement, which in turn rests upon higher promises. If **7**
the first agreement had proved satisfactory there would have been
no need for the second.

Actually, however, God does show himself dissatisfied for he **8**
says to those under the first agreement:

>   Behold the days come, saith the Lord,
>   That I will make a new covenant with the house of Israel and
>   with the house of Judah;
>   Not according to the covenant that I made with their fathers **9**
>   In the day that I took them by the hand to lead them forth out
>   of the land of Egypt;
>   For they continued not in my covenant,
>   And I regarded them not, saith the Lord.
>   For this is the covenant that I will make with the house of **10**
>   Israel
>   After those days, saith the Lord;
>   I will put my laws into their mind,
>   And on their heart also will I write them:
>   And I will be to them a God,
>   And they shall be to me a people:
>   And they shall not teach every man his fellow-citizen, **11**
>   And every man his brother, saying, Know the Lord:
>   For all shall know me,
>   From the least to the greatest of them.
>   For I will be merciful to their iniquities. **12**
>   And their sins will I remember no more.

The mere fact that God speaks of a new covenant or agree- **13**
ment makes the old one out of date. And when a thing grows
weak and out of date it is obviously soon going to be dispensed
with altogether.

CHAPTER 9

The sanctuary under the old agreement

1 Now the first agreement had certain rules for the service of
God, and it had a sanctuary, a holy place in this world for the
2 eternal God. A tent was erected: in the outer compartment were
3 placed the lamp-standard, the table and the sacred loaves. Inside,
beyond the curtain, was the inner tent called the Holy of Holies,
4 in which were the golden incense-altar and the gold-covered ark of
the agreement, containing the golden jar of manna. Aaron's bud-
ding staff and the stone tablets inscribed with the words of the
5 actual agreement. Above these things were fixed representations
of the cherubim of glory, casting their shadow over the ark's
covering, known as the mercy seat. (All this is full of meaning but
we cannot enter now into a detailed explanation.)
6 Under this arrangement the outer tent was habitually used by
7 the priests in the regular discharge of their religious duties. But
the inner tent was entered once a year only, by the High Priest,
alone, bearing a sacrifice of shed blood to be offered for his own
sins and those of the people.

The old arrangements stood as symbols until Christ, the truth, came

8 By these things the Holy Spirit means us to understand that the
way to the holy of holies was not yet open, that is, so long as the
9 first tent and all that it stands for still exist. For in this outer tent
we see a picture of the present time, in which both gifts and sacrifices are offered and yet are incapable of cleansing the soul of the
10 worshipper. The ceremonies are concerned with food and drink,
various washings and rules for bodily conduct, and were only
intended to be valid until the time when Christ should establish
11 the truth. For now Christ has come among us, the High Priest of
the good things which were to come, and has passed through a
greater and more perfect tent which no human hand had made
12 (for it was no part of this world of ours). It was not with goats'
or calves' blood but with his own blood that he entered once and
for all into the Holy of Holies, having won for us men eternal
13 reconciliation with God. And if the blood of bulls and goats and
the ashes of a burnt heifer were, when sprinkled on the unholy,
14 sufficient to make the body pure, then how much more will the
blood of Christ himself, who in his eternal spirit offered himself

to God as the perfect sacrifice, purify our souls from the deeds of death, that we may serve the living God!

The death of Christ gives him power to administer the new agreement

Christi is consequently the administrator of an entirely new 15 agreement, having the power, by virtue of his death, to redeem transgressions committed under the first agreement: to enable those who obey God's call to enjoy the promises of the eternal inheritance. For, as in the case of a will, the agreement is only 16 valid after death. While the testator lives, a will has no legal 17 power. And indeed we find that even the first agreement of God's 18 will was not put into force without the shedding of blood. For 19 when Moses had told the people every command of the Law he took calves' and goats' blood with water and scarlet wool, and sprinkled both the book and all the people with a sprig of hyssop, saying: "This is the blood of the agreement God makes with you." 20 Moses also sprinkled with blood the tent itself and all the sacred 21 vessels. And you will find that in the Law almost all cleansing is 22 made by means of blood—as the common saying has it: "No shedding of blood, no remission of sin."

Christ has achieved the real appearance before God for us

It was necessary for the earthly reproductions of heavenly 23 realities to be purified by such methods, but the actual heavenly things could only be made pure in God's sight by higher sacrifices than these. Christ did not therefore enter into any holy places 24 made by human hands (however truly these may represent heavenly realities), but he entered Heaven itself to make his appearance before God as High Priest on our behalf. There is no 25 intention that he should offer himself regularly, like the High Priest entering the holy of holies every year with the blood of another creature. For that would mean that he would have to 26 suffer death every time he entered Heaven from the beginning of the world! No, the fact is that now, at this point in time, the end of the present age, he has appeared once and for all to abolish sin by the sacrifice of himself. And just as surely as it is appointed 27 for all men to die once, and after that pass to their judgment, so 28 it is certain that Christ was offered once to bear the sins of many and after that, to those who look for him, he will appear a second time, not this time to deal with sin, but to bring to full salvation those who eagerly await him.

CHAPTER 10

Sacrifices under the Law were "typical" not final

1 THE Law possessed only a dim outline of the benefits Christ
would bring and did not actually reproduce them. Consequently
it was incapable of perfecting the souls of those who offered their
2 regular annual sacrifices. For if it had, surely the sacrifices would
have been discontinued—on the grounds that the worshippers,
having been really cleansed, would have had no further conscious-
3 ness of sin. In practice, however, the sacrifices amounted to an
4 annual reminder of sins; for the blood of bulls and goats cannot
really remove the guilt of sin.

Christ, however, makes the old order obsolete and makes the perfect sacrifice

5   Therefore, when Christ enters the world, he says:
        Sacrifice and offering thou wouldest not,
        But a body didst thou prepare for me;
6   In whole burnt offerings and sacrifices for sin thou hadst no
          pleasure:
7   Then said I, Lo, I am come
        (In the roll of the book it is written of me)
        To do thy will, O God.
8   After saying that God has "no pleasure in sacrifice, offering and
9 burnt-offering" (which are made according to the Law), Christ
then says, "Lo, I am come to do thy will." That means that he is
dispensing with the old order of sacrifices, and establishing a new
10 order of obedience to the will of God, and in that will we have
been made holy by the single unique offering of the body of Jesus
Christ.
11   Every human priest stands day by day performing his religious
duties and offering time after time the same sacrifices—which can
12 never actually remove sins. But this man, after offering one
13 sacrifice for sins for ever, took his seat at God's right hand, from
that time offering no more sacrifice, but waiting until "his
14 enemies be made his footstool". For by virtue of that one offering
15 he has perfected for all time every one whom he makes holy. The
Holy Spirit himself endorses this truth for us, when he says, first:
16   This is the covenant that I will make with them
        After those days, saith the Lord;

I will put my laws on their heart,
And upon their mind also will I write them.
And then, he adds:

And their sins and their iniquities will I remember no more. *17*
Where God grants remission of sin there can be no question of *18*
making further atonement.

Through Christ we can confidently approach God

So, by virtue of the blood of Jesus, you and I, my brothers, *19*
may now have confidence to enter the Holy of Holies by a fresh *20*
and living way, which he has opened up for us by himself passing
through the curtain, that is, his own human nature. Further, since *21*
we have a great High Priest set over the household of God, let us *22*
draw near with true hearts and fullest confidence, knowing that
our inmost souls have been purified by the sprinkling of his blood
just as our bodies are cleansed by the washing of clean water. In *23*
this confidence let us hold on to the hope that we profess without
the slightest hesitation—for he is utterly dependable—and let us *24*
think of one another and how we can encourage each other to love
and do good deeds. And let us not hold aloof from our church *25*
meetings, as some do. Let us do all we can to help one another's
faith, and this the more earnestly as we see the final day drawing
ever nearer.

A warning: let us not abuse the great sacrifice

Now if we sin deliberately after we have known and accepted *26*
the truth, there can be no further sacrifice for sin for us but only *27*
a terrifying expectation of judgment and the fire of God's indignation, which will one day consume all that sets itself against him.
The man who showed contempt for Moses' Law died without *28*
hope of appeal on the evidence of two or three of his fellows.
How much more dreadful a punishment will he be thought to *29*
deserve who has poured scorn on the Son of God, treated like
dirt the blood of the agreement which had once made him holy,
and insulted the very Spirit of grace? For we know the one who *30*
said:

Vengeance belongeth unto me, I will recompense.
And, again:

The Lord shall judge his people.
Truly it is a terrible thing for a man who has done this to fall into *31*
the hands of the living God!

Recollect your former faith, and stand firm today!

32 You must never forget those past days when you had received
33 the light and went through such a great and painful struggle. It
was partly because everyone's eye was on you as you endured harsh
words and hard experiences, partly because you threw in your lot
34 with those who suffered much the same. You sympathised with
those who were put in prison and you were cheerful when your
own goods were confiscated, for you knew that you had a much
35 more solid and lasting treasure in Heaven. Don't throw away your
trust now—it carries with it a rich reward in the world to come.
36 Patient endurance is what you need if, after doing God's will,
you are to receive what he has promised.

37 For yet a very little while,
He that cometh shall come, and shall not tarry.
38 But my righteous one shall live by faith;
And if he shrink back, my soul hath no pleasure in him.

39 Surely we are not going to be men who cower back and are
lost, but men who maintain their faith until the salvation of their
souls is complete!

CHAPTER 11

1 Now faith means putting our full confidence in the things we
2 hope for, it means being certain of things we cannot see. It was
this kind of faith that won their reputation for the saints of old.
3 And it is after all only by faith that our minds accept as fact that
the whole scheme of time and space was created by God's command—that the world which we can see has come into being
through principles which are invisible.

Faith is the distinctive mark of the saints of the old agreement

ABEL

4 It was because of his faith that Abel made a better sacrifice to
God than Cain, and he had evidence that God looked upon him
as a righteous man, whose gifts he could accept. And though Cain
killed him, yet by his faith he still speaks to us today.

ENOCH

5 It was because of his faith that Enoch was promoted to the
eternal world without experiencing death. He disappeared from

470

this world because God promoted him, and before that happened his reputation was that "he pleased God". And without faith it **6** is impossible to please him. The man who approaches God must have faith in two things, first that God exists and secondly that it is worth a man's while to try to find God.

NOAH

It was through his faith that Noah, on receiving God's warning **7** of impending disaster, reverently constructed an ark to save his household. This action of faith condemned the unbelief of the rest of the world, and won for Noah the righteousness before God which follows such a faith.

ABRAHAM

It was by faith that Abraham obeyed the summons to go out **8** to a place which he would eventually possess, and he set out in complete ignorance of his destination. It was faith that kept **9** him journeying like a foreigner through the land of promise, with no more home than the tents which he shared with Isaac and Jacob, co-heirs with him of the promise. For Abraham's eyes **10** were looking forward to that city with solid foundations of which God himself is both architect and builder.

SARAH

It was by faith that even Sarah gained the physical vitality to **11** become a mother despite her great age, and she gave birth to a child when far beyond the normal years of child-bearing. She could do this because she believed that the one who had given the promise was utterly trustworthy. So it happened that from one **12** man, who as a potential father was already considered dead, there arose a race "as numerous as the stars", as "countless as the sands of the sea-shore".

All the heroes of faith looked forward to their true country

All these whom we have mentioned maintained their faith but **13** died without actually receiving God's promises, though they had seen them in the distance, had hailed them as true and were quite convinced of their reality. They freely admitted that they lived on this earth as exiles and foreigners. Men who say that mean, of **14** course, that their eyes are fixed upon their true home-land. If they **15** had meant the particular country they had left behind, they had ample opportunity to return. No, the fact is that they longed for **16** a better country altogether, nothing less than a heavenly one. And because of this faith of theirs, God is not ashamed to be called their God for in sober truth he has prepared for them a city.

Abraham's faith once more

17 It was by faith that Abraham, when put to the test, offered Isaac for sacrifice. Yes, the man who had heard God's promises
18 was prepared to offer up his only son of whom it had been said
19 "In Isaac shall thy seed be called." He believed that God could raise his son up, even if he were dead. And he did, in a manner of speaking, receive him back from death.

The faith of Isaac, Jacob and Joseph

20 It was by faith that Isaac gave Jacob and Esau his blessing, for
21 his words dealt with what should happen in the future. It was by faith that the dying Jacob blessed each of Joseph's sons as he
22 bowed in prayer over his staff. It was by faith that Joseph on his death-bed spoke of the exodus of the Israelites, and gave confident orders about the disposal of his own mortal remains.

Moses

23 It was by faith that Moses was hidden by his parents for three months after his birth, for they saw that he was a beautiful child
24 and refused to be daunted by the king's decree. It was also by faith that Moses himself when grown up refused to be called the
25 son of Pharaoh's daughter. He preferred sharing the burden of God's people to enjoying the temporary advantages of alliance
26 with a sinful nation. He considered the "reproach of Christ" more precious than all the wealth of Egypt, for he looked steadily at the ultimate, not the immediate, reward.
27 By faith he left Egypt; he defied the king's anger with the strength that came from obedience to the invisible king.
28 By faith Moses kept the first Passover and made the blood-sprinkling, so that the angel of death which killed the first-born should not touch his people.
29 By faith the people walked through the Red Sea as though it

were dry land, and the Egyptians who tried to do the same thing were drowned.

Rahab

It was by faith that the walls of Jericho collapsed, for the people had obeyed God's command to encircle them for seven days. It was because of her faith that Rahab the prostitute did not share the fate of the disobedient, for she welcomed the Israelites sent out to reconnoitre. *30 31*

The Old Testament is full of examples of faith

And what other examples shall I give? There is simply not time to continue by telling the stories of Gideon, Barak, Samson and Jeptha; of David, Samuel and the prophets. Through their faith these men conquered kingdoms, ruled in justice and proved the truth of God's promises. They shut the mouths of lions, they quenched the furious blaze of fire, they escaped from death itself. From being weaklings they became strong men and mighty warriors; they routed whole armies of foreigners. Women received their dead raised to life again, while others were tortured and refused to be ransomed, because they wanted to deserve a more honourable resurrection in the world to come. Others were exposed to the test of public mockery and flogging, and to the torture of being left bound in prison. They were killed by stoning, by being sawn in two; they were tempted by specious promises of release and then were killed with the sword. Many became refugees with nothing but sheepskins or goatskins to cover them. They lost everything and yet were spurned and ill-treated by a world that was too evil to see their worth. They lived as vagrants in the desert, on the mountains, or in caves or holes in the ground. *32 33 34 35 36 37 38*

All these won a glowing testimony to their faith, but they did not then and there receive the fulfilment of the promise. God had something better planned for our day, and it was not his plan that they should reach perfection without us. *39 40*

CHAPTER 12

We should consider these examples and Christ the perfect example

SURROUNDED then as we are by these serried ranks of witnesses, let us strip off everything that hinders us, as well as the sin which *1*

dogs our feet, and let us run the race that we have to run with
2 patience, our eyes fixed on Jesus the source and the goal of our
faith. For he himself endured a cross and thought nothing of its
shame because of the joy he knew would follow his suffering;
3 and he is now seated at the right hand of God's throne. Think
constantly of him enduring all that sinful men could say against
him and you will not lose your purpose or your courage.

Look upon suffering as heavenly discipline

4 After all, your fight against sin has not yet meant the shedding
5 of blood, and you have perhaps lost sight of that piece of advice
which reminds you of your sonship in God:

My son, regard not lightly the chastening of the Lord,
Nor faint when thou art reproved of him;
6 For whom the Lord loveth he chasteneth,
And scourgeth every son whom he receiveth.

7 Bear what you have to bear as "chastening"—as God's dealing
with you as sons. No true son ever grows up uncorrected by his
8 father. For if you had no experience of the correction which all
sons have to bear you might well doubt the legitimacy of your
9 sonship. After all, when we were children we had fathers who
corrected us, and we respected them for it. Can we not much more
readily submit to the discipline of the Father of men's souls, and
learn how to live ?
10 For our fathers used to correct us according to their own ideas
during the brief days of childhood. But God corrects us all our
11 days for our own benefit, to teach us his holiness. Now obviously
no "chastening" seems pleasant at the time: it is in fact most
unpleasant. Yet when it is all over we can see that it has quietly
produced the fruit of real goodness in the characters of those who
12 have accepted it in the right spirit. So tighten your loosening grip
13 and steady your wavering stand. Don't wander away from the
path but forge steadily onward. On the right path the limping
foot recovers strength and does not collapse.

In times of testing be especially on your guard against certain sins

14 Let it be your ambition to live at peace with all men and to
15 achieve holiness "without which no man shall see the Lord". Be
careful that none of you fails to respond to the grace which God
gives, for if he does there can very easily spring up in him a bitter

spirit which is not only bad in itself but can also poison the lives of many others. Be careful, too, that none of you falls into impurity *16* or loses his reverence for the things of God and then, like Esau, is ready to sell his birthright to satisfy the momentary hunger of his body. Remember how afterwards, when he wanted to have *17* the blessing which was his birthright, he was refused. He never afterwards found the way of repentance though he sought it desperately and with tears.

Your experience is not that of the old agreement but of the new

You have not had to approach things which your senses could *18* experience as they did in the old days—flaming fire, black darkness, rushing wind and out of it a trumpet-blast, a voice speaking *19* human words. So terrible was that voice that those who heard it begged and prayed that it might stop speaking, for what it had *20* already commanded was more than they could bear—that "if even a beast touch this mountain it must be stoned". So fearful *21* was the spectacle that Moses cried out, "I am terrified and tremble at this sight!"

No, you have been allowed to approach the true Mount Zion, *22* the city of the living God, the heavenly Jerusalem. You have drawn near to the countless angelic army, the festal assembly of *23* Heaven and the Church of the first-born whose names are written above. You have drawn near to God, the judge of all, to the souls of good men made perfect, and to Jesus, mediator of a new *24* agreement, to the cleansing of blood which tells a better story than the age-old sacrifice of Abel.

So be sure you do not refuse to hear the voice of God! For if *25* they who refused to hear those who spoke to them on earth did not escape, how little chance of escape is there for us if we refuse to hear the one who speaks from Heaven. Then his voice shook *26* the earth, but now he promises:

> Yet once more will I make to tremble
> Not the earth only, but also the heaven.

This means that in this final "shaking" all that is impermanent *27* will be removed, that is, everything that is merely "made", and only the unshakable things will remain. Since then we have been *28* given a kingdom that is "unshakable", let us serve God with thankfulness in the ways which please him, but always with reverence and holy fear. For it is perfectly true that our God is *29* a burning fire.

CHAPTER 13

Some practical instructions for Christian living

1, 2 NEVER let your brotherly love fail, nor refuse to extend your hospitality to strangers—sometimes men have entertained angels
3 unawares. Think constantly of those in prison as if you were prisoners at their side. Think too of all who suffer as if you shared their pain.

4 Both honourable marriage and chastity should be respected by all of you. God himself will judge those who traffic in the bodies
5 of others or defile the relationship of marriage. Keep your lives free from the lust for money: be content with what you have.

God has said:

I will in no wise fail thee,
Neither will I in any wise forsake thee.

6 We, therefore, can confidently say:
The Lord is my helper; I will not fear:
What shall man do unto me?

Be loyal to your leaders and, above all, to Christ

7 Never forget your leaders, who first spoke to you the Word of God. Remember how they lived, and imitate their faith.

8 Jesus Christ is always the same, yesterday, today and for ever.
9 Do not be swept off your feet by various peculiar teachings. Spiritual stability depends on the grace of God, and not on rules of diet—which after all have not spiritually benefited those who
10 have made a speciality of that kind of thing. We have an Altar from which those who still serve the tabernacle have no right to eat.
11 When the blood of animals was presented as a sin-offering by the High Priest in the sanctuary, their bodies were burned outside
12 the precincts of the camp. That is why Jesus, when he sanctified men by the shedding of his own blood, suffered and died outside
13 the city gates. Let us go out to him, then, beyond the boundaries
14 of the camp, proudly bearing his "disgrace". For we have no permanent city here on earth, we are looking for one in the world
15 to come. Our constant sacrifice to God should be the praise of
16 lips that give thanks to his name. Yet we should not forget to do good and to share our good things with others, for these too are the sort of sacrifices God will accept.

Obey your rulers and recognise their authority. They are like **17** men standing guard over your spiritual good, and they have great responsibility. Try to make their work a pleasure and not a burden—by so doing you will help not only them but yourselves.

Personal: our blessing and our greetings

Pray for us. Our conscience is clear before God, and our great **18** desire is to lead a life that is completely honest. Please pray **19** earnestly that I may be restored to you the sooner.

Now the God of peace, who brought back from the dead that **20** great shepherd of the sheep, our Lord Jesus, by the blood of the everlasting agreement, equip you thoroughly for the doing of his **21** will! May he effect in you everything that pleases him through Jesus Christ, to whom be glory for ever and ever.

All I have said, my brothers, I ask you to accept as though it **22** were an appeal in person, although I have compressed it into a short letter.

You will be glad to know that brother Timothy is now at liberty. **23** If he comes here soon, he and I will perhaps visit you together.

Greetings to all your leaders and all your church members. **24** The Christians of Italy send their greetings. **25**

Grace be with you all.

The Letter of James

AUTHOR. *Quite probably James, brother or step-brother of Jesus. He had a high reputation and was known as "the Just". Paul calls him a messenger (Galatians 1, 19). Some think he was the first bishop of Jerusalem, and he was certainly the head of the church there at Paul's last visit (Acts 21, 18).*

DATE. *Possibly early, about 50, making it the earliest letter of the New Testament. Some suggest a date as late as "after 100". If this is so it cannot be the work of James, who died about 62.*

DESTINATION. *The displaced Jews, or the "Dispersion", i.e. Christian Jews who had been scattered by persecution or force of circumstance.*

THEME. *The teaching closely follows that of Jesus' Sermon on the Mount and reads like a collection of short homilies. It deals particularly with the dangers of an uncontrolled tongue, snobbery, belief in God unaccompanied by Christian conduct, and trusting in material prosperity. The emphasis in this letter on behaviour has sometimes been supposed to contradict Paul's teaching on "justification by faith". In fact it does not contradict but complement. Paul says that a man is "justified" before God not by achievement but by a real faith: James says that the test of a real faith is whether it issues in appropriate behaviour.*

CHAPTER 1

1 JAMES, a servant of God and of the Lord Jesus Christ, sends greeting to the twelve dispersed tribes.

The Christian can even welcome trouble

2 When all kinds of trials and temptations crowd into your lives, my brothers, don't resent them as intruders, but welcome them
3 as friends! Realise that they come to test your faith and to produce
4 in you the quality of endurance. But let the process go on until that endurance is fully developed, and you will find you have become men of mature character with the right sort of indepen-
5 dence. And if, in the process, any of you does not know how to meet any particular problem he has only to ask God—who gives generously to all men without making them feel foolish or guilty —and he may be quite sure that the necessary wisdom will be
6 given him. But he must ask in sincere faith without secret doubts as to whether he really wants God's help or not. The man who trusts God, but with inward reservations, is like a wave of the sea, carried forward by the wind one moment and driven back
7 the next. That sort of man cannot hope to receive anything from
8 the Lord, and the life of a man of divided loyalty will reveal instability at every turn.

Rich and poor can be glad—for different reasons!

9 The brother who is poor may be glad because God has called
10 him to the true riches. The rich may be glad that God has shown him his spiritual poverty. For the rich man, as such, will wither
11 away as surely as summer flowers. One day the sunrise brings a scorching wind; the grass withers at once and so do all the flowers

—all that lovely sight is destroyed. Just as surely will the rich man and all his extravagant ways fall into the blight of decay.

No temptation comes from God, only highest good

The man who patiently endures the temptations and trials that *12* come to him is the truly happy man. For once his testing is complete he will receive the crown of life which the Lord has promised to all who love him.

A man must not say when he is tempted, "God is tempting me." *13* For God cannot be tempted by evil, and does not himself tempt anyone. No, a man's temptation is due to the pull of his own *14* inward desires, which can be enormously attractive. His own *15* desire takes hold of him, and that produces sin. And sin in the long run means death—make no mistake about that, brothers of *16* mine! But every good endowment that we possess and every *17* complete gift that we have received must come from above, from the Father of all lights, with whom there is never the slightest variation or shadow of inconsistency. By his own wish he made *18* us his own sons through the Word of truth, that we might be, so to speak, the first specimens of his new creation.

Hear God's Word and put it into practice: that is real religion

In view of what he has made us then, dear brothers, let every *19* man be quick to listen but slow to use his tongue, and slow to lose his temper. For man's temper is never the means of achieving *20* God's true goodness.

Have done, then, with impurity and every other evil which *21* touches the lives of others, and humbly accept the message that God has sown in your hearts, and which can save your souls. Don't I beg you, only hear the message, but put it into practice; *22* otherwise you are merely deluding yourselves. The man who *23* simply hears and does nothing about it is like a man catching the reflection of his own face in a mirror. He sees himself, it is true, *24* but he goes on with whatever he was doing without the slightest recollection of what sort of person he saw in the mirror. But the *25* man who looks into the perfect mirror of God's law, the law of liberty, and makes a habit of so doing, is not the man who sees and forgets. He puts that law into practice and he wins true happiness.

If anyone appears to be "religious" but cannot control his *26*

tongue, he deceives himself and we may be sure that his religion
27 is useless. Religion that is pure and genuine in the sight of God
the Father will show itself by such things as visiting orphans and
widows in their distress and keeping oneself uncontaminated by
the world.

CHAPTER 2

Avoid snobbery: keep the royal law

1 DON'T ever attempt, my brothers, to combine snobbery with
2 faith in our glorious Lord Jesus Christ! Suppose one man comes
into your meeting well-dressed and with a gold ring on his finger,
3 and another man, obviously poor, arrives in shabby clothes. If
you pay special attention to the well-dressed man by saying,
"Please sit here—it's an excellent seat", and say to the poor man,
"You stand over there, please, or if you must sit, sit on the floor",
4 doesn't that prove that you are making class-distinctions in your
mind, and setting yourselves up to assess a man's quality ?—a very
5 bad thing. For do notice, my brothers, that God chose poor men,
whose only wealth was their faith, and made them heirs to the
6 kingdom promised to those who love him. And if you behave as
I have suggested, it is the poor man that you are insulting. Look
around you. Isn't it the rich who are always trying to "boss"
7 you, isn't it the rich who drag you into litigation ? Isn't it usually
the rich who blaspheme the glorious name by which you are
known ?

8 If you obey the royal law, expressed by the scripture, "Thou
9 shalt love thy neighbour as thyself", all is well. But once you
allow any invidious distinctions to creep in, you are sinning, you
10 have broken God's Law. Remember that a man who keeps the
whole Law but for a single exception is none the less a law-
11 breaker. The one who said, "Thou shalt not commit adultery",
also said, "Thou shalt do no murder". If you were to keep clear of
adultery but were to murder a man you would have become a
breaker of God's whole Law.

12 Anyway, you should speak and act as men who will be judged
13 by the law of freedom. The man who makes no allowances for
others will find none made for him. It is still true that "mercy
smiles in the face of judgment".

The relation between faith and action

14 Now what use is it, my brothers, for a man to say he "has faith'

if his actions do not correspond with it? Could that sort of faith save anyone's soul? If a fellow man or woman has no clothes to 15 wear and nothing to eat, and one of you say, "Good luck to you 16 I hope you'll keep warm and find enough to eat", and yet give them nothing to meet their physical needs, what on earth is the good of that? Yet that is exactly what a bare faith without a 17 corresponding life is like—useless and dead. If we only "have 18 faith" a man could easily challenge us by saying, "You say that you have faith and I have merely good actions. Well, all you can do is to show me a faith without corresponding actions, but I can show you by my actions that I have faith as well."

To the man who thinks that faith by itself is enough I feel inclined to say, "So you believe that there is one God? That's fine. 19 So do all the devils in hell, and shudder in terror!" For, my dear 20 short-sighted man, can't you see far enough to realise that faith without the right actions is dead and useless? Think of Abraham, 21 our ancestor. Wasn't it his action which really justified him in God's sight when his faith led him to offer his son Isaac on the altar? Can't you see that his faith and his actions were, so to speak, 22 partners—that his faith was implemented by his deed? That is 23 what the scripture means when it says:

And Abraham believed God,
And it was reckoned unto him for righteousness;
And he was called the friend of God.

A man is justified before God by what he does as well as by what 24 he believes. Rahab, who was a prostitute and a foreigner, has been 25 quoted as an example of faith, yet surely it was her action that pleased God, when she welcomed Joshua's reconnoitring party and sent them safely back by a different route.

Yes, faith without action is as dead as a body without a soul. 26

CHAPTER 3

The responsibility of a teacher's position

DON'T aim at adding to the number of teachers, my brothers, 1 I beg you! Remember that we who are teachers will be judged by a much higher standard.

The danger of the tongue

We all make mistakes in all kinds of ways, but the man who 2

can claim that he never says the wrong thing can consider himself perfect, for if he can control his tongue he can control every other
3 part of his personality! Men control the movements of a large
4 animal like the horse with a tiny bit placed in its mouth. Ships too, for all their size and the momentum they have with a strong wind behind them, are controlled by a very small rudder accord-
5 ing to the course chosen by the helmsman. The human tongue is physically small, but what tremendous effects it can boast of!
6 A whole forest can be set ablaze by a tiny spark of fire, and the tongue is as dangerous as any fire, with vast potentialities for evil. It can poison the whole body, it can make the whole of life a blazing hell.

7 Beasts, birds, reptiles and all kinds of sea-creatures can be, and
8 in fact are, tamed by man, but no one can tame the human tongue. It is an evil always liable to break out, and the poison it spreads
9 is deadly. We use the tongue to bless our Father, God, and we use the same tongue to curse our fellow-men, who are all created in
10 God's likeness. Blessing and curses come out of the same mouth— surely, my brothers, this is the sort of thing that never ought
11 to happen! Have you ever known a spring to give sweet and
12 bitter water simultaneously? Have you ever seen a fig-tree with a crop of olives, or seen figs growing on a vine? It is just as impossible for a spring to give fresh and salt water at the same time.

Real, spiritual, wisdom means humility, not rivalry

13 Are there some wise and understanding men among you? Then your lives will be an example of the humility that is born of true
14 wisdom. But if your heart is full of rivalry and bitter jealousy, then do not boast of your wisdom—don't deny the truth that you
15 must recognise in your inmost heart. You may acquire a certain superficial wisdom, but it does not come from God—it comes from this world, from your own lower nature, even from the
16 devil. For wherever you find jealousy and rivalry you also find
17 disharmony and all other kinds of evil. The wisdom that comes from God is first utterly pure, then peace-loving, gentle, approach-able, full of tolerant thoughts and kindly actions, with no breath
18 of favouritism or hint of hypocrisy. And the wise are peace-makers who go on quietly sowing for a harvest of righteousness— in other people and in themselves.

CHAPTER 4

Your jealousies spring from love of what the world can give

BUT what about the feuds and struggles that exist among you **1**
—where do you suppose they come from ? Can't you see that they
arise from conflicting passions within yourselves ? You crave for **2**
something and don't get it; you are murderously jealous of what
others have got and which you can't possess yourselves; you
struggle and fight with one another. You don't get what you want
because you don't ask God for it. And when you do ask he doesn't **3**
give it to you, for you ask in quite the wrong spirit—you only want
to satisfy your own desires.

You are like unfaithful wives, flirting with the glamour of this **4**
world, and never realising that to be the world's lover means
becoming the enemy of God! Anyone who deliberately chooses
to be the world's friend is thereby making himself God's enemy. **5**
Do you think what the scriptures have to say about this is a mere
formality ? Or do you imagine that this spirit of passionate jealousy
is the Spirit he has caused to live in us ? No, he gives us grace **6**
potent enough to meet this and every other evil spirit, if we are
humble enough to receive it. That is why he says:

God resisteth the proud,
But giveth grace to the humble.

You should be humble, not proud

Be humble then before God. But resist the devil and you'll find **7**
he'll run away from you. Come close to God and he will come **8**
close to you. Realise that you have sinned and get your hands
clean again. Realise that you have been disloyal and get your
hearts made true once more. As you come close to God you should **9**
be deeply sorry, you should be grieved, you should even be in
tears. Your laughter will have to become mourning, your high
spirits will have to become heartfelt dejection. You will have to **10**
feel very small in the sight of God before he will set you on your
feet once more.

It is for God to judge, not for us

Never pull each other to pieces, my brothers. If you do you **11**
483

are judging your brother and setting yourself up in the place of God's Law; you have become in fact a critic of the Law. Yet if you start to criticise the Law instead of obeying it you are setting

12 yourself up as judge, and there is only one judge, the one who gave the Law, to whom belongs absolute power of life and death. How can you then be so silly as to imagine that you are your neighbour's judge?

It is still true that man proposes, but God disposes

13 Just a moment, now, you who say, "We are going to such-and-such a city today or tomorrow. We shall stay there a year doing

14 business and make a profit"! How do you know what will happen even tomorrow? What, after all, is your life? It is like a puff of smoke visible for a little while and then dissolving into thin air.

15 Your remarks should be prefaced with, "If it is the Lord's will,

16 we shall still be alive and will do so-and-so." As it is, you get a certain pride in yourself in planning your future with such confidence. That sort of pride is all wrong.

17 No doubt you agree with the above in theory. Well, remember that if a man knows what is right and fails to do it, his failure is a real sin.

CHAPTER 5

Riches are going to prove a liability, not an asset, to the selfish

1 AND now, you plutocrats, is the time for you to weep and moan
2 because of the miseries in store for you! Your richest goods are
3 ruined, your hoard of clothes is moth-eaten, your gold and silver are tarnished. Yes, their very tarnish will be the evidence of your wicked hoarding and you will shrink from them as if they were red-hot. You have made a fine pile in these last days, haven't you?
4 But look, here is the pay of the reaper you hired and whom you cheated, and it is shouting out against you! And the cries of the other labourers you swindled are heard by the Lord of Hosts him-
5 self. Yes, you have had a magnificent time on this earth, and have indulged yourselves to the full. You have picked out just what
6 you wanted like soldiers looting after battle. You have condemned and ruined innocent men in your career, and they have been powerless to stop you.

Ultimate justice will surely come: be patient meanwhile

But be patient, my brothers, as you wait for the Lord to come. 7
Look at the farmer quietly awaiting his precious harvest. See how
he has to possess his soul in patience till the land has had the early
and late rains. So must you be patient, resting your hearts on the 8
ultimate certainty. The Lord's coming is very near.

Don't make complaints against each other in the meantime, 9
my brothers—you may be the one at fault yourself. The judge
himself is already at the door.

For our example of the patient endurance of suffering we can 10
take the prophets who have spoken in the Lord's name. Remember 11
that it is usually those who have patiently endured to whom we
accord the word "blessed". You have heard of Job's patient
endurance and how God dealt with him in the end, and therefore
you have seen that the Lord is merciful and full of understanding
pity for us men.

Don't emphasise with oaths: speak the plain truth

It is of the highest importance, my brothers, that your speech 12
should be free from oaths (whether they are "by" heaven or earth
or anything else). Your yes should be a plain yes, and your no a
plain no, and then you cannot go wrong in the matter.

Prayer is a great weapon

If any of you is in trouble let him pray. If anyone is flourishing 13
let him sing praises to God. If anyone is ill he should send for 14
the church elders. They should pray over him, anointing him
with oil in the Lord's name. Believing prayer will save the sick 15
man; the Lord will restore him and any sins that he has committed
will be forgiven. You should get into the habit of admitting your 16
sins to each other, and praying for each other, so that if sickness
comes to you you may be healed.

Tremendous power is made available through a good man's
earnest prayer. Do you remember Elijah? He was a man like us 17
but he prayed earnestly that it should not rain. In fact, not a drop
fell on the land for three and a half years. Then he prayed again, 18
the heavens gave the rain and the earth sprouted with vegetation
as usual.

A concluding hint

19 My brothers, if any of you should wander away from the truth
20 and another should turn him back on to the right path, then the
latter may be sure that in turning a man back from his wandering
course he has rescued a soul from death, and his loving action
will "cover a multitude of sins".

JAMES.

The First Letter of Peter

AUTHOR. *Peter, one of the original Twelve, writing probably from
Rome, symbolically described as "Babylon". It is thought that
Silvanus, or Silas, did the actual writing of the letter.*

DATE. *Almost certainly 64.*

DESTINATION. *This letter, like that of James, is addressed to the
Christian Jews scattered, by persecution or force of circumstance,
to various parts of Asia Minor.*

THEME. *We are here largely concerned with the Christian's attitude
towards undeserved suffering, possibly because persecution of
Christians was becoming common. It also contains advice to
Christian husbands and wives and direction for Christian servants
and Christian citizens.*

*The passage in 3, 18–21, about Christ preaching to "im-
prisoned spirits", is obscure, and many speculations have arisen
from it.*

CHAPTER 1

1 PETER, a messenger of Jesus Christ, sends this letter to the exiles
of the dispersed tribes (in Pontus, Galatia, Cappadocia, Asia and
2 Bithynia), whom God the Father knew and chose long ago to
be made holy by his Spirit, that they might obey Jesus Christ and
be cleansed by his blood: may you know more and more of
God's grace and peace.

Your faith is being tested, but your future is magnificent

3 Thank God, the God and Father of our Lord Jesus Christ, that

486

in his great mercy we men have been born again into a life full of hope, through Christ's rising again from the dead! You can **4** now hope for a perfect inheritance beyond the reach of change and decay, "reserved" in Heaven for you. And in the meantime **5** you are guarded by the power of God operating through your faith, till you enter fully into the salvation which is all ready for the dénouement of the last day. This means tremendous joy to **6** you, I know, even though at present you are temporarily harassed by all kinds of trials and temptations. This is no accident—it **7** happens to prove your faith, which is infinitely more valuable than gold, and gold, as you know, even though it is ultimately perishable, must be purified by fire. This proving of your faith is planned to result in praise and honour and glory in the day when Jesus Christ reveals himself. And though you have never seen him, **8** yet I know that you love him. At present you trust him without being able to see him, and even now he brings you a joy that words cannot express and which has in it a hint of the glories of Heaven; and all the time you are receiving the result of your faith **9** in him—the salvation of your own souls. The prophets of old did **10** their utmost to discover and obtain this salvation. They did not find it, but they prophesied of this grace that has now come to you. They tried hard to discover to what time and to what sort **11** of circumstances the Spirit of Christ working in them was referring. For he foretold the sufferings of Christ and the glories that should follow them. It was then made clear to them that they **12** were dealing with matters not meant for themselves, but for you. It is these very matters which have been made plain to you by those who preached the gospel to you by the Holy Spirit sent from Heaven—and these are facts to command the interest of the very angels!

Consider soberly what God has done for you

So brace up your minds, and, as men who know what they **13** are doing, rest the full weight of your hopes on the grace that will be yours when Jesus Christ reveals himself. Live as obedient **14** children before God. Don't let your character be moulded by the desires of your ignorant days, but be holy in every department **15** of your lives, for the one who has called you is himself holy. The **16** scripture says:

Ye shall be holy; for I am holy

17 If you pray to a Father who judges men by their actions without the slightest favouritism, then you should spend the time of
18 your stay here on earth with reverent fear. For you must realise all the time that you have been "ransomed" from the futile way of living passed on to you by your fathers' traditions, not with some money payment of transient value, but by the costly shed-
19 ding of blood. The price was in fact the life-blood of Christ, the
20 unblemished and unstained lamb of sacrifice. It is true that God chose him to fulfil this part before the world was founded, but
21 it was for your benefit that he was revealed in these last days—for you who found your faith in God through Christ. And God raised him from the dead and gave him unimaginable splendour, so that all your faith and hope might be centred in God.

Let your life match your high calling

22 Now that you have, by obeying the truth, made your souls clean enough for a genuine love of your fellows, see that you do love
23 each other, fervently and from the heart. For you are sons of God now; the live, permanent Word of the living God has given you
24 his own indestructible heredity. It is true that:

All flesh is as grass,
And all the glory thereof as the flower of grass.
The grass withereth, and the flower falleth:
25 But the word of the Lord abideth for ever.

The Word referred to, as far as you are concerned, is the message of the gospel that was preached to you.

CHAPTER 2

1 HAVE done, then, with all evil and deceit, all pretence and jealousy
2 and slander. You are babies, new-born in God's family, and you should be crying out for unadulterated spiritual milk to make you
3 grow up to salvation! And so you will, if you have already tasted the goodness of the Lord.
4   To change the metaphor, you come to him, as living stones to the immensely valuable living stone (which men rejected but God
5 chose), to be built up into a spiritual House of God, in which you, like holy priests, can offer those spiritual sacrifices which are

acceptable to God by Jesus Christ. There is a passage to this effect **6** in scripture, and it runs like this:

> Behold I lay in Zion a chief corner stone, elect, precious:
> And he that believeth on him shall not be put to shame.

It is to you who believe in him that he is "precious", but to those **7** who disobey God, it is true that:

> The stone which the builders rejected,
> The same was made the head of the corner.

And he is, to them, **8**

> A stone of stumbling and a rock of offence.

Yes, they stumble at the Word of God for in their hearts they are unwilling to obey it—which makes stumbling a foregone conclusion. But you are God's "chosen generation", his "royal **9** priesthood", his "holy nation", his "peculiar people"—all the old titles of God's people now belong to you. It is for you now to demonstrate the goodness of him who has called you out of darkness into his amazing light. In the past you were not "a **10** people" at all: now you are the people of God. In the past you had no experience of his mercy, but now it is intimately yours.

Your behaviour to the outside world

I beg you, as those whom I love, to live in this world as **11** strangers and "temporary residents", to keep clear of the desires of your lower natures, for they are always at war with your souls. Your conduct among the surrounding peoples in your different **12** countries should always be good and right, so that although they may in the usual way slander you as evil-doers yet when disasters come, they may glorify God when they see how well you conduct yourselves.

Obey every man-made authority for the Lord's sake—whether **13** it is the emperor, as the supreme ruler, or the governors whom he **14** has appointed to punish evil-doers and reward those who do good service. It is the will of God that you may thus silence the ill- **15** informed criticisms of the foolish. As free men you should never **16** use your freedom as an excuse for doing something that is wrong, for you are at all times the servants of God. You should have **17** respect for everyone, you should love our brotherhood, fear God and honour the emperor.

A word to household servants

You who are servants should submit to your masters with **18**

19 proper respect—not only to the good and kind, but also to the difficult. A man does something valuable when he endures pain, as in the sight of God, though he knows he is suffering unjustly.

20 After all, it is no credit to you if you are patient in bearing a punishment which you have richly deserved! But if you do your duty and are punished for it and can still accept it patiently, you

21 are doing something worthwhile in God's sight. Indeed this is your calling. For Christ suffered for you and left you a personal

22 example, and wants you to follow in his steps. He was guilty of

23 no sin nor of the slightest prevarication. Yet when he was insulted he offered no insult in return. When he suffered he made no threats of revenge. He simply committed his cause to the one who

24 judges fairly. And he personally bore our sins in his own body on the cross, so that we might be dead to sin and be alive to all that is

25 good. It was the suffering that he bore which has healed you. You had wandered away like so many sheep, but now you have returned to the shepherd and guardian of your souls.

CHAPTER 3

A word to married Christians

1 IN the same spirit you married women should adapt yourselves to your husbands, so that even if they do not obey the Word of God they may be won to God without any word being spoken,

2 simply by seeing the pure and reverent behaviour of you, their

3 wives. Your beauty should not be dependent on an elaborate

4 coiffure, or on the wearing of jewellery or fine clothes, but on the inner personality—the unfading loveliness of a calm and gentle

5 spirit, a thing very precious in the eyes of God. This was the secret of the beauty of the holy women of ancient times who trusted

6 in God and were submissive to their husbands. Sarah, you will remember, obeyed Abraham and called him her lord. And you have become, as it were, her true descendants today as long as you too live good lives and do not give way to hysterical fears.

7 Similarly, you husbands should try to understand the wives you live with, honouring them as physically weaker yet equally heirs with you of the grace of life. If you don't do this, you will find it impossible to pray properly.

Be good to each other—and to all men

8 To sum up, you should all be of one mind living like brothers

490

with true love and sympathy for each other, generous and courteous at all times. Never pay back a bad turn with a bad turn or 9
an insult with another insult, but on the contrary pay back with good. For this is your calling—to do good and one day to inherit all the goodness of God. For: 10

He that would love life,
And see good days,
Let him refrain his tongue from evil,
And his lips that they speak no guile: 11
And let him turn away from evil, and do good;
Let him seek peace and pursue it.
For the eyes of the Lord are upon the righteous, 12
And his ears unto their supplication:
But the face of the Lord is against them that do evil.

Do good, *even if you suffer for it*

After all, who in the ordinary way is likely to injure you for 13
being enthusiastic for good? And if it should happen that you 14
suffer "for righteousness' sake", that is a privilege. You need
neither fear their threats nor worry about them; simply con- 15
centrate on being completely devoted to Christ in your hearts.
Be ready at any time to give a quiet and reverent answer to any
man who wants a reason for the hope that you have within you.
Make sure that your conscience is perfectly clear, so that if men 16
should speak slanderously of you as rogues they may come to feel
ashamed of themselves for libelling your good Christian behaviour.

If it is the will of God that you should suffer it is really better 17
to suffer unjustly than because you have deserved it. Remember 18
that Christ the just suffered for us the unjust, to bring us to God.
That meant the death of his body, but he came to life again in
the spirit. It was in the spirit that he went and preached to the 19
imprisoned souls of those who had been disobedient in the days of 20
Noah—the days of God's great patience during the period of the
building of the ark, in which eventually only eight souls were
saved in the flood. And I cannot help pointing out what a 21
perfect illustration this is of the way you have been admitted to
the safety of the Christian "ark" by baptism, which means, of
course, far more than the mere washing of a dirty body: it means
the ability to face God with a clear conscience. For there is in
every true baptism the virtue of Christ's rising from the dead. And 22
he has now entered Heaven and is at God's right hand, with all
angels, authorities and powers subservient to him.

CHAPTER 4

Following Christ will mean pain

1 SINCE Christ had to suffer physically for you, you must fortify yourselves with the same inner attitude that he must have had. You must realise that to be dead to sin inevitably means pain, and
2 you should not therefore spend the rest of your time here on earth
3 indulging your physical nature, but in doing the will of God. Our past life may have been good enough for pagan purposes, though it meant sensuality, lust, drunkenness, orgies, carousals and wor-
4 shipping forbidden gods. Indeed your former companions may think it very queer that you will no longer join with them in their riotous excesses, and accordingly say all sorts of unpleasant things
5 about you. Don't worry: they are the ones who will have to explain their behaviour before the one who is prepared to judge
6 all men, whether living or dead. (For that is why the dead also had the gospel preached to them—that it might judge the lives they lived as men and give them also the opportunity to share the eternal life of God in the spirit.)

Your attitude in these last days

7 We are near the end of all things now, and you should therefore
8 be calm, self-controlled men of prayer. Above everything else be sure that you have real deep love for each other, remembering
9 how love can "cover a multitude of sins". Be hospitable to each
10 other without secretly wishing you hadn't got to be! Serve one another with the particular gifts God has given each of you, as
11 faithful dispensers of the magnificently varied grace of God. If any of you is a preacher then he should preach his message as from God. And in whatever way a man serves the Church he should do it recognising the fact that God gives him his ability, so that God may be glorified in everything through Jesus Christ. To him belong glory and power for ever, amen!

Your attitude to persecution

12 And now, dear friends of mine. I beg you not to be unduly alarmed at the fiery ordeals which come to test your faith, as
13 though this were some abnormal experience. You should be glad,

492

because it means that you are called to share Christ's sufferings. One day, when he shows himself in full splendour to men, you will be filled with the most tremendous joy. If you are reproached **14** for being Christ's followers, that is a great privilege, for you can be sure that God's Spirit of glory is resting upon you. But take **15** care that none of your number suffers as a murderer, or a thief, a rogue or a spy! If he suffers as a Christian he has nothing to be **16** ashamed of and may glorify God in Christ's name.

The time has evidently arrived for God's judgment to begin, **17** and it is beginning at his own House. And if it starts with us, what is it going to mean to those who refuse to obey the gospel of God? If even the good man is only just saved, what will be the **18** fate of the wicked and the sinner? And if it is true that we are **19** living in a time of judgment, then those who suffer according to God's will can only commit their souls to their faithful creator, and go on doing all the good they can.

CHAPTER 5

A word to your leaders

Now may I who am myself an elder say a word to you my **1** fellow-elders? I speak as one who actually saw Christ suffer, and as one who will share with you the glories that are to be unfolded to us. I urge you then to see that your "flock of God" is properly **2** fed and cared for. Accept the responsibility of looking after them willingly and not because you feel you can't get out of it, doing your work not for what you can make, but because you are really concerned for their well-being. You should aim not at being **3** "little tin gods" but as examples of Christian living in the eyes of the flock committed to your charge. And then, when the chief **4** shepherd reveals himself, you will receive that crown of glory which cannot fade.

Learn to be humble and to trust

You younger members must also submit to the elders. Indeed **5** all of you should defer to one another and wear the "overall" of humility in serving each other. God is always against the proud, but he is always ready to give grace to the humble. So, humble **6** yourselves under God's strong hand, and in his own good time he will lift you up. You can throw the whole weight of your **7** anxieties upon him, for you are his personal concern.

Resist the devil: you are in God's hands

8 Be self-controlled and vigilant always, for your enemy the devil is always about, prowling like a lion roaring for its prey.
9 Resist him, standing firm in your faith and remember that the strain is the same for all your fellow-Christians in other parts of
10 the world. And after you have borne these sufferings a very little while, the God of all grace, who has called you to share his eternal splendour through Christ, will himself make you whole
11 and secure and strong. All power is his for ever and ever, amen!

Final greetings

12 I am sending this short letter by Silvanus, whom I know to be a faithful brother, to stimulate your faith and assure you that the above words represent the true grace of God. See that you stand fast in that grace!
13 Your sister-church here in "Babylon" sends you greetings, and
14 so does my son Mark. Give each other a handshake all round as a sign of love.

Peace be to all true Christians.

PETER.

The Second Letter of Peter

AUTHOR. *The authenticity of this letter was sharply disputed by the early Church, and it is still viewed with suspicion by many. This is partly because one section appears to be copied from the letter of Jude, partly because the general character is different from the first letter of Peter, and partly because competent scholars consider there are references in it to events which happened after Peter's death in approximately 64. It is, of course, possible that we have here parts of a genuine letter of Peter with considerable later additions.*

DATE. *About 130 ? (very uncertain.)*

DESTINATION. *A particular, but unknown, church.*

THEME. *The letter stresses the observed facts upon which the Christian faith rests. It contains a stern warning and violent attack against false teachers, and a reminder that Christ will certainly return in person, even though his coming appears to men to be long delayed.*

494

CHAPTER 1

SIMON PETER, a servant and messenger of Jesus Christ, sends this *1*
letter to those who have been given a faith as valuable as ours in
the righteousness of our God, and saviour Jesus Christ. May you *2*
know more and more of grace and peace as your knowledge of
God and Jesus our Lord grows deeper.

God has done his part: see that you do yours

He has by his own action given us everything that is necessary *3*
for living the truly good life, in allowing us to know the one who
has called us to him, through his own glorious goodness. It is *4*
through him that God's greatest and most precious promises have
become available to us men, making it possible for you to escape
the inevitable disintegration that lust produces in the world and
to share in God's essential nature. For this very reason you must *5*
do your utmost from your side, and see that your faith carries
with it real goodness of life. Your goodness must be accompanied
by knowledge, your knowledge by self-control, your self-control *6*
by the ability to endure. Your endurance too must always be
accompanied by devotion to God; that in turn must have in it *7*
the quality of brotherliness, and your brotherliness must lead on
to Christian love. If you have these qualities existing and growing *8*
in you then it means that knowing our Lord Jesus Christ has not
made your lives either complacent or unproductive. The man *9*
whose life fails to exhibit these qualities is short-sighted—he can
no longer see the reason why he was cleansed from his former sins.
Set your minds, then, on endorsing by your conduct the fact *10*
that God has called and chosen you. If you go along the lines I
have indicated above, there is no reason why you should stumble,
and if you have lived the sort of life I have recommended God *11*
will open wide to you the gates of the eternal kingdom of our
Lord and saviour Jesus Christ.

Truth will bear repetition

I shall not fail to remind you of things like this although you *12*
know them and are already established in the truth. I consider it *13*
my duty, as long as I live in the temporary dwelling of this body,
to stimulate you by these reminders. I know that I shall have to *14*
leave this body at very short notice, as our Lord Jesus Christ made

15 clear to me. Consequently I shall make the most of every opportunity, so that after I am gone you will remember these things.

16 We were not following a cleverly written-up story when we told you about the power and coming of our Lord Jesus Christ

17 —we actually saw his majesty with our own eyes. He received honour and glory from God the Father himself when that voice said to him, out of the sublime glory of Heaven, "This is my

18 beloved Son, in whom I am well pleased." We actually heard that voice speaking from Heaven while we were with him on the

19 sacred mountain. The word of prophecy was fulfilled in our hearing! You should give that word your closest attention, for it shines like a lamp amidst all the dirt and darkness of the world, until the day dawns, and the morning star rises in your hearts.

False prophets will flourish, but only for a time

20 But you must understand this at the outset, that no prophecy of scripture arose from an individual's interpretation of the truth.

21 No prophecy came because a man wanted it to: men of God spoke because they were inspired by the Holy Spirit.

CHAPTER 2

1 BUT even in those days there were false prophets, just as there will be false teachers among you today. They will be men who will subtly introduce dangerous heresies. They will thereby deny the Lord who redeemed them, and it will not be long before they

2 bring on themselves their own downfall. Many will follow their pernicious teaching and thereby bring discredit on the way of

3 truth. In their lust to make converts these men will try to exploit you too with their bogus arguments. But judgment has been for

4 some time hard on their heels and their downfall is inevitable. For if God did not spare angels who sinned against him, but banished

5 them to the dark imprisonment of hell till judgement day: if he did not spare the ancient world but only saved Noah (the solitary voice that cried out for righteousness) and his seven companions when

6 he brought the flood upon the world in its wickedness; and if God reduced the entire cities of Sodom and Gomorrah to ashes (when he sentenced them to destruction as a fearful example to those who

7 wanted to live in defiance of his laws), and yet saved Lot the righteous man, in acute mental distress at the filthy lives of the

8 godless—Lot, remember, was a good man suffering spiritual

496

agonies day after day at what he saw and heard of their lawlessness —then you may be absolutely certain that the Lord knows how to rescue a good man surrounded by temptation, and how to reserve his punishment for the wicked until his day comes. *9*

Let me show you what these men are really like

His judgment is chiefly reserved for those who have indulged all *10* the foulness of their lower natures, and have nothing but contempt for authority. These men are arrogant and presumptuous—they think nothing of scoffing at the glories of the unseen world. Yet *11* even angels, who are their superiors in strength and power, do not bring insulting criticisms of such things before the Lord.

But these men, with no more sense than the unreasoning brute *12* beasts which are born to be caught and killed, scoff at things outside their own experience, and will most certainly be destroyed in their own corruption. Their wickedness has earned them an *13* evil end and they will be paid in full.

These are the men who delight in daylight self-indulgence; they are foul spots and blots, playing their tricks at your very dinner-tables. Their eyes cannot look at a woman without lust, they *14* captivate the unstable ones, and their technique of getting what they want is, through long practice, highly developed. They are born under a curse, for they have abandoned the right road and *15* wandered off to follow the old trail of Balaam, son of Beor, the man who had no objection to wickedness as long as he was paid for it. But he, you remember, was sharply reprimanded for his *16* wickedness—by a donkey, of all things, speaking with a human voice to check the prophet's wicked infatuation!

These men are like wells without a drop of water in them, like *17* the changing shapes of whirling storm-clouds, and their fate will be the black night of utter darkness. With their high-sounding *18* nonsense they use the sensual pull of the lower passions to attract those who were just on the point of cutting loose from their companions in misconduct. They promise them liberty. Liberty! *19* —when they themselves are bound hand and foot to utter depravity. For a man is the slave of whatever masters him. If men *20* have escaped from the world's contaminations through knowing our Lord and saviour Jesus Christ, and then become entangled and defeated all over again, their last position is far worse than their first. It would be better for them not to have known the *21* way of goodness at all, rather than after knowing it to turn their

22 backs on the sacred commandments given to them. Alas, for them, the old proverbs have come true about the "dog returning to his vomit", and "the sow that had been washed going back to wallow in the muck".

CHAPTER 3

God delays the last day, in his mercy

1 THIS is the second letter I have written to you, dear friends of mine, and in both of them I have tried to stimulate you, as men with minds uncontaminated by error, by simply reminding you

2 of what you really know already. For I want you to remember the words spoken of old by the holy prophets as well as the commands of our Lord and saviour given to you through his messengers.

3 First of all you must realise that in the last days mockers will undoubtedly come—men whose only guide in life is what they

4 want for themselves—and they will say, "What has happened to his promised coming? Since the first Christians fell asleep, everything remains exactly as it was since the beginning of creation!"

5 They are deliberately shutting their eyes to a fact that they know very well, that there were, by God's command, heavens in the old days and an earth formed out of the water and surrounded

6 by water. It was by water that the world of those days was deluged

7 and destroyed, but the present heavens and earth are, also by God's command, being carefully kept and maintained for the fire of the day of judgment and the destruction of wicked men.

8 But you should never lose sight of this fact, dear friends, that time is not the same with the Lord as it is with us—to him a day

9 may be a thousand years, and a thousand years only a day. It is not that he is dilatory about keeping his own promise as some men seem to think; the fact is that he is very patient towards you. He has no wish that any man should be destroyed. He wishes

10 that all men should come to repent. Yet it remains true that the day of the Lord will come as suddenly and unexpectedly as a thief. In that day the heavens will disappear in a terrific tearing blast, the very elements will disintegrate in heat and the earth and all that is in it will be burnt up to nothing.

Never lose sight of the eternal world

11 In view of the fact that all these things are to be dissolved, what

498

sort of people ought you to be? Surely men of good and holy
character, who live expecting and earnestly longing for the coming   12
of the day of God. True, this day will mean that the heavens will
disappear in fire and the elements disintegrate in fearful heat, but   13
our hopes are set not on these but on the new Heavens and the
new earth which he has promised us, and in which nothing but
good shall live.

Because, my dear friends, you have a hope like this before   14
you, I urge you to make certain that such a day would find you
at peace with God and man, clean and blameless in his sight.
Meanwhile, consider that God's patience is meant to be man's   15
salvation, as our dear brother Paul pointed out in his letter to you,
written out of the wisdom God gave him. In that letter, as indeed   16
in all his letters, he referred to these matters. There are, of course,
some things in his letters which are difficult to understand, and
which, unhappily, ill-informed and unbalanced people distort (as
they do the other scriptures), and bring disaster on their own heads.

But you, my friends whom I love, are forewarned, and should   17
therefore be very careful not to be carried away by the errors of
wicked men and so lose your proper foothold. On the contrary,   18
you should grow in grace and in your knowledge of our Lord
and saviour Jesus Christ—to him be glory now and until the
dawning of the day of eternity!

The First Letter of John

AUTHOR. *John, one of the original Twelve, or John the Elder, a close
companion of his. It is believed that he wrote it from Ephesus,
when a very old man.*

DATE. *Uncertain, possibly about* 90.

DESTINATION. *Augustine refers to this letter as "The Epistle of John
to the Parthians", but there is no other evidence of a church in what
would now be called Persia or Iran. Many scholars think that this
letter is addressed to the local churches round about Ephesus.*

THEME. *This letter emphasises the fact that Christ really did become
man, and did not merely "appear" to be human as the heresy of
"docetism" maintained. It speaks in the strongest possible language
of men being able to live "in" God, and of the fact of God being
"in" those who believe in him. God is light and love and life.*

CHAPTER 1

1 WE are writing to you about something which has always existed yet which we ourselves actually saw and heard: something which we had opportunity to observe closely and even to hold in our hands, and yet, as we know now, was something of the very Word

2 of life himself! For it was *life* which appeared before us: we saw it, we are eye-witnesses of it, and are now writing to you about it. It was the very life of all ages, the life that has always existed with the Father, which actually became visible in person to us

3 mortal men. We repeat, we really saw and heard what we are now writing to you about. We want you to be with us in this —in this fellowship with the Father, and Jesus Christ his Son.

4 We must write and tell you about it, because the more that fellowship extends the greater the joy it brings to us who are already in it.

Experience of living "in the light"

5 Here, then, is the message which we heard from him, and now proclaim to you: GOD IS LIGHT and no shadow of darkness

6 can exist in him. Consequently, if we were to say that we enjoyed fellowship with him and still went on living in darkness, we should

7 be both telling and living a lie. But if we really are living in the same light in which he eternally exists, then we have true fellowship with each other, and the blood which his Son shed for us

8 keeps us clean from all sin. If we refuse to admit that we are sinners, then we live in a world of illusion and truth becomes a

9 stranger to us. But if we freely admit that we have sinned, we find God utterly reliable and straightforward—he forgives our sins and

10 makes us thoroughly clean from all that is evil. For if we take up the attitude "we have not sinned", we flatly deny God's diagnosis of our condition and cut ourselves off from what he has to say to us.

CHAPTER 2

Love and obedience are essentials for living in the light

I WRITE these things to you (may I call you "my children"—for *1*
that's how I think of you), to help you to avoid sin. But if a man
should sin, remember that our advocate before the Father is Jesus
Christ the righteous, the one who made personal atonement for *2*
our sins (and for those of the rest of the world as well). It is only *3*
when we obey God's laws that we can be quite sure that we really
know him. The man who claims to know God but does not obey *4*
his laws is not only a liar but lives in self-delusion. In practice, the *5*
more a man learns to obey God's laws the more truly and fully
does he express his love for him. Obedience is the test of whether
we really live "in God" or not. The life of a man who professes *6*
to be living in God must bear the stamp of Christ.

I am not really writing to tell you of any new command, *7*
brothers of mine. It is the old, original command which you had
at the beginning; it is the old message which you have heard
before. And yet as I give it to you again I know that it is true—in *8*
your life as it was in his. For the darkness is beginning to lift and
the true light is now shining in the world. Anyone who claims to *9*
be "in the light" and hates his brother is, in fact, still in complete
darkness. The man who loves his brother lives and moves in the *10*
light, and has no reason to stumble. But the man who hates his *11*
brother is shut off from the light and gropes his way in the dark
without seeing where he is going. To move in the dark is to move
blindfold.

As I write I visualise you, my children

I write this letter to you all, as my dear children, because your *12*
sins are forgiven for his name's sake. I write to you who are *13*
now fathers, because you have known him who has always
existed. And to you vigorous young men I am writing because
you have been strong in defeating the evil one. Yes, I have written
these lines to you all, dear children, because you know the Father;
to you fathers because of your experience of the one who has *14*
always existed, and to you young men because you have all the
vigour of youth, because you have a hold on God's truth and
because you have defeated the evil one.

See "the world" for what it is

15 Never give your hearts to this world or to any of the things in
it. A man cannot love the Father and love the world at the same
16 time. For the whole world-system, based as it is on men's primitive
desires, their greedy ambitions and the glamour of all that they
think splendid, is not derived from the Father at all, but from the
17 world itself. The world and all its passionate desires will one day
disappear. But the man who is following God's will is part of the
permanent and cannot die.

Little anti-christs are abroad already

18 Even now, dear children, we are getting near the end of things.
You have heard, I expect, the prophecy about the coming of
anti-Christ. Believe me, there are anti-christs about already, which
19 confirms my belief that we are near the end. These men went out
from our company, it is true, but they never really belonged to it.
If they had really belonged to us they would have stayed. In fact,
their going proves beyond doubt that men like that were not
"our men" at all.

Be on your guard against error

20, 21 God has given you all a certain amount of spiritual insight, and
indeed I have not written this warning as if I were writing to men
who don't know what error is. I write because your eyes are clear
22 enough to discern a lie when you come across it. And what, I
ask you, is the crowning lie? Surely the denial that Jesus is God's
anointed one, his Christ. I say, therefore, that any man who refuses
23 to acknowledge the Father and the Son is an anti-christ. The man
who will not recognise the Son cannot possibly know the Father;
yet the man who believes in the Son will find that he knows the
Father as well.

24 For yourselves I beg you to stick to the original teaching. If
you do, you will be living in fellowship with both the Father and
25 the Son. And that means sharing his own life for ever, as he has
promised.

26 It is true that I felt I had to write the above about men who
27 would dearly love to lead you astray. Yet I know that the touch
of his Spirit never leaves you, and you don't really need a human
teacher. You know that his Spirit teaches you about all things,
always telling you the truth and never telling you a lie. So, as he
28 has taught you, live continually in him. Yes, now, little children

remember to live continually in him. So that if he were suddenly to reveal himself we should still know exactly where we stand, and should not have to shrink away from his presence.

What it means to be sons of God

You all know that God is really good. You may be just as sure that the man who leads a really good life is a true child of God. *29*

CHAPTER 3

CONSIDER the incredible love that the Father has shown us in allowing us to be called "children of God"—and that is not just what we are called, but what we *are*. Our heredity on the God-ward side is no mere figure of speech—which explains why the world will no more recognise us than it recognised Christ. *1*

Oh, dear children of mine (forgive the affection of an old man!), have you realised it? Here and now we *are* God's children. We don't know what we shall become in the future. We only know that, if reality were to break through, we should reflect his like-ness, for we should see him as he really is! *2*

Everyone who has at heart a hope like that keeps himself pure, for he knows how pure Christ is. *3*

Conduct will show who is a man's spiritual father

Everyone who commits sin breaks God's law, for that is what sin is, by definition—a breaking of God's law. You know, moreover, that Christ became man for the purpose of removing sin, and that he himself was quite free from sin. The man who lives "in Christ" does not habitually sin. The regular sinner has never seen or known him. You, my children, are younger than I am, and I don't want you to be taken in by any clever talk just here. The man who lives a consistently good life is a good man, as surely as God is good. But the man whose life is habitually sin-ful is spiritually a son of the devil, for the devil is behind all sin, as he always has been. Now the Son of God came to earth with the express purpose of liquidating the devil's activities. The man who is really God's son does not practise sin, for God's nature is in him, for good, and such a heredity is incapable of sin. *4* *5* *6* *7* *8* *9*

10   Here we have a clear indication as to who are the children of
God and who are the children of the devil. The man who does
not lead a good life is no son of God, nor is the man who fails
11   to love his brother. For the original command, as you know, is that
12   we should love one another. We are none of us to have the spirit
of Cain, who was a son of the devil and murdered his brother.
Have you realised his motive? It was just because he realised the
13   goodness of his brother's life and the rottenness of his own. Don't
be surprised, therefore, if the world hates you.

Love and life are inter-connected

14   We know that we have crossed the frontier from death to life
because we do love our brothers. The man without love for his
15   brother is living in death already. The man who actively hates his
brother is a potential murderer, and you will readily see that the
eternal life of God cannot live in the heart of a murderer.
16   We know and, to some extent realise, the love of God for us
because Christ expressed it in laying down his life for us. We must
in turn express our love by laying down our lives for those who
17   are our brothers. But as for the well-to-do man who sees his
brother in want but shuts his eyes—and his heart—how could
18   anyone believe that the love of God lives in him? My children,
let us love not merely in theory or in words—let us love in
sincerity and in practice!

Living in love means confidence in God

19   If we live like this, we shall know that we are children of the
20   truth and can reassure ourselves in the sight of God, even if our
own hearts make us feel guilty. For God is infinitely greater than
21   our hearts, and he knows everything. And if, dear friends of mine,
when we realise this our hearts no longer accuse us, we may have
22   the utmost confidence in God's presence. We receive whatever
we ask for, because we are obeying his orders and following his
23   plans. His orders are that we should put our trust in the name of
his Son, Jesus Christ, and love one another—as we used to hear
him say in person.
24   The man who does obey God's commands lives in God and
God lives in him, and the guarantee of his presence within us is
the Spirit he has given us.

504

CHAPTER 4

I repeat my warning against false teaching

DON'T trust every spirit, dear friends of mine, but test them to *1*
discover whether they come from God or not. For the world is
full of false prophets. You can test them in this simple way: every *2*
spirit that acknowledges the fact that Jesus Christ actually became
man, comes from God, but the spirit which denies this fact does *3*
not come from God. The latter comes from the anti-Christ,
which you were warned would come and which is already in the
world.

You, my children, who belong to God have already defeated *4*
this spirit, because the one who lives in you is far stronger than the
anti-Christ in the world. The agents of the anti-Christ are children *5*
of the world, they speak the world's language and the world, of
course, pays attention to what they say. We are God's children *6*
and only the man who knows God hears our message; what we
say means nothing to the man who is not himself a child of God.

This gives us a ready means of distinguishing the true from the
false.

Let us love: God has shown us love at its highest

To you whom I love I say, let us go on loving one another, *7*
for love comes from God. Every man who truly loves is God's
son and has some knowledge of him. But the man who does not *8*
love cannot know him at all, for God is love.

To us, the greatest demonstration of God's love for us has been *9*
his sending his only Son into the world to give us life through
him. We see real love, not in the fact that we loved God, but that *10*
he loved us and sent his Son to make personal atonement for our
sins. If God loved us as much as that, surely we, in our turn, *11*
should love each other!

It is true that no human being has ever had a direct vision of *12*
God. Yet if we love each other God does actually live within us,
and his love grows in us towards perfection. And, as I wrote *13*
above, the guarantee of our living in him and his living in us
is the share of his own Spirit which he gives us.

Knowing Christ means more love and confidence, less and less fear

We ourselves are eye-witnesses able and willing to testify to the *14*

15 fact that the Father did send the Son to save the world. Everyone
who acknowledges that Jesus is the Son of God finds that God
16 lives in him, and he lives in God. So have we come to know and
trust the love God has for us. God *is* love, and the man whose life
is lived in love does, in fact, live in God, and God does, in fact, live
17 in him. So our love for him grows more and more, filling us
with complete confidence for the day when he shall judge all
men—for we realise that our life in this world is actually his life
18 lived in us. Love contains no fear—indeed fully-developed love
expels every particle of fear, for fear always contains some of the
torture of feeling guilty. This means that the man who lives in
fear has not yet had his love perfected.
19, 20 Yes, we love him because he first loved us. If a man says, "I love
God" and hates his brother, he is a liar. For if he does not love the
brother before his eyes how can he love the one beyond his sight?
21 And in any case it is his explicit command that the one who loves
God must love his brother too.

CHAPTER 5

*Only real faith in Christ as God's son can make a man confident,
obedient and loving*

1 EVERYONE who really believes that Jesus is the Christ proves
himself one of God's family. The man who loves the Father cannot help loving the Father's own Son.
2 The test of the genuineness of our love for God's family lies
in this question—do we love God himself and do we obey his
3 commands? For loving God means obeying his commands, and
4 these commands of his are not burdensome, for God's "heredity"
within us will always conquer the world outside us. In fact, this
faith of ours is the only way in which the world has been con-
5 quered. For who could ever be said to conquer the world, in the
true sense, except the man who really believes that Jesus is God's
6 Son? Jesus Christ himself is the one who came by water and by
blood—not by the water only, but by the water and the blood.
7 The Spirit bears witness to this, for the Spirit is the truth. The
8 witness therefore is a triple one—the Spirit in our own hearts,
the signs of the water of baptism and the blood of atonement—

506

and they all say the same thing. If we are prepared to accept 9
human testimony, God's own testimony concerning his own Son
is surely infinitely more valuable. The man who really believes in 10
the Son of God will find God's testimony in his own heart. The
man who will not believe God is making him out to be a liar,
because he is deliberately refusing to accept the testimony that
God has given concerning his own Son. This is, that God has 11
given men eternal life and this real life is to be found only in his 12
Son. It follows naturally that any man who has genuine contact
with Christ has this life; and if he has not, then he does not
possess this life at all.

I have written like this to you who already believe in the name 13
of God's Son so that you may be quite sure that, here and now,
you possess eternal life. We have such confidence in him that we 14
are certain that he hears every request that is made in accord with
his own plan. And since we know that he invariably gives his 15
attention to our prayers, whatever they are about, we can be
quite sure that our prayers will be answered.

Help each other to live without sin

If any of you should see his brother committing a sin (I don't 16
mean deliberately turning his back on God and embracing evil),
he should pray to God for him and secure fresh life for the sinner.
It is possible to commit sin that is a deliberate embracing of evil
and that leads to spiritual death—that is not the sort of sin I have
in mind when I recommend prayer for the sinner. Every failure 17
to obey God's laws is sin, of course, but there is sin that does not
preclude repentance and forgiveness.

Our certain knowledge

We know that the true child of God does not sin, he is in the 18
charge of God's own Son and the evil one must keep his distance.
We know that we ourselves are children of God, and we also 19
know that the world around us is under the power of the evil
one. We know too that the Son of God has actually come to this 20
world, and has shown us the way to know the one who is true.
We know that our real life is in the true one, and in his Son
Jesus Christ. This is the real God and this is real, eternal life.

But be on your guard, my dear children, against every false god! 21

JOHN.

The Second Letter of John

AUTHOR. *Although the author calls himself simply "the Elder" there is no real reason to suppose that he is not the same person as the author of the first letter. An old "retired apostle" might in his humility call himself by such a title.*

DATE. *Uncertain, possibly 90.*

DESTINATION. *Either a Christian lady and her family, or a church and its members. Nobody now knows which.*

THEME. *This brief letter expresses the writer's joy at the true faith exhibited by some members of the family he has met. He urges them to continue in Christian love and to set their faces sternly against teachers of a false Christianity.*

1 THIS letter comes from the Elder to a certain Christian lady and her children, held in the highest affection not only by me but by
2 all who know the truth. For that truth's sake (which even now we
3 know and which will be our companion for ever) I wish you, in all love and sincerity, grace, mercy and peace from God the Father and the Lord Jesus Christ, the Father's Son.

Let us love, but have no dealings with lies

4 I was overjoyed to find some of your children living the life of
5 truth, as the Father himself instructed us. I beg you now, dear lady, not as though I were issuing any new order but simply reminding you of the original one, to see that we continue to
6 love one another. Real love means obeying the Father's orders, and you have known from the beginning that you must live in
7 obedience to him. For the world is becoming full of impostors—men who will not admit that Jesus the Christ really became man.
8 Now this is the very spirit of deceit and is anti-Christ. Take care of yourselves; don't throw away all the labour that has been spent on you, but persevere till God gives you your reward.

Have nothing to do with false teachers

9 The man who is so "advanced" that he is not content with what

508

Christ taught, has in fact no God. The man who bases his life on Christ's teaching, however, has both the Father and the Son as his God. If any teacher comes to you who is disloyal to what **10** Christ taught, don't have him inside your house. Don't even wish him "God-speed", unless you want to share in the evil that he is **11** doing.

Personal

I have a lot that I could write to you, but somehow I find it **12** hard to put down on paper. I hope to come and see you personally, and we will have a heart-to-heart talk together—and how we shall enjoy that! Your sister's children send their love.

JOHN.   **13**

The Third Letter of John

AUTHOR. *The same author as the Second Letter of John.*
DATE. *Uncertain, possibly about* 90.
DESTINATION. *The letter is addressed personally to Gaius, possibly the leader of a small church in Asia Minor. Gaius was such a common name that it is impossible to say whether the reference is to any of those of that name mentioned elsewhere in the New Testament.*
THEME. *The letter deals with the Christian duty and privilege of entertaining those who are busy carrying the Gospel from place to place. It roundly condemns the conceited behaviour of Diotrephes and commends the excellent character of Demetrius.*

THE ELDER sends this personal letter to his very dear friend Gaius **1** with love in the truth.

I thank God for you and pray for you

My heartfelt prayer for you, my very dear friend, is that you **2** may be as healthy and prosperous in every way as you are in soul. I was delighted when the brothers arrived and spoke so **3** highly of the sincerity of your life—obviously you are living in the truth. Nothing brings me greater joy nowadays than hearing **4** that "my children" are living "in the truth".

Your actions have been just right

5 You are doing a fine faithful piece of work, dear friend, in looking after the brothers who come your way, especially when
6 you have never seen them before. They have testified to your love before the Church. It is a fine thing to help them on their way—
7 it shows you realise the importance of what they are doing. They set out on this work, as you know, for the sake of "the name" and
8 they accept no help from non-Christians. We ought to give such men a real welcome and prove that we too are co-operating with the truth.

I know about Diotrephes

9 I did write a letter to the church, but Diotrephes, who wants
10 to be head of everything, does not recognise us! If I do come to you, I shall not forget his actions nor the slanderous things he has said against us. And it doesn't stop there, alas, for although he wants to be leader he refuses the duty of welcoming the brothers himself, and stops those who would like to do so—he even excommunicates them!

A little piece of advice: and I shall soon be seeing you personally

11 Never let evil be your example, dear friend of mine, but always good. The man who does good is God's man, but the man who does evil does not know God at all.
12 Everyone has a good word to say for Demetrius, and the very truth speaks well of him. He has our warm recommendation also, and you know you can trust what we say about anyone.
13 There is a great deal I want to say to you but I can't put it
14 down in black and white. I hope to see you before long, and we will have a heart-to-heart talk. Peace be with you. All our friends here send love: please give ours personally to all our friends at your end.

JOHN.

510

The Letter of Jude

AUTHOR. *It may still reasonably be held that this letter was written by Jude (Judas), the brother or step-brother of Jesus. Like his brother James, he did not believe in the divinity of Jesus until after the Resurrection.*

DATE. *Between 70 and 80, or, if not written by Jude, possibly as late as 2nd century.*

DESTINATION. *Some unknown church, where false teaching was prevalent, or possibly for general circulation.*

THEME. *This letter is almost entirely a terrific condemnation of false teachers, with scathing comparisons with evil characters in the Old Testament. It concludes with an exhortation to loyalty to the truth, and with the well-known "doxology".*

JUDE, a servant of Jesus Christ and brother of James, to those 1 who have obeyed the call, who are loved by God the Father and kept in the faith by Jesus Christ—may you ever experience more 2 and more of mercy, peace and love!

The reason for this letter

I fully intended, dear friends, to write to you about our common 3 salvation, but I feel compelled to make my letter to you an earnest appeal to put up a real fight for the faith which has been once and for all committed to those who belong to Christ. For there are 4 men who have surreptitiously entered the Church but who have for a long time been heading straight for the condemnation I shall plainly give them. They have no real reverence for God, and they abuse his grace as an opportunity for immorality. They will not recognise the only master, Jesus Christ our Lord.

Past history warns us that the unfaithful have mingled with the faithful

I want to remind you of something that you really know already: 5 and although the Lord saved all the people from the land of

Egypt, yet afterwards he brought to their downfall those who
6 would not trust him. And the very angels who failed in their high
duties and abandoned their proper sphere have been deprived by
God of both light and liberty until the judgment of the great day.
7 Sodom and Gomorrah and the adjacent cities who, in the same
way as these men today, gave themselves up to sexual immorality
and perversion, stand in their punishment as a permanent warning
8 of the fire of judgment. Yet these men are defiling their bodies
by their filthy fantasies in just the same way; they show utter
contempt for authority and make a jest of the heavenly glories.
9 But I would remind you that even the archangel Michael when
he was contending with the devil in the dispute over the body of
Moses did not dare to condemn him with mockery. He simply
said, the Lord rebuke you!
10 These fellows, however, are ready to mock at anything that is
beyond their immediate knowledge, while in the things that they
know by instinct like unreasoning beasts they have become utterly
11 depraved. I say, Woe to them! For they have taken the road of
Cain; for what they could get they have rushed into the same error
as Balaam; they have destroyed themselves by rebelling against
God as did Korah long ago.

Be on your guard against these wicked men

12 These men are a menace to the good-fellowship of your feasts,
for they eat in your company without a qualm yet they care for
no one but themselves. They are like clouds driven up by the wind,
but they bring no rain. They are like trees with the leaves of
autumn but without a single fruit—they are doubly dead for they
13 have no roots either. They are like raging waves of the sea producing only the spume of their own shameful deeds. They are
like stars which follow no orbit, and their proper place is the
14 everlasting blackness of the regions beyond the light. It was of
men like these that Enoch (seventh descendant from Adam)
prophesied when he said:
Behold, the Lord came with ten thousands of his holy ones,
15 to execute judgment upon all, and to convict all the ungodly
of all their works of ungodliness which they have ungodly
wrought, and of all the hard things which ungodly sinners
have spoken against him.
16 These are the men who complain and curse their fate while trying
all the time to mould life according to their own desires. They

"talk big" but will pay men great respect if it is to their own advantage.

Forewarned is forearmed

Now do remember, dear friends, the words that the messengers [17] of Jesus Christ gave us beforehand when they said "there will [18] come in the last days mockers who live according to their own Godless desires". These are the men who split communities, for [19] they are led by human emotions and never by the Spirit of God.

Look after your own faith: save whom you can

But you, dear friends of mine, build yourselves up on the [20] foundation of your most holy faith and by praying through the Holy Spirit keep yourselves within the love of God. Wait patiently [21] for the mercy of our Lord Jesus Christ which will bring you to the life eternal. For some of these men you can feel pity and you can [22] treat them differently. Others you must try to save by fear, snatch- [23] ing them as it were out of the fire while hating the very garments their deeds have befouled.

Ascription

Now to him who is able to keep you from falling and to present [24] you before his glory without fault and with unspeakable joy, to [25] the only God, our saviour, be glory and majesty, power and authority, through Jesus Christ our Lord, before time was, now, and in all ages to come, amen.

JUDE.

THE YOUNG CHURCHES

DALMATIA

ROME
A.D. 57

MACEDONIA

THESSALONICA
A.D. 50-51

PHILIPPI
A.D. 62

Troas

Nicopolis

CORINTH A.D. 56,57

Cenchrea

ACHAIA

CRETE
(To Titus)
A.D. 66

BITHYNIA AND PONTUS

CAPPADOCIA

ASIA

GALATIA
A.D. 56 OR 57

EPHESUS
A.D. 62
(To Timothy)
A.D. 66

• Lystra
• Antioch of Pisidia

• Hierapolis

Laodicea •

COLOSSAE
A.D. 62 (Philemon)

Tarsus •

Miletus •

• Antioch

• Jerusalem

Miles

0   100   200   300   400   500

THE BOOK OF REVELATION

The Revelation of John

AUTHOR. *John the Apostle, John the Elder or another leading Christian by the name of John.*

(Justin Martyr in his "Dialogue with Trypho the Jew", written about 140, appears to ascribe the authorship of this book to John the Apostle. But Dionysius, Bishop of Alexandria from 249 to 265, a learned and holy man, could not accept John the Apostle as the author of this Revelation, and gave almost conclusive reasons for his opinion. Since those early days there has been much argument, and much research has gone into the problem of establishing authorship but without conclusive result. It is essential that the reader should study a good commentary on the subject of authorship, so that he may appreciate the difficulties involved.)

DATE. *Probably about 95, but some hold to an earlier date.*

DESTINATION. *This book is plainly intended primarily for the seven Churches of Asia. But since the message of the book is relevant to all Christians under persecution, and since the book treats of divine judgments upon the whole world, the author must surely have intended it to be circulated among all Christian communities.*

THEME. *This book consists of a series of visions granted to John while in exile for his Christian witness. The language is highly symbolic and figurative, and attempts in modern days to fit its prophecies into contemporary situations have led interpreters into all kinds of difficulties. It is thought by many that the symbols and figures of the book would be understood by the Christians to whom the book was first sent, but that the key to their interpretation has now been lost. However, certain themes emerge distinctly for the modern reader's profit:*

(1) *The absolute sovereignty of God, and his ultimate purpose to destroy all forms of evil.*

(2) *The inevitable judgments of God upon evil, upon the worship of false gods, which include riches, power and success.*

(3) *The necessity for patient endurance, the ultimate security being the knowledge that God is in control of history.*

516

(4) *The existence of reality, represented here under such symbols as the New Jerusalem, apart and secure from the battles and tribulations of earthly life, promises complete spiritual security to those who are faithful to God and his Christ.*

(5) *The glimpses of worship and adoration, constantly offered to God and the Lamb, are a kind of pattern of man's ultimate acknowledgment of the character of God when he sees him as he is.*

But for any proper appreciation of the themes of this mysterious book it is imperative that the reader should make use of one or more commentaries.

CHAPTER 1

Concerning this book

THIS is a Revelation from Jesus Christ, which God gave him so 1 that he might show his servants what must very soon take place. He made it known by sending his angel to his servant John, who 2 is the witness of all that he saw—the message of God, and the testimony of Jesus Christ.

Happy is the man who reads this prophecy and happy are those 3 who hear it read and pay attention to its message; for the time is near.

John's greeting and ascription

John, to the seven Churches in Asia: 4

Grace and peace be to you from him who is and who was and who is coming, from the seven Spirits before his throne, and from 5 Jesus Christ the faithful witness, first-born of the dead, and ruler of kings upon earth. To him who loves us and has set us free from our sins through his own blood, who has made us a kingdom of 6 priests to his God and Father, to him be glory and power for timeless ages, amen!

See, he is coming in the clouds and every eye shall see him, 7 even those who pierced him, and his coming will mean bitter sorrow to every tribe upon the earth. So let it be!

"I am Alpha and Omega," says the Lord God, "who is and 8 who was and who is coming, the Almighty."

The message to the seven Churches

I, John, who am your brother and your companion in the 9

distress, the kingdom and the faithful endurance to which Jesus calls us, was on the island called Patmos because I had spoken

10 God's message and borne witness to Jesus. On the Lord's day I knew myself inspired by the Spirit, and I heard from behind me

11 a voice loud as a trumpet-call, saying,

"Write down in a book what you see, and send it to the seven Churches—to Ephesus, Smyrna, Pergamum, Thyatira, Sardis, Philadelphia and Laodicea!"

12 I turned to see whose voice it was that was speaking to me and

13 when I had turned I saw seven golden lampstands, and among these lampstands I saw someone like a Son of Man. He was dressed in

14 a long robe with a golden girdle around his breast; his head and his hair were white as snow-white wool, his eyes blazed like fire,

15 and his feet shone as the finest bronze glows in the furnace. His

16 voice had the sound of a great waterfall, and I saw that in his right hand he held seven stars. A sharp two-edged sword came out of his mouth, and his face was ablaze like the sun at its height.

17 When my eyes took in this sight I fell at his feet like a dead man. And then he placed his right hand upon me and said,

18 "Do not be afraid. I am the first and the last, the living one. I am he who was dead, and now you see me alive for timeless ages!

19 I hold in my hand the keys of death and the grave. Therefore, write down what you have seen, both the things which are now,

20 and the things which are to be hereafter. The secret meaning of the seven stars which you saw in my right hand, and of the seven golden lampstands is this: the seven stars are the angels of the seven Churches and the seven lampstands are the Churches themselves."

CHAPTER 2

(i) To the loveless Church

1 "WRITE this to the angel of the Church in Ephesus:

These words are spoken by the one who holds the seven stars safe in his right hand, and who walks among the seven golden

2 lampstands. I know what you have done; I know how hard you have worked and what you have endured. I know that you will not tolerate wicked men, that you have put to the test self-styled 'apostles', who are nothing of the sort, and have found them to

3 be liars. I know your powers of endurance—how you have suffered

4 for the sake of my name and have not grown weary. But I hold

this against you, that you do not love as you did at first. Remem- 5
ber then how far you have fallen. Repent and live as you lived
at first. Otherwise, if your heart remains unchanged, I shall come
to you and remove your lampstand from its place.

Yet you have this to your credit, that you hate the practices of 6
the Nicolaitans, which I myself detest. Let every listener hear what 7
the Spirit says to the Churches:

To the victorious I will give the right to eat from the tree of
life which grows in the paradise of God.

(ii) To the persecuted Church

"Write this to the angel of the Church in Smyrna: 8

These words are spoken by the first and the last, who died and
came to life again. I know of your tribulation and of your poverty 9
—though in fact you are rich! I know how you are slandered by
those who call themselves Jews, but in fact are no Jews but a
synagogue of Satan. Have no fear of what you will suffer. I tell 10
you now that the devil is going to cast some of your number into
prison where your faith will be tested and your distress will last
for ten days. Be faithful in the face of death and I will give you
the crown of life. Let every listener hear what the Spirit says to 11
the Churches:

The victorious cannot suffer the slightest hurt from the second
death.

(iii) To the over-tolerant Church

"Write this to the angel of the Church in Pergamum: 12

These words are spoken by him who has the sharp two-edged
sword. I know where you live—where Satan sits enthroned. I 13
know that you hold fast to my name and that you never denied
your faith in me even in the days when Antipas, my faithful
witness, was martyred before your eyes in the very house of Satan.

Yet I have a few things against you—some of your number 14
cling to the teaching of Balaam, the man who taught Balak how
to entice the children of Israel into eating meat sacrificed to idols
and into sexual immorality. I have also against you the fact that 15
among your number are some who hold just as closely to the
teaching of the Nicolaitans. Repent then, or else I shall come to 16
you quickly and make war upon them with the sword of my
mouth. Let the listener hear what the Spirit says to the Churches: 17

I will give the victorious some of the hidden manna, and I will also give him a white stone with a new name written upon it which no man knows except the man who receives it.

(iv) To the compromising Church

18 "Write this to the angel of the Church in Thyatira:

These are the words of the Son of God whose eyes blaze like fire and whose feet shine like the finest bronze:

19 I know what you have done. I know of your love and your loyalty, your service and your endurance. Moreover, I know that
20 you are doing more than you did at first. But I have this against you, that you tolerate that woman Jezebel who calls herself a prophetess, but who by her teaching deceives my servants into
21 sexual immorality and eating idols'-meat. I have given her time to repent but she has shown no desire to repent of her immorality.
22 See, now, how I throw her into bed and her lovers with her, and I will send them terrible suffering unless they repent of what she
23 has done. As for her children, I shall strike them dead. Then all the Churches will know that I am the one who searches men's hearts and minds, and that I will reward each one of you according to your deeds.

24 But for the rest of you at Thyatira, who do not hold this teaching, and have not learned what they call 'the deep things of
25 Satan', I will lay no further burden upon you, except that you hold on to what you have until I come!

26 To the one who is victorious, who carries out my work to the
27 end, I will give authority over the nations, just as I myself have
28 received authority from my Father, and I will give him the morning star. He shall 'shepherd them with a rod of iron'; he shall
29 'dash them in pieces like a potter's vessel'. Let the listener hear what the Spirit says to the Churches.

CHAPTER 3

(v) To the sleeping Church

1 "Write this to the angel of the Church in Sardis:

These are the words of him who holds in his hand the seven Spirits of God and the seven stars:

I know what you have done, that you have a reputation for
2 being alive, but that in fact you are dead. Now wake up! Strengthen what you still have before it dies! For I have not found any

of your deeds complete in the sight of my God. Remember then   **3**
what you were given and what you were taught. Hold to those
things and repent. If you refuse to wake up, then I will come to you
like a thief, and you will have no idea of the hour of my coming.

Yet you still have a few names in Sardis of people who have   **4**
not soiled their garments. They shall walk with me in white, for
they have deserved to do so. The victorious shall wear such white   **5**
garments, and never will I erase his name from the book of life.
Indeed, I will speak his name openly in the presence of my Father
and of his angels. Let the listener hear what the Spirit says to the   **6**
Churches.

(vi) To the Church with opportunity

"Then write this to the angel of the Church in Philadelphia: **7**
These are the words of the holy one and the true, who holds the
key of David, who opens and no man shall shut, and who shuts
and no man shall open. I know what you have done. See, I have   **8**
given you a door flung wide open, which no man can close! For
you have some little power and have been faithful to my message
and have not denied my name. See how I deal with those of   **9**
Satan's synagogue, who claim to be Jews, yet are no Jews but
liars! Watch how I make them come and bow down before your
feet and acknowledge that I have loved you. Because you have   **10**
obeyed my call to patient endurance I will keep you safe from the
hour of trial which is to come upon the whole world, to test all
who live upon the earth. I am coming soon; hold fast to what you   **11**
have—let no one deprive you of your crown. As for the victorious,   **12**
I will make him a pillar in the Temple of my God, and he will
never leave it. I will write upon him the name of my God, and
the name of the city of my God, the new Jerusalem which comes
down out of Heaven from my God. And I will write upon him
my own new name. Let the listener hear what the Spirit says to   **13**
the Churches.

(vii) To the complacent Church

"Then write this to the angel of the Church in Laodicea: **14**
These are the words of the Amen, the faithful and true witness,
the beginning of God's creation:

I know what you have done, and that you are neither cold nor   **15**
hot. I could wish that you were either cold or hot! But since you   **16**
are lukewarm and neither hot nor cold, I intend to spit you out

17 of my mouth! While you say, 'I am rich, I have prospered, and there is nothing that I need', you have no eyes to see that you are
18 wretched, pitiable, poverty-stricken, blind and naked. My advice to you is to buy from me that gold which is purified in the furnace so that you may be rich, and white garments to wear so that you may hide the shame of your nakedness, and salve to put on your
19 eyes to make you see. All those whom I love I correct and dis-
20 cipline. Therefore, shake off your complacency and repent. See, I stand knocking at the door. If anyone listens to my voice and opens the door, I will go into his house and dine with him, and
21 he with me. As for the victorious, I will give him the honour of sitting beside me on my throne, just as I myself have won the victory and have taken my seat beside my Father on his throne.
22 Let the listener hear what the Spirit says to the Churches."

CHAPTER 4

The vision of Heaven

1 LATER I looked again, and before my eyes a door stood open in Heaven, and in my ears was the voice with the ring of a trumpet, which I had heard at first, speaking to me and saying,

"Come up here, and I will show you what must happen in the future."

2 Immediately I knew myself to be inspired by the Spirit, and in my vision I saw that a throne had been set up in Heaven, and there
3 was someone seated upon the throne. His appearance blazed like diamond and topaz, and all around the throne shone a halo like
4 an emerald rainbow. In a circle around the throne there were twenty-four thrones and seated upon them twenty-four elders
5 dressed in white with golden crowns upon their heads. From the central throne come flashes of lightning, noises and peals of thunder. Seven lamps are burning before the throne, and they are
6 the seven Spirits of God. In front of the throne there appears a sea of glass as clear as crystal. On each side, encircling the throne, are four living creatures covered with eyes in front and behind.
7 The first living creature is like a lion, the second is like a calf, the third has a face like a man, and the fourth living creature appears
8 like an eagle in flight. These four creatures have each of them six wings and are covered with eyes, all around them, and even within them. Day and night they never cease to say,

"Holy, holy, holy is the Lord God, the Almighty, who was and who is and who is coming."

The ceaseless worship of Heaven

And whenever the living creatures give glory and honour and
thanksgiving to the one who sits upon the throne, who lives for
timeless ages, the twenty-four elders prostrate themselves before
him who is seated upon the throne and worship the one who lives
for timeless ages. They cast their crowns before the throne and say,

"Thou art worthy, O Lord our God, to receive glory and
honour and power, for thou didst create all things; by thy will
they existed and were created."

CHAPTER 5

The sealed book of future events

THEN I noticed in the right hand of the one seated upon the
throne a book filled with writing both inside and on its back, and
it was sealed with seven seals. And I saw a mighty angel who
called out in a loud voice,

"Who is fit to open the book and break its seals?"

And no one in Heaven or upon earth or under the earth was
able to open the book, or even to look at it. I began to weep
bitterly because no one could be found fit to open the book, or
even to look at it, when one of the elders said to me,

"Do not weep. See, the lion from the tribe of Judah, the root
of David, has won the victory and is able to open the book and
break its seven seals."

Then, standing in the very centre of the throne and of the four
living creatures and of the elders, I saw a Lamb that seemed to
have been slaughtered. He had seven horns and seven eyes, which
are the seven Spirits of God and are sent out into every corner of
the earth. Then he came and took the book from the right hand
of him who was seated upon the throne.

The new hymn of the created and of the redeemed

When he had taken the book, the four living creatures and the
twenty-four elders prostrated themselves before the Lamb. Each
of them had a harp, and they had golden bowls full of incense,
which are the prayers of the saints. They sang a new song and
these are the words they sang,

523

"Worthy art thou to take the book and break its seals, for thou hast been slain and by thy blood hast purchased for God men from every tribe, and tongue, and people, and nation! Thou hast made them a kingdom of priests for our God, and they shall reign as kings upon the earth."

The hymn of the whole company of Heaven

11 Then in my vision I heard the voices of many angels encircling the throne, the living creatures and the elders. There were myriads
12 of myriads and thousands of thousands, crying in a great voice,

"Worthy is the Lamb who was slain, to receive power and riches and wisdom, and strength and honour and glory and blessing!"

13 Then I heard the voice of everything created in Heaven, upon earth, under the earth and upon the sea, and all that are in them saying,

"Blessing and honour and glory and power be given to him who sits upon the throne, and to the Lamb, for timeless ages!"

14 The four living creatures said, "Amen", while the elders fell down and worshipped.

CHAPTER 6

THE LAMB BREAKS THE SEALS

The first rider: Conquest

1 THEN I watched while the Lamb broke one of the seven seals, and I heard one of the four living creatures say in a voice of thunder, "Come out!"

2 I looked, and before my eyes was a white horse. Its rider carried a bow, and he was given a crown. He rode out conquering and bent on conquest.

The second rider: War

3 Then, when the Lamb broke the second seal, I heard the second living creature cry,
"Come out!"

4 And another horse came forth, red in colour. Its rider was given power to deprive the earth of peace, so that men should kill each other. A huge sword was put into his hand.

The third rider: Famine

When the Lamb broke the third seal, I heard the third living 5
creature say,
"Come out!"
I looked again and there before my eyes was a black horse.
Its rider had a pair of scales in his hand, and I heard a voice which 6
seemed to come from the four living creatures, saying,
"A quart of wheat for a shilling, and three quarts of barley for
a shilling—but no tampering with the oil or the wine!"

The fourth rider: Death

Then, when he broke the fourth seal I heard the voice of the 7
fourth living creature cry,
"Come out!"
Again I looked, and there appeared a horse sickly green in 8
colour. The name of its rider was death, and the grave followed
close behind him. A quarter of the earth was put into their power,
to kill with the sword, by famine, by violence, and through the
wild beasts of the earth.

The cry of the martyrs in Heaven

When the Lamb broke the fifth seal, I could see, beneath the 9
altar, the souls of those who had been killed for the sake of the
Word of God and because of the faithfulness of their witness.
They cried out in a loud voice, saying, 10
"How long shall it be, O Lord of all, holy and true, before thou
shalt judge and avenge our blood upon the inhabitants of the
earth?"
Then each of them was given a white robe, and they were told 11
to be patient a little longer, until the number of their fellow-
servants and of their brethren, who were to die as they had died,
should be complete.

The awe-full wrath of God

Then I watched while he broke the sixth seal. There was a 12
tremendous earthquake, the sun turned dark like coarse black
cloth, and the full moon was red as blood. The stars of the sky 13
fell upon the earth, just as a fig-tree sheds unripe figs when shaken

14 in a gale. The sky vanished as though it were a scroll being rolled
up, and every mountain and island was jolted out of its place.
15 Then the kings of the earth, and the great men, the captains, the
wealthy, the powerful, and every man, whether slave or free,
16 hid themselves in caves and among mountain rocks. They called
out to the mountains and the rocks,
"Fall down upon us and hide us from the face of him who sits
17 upon the throne, and from the wrath of the Lamb! For the great
day of their wrath has come, and who can stand against it?"

CHAPTER 7

Judgment stayed for the sealing of God's people

1 LATER I saw four angels standing at the four corners of the earth
holding in check the four winds of the earth that none should
2 blow upon the earth or upon the sea or upon any tree. Then I
saw another angel ascending out of the east, holding the seal of
the living God. He cried out in a loud voice to the four angels
who had the power to harm the earth and the sea:
3 "Do no harm to the earth, nor to the sea, nor to the trees until
we have sealed the servants of our God upon their foreheads."
4 I heard the number of those who were thus sealed and it was
5 144,000, from every tribe of the sons of Israel. Twelve thousand
were sealed from the tribe of Judah; twelve thousand from the
6 tribe of Reuben; twelve thousand from the tribe of Gad; twelve
thousand from the tribe of Asher; twelve thousand from the tribe
7 of Naphtali; twelve thousand from the tribe of Manasseh; twelve
thousand from the tribe of Simeon; twelve thousand from the
8 tribe of Levi; twelve thousand from the tribe of Issachar; twelve
thousand from the tribe of Zebulun; twelve thousand from the
tribe of Joseph; and twelve thousand were sealed from the tribe of
Benjamin.

The countless host of the redeemed

9 When this was done I looked again, and before my eyes
appeared a vast crowd beyond man's power to number. They
came from every nation and tribe and people and language, and
they stood before the throne of the Lamb, dressed in white robes
10 with palm-branches in their hands. With a great voice they
shouted these words:
"Salvation belongs to our God who sits upon the throne and
to the Lamb!"

Then all the angels stood encircling the throne, the elders and **11**
the four living creatures, and prostrated themselves with heads
bowed before the throne and worshipped God, saying, **12**

"Amen! Blessing and glory and wisdom and thanksgiving and
honour and power and strength be given to our God for timeless
ages!"

The countless host explained

Then one of the elders addressed me and asked, **13**
"These who are dressed in white robes—who are they, and
where do they come from?"

"You know, my Lord," I answered him. **14**
Then he told me,
"These are those who have come through the great oppression:
they have washed their robes and made them white in the blood
of the Lamb. That is why they now have their place before the **15**
throne of God, and serve him day and night in his temple. He
who sits upon the throne will be their shelter. They will never **16**
again know hunger or thirst. The sun shall never beat upon them,
neither shall there be any scorching heat, for the Lamb who is in **17**
the centre of the throne will be their shepherd and will lead them
to springs of living water. And God will wipe away every tear
from their eyes."

CHAPTER 8

The seventh seal: Complete silence

THEN, when he had broken the seventh seal, there was utter **1**
silence in Heaven for what seemed to me half-an-hour.

The vision of the seven trumpeters

Then I saw the seven angels who stand in the presence of God, **2**
and seven trumpets were put into their hands.

Then another angel came and stood by the altar holding a **3**
golden censer. He was given a great quantity of incense to add to
the prayers of all the saints, to be laid upon the golden altar before
the throne. And the smoke of the incense rose up before God from **4**
the angel's hand, mingled with the prayers of the saints. Then the **5**
angel took the censer, filled it with fire from the altar, and hurled
it upon the earth. And at that there were thunderings and noises,
flashes of lightning and an earthquake.

6   Then the seven angels who were holding the seven trumpets prepared to blow them.

The first trumpet: Hail and fire

7   The first angel blew his trumpet. Hail and fire mingled with blood appeared, and were hurled upon the earth. One-third of the earth was burnt up, one-third of all the trees was burnt up, and every blade of green grass was burnt up.

The second trumpet: The blazing mountain

8   The second angel blew his trumpet, and something like a vast mountain blazing with fire was thrown into the sea. A third-part
9   of the sea turned into blood, a third of all live creatures in the sea died, and a third-part of all shipping was destroyed.

The third trumpet: The poisonous star

10   Then the third angel blew his trumpet and there fell from the sky a huge star blazing like a torch. It fell upon a third of the rivers
11   and springs of water. The name of the star is said to be Apsinthus (Wormwood). A third of all the waters turned into wormwood, and many people died because the waters had become so bitter.

The fourth trumpet: Light from the sky diminishes

12   The fourth angel blew his trumpet, and a third-part of the sun, a third-part of the moon and a third of the stars were struck. A third-part of the light of each of them was darkened, so that light by day and light by night were both diminished by a third-part.

The cry of pity from mid-heaven

13   Then in my vision I saw a solitary eagle* flying in mid-heaven, crying in a loud voice,
    "Alas, alas, alas for the inhabitants of the earth for there are three more trumpet blasts which the three angels shall sound!"

    * Not "angel", as in A.V.

CHAPTER 9

The fifth trumpet: The fathomless pit

THE fifth angel blew his trumpet. I saw a star that had fallen **1**
down from Heaven to earth, and he was given the key to the
fathomless pit. Then he opened the pit and smoke like the smoke **2**
of a vast furnace rose out of it, so that the light of the sun and the
air itself grew dark from the smoke of the pit.

Then out of the smoke emerged locusts to descend upon the **3**
earth. They were given powers like those of earthly scorpions.
They had orders to do no harm to any grass, green thing or tree **4**
upon the earth, but to injure only those human beings who did
not bear the seal of God upon their foreheads. They were given no **5**
power to kill men, but only to torture them for five months. The
torture they could inflict was like the pain of a scorpion's sting.
In those days men will seek death but they will never find it; **6**
they will long to die but death will elude them. These locusts **7**
looked to me in my vision like horses prepared for battle.
On their heads were what appeared to be crowns like gold;
their faces were like human faces, and they had long hair like **8**
women. Their teeth were like lion's teeth, their breasts were **9**
like iron-breastplates, and the noise of their wings was like the
noise of a host of chariots and horses charging into battle. They
have tails and stings like scorpions, and it is in their tails that they **10**
possess the power to injure men for five months. They have as
their king the angel of the pit, whose name in Hebrew is Abaddon **11**
and in Greek Apollyon, (meaning the destroyer).

The first disaster is now past, but I see two more approaching. **12**

The sixth trumpet: The destroying angels

Then the sixth angel blew his trumpet, and I heard a solitary **13**
voice speaking from the four corners of the golden altar that
stands in the presence of God. And it said to the sixth angel who **14**
held the trumpet,

"Release the four angels who are bound at the great river
Euphrates!"

Then these four angels who had been held ready for the hour, **15**
the day, the month and the year, were set free to kill a third-part
of all mankind. The number of their horsemen was two hundred **16**

17 million—I heard what their number was. In my vision I saw these horses and their riders, and their breastplates were fiery-red, blue and yellow. The horses' heads looked to me like the heads of lions, and out of their mouths poured fire and smoke and sulphur.

18 A third of all mankind died from the fearful effects of these three, the fire, the smoke and the sulphur which pours out of their

19 mouths. For the power of these horses lies in their mouths and in their tails. Indeed their tails are like serpents with heads, and with these they inflict injury.

20 The rest of mankind, who did not die in this fearful destruction, neither repented of the works of their own hands nor ceased to worship evil powers and idols of gold, silver, brass, stone or wood,

21 which can neither see nor hear nor move. Neither did they repent of their murders, their sorceries, their sexual sins, nor of their thieving.

CHAPTER 10

The angel with the little book

1 THEN I saw another mighty angel descending from Heaven. He was clothed in a cloud, and there was a rainbow around his

2 head. His face blazed like the sun, his legs like pillars of fire, and he had a little book lying open in his hand. He planted his right

3 foot on the sea and his left foot on the land, and then shouted with a loud voice like the roar of a lion. And when he shouted the

4 seven thunders lifted their voices. When the seven thunders had rolled I was on the point of writing but I heard a voice from Heaven, saying,

"Seal up what the seven thunders said, but do not write it down!"

5 Then the angel whom I had seen bestriding the sea and the

6 land raised his right hand to Heaven and swore by the living one of the timeless ages, who created Heaven, earth and sea and all that is in them:

7 "There shall be no more delay! In the days which shall soon be announced by the trumpet-blast of the seventh angel the mysterious purpose of God shall be completed, as he assured his servants the prophets."

8 Then the voice which I had heard from Heaven was again in my ears, saying,

"Go and take the little book which lies open in the hand of the angel whose feet are planted on both sea and land."

So I went off towards the angel, asking him to give me the   *9*
little book.

"Take it," he said to me, "and eat it up. It will be bitter to your
stomach, but sweet as honey in your mouth."

Then I took the little book from the angel's hand and swallowed   *10*
it. It was as sweet as honey to the taste but when I had eaten it
up it was bitter to my stomach.

John is instructed to prophesy

Then they said to me, "It is again your duty to prophesy about   *11*
many peoples, nations, languages and kings."

CHAPTER 11

AND I was given a measuring rod like a staff, and I was told,   *1*
"Get up and measure the Temple of God, and the altar, and count
those who worship there. But leave out of your measurement the   *2*
courtyard outside the Temple—do not measure that at all. For it
has been given over to the nations, and they will trample over the
holy city for forty-two months."

God's two witnesses

"And I will give authority to my two witnesses to proclaim   *3*
the message, clothed in sackcloth for twelve hundred and sixty
days."

These are the two olive trees and the two lampstands which   *4*
stand before the Lord of the earth. If anyone tries to harm them,   *5*
fire issues from their mouths and consumes their enemies. Indeed,
if anyone should try to hurt them, this is the way in which he
will certainly meet his death. These witnesses have power to shut   *6*
up the sky and stop any rain from falling during the time of their
preaching. Moreover, they have power to turn the waters into
blood, and to strike the earth with any plague as often as they wish.

The emergence of the animal

Then, when their work of witness is complete, the animal will   *7*
come up out of the pit and go to war with them. It will conquer
and kill them, and their bodies will lie in the street of the great   *8*

city, which is called by those with spiritual understanding, "Sodom" and "Egypt"—the very place where their Lord himself
9 was crucified. For three and a half days men from all peoples and tribes and languages and nations will gaze upon their bodies and
10 will not allow them to be buried. The inhabitants of the earth will gloat over them and will hold celebrations and send one another presents, because these two prophets had brought such misery to the inhabitants of the earth.

The resurrection and ascension of the two witnesses

11 But after three and a half days the Spirit of life from God entered them and they stood upright on their feet. This struck
12 terror into the hearts of those who were watching them, and they heard a tremendous voice speaking to these two from Heaven, saying,

"Come up here!"

And they went up to Heaven in a cloud in full view of their
13 enemies. And at that moment there was a great earthquake, a tenth-part of the city fell in ruins and seven thousand people were known to have been killed in the earthquake. The rest were terrified and acknowledged the glory of the God of Heaven.

The seventh trumpet: (i) The worship of Heaven

14 The second disaster is now past, and I see the third disaster
15 following hard upon the heels of the second. The seventh angel blew his trumpet. There arose loud voices in Heaven and they were saying,

"The kingship of the world now belongs to our Lord and to his Christ, and he shall be king for timeless ages!"

16 Then the twenty-four elders, who sit upon their thrones in the presence of God, prostrated themselves and, with bowed
17 heads, worshipped God, saying:

"We thank thee, O Lord who art God the Almighty, who art and who wast, that thou hast assumed thy great power and hast
18 become king. The nations were full of fury, but now thy wrath has come and with it the time for the dead to be judged and for reward to be given to thy servants, the prophets and the saints, and all who fear thy name, both small and great. Now is the time for destroying the destroyers of the earth!"

19 Then the Temple of God in Heaven was thrown open and the

ark of his agreement within his Temple could be clearly seen. Accompanying this sight were flashes of lightning, loud noises, peals of thunder, an earthquake and a violent storm of hail.

CHAPTER 12

The seventh trumpet: (ii) The sign of the woman

THEN a huge sign became visible in the sky—the figure of a 1 woman clothed with the sun, with the moon under her feet and a crown of twelve stars upon her head. She was pregnant, and 2 cried out in her labour and in the pains of bringing forth her child.

The seventh trumpet: (iii) The dragon, the enemy of the woman

Then another sign became visible in the sky, and I saw that it 3 was a huge red dragon with seven heads and ten horns, with a diadem upon each of his heads. His tail swept down a third of 4 the stars in the sky and hurled them upon the earth. The dragon took his place in front of the woman who was about to give birth to a child, so that as soon as she did so he might devour it. She 5 gave birth to a male child who is to shepherd all the nations "with a rod of iron". Her child was snatched up to God and to his throne, while the woman fled into the desert where she has a place pre- 6 pared for her by God's command. There they will take care of her for twelve hundred and sixty days.

War in Heaven

Then war broke out in Heaven. Michael and his angels battled 7 with the dragon. The dragon and his angels fought back, but they 8 did not prevail and they were expelled from Heaven. So the huge 9 dragon, the serpent of ancient times, who is called the devil and Satan, the deceiver of the whole world, was hurled down upon the earth, and his angels were hurled down with him.

The victory of Heaven proclaimed

Then I heard a great voice in Heaven cry: 10
"Now the salvation and the power and kingdom of our God, and the authority of his Christ have come! For the accuser of our brethren has been thrown down from this place, where he stood

11 before our God accusing them day and night. Now they have conquered him through the blood of the Lamb, and through the Word to which they bore witness. They did not cherish life even in the face of death!

12 "Therefore, rejoice, O Heavens, and all you who live in the Heavens! But alas for the earth and the sea, for the devil has come down to you in great fury, knowing that his time is short!"

The dragon's enmity against the woman

13 And when the dragon saw that he had been cast down upon the earth, he began to pursue the woman who had given birth
14 to the male child. But she was given two great eagle's wings so that she could fly to her place in the desert, where she is kept safe
15 from the serpent for a time and times and half a time. Then the serpent ejected water from his mouth, streaming like a river in
16 pursuit of the woman, to drown her in its flood. But the earth came to the woman's rescue, opened its mouth and swallowed up
17 the river which the dragon had emitted from his mouth. Then the dragon raged with fury against the woman and went off to make war against the rest of her children—those who keep the commandments of God and bear their witness to Jesus.

CHAPTER 13

The animal from the sea

1 THEN, as I stood on the sand of the sea-shore, there rose out of the sea before my eyes an animal with seven heads and ten horns. There were diadems upon its horns and blasphemous names upon
2 its heads. The animal which I saw had the appearance of a leopard, though it had the feet of a bear and a mouth like the mouth of a lion. Then the dragon gave it his own power and throne and great
3 authority. One of its heads appeared to have been wounded to death but the mortal wound had healed.
4 The whole earth followed the animal with wonder, and they worshipped the dragon because he had given authority to the animal. Then they worshipped the animal, too, saying,

"Who is like the animal? Who could make war against it?"

5 It was allowed to speak monstrous blasphemies and to exert its authority for forty-two months.
6 So it poured out blasphemies against God, blaspheming his

name and his dwelling-place and those who live in Heaven.
Moreover, it was permitted to make war upon the saints and to   *7*
conquer them; the authority given to it extended over every
tribe and people and language and nation. All the inhabitants of   *8*
the earth will worship it—all those whose names have not been
written in the book of life which belongs to the Lamb slain from
the foundation of the world.

Parenthetical: a word to the reader

Let the listener hear this: *9*
If any man is destined for captivity he will go into captivity.   *10*
If any man kills with the sword he must himself be killed with
the sword. Amid all this stands the endurance and faith of the
saints.

The animal from the earth

Then I saw another animal rising out of the earth, and it had   *11*
two horns like a lamb but it spoke in the voice of a dragon. It   *12*
uses the full authority of the first animal in its presence. It compels
the earth and all its inhabitants to worship the first animal—the
one with the mortal wound which had healed. It performs great   *13*
signs: before men's eyes it makes fire fall down from heaven to
earth. It deceives the inhabitants of the earth by the signs which   *14*
it is allowed to perform in the presence of the animal, and it tells
them to make a statue in honour of the animal which received the
sword-thrust and yet survived. Further, it was allowed to give the   *15*
breath of life to the statue of the animal so that the statue could
speak and condemn to death all those who do not worship its
statue. Then it compels all, small and great, rich and poor, free   *16*
men and slaves, to receive a mark on their right hands or on their
foreheads. The purpose of this is that no one should be able to   *17*
buy or sell unless he bears the mark of the name of the animal
or the number of its name. Understanding is needed here: let every   *18*
thinking man calculate the number of the animal. It is the number
of a man, and its number is six hundred and sixty-six.

CHAPTER 14

The vision of the Lamb and the first of the redeemed

THEN I looked again and before my eyes the Lamb was standing   *1*
on Mount Sion, and with him were a hundred and forty-four

thousand who had his name and his Father's name written upon
2 their foreheads. Then I heard a sound coming from Heaven like
the roar of a great waterfall and the heavy rolling of thunder.
Yet the sound which I heard was also like the music of harpists
3 sweeping their strings. And now they are singing a new song of
praise before the throne, and before the four living creatures and
the elders. No one could learn that song except the one hundred
and forty-four thousand who had been redeemed from the earth.
4 These are the men who have never defiled themselves with
women, for they are celibate. These are the men who follow the
Lamb wherever he may go; these men have been redeemed from
5 among mankind as first-fruits to God and to the Lamb. They have
never been guilty of any falsehood; they are beyond reproach.

The angel with the gospel

6   Then I saw another angel flying in mid-heaven, holding the
everlasting gospel to proclaim to the inhabitants of the earth—
7 to every nation and tribe and language and people. He was crying
in a loud voice,
"Reverence God, and give glory to him; for the hour of his
judgment has come! Worship him who made Heaven and earth,
the sea and the springs of water."

The angel of doom

8   Then another, a second angel, followed him crying,
"Fallen, fallen is Babylon the great! She who made all nations
drink the wine of her passionate unfaithfulness!"

The angel of judgment

9   Then a third angel followed these two, crying in a loud voice,
"If any man worships the animal and its statue and bears its
10 mark upon his forehead or upon his hand, then that man shall
drink the wine of God's passion, poured undiluted into the cup of
his wrath. He shall be tortured by fire and sulphur in the presence
11 of the holy angels and of the Lamb. The smoke of such men's
torture ascends for timeless ages, and there is no respite from it
day or night. Such are the worshippers of the animal and its statue
and among their number are all who bear the mark of its name."

The call to stand fast

In all this stands the endurance of the saints—those who keep   *12*
the commandments of God and their faith in Jesus.

The security of the saints

Then I heard a voice from Heaven, saying,   *13*
"Write this! From henceforth happy are the dead who die in
the Lord!"

"Happy indeed," says the Spirit, "for they rest from their
labours and their deeds go with them!"

The harvest of God's wrath

Once again I looked, and a white cloud appeared before me   *14*
with someone sitting upon the cloud with the appearance of a
man. He had a golden crown on his head, and held a sharp sickle
in his hand. Then another angel came out from the Temple,   *15*
calling in a loud voice to the one sitting on the cloud,

"Thrust in your sickle and reap, for the time of reaping has
come and the harvest of the earth is fully ripe!"

Then the one sitting upon the cloud swung his sickle upon the   *16*
earth, and the reaping of the earth was done.

Then another angel came out from the Temple in Heaven, and   *17*
he also had a sharp sickle. Yet another angel came out from the   *18*
altar where he has command over the fire, and called out in a
loud voice to the angel with the sharp sickle,

"Thrust in your sharp sickle and harvest the clusters from the
vineyard of the earth for the grapes are fully ripe!"

Then the angel swung his sickle upon the earth and gathered   *19*
the harvest of the earth's vineyard, and threw it into the great
winepress of the wrath of God. The grapes were trodden outside   *20*
the city, and out of the winepress flowed blood for two hundred
miles in a stream as high as the horses' bridles.

CHAPTER 15

The seven last plagues prepared

THEN I saw another sign in Heaven, vast and awe-inspiring: *1*
seven angels are holding the seven last plagues, and with these the
wrath of God is brought to an end.

The hymn of the redeemed

2 And I saw what appeared to be a sea of glass shot through with fire, and upon this glassy sea were standing those who had emerged victorious from the fight with the animal, its statue and the number which denotes its name. In their hands they hold harps which God 3 has given them, and they are singing the song of Moses the servant of God, and the song of the Lamb, and these are the words they sing:

"Great and wonderful are thy works, O Lord God, the Almighty! Just and true are thy ways, thou king of the nations! 4 Who should not reverence thee, O Lord, and glorify thy name? For thou alone art holy; therefore all nations shall come and worship before thee, for thy just judgments have been made plain!"

The angels leave the Temple of God—

5 Later in my vision I saw the Temple of the tabernacle of testi-
6 mony in Heaven wide open, and out of the Temple came forth the seven angels who hold the seven plagues. They were dressed in spotless shining linen, and they were girded round their breasts with golden girdles.

7 Then one of the four living creatures gave to the seven angels seven golden bowls filled with the wrath of God who lives for
8 timeless ages. The Temple was filled with smoke from the glory and power of God, and no one could enter the Temple until the seven plagues of the seven angels were past and over.

CHAPTER 16

—and are ordered to pour out the bowls of his wrath

1 THEN I heard a loud voice from the Temple saying to the seven angels,

"Go and pour out upon the earth the seven bowls of the wrath of God!"

The first bowl: Ulcers

2 The first angel went off and emptied his bowl upon the earth. Whereupon loathsome and malignant ulcers attacked all those who bore the mark of the animal and worshipped its statue.

The second bowl: Death in the sea

The second angel emptied his bowl into the sea, which turned *3* into a fluid like the blood of a corpse, and every living thing in it died.

The third bowl: Water becomes blood

Then the third angel emptied his bowl into the rivers and *4* springs of water, and they turned into blood. And I heard the *5* angel of the waters say,
"Just art thou in these thy judgments, thou who art and wast the holy one! For they have spilled the blood of saints and *6* prophets, and now thou hast given them blood to drink. They have what they deserve."
And I heard the altar say, *7*
"Yes, O Lord, God Almighty, thy judgments are true and right."

The fourth bowl: Scorching heat

The fourth angel emptied his bowl over the sun, and the sun *8* was given power to scorch men in its fiery blaze. Then men were *9* terribly burned in the heat, and they blasphemed the name of God who has control over these afflictions; but they neither repented nor gave him glory.

The fifth bowl: The plague of darkness

Then the fifth angel emptied his bowl upon the throne of the *10* animal. Its kingdom was plunged into darkness; men gnawed their tongues in agony, cursed the God of Heaven for their pain *11* and their ulcers, but refused to repent of what they had done.

The sixth bowl: The great river dried up

Then the sixth angel emptied his bowl upon the great river *12* Euphrates. The waters of that river were dried up to prepare a road for the kings from the east. And then I noticed three foul *13* spirits, looking like frogs, emerging from the mouths of the dragon, the animal and the false prophet. They are diabolical *14* spirits performing wonders and they set out to muster all the kings of the world for battle on the great day of God, the Almighty.
So they brought them together to the place called, in Hebrew, *16* Armageddon.

The words in the background

15 "See, I am coming like a thief! Happy is the man who stays awake and keeps his clothes at his side, so that he will not have to walk naked and men see his shame."

The seventh bowl: Devastation from the air

17 The seventh angel emptied his bowl into the air. A loud voice came out of the Temple, from the throne, saying,
"The end has come!"

18 Then followed flashes of lightning, noises and peals of thunder. There was a terrific earthquake, the like of which no man has ever seen since mankind began to live upon the earth—so great

19 and tremendous was this earthquake. The great city was split into three parts, and the cities of all the nations fell in ruins. And God called to mind Babylon the great and made her drink the cup of

20 the wine of his furious wrath. Every island fled and the mountains

21 vanished. Great hailstones like heavy weights fell from the sky, and men blasphemed God for the curse of the hail, for it fell upon them with savage and fearful blows.

CHAPTER 17

The judgment of the evil woman announced

1 THEN came one of the seven angels who held the seven bowls, and said to me,
"Come, and I will show you the judgment passed upon the

2 great harlot who is seated upon many waters. It is with her that the kings of the earth have debauched themselves and the inhabitants of the earth have become drunk on the wine of her filthiness."

The gorgeous mother of evil

3 Then he carried me away in spirit into the desert. There I saw a woman riding upon a scarlet animal, covered with blasphemous

4 titles and having seven heads and ten horns. The woman herself was dressed in purple and scarlet, glittering with gold, jewels and pearls. In her hand she held a golden cup full of the earth's filthi-

5 ness and her own foul impurity. On her forehead is written a name with a secret meaning—BABYLON THE GREAT, MOTHER OF ALL HARLOTS AND OF THE EARTH'S ABOMINATIONS.

The vision explained

Then I noticed that the woman was drunk with the blood of **6**
the saints and of the martyrs for Jesus. As I watched her, I was
filled with utter amazement, but the angel said to me, **7**

"Why are you amazed? I will explain to you the mystery of
the woman and of the animal with seven heads and ten horns
which carries her. The animal, which you saw, once lived but **8**
now is no more—it will come up out of the pit only to meet with
destruction. The inhabitants of the earth, whose names have not
been written in the book of life from the foundation of the world,
will be utterly astonished when they see that the animal was, and
is not, and yet is to come. (Here we need a mind with under- **9**
standing.)

"The seven heads are seven hills on which the woman takes her
seat. There are also seven kings; five have been dethroned, one **10**
reigns and the other has not yet appeared—when he comes he
must remain only for a short time. As for the animal which once **11**
lived but now lives no longer, it is an eighth king which belongs
to the seven, but it goes to utter destruction. The ten horns which **12**
you saw are ten kings who have not yet received their power to
reign, but they will receive authority to be kings for one hour in
company with the animal. They are of one mind, and they will **13**
hand over their power and authority to the animal. They will **14**
all go to war with the Lamb, and the Lamb, with his called, chosen
and faithful followers, will conquer them. For he is Lord of lords
and king of kings."

Then he said to me, **15**

"As for the waters which you saw, on which the woman took
her seat, they are peoples and vast crowds, nations and languages.
The ten horns and the animal which you saw will loathe the harlot, **16**
and leave her deserted and naked. Moreover, they will devour
her flesh, and then consume her with fire. For God has put it into **17**
their hearts to carry out his purpose by making them of one mind,
and by handing over their authority to the animal, until the words
of God have been fulfilled.

"The woman that you saw is the great city which dominates **18**
the kings of the earth."

CHAPTER 18

The final overthrow of Babylon

1 LATER I saw another angel coming down from Heaven, armed with great authority. The earth shone with the splendour of his
2 presence, and he cried in a mighty voice,

"Fallen, fallen is Babylon* the great! She has become a haunt of devils, a prison for every unclean spirit, and a cage for every
3 foul and hateful bird. For all nations have drunk the wine of her passionate unfaithfulness and have fallen thereby. The kings of the earth have debauched themselves with her, and the merchants of the earth have grown rich from the extravagance of her dissipation!"

4 Then I heard another voice from Heaven, crying,

"Come out from her, O my people, lest you become accom-
5 plices in her sins and must share in her punishment. For her sins have mounted up to the sky, and God has remembered the tale
6 of her wickedness. Pay her back in her own coin—yes, pay her back double for all that she has done! In the cup which she mixed
7 for others mix her a drink of double strength! For the pride in which she flaunted herself give her torture and misery! Because she says to herself, 'Here I sit a queen on a throne; I am no woman
8 who lacks a man and I shall never know sorrow!' So in a single day her punishments shall strike her—death, sorrow and famine and she shall be burned in the fire. For mighty is the Lord God who judges her!"

The lament over the city

9 Then the kings of the earth, who debauched and indulged
10 themselves with her, will wail and lament over her. Standing at a safe distance through very fear of her torment, they will watch the smoke of her burning and cry,

"Alas, alas for the great city, Babylon the mighty city, that your judgment should come in a single hour."

11 The merchants of the earth shall also wail and lament over her,
12 for there is no one left to buy their goods—cargoes of gold and silver, jewels and pearls, fine linen, purple, silk and scarlet, all kinds of scented wood, every sort of ivory vessel, every kind of

* Referring to Rome, but prophetically to any great, prosperous but Godless city.

vessel of precious wood, of bronze, iron and marble; cinnamon, 13*
spice, incense, myrrh, frankincense, wine, oil, fine flour and corn;
cattle, sheep and horses; chariots, slaves, the very souls of men.

Those who bought and sold these things, who had gained their 15
wealth from her, will stand afar off through fear of her punishment, weeping and lamenting and saying, 16

"Alas, alas for the great city that was dressed in fine linen,
purple and scarlet, and was bedecked with gold and jewels and
pearls—alas that in a single hour all that wealth should be 17
destroyed!"

Then every shipmaster and seafarer—sailors and all whose
business is upon the sea—stood and watched the smoke of her 18
burning from afar, and cried out,

"What city was ever like the great city?"

They even threw dust on their heads and cried aloud as they 19
wept, saying,

"Alas, alas for the great city where all who had ships on the
sea grew wealthy through the richness of her treasure! Alas that
in a single hour she should be ruined!"

A comment in the background

"Rejoice over her fate, O Heaven, and all you saints, apostles 20
and prophets! For God has pronounced his judgment for you
against her!"

The words of Babylon's doom

Then a mighty angel lifted up a stone like a huge mill-stone and 21
hurled it into the sea, saying,

"So shall Babylon the great city be sent hurtling down to disappear for ever! Never more shall the sound of harpists and 22
musicians, flute-players and trumpeters be heard in you again!
Never again shall a craftsman of any craft be found in you; never
again will the sound of the mill-stone's grinding be heard in you!
No light of a lamp shall ever shine in you again, and the voices of 23
bridegroom and bride shall be heard in you no more! The fruit
of your soul's desire is lost to you for ever. All your luxuries and
brilliance are lost to you and men will never find them in you
again!

"For your merchants were the great ones of the earth, and all
nations were seduced by your witchery!"

* Verse 14 has been incorporated with verse 23, which seems to
be its natural place.

24   For in her was discovered the blood of prophets and saints, indeed the blood of all who were ever slaughtered upon the earth.

CHAPTER 19

Rejoicing in Heaven

1   AFTERWARDS I heard what sounded like the mighty roar of a vast crowd in Heaven, crying,
    "Alleluia! Salvation and glory and power belong to our God,
2 for his judgments are true and just. He has judged the great harlot who corrupted the earth with her wickedness, and he has avenged upon her the blood of his servants!"
3   Then they cried a second time,
    "Alleluia! The smoke of her destruction ascends for timeless ages!"
4   Then the twenty-four elders and the four living creatures prostrated themselves and worshipped God who is seated upon the throne, saying,
    "Amen, alleluia!"
5   Then out of the throne came a voice, saying,
    "Praise our God, all you who serve him, all you who reverence him, both small and great!"
6   And then I heard a sound like the voices of a vast crowd, the roar of a great waterfall and the rolling of heavy thunder, and they were saying,
    "Alleluia! For the Lord our God, the Almighty, has come into
7 his kingdom! Let us rejoice, let us be glad with all our hearts. Let us give him the glory, for the wedding-day of the Lamb has
8 come, and his bride has made herself ready. She may be seen dressed in linen, gleaming and spotless—for such linen is the righteous living of the saints!"

Instruction to John

9   Then he said to me,
    "Write this down: Happy are those who are invited to the wedding-feast of the Lamb!"
    Then he added,
    "These are true words of God."
10   At that I fell at his feet to worship him, but he said to me,

"No! I am your fellow-servant and fellow-servant with your brothers who are holding fast their witness to Jesus. Give your worship to God!"

(This witness to Jesus inspires all prophecy.)

The Word of God on the white horse

Then I saw Heaven wide open, and before my eyes appeared 11 a white horse, whose rider is called faithful and true, for his judgment and his warfare are just. His eyes are a flame of fire 12 and there are many diadems upon his head. There is a name written upon him, known only to himself. He is dressed in a 13 cloak dipped in blood, and the name by which he is known is the Word of God.

The armies of Heaven follow him, riding upon white horses 14 and clad in white and spotless linen. Out of his mouth there comes 15 a sharp sword with which to strike the nations. He will shepherd them "with a rod of iron", and alone he will tread the winepress of the furious wrath of God the Almighty. Written upon his 16 cloak and upon his thigh is the name, KING OF KINGS AND LORD OF LORDS.

The feast of death after battle

Then I saw an angel standing alone in the blazing light of the 17 sun, and he shouted in a loud voice, calling to all the birds flying in mid-air,

"Come, flock together to God's great feast! Here you may eat 18 the flesh of kings and captains, the flesh of strong men, of horses and their riders—the flesh of all men, free men and slaves, small and great!"

And I saw the animal with the kings of the earth and their 19 armies massed together for battle against the rider upon the horse and his army. The animal was captured and with it the false 20 prophet who had performed marvels in its presence, which he had used to deceive those who accepted the mark of the animal and worshipped its statue. These two were thrown alive into the lake of fire which burns with sulphur.

The rest were killed by the sword which issues from the mouth 21 of the rider upon the horse; and all the birds gorged themselves on their flesh.

CHAPTER 20

Satan bound for a thousand years

1 THEN I saw an angel coming down from Heaven with the key
2 of the pit and a huge chain in his hand. He seized the dragon,
the serpent of ancient days, who is both the devil and Satan, and
3 bound him fast for a thousand years. Then he hurled him into
the pit, and locked and sealed it over his head, so that he could
deceive the nations no more until the thousand years were past.
But then he must be set free for a little while.

The first resurrection

4   And I saw thrones, with appointed judges seated upon them.
Then I saw the souls of those who had been executed for their
witness to Jesus and for proclaiming the Word of God—those who
never worshipped the animal or its statue, and had not accepted
its mark upon their foreheads or their hands. They came to
5 life and reigned with Christ for a thousand years. (The rest of
the dead did not come to life until the thousand years were over.)
6 This is the first resurrection. Happy and holy is the one who
shares in the first resurrection! The second death cannot touch
such men; they shall be priests of God and of Christ, and shall
reign with him for the thousand years.

Satan finally destroyed

7   Then, when the thousand years are over, Satan will be released
8 from his prison, and will set out to deceive the nations in the four
corners of the earth, Gog and Magog, and to lead them into battle.
They will be as numerous as the sand of the seashore.
9   They came up and spread over the breadth of the earth; they
encircled the army of the saints defending the beloved city. But
10 fire came down from the sky and consumed them. The devil who
deceived them was hurled into the lake of fire and sulphur to
join the animal and the false prophet. And there they shall be
tortured day and night for timeless ages.

The final judgment

11   And then I saw a great white throne, and one seated upon it
from whose presence both earth and sky fled and vanished.

546

Then I saw the dead, great and small, standing before the *12* throne and the books were opened. And another book was opened, which is the book of life. And the dead were judged by what was written in the books concerning what they had done. The sea gave *13* up its dead, and death and the grave gave up the dead which were in them. And men were judged, each according to what he had done.

Then death and the grave were themselves hurled into the lake *14* of fire, which is the second death. If anyone's name was not found *15* written in the book of life he was thrown into the lake of fire.

CHAPTER 21

All things made new

THEN I saw a new Heaven and a new earth, for the first Heaven *1* and the first earth had disappeared and the sea was no more. I *2* saw the holy city, the new Jerusalem, descending from God out of Heaven, prepared as a bride dressed in beauty for her husband. Then I heard a great voice from the throne crying, *3*

"See! The home of God is with men, and he will live among them. They shall be his people, and God himself shall be with them, and will wipe away every tear from their eyes. Death shall *4* be no more, and never again shall there be sorrow or crying or pain. For all those former things are past and gone."

Then he who is seated upon the throne said, *5*

"See, I am making all things new!"

And he added,

"Write this down for my words are true and to be trusted."

Then he said to me, *6*

"It is done! I am Alpha and Omega, the beginning and the end. I will give to the thirsty water without price from the fountain of life. The victorious shall inherit these things, and I will be God to *7* him and he will be son to me. But as for the cowards, the faithless *8* and the corrupt, the murderers, the traffickers in sex and sorcery, the worshippers of idols and all liars—their inheritance is in the lake which burns with fire and sulphur, which is the second death."

The vision of the new Jerusalem

Then one of the seven angels who hold the seven bowls which *9* were filled with the seven last plagues, came to me and said,

"Come, and I will show you the bride, the wife of the Lamb."
10 Then he carried me away in spirit to the top of a vast mountain,
and pointed out to me the city, the holy Jerusalem, descending
11 from God out of Heaven, radiant with the glory of God. Her
brilliance sparkled like a very precious jewel with the clear light
12 of crystal. Around her she had a vast and lofty wall in which
were twelve gateways with twelve angels at the gates. There were
twelve names inscribed over the twelve gateways, and they are the
13 names of the twelve tribes of the sons of Israel. On the east there
were three gateways, on the north three gateways, on the south
14 three gateways and on the west three gateways. The wall of the
city had twelve foundation-stones, and on these were engraved
the names of the twelve apostles of the Lamb.

The measurement of the city

15 The one who was talking to me had a golden rod in his hand
16 with which to measure the city, its gateways and its wall. The
city lies foursquare, its length equal to its breadth. He measured
the city with his rod and it was twelve thousand furlongs in each
17 direction, for its length, breadth and height are all equal. Then he
measured its wall, and found that to be one hundred and forty-four
half-yards high by human measurement, (which the angel was
using).

The splendour of the city's building

18 The wall itself was built of translucent stone, while the city
19 was of purest gold, with the brilliance of glass. The foundation
stones of the wall of the city were fashioned out of every kind of
precious stone. The first foundation-stone was jasper, the second
20 sapphire, the third agate, the fourth emerald, the fifth onyx, the
sixth cornelian, the seventh goldstone, the eighth beryl, the ninth
topaz, the tenth green goldstone, the eleventh zircon, and the
21 twelfth amethyst. The twelve gates were twelve pearls, each gate
made of a single pearl. The street of the city was purest gold
gleaming like glass.

The splendour within the city

22 I could see no Temple in the city, for the Lord, the Almighty
23 God, and the Lamb are themselves its Temple. The city has no

need for the light of sun or moon, for the splendour of God fills
it with light and its radiance is the Lamb. The nations will walk   24
by its light, and the kings of the earth will bring their glory into
it. The city's gates shall stand open day after day—and there will   25
be no night there. Into the city they will bring the splendours and 26
honours of the nations.

But nothing unclean, no one who deals in filthiness and lies,   27
shall ever at any time enter it—only those whose names are written
in the Lamb's book of life.

CHAPTER 22

A further glimpse of the city

THEN he showed me the river of the water of life, sparkling like   1
crystal as it flowed from the throne of God and of the Lamb. In   2
the middle of the street of the city and on either bank of the river
grew the tree of life, bearing twelve fruits, a different kind for
each month. The leaves of the tree were for the healing of the
nations.

Nothing that has cursed mankind shall exist any longer; the   3
throne of God and of the Lamb shall be within the city. His
servants shall worship him; they shall see his face, and his name   4
will be upon their foreheads. Night shall be no more; they have no   5
more need for either lamplight or sunlight, for the Lord God will
shed his light upon them and they shall reign as kings for timeless
ages.

The angel endorses the revelation

Then the angel said to me,   6
"These words are true and to be trusted, for the Lord God,
who inspired the prophets, has sent his angel to show his servants
what must shortly happen."

"See, I come quickly! Happy is the man who pays heed to the   7
words of the prophecy in this book."

John's personal endorsement

It is I, John, who have heard and seen these things. At the   8
time when I heard and saw them I fell at the feet of the angel
who showed them to me and I was about to worship him. But   9
he said to me,

"No! I am fellow-servant to you and to your brothers, to the prophets and to those who keep the words of this book. Give your worship to God!"

10 Then he added,

"Do not seal up the words of the prophecy in this book, for
11 the time of their fulfilment is near. Let the wicked man continue his wickedness and the filthy man his filthiness; let the good man continue his good deeds, and the holy man continue in holiness."

The interjected words of Christ

12 "See, I come quickly! I carry my reward with me, and repay
13 every man according to his deeds. I am Alpha and Omega,
14 the first and the last, the Beginning and the End. Happy are those who wash their robes, for they have the right to the tree of life
15 and the freedom of the gates of the city. Shut out from the city shall be the depraved, the sorcerers, the impure, the murderers and the idolaters, and everyone who loves and practises a lie!
16 "I, Jesus, have sent my angel to you with this testimony for the Churches. I am both the root and stock of David, and the bright star of the morning!"

The invitation of the Church and the Spirit

17 The Spirit and the bride say, "Come!"
Let everyone who hears this also say, "Come!"
Let the thirsty man come, and let everyone who wishes take the water of life as a gift.

John's testimony to this book

18 Now I bear solemn witness to every man who hears the words of prophecy in this book:
If anyone adds to these words God will add to him the disasters
19 described in this book; if anyone takes away from the words of prophecy in this book, God will take away from him his share in the tree of life and in the holy city which are described in this book.
20 He, who is witness to all this, says,
"Yes, I am coming very quickly!"
"Amen, come, Lord Jesus!"
21 The grace of the Lord Jesus be with all his people.

Notes

Note 1.

"Scribes."

There is no modern English word by which "scribes" can be fairly translated. It is therefore necessary to explain that the "scribes" of the Gospels were the interpreters of the Divine Law (or Torah), for the people of Israel. The Torah was a kind of textbook for both the religious and civil functions of the community. Since in process of time this had become a highly complex matter, the scribes had to be expert both in knowledge, interpretation and administration. Consequently their position was one of considerable authority and, though there were doubtless noble exceptions, they tended to become both legalist and theological in outlook, and were therefore unprepared to accept the revolutionary teaching of Jesus.

"Pharisees."

The Pharisees were a class of zealous Jews whose chief characteristic lay in their separation from the heathen and from all that they considered evil. They were the Puritans of their day, and emphasised the spiritual rather than the nationalistic side of Judaism. We might fairly say that they were Churchmen rather than statesmen. And, again, though there were good men among them, they tended to concentrate upon rigid outward observances, to the exclusion of human sympathy and understanding. It was this tendency, and the conviction that they alone were right, which brought them into conflict with Jesus.

"Sadducees."

The Sadducees represented the aristocratic conservative element in the Jewish priesthood. Their conservatism, with its desire to maintain things as they were, led them to compromise politically with the Roman occupying power, and thus their moral authority became weakened. Moreover, in clinging to the tenets of the past, they failed to develop in their religion and did not, for example, believe, as the Pharisees did, in the coming Kingdom of God, and only in a very shadowy way did they believe in the immortality of the human soul.

Note 2.

Matthew 5, 22—Raca.

"Raca" means a fool or empty-headed fellow, but the Greek word used in the previous sentence means much the same thing.

551

If however it is, as some suggest, a transliteration of the Hebrew "moreh", then we have a further stage of uncharitable condemnation, for this word means "a persistent rebel against God", and thus makes much better sense.

Note 3.

Matthew 16, 19 and 18, 18—"forbidding" and "permitting". There is a very curious Greek construction here, viz. a simple future followed by the perfect participle passive. If Jesus had meant to say quite simply, "Whatever you forbid on earth will be forbidden in Heaven", can anyone explain why the simple future passive is not used? It seems to me that if the words of Jesus are accurately reported here, and I have no reason to doubt it, then the force of these sayings is that Jesus' true disciples will be so led by the Spirit that they will be following the heavenly pattern. In other words what they "forbid" or "permit" on earth will be consonant with the Divine rules.

If a simple future passive had been used it would mean an automatic heavenly endorsement of the Church's actions, which to me, at least, is a very different thing.

In the pertinent verses of John's Gospel (chapter 20, 22, 23), it is quite plain that "holy spirit", of which Christ is giving his disciples a first breath, so to speak, (for the Holy Spirit in person was not given until Pentecost), would be the factor by which alone human beings could perform the Divine function of forgiving or not forgiving sins. There is again no ground for supposing that celestial endorsement automatically follows human action, however exalted.

Note 4.

John 7, 53 to 8, 11—The Woman taken in Adultery. This passage has no place in the oldest manuscripts of John, and is considered by most scholars to be an interpolation from some other source. Almost all scholars would agree that, although the story is out of place here, it is part of a genuine apostolic tradition.

Note 5.

This is the sole instance of the translator's departing from the accepted text. He felt bound to conclude, from the sense of the next three verses, that we have here either a slip of the pen on the part of Paul, or, more probably, a copyist's error.

SHORT INDEX OF NAMES, PLACES AND EVENTS

NOTE: *This index is in no sense a substitute for a New Testament concordance. It is simply designed to help the reader to find quickly a significant incident, a person who plays some part in the New Testament story, or a place which is important because of events which happened there. In addition this index will make it easy to find the many parables of Jesus, for example, or the passages which refer to the journeys of St. Paul.*

It is obvious that some words such as "God", "Christ", "Law", as well as the proper names of some important people and places, occur too frequently for inclusion in a simple index. Such words are therefore omitted altogether.

The New Testament student who wants to make a detailed study of particular themes or the growth of certain doctrines will find himself bound to consult a comprehensive concordance.

J. B. P.